Johann J. Ignaz von Döllinger, Henry Nutcombe Oxenham

**The first Age of Christianity and the Church**

Johann J. Ignaz von Döllinger, Henry Nutcombe Oxenham

**The first Age of Christianity and the Church**

ISBN/EAN: 9783743329904

Manufactured in Europe, USA, Canada, Australia, Japa

Cover: Foto ©ninafisch / pixelio.de

Manufactured and distributed by brebook publishing software (www.brebook.com)

Johann J. Ignaz von Döllinger, Henry Nutcombe Oxenham

**The first Age of Christianity and the Church**

# THE FIRST AGE OF THE CHURCH.

*This Translation is published with the Author's exclusive Approbation.*

# THE FIRST AGE OF CHRISTIANITY

AND

# THE CHURCH.

BY

JOHN IGNATIUS DÖLLINGER, D.D.,

PROFESSOR OF ECCLESIASTICAL HISTORY IN THE UNIVERSITY OF MUNICH;
PROVOST OF THE CHAPEL ROYAL AND THEATINE CHURCH, ETC.

TRANSLATED BY

HENRY NUTCOMBE OXENHAM, M.A.,

LATE SCHOLAR OF BALLIOL COLLEGE, OXFORD.

"Attendite ad petram unde excisi estis, et ad cavernam laci de quâ præcisi estis."

SECOND EDITION.

LONDON:
WM. H. ALLEN & Co., 13, WATERLOO PLACE,
PALL MALL, S.W.
1867.

*All Rights reserved.*

TO

THE VERY REVEREND

# JOHN HENRY NEWMAN, D.D.,

WHOSE ILLUSTRIOUS NAME

IS ALONE

A PASSPORT TO THE HEARTS

AND

A SECURE CLAIM ON THE INTELLECTUAL RESPECT

OF HIS COUNTRYMEN

BOTH WITHIN AND WITHOUT THE CHURCH,

THIS TRANSLATION

OF A WORK

BY THE GREAT CATHOLIC DIVINE OF THE CONTINENT,

IS, WITH HIS KIND PERMISSION,

Very respectfully Dedicated, by

THE TRANSLATOR.

TRANSLATOR'S PREFACE
# TO THE SECOND EDITION.

The favourable notice which this Translation has met with in so many quarters, and the demand for a Second Edition within six months of its appearance, afford a gratifying confirmation of the belief I had been led to entertain, that Dr. Döllinger's name would carry its own recommendation with it in this country, as in his own, and would at once secure attention to the intrinsic merits of a work proceeding from his pen. It is hoped that the issue of a new Edition, in one volume, and at little above half the original price, may bring it within the reach of many, especially among the Clergy, to whom it might otherwise be less accessible.

The Translation has been carefully revised throughout, and is now (I trust) presented in a form more worthy the kindly reception already accorded to it. The Table of Contents has also been revised and enlarged, and an Index added at the end of the volume, adapted from the original. 1 have thought it well to adapt the English usage, which differs from the German, as from the Latin, in ordinarily prefixing to the names of Apostles and other personages held in reverence in the Church, their title of "Saint." Through the Author's kindness I have now been enabled to incorporate the corrections and additions of the Second

Edition of the original, so far as it is yet in type, *i.e.*, up to p. 200 of the present volume.

Since the earlier sheets of this volume were struck off, I observe, in reference to the disputed dates of the Cleansing of the Temple and the Passover, (infr. pp. 34, 35) that Neander considers the former event to have occurred once only, at the beginning of our Lord's ministry, as recorded by St. John; and that he makes the Feast of the Passover, in accordance with St. John's Gospel, commence on the Sabbath, *i.e.*, the Friday evening, so that both the Last Supper and the Crucifixion would take place on the day before the Feast.[1] This view, which is almost required by John xviii. 28; xix. 31; Luke xxiii. 54, seems on the whole to present fewest difficulties.[2] Neander supposes the institution of the Eucharist, which is omitted by St. John, to occur between v. 32 and 33 of ch. xiii. in his narrative.[3]

In conclusion, I would venture to express the hope that, by its calm uncontroversial enunciation of Catholic truth, its habitual moderation of statement and conciliatory tone, and the friendly reception it has met with among English readers of such various schools of religious thought,—this work of Dr. Döllinger's may, in a very real, though indirect sense, be subserving the ends of an Eirenicon in our divided Christendom.

H. N. O.

New Year's Day, 1867.

---

[1] See Neander's *Life of Christ*, p. 178, note j; and pp. 425 sqq., note t., *Eng. Trans.*

[2] The same view is maintained in Ellicott's *Lectures on the Life of our Lord*, p. 322, notes 1, 2, 3, (2nd Ed., 1861).

[3] Neander's *Life of Christ*, p. 430, note b.

# TRANSLATOR'S PREFACE TO THE FIRST EDITION.

No apology can be needed for introducing to English readers what is considered by competent judges one of the ablest and most instructive works of the first divine and Ecclesiastical historian of Catholic Germany. The words used in 1840, in the Preface to his translation of an earlier work of Dr. Döllinger's, by the late Dr. Cox, President of St. Edmund's College, Herts—who has the high credit of having called the attention of his countrymen to the rich stores of German theological literature, at a period when such knowledge was far less common, both among Catholics and Protestants, even than it is now,—may well be repeated here, when their truth has been so abundantly illustrated by the superadded testimony of twenty-six intervening years. "The name of the learned Professor, the author of this history, may stand as its only, its sufficient recommendation. The works already published by Dr. Döllinger, in the cause of literature and religion, have spread his fame widely through the nations of Europe."[1] If his name was a sufficient recommendation then, it is more than sufficient now.

But a few words will be in place, to explain the main scope and design of the present work. It is, properly speaking, a sequel to the Author's *Heidenthum und Judenthum*—of which an admirable and scholarly Translation

---

[1] Preface to Cox's *Translation of Döllinger's History of the Church.* (Dolman, 1840).

appeared four years ago, from the pen of the Rev. N. Darnell, late Fellow of New College, Oxford[1]—and a first instalment of what, if life and health be spared him, will be a complete Ecclesiastical History, destined to supersede the earlier and less matured work already referred to. It must be remembered, however, that the Apostolic Age, while it forms, so to say, the first Chapter in the life of the Catholic Church, is in many respects an exceptional period, standing alone and isolated from all later epochs of Christian history. It is no mere portion, however integral, of the edifice of that new Society which Christ set up on earth, but the foundation of the entire building. It is, therefore, a period capable of separate treatment; and the description of it may be viewed as a whole in itself, not, indeed, as having no relation to the later history, but as containing the fundamental axioms for its right interpretation. To use the Author's words, in another work; "The Catholic theologian cannot but regard the whole course of the Church in the light of a grand process of development, a continual growth from within, not the growth of a tape-worm, but of a tree, into which the mustard seed of the Apostolic age has expanded. He cannot arbitrarily choose a period here or there, and content himself with studying that, but must investigate the Church in the entirety of her outward life and historical continuity from the beginning until now, and do his best to exhibit it adequately to others; and this is the work of a lifetime."[2] We are to examine in the present treatise the sources of this development, the seed from which the tree has grown.

[1] *The Gentile and the Jew in the Courts of the Temple.* 2 vols. (Longman. 1862). When the Author has occasion to refer to the original, a reference to this Translation is here added in brackets.

[2] *Rede über Vergangenheit und Gegenwart der katholischen. Theologie.* p. 21.

1. Among its peculiar excellences not the least is, that the Author has described the Apostolic age, as far as possible, from the stand-point of a contemporary observer, and by the light of contemporary documents; excluding all reference to the traditions or usages, still more to the prepossessions, of a later period. The Church of the Apostles is the Church of the New Testament; and he accordingly traces in the Apostolic writings the moral and dogmatic aspects of Apostolic Christianity. The Second Book, which is concerned with doctrine, consists chiefly of a comment on those writings. The truths presented to our notice are, indeed, substantially identical with those we are familiar with in the creeds and definitions of the Church from Nicæa to Trent; but they come before us here, not in their ultimate development, which was the growth of centuries, and in that technical and systematic shape which the pressure of heresy ultimately compelled them to assume, but in the freshness of their first utterance, as they fell from the lips of Apostles and Evangelists, and in the devotional or hortatory form natural to Epistles addressed, for the most part, to particular individuals or communities, and called forth by special exigencies of time or place. To take one instance; the doctrine of Justification, of which our Author gives a full and luminous exposition, is handled at length in several of St. Paul's Epistles, especially in the Epistle to the Romans, and the Tridentine definitions explain and summarise his teaching. Here, it is put before us, not in the words of the Tridentine formula, but as gathered from the fuller, though, at first sight, less explicit, statements scattered through the writings of the great Apostle himself. We are thus reminded of the fundamental harmony between the language of Scripture and of Theology, and of those needs and capabilities of the human mind which are the

ground and justification, within certain limits, of doctrinal development in the Church; "the text of Scripture being addressed principally to the affections, and though definite according to the criterion of practical inference, vague and incomplete in the judgment of the intellect."[1]

2. Dr. Döllinger has not thrown this work into a controversial shape, but it has none the less obviously its bearings on Strauss's estimate of the Life of Christ[2]—lately re-published by the Author with little material alteration—and still more on Baur's conception of the history and doctrinal position of the Apostolic Church. Indeed, the favourite theory of the Tübingen school, of a threefold division of Apostolic Christianity, ranging itself under the rival banners of the three leading Apostles, St. Peter, St. Paul and St. John, is more than once directly animadverted upon; while those familiar with the destructive criticism of Germany—which has incidentally rendered important services to the cause of Truth[3]—will often recognise a special meaning in passages where it is not expressly named. Recent legislation in this country will have invested the discussion, in the Third Book and the final Appendix, on the Scriptural doctrine of Marriage and Divorce with peculiar interest for many English readers. And if there are any besides Dr. Cumming who still retain a lingering respect for the Protestant tradition about Antichrist and the "Man of Sin," they will find in the first Appendix an exhaustive account of its origin and growth.

[1] Newman's *Arians of the Fourth Century*, p. 161.

[2] Rénan's *Vie de Jésus*, which has evidently exerted an important influence on the composition of a remarkable book lately published in this country, *Ecce Homo* (Macmillan, 1866), did not appear till after the publication of the present work.

[3] It is a remarkable circumstance that, for some years past, the most distinguished Faculty of Catholic Theology in Germany has been that of Tübingen, where Möhler was reared and remained as theological Professor till 1835, and where he published, in 1832, his most important work, the *Symbolik*. Dr. Kühn, the present occupant of his Chair, is regarded as *facilé secundus* among German Catholic divines.

3. A further remark, of more general application to Dr. Döllinger's writings, will probably suggest itself to the reader. While he is a strenuous upholder of the Catholic and dogmatic principle, his manner of explaining and recommending it differs in some important respects from what is not unfrequently in the present day, to our great misfortune, treated by friend and foe alike, as the only legitimate or intelligible championship of orthodoxy. There is no need to enter on a detailed examination of those differences here, and it would be a mere impertinence to defend them.[1] But the fact deserves a passing recognition, when among those who claim to be the spokesmen and apologists of Catholicism in modern Europe there are not a few who seem to regard as little better than heretics or infidels, men (such as Döllinger and Rosmini) who have dedicated their highest intellectual energies and the toils of a lifetime to the service of the Church of God, but who shrink instinctively from a method of serving her cause which appears to them the most fatal, because least intentional, contribution to the progress of unbelief. No reader, of whatever school of thought, or however widely he may dissent from the Author's views, need fear to encounter in Dr. Döllinger a narrow dogmatist, or an adroit special pleader, or a fierce and indiscriminate partizan. If, on the one hand, he regards it as "the mark of a true theologian to dig deep, to examine with restless assiduity, and not to draw back in terror, should his investigation lead to conclusions that are unwelcome or inconsistent with preconceived notions or favourite views;" he would certainly be the last to claim for himself any infallibility, in forgetfulness of his own emphatic statement, that "it is a law, as valid for

---

[1] The reader may be referred on this subject to the Speech delivered before the Munich Congress, from which my last extract was taken.

the future as for the past, that in theology we can only through mistakes attain to truth."[1] Few, indeed, have known so well as himself how to act in the spirit of his own memorable advice at the closing of the Munich Congress of 1863; "to make a firm resolution for the future, to use none but scientific weapons in philosophical and theological inquiries; to banish from literature, as un-German [let us add un-English] and un-Catholic, all denunciation and holding up to suspicion of those who differ from us, and rather to take for our model in dealing with them the grave and truly Evangelical gentleness of Augustine and the enlightened teachers of the ancient Church."[2]

To speak now of the Translation;—it has been my aim throughout to present an idiomatic rendering of the exact *sense*, not always necessarily the exact words of the original. The following admirable remarks by one of the greatest living masters of the English language may be fitly quoted here, not in deprecation of criticism, but in explanation of the method pursued, and in extenuation of defects more or less incidental to a task the difficulty of which has been so keenly felt by a writer who has so successfully surmounted it. "It should be considered that translation in itself is, after all, but a problem, how, two languages being given, the nearest approximation may be made in the second to the expression of ideas already conveyed through the medium of the first. The problem almost starts with the assumption that something must be sacrificed, and the chief question is, what is the least sacrifice? .... Under these circumstances, perhaps, it is fair to lay down that, while every care must be taken against the introduction of new, or the omission of existing ideas in the original text, yet in

---

[1] *Verhandl. der Versammlung kathol. Gelehrt. in München*, pp. 50, 58.
[2] *Ib.* p. 133.

a book intended for general reading faithfulness may be held simply to consist in expressing in English the *sense* of the original, the actual words of the latter being viewed as *directions into* its meaning, and scholarship being necessary in order to gain the full insight which they afford; and next, that where something must be sacrificed, precision or intelligibility, it is better in a popular work to be understood by those who are not critics than to be applauded by those who are."[1] In describing what he has himself, in fact, attained, Dr. Newman has described what I have aimed at. I have always tried to keep in mind what appears to me the true idea of a translation—that it should read like an original composition, so far as is consistent with fidelity to the sense of the text. How inadequately that standard has been realised here, I am well aware; and it is only right to add that the fault, where I have failed, is not my Author's but my own. Those who are acquainted with Dr. Döllinger's writings will have observed how markedly the clear and luminous simplicity of his style contrasts with the long and involved sentences often so perplexing to us in German writers, the more so as their obscurity of language seems not unfrequently to spring from obscurity of thought. In this respect the two great leaders, on the Christian and the infidel side, Döllinger and Strauss, stand pre-eminently distinguished from the majority of their countrymen.

I need scarcely observe, what is obvious, that the office of a translator is to translate, not to criticise. The few notes I have added of my own are simply designed to explain or illustrate the text, and occasionally to point out a difference between high authorities on some question of fact. In one or two instances, where the sense assigned to

[1] Preface to *Church of the Fathers*, pp. 8, 9.

a word or passage in the Greek Testament seemed doubtful, I have added a literal translation at the bottom of the page. I have also ventured, for the greater convenience of my readers, to break up each of the three books into chapters; and have re-arranged, and considerably enlarged, the Table of Contents. The quotations from Scripture are not taken ordinarily from any English version with which the reader, Catholic or Protestant, may be familiar; Old Testament passages are translated from the Vulgate, New Testament passages from the Greek text, regard being had in doubtful cases to the rendering of the Vulgate. As a general rule, however, the Author does not quote Scripture but paraphrases it; and even in quotations he does not always follow the precise wording of the original. Where the nomenclature or arrangement of the Vulgate differs from that of the English "Authorised Version" (as in the Psalter) a reference to the latter is added in brackets, for the convenience of those who use it.

To the Translator himself it has been a privilege thus to sit, as it were, for awhile at the feet of so great and good a man. And, should the appearance of this work in an English dress lead any of our countrymen hitherto unacquainted with Dr. Döllinger's writings to study them, or any who know something of them already to seek to know more; and thus contribute, in an age of bitterness and contradiction, to make the influence of his calm, fearless wisdom, truth-loving spirit, and large-hearted charity more widely felt, the time and labour expended on the work of translation for the benefit of others will not have been spent in vain.

H. N. O.

Feast of St. Gregory the Great, 1866.

# AUTHOR'S PREFACE.

This work deals with the history of a period of only seventy years, and indeed with one event and institution only, which to far the greater number of those living at the time either remained unknown or seemed much too insignificant for it to be worth their while to trouble themselves further about the matter. Yet this mere span of time is the most important in the history of mankind. The foundation of the Christian Church closes a preparation and development of many thousand years, and is the starting point of a new order in the world. The world before Christ, and the world after Christ—that is, and ever must be, the simplest and truest division of history.

It is but the beginnings and simple form of the original Apostolic Church, self-contained like a seed-corn, and hiding its inner reality from strangers, that we are here concerned with. But these beginnings contain the powers and secrets of a culture which, embracing the whole of humanity in its universal scope, is still, after eighteen centuries, ever receiving new life and in constant growth; there is laid up in them a wealth of creative ideas, a fulness of new forms in Church, in State, in Art, in Knowledge and in Manners, which are far, indeed, from being exhausted; nay, more, which in time to come will bring to light developments in knowledge and in life that as yet we can scarcely conjecture.

The sharpest and most concentrated gaze of the naturalist, who opens and dissects a seed-corn, cannot discern the forms potentially and substantially contained in it, or suggest what it will grow into. And just so, the acutest Greek or Roman, had he scrutinised ever so carefully and impartially the young Christian communities at his side, would either have refused to predict anything of their future progress and place in history, or would have given an entirely wrong account of what actually followed, not to say exactly the reverse of the true one. Nor only so; Christians themselves were very far from appreciating the reach, and the force for the world's culture, of those spiritual and moral powers laid up in the bosom of their Society, and entrusted to their care and administration. On the other hand, nearly two thousand years of Christian history are spread before our eyes; we are in a position to embrace and measure the process of development working itself out by an internal law of necessary sequence, a continually advancing and constructive process, never, indeed, transcending the original fulness of its internal being, but far surpassing the simple outlines and primitive forms of thought and life in the Apostolic age. In the light of this long experience, where every age is a commentary to illustrate the preceding one, we can pierce more deeply into the spirit of the Apostolic Church, and exhibit all its bearings more fully than former generations could. The reader, then, will easily comprehend the scope and nature of the present work, as it floated before the Author's mind; he readily admits that it has not been adequately realised here.

MUNICH, *Sept.* 18, 1860.

# CONTENTS.

## BOOK I.—CHRIST AND THE APOSTLES.

### Chap. I.—Ministry and Teaching of Christ.

|  | PAGE |
|---|---|
| St. John Baptist, the Precursor of Christ | 1 |
| Early Life and Baptism of Christ | 2 |
| His Answer to the Messengers of the Baptist | 4 |
| His first Disciples | 5 |
| First Cleansing of Temple | 6 |
| Conversation with Nicodemus | 7 |
| Conversation with Samaritan Woman | 7 |
| His Ministry in Galilee | 8 |
| Call of the Apostles | 10 |
| His Relation to the Jews and their Authorities | 11 |
| Relation to His own Followers | 12 |
| His Miracles | 14 |
| His Prophecies | 16 |
| *His Teaching*—On the Fatherhood of God | 16 |
| On His own Person as God and Man and on the Holy Ghost | 16 |
| His Example | 19 |
| *His Teaching*—On Sin, the World, and Satan | 20 |
| On Redemption | 20 |
| On Faith and Repentance | 21 |
| On Love, True Righteousness, and Fulfilling the Law | 22 |
| On the Church, or Kingdom of God | 25 |
| On the Primacy of Peter | 28 |
| On the Plenary Powers of the Apostles | 30 |
| On the Mixture of Good and Evil in the Church | 32 |
| The Transfiguration | 33 |
| Raising of Lazarus, Entry into Jerusalem, and Second Cleansing of Temple | 33 |
| The Last Supper, and Institution of the Eucharist | 35 |
| The Agony, Trial, and Crucifixion | 37 |
| The Resurrection and Ascension | 39 |

CHAP. II.—ST. PETER AND ST. PAUL.

|  | PAGE |
|---|---|
| The First Disciples | 41 |
| Election of St. Matthias | 41 |
| Descent of Holy Ghost at Pentecost | 42 |
| St. Peter—His Preaching at Jerusalem and Imprisonment; the Infant Church | 43 |
|     Appointment of Seven Deacons; St. Stephen's Martyrdom | 46 |
|     St. Philip preaches at Samaria; St. Peter confirms there with St. John, and rebukes Simon Magus | 47 |
|     The Conversion of Cornelius | 48 |
|     Founding of the Gentile Church at Antioch; Labours of St. Barnabas there | 50 |
| St. Paul—His conversion | 50 |
|     Journeys to Arabia and Jerusalem (Martyrdom of St. James) | 52 |
|     Divine Call to the Apostolate with St. Barnabas | 55 |
|     The Dispute about the Jewish Law | 57 |
|     The Council of Jerusalem | 59 |
|     St. Peter and St. Paul at Antioch | 61 |
|     St. Paul's Journeys and Epistles (1, 2 Thess.; Gal. 1, 2 Cor.; Rom.), till his first Imprisonment at Rome | 64 |
|     His arrival and sojourn at Rome | 76 |
|     His Epistles written in Prison (Col., Eph., Philem., Philipp.) | 77 |
|     His Liberation | 78 |
|     His Pastoral Epistles | 80 |
|     His second Imprisonment at Rome | 81 |
| The Epistle to the Hebrews | 82 |
| St. Paul's Character and Teaching | 84 |
|     His Relation to the other Apostles | 90 |
| St. Peter's Epistles | 92 |
|     His Relation to the Roman Church | 94 |
|     Martyrdom of St. Peter and St. Paul at Rome | 98 |
|     Burning of Rome and Neronian Persecution | 100 |

CHAP. III.—ST. JAMES, ST. JUDE, ST. JOHN, AND THE REMAINING APOSTLES.

| | |
|---|---|
| St. James—Son of Alphæus, the Lord's Brother and Bishop of Jerusalem | 102 |
|     His Observance of the Jewish Law and Ascetic Life | 104 |
|     His Martyrdom | 105 |
|     His Epistle | 106 |
| St. Jude, and his Epistle | 107 |
| Destruction of Jerusalem, and its results for Judaism and the Church | 108 |
| St. John, Apostle and Evangelist | 111 |
|     His Epistles | 112 |
|     The Apocalypse, its Authorship and Date | 113 |
|     Contents of Apocalypse | 117 |

## CONTENTS.

|  | PAGE |
|---|---|
| *The Beginnings of Heresy*, combated in Apostolic Writings | 123 |
| Platonic Judaism | 123 |
| Various forms of Gnosticism | 125 |
| Simon Magus, the Father of Heresy | 127 |
| The Nicolaitans | 128 |
| The Balaamites | 128 |
| The Synoptic Gospels and Acts of the Apostles | 129 |
| St. John's Gospel, and its Relation to the Synoptics | 132 |
| Gospel of the Hebrews, and its Relation to St. Matthew's | 135 |
| The Remaining Apostles and Evangelists | 137 |
| Epistle of Barnabas | 137 |

### BOOK II—DOCTRINE OF THE APOSTLES.

#### CHAP. I.—SCRIPTURE AND TRADITION.

|  | |
|---|---|
| *Scripture*—Occasion and Object of the Apostolic Writings | 139 |
| Fragmentary Nature of their Doctrinal Contents | 140 |
| Varieties of Individual Character | 142 |
| Use of Greek Language | 143 |
| Old Testament inherited by Christian Church from Judaism | 144 |
| How used by Christ and the Apostles; its Inspiration | 145 |
| Septuagint Version generally followed; its Character | 147 |
| Uncanonical Writings used | 149 |
| Canon and Inspiration of New Testament | 150 |
| *Tradition*—Oral Teaching anterior to New Testament Scriptures | 152 |
| But embodied in them | 152 |
| Jewish Tradition passed into the Christian Church | 153 |
| Relation of Tradition and Scripture to Christian Belief | 155 |
| First Fixing of Tradition | 157 |
| Development of Doctrine | 158 |
| Its Continuity | 160 |

#### CHAP. II.—THE TRINITY, INCARNATION, AND REDEMPTION.

|  | |
|---|---|
| Divinity of Christ; the Logos of St. John (and of Philo) | 162 |
| The Holy Ghost; His Mission, Office, and Work | 165 |
| The Holy Trinity | 168 |
| The Kingdom of Good Angels | 168 |
| The Kingdom of Evil Angels | 170 |
| The Incarnation, Atonement, and Redemption | 172 |
| Sin and the Law, Justification and Sanctification | 176 |
| The Offer of Salvation universal, Election and Reprobation | 206 |

#### CHAP. III.—THE CHURCH AND THE SACRAMENTS,

|  | |
|---|---|
| The Church, Catholic *in extension;* composed of Jews and Gentiles, an aggressive Kingdom | 210 |

| | PAGE |
|---|---|
| The Church, Catholic in internal *comprehension*; as mustard seed, leaven, and Body of Christ | 213 |
| Holiness of Church, as worthy Bride of Christ | 214 |
| Unity; Combination of visible and invisible elements | 215 |
| Indefectibility and Infallibility | 216 |
| Threefold Office of Christ administered by the Church | 218 |
| Universal Priesthood of Christians | 220 |
| Special Priesthood, transmitted through Ordination | 222 |
| Divine Origin of all Church Offices | 223 |
| The right Manner of discharging them | 224 |
| Teaching Office; duty and unity of profession of Faith, and exclusion of every Heresy | 225 |
| Pastoral Office; relations of Freedom and Obedience in the Church | 227 |
| Office of the Church for Education and Salvation | 228 |
| Privileges of her Members | 230 |
| The Sacraments in general | 231 |
| Baptism | 232 |
| Confirmation | 233 |
| Ordination | 234 |
| Unction of the Sick | 235 |
| The Eucharist, as a Sacrament and a Sacrifice | 235 |

### CHAP. IV.—THE LAST THINGS AND THE FUTURE OF THE CHURCH AND THE WORLD

| | |
|---|---|
| Death | 246 |
| Beatitude | 246 |
| Purification | 248 |
| Hades | 249 |
| Heaven | 250 |
| The Church Visible and Invisible | 250 |
| The Disembodied Soul | 251 |
| Gehenna | 252 |
| Resurrection, and the Resurrection Body | 253 |
| Return of Christ to Judgment | 255 |
| Regeneration of the World | 255 |
| God All in All | 257 |
| Christ's Prophecies of His Second Coming; time uncertain | 257 |
| The Antichrist of St. John and St. Paul; the Abomination in the Temple; the Apostasy | 261 |

## BOOK III.—CONSTITUTION, WORSHIP, AND LIFE OF THE APOSTOLIC CHURCH.

### CHAP. I.—ORDERS AND OFFICES OF MINISTRY AND SPIRITUAL GIFTS.

| | |
|---|---|
| Relation of Apostles to the Community | 276 |
| Position of St. Peter | 278 |

|   | PAGE |
|---|---|
| First Division of Offices; Period of Extraordinary Gifts | 281 |
| Institution of the Diaconate | 285 |
| Elders or Overseers; the Presbyterate | 286 |
| The Episcopate; its gradual Development | 287 |
| St. Peter's Labours and Martyrdom at Rome | 296 |
| Succession of Bishops in Roman See | 298 |
| St. Clement of Rome | 301 |
| Ebionite Testimonies | 302 |
| Epiphanius' View of two Bishops in one See | 304 |
| Deaconesses | 306 |
| Qualifications for the Ministry | 308 |
| Method of choosing Persons for it | 310 |
| Means of supporting them | 310 |
| Spiritual Gifts; their Diversity | 312 |
| The Gift of Tongues | 314 |

CHAP. II.—ORDINANCES OF DISCIPLINE AND WORSHIP AND RELIGIOUS IDEAS.

|   |   |
|---|---|
| Baptism | 318 |
| Baptism for the Dead | 321 |
| Penance, a Divine Institution | 321 |
| Its twofold Object | 322 |
| Confession, private and public | 324 |
| Church Discipline | 325 |
| Christian Worship, connected with Jewish, but independent of it | 327 |
| Its general Character | 328 |
| The *Agape* and the Eucharist | 328 |
| Frequent assemblies for reading Scripture, Psalmody, and Intercession | 330 |
| The Jewish Sabbath | 331 |
| The Christian Sunday | 332 |
| Annual Festivals | 333 |
| Nature and frequency of Christian Prayer | 334 |
| The Lord's Prayer | 335 |
| Influence of Prayer on Life | 338 |
| Christian Aspect of Suffering and Patience | 339 |
| Christian Estimate of Martyrdom | 341 |

CHAP. III.—ECCLESIASTICAL INSTITUTIONS AND CUSTOMS.

|   |   |
|---|---|
| The Principle and Practice of Fasting | 344 |
| True and False Asceticism distinguished | 346 |
| The Law of Conscience | 347 |
| Virginity | 348 |
| Clerical Celibacy | 353 |
| Religious Vows | 357 |
| Position of Women in the Church | 358 |

|  | PAGE |
|---|---|
| Chastity | 359 |
| Christian Marriage | 360 |
| Its Indissolubility, according to Christ's teaching | 362 |

### Chap. IV.—Social and Political Relations.

|  | |
|---|---|
| Poverty and Wealth | 373 |
| Dignity of Labour | 374 |
| Property and Almsgiving | 375 |
| Love of Our Neighbour | 376 |
| Intercourse of Christians with the Heathen | 377 |
| Respect for Human Personality | 378 |
| Christian Humility | 379 |
| Christianity and Slavery | 380 |
| Christian Idea of Liberty | 381 |
| Duties of Christians towards the Civil Power | 384 |
| Position of Christians in the Roman Empire | 387 |
| Christian Equality | 389 |
| Oaths | 389 |
| Death and Burial | 390 |
| Conclusion | 391 |

Appendix I.—History of the Interpretation of 2 Thess. ii. 12, on the Man of Sin . . . . . . . . . 393
Appendix II.—Right of the Sanhedrim over Life and Death . . 420
Appendix III.—The Teaching of Christ on Marriage and Divorce . 424

# FIRST BOOK.

## CHRIST AND THE APOSTLES.

### CHAPTER I.

THE PUBLIC MINISTRY AND TEACHING OF CHRIST.

THE Jewish kingdom united under Herod was again broken up at his death, and in 779, A.U.C., the procurator, Pontius Pilate, ruled in what had become the Roman province of Judæa. The Emperor was a voluntary exile in Capreæ, where he disgraced his old age by the most shameful vices, while his favourite Sejanus made the trembling inhabitants of the capital feel how powerless and defenceless they were against the new imperial power, now turned into a murderous despotism. At this time there appeared in the remotest and south-easternmost corner of the empire, in that desolate region stretching westwards from the Dead Sea and reaching up to the mouth of the Jordan, a preacher of repentance, John, the son of the Jewish priest Zachariah.[1]

In him was renewed the old race of Prophets—extinguished for centuries—of whom he was the last and greatest. It was his office to proclaim what none of the earlier prophets could, that the Promised One and His kingdom were close at hand, and to prepare the way before Him. He was to be the last and immediate messenger of the new

[1] Luke iii. 1 sqq.

kingdom of faith, and the herald of its Founder, who was already on earth, but as yet hidden and unknown.

On him rested the zeal and the avenging fiery spirit of Elias. He denounced in the sharpest words the ruling sins of the ruling classes; nay, the whole nation seemed to him unclean, and unworthy the high destiny now awaiting it. He announced not only the setting up of Messiah's kingdom, but that a separation and a great judgment was to accompany His appearance.[1]

For six months he worked on the people by his preaching, before calling them to be baptized in the Jordan. This baptism was an outward and prophetic one. John baptized with water only; He, of whom he spoke, was first to bring in a baptism with the Spirit and with fire, bestowing higher powers.[2] For the present, men were to testify by laying aside their clothes at the water baptism their willingness to put off the old man, and by their immersion their willingness to be cleansed from moral defilement.

John waited, baptizing at the Jordan, for Him whom he preached, but as yet knew not. For he had been promised a miraculous sign from heaven to point out Him for whom he was looking.[3] A youth approached him in whom he recognised a near relative on the mother's side. This young man, Jesus, was the son of a poor woman who lived in the little Galilean town of Nazareth, and the secret of His fatherless conception had not got beyond the walls of the house at Nazareth; before the world He passed for the son of the carpenter, who had married His mother. He had first seen the light of day in a stall at Bethlehem, and a manger had been His cradle. His foster-father and His mother had fled with the Child into Egypt from the murderous attack of Herod. On His return from thence He had been brought up to His foster-father's trade, and had lived, as the "carpenter," at Nazareth, quiet and unobserved; only once, as a Boy twelve years old, when He accompanied His parents to Jerusalem at the festival, He had attracted passing notice by His premature knowledge of the Scriptures. But that had been long forgotten; His immediate neighbourhood had perceived nothing remark-

---

[1] Matt. xi. 14; iii. 7 sqq. Luke i. 17; iii. 7 sqq.
[2] Matt. iii. 11. John i. 26, 33.     [3] John i. 33.

able in Him; so far from it that, when He afterwards began to teach in public, His relations thought Him mad, and wished to lay hands on His person.[1]

The Baptist felt an immediate presentiment that this and no other was the object of universal desire, the long expected Messiah, that Greater One, whose shoe latchet, as he had already said, he himself was not worthy to unloose. He knew that this Youth had no need of his baptism, the baptism of repentance; that he, the unclean, had nothing to offer to the Holy One. He drew back and said, " It is I that have need of Thy baptism, and comest Thou to receive of me this token of sin and repentance?" But the Son of Mary insisted on being baptized by him, " for so it becometh us," He said, "to fulfil all righteousness." It was right, that is to say, for Him to put the seal on the divine mission of His forerunner, and the sacred institution of the baptism he administered, by Himself receiving it; it was right, too, for Him, whose office it was become to bear the burden of His people, that He should submit, as a son of that people, to the token of national guilt and defilement. Moreover, this baptism had in Him the meaning of a vow for the future, to lead a life entirely devoted to fulfilling the will of God.

His voluntary abasement was turned into an occasion of glory for Him—to John it was the promised sign by which he recognised the Messiah. Both of them at the baptism heard the voice from heaven, " This is My beloved Son, in whom I am well pleased;" both saw the heavens opened, and the dove descend, and rest upon Jesus.[2] Thus the baptism, and what accompanied it, were the initiation of Christ to His Messianic office. He had received His consecration as King, Prophet, and High Priest of the new kingdom through this baptism and the over-shadowing of the Holy Ghost, as under the old law the high priests were consecrated by washing with water and the unction poured on their head.[3]

St. John looked much further and deeper than the mass of the people to whom the idea of a suffering, self-sacri-

---

[1] Mark iii. 21.
[2] Matt. iii. 13 sqq. Mark i. 9—11. Luke iii. 21—23. John i. 32.
[3] Exod. xxix. 4, 7.

ficing Messiah was then a strange one, and had already pointed out Christ to his disciples as the Lamb devoted to God and destined to offer Himself for the sins of the whole world. He had already declared to the messengers of the Sanhedrim, the highest spiritual tribunal, when questioned about his office and credentials, that not he but another already standing among them was the Messiah, and by this saying he brought Christ His first disciples. Though he still continued to baptize, his office closed, properly speaking, with the baptism of Jesus. He said that Christ's influence must increase while his own decreased.[1]

Herod Antipas tetrarch of Galilee had at first paid some attention to the severe preacher of repentance who held up his sins as in a mirror before him, but when the prophet denounced his incestuous connection with Herodias, his own niece and his brother's wife, he imprisoned him in the castle of Machar, partly to protect him from Herodias's anger, partly fearing his influence over an excitable people.[2]

The news of the attitude and works of Christ which reached the Baptist in prison, roused his suspicions. The worker of so many miraculous cures seemed to him more like one of the prophets and a herald of the coming kingdom than one introducing it as himself its king. He had not expected this reserved and unobtrusive line, but rather an immediate display of Messianic dignity and judicial power, such as he had himself threatened the terrified Jews with as close at hand. He therefore sent two of his disciples to Jesus to ask, "Art thou the Messiah that was to come, or must we wait for another?" This question clearly implied the wish and expectation that, on being thus pressed, Jesus would openly assume his Messianic title and office, for the consolation of all eagerly looking for the moment.

The messengers found Him surrounded by those miraculously healed, and He referred them to His works; they were to tell their master what they had seen and heard, how by Christ's power the blind saw, the lame walked, the deaf heard, the lepers were cleansed, the dead raised, the poor—whether spiritually or from bodily want—had the

---

[1] John i. 19—29; iii. 30.
[2] Matt. xiv. 1 sqq. Mark vi. 14—29. Luke iii. 19, 20.

Gospel preached to them. He could not but remember that this fulfilled the Messianic promises of the old Prophets; and thus his question received the most emphatic reply.[1]

Christ was led to give a solemn attestation to the dignity and greatness of John before the people, from observing that, though they had eagerly sought him out as a prophet, they now esteemed him lightly when in prison, and made small account of his person, his mission, and his words. He therefore declared him the greatest among the prophets or those born of women, and more than a prophet, for he had proclaimed what they could not—the actual presence of the Promised One and the kingdom of God. He knew more of the Messiah, and had drawn a fuller and clearer picture of Him, than the old Prophets and the whole people after them.[1]

Christ had found His first disciples among the followers of the Baptist. By his testimony Andrew and another—by whom the fourth Evangelist means himself—had joined Him. Andrew brought his brother Simon, in whom Jesus recognised at the first glance that type of character which specially fitted him to become the rock of the Church, and He therefore gave him the prophetic name of Rock, Peter or Cephas. On the way towards Galilee, a fourth, named Philip, was called by Jesus to follow Him, coming, like Andrew and Simon, from Bethsaida. Then came Nathanael or Bartholomew, who, when Philip first told him that he had found the true Messiah in the carpenter's son of Nazareth, inquired doubtfully if any good could come out of a town so ill-reputed of as Nazareth? But this doubt vanished when Jesus showed knowledge of an important moment in his life which he thought only known to himself. Jesus promised him and the rest that they should see greater things than these; in His school and service they would be allowed to gaze into the open heavens, the depth of the divine counsels; they would witness His constant intercourse with God, as it were through angels ascending and descending upon Him, and those higher powers which He had brought with Him as a

---

[1] Isa. xxxv. 4—6, xvi. 1. Matt. xi. 1—6. Luke vii. 18—23.
[2] Matt. xi. 7 sqq.

heavenly gift to the earth. Of those powers He gave the first proof at the marriage feast in Cana of Galilee, which He attended with His mother and disciples, by turning water into wine.[1]

During His stay in Judæa, when He went with His disciples to Jerusalem for the Passover of 780, A.U.C., Jesus performed an act, which in itself any zealot for the law might have undertaken, but which in Him was a proclamation at once of His high dignity and His Messiahship;—He cleansed His Father's house, using His right as the Son of Him whose the temple was to drive out the buyers and sellers. He thus declared Himself to be the promised Messiah, who should reform and cleanse the temple. It was not from men recognising His dignity and claim that He was not opposed, but from surprise at the suddenness and boldness of the procedure, and still more from something about His presence, which overawed them, as when afterwards the majesty of His nature broke forth from its accustomed veil, it disarmed the soldiers sent to seize Him, and cast them to the ground.[2]

This act was a reflection on the priesthood who had before favoured this disorder in the temple, and thus, while it reminded the disciples of that devouring zeal for the House of God spoken of in the Messianic psalm, the Pharisees required Him to justify it by a miracle, showing Him to be either a prophet divinely commissioned, or the Messiah. He replied, "Destroy this temple, and in three days I will raise it up again," referring to His own body as the true temple, where the Godhead dwelt, and thus giving the sign at once of a double prophecy, of His death and resurrection. But they, who of course could not understand His meaning, asked contemptuously whether He would rear in three days an edifice which took forty-six years to build?[3]

The frequent cures which Christ then wrought in Jerusalem led to a belief in many that He was either a true prophet, or the expected Messiah himself; but He saw through the untrustworthiness of this merely external half-

---

[1] John i. 35—51; ii 1 sqq.
[2] John ii. 14 sqq.; vii. 46; xviii. 6. Mal. iii. 1—3.
[3] Ps. lxviii. 12 (lxix. 9, E. V.). John ii. 18—20.

belief produced by miracles, and confided neither His person nor His secret doctrine to such men, knowing that those who had a deeper and more living faith would follow after Him, and never rest till received among His disciples. Nicodemus, a member of the Sanhedrim, came to visit Him by night, in order to gain a deeper insight into His mission and real teaching. This interview, in which Nicodemus wanted to ascertain whether Jesus was the Messiah, showed how hard it was for a Pharisee, influenced by the Jewish notions then prevalent, even to understand the great truths on which His teaching was based.

He declared to the astonished Jewish Rabbi, "No mortal has yet ascended into heaven to search out the counsels of God; I alone was there, though appearing now as Son of Man; from thence I came down upon earth to be a man among men, and as the surest evidence of it I proclaim to them what I there saw, the divine plan of salvation. Though now on earth in human form, I am in abiding communion with God, and have also a more than earthly being. In his pitying love for man God has sent Me, His Only-Begotten, to be lifted up as a public spectacle on the gibbet, and thereby to become a source of redemption to all who rely in faith on this divine means of healing, as of old the brazen serpent was lifted up in the wilderness, that those bitten of serpents might look on it in faith and be healed.[1] From My death flows the power of that baptism of water and the Spirit whereby men shall be born again to a new life, and received into the kingdom of God I am come to found."

When Jesus saw that His influence with the people had drawn on Him the suspicious watchfulness of the Pharisee party, He resolved, late in the autumn of 780, to withdraw into Galilee, where He would be less exposed to their observation and the snares they laid for Him. His way led through Samaria, which the strict zealots of the Law used to avoid, out of hatred for the Samaritans, by taking a circuitous route through Peræa. At Sichem He got into conversation with a Samaritan woman, and, while maintaining the just claim of the Jewish worship against the arbitrarily devised Samaritan rite, took occasion to point out

[1] Numb. xxi. 9.

the temporary character of both forms, and the speedy introduction of a new and no longer local worship in their stead. "You Samaritans," He said, "honour God by sacrifices you have invented or adopted for yourselves, but which for you, who reject the Prophets and the whole course of that increasing revelation which points entirely to the Messiah, have no force or inward meaning. But we in Judæa, from whom comes salvation by the Messiah, celebrate the typical sacrifices of the Law on Sion. This quarrel, however, between Gerizim and Sion will soon have an end, for the time is come when the true worshippers of God will serve Him, not with the legal and typical ceremonies belonging to this or that place or temple, not with the blood of goats and lambs, but with a sacrifice suited to the spiritual nature of God, itself spirit and truth, and accompanied by the purely spiritual acts of prayer, adoration, love, and hope,—the one mystical unbloody sacrifice of the New Covenant, to be offered everywhere throughout the whole extent of the Church."[1]

Thus Jesus did in Samaria what He had not yet done in Jerusalem or Judæa or Galilee; He told the woman plainly that He was the Messiah, and having sent for the inhabitants of Sichem devoted two days to confirming their belief in Him. This He could do safely among a people with whom the Jews held no intercourse, where no Scribes and Pharisees were spies on Him, and where there was no fear lest a recognition of His claims should kindle an insurrection against the Roman Government.

From Samaria He went into Galilee, and was better received there than before, for the Galileans returned from Jerusalem had already spread the fame of His deeds and teaching. Thenceforward He spent great part of His public life in this fertile and populous region. In Jerusalem and Judæa a hostile feeling against Him had already grown up among the influential classes and leaders of the people, and especially since He healed a sick man on the Sabbath during the Feast of Tabernacles, and defended Himself as being the Son of God, they had sought after His life as a Sabbath-breaker and blasphemer. He, therefore, preferred to live and work in Galilee rather than where the Pharisees

[1] John iv. 1 sqq.

and lawyers were strongest. There He dwelt among Gentiles in that part of Israel most slighted and abandoned to itself. It was a saying of the Pharisees that no prophet could come out of Galilee. But as He wished to fulfil all righteousness as a Jew, and to show Himself a loyal and strictly conscientious son of His nation, He always came for a short time to Jerusalem on the high festivals.[1]

He fixed His abode in the little town of Capernaum, separating Himself finally from His family in the distant Nazareth, and thence made His journeys, passing gradually through all Galilee and teaching everywhere in the synagogues. But the neighbourhood of the Sea of Tiberias was His most frequent resort. He avoided the more important towns, such as Tiberias, where Herod the tetrarch lived, Sephoris, Gadara and the fortified Giskala, only teaching and working in the smaller towns and villages, true to His plan of not courting danger before the time, and avoiding an uproar which would be sooner excited among the masses in the larger towns. He shunned the interior of the country where the really Jewish population was, seeking rather the frontier mountains and remote regions, partly for undisturbed prayer, partly to avoid a populace craving for miracles and a political Messiah, who at one time wanted to proclaim Him king, while at another—so sudden was their revulsion of feeling—they were ready to surrender Him as a criminal.[2]

His public ministry lasted two years and some months. Certain women, some of them relatives, accompanied Him on His journeys besides the Twelve. The larger body of seventy disciples seem only now and then to have been with Him, and at other times despatched on the business He gave them. Out of loving condescension to the capacities of the poor in spirit and spiritual infants, He clothed his teaching in proverbs and parables and examples drawn from nature and human life. He used the Old Testament and appealed to prevalent popular belief, but He handled the sacred books as a Lord and Master who had learnt from no human teacher and received the impress of no school or party, but who was exalted above such limitations and brought to those books a light and clearness de-

---

[1] John iv. 43 sqq.; v. 1—18; vii. 52.   [2] Matt. iv. 13. John vi. 15.

rived from His own higher wisdom. He showed Himself fully and in all respects a true and genuine member of the Jewish nation and Church. As He received in childhood the national covenant sign of circumcision, so from the opening of His public ministry He observed the ritual law. He kept the Sabbath, though refusing to be bound by the later glosses put upon the rule. In the Sermon on the Mount He insisted on a stricter righteousness in observing the moral law than was found in the letter of the commandment or the prevalent opinions and practice of the Jews, but the works of this law were to grow spontaneously, like the fruits of a good tree, out of the pure root of a sanctified will wholly given up to God. The righteousness of His kingdom was to be the reverse of that dark, self-pleasing, often hypocritical righteousness of works which He denounced so sharply in the Pharisees. Full well did He foresee that the majority of His people at last would reject Him and His teaching. They took offence at His humble birth, His intercourse with publicans and sinners, and His not sharing the common hatred of the Roman Government and the desire to get rid of it. The Scribes and Pharisees saw in Him a dangerous rival who would injure their credit and influence with the people. His whole life was such that He could challenge even His enemies to accuse Him of one sin or error. The spies and watchers, who at last followed Him everywhere, could discover nothing which cast the slightest shadow on Him. But He taught and worked from the first with the full consciousness that He was rousing or augmenting the hatred of men, and that He must give up His life as a sacrifice to it.[1]

He announced during his first journeys that the kingdom of heaven was at hand, and His work on earth was to found it. He now first called to a lifelong and undivided activity in his service those four fishermen who had previously joined him, Andrew and Simon, John and James. Thomas and Nathanael now again joined Him. From the crowd of disciples and adherents who gradually collected round Him Jesus chose out an inner circle of men with whom to hold a more confidential intercourse, and who should form, as it were, His own family. These Twelve, all of them Galilean

---

[1] Matt. xiii. 55; ix. 11. John viii. 46.

fishermen, peasants, and publicans, were to be the foundation stones of His future Church, the twelve patriarchs of the new Israel corresponding to the twelve tribes. He had prepared for the great work of choosing them by a night of solitary prayer. He named them Apostles, that is—Sent. Six of them had attended Him from the beginning of His ministry, the brothers Peter and Andrew, James and John the sons of Zebedee, Philip and Bartholomew, or Nathanael. To these were now added Thomas (Didymus), and Matthew (Levi) the publican, James and Jude, or Thaddeus, sons of Alpheus and cousins of Jesus, Simon, whose surname, Zelotes, shows that he had once belonged to the party of zealots against foreign rule, and lastly, Judas Iscariot, who seems to have been the only one not a Galilean.[1]

The poor carpenter's Son and His Galilean fishermen and publicans—these were the powers for working the greatest revolution the world had yet seen. From the time He began His public teaching He could have no safe home anywhere. When He appeared as a teacher in the synagogue at His native Nazareth, the enraged inhabitants wanted to throw Him down from the steep rock their town stands on, and He only escaped by a miracle. So He travelled from town to town, from village to village, in Galilee, attended by His chosen band of disciples and by women who ministered of their means to the wants of the Lord and His followers. The people everywhere regarded His appearance as extraordinary and significant, and connected Him as a forerunner with the expected Messiah. Some thought John the Baptist, whom Herod Antipas had beheaded, was risen again, others that Elias or one of the old prophets had returned to life. While these carnal expectations and seditious ideas were popularly connected with the Messiah, Jesus could have no wish to be recognised as such before His Passion, and forbade His disciples to speak of it.[2]

He recognised the Scribes and Pharisees of his day as sitting in Moses' seat and having lawful authority to teach; but the whole condition of the people impressed Him with their being untaught, neglected, given over to false teachers, sheep without a shepherd. His compassion for them made

[1] Matt. iv. 18—22. Mark i. 16—20; iii. 14—19. Luke vi. 13—16.
[2] Luke iv. 28—30; viii. 1—3. Matt. xvi. 14—20.

Him send the Apostles on a preliminary mission to go two and two through the country, with power to heal diseases, to preach everywhere the tidings of His coming, and of the near approach of God's kingdom. At another time He sent out a larger body of disciples trained by Himself, the Seventy, to go into all the places He meant to visit and prepare the people for His appearance and teaching.[1]

More than once His life was endangered by a popular tumult. The Pharisees watched and spied after Him everywhere. But His presence inspired a kind of awe which long kept them from laying hands on Him. Once the Sanhedrim sent their servants to seize and bring Him before them, but they were disarmed by the power of His words, and could not fulfil their commission. Scribes were sent from Jerusalem with orders to follow and watch Him. The Pharisees scattered over Galilee and Judæa used their influence everywhere with the people to counteract His. There were those amongst the priests and scribes in the capital who judged Him worthy of death as a breaker of the law, and urged His being quietly made away with. He seemed to them to display a studied contempt of their maxims; He taught men that their righteousness must be other and better than that of the Pharisees, outward and fictitious with its show of scrupulous obedience. They saw in Him a dangerous enemy who threatened and undermined their whole influence and credit with the people. He had not studied in their school, paid no regard to their traditional glosses on the Law, and ventured sometimes to put them to shame before the people by His striking answers. He knew men's hearts, and often replied more to their thoughts than their words, which made them the more indignant at seeing their inward nakedness so cuttingly exposed.[2]

He had much to bear patiently even from His Apostles, with their want of insight, their national prejudices, their carnal expectations and wishes, and their consequently always misconceiving His office. What He said about His future kingdom, eating and drinking His flesh and blood, and His return to the Father, was a pure enigma to them.

---

[1] Matt. xxiii. 2; ix. 36. Luke x. 1 sqq.
[2] John v., vii., viii., xi. Matt. v., xxi., xxiii., xxvi.

At last they got so far that Peter could express in his own name and theirs the firm belief that He alone was the Messiah, the Son of God. Thenceforth He tried to familiarize them with the thought that they would lose Him through a violent death endured in the discharge of His office. He no longer busied himself chiefly with the miracle-loving crowds who were always thronging and pressing upon Him, but always fickle, carried about, as it were, by opposite winds, at one time from the influence of the Pharisees, at another from the impression produced by His own presence and acts. From this time He withdrew Himself more from public view, and only wrought miraculous cures on special occasions. He occupied Himself, on the other hand, all the more carefully with His disciples; His chief work now was to prepare them for their office, to train them for His representatives and successors in the mission He had undertaken.

So infinitely was Christ exalted above all human teachers, that in Him word and deed, the idea and its realisation, were always one. What He taught referred principally to Himself, His mission, His work; the mere fact of His appearance among men was the most eloquent sermon; His very presence, His acts, His sufferings, and His death, were the living, energizing commentary on His teaching, and its most superabundant confirmation. He put forth no detailed doctrine about God, His being, His attributes and tokens; but He offered Himself directly as the Image of the Father, so that whoever knew Him knew the Father. He spoke little about God being merciful toward men, and loving them as a father loves his children; but He presented Himself to them as the living embodiment of mercy, in whose person God had humbled Himself to man's estate. When He said, " All power is given to Me in heaven and upon earth,"[1] it was but a description of His own acts, for where He worked, the blind saw, the lame walked, and the dead were raised. In that fulness of power which He exercised on earth, as the mighty Ruler of nature and of natural forces, men were able and were bound to recognise that the Supreme Lord and Lawgiver of all had appeared in His Person. He not only, like the Baptist, exhorted men

[1] John xii. 45; xiv. 7—10. Matt xxviii. 18.

to repentance, He not only spoke of the righteousness of God, and His displeasure against sin; but He took also on Himself the greatest of all penances, He showed through His sufferings and His voluntary death what an offering the holiness of God and the sinfulness of men required. What gave to His teaching about the powerlessness of death, the indestructibility of life, and the future resurrection of man its convincing power, was the fact of His appearing among men Himself for forty days as the Conqueror of death and the First-fruits of the resurrection.

Thus, then, His works, like His words, had a stamp peculiarly their own. To work miracles was His natural, His normal state; He showed Himself in His miracles as the Lord and Ruler of nature. He commanded the winds and they were still; He walked upon the waves; He attested His power over nature and His human kindliness, by turning water into wine; He fed thousands with a few loaves and fishes; He freed those possessed with devils; He healed multitudes of the sick. Even in the earlier period of His ministry the fame of His wonderful healings had spread through Galilee, and the sick streamed together to Him.[1] He fanned into a new flame the spark of life when already quenched, and raised the daughter of Jairus, the youth of Nain, His friend Lazarus. In remoter regions, also, He performed healings, as on the servant at Capernaum, the son of the royal officer there, and the daughter of the Canaanitish woman. Thus was every step of His way marked by deeds of mercy, not wrought through human means, through gold or goods, but by the divine powers He possessed in Himself to form, to uphold, to heal. He was busied till late into the night with healing the sick, who were brought to Him in great numbers.[2] 'It seemed as if an atmosphere of health and blessing breathed around Him. Diseases of the body, sins and errors of the mind, fled at His approach. A healing virtue streamed from the very touch of His garment, as indeed what took place in His own case, His transfiguration, and at last His resurrection and ascension, showed that His very bodily nature was permeated and ruled by the divine. He could likewise endue His disciples with the gift of working miracles.

[1] Matt. iv. 24.    [2] Luke iv. 40. Mark ii. 4.

He usually wrought His cures by the laying on of hands, for in the hand the whole power of man's will is concentrated; but often the effect followed immediately on a word from Him, a command, or a prayer. The miracles by which He freely encroached on the life of nature were almost always of help, and not of punishment; one only was destructive, the curse of the barren fig-tree, to give a typical sign of His judicial power over mankind.

These miracles often took place before a crowd of spectators, and before men of the most hostile disposition, opponents who had only one way of evading their force, by objecting that they were wrought through the aid of diabolical powers.[1] Some were actually submitted to judicial examination.[2] He was wont to call on the Father to prosper a miracle He was just about to work[3], and to thank Him, before it was wrought, for the result confidently anticipated; to the Father He bade those healed to offer their thanksgiving.[4] To those "works" he referred both the Jews and His own disciples as proofs of His divine mission;[5] they bore a greater witness to Him than that of the Baptist,[6] for they were to publish His mission before the eyes of those who had no ears to hear His message, and to prepare the way for its acceptance; help and redemption in the natural order were to point to that redemption of the spirit which was His proper office. He freed some men from the mediate or immediate consequences of sin in the bodily life, that all might recognise His power and will to free them from its natural consequences, the perversion of the will and the darkening of the intellect. He wrought many miracles with the professed object that the Son of God might gain honour by them, and His dignity and mission be acknowledged. And if in some cases He forbade His miracles being made known,[7] this was partly because the time had not yet come when their publication could take place with advantage, partly because He wished to avoid a popular tumult, which would at once have assumed a political character, and led to His being proclaimed as king; and, further, that a quiet demeanour in those healed

---

[1] Luke xi. 15.   [2] John xi. 18 sqq.   [3] Mark vi. 41. John xi. 41 sqq.
[4] Mark v. 19. Luke xvii. 18.   [5] John x. 25 sqq.
[6] John v. 36.   [7] Mark vii. 36.

might confirm the influence of the teaching they had received. The only condition He required for healing men was faith, a trustful surrender of the will to His mighty power; whence it is said that He *could* not work many miracles where He found no faith. A carnal hankering after miracles He always repulsed. He withdrew from those who, out of mere idle curiosity, expected or desired a sign from heaven, a wonderful spectacle to gaze at.[1]

To His power over external nature was joined His prophetic power of gazing into the future. He foretold the destruction of Jerusalem, the fall of the temple, and the permanent dispersion of the Jews among all nations.[2] So, too, He declared that His being lifted up to die on the cross would draw men to Him with a powerful attraction; and that God's children among both Jews and Gentiles would be united, under His Shepherd's staff, in one fold. He foretold that before the end, the Gospel of the kingdom of God would be preached to all peoples in the whole world, and that His Church, at first, like the grain of mustard seed, small and invisible, would grow in process of time to a mighty tree, overshadowing all things.[3]

Christ was the first who distinctly and clearly taught men to look upon God as a Father, as One in whom is united the whole fulness of what is called love. In the Old Testament, indeed, God was represented as a Father, but chiefly in relation to the people He had chosen out and educated; and the contemporaries of Jesus, if they declared themselves to be the children of God, had before their eyes simply the fact of their belonging to the chosen people. But He taught men to acknowledge God as a Father, and themselves as His children, because they were designed to attain a moral and spiritual likeness to this Father of theirs through love, and thereby to inherit His kingdom; because the love which God has from eternity for His Son is also extended to those who believe in Him.[4]

While He represented Himself as the Lord of the angel world, He declared this earth to be the field where He sowed His seed, and on which He was to reap His harvest.

---

[1] Matt. xii. 38 sqq. Luke xxiii. 8, 9.   Matt. xxiv. 2 sqq. Luke xix. 41—4.
[3] John x. 16; xii. 32. Matt. xxiv. 14; xiii. 31, 32.
[4] Matt. v. 48. John viii. 41; xvii. 26.

The future history of mankind was to be measured by His departure and His return, His second coming was to be the end of the course of this world. Just as, in the Old Testament, the bond which united the Jewish nation to God was represented under the marriage relation, so Christ described Himself as the Bridegroom, but at the same time Lord and Lawgiver, of all mankind who are called to believe in Him. He wished men to regard themselves as His servants, stewards and subjects, and so much the more, since He would one day be their Judge, and, as the Father had given Him to have life in Himself, would, by His almighty voice call the dead to rise out of their graves.[1]

He claimed the same devotion, generally, for Himself as for the Father. All were to honour the Son as they honoured the Father, for He is the Fountain of life to all who believe in Him, the Vine of which all believers are living and fruitful branches, and possesses in Himself an everlasting, unbeginning life, exalted above all change and possibility of decay. From heaven had He come down, for in heaven He had dwelt of old with the Father before He appeared on earth; yea, before the world was, had the Father loved Him and given to Him the full enjoyment of glory.[2] He said to His enemies, "Before Abraham was, I am," to indicate the unchangeableness of His divine life, which excluded all notion of beginning or of ceasing to be.[3] By the Father's gift He had an independent fountain of life in Himself, from which, henceforth, all men were to obtain life.[4] To Him, who was the Son of the Father in a sense belonging only to Himself, the Father had entrusted the whole work of human salvation, so that no man could come to the Father but through Him, and to Him soon would all power in heaven and on earth be given. The Father made Him the all-wise Judge of the world, so that those He pardoned would rise to the resurrection of life, and those He rejected to the resurrection of judgment.[5] He and the Father were one, not only in will, but by the most intimate union of mutual life in each other, so that the Father dwelt in Him, and whoever had seen Him had

---
[1] Matt. xiii., xxiv., xxv. 1—30. Luke xix. 11—27.
[2] John v. 23; xx. 1—8; xvi. 28; xvii. 5, 24.
[3] John viii. 56.  [4] John v. 26.
[5] Matt. xi. 27. Luke x. 22. John xvi. 6; v. 27 sqq.

seen the Father. His Person was the mirror of the Godhead, the majesty and the condescending love of the divine nature shone out of His words and works.[1]

On the last evening which He spent with His disciples, He revealed to them that there was a Third Person in the Godhead, the Holy Ghost. This Spirit, the Spirit of truth, who proceeds from the Father, and will testify of Jesus, He meant to send them.[2] As the Son was sent by the Father because He derives from the Father the origin of His life and being, so would the Holy Ghost be sent by both the Son and the Father, because He derives His origin from Both, and is therefore called the Spirit of the Father and the Son. Thus the Son is the Fountain, not only of finite and created, but also of infinite life, and so far like in being to the Father. But it was only after His resurrection, and at the close of His earthly pilgrimage, that Jesus spoke out fully the threefold personality of God, when He bade His disciples baptize in the Name of the Father, and the Son, and the Holy Ghost, and thereby taught them that Each of those Three is of divine nature, and of like substance, Each the source of salvation to men.[3]

At the same time, He named Himself with peculiar emphasis and predilection the "Son of Man." This expression He had borrowed from the prophet Daniel, who after the fall of the four empires saw One, like the Son of Man, coming with the clouds of heaven, and brought before the Ancient of Days, and dominion, glory, and an everlasting kingdom were given Him.[4] Therefore, in that solemn and decisive moment when the High Priest adjured Him to say if He were the Son of God, while replying that He was, He called Himself also the "Son of Man," who would hereafter appear, sitting on the right hand of God, and coming in the clouds of heaven.[5] He meant, by His frequent use of this name, to make them understand, that He was the true, ideal, long-expected Man, the Second Adam, the Flower and Centre-point of Humanity; and finally, He loved the name because, while intimating His dignity, it yet concealed it from the unthinking multitude.

As true, genuine, perfect Man, like in all points to His

---

[1] John xiv. 7—10.    [2] John xv. 26; xvi. 7.    [3] Matt. xxviii. 19.
[4] Dan. vii. 13, 14. Cf. Matt. xxvi. 64.    [5] Matt. xxvi. 63, 64.

earthly brothers, He was subject in every respect to the needs, the mental emotions, the dispositions of soul which belong to humanity. Those means and exercises which man requires to assure the mastery of spirit over matter, and to cherish communion of soul with God, He, too, made use of. He prepared by a forty days' fast for entering on His ministry, and overcame the temptations of the devil which then assailed Him;[1] He prayed much, and for long at a time; even when working miracles He prayed for the power, and ascribed the performance to God's having heard His prayer.[2] He felt a holy indignation at seeing the temple desecrated by buyers and sellers; He was bound to one of His disciples in a tender friendship; He felt a deep sympathy with the sorrows of others, which moved Him even to tears; He was constrained to shed tears as He foresaw the fate of Jerusalem. He wept over the closed grave of Lazarus, over the grave opened for His city. The foresight of His impending sufferings filled Him with bitter anguish.[3] He felt, as a man capable of suffering, that horror at the approach of a painful death which is natural to flesh and blood. Thus He took on Himself in the completest sense the nature of man, pure and simple, only uncorrupted by sin. Never had the idea of man, as it existed in the Divine Mind, been so absolutely realised. This form is held up for all times as the ideal, unattainable indeed, but which all must strive after, as the one and highest specimen of humanity.

Above all, He was not only the Teacher but the Model of love, such love as men had never known before, not sensuous and self-seeking, but a pure love exalted above all carnal impulses, and all selfishness, (*Charity*). There were some, indeed, for whom He felt a more special love, as St. John and Lazarus; but His affection had nothing of instinct or mere habit about it, it was one with His holiness, it was a virtue. What was outward, accidental, self-interested, had no place in it; it was the love which pierces through all veils and bars of flesh or sense, and unites the immortal, soul to soul; that love, in a word, which as He Himself said, gave its life for its friends in proof of its irre-

---

[1] Matt. iv. 1 sqq. Luke iv. 1 sqq.    [2] Mark vii. 34. John xi. 41 sqq.
[3] John xi. 35; xii. 27. Luke xix. 41; xii. 50.

sistible force, and treating sinners as already friends, died for them.¹

It was not only, however, by His appearance and whole course of life that Jesus reminded men how far gone they were from the original type of manhood; He spoke it out shortly and energetically in the form of doctrine. He declared man to be a creature of carnal mind naturally, and morally imperfect, one in whose very nature sinful inclination was ingrained.² That sinfulness which is dominant and overpowering in the whole race of man, that collective common life of sin, depending on spiritual infection and evil example, which then ruled supreme in the earthly order and corrupted it to the heart's core—He summed up under the name of "the world," as contradistinguished from the believers chosen out of it.³ But, then, there is also, as He said, a Prince of this world, that fallen ruler of spirits, that murderer and liar from the beginning, who has estranged himself from divine truth, and set himself in chronic antagonism to it, that first author of man's sin, the murderous enemy of his spiritual and natural life, through whom death came into the world; namely, Satan.⁴ He is the lord of a wide and graduated kingdom, with his angels, whom he uses as instruments.⁵ He is an all too powerful ruler, through the universal sinfulness, which, up to that time, had displayed itself in the order of the world: and Christ pointed out that to break his dominion, to judge the Prince of this world, was a work directly belonging to Himself as the Son of Man.⁶

The Baptist had called Jesus the Lamb of God that taketh away the sins of the world. He meant to say that He was the anti-type of that Paschal Lamb whose blood was sprinkled on the door-posts of the houses of the Israelites, so that the first-born who dwelt there might be spared; that He was that gentle patient Lamb, appointed for the slaughter-house, who, after the prophecy of Isaiah, was to take on Himself the sins of His people.⁷ He Himself, however, up to the close of His public ministry, only spoke in hints and figuratively of His mission as Redeemer. He

---

¹ John xv. 13.   ² John iii. 6.   ³ Matt. xviii. 7. John vii. 7; viii. 23.
⁴ John xii. 31; viii. 44.   ⁵ Matt. xxv. 41; xii. 24—26.
⁶ John xvi. 11; xii. 31.   ⁷ Exod. xii. 13. Isa. liii. 7.

said He was the Physician of the spiritually sick, come to seek and to save that which was lost, not come to be ministered unto but Himself to minister.[1] He spoke of the Son of Man having to be lifted up, as the brazen serpent was lifted up by Moses.[2] Later again He described Himself as the good Shepherd, who giveth His life for the sheep.[3] For the first time, just before His Transfiguration, and for the last time, soon after it, on His last journey to Jerusalem, He said plainly that He would give His life a ransom for many.[4] After His entrance into Jerusalem He spoke again enigmatically and prophetically about the corn of wheat which must first be laid in the ground and die, that it may bear much fruit, adding that if He were lifted up from the earth He would draw all men to Him, Gentile and Jew alike. And by this He signified that His death, that act of self-sacrificing love, would exert the greatest power of attraction over men, and His deepest abasement turn to His highest honour and glorification; that from all nations, and all over the world, those disposed to receive Him would gather themselves to Him, and be united as one fold under one Shepherd.[5] Yet it was only on the eve of His death, at the institution of the Eucharist, that He first spoke, quite clearly and openly, in a way every one could understand, of the necessity and significance of His death. Then it was that He declared He had devoted Himself as the new Paschal Lamb, and that by His blood, which he would shed for the world, the new Covenant, a covenant of perfect reconciliation and most intimate union with God, would be sealed and dedicated, and that so His death was a sacrifice offered for the sins of men, His blood the means to secure the remission of their sins.[6]

Jesus required faith and repentance as conditions of sharing the benefits of His kingdom. Men were to believe on Him, that is, to acknowledge His Person and dignity with lively joy, to receive and appropriate His words as the purest utterance of divine truth, to trust Him as the Surety

---

[1] Matt. ix. 12; xviii. 11; xx. 28. Luke xix. 10.
[2] John iii. 14.   [3] John x. 11.
[4] Matt. xvi. 21; xvii. 22; xx. 18, 28. Luke xxiv. 46. John x. 17.
[5] John xii. 24, 32; x. 16.
[6] Matt. xxvi. 26 sqq. Luke xxii. 19, 20. John xvii. 1 sqq.

and Mediator of divine grace through whom they had access to God. But this belief God must work in us; through Him we were to be made partakers of all divine graces, and especially was it His will that eternal life should be the reward of faith in His Son. Without repentance, however, this faith is neither possible nor availing to salvation. Those alone are real believers who unite a humble confession of their own guilt and strong hatred of sin, as the cause of their alienation from God, with a conviction of the inadequacy of their own moral powers, and come to Christ in earnest self-abasement, weary and heavy laden, with a lively yearning to be delivered, hungering and thirsting after righteousness, and with hearts full of love to Him and of forgiveness and mercy towards men. To such only He offered pardon, justification, and restoration to the state of God's children lost by sin.[1]

The commandment found in Deuteronomy, to love God above all, Christ declared to be the first and great commandment, and by this love He meant the fixing our whole mind, soul, and will upon God as the Embodiment and Archetype of perfection, and the Highest Good, who first loved us, and is the Giver of all happiness. He did not represent this as like other commandments, but as controlling them, because, where this love to God, this unconditional surrender of the whole will and all its powers to Him preponderates, every other love is sanctified and ennobled, and this becomes the guiding and determining principle of the whole will, conduct, and feelings. Christ placed on a par with this the command to love our neighbour, for he who really loves God loves his brother also for God's sake, not more, or less, or otherwise than he loves himself. This love, as He elsewhere taught, sees a neighbour in every man as such, without regard to national or social differences, and therefore does as it would be done by.[2]

He insisted strongly, that all true love to Him must be shown in keeping His commandments, and that all who would be His disciples, and share His promised blessings,

---

[1] Matt. iv. 17; v. 3—7; vi. 12; xi. 28. Mark i. 15; xi. 25, 26. John iii. 16; vi. 29; xi. 25, 26. Luke vii. 47; xv., xviii. 13, 14.
[2] Deut. vi. 5. Matt. xxii. 37, 38; vii. 12. Luke x. 29 sqq.

must follow Him in self-denial and love to God and man. That He called a better righteousness than the Scribes and Pharisees had, not taking shelter, as was then frequent, under the letter of the law in its narrowest sense, as accordant with selfish interests, but fulfilling the commandment in its inward meaning and fullest extent. He further declared that those who believed on Him must love God and Himself above all, and must loosen the firmest and dearest ties of blood and relationship, if hindering the singleness of their love to Him. But He assured His followers of strength to fulfil this command, to make the hard soft and the difficult easy to them, and give them rest and refreshment. He pronounced them happy, and bade them rejoice that their names were written in heaven.[1]

For Jesus pointed to another world as their real home and only true life, His Father's house, wherein He reveals His essential glory, and where are many mansions, "everlasting habitations," whither He was going to prepare a place for them, that they might share His glory.[2]

At the beginning of His ministry He opposed the notion of His meaning to overthrow the old Covenant, and weaken or abolish the Law and the Prophets. He said He was come not to remove or destroy, but to fulfil Law and Prophets, command and promise, word and ordinance, the combined ingredients of the old Covenant. He would fulfil the law by making it spiritual, being the first to fulfil the whole circle of its requirements in His holy and spotless life, and by committing to His Church those higher powers which would enable all believers to keep it perfectly. The promises would be realised, partly in His own Person, partly in the Church He founded, so that what was promised would be visibly accomplished. He told them that the law comprehended in word and deed would last till the end of the present order of the world, adding afterwards that His own word would outlast it, and be eternal.[3]

He, therefore, submitted to the Jewish law and institutions. He attended the synagogues on the Sabbath, and went, like other Jews, to Jerusalem on the high festivals. He ate the Paschal lamb with His disciples, and com-

---
[1] John xiv. 15; viii. 12; xii. 26. Matt. v.; x. 37; xi. 28—30. Luke ix. 23.
[2] John xiv. 2; xvii. 24. Luke xvi. 9. [3] Matt. v. 17, 18; xxiv. 35.

manded the lepers He cleansed to go and show themselves to the priests, and offer the gift commanded in the Law.[1] He pointed out to the Pharisees that the Law was a simple, organic, coherent whole, not a stray collection of single, disconnected precepts, and that the real scope and aim of its contents was the love of God and of our neighbour.[2] He reproached them with having made void the divine law through their arbitrary and new-fangled rules, notwithstanding all their outward parade of zeal for it, and referred in proof of it to their decisions about the Corban, or gifts to the sanctuary, which, according to Rabbinical teaching, freed the son from all duty to his parents.[3]

In the same way He set aside the strict Pharisaic regulations about the observance of the Sabbath, by laying down the simple principle, that the Sabbath was made for man, and not man for the Sabbath, and by declaring that He, the Son of Man, was Lord also of the Sabbath, and had power to destroy or to spiritualise it, as His Church has since done through the plenary power given by Him.[4] He declared plainly that He was higher and holier than the temple,[5] though He Himself honoured it, and wished to see it honoured, and therefore zealously cleansed it from being desecrated by merchandise. He confirmed the high rank of the Jews as chosen out by God before all peoples of the earth; He said that of them was salvation, and theirs was the place appointed for it; they knew what they worshipped, while the Samaritans knew not, for their worship was grounded on no divine ordinance. Yet the Jewish worship would undergo a great revolution; the hour was already come when God would show that His service was confined within no local limits, and that He would no more be exclusively worshipped on Gerizim, the holy mountain of Samaria, or on Moriah, and in the sanctuary of Jerusalem, but without any such limits of place, as a Spirit, in spirit and in truth.[6]

While Christ affirmed in His Sermon on the Mount that it was His office to fulfil the law completely, He also opposed His, "I say unto you," not only to the false glosses

---

[1] Matt. viii. 4. Luke xvii. 14.
[2] Matt. xxii. 36 sqq. Luke x. 25 sqq. Mark xii. 28 sqq.    [3] Matt. xv. 3 sqq.
[4] Mark ii. 27, 28.    [5] Matt. xii. 6.    [6] John iv. 21—24.

of the Pharisees, but to the express verbal statements of the old Law with all the dignity of a lawgiver, and the authority of a messenger sent from God.[1] He thereby showed what He meant by fulfilling the law, and that, as with the form of divine worship, so with the moral law itself, the time was come for breaking through the narrow bounds of nationality, for divesting the law, which had been given as a civil and religious bond, and an ordinance for holding together and ruling the nations, of its juridical character, so that for the sanction of judicial and police regulations might be substituted the higher and more universal rule of the holiness and righteousness of God. Whatever was unsuited to continue, as being a temporary condescension on God's part to the childhood of a people composed of sinful and carnally-minded men, Jesus abolished, and in so doing fulfilled and perfected the law, by making it correspond as an utterance of the divine will with the stage of development on which the world was entering. Thus He declared that the love of one's neighbour, which was enjoined by the old Law, was no longer limited to one's countrymen, but must include one's enemies, in the widest extent of the term,—the enemies of one's nation, and all the Heathen.

It was impossible for Him to announce openly and distinctly to the great multitude who listened to His words, that He had come to tear asunder the narrow limitations of the Jewish religious community, and to found a world-kingdom. He, therefore, never used the word Church (*Ecclesia*) in His public addresses. Only before His disciples, and only latterly before them—for even they very imperfectly comprehended the matter—did He speak more clearly about His Church. What He almost always spoke of, and that in a way often very enigmatical to His hearers, was the kingdom of God, or kingdom of heaven, which was close at hand, or actually come, confining Himself to the expression used previously by the Prophets, and adopted by the Baptist.[2] He said He was come "to preach the Gospel of the Kingdom;"[3] and this kingdom formed now the basis of His teaching. He said the time of the Old Testament economy, the Law and the Prophets, lasted till

[1] Matt. v. 27 sqq.   [2] Dan. ii. 24. Matt. iii. 2.   [3] Luke iv. 43.

John the Baptist; since then the time of the kingdom of God was begun, and every one pressed into it by the force of his belief.¹ St. John himself had but pointed to the kingdom about to appear, as one standing outside it. But as most of His hearers only understood by God's kingdom a kingdom of earthly power and worldly greatness, Christ soon began to utter His doctrine about the kingdom of heaven, but only in the form of parables, which served the double object of concealing the truth they would only have misused from the carnally-minded Jews, and of presenting to His disciples expressive images to convey a doctrine, even they could not fully understand till afterwards. Hence the parables of the field, of the public feast or great marriage supper, of the virgins, and of the labourers in the vineyard, in which He taught them about His Church.² Under the veil of those similes He could say, what if openly spoken would hardly have been endured, that He had other sheep besides those of His own nation to come from the East and from the West; that He would have men invited, as from the streets, without distinction; and finally, that the Gospel would be preached in the whole world.³

By the kingdom of heaven, or of God, He understood generally that divine order of things which He had come to establish. It was a kingdom, not of this world, though in the world, to which, as a kingdom revolted from God and ruled by Satan, His own stood directly opposed.⁴ And so He answered the question of the Pharisees, when the kingdom of God would come, that it was already in the midst of them; its first germs and beginnings, that is, were already present in the persons of Himself and His disciples.⁵ But He also predicted that a great part of His people would have no share in this kingdom, and gave them to understand in parables that the kingdom of God would no longer be entrusted to His people, as such, but other nations would be called to take their place.⁶

This kingdom, moreover, embraces in the words of Jesus heaven and earth, and the whole course of human history

---

¹ Matt. xi. 12. Luke xvi. 16.
² Matt. xiii. 24 sqq.; xx. 1—16; xxii. 2, 14; xxv. 1—13. Luke xx. 9—16.
³ Matt. viii. 11—13; xxiv. 14. Luke xiv. 15—24. John x. 16.
⁴ John xviii. 36; xii. 31; xiv. 30; xvi 11, 33. Mark xiii. 10.
⁵ Luke xvii. 20, 21.     ⁶ Matt. xxi. 33 sqq.

from His time onwards. He represented the growth and spread of His kingdom under the images of the seed developing till it bore fruit an hundredfold, and of the little mustard seed growing up into a lofty over-shadowing tree. A flock of sheep with its shepherd, whose voice it knows,—a family with its master, its men servants and women servants, a town, a nation, a kingdom, whose king He was Himself,—these were the images by which He exhibited the organic coherence of His Church, the power and authority belonging in this His kingdom to Himself and His representatives.[1] The ministry He meant to establish in His Church, its duties and privileges, He described under the simile of a gardener, a fisherman and a shepherd. The ministers of His Church were to be His stewards, set over the other servants; and He promised to His Apostles and their successors a special gift for the right administration of their office.[2] When there was a strife among His disciples as to which of them should be the greatest in His kingdom, He taught them that those who would be greatest and first in the Church, must be the humblest, the willing servants of the rest.[3] Closely connected with this was the solemn announcement at the last farewell supper, that in return for the loyalty with which they had hitherto followed and served Him, He left them for an inheritance His kingdom, the Church, as the Father had given it to Him. In that kingdom they were to celebrate continually a holy feast at His table, sitting on twelve thrones, to judge as kings the tribes of Israel, to decide on their acceptance or rejection, and to exercise the priestly and royal power conferred upon them. It was prophesied of Christ that He should sit upon the throne of David. So, too, were they, as His representatives, to sit upon thrones in His kingdom. Their power and authority was to be equal to His who appointed them. "He that receiveth you receiveth Me, and he that receiveth Me receiveth Him that sent Me."[4]

Christ wished to verify in the widest sense the saying that "He was come not to destroy the law, but to fulfil it." His Church had been conceived and hitherto preserved in the womb of the Jewish State and Church, as the embryo

---
[1] Matt. xiii. 3—8.  Mark iv. 26—29.  John x. 1—16.  Matt. v. 14.  John xviii. 37.
[2] Luke xii. 42 sqq.; xvi. 1 sqq.   [3] Luke xxii. 25—30.   [4] Matt. x. 40.

of the future Church of the New Covenant. The time was not yet come for the daughter to be fully delivered. He Himself attested the authority of the Synagogue in Jerusalem before the people, saying that they sat on Moses' seat, having lawful authority to teach and rule the Church. "What they teach do, but do not after their works." He knew the Synagogue would soon condemn Him to death as a blasphemer, but its authority was not yet abrogated, nor the moment for renouncing all obedience to it come; the chair of Moses was still standing. When the time came, that tribunal would be transplanted into His Church. For He had already arranged for the establishment of an authority, flowing from and supplementing His own, commensurate with that universal Church, which would supersede a national Synagogue. In Him were combined the characters of Prophet, Priest, and King; by Him the Chair of Moses would be changed into the Chair of the Apostles as the eternal centre and point of unity in His Church.

He spent two years in carefully training His disciples for the office to be laid upon them, and for that end sent them out to preach, and gave them power to heal the sick. He said that He sent them as sheep among wolves, and foretold their lot among Jews and Gentiles in their future ministry. He tried to inspire them with sure confidence in God, whose Spirit would put the right word into their mouths in critical moments, when they stood before the rulers of the world.[1]

At the turning point, when His ministry was closing and His sufferings about to begin, Peter made confession that Jesus Christ was the Son of the living God. For this he was repaid by four closely allied promises of future power and pre-eminence in the Church. First; he should be the Rock whereon Christ would build it; secondly, the Church built on him should never fail; thirdly, Christ would give him the keys of His kingdom or Church; fourthly, what he bound or loosed on earth would be bound or loosed in heaven.[2]

Peter alone here spoke; he was not commissioned by the

---

[1] Matt. x. 16 sqq.
[2] Matt. xvi. 18, 19. The Greek translator of the Aramaic text was obliged to use πέτρος and πέτρα: in the original Cephas stood in each place without change of gender. "Thou art stone, and on this stone," &c., Cephas being both name and title.

other apostles, and stood foremost among them through the faith given him by his heavenly Father. That faith, firm as a rock, fitted him to be the foundation of the Church, which Christ had compared to a house. Now first Simon Bar Jona perceived why the Lord originally named him Cephas, the rock. And thus Christ, like St. Paul afterwards, has combined the two similes of a home, and of family life. He wills to build His house, the imperishable Church, never to be overcome by the powers of death, on the believing and confessing Simon, who again is to be its foundation in the same sense as all the Apostles are according to St. Paul or St. John, though excelling all others in his speciality as chief foundation stone.[1] And in this house built upon him, Peter is to have the duties and powers, not of the master of the house—that Christ is, and remains —but of the steward. These were promised him under the symbol of the keys, whereby he is enabled to open the treasuries of the house, to guard the spiritual stores and possessions of the Church, doctrine and means of grace.

What is here first, according to St. Matthew's account, only *promised* to Peter, was after the resurrection bestowed upon him, at the third appearance of Jesus, to three apostles and three disciples only besides himself. As He had before assured him of his future exaltation on the evidence of his divinely inspired strength of faith, so now He taught him by a question, thrice solemnly repeated, that he must also surpass the other apostles in love to Him, and be a Rockman in love as in faith, giving him thereby an opportunity of retracting his three denials, and adding the charge thrice repeated; "Feed my lambs; feed my sheep." Thereby a chief shepherd was given to the whole Church, including the Apostles, and Peter was placed in the same relation as Christ had been before to the collective body of believers, as the good shepherd who cares for his sheep and gives himself for them out of love, not like a hireling for his own advantage.[2]

When Christ prophesied to St. Peter, just before the beginning of His Passion, that on the same night he would deny Him thrice, He also assured him that, by virtue of a special prayer offered for him to the Father, his weakness

[1] Eph. ii. 19, 20. Apoc. xxi. 14.   [2] John xxi. 15—17; x. 12.

in faith should not sink as low as complete apostasy, or determinate unbelief. And he exhorted him, when recovered from his own fall, to strengthen his brethren, the apostles and other disciples, in their wavering faith; to sustain them in their discouragement, and console them with the hope of His sure and speedy resurrection.[1]

St. Peter is so uniformly marked out in the Gospels, and placed in such immediate proximity to Jesus, as the shadow accompanying Him; the one who possessed His confidence and mediated between Him and the other disciples, that in this respect no other apostle comes near him. Where only the apostles are enumerated or mentioned he always stands first. All the critical moments in the life of Jesus are placed in a certain relation to him, and to him alone. To him individually Jesus ordered His resurrection to be made known; the New Testament narrative records only his failings and humiliations, not those of the other apostles; while it mentions the strength of his faith and love, and the dignity conferred in return for it, it carefully marks the depth of his fall. There is no other to whose education and training Christ devoted so much labour. Much of grave import he communicated only to him directly, as his future martyrdom, and his elevation to the highest dignity. And again, in his death he was to be like his Lord.

It was only in common with the other Apostles that St. Peter received the remaining powers left by Christ to His Church: viz., the power to bind and loose in a manner availing in heaven as on earth, which means to forbid and command; and finally, after the resurrection, the communication of the Spirit with power to remit and retain. Three prerogatives were left to him. He was chosen before all other Apostles, and in a peculiar sense, as the foundation of the Church; to him alone were the keys given in Christ's house; he alone was to have power as shepherd of the whole flock.

For two years Jesus had laboured with unwearied love in moulding the obstinate and uncongenial material of human nature in those twelve men chosen out as the instruments for founding His Kingdom, the pillars, teachers, and rulers of His Church. But the actual mission, the

[1] Luke xxii. 31, 32.

conferring of the powers allotted to them, was His last concern, the decisive act which He deferred till after His resurrection, till the close of His earthly course and the moment of His departure. The powers and commissions which He now gave and left to the apostles collectively He introduced in the most solemn manner and with weighty words, clenching them with promises which only He could give who had before His eyes the most distant future of His Church. In His prayer as High Priest He had said to the Father, "As Thou hast sent Me into the world, so have I sent them also into the world."[1] Now He spoke out more distinctly the similarity of this twofold mission, and renewed His declaration that the mission given Him by the Father devolved upon them. He spoke of His own fulness of power; He, to whom was given all power in heaven and on earth, gave full power to them to carry into all the world the preaching of His doctrine, to offer to all nations baptism and entrance into His Kingdom, on the condition of keeping His commandments.[2] He gave them at the same time a judicial authority over men, with power to remit or retain sins. They were to teach everywhere, to baptize, to found Churches, to bind and loose, to remit and retain sins. That whoever would not hear the Church must be treated as a publican and sinner and shut out of it, He had already declared.[3] And for these ministries He promised them His abiding presence and powerful aid "always, to the end of the world,"—a promise which reached beyond their earthly life and applied to their heirs and successors. He promised them the Spirit of truth to preserve them from all doctrinal error, and lead them into all the truth, to conduct them and those that came after them continually into a deeper appreciation of the whole connection of His teaching, and to guide the organic development of that teaching in His Church.[4] Thus had He given its Magna Charta to His Church. It was to be built on a rock; indestructible permanence, indefectibility, uniform teaching and administration of the means of grace were to belong to it securely for all time, through the assistance of Christ raised to the right hand of the Father,

[1] John xvii. 18.   [2] Matt. xxviii. 18—20.  Mark xvi. 15.  John xx. 21—23.
[3] Matt. xviii. 17.        [4] John xvi. 13.

and of the Holy Ghost sent by Him to abide and dwell in the Church. Henceforth no one could separate himself from the Church without separating himself from Christ, for the Church had the assurance of His perpetual presence.

He meant to remain the true, though invisible, King of His Church; the Apostles were to be only His representatives in His absence; their power was not their own but derived from Him, and they were responsible to Him for their administration of it. "Ye shall not be called Master, or Rabbi, or Father; One is your Master, even Christ; One is your Father, He who is in Heaven; but ye are all brethren."[1] They were only to be His instruments, and He would govern His Kingdom in every age, as the One Lord and High Priest, according to His own good pleasure. And, therefore, the powers and privileges given to them did not die with them, for they had never belonged to them as their own.

He had foreseen that there would be no lack of scandals in His Church, that the evil would be constantly mixed with the good, and must often be patiently borne with by the ecclesiastical authorities, and had accordingly instructed His disciples that it was the will of God it should be so in the Church. He pointed out to them in parables, how in the field of His Church the tares would spring up among the wheat, and how both must be left to grow together till the harvest, when the Lord Himself would undertake a full sifting and separation, because else very often, from the close intertwining of wheat and tares together, the one would be rooted up with the other, and more harm than good follow from a premature separation of the bad from the good in His Church.[2]

Every day brought matters nearer and nearer to a final crisis. The position which Jesus had assumed among His people made only two solutions possible, either the conversion of the whole nation to belief in Him as the true Messiah, or His condemnation and execution as a blasphemer, falsely claiming to be the promised Messiah. The temper and attitude of the most influential and powerful part of the nation, the Priests and Pharisees, placed it

---

[1] Matt. xxiii. 8—10.  [2] Matt. xiii. 24—30.

beyond a doubt that the latter alternative would be chosen, unless He withdrew Himself from it. The rulers of the Sanhedrim had already agreed that all who received Him openly as the Messiah should be put under ban and cast out of the Synagogue.[1] But at that time, "His hour was not yet come;" His earthly work was not yet finished; and accordingly, when He came to Jerusalem for the festivals, He always left the capital soon afterwards, and withdrew from those who wanted to use violence to imprison Him.

He allowed those three disciples who had all along enjoyed His closer intimacy and more particular confidence, Peter, James, and John,—the same who were afterwards present at the bitterest of all His sufferings, the Agony in Gethsemane,—to witness His Transfiguration, which took place on a mountain, shortly before His last journey to Jerusalem. There His countenance shone like the brightness of the sun, and His raiment became glittering white, as though suffused with light, and to the two earthly witnesses were added two heavenly ones, the two greatest Prophets of the Old Law, who spoke with Him of His impending death, while a voice from above, as before at His baptism, gave solemn attestation to His Messianic dignity. For Him this Transfiguration was a dedication to His approaching sufferings, an anticipation of the glory to come after; for His disciples, who were seized with fear, and fell into a deep sleep as drunken men at the sight, crushed under the feeling of their weakness in presence of the majesty of a Teacher hitherto only seen in the form of a servant, the spectacle was a visible sign of the unity of principle between the Old and New Dispensation, and of the capability of the human body for being glorified.[2]

When, after staying and working a long while in Peræa, Jesus raised Lazarus from the dead at Bethany, before many witnesses, the miracle created a great sensation among the people. The Sanhedrim, on the motion of the High Priest, Caiaphas, came to a further resolution that He should be seized and brought to trial as a deceiver of the people.[3] Then for the third time He foretold His Passion, now close at hand, to the disciples, who were still con-

---

[1] John ix. 22.   [2] Matt. xvii. 1 sqq. Luke ix. 28—36. Mark ix. 2—9.
[3] John xi. 47- 53.

stantly dreaming of the immediate setting up of a Jewish Messianic kingdom in all earthly splendour, and thereupon made His public entry into Jerusalem.[1] For, now that the hour was come, there was no longer any ground for a prudential holding back. He entered the capital, saluted as Son of David and Messiah by the Hosannahs of the multitude coming to the Easter festival.[2] In vain the Pharisees urged Him to forbid the vociferous homage of the people. He now taught and healed openly in the temple, which He yet once more cleansed of buyers and sellers, not without symbolic reference to His own mission of purifying Israel itself.[3] In the temple, so strong a feeling of horror came over Him at the thought of His Passion, now close at hand, that He first prayed to be "delivered from this hour;" but immediately afterwards, in the triumphant consciousness of His lofty destiny, He made a complete offering of His will to that of the Father, and only prayed that the Father would glorify His name through His suffering of death. On this, a voice from heaven, which sounded like thunder, proclaimed that the Father accepted the offering of His Son, and would make it serve for His glorification.[4] By day He worked in the capital, spending every night till Thursday in the neighbouring village of Bethany, for Jerusalem was full of strangers, and He wished, too, to withdraw from His enemies. His public teaching closed with the woes pronounced upon the hypocritical guides of the people, upon the city and its inhabitants, whom He had so often and so constantly sought in vain to draw to Himself, and upon the temple devoted to speedy destruction, coupled with the prophecy that they would now fill up the measure of their fathers' sins, and bring the whole burden of their blood guiltiness on themselves and on their people.[5]

---

[1] Matt. xx. 17—19. Mark x. 32—34.
[2] Matt. xxi. 1—11. Mark xi. 1—10. Luke xix. 29—40. John xii. 12—19.
[3] Matt. xxi. 12—16. Mark xi. 15—17. Luke xix. 45, 46. [Cf. supr. p. 6. The reader will of course remember that the cleansing of the temple is placed by St. John at the commencement, by the synoptic Gospels at the conclusion of our Lord's public ministry. Whether He performed the act twice, as Dr. Döllinger here implies; or whether all the Evangelists refer to the same event, though in a different connection, as others suppose; and which date we are in the latter case to adopt, are questions disputed among modern critics in Germany. There seem strong reasons for preferring the opinion adopted by our Author.—TR.]
[4] John xii. 27—30.          [5] Matt. xxiii. 13 sqq.

On the day before the Paschal feast,[1] at a supper held with His disciples, Jesus performed, in token of loving humility, an act which only slaves or the lowest of the company were wont to perform;—He washed His disciples' feet. He now foretold that one of them, and that one Judas, would betray Him, that Peter would deny Him, and that on the night He was taken prisoner, all would forsake Him. On Thursday He ate the Passover with the Twelve, and in doing so ordained the Sacrament of His Body and Blood, which was to take its place in His Church.[2] He wished to open the eyes of His disciples to the necessity of His death as a free-will offering for them and for the whole human race; He wished to associate them with Himself in the communion of His death, and at the same to give them the highest proof of His love.[3] He had pointed out the necessity of laying down His life for the redemption of the world on the actual day of the Passover, and had therefore taken care that His entry into Jerusalem should fall on the very day when, according to the ordinance of Moses, the Paschal lamb was chosen. The communion of the Paschal lamb, as the characteristic offering of the Old Law, had formed the foundation and centre of the whole sacrificial system of the Old Testament, and now the time was come when He was about actually to offer up His life as a Victim, in place of the Paschal Sacrifice and all the others connected with it, and also to establish in His Church an abiding sacrificial mystery, exalted high above the mere fragmentary and shadowy system of animal sacrifices.

Since the Fall, men had become incapable of offering to God of themselves the right and proper sacrifice, viz., their own persons. Since their persons had been defiled by sin, and a separation brought about between God and man, all

---

[1] John xiii. 1 sqq. πρὸ δὲ τῆς ἑορτῆς τοῦ πάσχα. [The author here supposes the supper described by St. John (ch. xiii.—xvii.), to have taken place on the Wednesday evening, and to be distinct from that mentioned in the synoptic Gospels at which the Eucharist was instituted. But this method of reconciliation creates more difficulties than it removes. And it is quite clear, however the difference be explained, that St. John assumes the feast of the Passover to have commenced on the *Friday* evening, the day of the crucifixion (John xviii. 28), while the synoptic Gospels make our Lord eat it on the *Thursday* evening, the day of the Last Supper. (Matt. xxvi. 17, 19; Mark xiv. 12, 16; Luke xxii. 7, 13). For patristic explanations of the difficulty, see Wordsworth's *Gr. Test.*, and for modern explanations Alford's *Gr. Test.* on Matt. xxvi. 17, and John xviii. 28.—Tr.]

[2] Matt. xxvi. 26—28. Mark xiv. 22—24. Luke xxii. 19, 20. 1 Cor. xi. 23—25.
[3] John xiii. 1 sqq.

sacrifices were essentially insufficient, they "could not cleanse the conscience;"[1] they only pointed to the offering of a future sacrifice, from which they derived their light, their strength, and their meaning. But now He, in whom was realised the ideal of humanity, was to accomplish the one great sacrifice, all-sufficient for time and eternity, by freely giving His life for the whole race of whom He had made Himself a member: and, by at once disclosing and repairing the defectiveness of all previous sacrifices, to put His own in their place. As the Passover was a feast of life and deliverance to the people, a meal at which the people exhibited and ratified their communion with God and rejoiced in it; so was this transfigured Passover to be to them the sacrificial feast of the New Testament, wherein the faithful, by feeding on His Body, would be brought into substantial communion with the great Sacrifice, would receive remission of their sins, be cleansed and sanctified, and united as members to the body of which Christ is the Head, and thus be able to offer themselves as a sacrifice to their reconciled God.

When He blessed the Bread and Wine, His eye was fixed on His approaching death upon the Cross on the morrow, and on the whole course of earthly time, and the development of the human race. His priesthood, which He began with His assumption of human nature, was not to terminate and be laid aside with one act of sacrifice once offered; He meant to exercise it continually in the world above before the Father, and here below through human representatives, who under the veil of bread and wine were to offer Himself, His glorified Body, His spiritualised Blood, and with Him those who fed upon Him, as the uninterrupted offering of the Church constantly realising itself yet ever one and the same.

What He was in no position to testify to the world on the following day, when the soldiers laid their rude hands upon Him and bound Him—that His death was really an offering, a free-will surrender of Himself—that He testified now; "What I give you to eat is My Body which is broken for you, what ye drink is My Blood which I shed for you." Thus were the altars of His Church for the future to be

[1] Heb. ix. 9.

one with the Cross, the same Body, the same Sacrifice here as there, one great and single offering, not repeated, but extended in time to be co-extensive with the duration of His Church; this was the one oblation truly worthy of the divine Majesty, and the solemn worship of the New Covenant, which would not be less but far more real in His Church than that preparatory and typical system of sacrifices and ceremonies administered hitherto by the sons of Aaron.

So did He attain in the simplest manner the double object of giving to His Church a continual sacrifice and a centre-point of common worship, and at the same time of giving to believers a food which would convey to the whole man, body and soul, the benediction and the sanctifying power of His own Humanity and plant in them the germs of future immortality. This was done by His elevating bread and wine, as representing the most elementary ingredients of man's bodily food, by a substantial change, but in a sphere removed from all cognisance of sense, to the dignity of His glorified Body and Blood, penetrated with the powers of His divine life. Thus the Eucharist was the fulfilment of what He had begun in the Incarnation, and thus He provided for the incorporation of His Church in all future generations, so that it might continually be able to appear before God as an acceptable sacrifice, being inseparably united to Himself.

While Jesus was awaiting the moment of His seizure in the Garden of Gethsemane, an overpowering feeling of agony and dereliction came over Him. He felt, as no other man has felt it, the bitterness of death as the wages of sin, in the consciousness that the sins of the whole world were laid upon Him as the Sin-offering. His horror of death was in Him, above all, a horror of sin; and His human nature, sinking under this feeling, required the support of an angel sent to strengthen Him. A passing wish came over Him that, if it were possible, this chalice of agony might pass from Him; this greatest of all crimes be spared His people, and a pain be removed in which none could even distantly resemble Him. But the next instant, the clear returning consciousness of the irrevocable counsel of God triumphed in Him.[1]

[1] Matt. xxvi. 36—44. Mark xiv. 32—39. Luke xxii. 39—44.

After the mental struggle in Gethsemane, He was betrayed by Judas with a kiss, and seized by the soldiers sent from the Supreme Council. Before surrendering Himself into their hands to be bound, He made them feel His greatness, and they sank to the earth before the majesty that shone out of Him.[1] The way the Sanhedrim dealt with Him was short and simple. When the depositions of the witnesses about Him did not agree together, as the Law required, the High Priest, Caiaphas, challenged Him to declare on oath whether He was the Son of God. His calm reply, that He was, left to His judges only the alternative of either acknowledging their belief in His being what He professed to be, or condemning Him to death as a blasphemer. They did not hesitate to do the latter, and, to express abhorrence at the blasphemy he had heard, the High Priest rent his garments.[2] But, to avoid taking the odium of His execution on themselves with the people who were still greatly attached to Him, and to procure His crucifixion instead of the stoning ordered by the Law, they impeached Him as guilty of high treason before the Roman procurator, Pilate, forgetting that they had already sentenced Him to death themselves.[3] His answers to Pilate impressed him with a conviction of his innocence, but when the Jews pressed their accusation, Pilate tried to relieve himself from a disagreeable demand by sending Jesus as a Galilean to His native prince, Herod Antipas, who was then in Jerusalem. The wanton Herod, who saw in Christ only an obstinate but harmless enthusiast, not a subject for death but for contempt and mockery, sent Him back to Pilate, who sought in vain to deliver Him by the custom of the feast which required the release of one condemned criminal, for the people, at the Pharisees' instigation, preferred the robber and murderer, Barabbas. Then Pilate sentenced Him to be scourged and crucified, while declaring that He was an innocent and righteous man. Even his last attempt to rouse the compassion of the people by bringing Jesus forward scourged and bleeding, and clothed in mockery in

---

[1] John xviii. 4—9.
[2] Matt. xxvi. 59—66. Mark xiv. 55—64. Luke xxii. 66—71.
[3] John xviii. 31. [See Appendix II. on the power of life and death in the Sanhedrim.—TR.]

the insignia of royalty, was a failure. Intimidated at the threatening reference made by the Priests to the Emperor, designating Christ as a political conspirator, he ordered the sentence of crucifixion to be executed.

The Cross of the Lord was set up on Calvary between two malefactors. While the guard were dividing His garments among them, the priests and people and even one of those crucified with Him mocking and blaspheming Him, He prayed that they might be forgiven, because they knew not what they did. He had rejected the stupifying potion offered Him, that He might die with full and clear consciousness His death of sacrifice. All His disciples had left Him and were fled; Peter had thrice denied Him; only His favourite John stood beneath the Cross. As a reward, the care of the Lord's Mother was entrusted to him. At that supreme moment of almost intolerable suffering, when His whole soul was as it were overpowered, and for an instant crushed, the cry of agony broke from Him at being forsaken of God, in the words of that Psalm which predicts His Passion and which He thus made His own.[1] Then He testified that His work of redemption was finished, and died, commending His Spirit into the hands of His Father, on Friday, the 15th Nisan, or 7th April, 783, A.U.C., the year 30 of the Christian era. The extraordinary phenomena of nature at His death, the darkening of the sun, and the earthquake, were indications that the whole of nature was drawn into passionate sympathy with the death of its Lord, and the rending of the veil of the temple that concealed the Most Holy place showed that by the Redeemer's death the wall of partition was thrown down, and the entrance to the Most Holy, the kingdom of God on earth, laid open to all mankind.

The corpse, which for greater security had been pierced with a lance, was guarded by a watch of soldiers in its sealed grave. But He had declared that, as He laid down His life of His own free will, so He would take it again by His own power,[2] and would only remain three days among the dead. This coming forth from the grave was to be the great and decisive sign given even to those who would not

---

[1] Matt. xxvii. 46. Cf. Ps. xxi. 1; (xxii. 1. E.V.)
[2] John x. 17, 18.

believe the other evidences of His power.¹ On the day of His resurrection He appeared to Mary Magdalene, to Peter, to two disciples on the way to Emmaus, and late at night to the assembled apostles. So little could they at first take in the fact and trust their senses, notwithstanding His predictions, that the Lord was obliged to convince them of the reality of His body come forth from the grave, by letting them touch it, and by eating some food. Eight days later, when Thomas, who had before been away, and was still unbelieving, was present, He appeared again among them, and this time the apostle convinced himself and acknowledged his Lord and his God.² But it was not in Jerusalem, or by His enemies, that He chose to be seen; in Galilee, where He had carried on His ministry and found the greatest number of followers, it was His will to appear to this multitude of believers, and at the same time to prepare His apostles for the discharge of their ministry after His departure. By His command they went directly after Easter from Jerusalem into Galilee, and here He appeared first to seven of them on the lake of Tiberias, where Peter was declared to be the Head of His Church.³ More than five hundred disciples saw Him there and heard His words.⁴ Shortly before Pentecost, the apostles returned to Jerusalem, and were there also strengthened and taught by repeated visits of Jesus. His appearance, His form, His demeanour convinced them that He had indeed a true body and was no unsubstantial spirit, but that His Body was no longer subject to the limits and conditions of earthly and corporeal existence, that it was glorified. In a room with closed doors, He stood suddenly in the midst of them; sometimes His form was known to them; sometimes it was strange and could not be recognised. Finally, on a Thursday, the fortieth day after His resurrection, He appeared for the last time to His Apostles on the Mount of Olives, near Bethany; He commanded them to tarry in Jerusalem for the outpouring of the Holy Ghost; and then, while a cloud withdrew Him from their gaze, He ascended and returned to the glory of the Father.⁵

---

[1] Matt. xii. 38—40. [2] Luke xxiv. John xx; xxi. 12—14.
[3] Matt. xxviii. 10, 16. John xxi. [4] 1 Cor. xv. 6.
[5] Mark xvi. 19. Luke xxiv. 50, 51. Acts i. 4—9.

## CHAPTER II.

### ST. PETER AND ST. PAUL.

When Jesus departed from the earth, He left only small and scanty beginnings of a new Church. He had appeared in Galilee to five hundred brethren after His resurrection; one hundred and twenty disciples, including the Apostles, were now assembled in Jerusalem. It was natural that those only should believe on Him who had seen and heard Him since His resurrection, and these amounted to at most about six hundred. This was the hidden mustard seed, and nothing could be unlikelier in all human estimation, than that out of this little gathering of peasants and craftsmen, fishers and publicans, among whom there was not even one man of cultivation, who were alike unacquainted with the world and unknown by it, should grow that mighty tree overshadowing the world, a Church embracing millions, and from nations the most widely separated.

The first thing to be done was to fill up the number of the Apostolic College. Christ had appointed twelve Apostles, according to the original number of the family from which the people of Israel were descended. Before the outpouring of the Holy Ghost this number had to be restored, and the vacancy caused by the fall of Judas to be filled, and that by a man who had been an eyewitness and disciple of Jesus during the whole time of His earthly ministry. This was done under St. Peter's direction in an assembly of the little community. Christ Himself was to decide by the lot between the two proposed, for He alone could confer the apostolic office. Thus Matthias became one of the Twelve.

On the feast of Pentecost, in the year 783, ten days after the Ascension of Jesus, the feast when the Jews brought bread and meal into the temple as first fruits of the harvest to consecrate to Jehovah, the outpouring of the Holy Ghost took place. The first fruits of the new harvest of the Spirit, the disciples, were assembled in a house. Long ago had the Prophets promised a great and mighty outpouring of the divine Spirit upon whole communities, upon every sex and age, and that God would write His law upon their heart and mind, and give them a new heart and a new spirit.[1] Christ Himself had repeatedly promised this outpouring to His disciples, adding, however, that it could not take place till after His departure from the earth, that His human form and appearance to which they had too carnal an attachment must be removed from them, before their hearts would be a fitting soil to receive the gifts of the Spirit.[2] Thus, then, came that outpouring, the baptism of the Spirit and of fire, which St. John the Baptist had already announced as the work of Christ. As fire pierces through to the marrow while water remains on the surface, so was the Spirit from on high of whom that fire is a type to penetrate the Apostles and disciples to their very inmost soul, and fill them with His gifts; He was, as Jesus said, to clothe them with power from on high.[3] The sound of a mighty wind and the appearance of tongues of flame, symbols of the Spirit and of the new gift of tongues, over the heads of the assemblage, including the women who were present, announced the communication of the Holy Ghost. Its first result was a state of ecstasy, in which the possessed spoke in foreign languages, hitherto unknown to them, especially the Greek and Persian, and in various dialects, and were understood by the Hellenistic Jews from the dispersion, who had come to Jerusalem for the feast, and by the Proselytes, while the native Israelites, who did not know these languages, mocked them, thinking they were already drunken with wine early in the morning. This was the beginning and inauguration of the great work, destined to re-unite in one vast communion the human race which had been split up and divided into hostile

---

[1] Joel ii. 28, 29. Ez. xi. 19 sqq.  [2] John xvi. 7.
[3] Luke xxiv. 49 ($ἐνδύσησθε$).

nations since the confusion of tongues, to exalt all languages into instruments of the one uniform truth, and bind together the peoples hitherto sharply sundered from each other in the higher unity of the Church. Sometimes after this, the communication of the Holy Ghost, or rather the renewal of the occurrence of Pentecost, took place in the same striking and sensible manner. The first time was when another outpouring of the Spirit on those assembled, accompanied by the same sign of shaking the house, followed the thanksgiving offered by the apostles Peter and John, when they returned to their friends after being released from imprisonment.[1] The second time was when the first Proselytes of the gate were received into the Church, and the phenomenon of speaking with tongues was repeated.[2] The same thing occurred with the Samaritans, and with those disciples of John on whom St. Paul laid his hands at Ephesus.[3]

St. Peter's address on the occurrence of the Pentecostal miracle had a powerful effect. The impression of what they had seen and heard had already prepared the hearts of many to receive his words; "An old promise is here fulfilled before your eyes. All those who are the subjects of this miracle believe firmly that He whom ye, the nation, crucified fifty days ago through your Sanhedrim is the Messiah. Him ye have dared to slay, as was permitted in the counsels of God, but He, as David's Son, and in fulfilment of a promise, has overcome death; He is risen, and has endued us, the witnesses of His resurrection, with these gifts of the Spirit, as a guarantee of the truth." Then were fulfilled those words of the Prophet: "they shall look on Him whom they have pierced, and shall mourn for Him as for an only Son."[4] Three thousand were at once baptized.

The first fair days of the young Church had begun. But the believers were still in a quite peculiar and expectant transition state; the Church, so to speak, was but halfborn, the other half was still in the womb of the Synagogue. The followers of Jesus were under the guidance of the Apostles, but they continued to acknowledge the authority of the chair of Moses in Jerusalem. God had not yet

[1] Acts iv. 31.  [2] Acts x. 46.  [3] Acts viii. 18; xix. 6.  [4] Zech. xii. 10.

abolished the Synagogue; the Sanhedrim still asserted a rightful jurisdiction over the Jewish Church, and the believers submitted to it on all points but one, where they "must obey God rather than man." They were still members of the great politico-religious organisation of their people, and were willing to fulfil all the obligations of membership; they resorted to the temple, as still being the one Sanctuary of the one God, they joined in the public solemnities and public prayer, but they also frequently met among themselves to hear the Apostles, to pray, and "to break bread," *i.e.*, to celebrate the Communion of the Body and Blood of Christ. Their abiding inspiration, the example of Christ and the Apostles, and also the expectation of the approaching judgment on Jerusalem and Judæa, acted so powerfully, that the multitude of their own accord introduced a community of goods among themselves, so that every man regarded and used his private purse as what the brethren had a right to share, and many who had real estates sold them, that the proceeds might be applied by the apostles to the common wants of all. This example, however, was not followed by any of the daughter Churches. When Ananias and Sapphira, through their hypocrisy and avaricious attempt at deception, had made the first assault on the authority of the Apostles and the Holy Ghost ruling in the Church, St. Peter inflicted a terrible punishment upon them.[1]

The event of Pentecost, and its consequences, had left the authorities in Jerusalem outwardly quiet and inactive. Many meantime were indignant or alarmed at the dangerous sect, which they thought to have trodden down like a worm by the death of its Founder, suddenly lifting its head again, and preaching the resurrection of the Crucified One, while thrusting His death in the teeth of the nation, as a great wickedness. Then followed the public healing of the lame man at the gate of the temple by St. Peter, and a second speech of the Apostle, addressed this time to the crowd of worshippers assembled. It is not we, he told them, who have performed this cure; it is Jesus, whom ye through ignorance have killed, in whose Name this man is made whole.[2] His summons, which followed, to turn to

[1] Acts v. 1—10.  [2] Acts iii. 12—26.

Jesus with penitent conversion, was interrupted by the soldiers of the temple guard sent from the priests and Sadducees, who seized him and his companion St. John. Peter declared before the Sanhedrim that there was no other name given whereby men could be saved, but only the name of Jesus; and appealed against their prohibition to preach this Name to the higher will of God; they could not but proclaim what they had seen and heard.[1] This occurrence was again followed by a great increase of the new community, so that the number of its members had already advanced to five thousand. A close bond of mutual love bound together the daily growing society who were wont to assemble in Solomon's Porch, regarded by tradition as a relic of the old temple. They were looked upon by the people with a kind of shrinking awe.[2] The fame of the extraordinary events of Pentecost, and of the numerous healings which surrounded the path of the infant Church, as of its Divine Founder, encircled them in public estimation with a halo which even their enemies for a time scrupled to touch. As St. Peter on all occasions took the precedence, acting and speaking first, as being the head of the young Church, on him, too, the gift of healing chiefly rested. Already the sick were brought from the neighbouring towns, and the pressure on him was so great that they had to be placed on their beds in the streets, that only the shadow of the Apostle as he passed might fall upon them.[3]

The Apostles having been imprisoned anew, at the suggestion of the Sadducees in concert with the High Priest Annas, were miraculously set free and preached again immediately in the temple. Then Gamaliel, a Pharisee of great reputation, advised in the high Council a wise and merciful policy of delay. It was best to see first what would come of the thing. This advice prevailed so far that the Sanhedrim dismissed the apostles after they had been punished with scourging, and again forbidden to preach Jesus. With the principle of this order they did not comply, and now broke out the storm of a general and systematic persecution.[4]

---

[1] Acts iv. 1 sqq.
[2] Acts v. 12, 13.
[3] Acts v. 15, 16.
[4] Acts v. 17—42.

Among the seven men who had been entrusted with the newly-established office of the diaconate, for the care of the poor, Stephen ranked first in power and in spiritual gifts. Himself a Hellenist, he had come into contact as a messenger of Christ with Hellenistic Jews from Italy, Cyrene, Egypt, Cilicia and the coasts of Asia, and had exercised a powerful influence over them. His adversaries among these Hellenists accused him before the Sanhedrim, bringing witnesses to prove that he had blasphemed the law and the temple; that is, he had spoken of the approaching fall of the temple and the abolition or reformation of the ceremonial law by a Divine judgment. In his defence he drew a picture of the past history and divine guidance of Israel, that he might exhibit to them, as in a mirror, their own conduct in that of their forefathers against the prophets sent from God, and at the same time point out how the preparatory course of God's counsels had found its destined end in the mission of the Messiah. But when he passed on to a fiery exhortation to repentance, and told them the same spirit of obstinate disobedience and faithlessness which their fathers showed ruled in them too, and had driven them to betray and murder the Righteous One; when he cried out in an ecstatic vision of the glory of Christ, "I see the heavens opened, and the Son of Man standing at the right hand of God," they treated this as a fresh blasphemy, and dragged him forth in wild tumult, without any formal sentence, to be stoned, according to the law of the Zealots. Thus died the first Martyr, praying for his enemies after his Master's example.[1]

The favour they had before found with the people could now no longer protect any disciple of Christ; when once the word "blasphemy" had gone forth, the Pharisees regained all their old influence over the people, who were ready to give up the Christians to their will, or even to help in executing punishment on them. The great persecution in Jerusalem dispersed most of the believers over the provinces of Judæa and Samaria, and even drove them further to Phœnicia, Cyprus, and Antioch; that the Apostles, who were chiefly threatened, remained at Jerusalem, showed that they had received a special command of Christ to do

[1] Acts vi., vii.

so.[1] The Samaritans, that mongrel race, half Jew half Gentile, hated and shunned as unclean by the Jews, were the first to benefit by the dispersion of the Christians; their country was the first stage of a mission now for the first time over-stepping the limits of Jewish nationality. The deacon, Philip, who baptized a foreign proselyte of the gate, the chamberlain of the queen of Meroe, worked among them with very happy results, and reaped the harvest which Christ Himself had sown earlier.[2] Peter and John were sent by the Apostolic College to impart confirmation to those he baptized, through prayer and the laying on of hands, and with it the visible gifts of the Holy Ghost which then so often accompanied it. Without such a testimony the Jewish believers would have been very slow to understand that this bastard brother of the chosen people was called to enter the Church. The extraordinary effects of this communication of the Spirit led the Samaritan magician, Simon, to imagine that the Apostles possessed a magical power, exercised through the laying on of hands, the use of which they could impart to others, and that they would sell the secret of it for money. St. Peter's threatening rebuke so terrified him that he besought them to pray to God for him.[3] But it must not be supposed that this was any real conversion; he played the part of a miracle-monger and head of a sect to the last.

With the exception of its being received in Samaria, the Gospel as yet was only preached to the children of Abraham. There was no beginning even made as yet of a fulfilment of the promises given long before Christ that the heathen also were to enter into the kingdom of God, and of His own general command to the apostles to teach and baptize all peoples. It must have seemed to those who considered the events taking place in the bosom of Judaism, as though the whole of that great movement which had originated with Christ were to be confined within the limits of Israel, and the impenetrable wall of partition which temporary custom, even more than the written law, had built up between the Jews and the rest of mankind, was to remain even for the disciples of Jesus.

The Apostles knew, in a general way, God's decree as

[1] Acts viii. 1; xi. 19. [2] John iv. 35—38. [3] Acts viii. 14—24.

to the call of the Gentiles: but they were not clear as to its precise time or conditions. Were those Gentiles only to be received who were already "proselytes of righteousness," or those who had submitted to circumcision and the whole Jewish law? The law of Moses had enjoined circumcision as a permanent and constantly binding obligation; the uncircumcised was to be rooted out of the people of God. And the Apostles foresaw that to relax this condition by admitting him to communion among born Jews would certainly give the greatest offence, and be a serious hindrance to the further spread of the faith among them. It needed a special divine revelation to overcome their scruples and hesitation, and accordingly one was given to St. Peter, who was destined, as head of the Church, to admit the first Gentiles.

There were at that time many Gentiles everywhere who, in the eyes of the Jews, were half converts, like those earlier "proselytes of the gate," who were not required to observe the whole law, but only to abstain from certain heathen practices. These "God-fearing" Gentiles used to observe the hours of prayer in the temple, and attended the service at the Synagogues, but, being uncircumcised, were regarded and treated by the Jews as unclean, and they would not eat or drink or hold any familiar intercourse with them. Such a half proselyte was the centurion Cornelius, who belonged to the Italian cohort quartered at Cæsarea. He had already won the very highest character among the Israelites far and near by his unfeigned piety, which his whole family shared, and by his gentleness. This was the man chosen out by Divine Providence to be an example and evidence of the breaking down and entire removal of the partition-wall between different nations. And so, while Cornelius was warned by an angel to send for St. Peter, the apostle, too, was set free, by a special divine interposition, from the notion sucked in from his youth—on which the separation of Jew and Gentile chiefly rested—that every uncircumcised man was unclean and all intercourse with him defiling. For it was the law about food, which discriminated between clean and unclean meats, that kept alive the aversion of the Jews for any intercourse with foreigners, who through tasting unclean animals had themselves become unclean.[1] Therefore, when Peter was hungry, a sheet coming down from heaven was shown to him in vision full of clean and unclean animals, and when he hesitated to comply with the command, "Kill and eat," because he had never eaten anything unclean, he was told that what God had cleansed he must not treat as unclean; and thus he learnt that the Supreme Lawgiver Himself, who had before marked out and given for food only certain kinds of animals, now withdrew that distinction, and allowed all animals indifferently to be eaten. The further meaning of the vision was clear to him, when the messengers of Cornelius appeared directly afterwards, and so he had no scruple about accepting their invitation. When he found from the words of Cornelius how wonderfully the two visions fitted into each other, it became clear to him for the first time that God did not vouchsafe His grace only to the children of Abraham, as he had hitherto believed with his countrymen, but that among other nations, too, the fear of God and practical piety were pleasing to Him, and that He was calling those who served Him, though not Jews, to believe and enter His Church. And now followed an occurrence which could not but remove the last lingering scruples of St. Peter's Jewish attendants; God Himself showed that He had made these Gentiles members of Christ, independently of the ministry of the apostle who was summoned for the purpose. For, before they were baptized and had received the laying on of hands, while they were listening to his words, the Holy Ghost came upon them, and they spoke with tongues and praised God. Thus was the same privilege accorded to the first fruits of the Gentiles, which had been the glory of the first fruits of Israel at Pentecost. They were at once baptized by St. Peter's direction; and thus God had Himself reversed in some sense the usual order of His grace, by bestowing on the unbaptized the gifts of the Holy Ghost, to meet the popular error of the Jews that the promises were given only to them to the exclusion of the Gentiles, and to show that He had called these, too, to the faith and privileges of the New Testa-

---

[1] So the Jews themselves explained the aim and operation of the Mosaic law about meats. See Eleazer's speech, Euseb. *Præp. Ev.* viii. 9.

ment.¹ When the believers at Jerusalem received Peter with reproaches for having associated and eaten with the uncircumcised, he justified himself by simply relating what had occurred, which showed clearly the immediate interposition of God, and by reminding them of Christ's promise, that His followers should be baptized with the Holy Ghost, which was here fulfilled.

If the conversion of the Gentile family at Cæsarea was an isolated event, a whole community of Gentile converts was founded at the same time in the Eastern capital of the Empire, which had also a great number of Jewish inhabitants, and thus the admission of the uncircumcised into the Church of Christ became a recognised procedure. The Cyprian and Cyrenaic Hellenists, driven out of Jerusalem by the persecution, preached Christ with great success to the Greeks of Antioch on the Orontes. Barnabas, of Cyprus, who was sent from Jerusalem to take charge of these first instalments of a Gentile Christian community, perceived that a wide field for work lay open there, and therefore fetched an assistant from Tarsus, whose marvellous greatness and importance in the world's history he himself did not yet conjecture. They worked together there for a year. Antioch, from the size of the city and the personal standing of the men who laboured there to build up the Christian society, became the second Christian metropolis and Mother Church, which, consisting chiefly of Gentile converts, took its place beside the Mother Church of Jerusalem, consisting wholly of Jewish converts. Here the name of Christian was first given to believers, probably by the Latin portion of the Gentile population, in derision.²

Meanwhile the Church had obtained through a miraculous call and conversion the man chosen above all to break down the partition wall between Jew and Gentile, and to bring the latter in a body into the new communion. A young man of Tarsus, Saul by name, had distinguished himself above all by his burning zeal against the disciples of Christ, and his unwearied energy in extirpating them. The son of a Pharisee, he had been educated at Jerusalem in the school of Gamaliel, the most learned and pious doctor of the Law of the day, and was firmly grounded in the preva-

¹ Acts x.  ² Acts xi. 26.

lent doctrine about the approaching glorification of the Law and erection of the Kingdom of Israel. He had inherited from his father the important and valuable privileges of Roman citizenship; and, belonging as he did to a city which could even compete with Athens and Alexandria as a chief seat of Greek civilisation and science, was not unacquainted with Greek literature, though it had done nothing to subdue the rigour of his Pharisaic zeal for the Law.

Saul, as he was called in Hebrew, or Paul after the Hellenistic form of his name, was a witness of the heroic resignation and magnanimous constancy with which St. Stephen had suffered death. And that event may have left a sting in his breast which afterwards contributed to his conversion, though for the time it only confirmed him in the conviction that a sect which produced such martyrs constituted a grave danger to pure Judaism, distracted as it was otherwise from within and threatened more and more seriously from without, and that it must, therefore, be extirpated. He hastened to Damascus, whither many Christians had fled, with full powers from the High Priest, the president of the Sanhedrim, to superintend the imprisonment of the apostates.

But in the persecutor of to-day was hidden the Apostle of to-morrow, as the generous fruit is hidden in its rough shell. When he was certain that the promised Deliverer of Israel, whom he with all his people was looking for, had already come, and come in the person of Jesus, then that stream of fiery zeal poured itself into the bed of the young Church; that fulness of acquirements, that strength of mind and will, came over to the service of the cause he had hitherto hated and persecuted. This certainty he gained on his way to Damascus; he suddenly heard the voice of the Lord and saw His countenance, and the favour granted during the forty days to the apostles and disciples was also conferred on him; the risen Jesus appeared to him, not, as to them, with shrouded majesty, but in the splendour and brightness of His glorified Humanity. To him alone was this sight vouchsafed, while his companions perceived, indeed, the light outshining the mid-day sun and heard the sound of a voice, but neither saw Jesus nor understood the words spoken. Saul, struck to the ground at the presence of the Lord, and then raised up again by His word, learnt now that he, the former persecutor, was ordained to preach and testify what he had hitherto denied and abhorred as blasphemy. When the vision was over, he observed that he had lost his sight. He was led on by his attendants the little way still left to Damascus, and remained three days blind, eating and drinking nothing; but his spiritual sight was all the keener in this night of his outward senses. The illusions which had before held captive this lofty and powerful spirit vanished now; the prophetic passages of Scripture became clear to him, and the look of the dying Stephen rose before his soul. In those three days he lived whole years of penitence, and recognised himself as the chief of sinners;[1] the proud self-righteousness of the Pharisee, which deemed itself blameless in observing all the externals of the Law, fell, like a hard crust, from his heart; belief in Jesus, whose disciples he had compelled to blaspheme Him, entered and began at once to transform His whole consciousness. A believer at Damascus, named Ananias, to whom even the Jews bore testimony as a conscientious observer of the Law, had already been commanded in a vision to restore sight, by laying on of hands, to the enemy and threatening persecutor, whose mere name filled him with fear and anxiety, but who was even now absorbed in prayer, and thus showed that he had grown humble and obedient. As St. Peter and Cornelius had been prepared for their intercourse with each other by similar visions, so, while Ananias received this summons, Saul was instructed by a vision that Ananias would come and cure him of his blindness. And thus he was received into the bosom of the Church by baptism, and preached Jesus in the synagogue of the city.[2]

Not for long however—that the Jews at Damascus, where they had full power against an apostate from their own ranks, would not have tolerated.. Saul did not return to Jerusalem, but went into Arabia,[3] either that part of the Arabian desert which stretches to the Gardens of Damascus, or into Arabia Petræa touching on Syria and Egypt, not to preach there, but to prepare in solitary intercourse with God for the duties of his future life, to obtain through con-

---

[1] 1 Tim. i. 15. Eph. iii. 8.    [2] Acts ix. 1—22.    [3] Gal. i. 17.

verse with his glorified Redeemer that fitness for the apostolate which the other Apostles had gained from their converse with Christ on earth. Even the Lord Himself, after His baptism and before entering on His ministry, had been driven by the Spirit into the wilderness. When Saul after a short absence re-appeared in Damascus, the Jews sought to kill him. They had won over the governor under King Aretas who then ruled the city, and he gave orders to arrest him, while they watched the gates that the hated renegade might not escape. But the believers let him down over the walls by night in a basket. And now, in the third year after his conversion, he went for the first time to Jerusalem.[1]

St. Paul himself insisted afterwards on the fact that he had not after his miraculous enlightening submitted to human influence or to human trial and approval, and had on that account not gone sooner to Jerusalem, because, being under the personal teaching and guidance of the glorified Jesus, he had no need of such aid, or of any earthly attestation.[2] His gospel, as he had received it immediately from God, left no room for doubt or for correction or addition from men, not even from the Apostles themselves. What took him now to Jerusalem was the desire to become better acquainted with the first and chiefest of them, whom Christ Himself had made the shepherd of His flock, and to hold converse with him. It was the Cyprian Barnabas who introduced him to the apostles, that is to Peter and James, the bishop of Jerusalem; the rest he did not then see. The believers there had heard nothing of the events at Damascus, and accordingly looked with fear and suspicion on a man who shortly before was their bitter enemy, but now gave himself out as one of them. They were convinced, however, of the earnestness and reality of his conversion by the word of St. Barnabas, and not less by the hatred which instigated the Hellenistic Jews to seek his life. After spending fifteen days with St. Peter, he left Jerusalem and went to Tarsus, accompanied as far as Cæsarea by friends who were apprehensive for his life; soon after, on a summons from St. Barnabas, he went to Antioch.

A common contribution which the new converts at Antioch sent to their Jewish fellow Christians at Jerusalem, in

[1] 2 Cor. xi. 32, 33.   [2] Gal. i. 15—17.

consequence of a famine, took Barnabas and Saul again to the capital of Judæa.[1] The hatred of the Synagogue against the poor and insignificant little flock of believers was in full force there; but they avoided exciting observation, and were the better able to remain concealed as they assiduously attended the temple and joined in the religious solemnities of the Jews. The High Priests and Sanhedrim were willing enough then to avoid attracting the attention of the Roman authorities to their own internal affairs by persecuting others; and were otherwise sufficiently occupied and kept on the stretch, first by the attempt of Caligula to put up his image in the temple, and then by the policy of the Roman governor of not leaving the same High Priest long in office but changing them oftener, so as to keep alive the jealousy between Pharisees and Sadducees. But when St. Paul came the second time to Jerusalem (A.D. 44), they had again a king of their own, Herod Agrippa, grandson of Herod the Great, who might be regarded as belonging to their nation, for he had the blood of the old Hasmoneans in his veins. He wished to solve the difficult problem of at once making himself popular with his people and standing well with the Roman authorities; and therefore he, too, kept the High Priests strictly dependent on him by frequent changes, but gave over the believers to the hatred of priests and people. Again was the Easter season the time selected for the execution of punishment; James, the son of Zebedee and brother of John, was the first martyr among the Apostles; Peter was kept in prison, that his death might serve as a welcome spectacle at the close of the festival. But he was set free at night by an angel, and showed himself to the assemblage of believers who were praying for him in Mary's house and were seized with joyful astonishment, bade them inform James the son of Alphæus and the rest of the brethren of his release, and immediately left Jerusalem, where from this time St. James alone remained, as bishop of the community. The Church, however, was soon delivered from the enmity of Herod by a death which, from its terrible circumstances, appeared to the believers a judgment of God on the persecutor.[2]

Several years had now elapsed since St. Paul's conver-

---

[1] Acts xi. 27—30.      [2] Acts xii. 1—23.

sion, yet he never took more than a subordinate position in the Church, and in the rank of those engaged in the ministry. The enlightened prophets and teachers who were then in the Church at Antioch are named in the Acts of the Apostles; first Barnabas, then Simeon Niger, Lucius of Cyrene, Manaen, foster brother of Herod the tetrarch, and lastly, Saul. It was some time after his return from his second journey to Jerusalem with St. Barnabas that he was first raised, together with him, to the apostolic office, according to previous announcement. While the persons just named were keeping a fast and discharging their priestly functions, the divine command went forth, either by the mouth of one of the prophets present or by an inspiration of several, to separate Barnabas and Saul for the work to which the Lord had called them; and this was done by prayer and the laying on of hands. This was no conferring of apostleship on their part; the apostles themselves had received no power from Christ to do that. Both the vocation to the apostolate and its bestowal, could only come direct from God. In the election of St. Matthias, the only matter dealt with was the filling up the complete number of the Twelve which had been so appointed and fixed by Christ.[1] Nor can we say that Saul and Barnabas were called to a new and hitherto non-existent kind of apostolate, that of the Gentiles; for there was no such division of apostolic action for Jews and Gentiles, and the new apostles themselves always turned first to the Jews. The most probable account to be given of the matter is this:—Barnabas and Saul were appointed to fill up two vacant places in the Apostolic College, one caused by the sword of Herod in the execution of James, son of Zebedee, the other by James, son of Alphæus, being withdrawn from the peculiar work of an apostle, without of course losing the dignity, through his position as bishop of Jerusalem, after all the other apostles had left the city to carry the preaching of the gospel into more distant lands. And thus, by the entrance of Saul and Barnabas into their body, the number of those exercising the apostolic mission was restored to its normal condition of Twelve,

[1] Matt. xix. 28.

That St. Barnabas in particular was made an apostle in just as strict a sense of the word as St. Paul, is a matter there can be no mistake about. St. Paul places him with himself on a par with the other apostles.[1] St. Luke never gives St. Paul alone the title of Apostle, but always with St. Barnabas, and that first after the ordination at Antioch, which so far constitutes a turning-point in his narrative that, whereas before it he always mentions Barnabas first, afterwards he mentions Paul first.[2] The Greek no less than the Western Church honours St. Barnabas as an Apostle, and St. Jerome reckons him and St. Paul as the thirteenth and fourteenth apostles. And thus the Apostolic College has always consisted of Twelve only at a time, but of fourteen men successively;[3] and therefore the Apocalypse knows only of Twelve Apostles as foundation stones of the walls of the holy City.[4]

Since the call to the apostolate must come immediately from God, St. Paul received his appointment to preach the gospel to the Gentiles in another appearance and revelation of Christ, vouchsafed to him in an ecstasy in the temple during his second visit to the Jewish capital, and in this apostolate St. Barnabas was united to him through a manifestation of the Divine will at Antioch. Hence he appeals, as against the objections of the Galatians, to the direct bestowal of his apostolic office by God, and its consequent equality to that of the rest; he was to preach his gospel without having learnt it from any one, without asking any one first and getting his consent. If he sought out the apostle Peter during his short stay in Jerusalem, that was only to show honour to his primacy, not to receive instruction from him, which he needed not, or power and mission, which he already possessed.[5] St. Paul and St. Barnabas, though specially called to the Gentile apostolate, always recognised the prior right of the Jews by preaching Christ first to them on their journeys. The Synagogues were the places where St. Paul appeared, the rather since a number of "God-fearing" Gentiles, proselytes of the gate, were

---

[1] 1 Cor. ix. 5, 6.   [2] Acts xi. 30; xiii. 43, 46, 50; xv. 35.
[3] [Or rather of fifteen, reckoning Judas.—Tr.]
[4] Apoc. xxi. 14.   [5] Gal. i. 15—19.

always among their members, who formed the bridge whereby Christ's message might reach the unbelieving Gentiles also.[1]

In the year 45, immediately after entering on their apostleship, St. Paul and St. Barnabas undertook a first missionary journey to Cyprus and the Southern provinces of Asia Minor, which had great results.[2] But on their return to Antioch the quarrel with the Judaizers broke out, which henceforth through the whole Apostolic age was the sorest trial of the infant church and the grand difficulty especially which St. Paul had to contend with. The conduct of both apostles in inviting Gentiles at once to enter the Jewish Christian community, without any regard to law, defilement, or separation, was something shocking and intolerable to the great body of Jews as then minded. The sons of Abraham and their lofty privileges would be swallowed up, as it were, at no distant period by the mass of Gentile believers. This anxiety was felt above all in Jerusalem, where the temple and Levitical service were constantly before men's eyes. The affair of Cornelius was an isolated case, an exception to the rule, acquiesced in as having received the seal of divine approval through the miraculous outpouring of the gifts of the Spirit on those Gentiles; but now that communities were being formed consisting wholly or chiefly of Gentile converts, the greatness of the danger was conspicuous. And certain "false brethren, who had crept in secretly" appeared at Antioch, intending to force the yoke of the Mosaic law on the new converts.

The Ceremonial Law had its stronghold and the guarantee of its continuance in the existence of the Jewish polity. So long as this and the temple stood, it was idle to think of abolishing the law; or at least its abolition could only have come about through a general and simultaneous entrance of the Jewish nation, as well its lower as its higher classes, into the Church. For the ceremonial was also a civil law; the Jew was bound to its observance not only as an individual, but above all as a member of the state and nation; nor was there any command of the Lord to the individual believer to separate from his people and its Church

---

[1] Acts xiii. 5, 14.   [2] Acts xiii., xiv.

and State organisation. Moreover, in Judæa and Galilee it was impossible to do so without emigrating. But even the Jews of the Dispersion always regarded themselves as members of the Commonwealth which had its seat and centre at Jerusalem, and sent their contributions thither. Thus it was not left to the caprice of believers in Judæa whether they would observe the ceremonial law or not, but was for them a necessity. Meanwhile, until the counsel of God was more, broadly and clearly developed, they remained in the fullest sense Israelites, only distinguished in the one point of their believing that Messiah had already come, but willingly conforming in all other respects to the existing order of the law.

The Apostles on their side did not venture to do anything which might impede the grand vocation of the whole nation to become pillars and instruments of the religion of Messiah—a vocation not yet definitively rejected, nor had the interval permitted for accepting it yet expired. They did not venture to introduce or abolish anything at the risk of needlessly repelling the great body of the Jews, and were bound to sustain carefully all the fibres by which the Christian community was attached to the great Jewish national Church and State. They accordingly continued to observe the law themselves, and tolerated and approved its observance in the Jewish Christian communities.

The Christian zealots for the law who came from Jerusalem to Antioch declared to the Gentile converts: "Unless you are circumcised, you cannot be saved."[1] This was going beyond even the prevalent Jewish view of the period, for there was a large body of "Proselytes of the gate" who were not required to keep the ceremonial law. But had it been announced in the name of the Synagogue that there was no salvation without being circumcised, of course no Gentile would have become a proselyte of this kind; he would either have remained a Heathen or become a "Proselyte of righteousness;" but this latter class was comparatively a small one. Only a few zealots among the Jews considered circumcision absolutely indispensable, like that Eleazer who represented to King Izates of Adiabene the danger to his soul of not being circumcised, while the Jewish

[1] Acts xv. 1.

merchant Ananias had dissuaded him from circumcision, because he could please God without it.¹ The view of these Pharisee converts was that not only belief in Christ as the promised Messiah but also observance of the ritual law was a condition of salvation, that Christ had come for the very purpose of confirming the Law and enlarging the circle of its adherents, and that since His kingdom had begun the time of patience and forbearance with "God-fearing" Gentiles was over; so that whoever would be saved must become a full citizen of Israel strengthened by the addition and incorporation of Gentile converts.

Here, then, was a very grave practical difficulty. It was not easy to see how a brotherly relationship and healthy intercourse of common life could grow up between Gentile and Jewish Christians, the circumcised and uncircumcised. For the strict ceremonialist would not eat and drink with the uncircumcised; the law of meats prevented him. This, in fact, was a knot which could not really be untied or cut, except by the direct intervention of Divine Providence. Meanwhile, as the claims of the two parties could not be thoroughly reconciled, some temporary accommodation had to be devised.

Paul and Barnabas, therefore, with certain others, including Titus, a learned Greek who had joined St. Paul, went to Jerusalem commissioned by the Church at Antioch to get this difficult question settled. It was St. Paul's third journey to the capital since his conversion, and fourteen years after it. He has given us an account of it in his Epistle to the Galatians, but only so far as regards the recognition of his apostolate and preaching of the Gospel by the chief apostles there. When representing himself to the Galatians, in proof of his apostolic authority, as being under the immediate guidance and enlightenment of the Lord, he refers this journey to a special revelation. It was resolved on St. Peter's proposal, in an assembly where he and St. James were present together with the presbyters of the Church, that the burden of circumcision and the law should not be laid on Gentile converts. But in order to facilitate a real fusion of Jews and Gentiles in the Church, the latter were to abstain from certain things peculiarly repul-

---

¹ Joseph. *Arch.* xxii. 2, 5.

sive to the Jews, viz., from sharing in Heathen sacrificial feasts, and eating blood or the flesh of strangled animals. The apostles felt the more bound to require the observance of these restrictions, as it was a matter causing offence to the Jews and making Christianity appear to them a religion beset with Heathen abominations. It was thought necessary in Jerusalem to add the prohibition of "fornication," because impurity and sins of the flesh were so common and so little regarded among the Heathen that much of this sort might also survive among converts from Heathenism.[1]

St. Paul had communicated to the three leading Apostles at a private interview his manner of procedure in preaching to the Gentiles, probably before the public meeting; not, as he says, to gain instruction from them—for he did what he did by divine inspiration—but to gain the confirmation and sanction of their authority. He had already successfully resisted the demands of the Christian Pharisees that his attendant, Titus, a converted Greek, should be circumcised. The apostles had nothing to object to St. Paul's conduct and teaching, which they found all perfectly regular, and made a brotherly covenant with him, acknowledging that, as Peter had been prepared and blessed by God for the work of converting the Jews, so Paul was a chosen instrument for winning the Gentiles. They agreed, therefore, to work according to a mutual understanding, Peter, James and John devoting themselves principally to preaching the gospel to the circumcised, while Paul and Barnabas worked as Apostles of the Gentiles.[2] But this did not hinder St. Paul from labouring with unwearied zeal to win his countrymen to faith in Christ, or withdraw St. Peter and St. John from preaching to the Gentiles when opportunity offered. All communities already founded, or now growing up beyond the limits of Judæa, were composed of both Jews and Gentiles, so that every apostle who did not remain in Judæa, like St. James, must attend to both. At the same time whatever communities St. Paul and St. Barnabas might found were to be connected with the Church at Jerusalem, and testify their relation to it as daughters by sending contributions for the poor there.

The worst was thus averted, and the Christian liberty of

[1] Acts xv. 1—29. Gal. ii. 1—10.   [2] Gal. ii. 1—9.

Gentile converts secured; but the main difficulty remained unsolved, and was purposely not touched upon at the Council. It was tacitly assumed that the Jewish Christians and the Apostles themselves would continue to observe the law. But how was a real Church communion to come about while the Israelite held a converted and baptized Greek for an unclean being, with whom it was defilement to eat and drink? Without doubt the Apostles intended the requirements of the Jewish law to yield here to the higher duties of Christian brotherly love, and the better claims of membership in the body of the Church. In Judæa, where the Christian societies were purely Jewish, there was no opportunity for exhibiting this in practice; but soon after the apostolic Council St. Peter had an opportunity of doing so while staying at Antioch with St. Paul and St. Barnabas. In that city, where the Jewish law was not the law of the land, he had no scruple about "living as a Gentile;" *i.e.*, associating at table and in domestic life with Gentiles, until some Jewish Christians arrived there from St. James' communion at Jerusalem. And then, to avoid offending them and damaging his influence among the Jews of Palestine, he thought it right to withdraw from eating with Gentile converts. All the Jewish Christians at Antioch—St. Barnabas among them—followed his example.[1] This was no violation of the rule laid down by the Council, for the whole question was left unsettled there, and whoever disregarded this part of the law was, in the eyes of all Jews, a complete breaker of the law. St. Peter, therefore, might well think that, being compelled to choose between the Gentiles and the Jews, he had better take the lesser evil of the two. As St. Paul says, he feared those of the circumcision. This was no want of moral courage, of which he had given abundant proof in more than once upbraiding all Jerusalem and its rulers with their sin against the Lord, in opening the Church's gates to the first Gentile family, and in being the first at the Council to recognise Gentile liberties. But he remembered that the Jewish Christians of Palestine belonged to the Jewish civil polity, still existing, though dependent on Rome, and based entirely on the Mosaic law; he knew that law,—social, ritual, and political,—to be the

---

Gal. ii. 11—14.

law of the land, from which Christians could not withdraw themselves while continuing to be citizens and residents in the country. He had rightly preferred regard for his Gentile brethren to observance of the law while living at Antioch beyond the jurisdiction of the Jewish state. But the arrival of Jewish Christians from Jerusalem placed him in a dilemma between opposite duties and relations, his old duty to his fellow-countrymen, converted chiefly by him, and bound by the law of separation, and his new duty to brethren gained over by others. As the shepherd appointed by Christ for the whole flock, he belonged to both, but he had hitherto been peculiarly the Apostle of Israel, and was not willing to give up his labours in Jerusalem and Judæa; he wished especially to preserve his authority and influence where born Jews predominated. He had, indeed, already broken through the partition wall by the baptism of Cornelius; and maintained his right to do so against the scruples of others; but then he could appeal to the fire baptism and miraculous gifts of the Spirit, whereby God Himself attested that the Gentiles were no more unclean or inferior to Jewish believers. No such event had occurred at Antioch.

But St. Peter had himself declared at the Council that the ritual law was a yoke neither the Jews nor their fathers had been able to bear; he had first, as St. Paul said, "though a Jew, lived as a Gentile," yet he now assumed an attitude which, from his position in the Church, amounted to putting on Gentile converts a moral compulsion to submit to the yoke of the law. For if he, the pillar of legitimate unity chosen by Christ as shepherd of the flock, showed by his actions that he held the uncircumcised unclean, their persons and their meats defiling, they could only infer that to be admitted to communion with the Head of the Church, they must sacrifice the liberty guaranteed to them by the Council and adopt the Jewish Law. That was intolerable to St. Paul as Apostle of the Gentiles and preacher of Evangelical freedom, and he thought, too, how the Pharisee zealots who wanted to impose the whole law on Gentiles would abuse this example of the chief Apostle. He openly and sharply censured St. Peter for building up again what he had pulled down, and, after he had already by his conduct vindicated Gentiles from the obligation of the law, acting now from fear of men against his better judgment; that was "hypocrisy." We are not told the reply; but there was no lasting quarrel, for in the thing itself both apostles were agreed. St. Paul never thought of urging Jews in general, especially those in Palestine, to renounce the law altogether, of requiring them, *e.g.*, not to circumcise their children; he acknowledged that they must keep it as long as the present State and Church organisation of the Jewish people lasted. The great separation was not yet come, the Jew who believed in Christ remained a member of his nation and shared its duties, as also its rights and privileges. When the key-stone which held all together was broken to pieces, when the national sanctuary of the temple was destroyed by a higher interposition, then the links of the chain would be severed and the converted son of Abraham would belong only to the Church, and no more to his people and to the Synagogue. St. Paul himself, therefore, felt no hesitation about observing the law, when it did not come into collision with the higher duties of his apostolate and his position towards the Gentile Christians, as when he had St. Timothy, the son of a Jewish mother and Greek father, circumcised, and bore the charges of a Nazarite vow.[1] He was only zealous against it when it was substituted for faith in Christ, and had a value given it in the conscience as the means of man's justification before God, and when, as was only possible from this false stand-point, its yoke was to be laid on the necks of Gentile Christians. Such an attempt he thought was involved indirectly in St. Peter's behaviour. On the other hand, St. Peter and St. Barnabas thought they had full freedom of conscience to observe or neglect the ritual law as a thing indifferent in itself, and in the impossibility of doing justice to both parties they believed that they ought to give the preference to their countrymen. This can be more naturally and easily justified in St. Peter than in Barnabas the Cypriote. For he saw in converted Israel the germ of the Church, to which the Gentile Christians belonged only as guests arrived later, and to their good all other considerations must yield; he knew that nothing could be more pre-

[1] Acts xvi. 3; xxi. 23—26.

judicial to the success of his work in Jerusalem and Judæa than his being known to have broken through the fence which guarded the ritual purity of Judaism.

This dispute appears to have led to a temporary separation between St. Paul and St. Barnabas, for when the latter wanted to take his kinsman, Mark, with him on the missionary journey arranged already between them, St. Paul opposed it because he had previously left them in Pamphylia from love of ease.[1] The fact of St. Mark, who was intimately allied to St. Peter, having followed his example and that of St. Barnabas, in separating from the Gentile Christians, may have helped to form St. Paul's decision. On this account the two apostles of the Gentiles, who had hitherto worked in union, parted. Barnabas went with St. Mark to his native Cyprus; St. Paul, accompanied by Silas, entered on his second great missionary journey. He visited the communities in Syria, Cilicia, and Lycaonia, took up the young Timothy in Lystra, and soon afterwards, as appears from the changed tone of the narrative, must have also been joined by the Evangelist St. Luke. St. Paul, who at Jerusalem had refused the requisition of the legal zealots to get Titus circumcised, on the other hand induced Timothy to undergo the rite:[2] for he wished to make use of him for preaching the Gospel in the Synagogues and Jewish houses. From this period the other Apostles for a long time retire into the background, and nothing is known to us of their operations. St. Paul is now the leading person whose history, up to his imprisonment at Rome, forms the subject of the second part of St. Luke's narrative.

After staying a long while in Galatia, St. Paul, being warned in a dream, went over with his three companions from Troas to Macedonia, and thus the Gospel for the first time touched the soil of Europe. In spite of the ill-treatment they suffered he founded flourishing communities at Philippi, Thessalonica, and Beroea; the first of these he named afterwards his joy and his crown.[3] In Thessalonica he was allowed to preach Jesus for three weeks in the Synagogue, but at last the Jews stirred up the multitude against him, and when the Jews at Beroea

---

[1] Acts xv. 36—41.    [2] Acts xvi. 3.    [3] Phil. i. 3—8; iv. 1.

showed more readiness to receive him, he was soon turned out from thence, too, in an uproar organised by Jews who came over from Thessalonica. The believers made him fly to Athens.[1] There, among a light-minded people, and surrounded by the highest artistic splendour of the Heathen world, he did not find a favourable soil; Epicureans and Stoics mocked him and his crucified Nazarene; some called him a babbler, others scornfully thought he wanted to introduce two new gods, Jesus and the Resurrection. Meanwhile his speech on the Areopagus was not without effect, where he alluded to an altar erected to the "unknown God," in order to proclaim to the Athenians this nameless, and as yet to them unknown, God. Some persons were converted, and among them Dionysius the Areopagite, first bishop of Athens.

He found a more productive field opened to him in the wealthy and luxurious commercial city of Corinth, where he staid a year and a half, living on his earnings as a carpet-maker in the house of the Jew Aquila, one of his own trade, which he had, according to the Jewish custom, learnt with his studies. A numerous community was the result of his preachings. In Corinth, as elsewhere, he turned first to the Jews and the proselytes belonging to their Synagogue; but he met with violent opposition from the majority. He, therefore, turned his back on the Synagogue, and held his meetings in the neighbouring house of a proselyte, Justus. His successes were great among the Gentiles, especially the lower classes; and the director of the Synagogue, Crispus, was himself converted with his whole family. It was in vain that the Jews brought him before the tribunal of the pro-consul, Gallio, as a troubler of their religion. They were driven away.

During his first stay at Corinth St. Paul wrote his first Epistle, that to the Thessalonians, about the year 52; and soon afterwards a second, full of desire to see them again. St. Timothy, who had been sent thither from Athens, had brought back a favourable report, on the whole, of their condition; their firmness in the faith under severe trials was already spoken of far and wide. St. Paul said they were models for the believers in Macedonia and Achaia;

[1] Acts xvii. 1—15.

their Church constitution was already in order; they had presbyters, and spiritual gifts, especially that of prophecy, were not wanting. But a dark side of the picture is, that the imagination of Christians there had fixed itself eagerly on the notion of the near approach of Christ's second coming; they thought this return of the Lord to accomplish His kingdom on earth was close at hand, and this expectation dominated their whole attitude of mind and kept other Christian truths in the background. The consequence was that not a few, giving themselves over to visionary anticipations, relinquished or neglected the business of their calling, and frittered away their energies in idleness or in busying themselves without any definite aim.[1] The Apostle attacked this error by representing to them in his First Epistle that the time of the Second Advent could not be fixed, for the Lord would come unexpectedly, as a thief in the night, but for the salvation of the watchful. He, at the same time, contradicted the notion that at the Second Coming the dead would be worse off than those alive.

Meanwhile, in Thessalonica itself, a forged letter of St. Paul's had been circulated to confirm this expectation;[2] and he therefore took pains in his Second Epistle to bring them back to a quiet and sensible state of mind, by pointing to certain signs which must precede the Second Coming of Christ. As he here referred to declarations he had made before by word of mouth, so his expressions in this Epistle are partly only dark hints, for he himself felt the hope recur to him that he might yet live to see the second appearance of Christ. Later he wrote to the Philippians, that he desired to die in order to be with Christ.[3]

After a stay of a year and a half St. Paul left Corinth, the greatest and most flourishing of the communities he had founded. He wished to perform a vow by bringing an offering to Jerusalem, for which reason he shaved his head at the harbour of Cenchrea, after the Jewish manner in such cases.[4] His road took him to the flourishing commer-

---

[1] 1 Thess. iv. 10, 11.  2 Thess. iii. 8—12.
[2] 2 Thess. ii. 2 Cf.; iii. 17.
[3] Phil. i. 23 Cf. 1 Thess. iv. 16, 17.
[4] Acts xviii. 18. No one who understands St. Luke's manner of speaking in the Acts can possibly refer the words in question to Aquila.

cial city of Ephesus, with its numerous Jewish population, who would gladly have detained him, but he wished to be at Jerusalem for the approaching feast on account of his vow; and he seems this time to have soon taken his departure, after a short stay and hasty salutation of the Church. But when he had visited Antioch and the previously converted Galatian communities, he returned for a longer stay to Ephesus. Not only was one of the most important Christian communities established there, principally by his means, but from this centre, which, from its commercial connections, offered abundant opportunities of intercourse, he propagated Christianity in other parts of Asia Minor, partly in person, partly through his assistants.

The Alexandrian Jew, Apollos, an eloquent man and well versed in the Scriptures, had already been at Ephesus before St. Paul; but he had only been instructed by St. John's disciples, and knew nothing of Christian baptism as distinct from that of John, though he preached Jesus as the Messiah. After receiving fuller instruction from St. Paul's friends, Aquila and Priscilla, he went to Corinth with letters of introduction, taught there with great success, and returned from thence to Ephesus in company with St. Paul.[1] In that city the Apostle found twelve disciples who had only received St. John's baptism, and knew nothing of the communication of the Holy Ghost and His gifts; he had them baptized, and confirmed them by the laying on of hands, on which they at once spoke with tongues and prophesied.[2]

Here, too, St. Paul was obliged after awhile to withdraw from the public Synagogue, and retire with his Christians into the private synagogue of Tyrannus. His personal presence, his teaching, the cures which here especially he worked on large numbers of the sick and the demoniacs,— all this created a great sensation at Ephesus, and it was increased by a remarkable occurrence which took place. Some Jewish exorcists, sons of the chief Rabbi Scevah, thought they could produce similar effects by using the name which St. Paul invoked, without any belief in Jesus. So they applied to a demoniac the formula, "I adjure thee by Jesus, whom Paul preaches." But they were insulted

[1] Acts xviii. 24—28. 1 Cor. i. 12.     [2] Acts xix. 1—7.

and severely handled by the demoniac and obliged to fly from the house. On this many conjurors and magicians were converted, and burnt their magical books. This became a serious matter for those who made their livelihood from the service of the gods, and Demetrius, who had a manufactory in which little silver images for the famous temple of Artemis were made, succeeded in exciting a popular uproar by the cry, "Great is Artemis of the Ephesians," in the hope of destroying St. Paul and his companions, or at least expelling them from the city; but it was appeased by the skilful address of the town clerk.[1]

From Ephesus St. Paul wrote two important Epistles,— that to the Galatians, and the First to the Corinthians. The communities he had founded in Galatia, chiefly of Gentile Christians but partly also of converted Jews, had been lately led astray by Judaizing teachers, so suddenly and so completely that it seemed to the Apostle like an enchantment.[2] These false guides recommended the Galatians to submit to circumcision, and to adopt several other usages of the Jewish law, and many followed their advice.

It has been thought strange that there is no appeal made in this Epistle to the decision of the Council at Jerusalem. But the Galatian Christians knew that decision well enough; St. Paul himself had brought it there. They knew that no one had any right to make their keeping the Law a condition of entering the Church or remaining in it, that to lay circumcision and the law on their necks as a compulsory yoke was forbidden. Nor do their false teachers appear to have meddled with this decision; they were not such zealots as those at Jerusalem, for they did not themselves keep the whole Law or require its observance from the Christians there, and they did not, like those at Jerusalem, threaten eternal damnation even to those who refused circumcision. Their chief ground was rather, according to St. Paul's own account, that they wished thereby to avert the persecutions of the Jews who were still powerful through the strength of their national and religious organisation, and to gain for the defenceless and unrecognised Christians the secure footing afforded by the Roman laws to Judaism.[3] For, as St. Jerome observes, all the circumcised, even if Christians,

[1] Acts xix. 8—41.   [2] Gal. iii. 1.   [3] Gal. vi. 12, 13.

were treated as Jews by the Heathen, while the uncircumcised Christians were equally persecuted by Jew and Heathen.[1] These men accordingly recommended circumcision and observance of certain legal usages, partly for the sake of security, partly on religious grounds. They appealed to the example of the chief Apostles in Judæa, who continued to observe the law themselves and make others observe it, which they certainly would not have done, had they not believed they were thereby offering an acceptable service to God. As the Jews of that day generally said to the Heathen: "It is enough for salvation to abjure the worship of the gods and become a proselyte of the gate, but of course it is better and more pleasing to God to be circumcised and become a proselyte of righteousness and member of the chosen people,"—so could the Galatian Judaizers represent the usages of the Law which they recommended to believers, as a higher stage, as something peculiarly meritorious and salutary. At the same time, these Judaizers made light of St. Paul's Apostolic office; he had not received his mission through the ordinary call from Christ Himself, he had not lived in the company of Jesus on earth, but had gained his first knowledge of the Gospel later from the real Apostles; these last, Peter, James, and John, continued to observe the ritual law, and he, with his teaching got second-hand, could not have the same authority as the original great Apostles.

To this St. Paul opposed himself with an energy and sharpness not to be found in any other Epistle. While unwillingly denouncing their fickleness, he protests that if an angel from heaven preached to them another doctrine he should be accursed; he shows by an account of his conversion and after life that he had received his Gospel and his mission directly from Christ, and not from men, that he had become a master without having ever been a learner, but that his doctrine was constantly recognised by the most influential Apostles as essentially one with their own. The remainder of this Epistle is occupied in pointing out that the Galatians were fools for wishing to exchange their Gospel liberty for the bondage of the Law, and he reminds them of their own experience, that they had received their spi-

---

[1] Hieron. *in Gal.* ii. 10.

ritual gifts, not through observance of the Law, but through faith.

About this time, whether before or after the Epistle to the Galatians is uncertain, St. Paul wrote his First Epistle to the Corinthians. While the former is addressed to a small community in an out-of-the-way little town in the interior of Asia Minor, the Church of Corinth was one set on a candlestick, in one of the most important cities of the old world, a great commercial centre, and point of contact between East and West, where believers from other lands were constantly coming and going. The evils to be combated here were also of a peculiar kind. The most conspicuous and mischievous of them was the encroachment of party spirit; some wanted to be Paulites, others followers of Apollos, who had appeared as a teacher in Corinth; while others again, probably Jewish Christians, gave themselves out for disciples of Peter, either because he had really been in Corinth, or because foreign Jewish Christian teachers had come there, and gained adherents by using his name. And lastly, there were some from Palestine who in opposition to these three parties professed to wish to hold to Christ only, whom they had known personally.[1] There was no question here of doctrinal differences, or the Apostle would have expressly named and combated them; but he treats these party watch-words merely as marking a defective sense of Church unity. St. Paul and Apollos were intimate friends, but the disciples of the latter prided themselves on the elevated form of teaching of one who was a master of Alexandrian philosophy and Scripture interpretation, and looked contemptuously on St. Paul's simple and unadorned preaching of the Cross of Christ. Meanwhile, these attempts to form particular schools had not gone to the length of any open rupture of Church communion.

St. Paul therefore had to combat the excessive value of human wisdom and philosophical speculations, partly with reference to the disciples of Apollos, partly to ward off errors sprung from Greek philosophy which threatened to become naturalised at Corinth. It was necessary to defend the doctrine of the resurrection against those Christians who denied the actual resurrection of the body, and explained

[1] 1 Cor. i. 12.

the doctrine figuratively of the spiritual awakening of men through faith;[1] and, in a city where the prevalent fashion made temptations to sins of the flesh so powerful, a general warning was needed against this error also and the evil consequences of a false liberty, for the Corinthian Christians were tolerating an incestuous man in their community. Lastly, they had to be reminded that it was unseemly for Christians to bring their litigations before the Heathen magistracy.

And here St. Paul examined with special care the question, how believers were to conduct themselves in the whole matter of partaking in sacrificial banquets and eating meats offered to idols. The Council of Jerusalem had forbidden this participation in general, but many difficulties arose in the application of the rule. Sacrificial banquets were often held in private houses as well as in the temples, and it was frequently impossible to know, in dining with a Heathen acquaintance, whether the meat put before you was of a sacrificed animal or not. It was hardly possible again to avoid buying such meat, for it was brought daily to the market. The Corinthians had asked about this, and the brief requirement of the Jerusalem Synod to abstain from things offered to idols, without any more precise definition, did not supply an answer. Strict Jewish Christians could extend it to cases which, from the nature of the thing, seemed to be left free to Gentile converts. St. Paul therefore did not appeal to it. He declared eating sacrificial meat, when bought in the market, or put before Christians at a Gentile banquet without any mention of what it was, to be indifferent in itself; but he desired Gentile Christians to refrain from using this liberty where there was danger of giving offence to their weaker brethren, the Jewish Christians, or leading them into sin. And he warned them against taking any formal part in a sacrificial banquet, for that always brought those who ate into communion with the demons to whom the Gentiles sacrificed.[2]

The news which Titus had brought the Apostle about the reception and consequences of the First induced him to send a Second Epistle to the Corinthians (after he had

[1] 1 Cor. xv. 12 sqq.   [2] 1 Cor. x. 14—32.

meanwhile been over Troas and Macedonia) which is a running personal apology of himself and his office, interspersed, however, with a great many admonitions. The intrusion of the Judaizing false teachers compelled him to take this course; they represented him as a man who had usurped the Apostolate on his own authority, who was changeable and unreliable, at one time defiant, at another despondent, and not deserving the confidence of the community in his vain self-exaltation.[1] Against this St. Paul urged that the national privileges on which those "superlative Apostles"[2] prided themselves belonged also to him, that he had done, striven, and suffered much more for God's cause than those dark and deceitful men, who falsely gave themselves out for apostles. He reminded them of the special proofs of divine power, visions and revelations, which had been given him in a state of ecstatic elevation; and he, therefore, required of the Corinthians a full recognition of his Apostolic authority.[3] He also earnestly recommended a contribution for the poor Christians in Jerusalem.[4]

St. Paul had already extended his labours as far as Illyria, on the coast of the Adriatic sea, when he again went into Greece, and paid another visit of three months to Corinth and its neighbourhood. His Epistle to the Roman Christians was written at this time, and he is able to boast of having preached the Gospel and secured its acceptance all round from Jerusalem to Illyria.[5] He had often felt a wish to visit the Christians in Rome, but had always abstained from doing so on his principle of not choosing a Church already founded by an Apostle as the field of his energies, not, as he says, building on another man's foundation. But though he had not himself been at Rome, he had many friends and followers there, among them Aquila and Priscilla. And so he wrote, for the first time, to a community not personally known to him. The Church there must already have been in a flourishing state; their faith in Christ was spoken of through the whole world,[6] as St. Paul says; though it consisted, of course, of a mixed body of Gentile and Jewish Christians, there were no

---

[1] 2 Cor. i. 17; iii. 1 sqq.; x. 1 sqq.; xi. 1 sqq.  [2] τῶν ὑπὲρ λίαν ἀποστόλων.
[3] 2 Cor. xi., xii.    [4] 2 Cor. viii. 1 sqq.    [5] Rom. xv. 19.    [6] Rom. i. 8.

parties and hostile principles at work, even if the difficulties of a complete fusion of Jewish and Gentile believers were felt there as elsewhere. The chief hindrances, however, were overcome when St. Paul wrote this Epistle; he testifies to the Romans that they are full of goodness, filled with all knowledge, and able to admonish one another.[1] He warns them not against the actual but the possible danger of being misled by false doctrine. He had already spent more than twenty years in apostolic labours when he composed this document, the fullest and ripest fruit of his spirit, the chief record of his theology. He had already in his Second Epistle to the Corinthians spoken of himself, in the full consciousness of his dignity and the triumphs he had won, as of a victorious general and mighty conqueror, before whose arms all errors fall like fortresses before a storming brigade, to whom all high things bow down, who takes captive all under the obedience of Christ.[2] He had in the main finished his work in the Eastern half of the Roman Empire, and he now turned his eyes to the West. He wanted to go to Spain and visit Rome on the way, but not till he had first brought the proceeds of a collection with his own hands to the Jewish capital, in order that the tie which connected the Western Church with the Mother Church of Jerusalem might not be loosened, and his true affection for his countrymen and brethren of the circumcision might be known there.

Jews and Gentiles have no right to reproach one another; sin rules universally on both sides, over the Jews in consequence of their own law; all are wanting in righteousness before God, which cannot be gained through the works of the Law in the broadest sense, but only through giving one's self up in faith to Christ, who as the Second Adam gives far more to those who believe on Him than they have lost through the first Adam. But a great part of the Jewish people reject this salvation. They hold fast to the Law, as the way of salvation, in proud, self-willed obduracy and enmity against Christ. While some of them walk in the true path of salvation, the great mass of the nation seems as if it lay under a sentence of rejection from God, but at the last God will make good the promises given

[1] Rom. xv. 14.  [2] 2 Cor. x. 3—5.

to His people. These are the leading ideas of this profound and out-spoken Epistle, so rich in contrasts, in decisive and startling passages, and in out-pourings of sorrowful love towards the writer's blinded people.

And now, in spite of many warnings, St. Paul carried out his resolution of paying a fifth visit to Jerusalem, this time as the bearer of a contribution for the Church. From Philippi, where he met St. Luke, he went to Troas, and found there the three companions who were to accompany him, one of whom was Timotheus. At Miletus he bade a last farewell to the presbyters of the communities on the coasts of Asia, commended to their care the Churches entrusted to them, and prophesied to them the near approach of false teachers, who would arise from among themselves. He knew well that, as he here said, bonds and affliction awaited him; Agabus, too, told him this in Cæsarea.[1] At Pentecost (of 58 or 59 A.D.) he came, probably after five years absence, to Jerusalem. He gave an account of the results of his apostolical labours to the Bishop James and the assembled presbyters. On this St. James advised him, as there were many thousand converted Israelites who were all zealous adherents of the Law, to do an act which would dispel the suspicion that he was a despiser of the ordinances of his nation and taught his countrymen to neglect them; namely, to associate himself in a Nazarite vow with four poor members of the Christian community by paying the costs of the offering. Finding himself here in the very central seat of the Law, where all, Jews and Christians alike, observed it, and where it controlled all public arrangements, as no sign had yet been given from God for breaking up the old edifice, St. Paul had no scruple in following this advice and appearing in the temple to make an offering. Not long before Agrippa, on coming from Rome to take possession of the throne, had adopted the same means to gain the favour of the Jews;[2] and the Apostle himself had laid it down as his principle to become a Jew to the Jews in order to win them, and had already performed a vow in Jerusalem.[3]

Scarcely had St. Paul set foot in the temple when the

---

[1] Acts xx. 17—38; xxi. 11.  [2] Joseph. Arch. xvii. 6, 1.
[3] 1 Cor. vii. 17—19; ix. 20.

Jews of Asia Minor, who knew him, raised an outcry against the man who everywhere taught against the people, the law, and the temple, which he had now come to desecrate. For he had been seen with the Greek Trophimus, one of his companions, and was supposed to have brought him into the temple. The Roman temple guard snatched him from the hands of the raving multitude, and he tried to change their feelings by a speech delivered from the steps of the castle of Antonia and a narration of his past life. They listened quietly till he mentioned the mission to the Gentiles imparted to him in the temple. Then the storm broke out; a Jew could bear any thing rather than the notion that the uncircumcised Gentiles should be made equal with the sons of Abraham. They cried out that such a wretch must be made away with from the earth. St. Paul appealed to his rights as a Roman citizen, against the design of the Roman commander to extort a confession by torture. When brought before the Sanhedrim, he skilfully threw a firebrand into the mixed assembly of Pharisees and Sadducees, by putting forward his Pharisaic descent and education, and his belief in the resurrection as the cause of his persecution by the Sadducees, to whom the High Priest himself inclined. He could truly say that his whole teaching was based on the resurrection of Christ and the future resurrection of all believers, especially as the first persecution of Christians proceeded from the Sadducee party who predominated in the Synagogue. An angry contention between the two parties was the consequence, and some Pharisees took the Apostle's side as an innocent and orthodox man, granting even the truth of the alleged vision. Set free for this time he was sent by the commander Lysias, who wished to save him from a murderous plot of forty Jews against his life, to Cæsarea to the procurator Felix, under a strong guard. There, after a few days, the High Priest Ananias made his appearance, with other members of the Sanhedrim as accusers, but neither Felix nor his successor Festus were willing to condemn him or give him up to the Jews. So he remained two years at Cæsarea in prison, not choosing to ransom himself with money. He vainly sought to touch or to shake King

Agrippa, Festus' guest. But as he had appealed to Cæsar he was to be sent, still as a prisoner, to Rome.

In the spring of 61 St. Paul landed on the coast of Italy. The Roman Christians went to meet him as far as Tres Tabernæ, and then was fulfilled his long cherished desire to work in the capital of the world, and the promise given him in a night vision at Jerusalem, that he should bear witness of the Lord also in Rome. He was allowed to live in a private house with a soldier chained to him, and so spent two years in Rome, closely guarded, but free to receive visits and preach Christ.[1] Early in the first year he sent for the principal men among the Jews there, thinking that hostile reports had probably reached them from Jerusalem. They assured him that they had heard nothing about him, but knew the Nazarene sect was everywhere spoken against. Here, too, his teaching had its usual result of leading them to mock him, and he hurled one word at them bitterer than death; "This salvation of God is sent to the Gentiles, and they will hear it."

What caused the Apostle's long detention was the delay of his accusers, who did not reach Rome till later, or perhaps allowed their charges to drop through non-appearance. If they really appeared, they would have to support their three charges against him—of exciting disturbance and party spirit among the Jews of the whole Empire, of being a ringleader of the Nazarenes, and of seeking to profane the temple—by numerous witnesses collected from various provinces. And as the Emperor Nero was in the habit of trying persons accused of several offences only at intervals, and taking each charge separately, that, too, would protract the process for a long time. But that it would end in acquittal might be seen from the conduct of Felix and Festus. Meanwhile St. Paul maintained through his messengers a constant intercourse with the Churches he had founded all over the Empire, and even with those he had not himself founded or visited in person. Many of his oldest and most faithful adherents surrounded him in Rome. St. Luke, St. Timothy, Tychicus, Demas, who afterwards left him, and St. Mark, who had caused the

[1] Acts xxviii. 30, 31.

former separation between him and St. Barnabas, were there and ministered to him. Two Macedonians, Aristarchus and Epaphras of Colossæ, were his fellow prisoners.[1]

He wrote three Epistles about the same time—the short one to Philemon in behalf of his faithless and runaway slave, that to the Colossians, and that to the Ephesians. The Church at Colossæ in Phrygia had not been founded by St. Paul, nor as yet visited by him. But he had learnt from its founder, Epaphras, who was now in Rome, that the faith of Christians there was in danger from false teachers, forerunners of the great Gnostic movement of the second century, who joined to Gnostic principles a zeal for the Jewish Law, especially its new moons and festivals. They taught abstinence from flesh and wine, cautioned men against defilement from touching or tasting unclean things, and boasting of a higher traditionary wisdom maintained, with a show of humility, that God was incomprehensible and out of reach, and must therefore be worshipped through intermediate beings, angels or higher spirits.[2]

Tychicus, who was the bearer of this Epistle, had also another short document to deliver, composed by the Apostle afterwards. It is inscribed to the Ephesians, but as the writer says nothing of his earlier labours for more than a year in Ephesus, and there are no personal allusions to members of that community, nor is even the name of Ephesus found in the older manuscripts, it clearly had a more general scope, and was a circular addressed to the Churches on the Asiatic coast, in whose assemblies it was to be read, though St. Paul had Ephesus chiefly in his eye.[3] The close similarity in the turn of thought shows this Epistle to have been written at the same time with that to the Colossians. It contains first a short abstract of Pauline doctrine, chiefly in the indirect form of a thanksgiving, special prominence being assigned to the abolition of the Mosaic Law, which implied the removal of separation between Jew and Gentile. The writer speaks of the fulness of grace given to them and the antithesis of their former Gentile life to their present one, of the unity of the Church

---

[1] Col. i. 1, 7; iv. 7, 10, 14. Philip. i. 1. Eph. vi. 21. Philem. 23, 24.
[2] Col. ii. 16—23. [3] Tertull. c. Marc. v. 11. Basil c. Eunom. i. 254. Opp. Ed. Garon.

where Gentiles are united with believing Israel in one temple of God, and of the exalted office God had conferred specially on him of calling the Gentile world into the Church. The second part includes a number of moral instructions and exhortations.

The Philippian Church, the first St. Paul had founded in Europe, had sent him a contribution by Epaphroditus, to support him in his imprisonment. Their messenger brought so favourable a report of their state, that in his letter of thanks he could praise them more highly than any other community. The whole Epistle accordingly is written in a tone of joyful exultation, and is pre-eminently an outpouring of warm and hearty affection for them. Here there were no internal divisions, but he thought it needful to warn them against his Jewish opponents and the false teachers who penetrated everywhere, and to show that he shared all the privileges boasted of by the false brethren of the circumcision who depreciated him.

It is the tradition of the whole ancient Church that St. Paul was released from prison, and, after working as an Apostle for two or three years more, was put to death in the Neronian persecution in the year 67. In recent times this release and second imprisonment have been sharply contested, and it has been assumed that the first imprisonment only ended with his death. But there is conclusive evidence of the truth of the old tradition. When the book of Acts, written by St. Paul's attendant, after the fullest and most detailed account of his journey and arrival at Rome suddenly closes with the statement that he remained two whole years at Rome under a military guard, this implies that with the two years his imprisonment ended. And it must have ended, either by his death or his release; clearly not by his death, for it would be inconceivable that St. Luke, who devotes the whole second part of his book to the biography of St. Paul, should not have added the coping-stone so gloriously crowning his hero's work. On the other hand, his silence as to what followed the two years' imprisonment is perfectly natural, for he was no longer the Apostles companion, and he wrote his narrative before the year 67, and therefore could not mention his death. St. Paul's release at that time is quite probable in itself, for the Jews, as Felix and Festus had already perceived, were obviously in no position to convict him of any capital crime according to Roman law: nor is it probable that a Roman citizen would be kept, not two, but four years in prison without any trial.

There is not a single witness in Christian antiquity to contradict the positive testimony of St. Clement, the Muratorian Canon, Eusebius, St. Chrysostom, and St. Jerome.[1] St. Clement, the Apostle's contemporary and disciple, says in his letter from Rome to Corinth, that St. Paul had preached the Gospel in East and West, and taught the whole world (*i. e.* the whole Roman world) righteousness, had gone to the extreme boundaries of the West, borne testimony before rulers, or suffered martyrdom, and thus been taken out of the world.[2] Here is a distinct geographical statement, and a writer in Rome cannot have understood Rome by the limits of the West. St. Clement had already mentioned generally St. Paul's having preached in the West, but he wishes to add something still greater, in order to bring out more conspicuously the all-embracing heroic energy of the Apostle, namely, that he had gone to the extremest limits of the West,[3] certainly meaning one of the western provinces of the Empire. The author of the Muratorian Canon, dating between 165 and 175, expressly asserts that this was Spain.[4] To this is added the weighty

---

[1] Euseb. ii. 22. Chrys. *in* 2 *Tim.* iv. 20. Hieron. *Catal. Script.*
[2] Clem. Rom. i. 5.
[3] Wieseler's notion of translating τὸ τέρμα τῆς δύσεως "the Rulers of Rome" would hardly deserve a refutation if Schaff (*Geschichte der apost. Kirche*, p. 348) had not adopted it, and translated "he appeared before the highest authority of the West;" but it is pure assumption that τέρμα anywhere means this. In the passage quoted κακῶν δ' ἀναψυχὰς θεοὶ βροτοῖς νέμουσ', ἀπάντων τέρμ' ἔχοντες αὐτοί. (Eur. Suppl. 616—618.) τέρμα means the goal or end (of sufferings), not highest power, as Schaff imagines. So in τέρμα σωτηρίας, Soph. *Œd. Col.* 725, Eur. *Orest.* 1343, (*metam salutis.*) No weight can be attached to the circumstance that there is no tradition in Spain of any Church founded there by St. Paul. We know almost nothing of the history of the Spanish Church for the first three centuries; two martyrs of a later date, the deposition of two Bishops in the third century mentioned in St. Cyprian's letters, and the Canons of the Synod of Elvira—that is all. The tradition of the Spanish Church reaches no further back than the third century; no Spanish Christians wrote anything before the end of the fourth.
[4] "Sicuti et (Lucas) semota passione Petri evidenter declarat seu (*or et*) profectione Pauli ab urbe ad Spaniam proficiscentis." Cf. Wieseler *in den theol. Studien*, 1856, p. 105. The author here infers from the omission of these two occurrences, St. Peter's death and St. Paul's Spanish journey, that St. Luke only records what took place in his own presence. He thus puts both facts in the same category of certainty.

testimony of the Pastoral Epistles, which can only be got rid of by the purely novel assumption of their being spurious; for they cannot be placed either before or during the first imprisonment without doing violence to the statements of fact contained in them, and they prove that St. Paul after that imprisonment visited Ephesus, Crete, Macedonia, and Nicopolis, and was then a second time imprisoned at Rome.[1]

St. Paul's three Pastoral Epistles were written within a few months of each other; they correspond in style, in matter, and in their account of the condition of the Church, and are essentially different in these points from the rest of his Epistles. All attempts to separate them in date have failed and must fail. A longer period, of about five years, must have elapsed between his Epistle to the Philippians, the last during his first imprisonment, and the first to St. Timothy, and it is most likely that this and the Epistle to St. Titus were written shortly before his last arrival in Rome. He had found Jewish proselytes in Spain to whom he could preach the Gospel in all the towns on the coast from Tarraco to Cadis. From Spain he seems to have gone to Ephesus about the year 66, where he found heretical teachers busy at work, the forerunners and first founders of Gnosticism. He did not, however, stay there long but hastened to other regions. The foreboding that he had but a short time to work, joined with the sense of bodily weakness and old age—several years earlier in his Epistle to the Philippians he had called himself an old man—drove him restlessly from place to place, to found as many new communities as possible, or visit and confirm for the last time those already founded. Thus he came first to Macedonia, then to Crete.[2] From Macedonia he sent his first Epistle to his beloved disciple Timothy, of whom he had before said that he did the Lord's work like himself.[3] This Epistle was to advise him as to the active administration of his episcopal office at Ephesus, and especially the appointment of Church ministers, and to put him in a condition to oppose the Judaizing Gnostic teachers at Ephesus with the Apostle's authority, and with greater success.

---

[1] 1 Tim. i. 3; 2 Tim. i. 17. Tit. i. 5; iii. 12.
[2] 1 Tim. i. 3. Tit. i. 5.    [3] 1 Cor. xvi. 10.

Soon afterwards St. Paul went by Ephesus to Crete, where, as many expressions in his Epistle to Titus indicate, he found Christian communities already founded, which had likewise been disturbed by false teachers, and had very little fixed organisation. He left behind him there his companion and disciple St. Titus, as his representative with full powers for ordering the community, and soon after, just before setting out for the West, sent him, probably from Ephesus, the Epistle in which he instructed him about the discharge of his office and his conduct towards the Judaizing false teachers. At Nicopolis in Epirus, where he meant to spend the winter, Titus was again to join him. On the way there he left his old companion Trophimus sick at Miletus, and Erastus at Corinth. It was probably during the winter at Nicopolis that he was seized and sent to stand his trial at Rome, as so conspicuous a Christian teacher could not long remain hidden in the then state of things. Fear of danger now scattered his companions and disciples. Demas, who had attended him faithfully in his first imprisonment, left him "from love for the world," and went to Thessalonica, Crescens turned to Galatia, Titus may have gone by his wish to Dalmatia. Only St. Luke held out and accompanied him to Rome.[1]

This second imprisonment of the Apostle at Rome was very different from the first, from which he was released at the beginning of the year 63. Then, he was left free to preach the Gospel in his hired dwelling to a numerous audience: every one could easily find the house where he lived for two years, and had free entry. Then, the widely-spread tidings of his freedom in preaching, notwithstanding his bonds, had filled the great body of Roman Christians with courage, so that they too preached Christ fearlessly.[2] But now, Onesiphorus, on coming to Rome, had much trouble to search him out; all his companions and assistants but one had deserted him. It was far too dangerous to show any interest in him, and every Christian had to fear for his own life.[3] He was not only chained now, but treated as a criminal, which had not been the case before. For, since then, the Christians had been accused of the burning

[1] 2 Tim. iv. 11.   [2] Phil. i. 13, 14.   [3] 2 Tim. i. 17; iv. 16.

of Rome, and horrible executions had taken place. St. Paul's trial came two years later, but the abhorrence of the new sect was nowise softened, and he was notorious as a leader of it. It laid a man open to so much suspicion, to give him even the ordinary legal assistance, that at his first hearing he had to dispense with the aid of counsel; this hearing was probably before the city prefect,[1] for the Emperor was in Greece. When St. Paul says he was at this time delivered from the lion's mouth,[2] he refers to his acquittal on the charge of participation in the burning of Rome, and his escape from the horrible death which condemnation on that score would have implied. He knew well that he had not been acquitted absolutely, and had not escaped death. He wrote after this first hearing to St. Timothy, that his blood would soon be poured out as a drink-offering and the time of his departure was at hand. The faithful Luke was with him, and he had found new disciples, Linus, Pudens, and Claudia, but he longed to see his beloved Timothy once more, and to give him his last charges; therefore he wrote this second Epistle, to beg him to come quickly. But as he was very uncertain whether Timothy would find him alive, he gave him many admonitions about the discharge of his office in the Church, exhorted him to steadfastness in persecution, and warned him again of the new false doctrine.

The Epistle to the Hebrews, *i.e.* the Jewish Christians of Palestine, coincides in date with the latter years of the Apostle's life. It is clear from internal evidence that it was not written before the year 63 or after 69. It is addressed to men familiar with the Levitical service and rites of the temple, and living in its neighbourhood, so that the Jewish worship and priesthood still exercise their full influence over them. Their Church had existed a long time; their original ministers and teachers were already dead; and their death could be held up as a pattern to survivors, from the unshaken constancy with which they died for their belief.[3] A second generation of Christians had grown up, but they were in imminent peril of falling away from

---

[1] St. Clement of Rome says ἐπὶ τῶν λεγομένων, which clearly cannot mean the Emperor.
[2] 2 Tim. iv. 17.   [3] Heb. v. 12; xiii. 7.

Christ and returning to Judaism. Some had already forsaken public worship. There is no reference in any other Apostolical Epistle to the danger here mentioned of apostasy to Judaism and blasphemy against Christ. This state of things had now appeared for the first time in Judæa, and especially at Jerusalem, caused apparently by the hostility of the unconverted Jews and the fear of exclusion from the temple worship. But it is a mistake to affirm, as has often been done of late, that the author of the Epistle required an entire separation from the Jewish religion.[1] He would not have done that incidentally in a couple of passing words, but have explained his grounds at length. As long as the temple stood, no Jewish Christian was required to abjure the Levitical worship. But the writer points out the superiority of the New to the Old Covenant, with its purely transitory and symbolical character, the dignity of Messiah and the prerogatives of the New as compared with the Old Testament revelation, and that the offering of Christ precludes all need of further offering for sin. The form of an Epistle only comes out towards the end of this document; the earlier portion is more like a treatise, carefully tracing out the chain of argument, and elaborating the subject with a more systematic arrangement than is found in any other Apostolical Epistle, not without some display of oratory. It was written originally, not in Aramaic, but in Greek; it bears no Apostle's name, and cannot in its present form be the work of St. Paul's hand, though breathing his spirit. We cannot, indeed, urge, as has often been done, the passage speaking of the salvation first proclaimed by the Lord being handed down to us by those that heard it, as conclusive against his authorship.[2] For that is said in the name of the community addressed, and it would have been very farfetched and gratuitous for the Apostle, who in fact had not heard the preaching of Jesus directly, to insert a saving clause; "I have indeed received an inward revelation from the Lord." But there are other proofs that he did not write the Epistle;—the author invariably follows the Alexandrian version, even where differing completely in sense from the Hebrew,[3] whereas St. Paul does not keep strictly

---

[1] As *e.g.* in Lünemann's and Delitzsch's erroneous interpretation of Heb. xiii. 13.
[2] Heb. ii. 3.     [3] See Heb. x. 5 especially.

to it but much oftener translates for himself;—secondly, St. Paul always names himself at the beginning of his Epistles; and lastly, the style is more polished, and flows more evenly and smoothly, but is less precise than St. Paul's, where the thought seems often to be struggling with the language. Moreover the tone is less dialectical and more rhetorical, betraying a philosophical education.

Nevertheless, the tradition of the Eastern Church, followed afterwards by the Western, has recognised the Apostle Paul as the principal author of the Epistle. It was attributed to him by the Syrian and Alexandrian Churches, those nearest the community it is addressed to, but the general belief was, that he had not written it with his own hand, but used the services of another, either Luke or Clement. Clement of Alexandria's idea, that St. Luke translated the Apostle's Hebrew into Greek, is quite untenable, for the Epistle betrays clearly enough its original Greek composition, and St. Paul's friend or disciple must have contributed more to the authorship than mere translation. Clement of Rome cannot be regarded as the writer, or joint writer, for then it would be the more unintelligible how the Epistle came to be so long rejected or ignored in the Roman Church, and the difference between this Epistle and his to the Corinthians is too great for both to be by the same author, besides that the use made in the latter of this one is further evidence against it. Tertullian's assertion, that St. Barnabas is the writer, stands quite alone. Nor is there any trace or hint in the Ancient Church of the conjecture that Apollos wrote it, and as nothing more distinct is known of Apollos it is a mere make-shift. It continues, therefore, to be the most probable view, that St. Luke wrote the Epistle under St. Paul's inspiration, and to this the most ancient tradition points.[1]

Of all the personages in the New Testament St. Paul is the one we know best; his form is brought visibly before us, not only in the narrative of his disciple and companion St. Luke, but in his own Epistles. His personal appearance seems not to have been striking; the Lycaonians took him for Hermes, and Barnabas for Zeus,

---

[1] Clem. Alex. *ap. Eus.* vi. 14. Tertull. *de Pudic.* 20. Origen *ap Eus.* vi. 25. Hieron. *Cat.* 5

clearly because the personal appearance of St. Barnabas was the more stately, that of St. Paul insignificant.[1] His letters, said his Corinthian opponents, are weighty and strong, but his bodily presence is feeble, and his speech contemptible;[2] they thought such bodily defects and weaknesses as were peculiar to him irreconcilable with the Apostolical authority he laid claim to. He himself felt most keenly the incongruity of his outward appearance and bodily powers with the high vocation entrusted to him. His want of eloquence even made him shy and embarrassed:—"I was with you in weakness, and in much fear and trembling," he writes to the Corinthians.[3] He compares his bodily state with its signs of infirmity, paleness and the like, to the condition of the Lord on the Cross. He speaks of a troublesome, depressing, unintermittent pain, whose recurring paroxysms he found a "thorn for the flesh,"[4] as though he were struck by a demon with his fists. Three times he had prayed that it might be taken away, but his prayer was not granted. To this were added the wounds and scars, which he received in his Apostolical office, but which he bore as honourable tokens, as marks of his Lord imprinted on him the servant of Christ.[5]

But in this feeble frame there dwelt a mighty spirit, a glowing enthusiasm that never slackened, a courage that never failed. And if all he accomplished was wrought in constant struggle with his frail and sickly body, if he had the consciousness of carrying the lofty treasure committed to him in an earthen vessel, this did not prevent him from glorying in his weakness, and finding in it a ground of joyful exultation, because when weak in himself then he was strong in God.[6] And if the depth and richness of his thoughts strove in vain for adequate expression, if his bold flight seemed to carry him away, yet he spoke "with power, and in the name of the Holy Ghost, and in great confidence."[7] For he had the profoundest conviction of possessing the Spirit of God, that Christ spoke through

---

[1] Acts xiv. 12.   [2] 2 Cor. x. 10.   [3] 1 Cor. ii. 3.
[4] [σκόλοψ τῇ σαρκί, literally "a stake." The Vulg. renders "stimulus carnis,']
[5] 2 Cor. iv. 10; xii. 7—9. Gal. vi. 17.
[6] 2 Cor. iv. 7; xii. 10.   [7] 1 Thess. i. 5.

him, or he in Christ, and that the Lord dwelt in him with His power.¹ And in fact Christ left him in no want of signs and proofs of His altogether exceptional guidance and enlightenment. Four times, so far as we know, in his Apostolical course the consolation of a special vision, with its illumination and encouragement, was vouchsafed him by the Lord. This took place, first in the temple at Jerusalem, soon after his conversion; secondly in Corinth, immediately after his being cast out of the Synagogue, when Jesus gave him in the night the same assurance He had given to the other Apostles,—"I am with thee;" a third time, in the castle of Antonia; and lastly, during the shipwreck.² Once it befel him in an ecstasy to feel himself suddenly transported into the seat of the glory of Christ, into the immediate presence of God, where he heard wonderful words that could not be repeated.³ And above all, He whom he saw on the way to Damascus was constantly with him; he called on Him, and was answered, and found in this personal converse and uninterrupted revelation the richest compensation and comfort for all the "infirmities, reproaches, necessities, persecutions, and distresses," to which he was a prey.⁴ He needed, indeed, that continual strengthening and support, for what he had to bear in the execution of his Apostolical office was beyond the powers of a man infirm in body, and the victim of severe suffering. When he wrote his Second Epistle to the Corinthians (A.D. 57), about ten years before his death, he had already been scourged five times by the Jews, and this punishment of the thirty-nine stripes, ordered by the Law, was so horrible that the victims sometimes died of it.⁵ Notwithstanding his rights of citizenship he had thrice endured the Roman punishment of whipping with rods, which also not unfrequently caused death. Once at Lystra the mob, incited by the Jews, had stoned him, so that he was taken for dead.⁶ Thrice he had suffered shipwreck, and had once in consequence been driven about a day and

---

¹ 1 Cor. vii. 40.   2 Cor. xiii. 3; ii. 17; xii. 9.
² Acts xxii. 17—21; xviii. 9, 10; xxiii. 11; xxvii. 23, 24.
³ 2 Cor. xii. 1—4.                               ⁴ 2 Cor. xii. 10.
⁵ Joseph. *Arch.* viii. 21, 23.                  ⁶ Acts xiv. 19.

a night on the sea with help of a wreck often covered by the waves. He had been seven times imprisoned before his death.[1]

The doctrine which St. Paul taught became flesh and blood in his person; it was bound up with his whole being, with his most personal and individual feelings and experiences. He was not only a disciple and imitator of Christ, but was completely possessed and inspired by Him. Since that one appearance of Christ, when He revealed Himself in His glory and Divine majesty, St. Paul had become quite another man, his very consciousness and life were different; he was now so inwardly united with Christ that the thought of Him and the consciousness of His presence was mixed up with every act and consideration, and his habitual condition was one of continual exaltation and, as compared with other men, of ecstasy.[2] He speaks of himself as so completely ruled by the love Christ, attested in His atoning death, that he is no more his own master, that he must follow the constraint of that love without regard to any personal considerations. He feels as one dead with Christ, to whom the world is crucified and he to the world.[3] His endeavour was to make his own life in actions and sufferings a worthy transcript of the life of Jesus. In his own sufferings he saw only a continuation and filling up of the sufferings of Christ.[4] Whether he shall glorify Christ by his life or death is the same to him;[5] he would prefer to die and be with Christ, if it were not his office to serve the Church.

The purely human many-sidedness[6] and spiritual mobility of Greek character was first transfigurated in his person into an entire self-surrender to the service of known truth, and raised to a saintly purity. To preach the Gospel is to him not a matter of free choice but a sacred duty and necessity. He only knows that he is a passive instrument in God's hand, that he has no power to restrain by his silence those mighty deeds and doctrines in their victorious course through the world. He cannot conceive the notion of the preacher's office entrusted to him remaining unful-

---

[1] Clem. Rom. *Ep.* i. 1, 5.   [2] Gal. ii. 20; vi. 14.  2 Cor. v 16.   Phil. iii. 20.
[3] Gal. vi. 14.   [4] Col. 1. 24.   [5] Phil. i. 21.
[6] [The εὐτραπελία of Thucydides.—Tr.]

filled. He feels, indeed, free from all earthly bonds, yet bound more than any man, for he is the servant of all, under an obligation to minister to all men with his Gospel.[1] And this ministry was moulded by his sincere geniality of character into a real art. He possessed a marvellous capability and readiness for putting himself in the place of others, for adapting his words and actions to the condition and comprehension of every body. With affectionate sympathy he completely merged himself in his converts, and took their feelings upon him; their joys and their sufferings were his, so thoroughly that in one of his Epistles two Pauls seem to speak interchangeably, the one absolutely identified with the feelings, views, and circumstances of his fellow believers, the other standing over them to instruct, to correct, and to punish in his Apostolic dignity. And thus he is able to say that he became all things to all men, to the Jews as a Jew, to the Gentiles as without law, that he might win them. He became for the whole Church the special model of that pastoral love which accommodates itself to all, yielding in indifferent matters, and gradually raising the weaker to itself. He first taught, by word and example, how genuine love should deny itself the use of a lawful freedom. "If eating offend my brother, I had rather eat no flesh all my life."[2]

He is accordingly present in all his instructions and ordinances to the Church he is guiding, with the whole force of his mind and energy of his will; where his letters go he goes with them, absent in body, as he says, but present in spirit. He always seems to reckon beforehand the effect of his words. With his mental eye sharpened by love and by rich experience and intuitive knowledge of human nature, he divines the feelings and dispositions of the new Christians and meets them with the right word. He is ever with them; he thinks, feels, lives, and suffers with them. Time and distance have no power over this fellowship of belief, joys, and sorrows. It is very seldom that he gives direct and simple commands, he rules his communities by drawing them into fellowship with his own judgment and will. While he takes on himself their views and trials, he merely lays before them in return his judg-

[1] 1 Cor. ix. 16, 19.  [2] 1 Cor. viii. 13.

ment and feelings. Instead of prescribing rigid laws, he strives to assimilate them to himself and to fuse his spirit into perfect unity with theirs.

It has often been thought strange that St. Paul's Epistles contain so extremely few references to the history of Jesus; but he wrote to those who were already believers, to whom, as he expressed it, he had discharged the office of mother and nurse.[1] Moreover, it is always the crucified and risen Lord who is before his mind; this double form he carries in himself, and speaks of one or the other to his converts. His Gospel is a Gospel of the glory of Christ, and a doctrine of the Cross; he rather looks forward to the future, and the approaching re-appearance of Jesus in His glory, than backwards to the time of His earthly pilgrimage.[2] There are, again, few express quotations of the sayings of Jesus to be found in St. Paul's writings, and those not in important questions. He is not wont to appeal to the words of the Lord, but to the fulness of his own Apostolic power, to the crucifixion and resurrection of the Lord. Yet he repeats the words used at the institution of the Eucharist, and mentions a saying of Jesus not found in the Gospels. He only twice appeals to precepts of Jesus, once in reference to the right of Apostles and missionaries to live of the Gospel, once in distinguishing between his own opinion and Christ's command, when he quotes the prohibition of divorce.[3] But it is clear enough that he had the Lord's declarations before his mind in his moral exhortations and his references to the things after death. His humility and ready admission that he, the persecutor of Christ and His disciples, was a great sinner, did not withhold him from boasting and testifying what great things God had wrought in him and through him, and referring to the signs and wonders he had worked as proofs of his real and legitimate Apostleship. That he considered due to his office, far as he was from all self-exaltation. Thus he reminds the Corinthians that he had vindicated his Apostolate among them by miracles and signs of Divine power, and in patient endurance of adversity; and he goes further in his Epistle to the Romans, where he boasts of

---

[1] 1 Thess. ii. 7. [2] Rom. vi. 9—11; vii. 4; x. 9. 2 Cor. iv. 4; xi. 30.
[3] 1 Cor. vii. 10; ix. 14.

having spread the Gospel of Christ from Jerusalem to Illyricum, through the power of his miracles wrought by the help of God.¹

Two expressions in the Epistle to the Galatians have been often alleged as implying a split, a great division and a stiffness between St. Paul and the elder Apostles, which in reality had no existence. Far from desiring to depreciate the authority and successful work of the other Apostles as compared with his own, he always speaks of them with full acknowledgment and respect, allying himself and making common cause with them. He feels and says that he and they are equal to each other, equal in the dignity of their office and mission, and in the reverence of mankind. "God hath set forth us the Apostles last, as it were condemned to death, a spectacle to the world, to angels, and to men."² He places the Apostles first in the Church; they are with the Prophets its foundations. They are his brethren, and men whose labours do honour to Christ.³ He names himself as the least of the Apostles, although he or rather the grace of God in him has laboured more than they all.⁴ St. Paul was not converted by an Apostle but by the immediate revelation and call of Christ; he received not from his colleagues but from Christ Himself his Apostolic office and mission. What he called his Gospel—that is the equality of the Gentiles in the Church through faith without observing the Mosaic Law with the Jewish converts who kept it, and their equal possession of hope and means of grace—was immediately made known to him through a special communication. In this certainty of his call and his doctrine, in the consciousness that God is with him giving testimony by His miraculous power, he uses the authoritative language of a mighty ruler in the spiritual Kingdom; he feels strong and well armed enough to pull down every fortress that exalts itself against the knowledge of God, to bend down every thought and imagination of men under the obedience of Christ, and to punish all disobedience.⁵

The other Apostles on their side must have been fully

---

[1] 2 Cor. xii. 12. Rom. xv. 19.
[2] 1 Cor. iv. 9.
[3] Eph. iv. 11; ii. 20. 2 Cor. viii. 23.
[4] 1 Cor. xv. 9, 10.
[5] 2 Cor. x. 4—6.

conscious of their high privilege as compared with St. Paul. Jesus Himself had pronounced them blessed in seeing what they saw; He had spoken of their seeing the day of the Son of Man as a great blessing, and had foretold that afterwards in their afflictions they would look back with earnest desire to one of those days.[1] How does St. John in his old age exult in the joy of the consciousness that he has seen with his eyes and handled with his hands Him who was from the beginning![2] But this consciousness led to no division on either side. If St. Peter and St. Paul agreed on a certain division of labour, this was grounded on St. Peter's feeling that he and the rest of the elder Apostles were more immediately fitted and called by their whole mental training to work among the Jews, and that it was their office to bring in the Gentiles at first only where a foundation had been previously laid of converted Jews and well-instructed communities of Jewish Christians. They could only act effectively on the Gentiles through the converted Jews of the Dispersion, who were already familiar with Heathen views and morals, while St. Paul was the right man to act immediately on them with the best success. But if St. Paul designated himself the Apostle of the Gentiles, he did not mean that he was to give preference to the Gentiles over the Jews in carrying out his vocation; on the contrary, his first duty and endeavours always belonged to the Jews. But he meant that the wide domain of the Heathen provinces of the Empire, (where the Jews were only scattered here and there), was the special field of his Apostolical energy, while the other Apostles were still devoting themselves to the communities in Judæa and Galilee, which contained only Jewish Christians or so few Gentiles that the Jewish element gave their dominant character to these societies, and the few Gentile converts had to adapt themselves to it. On the contrary, in the communities founded or visited by St. Paul, the Gentile character predominated from the beginning, and the Jewish Christians who chanced to be there were necessarily required to act accordingly, and to renounce the separatist element of the Law which forbade to eat with the uncircumcised.

[1] Luke x. 23, 24; xvii. 22.   [2] 1 John i. 1—4.

Nothing is known of the acts and events of St. Peter's life, from his meeting with St. Paul at Antioch till his martyrdom at Rome. But we have two Epistles of his, which probably belong to this period. He addressed the First, at a date which cannot be precisely fixed, to the communities in the north of Asia Minor, consisting partly of Jews, but chiefly of Gentile converts, to the believers living as strangers scattered among the Heathen in Pontus, Galatia, Cappadocia, Asia, and Bithynia,—communities partly founded by St. Paul. Silas, formerly a companion of St. Paul's, was its bearer.[1] The word, "dispersion," in the title does not at all mean that the Epistle was only addressed to the Christians of Jewish descent in those communities—a division St. Peter never dreamt of—but it suggested itself as the natural designation for Christians who, like the Jews before, were a "dispersion," and felt themselves a scattered body of strangers in the Roman Empire, yet inwardly united by the closest bonds.[2] There are several expressions in the Epistle which can only be understood of those who had formerly been Heathen.[3] Their past and future sufferings and persecutions gave occasion to the Apostle to strengthen the believers, by pointing to the promises they had received of future glory. Christian hope, and its proper influence over the whole life, is the ruling idea of his Epistle, which is hortatory, not dogmatic. He shows them how highly they have been favoured, as being redeemed and regenerate, and that it is their duty in consequence of that great gift to put to shame the reproaches of the Heathen by purity of life; to aim not only at individual sanctity, but at the glory and perfection of the whole Church, as the people now more than ever chosen by God for His own. A series of special admonitions are added bearing on particular details of daily life. It is obvious that St. Paul's Epistles to the Ephesians and Romans had left fixed impressions on St. Peter's mind which are reflected in his writings. At the same time this Epistle is interwoven with Old Testament words and

---

[1] 1 Peter v. 12.
[2] Cf. 1 Pet. ii. 11, where the Christians are called emphatically πάροικοι καὶ παρεπίδημοι as in the superscription παρεπίδημοι διασπορᾶς.
[3] 1 Peter iv. 3, 4.

phrases, in which it was natural to him to clothe his thoughts. Its whole line, both in what it says and what it does not say, proves that the original difficulties in the way of a complete coalescing of Jewish and Gentile Christians were already overcome, at least in those regions, and that the errors St. Paul had to combat in writing to the Galatians no longer presented themselves, while the seductions of Jewish Gnosticism had not yet appeared. The date of the composition must therefore be placed several years before the Apostle's death, before, indeed, St. Paul had written his Epistles to the Colossians, to Timothy, and Titus.

On the other hand, St. Peter's Second Epistle, addressed later to the same communities, is a kind of testament; he knows that his departure is at hand, and warns the Churches of the danger of erroneous doctrine, of Antinomian heretics who are spoken of partly as future, partly as already come, as men who on the ground of their *gnosis* and false spiritualism preached an indulgence of all the lusts of the flesh, and denied the Second Coming of Christ and the judgment. The remarkable agreement of this Epistle with that of St. Jude is not to be explained by the writer's using St. Jude's, but on the contrary by St. Jude having St. Peter's before him, and recognising in the erroneous teachers who had meantime actually appeared those whom St. Peter had foretold. Clearly as the Epistle reveals the hand of the Prince of the Apostles, it very slowly attained universal acknowledgment and use in the ancient Church. It is not found in the older Syrian *Peschito*, Origen and Eusebius reckon it among disputed writings; yet Hermas had already used it, Clement of Alexandria had commented on it in his Hypotyposes, Firmilian of Cæsarea had appealed to it, and from thenceforward, especially since the fourth century, it was universally accepted as canonical. According to St. Jerome,[1] the reason of the earlier doubt lay in the great difference of style observed between the first and unquestioned Epistle of St. Peter and this second. But St. Jerome has given the natural cause of this variety, namely, that St. Peter availed himself of different assistants, as not being sufficiently at home in the Greek

[1] Hier. *De Script. Eccl.* 1.

language to write it with ease. And in fact two such persons were recognised in the earliest ages, St. Mark, who is mentioned in the first Epistle as the Apostle's helper, and Glaucias.

Two questions are involved in deciding St. Peter's relation to the Church of Rome;—Did he found it? Did he die there? We must examine both. 1. The Roman Church must have been founded by an Apostle, and that Apostle can only have been Peter. St. Paul declares in his Epistle to the Romans that he had often withstood his longing to come to them, because he made a principle of only bringing the Gospel where Christ had not yet been preached, so as not to build on another man's foundation. But now, after the Church had been founded in the West, he was going into Spain, and would visit Rome on the way.[1] He was unwilling, then, at that time to undertake a regular Apostolic office in Rome, "because the foundation was already laid." By whom? St. Paul cannot possibly have meant by the chance visit of some nameless believer, or by those who returned from Jerusalem and related what they had heard there; he found irregular pre-announcements of that kind in most Churches, to which he none the less devoted his special energies. He cannot, in a word, mean that it was his principle only to teach where no one had preached the Gospel before him, for, on the one hand, no intelligible ground for such a rule can be imagined; on the other, the contrary is proved by his labours in Antioch and Cyprus, and his anxious care and earnest exhortations written to the community of Colossæ, which was unknown to him personally. He must refer, therefore, to his former agreement with the great Apostles at Jerusalem, and the position he took towards them, according to which he desired to abstain from meddling with their work or building on a foundation laid by them. There can be no doubt, then, that it was St. Peter, perhaps accompanied by St. John, who had laid the foundation in Rome.

The formation of a Church at Rome, in the centre of the Empire, where the number of Jews was greater and their position more important than at any other town out of Judæa, excepting Alexandria, was far too important a

[1] Rom. xv. 20—24.

matter to be left to chance. If St. Philip's work in Samaria determined the Apostles Peter and John to go there, to carry on and perfect what the deacon had begun, if the example of Alexandria showed them the expansive power of the Gospel and the importance and necessity of an ecclesiastical organisation in a great capital, it is inconceivable that at Jerusalem, where Jews from Rome appeared at every festival, the idea of planting the Gospel in the great capital of the world should not have been seriously entertained. While all the principal Churches have their tradition about the men to whom they owe their first foundation, Peter is marked out, both by the universal tradition of all Churches and the special tradition of the Roman, as the founder and first ruler of that Church, and is said—which comes to the same thing—to have first gone to Rome under Claudius. St. Dionysius of Corinth and St. Irenæus in the second century mention St. Peter as having laid the foundation of the Roman community. The planting of the Roman and Corinthian Churches, says the former, was by Peter and Paul;[1] *i.e.*, as St. Paul founded the Corinthian, St. Peter founded the Roman Church. St. Irenæus likewise ascribes to the two Apostles the founding and ordering of these Churches; and since all St. Paul did at Rome comes later it is St. Peter who always appears as the special father of the Church there.

The Roman Church, when St. Paul wrote his Epistle, was in a different state, and is addressed by him in a different tone from other Churches. It was already complete, so to speak, and its faith spoken of over all the world.[2] There were no quarrels and party-strifes, Jews and Gentiles lived together in the Church as brethren, and St. Paul speaks in turn to the one and the other, but he speaks with an apologetic respectfulness, found in none of his other Epistles;—he excuses his "boldness" in admonishing them, appealing to his lofty mission as a minister of Christ among the Gentiles, although the main contents of the Epistle concern the Jews more than the Gentiles. He knows well that the Roman Christians are already filled

---

[1] Dionysius (Eus. vi. 25) uses the word φυτείαν, and Irenæus says (Eus. v. 6.), θεμελιώσαντες καὶ οἰκοδομήσαντες. Cf. Eus. v. 8.
[2] Rom. i. 8; xvi. 19.

with all knowledge. It is impossible he could have written in such terms at a time when the most imperfect knowledge of the new doctrine was found in many communities, and among individuals, like Apollos, unless he had recognised in the person of its founder and first preacher a guarantee for the purity and perfection of the Gospel planted there. It is only at the end that he introduces a very short and generally-worded warning against divisions.[1] Neither, again, had he any Judaizing opponents at Rome, as in so many other communities; and if we consider that the Church there was clearly not founded by his disciples, while yet its unity implied a well-ordered ecclesiastical organisation, such as then could only be set up by an Apostle, we are brought back to Peter as the only founder who can be imagined. The notion of a gradual origin of the community without any particular founder, or of Aquila and Priscilla being its founders, or St. Paul himself, is self-evidently untenable.

The Jews had a particular quarter in the Transtiberine region of the city of Rome, where they had lived in part since 63 B.C., when Pompey brought thousands of them there as prisoners of war, and gave them their freedom. It was they who afterwards established the Synagogue of the Libertines at Jerusalem. At the death of the first Herod eight thousand of their fellow-countrymen living in Rome had joined the deputies sent from Jerusalem. Since then the number had increased, and many proselytes of the gate were added to it. In 49 A.D. they were banished from Rome, because, in the words of the Roman historian, they "excited an incessant disturbance instigated by one Chrestus."[2] That quarrels about the Messiahship of Christ and the disturbance caused by the formation of a Christian community are here meant, is so obvious an explanation that it is sure to be always recurred to. At the death of Claudius soon afterwards, the exiles returned. When St. Paul wrote to the Romans, Aquila and Priscilla, who had been expelled by the Edict, were again there. But when he came to Rome, about the year 62, in consequence of his appeal to Cæsar, the chief men among the Roman Jews expressed themselves with evident reserve about the

---

[1] Rom. xvi. 17, 18.     [2] Suet. Claud. 25.

Christian community;—"We wish to hear what thou thinkest, for this sect is known to us to be everywhere spoken against."[1] They had evidently been frightened and made cautious by the previous events and their sufferings under Claudius, and were unwilling to give any weapons against themselves to the man who was soon to be heard before the Emperor or his delegates, protected by his Roman citizenship. St. Paul himself seems to have seen through their mistrust, for he assures them that, in appealing to the Emperor, he has no intention of accusing his own people.[2] St. Peter's journey to Rome must, then, have preceded Claudius' decree of banishment.[3]

St. Peter's own testimony in his First Epistle raises to a certainty the fact of his having been at Rome. The letter is written from a city he calls Babylon. This cannot reasonably be understood of the Egyptian Babylon, a strong fortress and station of a Roman legion, and thus the question arises, whether it is Babylon on the Euphrates, or whether, according to a method of speech very natural to the Jews of that day from the usage of the Prophets, it means Rome. The latter is the belief of the ancient Church, following a tradition of the Apostolic age to which Papias bears witness. That St. Peter had passed over the boundaries of the Roman Empire into Parthia to Babylon on the Euphrates, that there was already a Christian community there, and that from thence the Apostle salutes the believers to whom he is writing—this is more than improbable. Strabo and Pliny mention Babylon as "a great desert" which, chiefly from the neighbourhood of Seleucia and Ctesiphon, had become emptied of inhabitants.[4] The towns of Nearda and Nisibis were the principal Jewish settlements in the Babylonian Satrapy; the Jews had

---

[1] Acts xxviii. 22.       [2] Acts xxviii. 17—19.
[3] The "Acts" are silent about St. Peter's doings and fate from Cornelius's baptism till his imprisonment by Herod Agrippa. (Acts xi. 18—xii. 3). There is thus an interval of full three years for his journey to Rome, to which tradition testifies, and his return to Jerusalem. (See Hug's *Introd.* ii. 273). His arrival at Rome comes in the beginning of Claudius' reign, not "secundo Claudii anno," as St. Jerome says, after the Chronicle of Eusebius; the better text of the Chronicle we now possess has not this date. (See Kunstmann, *Hist. Pol. Blättern*, 1857, ii. 596 sqq.). Orosius says more correctly (Hist. vii. 6) "Exordio regni Claudii." That St. Luke omits St. Peter's journey to Rome will surprise no one who remembers his omissions in the history of St. Paul.
[4] Plin. *Hist. Nat.* vi. 26. Strabo xvi. 738.

moved from Babylon to Seleucia several years befor
Peter could have come there, because they could not
out against the Heathen inhabitants who were host
them; and soon afterwards another emigration took
on account of a pestilence. Five years later more thar
thousand Jews were put to death in Seleucia by
Syrians and Greeks, and the remainder went, not ba
Babylon, but to Nearda and Nisibis;[1] the only infe
therefore to be drawn from Josephus' history is, that
date of St. Peter's Epistle there were no longer any
in Babylon, and so, too, Agrippa, in his speech at th
ginning of the Jewish war, knew of no Jews to
beyond the Jordan, except those in the province of
bene. That St. Mark, who was in "Babylon" wit
Apostle, was at Rome at the precise time when th
every reason to believe that this Epistle was writt
clear from St. Paul's mentioning him.[2] Soon after h
staying in Asia Minor, whence St. Paul recalled h
Rome shortly before his death.[3] There is nothing s
in St. Peter's designating Rome in an Epistle by the
used in the poetical prophecy of the Apocalypse. A
who had grown up in a country town of Galilee wi
language of the prophetic writings constantly in his
when he saw Rome with the abominations of Nero a
idolatry and moral corruptions prevalent there, cou
but be most vividly reminded of the Old Testament do
tions of Babylon; and thus it was natural enough
having at the beginning of his Epistle called the cc
nities of Asia Minor "elect pilgrims," he should at the
call the community, whose salutation he imparted
"fellow-elect in Babylon." And lastly, there are a
takable indications throughout the Epistle of the app
ing Neronic persecution, and St. Peter had good reas
using a local designation the Heathen would not
stand, in order to avoid the danger inevitable for h
and the Roman Christians if a copy of the document
fall into their hands, as it easily might.

St. Peter died as a Martyr in Rome under Nero b
cifixion, and Origen mentions the special circumsta

---

[1] Joseph. *Arch.* xviii. 9.     [2] Col. iv. 10. Philem. 24.
[3] 2 Tim. iv. 11.

his being nailed to the cross head downwards. This tradition is confirmed by the universal testimony of the whole ancient Church, and the grounds on which it has been assailed are not the result of historical criticism. St. John's Gospel leaves no doubt as to the Apostle's manner of death, for the Lord warned him prophetically in His last conversation with him of his end; in his old age his hands would be stretched and bound, and he would be carried whither he would not. The Evangelist adds that Jesus thereby signified by what manner of death he should glorify God.[1] And if, as this observation shows, St. Peter's martyrdom was a fact universally known in the Church at the end of the first century, so that the Evangelist found this mere intimation enough, it is impossible that the place where he glorified his Lord by his death, should not have been equally notorious. But no other town than Rome has ever been mentioned; there is not the least trace of any other Church having ever claimed to be the place of the Apostle's death. Dionysius of Corinth says (170 A.D.) that both the Apostles suffered martyrdom in Rome at the same time. The Roman Christian, Caius, says (A.D. 200), in his treatise against Proclus the Montanist, that he can point out on the Vatican and on the road to Ostia the memorials (trophies) of the Apostles (Peter and Paul) who founded this Church.[2] His contemporary Tertullian reckons among the prerogatives of the Roman Church, that "Peter was there conformed to the sufferings of the Lord."[3]

St. Peter suffered death either with St. Paul or after him. Clement of Rome fixes the time in saying, "Paul was executed under the rulers," for this points to the period of Nero's absence from Rome (A.D. 67) when the Prefect of the City, Helius Cæsarianus, and the pretorian Prefects, Nimphidius Sabinus and Tigellinus, were administering the government. The old tradition of St. Peter's twenty-five years episcopate in Rome arose from placing his journey thither in the year 42, the second of Claudius' reign, when he was set free from Agrippa's prison and escaped from Judæa; from then till his death in 67 is

---

[1] John xxi. 19.     [2] Euseb. ii. 25
[3] Tertull. *De Præscript.* 36.

twenty-five years. But, of course, it must not be inferred that he spent all that time in Rome.

The first Heathen persecution, to which St. Peter and St. Paul fell victims, was the baptism of blood of the Roman Church; it befitted her dignity and importance to shine forth as the first and most severely tried of all. Hitherto the Christians had passed in the eyes of the Heathen, especially the authorities at Rome, for a Jewish sect formed through some internal schism in the bosom of Judaism. As such they could only appear insignificant to the Romans. Tertullian expressly relates that Tiberius placed a motion before the Senate, on information received from Palestine, that Christ should be admitted among the Roman gods, and when the Senate rejected it still threatened punishment to those who accused Christians.[1] But this statement, improbable in itself, is contradicted by the silence of all other authorities. There seems never to have been any lack from the first of accusers of the Christians, partly Heathen, partly Jewish, for under Nero they were already "hated by the people on account of their shocking deeds," and taken for adherents of a new and criminal superstition, so that Christianity is first mentioned by Heathen historians as an abominable and corrupting misbelief, the Christians as "enemies of the human race;" and this was thenceforth the prevalent idea among educated Romans.[2] Even then had the enemies of Christianity spread those falsehoods about the *agape* and the Eucharist which afterwards demanded so many victims. The charge of misanthropy was their inheritance as a Jewish sect, for a similar reproach rested on the whole Jewish people, and the veil of mystery, in which the Christians shrouded their assemblies for divine service from the beginning, fostered the suspicion of their indulging in a criminal secret worship.

A frightful conflagration which broke out July 19, A.D. 64, had in six days and seven nights laid three of the fourteen quarters of Rome in ashes and destroyed the greater part of seven. It was known that during the fire, Nero, seated on a lofty tower, feasted his eyes on the magnificent spectacle of the sea of flame, and he was commonly believed to have been its author, though Tacitus leaves it undecided

---

[1] Tertull. *Apol.* 5.  [2] Tac. *Ann.* xv. 44. Suet. *Nero*, 16.

whether it was not accidental.[1] Terrified at the popular hatred, Nero looked for persons on whose shoulders the guilt could be laid; it was probably Jewish influence which suggested the Christians. For his wife, who then ruled him, Poppæa Sabina, was a proselyte, and he was himself surrounded by Jewish magicians and soothsayers who afterwards predicted in connection with the expectation of Messiah, that after his fall he would become ruler of Jerusalem, and live to see from thence the restoration of his former power.[2] At first some were seized who confessed themselves Christians, and on their statements, undoubtedly extorted by torture, a great number of others were taken and executed in a body. Some were crucified, some were sewn into animals' skins and torn to pieces by dogs, others were clothed in dresses dipped in combustible matter and burnt at night as torches in the Emperor's gardens. The persecution probably extended from Rome into some of the provinces, for when once the punishment of the alleged incendiaries had begun, others were executed, according to Tacitus, without being implicated in that charge, simply because through the universal hatred of Christians they were judged worthy of death.

---

[1] [The evidence for the whole story about Nero is questioned by Mr. Lewes. See *Cornhill Magazine* for July 1863.—TR.].
[2] Joseph. *Arch.* xx. 8. Suet. *Nero*, 40.

# CHAPTER III.

### ST JAMES, ST. JUDE, ST. JOHN, AND THE REMAINING APOSTLES AND EVANGELISTS.

ST. JAMES had already suffered martyrdom in the year 62. He is the James who ranked next to St. Peter and St. John in the original Apostolic College, and was surnamed "the Just." According to the old tradition, Christ had imparted to these three after his resurrection the *gnosis*, or deeper understanding of His doctrine, and they delivered it to their fellow Apostles.[1] The risen Jesus appeared separately to St. James,[2] and St. Paul names him with Cephas and John as a pillar of the Church.[3] He is called by pre-eminence "the Lord's brother;" his mother was the sister and namesake of the mother of Jesus, and had by her marriage with Clopas (Alphæus) four sons, James, Jude, Simon, and Joses, and one daughter. Clopas, in St. John's Gospel, is the same name as Alphæus in the Synoptics.[4] The two ways of writing it in Greek arise from the different pronunciations, hard or soft, of the first letter in the Aramaic names, as may be seen in several names of the Alexandrian translation. It seems that after Clopas's death Joseph, the foster father of Jesus, received the widow, his sister-in-law, with her children into his house, so that the two families were united, and the cousins of Jesus reckoned as his brothers and sisters, according to the more extended use of the word among the

---

[1] Clem. Alex. *ap. Euseb.* ii. 1.
[2] 1 Cor. xv. 7. The Apostle names "James" without further description, but the Gospel of the Hebrews says it was the son of Alphæus, not of Zebedee.
[3] Gal. ii. 9. [4] John xix. 25.

Jews.[1] Mary herself, the Virgin's sister, appears among the women who attended on Jesus during His last stay in Jerusalem. According to Hegesippus, Alphæus or Clopas was also Joseph's brother; if so, the two brothers had married two sisters, and it was the more agreeable to Jewish law and custom for Joseph to adopt his brother's children. Two of these brothers or cousins of Jesus, St. James and St. Jude, were taken into the number of the Apostles, the two others were not, clearly because for some time they would not believe on Him as the Messiah.[2] But they believed afterwards, and took part after the Ascension in preaching the Gospel, for St. Paul mentions after the Apostles the brothers of Jesus as availing themselves of the right to be attended by women as "sisters" on their missionary journeys,[3] and Simon was second bishop of Jerusalem.

There is then no third James, no brother of the Lord and bishop of Jerusalem distinct from the Apostle, the son of Alphæus. The oldest and most trustworthy tradition of the Church knows only of the sons of Zebedee and Alphæus. In the "Acts" of St. Luke there is certainly only one James spoken of after the son of Zebedee had been put to death;[4] but, if the one there named as head of the Mother Church was a different man from the Apostle, St. Luke would have let the latter disappear without any trace, and have brought "the brother of Jesus" into his place without any notice of it; and, above all, nothing would then be known of the Apostle—he would be a mere name in history.

Errors seem to have first crept into the Church tradition about St. James, through notices gathered from the apocryphal writings. In Hegesippus and Clement of Alexandria, it is still pure; they only know of two of that name, though Hegesippus says "many are mentioned." But he evidently identifies the bishop of Jerusalem with the son of Alphæus or Clopas. Confusion was caused by a notion Origen mentions which came very early into the Church, partly founded on a misapprehension of their true relation, that the brothers of Jesus were sons of Joseph by a former

---

[1] Matt. xiii. 55. Mark. vi. 3.     [2] John vii. 5.
[3] 1 Cor. ix. 5.     [4] Acts xv. 13; xxi. 18.

marriage.[1] This statement, which gained currency chiefly through the "Proto-Gospel of James," but was rejected as an apocryphal dream by St. Jerome, though seeming to be confirmed by the remark of Eusebius that James was equally called a son of Joseph, covered the fact that St. Joseph adopted his nephews after his brother's death. But the "Apostolic Constitutions," by completely separating the bishop of Jerusalem from the Twelve, did most to determine the later views of many in the Greek Church. In this work, belonging in its present form to the fourth century, James, son of Alphæus, is always mentioned apart as an Apostle, and next to him the Lord's brother and bishop of Jerusalem; we read in one place, "the thirteen Apostles were appointed by the Lord; I, James, I, Clement, and others, by the Apostles."[2] The appointment of St. James as first bishop of Jerusalem was made, according to an old tradition, by the three Apostles, Peter, and the sons of Zebedee, James and John.[3] Hegesippus says, that as long as the Apostles remained in the holy city he shared with them the government of the Church of Jerusalem.[4] He it was who in the Apostolic Council about the Gentile Christians spoke first after St. Peter, and got the resolutions carried as to what they were to abstain from. He with St. Peter and St. John gave his hand to St. Paul, in token of fellowship in the Apostolic office and belief. His mission and obligations towards the exclusively Jewish community at Jerusalem involved his being peculiarly the Apostle of the Jews.

As he took no part personally in the conversion of the Gentiles, and had no occasion to live with them, but was constantly in the neighbourhood of the temple, he could display that zeal in the wonted observance of the Law which made him appear to his contemporaries and to after ages the model of Jewish national piety, transfigured by the Gospel. After St. Peter's departure he was the ecclesiastical centre and final authority for the capital and for Palestine. He did not claim this high rank as "brother of the Lord," or as uniting that characteristic with the Apostolate, for his brother St. Jude, who equally combined

---

[1] Orig. *in Math.* Tom. xiii. 462.
[2] *Const. Apost.* ii. 55; vi. 16; viii. 46.
[3] Clem. Alex. *ap. Eus.* ii. 1.
[4] Eus. *Hist.* ii. 23.

both characters, calls himself "a servant of Christ and brother of James," regarding this last as a special privilege; St. Luke also calls him "Jude (brother) of James."[1]

He was so highly reverenced even by the unconverted Jews for his piety and asceticism, that the honourable name of "the Just" was universally given to him. Hegesippus, who had the older narratives of Jewish Christians before him, and whose account is in some places supplemented by Epiphanius, calls him a Nazarite who had been dedicated to God as such from his birth. He drank no wine or strong drink, he ate no flesh, and abstained from bathing and anointing with oil; he went barefoot, and wore no wool, but only one linen garment. His advice to St. Paul to associate himself in a Nazarite vow with some Jews makes this account of his being himself a strict Nazarite the more credible. He lived in perpetual virginity, so that the Ebionite sect exalted the state of voluntary celibacy solely on account of his example, a view they afterwards relinquished.[2] Latterly he was the only Christian allowed to enter the temple.[3] There he might often be found on his knees praying for the forgiveness of his people, and he did this so often, and so long, that his knees became as hard as a camel's. So great was the fame of his sanctity that the people thronged him, only to touch the hem of his garment.

As to his death, Josephus says shortly that James, the brother of Jesus, was stoned at the suggestion of the High Priest, Ananus, after the death of the Roman procurator, Festus, and before the arrival of his successor, Albinus, A.D. 62. In order to terrify him he was placed on the parapet of the temple, and asked which was the door of Jesus? *i.e.* what, according to the doctrine of Christ, was the entrance to eternal life? On his confession that Jesus sits in heaven on the right hand of Almighty power, and will come again, they cast him down from the pinnacle of the temple and stoned him beneath it; and, while he was

---

[1] Jude i. 1. Luke vi. 16. Acts. i. 13.    [2] Epiph. *Hær.* lxxviii. 13.
[3] εἰς τὰ ἅγια, as Hegesippus says, *i.e.*, where the priests performed their daily ministry. Epiphanius and Rufinus first made it "the most holy place," which is clearly inconceivable. See Ruinart, *not. ad Acta. MM.*, p. 4, Ed. Amstel. On that view St. James would have been the only person ever allowed, without being a priest, or member of a Levitical or priestly family, to enter this inner chamber of the temple.

yet praying for his murderers, a fuller killed him with his felt-stick. This account so far agrees with that of Josephus that the Jewish law orders a criminal condemned to stoning to be thrown down by the witnesses from a height; and, if he still lives, they are to cast a great stone on his heart, and the people around are to stone him till he dies.[1] After St. James' death, Ananias had several persons condemned by the Synagogue and stoned as breakers of the Law, that is Christians, till king Agrippa deposed him from the priesthood in consequence. We see that the death of St. James, and what immediately followed, was a result of the last great crisis in Jerusalem, shortly before the outbreak of the war and destruction of the City. Hegesippus observes that many even of the chief men among the people, were converted by his martyrdom; but the mass, both of people and rulers, persisted in their enmity against Christianity, and this brought on the catastrophe.

The Epistle of St. James is addressed to "the Twelve tribes in the Dispersion," the Jews already converted who lived scattered among the Heathen outside the borders of Palestine, and is thus strictly confined to Jewish Christians, with special reference to communities, such as there might be in Syria, composed wholly or principally of Jews. The readiness and easy flow of the original Greek style proves (unless St. James, like St. Peter, availed himself of the services of an Hellenistic Jew) how widely-spread was the power of writing Greek among the Jews of Palestine. The Epistle is further distinguished by a strength and richness of thought, a sententious, figurative, and often poetical elevation of speech, and a manifold and visible coincidence with the Sermon on the Mount. It is partly devoted to combating a doctrinal error (the misapprehension and misapplication of the doctrine of justification by faith), partly, and chiefly, to the censure and correction of moral faults, namely, the sharp distinction between rich and poor, and the preference given to the former in religious assemblies. The Apostle calls Christianity the law of freedom, the royal law of love which God writes on man's heart by faith; but otherwise the weightiest New Testament doctrines are not once touched

---
[1] Joseph. *Sanhedrin*, cap. 16 et 15.

on. Yet this Epistle contains more references to the discourses of Christ, and more quotations of His words, than all the other Apostolic Epistles put together.

During the first two centuries the Epistle was seldom quoted, though Hermas knew it; but it already had its place in the Syrian Peschito, and St. Clement of Alexandria had explained it with the rest.[1] Origen is the first who expressly assigns it to St. James.[2] In the Western Church it only came into use, so far as we know, at the end of the fourth century. Eusebius reckons it among disputed writings, but observes that it is read publicly in very many Churches, and gives as the reason for doubting its canonicity, that it is seldom quoted by earlier writers.[3] St. Jerome says that it only gained authority gradually, and in course of time.[4] The suspicion he mentions, that the Epistle had been published by another under the name of St. James, may have existed for some time in the West; there is no trace of it in the East, and no other author was ever named.

Another brother or cousin of Jesus, St. Jude, the brother of James and son of Clopas, Jesus' uncle, and Mary, was numbered among the Apostles by the name of Thaddæus or Lebbæus. The expression of Hegesippus, that he was called the Lord's brother "after the flesh," means that their relationship concerns only the Man Jesus, who as Son of God had no relations.[5] His short Epistle with a general superscription is, however, addressed specially to the communities of Asia Minor, and was composed after the death of St. Peter, St. Paul and St. James, to oppose the errors of the Gnostic Antinomian teachers there by the testimony of a surviving Apostle. It is mainly occupied with describing these seducers and false teachers, their carnal mind, their misuse of the Christian *agape*, and their blasphemies; and seeks to guard Christians against their enticements by reminding them of the predictions of

---

[1] Clem. *Ep.* i. 10. Herm. *Past.* viii. 6. Eus. vi. 14.
[2] Orig. *Opp.* iv. 306.     [3] Eus. iii. 25.     [4] Hieron. *De Virg. Ill.* 2.
[5] Eus. *Hist.* iii. 20. When the Apostle Jude is called (Luke vi. 16, Acts i. 13) Ἰούδας Ἰακώβου, this does not mean "a son of James," for then the writer of the Epistle would be a different person from the Apostle, but we must supply ἀδελφός; and we need have no scruple about it, since it was usual among the first Christians, as the title of the Epistle itself shows, to distinguish this Jude from his namesake, as brother of James, who was so celebrated and universally known.

the Apostles that such men would enter in and devastate the Church, as was now come to pass. And here St. Jude often recurs to the thoughts and even the words of St. Peter's Second Epistle, only that he clenches its more general intimations by the closer teaching of experience. The Epistle has always been received as genuine in the Church, and quoted from early times by name (as by Tertullian, Clement and Origen) and if Eusebius reckons it among disputed writings, and some doubts have been expressed about it, this arose only from the author having used two apocryphal Jewish writings of later date, the Book of Enoch, and the "Anabasis" of Moses.[1]

It seems as if with the martyrdom of St. James the time allowed for the conversion of the Jewish nation closed. For it was now clear that so long as Jerusalem and the temple stood, and the Jewish polity with its theocratic character survived, the mass of the Jews could not be brought to believe on their true Messiah. In fact, after St. James was put to death in Jerusalem, the state of the Christians grew daily more intolerable. The Epistle to the Hebrews describes a condition where not a few fell away, yielding to the enmity of their countrymen. The religious enthusiasm and the activity of the Pharisaic Zealots, which at last arrayed the whole people in war against the Romans, and indeed against all foreigners, made the peaceful continuance of the Christian community in Judæa and Galilee impossible, even though its members constantly testified their adherence to the Jewish polity in Church and State by observing the ceremonial law. The worshippers of a Messiah who came in poverty and loneliness, and died on a cross, could no longer dwell peacefully by the side of men who were even now looking with unbounded confidence and impatience for a Messiah armed with the sword, to lead them to victory over the Romans,—who still looked for Him, when the flames of the temple were crashing over their heads.

For the Jewish nation now drew more and more upon itself the fulfilment of the counsel and judgment of God. In the year 66 a tumult broke out against the Roman rule,

---

[1] The statement about the Archangel Michael and Satan came from this document, according to Origen. (*De Princip.* iii. 2).

which led to the siege and taking of Jerusalem. The Christian community there was not involved in this catastrophe. Christ had before warned His disciples, when they saw the abomination of desolation in the holy City, and Jerusalem surrounded by hostile armies, to quit the city and flee to the mountains.[1] Eusebius adds that, shortly before all egress was closed, a special revelation by the mouth of the most venerated among the Christians at Jerusalem commanded them to depart and settle at Pella in Peræa. The Christians in the country districts of Judæa and Galilee most likely followed the example of their brethren in Jerusalem. Pella was a Greek colony, and there accordingly the first Gentile influences may have been brought to bear on the hitherto exclusively Jewish Christians of Jerusalem.[2]

The fall of the temple was an event of critical importance for the young Church. Judaism required essentially and above all things a temple for its divine service and religious life, and this temple could be but one, and in one place only in the world. When the temple sunk in flames, the practice of the ritual law became impossible in its most integral parts, the sacrifices which were the holiest thing in Jewish religion had to cease, the priesthood was reduced to an honorary sinecure and empty name. The Christians did not share the delusion so many Jews clung to that God would suddenly restore the temple by miracle; they recognised in its destruction a providence of God and a sign that the end of the ceremonial law was come, that Christian doctrine was thereby completely taken out and separated from the maternal womb of Judaism. The Jewish people had lost everything that had once been their special prerogative. The last relics of common national polity and civil existence were annihilated, there was no longer centre or capital; the Law indeed remained, but a law which, so to speak, prohibited itself, for no single Israelite could observe its ritual ordinances without breaking it. This could not but appear to all Christians, surely also to many Jews, as a solemn rejection by God, declared in deeds, of the people He had formerly chosen out of all the nations of the earth.

[1] Matt. xxiv. 15, 16.   [2] Eus. *Hist.* iii. 5.  Epiph. *De Pond et Mens.* c. 5.

The majority of the people resolved, even after city and temple were destroyed, to persevere in their customary round of hopes and imaginations. The event was universally accepted as a terrible judgment of God upon the nation, but the real explanation of their guilt they had not discovered. That the catastrophe was the fulfilment of their own sentence on themselves, when they cried, "His blood be on us and on our children,"—that they understood not. Their teachers assured them this misfortune had come from their lack of zeal for the Law and their inadequate observance of it. The mass of Jews had no taste for a religion which met them on the very threshold with the admonition to renounce all their rights and privileges, to humble themselves to an equality with the uncircumcised, and to acknowledge that with all their legal righteousness they were sinners who, no less than the Gentiles, needed pardoning grace. Since the beginning of the great struggle the Gentiles had almost everywhere displayed a burning hatred against the Jews, who in many places had fallen victims to their bloodthirsty fury and been massacred in hundreds and thousands. So much the deeper and more inextinguishably did the feeling of hatred and vengeance against the uncircumcised glow within their breasts, and a faith whose first condition was a command of love for all men, and which sometimes bade them submit to an uncircumcised man as bishop or presbyter, was intolerable to them. That word—"the uncircumcised shall be rooted out of God's people"—was always before their minds, and to eat in company with one not a Jew was defilement. Their feasts, indeed, and much of their ceremonies had become an empty shell without a kernel, now that the temple and its sacrifices were at an end, but they waited long, from year to year, for the miraculous restoration of their fallen temple. Meanwhile the ruins of the ceremonial law were so much the more resolutely clung to as the bulwark behind which their nationality entrenched itself, and so firmly was it cemented by the common hope, the prejudice and pride, of the sons of Abraham, and their historical recollections, that all the blows of the Roman power, all the unexampled severity the Romans exercised over them alone of conquered nations, their being torn from their native soil and scattered over all lands, and the humiliation of paying tribute to the temple of Jupiter on the Capitol,—all this could not break it down.

All, henceforth, who became Christians ceased to belong to their nation, in whose eyes they were leaves and twigs fallen from the parent tree, while the tree lived on. The inexhaustible fruitfulness of this people richly supplied all such losses, and they had a fixed point of religious union in their Sanhedrim, which sat at Jamnia after the destruction of Jerusalem. And thus was developed that credulity and readiness to discover and adopt silly legends, flattering to the vanity, presumption, and carnal mind of the Jews, of which the Talmud literature, in its gradual formation, gives such abundant evidence. This attempt was natural with a people who possessed so rich and wonderful a past, while their present was so poor and empty, and who, therefore, would always be labouring to conceal the contradiction between their continued claim to be the one chosen people of God, and the fact that every token of Divine rejection pressed on this darling of the Deity among the nations, that it was the most severely maltreated and trodden down of all peoples. They had, moreover, a confident expectation that at the Messiah's advent all the oppressions they had endured would be richly compensated, and their imagination revelled in painting this compensation, according to their prevalent views, after a sufficiently carnal fashion.

From the destruction of Jerusalem, A.D. 70, all that we know of the Church for the last thirty years of the first century connects itself naturally with the Apostle, St. John. It was his lot long to survive his colleagues, so that the young Church should not want in those later days the high authority of an Apostle and eyewitness of Christ. Ecclesiastical tradition makes him a relation of Jesus, through his mother Salome; of all the disciples, none except St. Peter and St. James were so intimate with Jesus, he was the darling of the Lord who lay on His breast at the Last Supper, the one disciple present at the crucifixion, and whose loyalty Jesus rewarded by consigning His mother to his care. When he left Jerusalem for good is uncertain, but at St. Paul's last visit, in 58, he must already have gone.

St. John seems to have been closely united with St.

Peter, and, so long as we have any account of their common work, is always named with him as his companion; St. Paul designates them, together with St. James, pillars of the Church. He afterwards took Ephesus for his headquarters, and thence superintended the Churches on the coasts of Asia.[1] St. Polycarp and St. Ignatius were among the disciples he educated there. He was brought to Rome under Domitian, and there, as Tertullian and St. Jerome relate, thrown into boiling oil, and when he came out unhurt, banished to the island of Patmos, in the year 95. After Domitian's death he returned to Ephesus.[2] Three incidents are recorded of his later life;—the horror he expressed of the false teacher Cerinthus, on having gone into the same bath with him; his constant repetition of the words, "Children love one another," in the assemblies; and, lastly, his bringing back and converting the youth who, after being baptized, had fallen in with robbers and become leader of a robber band.[3] He died under Trajan, nearly a hundred years old, A.D. 100 or 101.

The first Epistle of St. John is a supplement, a kind of appendix to his Gospel. The Apostle reminds men, with evident reference to St. Paul, that it is the last hour, and that in token of it many Antichrists had appeared, Gnostic seducers, who dissolved the unity of Christ's Person,[4] dividing the man Jesus from the Divine Christ who had only temporarily dwelt in him. St. John insists against them that the Son of God has appeared in the flesh. The discourse passes at times into the tone of a treatise, but always reverts to the form of an address, and through its clear teaching on the Divine source of the Christian religion, and the foundations and blessedness of a Christian life expressing itself in active love, attains to universal interest as a doctrinal writing. This first Epistle was never questioned in the Church, or ascribed to any other than the Apostle, John, though the author has not named himself. But he characterises himself at the beginning as an eyewitness of the life of Jesus, and there are expressions which betray his

---

[1] Polyc. ap. *Eus.* v. 21. Iren. iii. 3, 4
[2] Eus. iii. 18. Orig. *Comm. in Matt. Opp.* iii. 729. Tert. *Præscr.* 36. Hieron. *adv. Jov.* i. 26. *Comm. in Matt.* xx. 22.
[3] Iren. iii. 3. Hieron. *Comm. in Gal.* vi. Clem. Alex. *Quis dives salv.* 42.
[4] [The Vulgate reads in 1 John iv. 3, "omnis spiritus *qui solvit Jesum.*"—TR.]

authorship.[1] The whole tone, the more contemplative habit of mind, and the use of abstract terms mark the author of the fourth Gospel.

On the other hand, doubts arose very early in the Church, as to whether the two short and very similar missives, called in the Canon the Second and Third Epistles of St. John, are really his. The author only designates himself "the Presbyter," but the use of the word in this Epistle shows that he cannot have understood this title in the usual ecclesiastical sense, as though he were only one among many presbyters of a community. Clearly the writer meant thereby to express the singular and lofty position he held in the circle around him, as the teacher venerable for his old age, and the last of the Apostles; for the use of this word in the Church, both then and later, combined the notion of office and of age. The Second Epistle gives us the impression of being addressed to a community, for, if a private family were signified by "the elect lady and her children," the writer could not have said that not only he but all who knew the truth loved the children of this elect one. It is then a community or part of one that is spoken of;[2] the Apostle rejoices that they walk in the truth, and warns them against false teachers who deny Christ's appearance in the flesh. The Third Epistle, to Caius, denounces the conduct of a bishop, Diotrephes, who was hostile to St. John, and had not only repulsed the brethren sent by him with a letter, but cast out of the communion of the Church those who were ready to receive them; the Apostle announces his intention of visiting the community in person.

To the Epistles of St. John are joined in the Canon his prophetical book, the "Revelation." It is unquestionably his work. The author calls himself John, and gives evidence of being a disciple of the Lord who at the time of writing the book held high official authority in the Churches on the Asiatic coast. Since another John was known of in the Church, a presbyter who was a contemporary of the Apostle's and a disciple of Jesus, and who also lived at Ephesus where his grave could be seen next to the Apostle's, it was

---

[1] 1 John i. 3, 5; iv. 14.
[2] The words εὕρηκα ἐκ τῶν τέκνων σοῦ (2 John, 4), obviously imply something more than a family consisting of mother and children.

an early conjecture that this presbyter might be the author of the Apocalypse. But this conjecture has no ground in history or tradition, and has merely arisen from the desire to ascribe this prophetical book to a different author from the Apostle, to whom the oldest tradition of the Church unmistakably attributes it. There is weight in the fact of Papias mentioning it as divinely inspired, and the testimony of Justin, Melito, Irenæus, Hippolytus, and the Muratorian Canon, is decisive. The Apostle lived till Trajan's time, at Ephesus; about forty years later, St. Justin in the same city mentions the Apocalypse as his undoubted work.[1] This implies that he was recognised as the author in his own Church, where the Apocalypse first appeared, and from whence it was circulated elsewhere. Shortly afterwards, Melito, bishop of Sardis, a Church to which one of the Apocalyptic messages is addressed, wrote a special treatise on the book, in which John is named, without being further described, as the author. The statement of Irenæus depends on his master Polycarp, St. John's disciple; and that he in calling the author, " John, the Lord's disciple," meant no other than the Apostle, is certain, from his appealing to the testimony of those who had seen St. John.[2] And it is clear that the Apocalypse was a book much read and talked of on the coasts of Asia, where those eyewitnesses lived, during their lifetime, from the dispute about the number 666, which St. Irenæus defends against the reading 616 on the evidence of these contemporaries. There can, then, have been but one tradition in the birthplace of the " Revelation " about its authorship, and this pointed only to the Apostle. Otherwise the writer would have been discriminated in that early age, either as the Apostle or as one who, though not an Apostle, was a disciple of Jesus and a presbyter. The Muratorian Canon and Hippolytus, who wrote a special treatise in defence of the Gospel and Revelation of St. John, prove that the Roman Church recognised it as the Apostle's work. Caius, therefore, cannot be taken as a witness of the Roman tradition on this point. Clement and Origen represent the tradition of the Alexandrian Church.[3] And thus, till the middle of

---

[1] Euseb. iv. 18. Justin. *Dial. contr. Tryph.* p. 308.  [2] Iren. v. 30.
[3] Clem. *Strom.* vi. p. 667; ii. p. 207. Orig. *ap. Eus.* vi. 25. *Comm. in Joann.* Opp. iv. 17.

the third century, Caius, at Rome, stands alone, who in his anti-millennial zeal ascribes the Apocalypse to the heretic Cerinthus.¹ The "Alogi"² in Asia Minor, who denied the Apostle's authorship of Gospel and Apocalypse, belong to a later period. Dionysius of Alexandria (247—264) was the first to shake somewhat the hitherto uniform tradition of the Church. Deceived by the obscurity of the book, and anxious to deprive the Egyptian Chiliasts of what seemed to be their most effective weapon, he affirmed, not on historical but on internal and negative grounds, that the Apocalypse could not be the Apostle's work, partly because he does not name himself in his Gospels or Epistles, whereas here the name is given, partly because there is too much difference in language, style, and thought from the Gospel and Epistles.³ He thence conjectured that another John, the presbyter at Ephesus, might be the author. From that time a doubt, and in some sense dislike, of the book appears in the Eastern Church; it was often omitted in lists of the canonical books, and in translations like the Peschito, while the Western Church continued to acknowledge it. Yet in the fourth century the fact of the Apostle's authorship was no longer doubted in the East.

According to Irenæus, who had the best opportunities of knowing through his master, Polycarp, St. John's disciple, the Apocalypse was composed towards the end of Domitian's reign, about 96 A.D.; and since he appeals, in connexion with the number 666, to persons who had seen St. John, his evidence about the date is trustworthy. The author himself says that he received the Revelation in Patmos, where he was, "for the word of God, and the testimony of Jesus."⁴ The frequent attempts to fix an earlier date for the book, under Nero, Galba, or Vespasian, rest on arbitrary interpretations of a few obscure passages. Its important variations of style from St. John's Gospel are explained by his having used a different translator for the one and the other. For it is highly probable that he, the son of a Galilean fisherman, was not sufficiently at home in Greek to put these writings into shape without the aid of Hellenists. Yet he may have had an assistant for his

¹ Caius *ap. Eus.* iii. 28. Theodoret *Hær. Feb.* ii. 3.
² [The Ἄλογοι were an early sect, only known from a passage of Epiphanius. They are discussed in Döllinger's *Hippolytus*.—Tr.]
³ Eus. vii. 24, 25. ⁴ Apoc. i. 9.

Epistles and Gospel, and have drawn up his last work, the Apocalypse, by himself.

The Apocalypse implies throughout a bitter persecution only just over. The blood of the Martyrs had flowed abundantly. One of them is mentioned by name, Antipas, who had been slain as a faithful witness among the Christians of Pergamos.[1] The prophet sees under the heavenly altar the souls of the witnesses slain for the word and testimony of God, who, after the Roman custom, were beheaded with the axe;[2] and they are told that their number shall become greater. In the Neronian persecution other and more cruel kinds of death were practiced. The Apostle calls himself a companion of the Churches in their tribulation;[3] and the angels, or bishops, of Pergamos and Philadelphia are especially praised for not having denied the faith of Christ.[4] The great harlot, Babylon or Rome, is already drunk with the blood of the Saints and the witnesses of Jesus, and the beast blasphemes God, and makes all the dwellers on the earth worship it.[5]

There can be no mistake here as to Domitian and his persecution being meant. He was the first after Caligula who claimed the formal title of "God," and began all his letters, "Our Lord and God commands;" he compelled every one to address him as such by word of mouth or in writing, and had statues put up to himself in the sanctuary of the temple, and whole herds of animals sacrificed to him.[6] We know very little of this persecution, but it is referred to by Dio Cassius who says that a cousin of the Emperor, the consul Flavius Clemens, and many others were condemned, some to death, some to confiscation of property, on the charge of atheism and for Jewish usages;[7] for Christians always passed with the Romans for a Jewish sect who combined denial of the gods with Judaism. It is certain that Domitian from political suspicion had the remaining members of David's family put to death, though he spared two relations of Jesus, who in proof of their poverty and innocence showed him the hardness of their hands.[8] The persecution meantime was so severe that

---

[1] Apoc. ii. 13. [2] Ib. xx. 4. [3] Ib. i. 9. [4] Ib. ii. 13; iii. 10.
[5] Apoc. xiii.; xvii. [6] Sueton. *Domit.* 13. Plin. *Paneg.* 33, 52.
[7] Dio. Cass. lxvii. 15. [8] Hegesip. *ap. Eus.* iii. 19, 20.

even a Heathen writer of the period, Bruttius, speaks of the number of Christians who suffered, and St. Clement of Rome mentions a great number of elect, even women, who, "through endurance of shameful penalties and tortures gave us the most glorious examples."[1]

During this persecution, or immediately after it and while the impression was still vivid on his mind, with the foresight of yet worse persecutions to come, St. John saw and wrote his Revelation. He recounts as a witness by Divine command what was shown him in a cycle of visions. He discloses the mysteries of the judgments and dispensations of God, hidden in a sealed book. The acts of the glorified Redeemer, the sufferings of believers, and the punishment of the powers of darkness and their instruments among Jews and Heathen, form the general subject of this book, designed primarily for the Churches of Asia Minor. Believers were thereby to be encouraged to patience and perseverance under their present and future dangers and persecutions, and to faithfulness and firmness in their profession. The prophet exhibits the Church triumphant in heaven, while he proclaims to the Church militant on earth the approach of most terrible trials. The whole book is full of references to the Old Testament, of allusions and reminiscences. Most of its imagery is borrowed from Ezekiel, Daniel, and other Old Testament Prophets.

It opens with seven Epistles addressed by the prophet in the name of Christ to the rulers of the Churches of Ephesus, Smyrna, Pergamos, Thyatira, Sardis, Philadelphia, and Laodicea, referring to the circumstances, defects, and dangers of those communities, or to the personal qualities, virtues, and faults of their bishops. In the series of visions which follows, great physical and political commotions and catastrophes, and all conceivable horrors of nature and plagues of the dwellers upon earth, are described under the richest and boldest symbolic imagery; and it soon becomes clear that any literal and concrete interpretation of these events is inadmissible. Four riders appear—Victory, War, Famine, Pestilence; earth, sea, rivers, fountains, the very heavenly bodies, are struck with horrible plagues; poisonous locusts and troops of destroying horsemen torment

---

[1] Eus. *Chron.* i. 2; *ad. Olymp.* 218. Clem. *Ep. ad Cor.* 6.

men. Meanwhile, the prophet opens his eyes on the Church in heaven, and shows how all that happens in and for the earthly Church has its ground in the counsels of God and the events of the unseen world, and how the Church invisible in heaven is in full enjoyment of its promised blessings, while on earth it must endure a painful and unceasing struggle.

The prophet represents in three successive periods the development and fulfilment of the Kingdom of God and of His judgment on the Church's enemies. First comes the time of the Heathen persecutions, whose temporary character is expressed by the number "three and a half," which is half the mystical seven. Then follows the long period of the victory of Christ and the Church, during which Satan is bound, and his influence over the powers of the world broken, while the Church under the dominion of Christ and the Saints in heaven flourishes and increases on earth; this is the reign of a thousand years. The last period succeeds, when Satan again makes war upon the Church with all his power; it is the time of a great strife, and of the dissolution of the present order of the world. The numbers are throughout symbolical, and they limit and fix all the rest. The number seven prevails throughout the whole book, linked together in the threefold cycle of the seven seals, trumpets, and vials of wrath. The Church purified through a sevenfold trial and persecution appears at last as Jerusalem coming down from heaven. The number of half seven borrowed from Daniel (three years and a half, forty-two months, one thousand two hundred and sixty days) stands for a more limited period, as a thousand years for one of unlimited duration. The attempt to extract fixed chronological dates from the Apocalypse, or to make a prophetic compendium of the history of the world or the Church out of it, rests on a radical misapprehension of the book. The whole time from the conquest of Christianity in the Roman Empire till the end of the present course of the world is presented under two aspects, the binding of Satan, and the rule of Christ and the Saints in heaven over the Church.

The Lamb that was slain and lives for evermore, the Lion of the tribe of Judah who hath overcome and by

His victory changed the fate and history of the world, He alone is worthy to open the book of the future closed with seven seals. And as He takes the book out of the Father's right hand all in heaven fall down to worship Him, praising God and the Lamb. Those slain in the persecution, whose souls St. John sees under the altar in heaven, are told that their number shall be increased by the victims of coming persecutions, and are already allowed to take part in the heavenly solemnity before God and the Lamb. At the same time, the believers delivered out of the great tribulation are sealed, as the Twelve tribes of the true Israel, and as being chosen out and placed under God's peculiar care; and the prophet beholds an innumerable multitude of blessed Martyrs out of all peoples, with palm branches in their hands, before the throne, praising God and the Lamb.[1]

The purification of the Church in the fire of Heathen persecution is now represented under another form. St. John is to measure the temple, the altar, and the worshippers; they are guarded as the inner sanctuary of the Church, and withdrawn from Heathen fury; but the outer court of the temple, and the holy city itself—the external Church—are given over to the Gentiles, who shall tread it under foot for the allotted period. At the same time, within the Empire, that great city which spiritually is called Sodom and Egypt, the Christian witnesses arise endued with power from on high and invincible.[2] And if the witnesses fall victims to the Heathen power of Rome, the beast from the abyss, if their corpses lie unburied for the scorn and joy of the many Gentile tribes and tongues, this Heathen triumph shall be turned into horror; the Christian testimony, seemingly destroyed in its instru-

---

[1] Apoc. v.; vi. 9—11; vii. 2 sqq.
[2] St. John clearly contrasts the holy city (the Church) with the great city (or Roman Empire), the spiritual Sodom and Egypt. That he is not speaking of any particular city, and cannot mean Jerusalem, appears from the comparison with a country, viz., Egypt; and again, he certainly would not describe Jerusalem in the same breath as holy and as Sodom. When it is said, that the Lord of the two witnesses was crucified in the great city, the reason for mentioning His death is to remind the witnesses (or preachers of the Gospel) that they can expect no other fate in the Roman Empire than what there befel their Lord. Nor could the prophet apply to an occurrence confined to the city of Jerusalem what is said (vv. 9, 10), that many of the peoples, kindreds, tongues and nations (so had he before called the inhabitants of the Roman Empire) should see their dead bodies, and that the dwellers upon earth who were tormented by the two Prophets should rejoice over their death.

ments, is raised again, the witnesses who were slain ascend into heaven, and the Roman Empire is simultaneously surprised by great catastrophes, civil wars and revolutions.[1]

St. John now describes under different imagery the same development of the Church, and the struggle of hostile powers against it and against Christ. He goes back to the birth of Christ. A woman clothed with the sun, and the moon beneath her feet, and a crown of twelve stars upon her head—the Church, represented in her earlier Jewish and present Christian form—gives birth to Messiah after bitter pains of labour. Satan, the great red dragon with seven heads, ten horns, and seven crowns upon his heads, waits to devour the Child as soon as it is born, through his instrument, Herod. But the Child was caught up to God and to His throne, while the mother (the Church), like the Synagogue before in the persecution of Antiochus, escapes for a fixed time into the wilderness. The great struggle with the arch enemies of the Church is now first decided in heaven. The dragon and his followers are overcome by the archangel Michael, the champion of the Church, and cast out of heaven upon the earth. If Michael is here represented as the Conqueror, so, too, are the believers themselves; they have overcome Satan, the constant accuser of the brethren, through the atoning blood of the Lamb, and through the testimony of their martyrdom, and the Church Triumphant in heaven rejoices over the victory of the combatants on earth.[2]

This conquest of the believers is followed by a long and severe struggle, which the prophet describes standing on the shore of the sea. The instruments of Satan appear. First rises from the sea a beast compounded of leopard, bear and lion, having seven heads and ten horns, and as many crowns, and on his heads a name of blasphemy. This is the Roman Empire, hostile to Christianity. The seven heads are seven mountains (the hills Rome stands on), and also seven rulers. The dragon (Satan) gives it power over the peoples of the earth, a throne, and great might to contend with the Saints. The dragon and the beast are worshipped by men. The beasts blasphemes God and oppresses believers, who are to wait patiently, and to keep their faith,

[1] Apoc. xi.     [2] Apoc. xii.

looking for the future recompense. Another beast comes up out of the earth, the false prophet. This is the new Heathen sects of philosophy, using magic and theurgy with the aim of confirming and restoring the Heathen religious institutions. This beast speaks like the dragon, and seduces men by his magical arts and wonders, so that they worship the first beast, and set up images to him.[1] Whoever will not worship the image of the beast is killed, and whoever does not receive the mark of the beast is excluded from all civil rights.[2]

The Lamb and a hundred and forty-four thousand with Him, marked with His own and His Father's name as children of God and Saints, stand on Mount Sion, over against the enemy. These are not the same who were before mentioned as sealed out of the Twelve tribes of Israel; they are "redeemed from among men" in general, and follow the Lamb whithersoever He goeth, as being pure, and undefiled with women. An angel flies through heaven with the everlasting Gospel of the fulfilment of the kingdom and approach of judgment; a second angel proclaims the fall of Babylon (Rome); a third threatens the worshippers of the beast with the wrath and chastisement of God. Under various figures of a harvest, a vintage with the wine-press, and of the seven vials of wrath poured out, the prophet describes the Divine judgment on Heathen idolatry and the triumph of Christianity.[3]

Then St. John sees in a wilderness a woman sitting on the beast (the Roman Empire) gorgeously arrayed and drunken with the blood of the holy Martyrs, having in her hand a golden cup full of abominations and filthiness. This is the seven-hilled Rome, the great Babylon, the mother of all idolatry. The beast has a deadly wound on his head which is healed again. Ten kings, represented by the ten horns, hate the harlot, but give their power and strength to the beast, and receive dominion for one hour with the beast; on the one hand, they shall lay waste Rome as instruments of God, on the other, they shall strive with the Lamb and be overcome. This apparently refers to the

---

[1] Compare *Heidenthum und Judenthum*, p. 614 [Vol. ii. pp. 166, 167, *Eng. Trans.*] on the prevalent worship of Emperors, living and dead, and of the goddess Rome, especially in the towns of Asia Minor, under the eye of St. John.

[2] Apoc. xiii. Cf. xvi. 13; xix. 20.    [3] Apoc. xiv., xv., xvi. Cf. vii. 4 sqq.

nations and kings who, after being for awhile dependent on Rome or allied to it, at length dismembered the Empire, took the capital, and, after oppressing the Christians, were converted to the Gospel. An angel from heaven now proclaims the fall of Babylon, the great city; the believers are to come out of her, for she is doomed to destruction. The kings who committed fornication with her shall bewail her, the merchants and shipmasters shall mourn for the desolation of the city of all riches, merchandise, and luxury. But the Saints, the Apostles, and the Prophets, rejoice in heaven. Then are the foreign kings overcome who had wrought judgment on the idolatrous city drunken with blood, and Christ Himself appears as King and Lord at the head of the armies of heaven, with the symbol and attributes of Judge of the world. The beast and the kings of the earth strive with Him; both beast and false prophet are cast into the lake of fire, but the kings that help the beast are slain with the sword that proceeds out of the mouth of Christ.[1]

Satan is now bound and cast into the pit for a long period of a thousand years; his power as ruler of this world is broken with the overthrow of Heathenism in the Roman Empire, and he can no longer seduce the nations to commit idolatry. Meanwhile the Martyrs and Saints who have not worshipped the beast reign with Christ in heaven; this is the first resurrection, figurative and not bodily, corresponding to the first death, and hence the Apostle sees only the *souls* of those who are risen, *i.e.*, passed from the Militant to the Triumphant Church. On earth this is the period of the increase and, in a sense, dominion of the Church; the sun-clothed woman is no more hidden in the wilderness, the three years and a-half of her trial are over, the Church possesses the countries, the peoples, and the property, which before belonged to her enemies.[2]

At the end of this long period (the present dispensation of the world), Satan will be unchained and go forth in person from his prison to deceive the nations—not the beast or the false prophet, for the old Heathen idolatry is long since passed away. He leads numberless hosts to war against the Church, the City of the Saints, but they are

[1] Apoc. xvii. xviii. xix.   [2] Apoc. xx. 1—6.

quelled, and Satan is cast for ever into the lake of fire, where are the beast and the false prophet. And now comes the real universal resurrection (the first was figurative and partial), and the judgment of the world results in the birth throes of a new and transfigured earth. Christ takes His Father's throne, and sits in judgment. They whose names are not written in the book of life incur eternal death, and lastly, death and Hell are cast into the lake of fire; the eternal separation of the two kingdoms is fulfilled.[1] St. John sees the new Jerusalem, the Church Triumphant, coming down from heaven in her glory as a bride adorned. The heavenly and the earthly Jerusalem henceforth are one, heaven is become earth, and earth is heaven. Sin and evil are destroyed and cast for ever out of the new Jerusalem, where God reveals Himself in light and glory. The book closes with a warning that none may add to the words of this prophecy or take from them, and with the promise that the Lord will come quickly.[2]

The messages to the seven Churches of Asia Minor point to internal disorders caused in some of them by those false doctrines whose beginnings St. Paul had already clearly spoken of, while he foretold their further development. From the first, there had advanced alongside of the outward enmity of Heathen powers an inward danger and affliction of the Church, through laboured attempts to disfigure the Apostolic deposit, to mix with it exoteric ideas, religious or philosophical, or, generally, to attach a strange doctrine to the Person of Jesus, however recognised in His Messianic, prophetic, or reforming character. The first heretical influences and ideas belonging to the Apostolic age passed from the Synagogue into the Church. As a Platonized Judaism had grown up in Egypt in the Alexandrian School, so, too, the numerous Jews scattered over Asia Minor, who were much less subject than their brethren in Palestine to the dominant Pharisaism which rejected all foreign elements, had derived from contact with Greek culture and speculation a good deal which held out to their taste pretensions of higher intellectual nourishment. With a desire to search out the secrets of the world of angels and demons was closely connected a longing for license and emancipation of the flesh, roused and cherished by the

---

[1] Apoc. xx. 7—15.     [2] Apoc. xxi. xxii.

seductive influence of Heathen morality. Men of this temper of mind were all the more ready to join the young Christian communion, because they found in it a new association, midway between Judaism and Heathenism, and a doctrine not shut up in fixed forms, but both capable of development and requiring it—what seemed like a shell they could fill according to their own mind.

The difficulty of the Apostles' work was essentially increased through the necessity of combating such attempts, whether the authors and adherents of these alien doctrines built upon maintaining their position within the Apostolic Communion, or laboured to effect a separation and form rival ecclesiastical bodies. St. Paul says of these divisions in their first beginnings that, as in the Divine order of the world evil is the unwilling instrument of good, so these separations and their causes are necessary in the higher dispensation of the Church, in order to prove and purify its members, and to exclude those who are found wanting.[1] The Apostle uses here the word, "Heresy," derived from the Greek philosophical schools, which has since passed into the language of the Church, to designate parties which separate themselves from her communion, or are excluded from it on account of doctrinal variations. But it was long before actual divisions occurred. St. Paul speaks oftener of "weak brethren" of Israel;[2] Jewish prejudices sucked in in childhood were powerful with them; they were neither willing nor able to form parties or sects, but stood alone, and it was to be expected that in time, under the influence of the new life of faith of their fellow Christians, especially Gentile converts, they would become completely identified with them. St. Paul treated such persons with tender and considerate forbearance. He says of them, "If in anything ye are otherwise minded, God shall reveal to you this also;" *i.e.* He will correct your views through the influence of the community, and your growth in the Spirit of Christ.[3]

But far more suspicious and threatening elements soon appeared in the newly founded communities. The ordinary Judaism in its Pharisaic form, to which nothing was so

---

[1] 1 Cor. xi. 19.     [2] Rom. xiv. 1, 2.   1 Cor. viii. 7; ix. 22.
[3] Phil. iii. 15.

dear as the universal force of the Law and the perpetual prerogatives of the Jewish nationality,—the Judaism St. Paul attacked so sharply, never succeeded in forming separate congregations, at least for any time, and in the later Apostolic period this danger seems to have been no longer important. On the other hand, a doctrine of far more seductive tendency crept increasingly into the communities —a Gnostic Judaism, producing serious disorders, and entailing on the Apostles and their first successors a difficult contest. It is uncertain when, and under what influences, this Gnostic tendency and admixture of Jewish and Gentile teaching found entrance among the Jews of the dispersion. In Palestine it only appeared among the Essenes, and there is no trace of their spreading or having influence out of Palestine. We can only say that the older Orphic Pythagorean ideas, and the notion long before brought into the West by the Babylonian magicians about various classes of demons, both higher and ministering spirits, and the conditions of influencing them, had gained admission also among the Jews of Asia Minor.[1]

The false teachers against whom St. Paul warned the believers of Colossæ were Jewish converts, who held to circumcision and the Law, and required an observance of the Old Testament rules about meats and of the Jewish feasts, new moons and Sabbaths. To this they added, against the body, as the defiling prison of the soul, a violent and unmeasured asceticism, and an angel-worship founded, as the Apostle says, on false humility. They made the angels, according to the Heathen idea, mediators whom men must apply to because the supreme God was incomprehensible and out of reach.[2] Without doubt they thus degraded the dignity of Christ, as a Prophet to whom only one of these cosmic angels—and an angel of a lower order —had revealed himself, whence St. Paul here insists so emphatically on the majesty of the Only-Born. His warning, "Beware that none rob you through philosophy and vain deceit, after the tradition of men," proves that this doctrine was drawn from a Heathen philosophy, as it was with the Essenes.[3]

The false teachers of Ephesus and its neighbourhood,

[1] Clem. Alex. *Strom.* iii. 6.  [2] Theodoret *ad Coloss.* ii. 18.  [3] Col. ii. 8.

against whom St. Paul's Pastoral Epistles are directed, were closely related to those of Colossæ. They were Jewish Gnostics; what they called *gnosis* was a pretended deeper and more secret insight into divine things, for which the mass of the uninitiated was unfit. They busied themselves with "myths and endless genealogies," *i.e.* with spinning out long catalogues of œons, whose limitation was purely arbitrary, and who might just as well have been multiplied. St. Paul calls the fables of these teachers, and their fantastic stories about the spirit-world, "Jewish myths,"[1] which shows that they had not come immediately from Judaism, but through the medium of a Judaism enriched with Heathen speculations. And he also foretells that to these errors will soon be added practical mistakes, the forbidding of marriage and of certain meats (namely, animal food,) from the essentially Gnostic view so foreign to Jewish traditions, that physical generation is something Satanic, and the use of sexual intercourse evil and defiling.[2] Two of these heretics, Hymenæus and Philetus, maintained that the resurrection was past already, meaning that it belonged to the present not to the future, and took place at the moment when man attained through *gnosis* to the consciousness of his higher, ante-natal existence and his true destiny.[3]

Another class of false teachers in Asia Minor, who threatened and partly laid waste the early Church, are mentioned in St. Peter's Second Epistle, and by St. Jude. The Gnostic idea seems to have been their predominant one, but their *gnosis* often had an Antinomian character. They boasted of their excesses, and exhibited them ostentatiously as a violation of the moral law at once authorized and well calculated to promote the interests of religion. They promised to conduct their followers to true freedom, appealing to St. Paul, whose teaching about Evangelical freedom and the abolition of the Law as a dead letter they twisted to their own ends.[4] They added in mockery, that the promise of Christ's Second Coming was still unfulfilled, and there was no appearance of the world being destroyed, nay, rather that everything continued as it had been since

---

[1] Tit. i. 14. [2] 1 Tim. iv. 3. [3] 2 Tim. ii. 18.
[4] 2 Pet. ii. 18, 19. Cf. iii. 15, 16.

the beginning of creation.¹ These false believers were in outward communion with the Church; for they took part in the *agape*, and profaned it for gratifying their animal desires.² But the Antichrists whose conduct St. John mentions in his first Epistle were separated, seemingly of their own will, from Church communion. They denied with the Gnostics the identity of Jesus and Christ, believed in no true Incarnation, and attributed to Jesus a merely apparent body, like the Docetæ. St. John calls them Antichrists, because he makes the denial of the Incarnation the fundamental lie which constitutes a real Antichrist, for whoever denies the Son, owing to the Son's essential union with the Father, denies the Father or God in the truth of His Being.³

Christian antiquity regards Simon Magus as the arch-heretic and father of all heresy. The magical powers, by which he supported his claim to a divine office and mission, probably consisted in his use of certain physical arts for adjuring spirits and demons, healing the sick and playing magical tricks. In his native country of Samaria he had gained over all the people from the least to the greatest, and he was universally believed to be an emanation from the Godhead come among them in human person, and, indeed, the highest of all, called for pre-eminence "the great power of God."⁴ Simon was undoubtedly a remarkable person; his conversion to Christianity was merely external and temporary, from a desire to partake in the extraordinary gifts of the Apostles. His name is involved, chiefly by the older heretics, in a network of fables; what is certain is, that afterwards he came to Rome and there again fell in with St. Peter. The oldest received tradition about his end is, that after preaching under a plane-tree he had himself buried alive, giving out that he should rise again, but, as was natural, rose no more.⁵ The document the Simonians had under his name, the "Great Apophasis," (or Annunciation) is certainly not his composition, and it is impossible, generally, to distinguish what belongs to the later development of the doctrine of their sect from the original dogmas of Simon himself.

¹ 2 Pet. iii. 3, 4. ² Jude 12. ³ 1 John ii. 18—23; iv. 3.
⁴ Acts viii. 10. ⁵ Hippol. *Philos.* p. 176, Miller.

The special severity of the author of the Apocalypse is directed against the Nicolaitan sect, whose works and life are characterized as hateful.¹ They gave out the deacon, Nicolas of Jerusalem, for their founder. There were two accounts of him, and of the occasion of connecting his name with the sect, current in the early Church. He had a very beautiful wife, from whom he separated, in order to lead a life of continence. According to one account, he after awhile took back his wife, from uxoriousness, and at last maintained that daily payment of the marriage debt is necessary for salvation. The Nicolaitans seem really to have taught this.² St. Clement gives an entirely different account, and he had much better sources of information, for he knew that the deacon's son and daughter lived to be very old in constant celibacy.³ According to this account, the Apostles reproached him with being too jealous about his wife, on which he sent for her and said thoughtlessly and in anger before the community, by way of getting rid of the reproach, that any one who would might marry her. And this was made a pretext of by men who wished to find a colour for their excesses, in connection with another saying of Nicolas, that one must maltreat one's flesh. Nicolas referred to taming the flesh by vigorous asceticism, but the heretics, who adorned themselves with his name, interpreted it of satisfying the lusts of the flesh by free indulgence. The Nicolaitans in Ephesus, Pergamos, and other cities of Asia Minor were, then, a Gnostic, Antinomian sect, who recommended acquiescence in Heathen idolatry, declared eating meats offered to the gods a thing indifferent after an exorcism had been pronounced over them, had community of wives, and made peace with those who practised impurity after an eight days' separation.⁴

The Balaamites, mentioned in the message to the Church of Pergamos, were different from the Nicolaitans; they are so named by the writer because they tempted Christians to Heathen licentiousness, as Balaam by his advice to Balak had tempted the Israelites. They also dispensed themselves from the Apostolic prohibition to eat meat offered to

---

¹ Apoc. ii. 6, 15.   ² Epiph. xxv. 1., p. 76.
³ Clem. Alex. *Strom.* iii. p. 436.
⁴ Iren. ii. 27; iii. 11. Theod. *Hær. Fab.* iii. 1.

idols, took part in Gentile sacrificial feasts, and suffered themselves to be thereby led into impurity. In Thyatira there were then adherents of a Gnostic prophetess whom the Apostle calls Jezabel, and who taught similar errors, devised to excuse immorality.[1]

Of the four Gospels received by the Church, St. John composed the last; and thus at the end of the history of the Apostles we are brought to the consideration of the historical literature emanating from them, consisting of five treatises. There were other narratives before the four we have, but nothing is now known of them beyond what St. Luke says at the commencement of his Gospel, that many had already undertaken to compose a Life of Jesus, or to relate what they knew of the facts concerning Him, of which the members of the Church were firmly convinced.[2] These written records, therefore, reach back to the time when most of the Apostles and many other eye-witnesses were still living, and when, therefore, any mistakes must at once have been set right.

But when Apostles, and eminent disciples of Apostles, undertook to narrate the life and teaching of Christ, these earlier essays of unknown authors perished. The first to do this was St. Matthew, formerly a publican on the Sea of Gennesareth, and then an Apostle. He wrote his Gospel in the Hebrew (*i.e.* Aramaic) language, primarily for the Christians of Palestine. This Aramaic original has long been lost; from the second century at least the Church knew and used only a Greek translation, the authorship of which was unknown even in ancient times; how far it gives an exact or a free rendering of the Aramaic text it is impossible to say. The quotations from the Old Testament frequently differ both from the Alexandrian version and the Hebrew text. The aim of the Evangelist is to show the Messianic dignity of Jesus, to convince the unbelieving Jews that the nation and its rulers had rejected and slain Him in manifest and judicial blindness, and to supply for the converted Jews an historical justification of their forming themselves into a distinct communion. He, therefore, presents the history of Jesus specially in connection with the Old Testament, and seizes every opportunity of pointing

[1] Apoc. ii. 14, 20.   [2] Luke i. 1, 2.

to His fulfilment of an Old Testament prophecy or type. Therefore, again, since he wrote for Jews who had still a vivid recollection of the facts, his narratives are much shorter, and the discourses more fully given; and in this careful account of long doctrinal discourses in their internal coherence he betrays his Apostolical character. On the other hand, he is often less explicit than St. Mark and St. Luke in describing facts and circumstances of time and place; he sometimes compresses the narrative portion into a few general statements; he groups together what is similar, and follows rather the order of relation than of time.

St. Matthew's is certainly the oldest of the canonical Gospels, and therefore it served as a pattern for the two others. That he wrote first, and wrote in Hebrew, is the tradition of the ancient Church, represented by a line of witnesses stretching back into Apostolic times and commencing with Papias, which was never questioned by any ancient authority.[1] St. Irenæus adds, that he wrote when intending to leave Palestine, at the time of the common labours of Peter and Paul in Rome, *i.e.* between 63 and 67 A.D.[2] His Gospel was at all events composed before the destruction of Jerusalem.

John Mark, son of a Christian named Mary who lived at Jerusalem and nephew of Barnabas, was converted by St. Peter, and acted as an assistant not only to St. Paul but to St. Barnabas and St. Peter also; he was with St. Paul in his first imprisonment at Rome, and accompanied St. Peter as interpreter or secretary to write down what he dictated.[3] He wrote his Gospel in Rome, and for the Roman Church principally, under St. Peter's inspiration, that is, from notes taken down in conversation with him, and from hearing his discourses. According to the oldest tradition, St. Peter neither hindered nor encouraged the publication of this Gospel; according to the account preserved by Eusebius, he expressly confirmed it.[4] St. Irenæus, on the contrary, affirms that it was not made public till after the death of Peter and Paul.

---

[1] Papias *ap. Eus.* iii. 39. Pantæn. *ap. Eus.* v. 10. Orig. *ap. Eus.* vi. 25. Euseb. iii. 24. Epiph. *Hær.* xxx. 3. Hieron. *Præf. in Matt.*  [2] Iren. iii. 1.

[3] Acts xii. 12. 1 Pet. v. 13. Col. iv. 10. Philem. 24. Papias *ap. Eus.* iii. 39. Tert. *c. Marc.* iv. 5. Iren. iii. 1. Eus. *Hist.* v. 8.

[4] Clem. Alex. *Hypot. ap. Eus.* vi. 14. Eus. ij. 15. *Dem. Evang.* iii. 5. Hieron. *ad Hedib.* cl. 11.

Papias who mentions this connection of St. Mark's Gospel with St. Peter on the authority of the Presbyter John, a disciple of the Lord, adds that he did not write things in the order of their occurrence, but in the order he heard them from St. Peter. Meanwhile, he made use of the Gospels of St. Matthew and St. Luke in his narrative, sometimes abbreviating, sometimes combining, sometimes expanding their statements, so that only six passages are peculiar to him. What he learnt from St. Peter supplied him with his rule in the use of the other Gospels, and the choice to be made of their contents. He mostly gives only facts, passing over the long discourses and the birth and youth of Jesus, beginning with the appearance of the Baptist. His omission of all which chiefly concerned the Jews, and his explanation of Jewish customs and localities, prove that he wrote specially for Gentile Christians.

Whether the Greek physician, Luke, was a convert from the Gentiles or from the Hellenistic Jews, is doubtful, but he shows an ample acquaintance with Jewish affairs and customs, and uses in the Acts of the Apostles the Jewish chronology. In his Gospel we are brought within the circle of Pauline influences, for St. Luke gave himself up to that Apostle with devoted loyalty; he attended him on his missionary journeys, and stuck fast to him during his imprisonment at Rome, whence he is specially praised by him.[1] St. Luke states that many before him had undertaken to write the Evangelical history, and that he had sought out everything from the beginning; he doubtless, therefore, examined and used the matter he found ready to his hand.[2] He wrote immediately for a Christian named Theophilus, probably a Roman of high rank, to show him the certainty of the instruction he had received. It is clear that St. Paul, or his manner of teaching, had a certain influence over this Gospel in its method of composition and choice of matter, so that Irenæus says distinctly, "Luke wrote down in his book the Gospel Paul preached."[3] The aspects of doctrine specially represented by St. Paul, as Apostle of the Gentiles, are conspicuously brought forward in St. Luke's parables and narratives—the call of the Gentiles, the universal scope of Christianity, and the forgiveness assured to believ-

---

[1] 2 Tim. iv. 10, 11.   [2] Luke i. 1—3.   [3] Iren. iii.1.

ing love and humility. No doubt was ever felt in the Church as to the authorship of this third Gospel, and the same may be said of St. Luke's second historical composition, the Acts of the Apostles, which is a continuation or second part of his Gospel. There is only a later and purely isolated notice of its being ascribed to St. Clement of Rome, and by others to St. Barnabas.[1] This book, too, was composed for Theophilus' instruction, the matter of the book being drawn from three sources, earlier narratives, information orally imparted by the Apostles and other witnesses, and the author's personal testimony. In the latter portion of the book he frequently indicates, by saying "we," that he was an eye-witness and took part in the events described.[2]

Widely different from the three older Gospels is the fourth and last, the work of the Apostle "whom Jesus loved," who alone stood by His Cross, and to whom He entrusted His Mother. This Gospel was published in Ephesus about 97 A.D., having been composed by St. John in his extreme old age, during or soon after his banishment to Patmos. It was written at the urgent entreaty of the Bishops of the Asiatic coast, and of deputies sent from several Churches, and many still surviving disciples of Christ, among whom is said to have been the Apostle, Andrew. There is a very old tradition reaching back to the time of Polycarp, St John's disciple, that he bade those who urged him to compose a new Gospel observe a three days' fast with him, in order that God might reveal His will to them. On this, it was revealed to the Apostle, Andrew, that St. John should write down every thing in his own name, and the rest examine it.[3] St. John had a double aim in composing his Gospel, both to supplement the narratives of the older Gospels, and to oppose the Jewish Gnosticism introduced by Cerinthus, which was trying even to establish itself in Ephesus, and especially its teaching about the Person of Christ. This is done, without any direct controversy or specific mention of the heresy, by a simple

---

[1] Phot. *Quæst. Amphil.* 145.
[2] Acts xvi. 10—17; xx. 5—15; xxi. 1—8; xxvii. 1—37.
[3] *Canon Murat.* St. Jerome relates in substance the same tradition (*Præf. Comm. in Matt.*) appealing to the *Ecclesiastica Historia*, which contains it, and putting forward the Prologue to the Gospel as a special result of the revelation then made to St. John.

statement of the opposite facts. It is an old tradition that St. John desired to write a spiritual Gospel, and as the other three Evangelists had mainly treated the bodily, the outward acts of Christ, so he wished to give special prominence to the spiritual element.[1]

The old tradition, that he meant to supplement the three other Gospels, is confirmed by comparing them with his. He generally pre-supposes their narratives and supplies omissions, nor is his own account intelligible without reference to the earlier Gospels. He only repeats three of the same events the three other Evangelists give, besides the history of the Passion, viz., the feeding of the five thousand, Jesus walking on the sea, and Mary anointing Him.[2] He purposely omits the most important things, the Birth of Jesus, the Baptism, Temptation, Transfiguration, and institution of the Eucharist (though he relates the washing of the disciples' feet which immediately preceded it), and the Agony in Gethsemane. Even in describing the Passion he passes over what was already known from the other Evangelists, where it is not rendered necessary by the context, or for the sake of making some addition to it; he makes his narrative dovetail into the others, omitting what they say, and giving what they omit. Once, he expressly corrects the chronology of the older Gospels.[3] He excels the other Evangelists in accuracy of dates, and greater freshness and more life-like method of description, repeatedly testifying to the truth of his narrative as being an eye-witness and ear-witness of what he tells.[4] Notwithstanding the limitations imposed on his choice of matter by his special objects, the order of narration is almost dramatic; the history marches on in sequence of time, and one sees the enmity of the Jews advancing to its final development in the closing catastrophe. The Gospel is a connected harmonious whole, in which clearness and depth, simplicity of expression and lofty elevation of thought, are united in equal measures, while the enthusiastic love of the writer for

[1] Eus. vi. 14.
[2] [This assumes the cleansing of the temple in St. John to be a different event from that in the Synoptics. Cf. supr. p. 34, note. Jesus walking on the sea is mentioned by St. Matthew and St. Mark, as also Mary's anointing Him at Bethany; the event recorded by St. Luke (vii. 37, 38) is clearly a different one. The feeding of the five thousand is mentioned by all four Evangelists.—TR.]
[3] John iii. 24.
[4] John i. 14; xix. 37.

Him on whose heart he rested is every where conspicuous; he knows how to interweave the very nicest shades of character into his portrait of his Lord. But the teachings of Jesus are with him the great thing; the acts he relates are often only a preface to a discourse of the Lord, and thus he only recounts five of His miracles. It is only for the sake of the introductory discourse of Jesus that he repeats His multiplication of the loaves, and walking on the sea, from the other Evangelists.

The scene of the history and most of its contents are different from those in the earlier Gospels. St. Matthew, the Galilean publican of Capernaum, and St. Mark and St. Luke, who follow him, relate the works of Jesus after the Baptist's imprisonment, among the fishermen, shepherds and little towns of Galilee. Here St. John comes in to supply what occurred between the Temptation of Jesus and the Baptist's apprehension, especially His first public appearance in Judæa.[1] His journeys to Jerusalem at the festivals were intimated and implied, but not described, in the earlier Gospels, no doubt because St. Matthew was hindered by his business from attending them. St. Luke, however, has given copious notices of the acts and teaching of Jesus in two journeys through Samaria towards Jerusalem, during which His ministry extended beyond the borders of Galilee; but he breaks off at the Lord's entrance into the capital.[2] St. John, on the other hand, who never left Him, relates each journey to Jerusalem and what took place there, as also His acts and teaching in Judæa and especially in the holy city. Hence, too, the great difference of form between the teaching and discourses of Jesus in the older Gospels and in this. The former relate principally addresses adapted for the Galilean populace in gnomes, parables, and moral precepts; St. John gives rather what Jesus said in the capital, when conversing with rulers, priests, and men learned in the Law; he narrates whole conversations and discourses, interrupted by objections and contradictions. The words of Jesus in this Gospel are often more solemn, mysterious, and hard to understand— undoubtedly because it is precisely such utterances of his Lord that were most deeply engraven on St. John's mind

[1] John i.—iv.  [2] Luke ix. 51 sqq; xix. 28 sqq.

from his natural temperament, and because it was part of his object to exhibit the Messiah as the Divine incarnate Logos, and, therefore, to bring forward those sayings of Jesus which point, in opposition to the unbelief of the Jews, to His Divine dignity and heavenly origin.

The author of the fourth Gospel indicates, without naming, himself so unmistakably that even apart from tradition there could be no doubt about him. He only describes himself in the narrative as "the disciple whom Jesus loved," or the "other disciple." He wrote, as he says, "that ye may believe that Jesus is the Christ, the Son of God," not for Jews or unconverted Gentiles, but for Gentile and Hellenistic Jewish converts. His first Epistle seems to be an accompaniment to his Gospel. When he says at the beginning of this Epistle, "What we have heard, and have seen with our eyes, and our hands have handled of the Word of Life .... that we declare unto you," and when again he uses the words, "I write unto you," of what he had written previously, this must refer to his Gospel.[1] Above all, the Epistle is most closely allied in spirit and tone with the Gospel. There is abundant proof of the Gospel being St. John's work, from the whole tradition of the Church, and from the influence it had from the first on the teaching, habits of thought and writings of Christians. "It is well known," says Eusebius, "to all the Churches under heaven, and the first line is conclusive evidence to every one."[2] Were it, as recent writers have tried to make out, a supposititious work of the middle of the second century, it must at once, as though by miracle, have come into universal use and veneration, at a time when other spurious Gospels were carefully rejected by the Christians. It is inconceivable, if so, that none of St. John's many disciples who were still living should have raised his voice against it, that no particular Churches (as happened in the case of the Epistle to the Hebrews and the Apocalypse) should have felt any suspicion or uncertainty about it for some time, and especially that the Churches of Asia Minor, over which St. John presided to the last, should have at once received it.

There are other Gospels on record besides these, among

---

[1] 1 John i. 1—3; ii. 12—14.   [2] Eus. iii. 24.

which the "Gospel of the Hebrews," in the Syro-Chaldaic language, was the oldest and most important. It was founded on the Aramaic original of St. Matthew, and existed in two forms, for both the Jewish Christian sects, Nazarites and Ebionites, possessed it, but each with special additions. Both parties, of course, maintained that their Gospel was the genuine production of St. Matthew, and the Ebionite, Symmachus, at the end of the second century, attacked the Greek version in his memoirs, naturally, as he assumed the Ebionite form to be the true one.[1] The Nazarites, who were nearer the Church, had it in its complete form, with the two first chapters, which are missing in the Ebionite Gospel.[2] It was probably known in this form to the Jewish Christian, Hegesippus, who occasionally quoted it.[3] St. Jerome was allowed by the Nazarites of Berœa to copy it, and he translated it into Greek and Latin. He shared the prevalent opinion that it was in substance the original draught of St. Matthew, but in a mutilated condition.[4] The Gospel was not, as has been recently maintained,[5] a corrupt translation from the Greek of St. Matthew, for, according to St. Jerome, all the Old Testament passages were quoted from the Hebrew text, not the Alexandrian version; and that Father, who knew well enough what he had twice translated, would easily have discovered its alleged Greek origin. But he always retained his belief that it came from the Hebrew original of St. Matthew, the version which the Apostle, Bartholomew, brought to South Arabia or Ethiopia, and which Pantœnus found there a century later.[6]

---

[1] Eus. vi. 17.     [2] Epiph. *Hær.* xxix. 9.
[3] Eus. iv. 22; iii. 20. Phot. *Bibl. Cod.* 232.
[4] Hier. *de Vir. Ill.* iii. *adv. Pelag.* iii. 1.
[5] Delitzsch *Zeitschrift für Luth. Theologie* 1850, p. 469.
[6] St. Jerome did not know two documents, an Aramaic Gospel of St. Matthew and a Nazarite Hebrew Gospel, but one document only, which the Nazarites lent him and which he transcribed and translated, of which there was also a copy in the Pamphilian library at Cæsarea. Of this he once says, that it is the original of St. Matthew, elsewhere that it was taken for such by many. He calls it the "Gospel the Nazarites use" (*ad Matt.* xii. 13; xxiii. 35, *Comm. in Ezech.* xxiv. 7), or "that written in Hebrew characters," (*Ep. ad Hedib.*) Thus the Nazarite Gospel of the Hebrews agreed for the most part with the Greek text of St. Matthew, except as regards the passages and additions marked by him; and he could both say that the Nazarite document *was* the Hebrew of St. Matthew (*i.e.* in substance), and that many so regarded it—those, namely, who knew only of the substantial agreement and not of the variations and interpolations. St. Jerome had no further knowledge of the Ebionite Gospel of the Hebrews, as neither had Epiphanius of the Nazarite (at least any more accurate knowledge).

Those of whose Apostolic labours history tells us are the "pillars of the Church," Peter, James, Alphæus, John, and after them Paul and Barnabas; of the work of the other eight Apostles the New Testament contains no trace, and later authorities supply only scanty and in part uncertain notices. Several of them are said to have visited distant lands as preachers of Christ, and, so far as Jewish communities in such regions gave them a centre and standpoint, this is credible. Origen says that Andrew worked in Scythia, and Thomas in Parthia, viz., the Western districts of the Parthian Kingdom between the Euphrates and Tigris.[1] There, in Edessa, was his sepulchre, and the graves of four Apostles only, Peter, Paul, John, and Thomas, were known in the fourth century.[2] St. Bartholomew went to "India"—which probably means Southern Arabia—and there, a century later, Pantænus found the Aramaic Gospel of St. Matthew, which he had brought.[3] All that is told of St. Matthew in the oldest authorities is, that he lived in strict continence and ate no flesh.[4] St. Philip taught in Phrygia and died in Hierapolis. His three daughters, some married, some unmarried, were highly reverenced long after his death, and Polycrates, bishop of Ephesus, in the second century speaks of them as venerated pillars of the Church of Asia.[5] Of St. Matthias there is only a saying preserved on the necessity of taming the flesh thoroughly by mortification.[6] Heracleon in the middle of the second century maintained that St. Matthias, St. Thomas, St. Philip, and St. Matthew died a natural death, and Clement quotes this without contradicting it.[7] Lastly, St. Barnabas, immediately called by Christ to the Apostolate like St. Paul, placed by St. Luke and the Apostolic Council before St. Paul, and rightly reckoned by St. Jerome the fourteenth Apostle, with St. Paul as thirteenth, seems to have died in Cyprus.

The Epistle to the Jewish Christians extant under his name and much read in the ancient Church is shown by clear grounds of internal evidence not to be his, but was

---

[1] Eus. *Hist.* iii. 1.  [2] Chrys. *Hom. in Heb.* xxvi.
[3] Eus. *Hist.* v. 10.  [4] Clem. Alex. *Pæd.* ii. 1, p. 114.
[5] Eus. *Hist.* v. 24.  [6] Clem. Alex. *Strom.* iii. p. 436.
[7] Clem. Alex. *Strom.* i. 4. p. 502. For Ματθαῖος we must read Ματθίας, for the Levi named afterwards is St. Matthew.

ascribed to him later; no doubt, through mere conjecture, and with no intent to deceive. It was obviously written after the destruction of Jerusalem, at a time when an attempt was made to restore the Jewish temple, which can only have been in the period between Nerva and the second destruction under Hadrian, from 97 to 135 A.D.[1] The harshness of judgment on everything Jewish, the unmeasured exaggeration in describing the moral character of the Apostles before their call, the number of forced typical and allegorical meanings, the unhistorical and unscriptural views, *e. g.*, about circumcision—all these things are fatal to the notion of a Levite and Apostle being the author of this Epistle. It is obviously the work of an unknown Alexandrian allegorist in the first half of the second century. That the name of Barnabas was given to it, occurred naturally from the learned allegorical explanation of the ceremonial law, combined with the anti-Jewish scope of the Epistle, suggesting a man who was both a Levite and an Apostle of the Gentiles as the writer. Yet Eusebius classed the document as a spurious production with other decidedly apocryphal writings.[2]

St. Mark planted the Christian Church at Alexandria, and, according to Eusebius, made Annianus first bishop there, A.D. 62.[3] For centuries his mantle was preserved, and every new bishop clothed with it at his enthronement, and in the fourth century pilgrims came from a distance to visit his tomb near the city.[4] Titus, whom St. Paul had finally sent to Dalmatia, returned to Crete, and died there.[5] Thaddæus or Adæus, a Jew of Edessa and one of the seventy disciples, was sent by the Apostle Thomas to his native city, where he converted King Abgar of Osroene, with some of his people. Eusebius found a report of this in the Archives of Edessa,[6] which may thus claim to be the first of all cities that became completely Christian, and the centre whence Christianity was propagated in the Persian kingdom.

---

[1] Ep. Barn. c. 16.  [2] Eus. *Hist.* iii. 25.  [3] Eus. ii. 16.
[4] *Literat. Brev.* c. 20. Pullad. *Hist. Laus.* c. 113.
[5] *Addita. Gr. ad Hieron. de Vir. Ill.* 12.
[6] Eus. *Hist.* i. 13. Cf. Asseman. *Bibl. Orient.* iii. P. ii. p. 3 sqq. *Acta. S. Thom. ill.* Thilo. p. 116.

# SECOND BOOK.

## THE DOCTRINE OF THE APOSTLES.

### CHAPTER I.

#### SCRIPTURE AND TRADITION.

It was inconsistent with the origin and dignity of the Founder of the Christian Religion to write Himself. He was too exalted to become a writer. It was not by a book, but by His acts, His words, the means of grace He ordained, and the Spirit whom He bestowed, that He chose to found His Church. Nor did He give His disciples a commission to write. They were to go from place to place, bearing witness everywhere personally by word of mouth and claiming to be heard, and so to carry His message and form communities. When He promised them the assistance of the Holy Ghost, He was not thinking of authorship, but of the cases where they would have to speak. And even in that solemn moment of departure, when He gave His last charges including all their Apostolic duties, there was no mention made of writing books. So, again, was it when St. Paul was called to the Apostolate. And among the *charismata* he reckons a prophetic gift, but no special gift of writing.[1]

Several Apostles, St. James, son of Zebedee, St. Philip, St. Thomas, St. Simon, and St. Matthias, have left no writings. A quarter of a century passed from the Ascension before anything was written at all. And those who then

[1] Rom. xii. 6. 1 Cor. xii. 10.

began to write were led to do so from special circumstances, and had no idea of leaving behind them religious documents or full confessions of faith,—books like those of Moses and the Prophets, or the original records of other religions, which claim to be divinely inspired codes of doctrine and practice. None of the Apostles held it necessary to collect and put on record in one or more written documents a summary of his oral teaching, nor have any done so; still less could there be any design of the writings of separate Apostles being made to supplement each other, and combined into a general statement of Christian doctrine. That could not be attempted, because there was no common understanding among them as to a previous arrangement and distribution of labour in their writings. Every one wrote as particular circumstances or local needs required, —to supply the want of personal intercourse, to confirm what he had taught already by word of mouth, to answer questions, resolve doubts, denounce errors and evil customs, in short to do the very thing which was best and oftenest done by word of mouth. St. Paul attached greater weight to his oral teaching, to sight and speech, than to his writings. While he addressed to the Roman Christians his most elaborate and dogmatic Epistle, he yet desired to see them, that from the fulness of his spirit he might impart some gift of grace to confirm their faith.[1] He wrote to the Thessalonians, that he prayed without ceasing to see them again, to supply the defects of their faith.[2] In all the Apostolic Epistles a previous knowledge of the matter of faith is implied. St. John says, "I have not written to you as though you knew not the truth."[3] The Apostles only meant to recall what had been orally taught, and the contents of their Epistles are chiefly practical. Moral exhortations, precepts and counsels about conduct in relations of life partly or wholly exceptional and of new occurrence, and censures of imminent or actual abuses and vices, constitute a great part of the matter.

If we examine the doctrinal drift of the Apostolic speeches and letters, we shall find the leading points of St. Peter's teaching to be the Messianic office of Christ, the atoning and purifying power of His sufferings and death,

---

[1] Rom. i. 11 sqq.     [2] 1 Thess. iii. 10.     [3] 1 John ii. 21.

His influence in the world unseen, and the three conditions of salvation and the hope of future blessedness, repentance, faith, and baptism, together finally with the Second Coming of the Lord and renewal of the world. These are asserted briefly and authoritatively by him. The fundamental idea in St. James' Epistle is, that the Law is elevated and transfigured into a law of liberty; beyond this he only interweaves into his moral exhortations and censures the doctrine that it is not faith alone, but faith with works, that justifies men before God. In St. John's writings, it is the Divine Word, the Only Born Son, who is Life and the Principle of life for all mankind, and who shows Himself the Deliverer from the power and defilement of sin through the threefold means and testimony of His blood, or death, the water (of baptism), and the Holy Ghost whom He bestows. The life He gives is above all the love of God, and with and through it the taking away of sin, the capacity of sanctification, the power to know God and keep His commandments, the confidence that our prayers are heard, and the sure and joyful hope that our salvation will be perfected.

St. Paul, as is natural, deals most largely in doctrine, partly grounded on an elaborate argumentation from passages of the Old Testament. At the same time, a great portion of his Epistles is occupied with hortatory matter. The whole of that to the Philippians is an out-pouring of heart in thankfulness and love, without any doctrinal significance. A good deal of his writing is only a defence of his office, and his conduct towards the Gentiles; in fact the whole Second Epistle to the Corinthians is devoted to maintaining his Apostolical authority against various attacks. Then, again, practical questions of Christian life and discipline chiefly occupy him in the First Epistle to the Corinthians, such as parties among Christians, the use of spiritual gifts, meat offered in sacrifice, immorality, marriage, the *agape*, women covering their heads. The Epistles to Timothy and Titus give advice about the pastoral and teaching offices; those to the Romans, Colossians, Galatians, and Ephesians, are mostly doctrinal. His chief Epistle, that to the Romans, lays down that the righteousness without which, owing to the common sinfulness, none can be saved, is vainly sought in observance of the Mosaic Law, but given by Christ through faith as a gift of grace. The Epistle to the Galatians, again, is to prove against the Jewish righteousness by works, that the Law was indeed to conduct us to Christ, but that salvation is independent of its observance. In the Epistle to the Colossians, he speaks briefly of two truths of faith, the Divinity of Christ, and redemption; in that to the Ephesians, of the privileges of the Church and the happiness of belonging to her communion. The Epistles to the Thessalonians refer only, together with much personal and hortatory matter, to the expectation of Christ's Second Coming, which is noticed in connection with the resurrection. Lastly, the Epistle to the Hebrews, the most doctrinal after that to the Romans, exhibits in an argument designed entirely for the Jews of that day, the infinite dignity of Christ's Person, the consequent superiority of the Christian to the Old Testament religion, and the distinction of priesthood and sacrifice under the Old and the New Law.

All this, in general and in detail, is widely different from a code of doctrine, or summary of faith. The very fundamental doctrine of Christianity, so strange and offensive to Jews of that day, so new to Gentiles—that of the Holy Trinity—the doctrine the Church was to be engaged for centuries in fixing and building up, is nowhere expressly affirmed, scarcely touched on in passing, only always assumed. Yet without this dogma, the whole fabric of Christianity, which rested on it, was insecure; every believer had to realise it as a fact, and to recognise and find the working out of his own salvation in the manifestation of the Father through His Incarnate Son and the action of the Son through the Holy Ghost, though Christians of that day were far from seeking to master the mystery in the form of any abstract theory or speculation.

Whatever common attributes belong to the Apostolic writings, the mental individuality and character of the writers always shows itself conspicuously. They are as unlike as possible to mere lifeless, impersonal instruments. Thus there is a striking contrast between St. John and St. Paul. St. John writes with calm assertion, without dialectical argument, his spiritual gaze fixed on God and the Incarnate Word, while the hurried movement of St. Paul's utterance, with its abrupt and pregnant statements, gives one the impression of his being often overpowered by the fulness of thoughts that crowd upon him. His many digressions, questions, exclamations, unfinished or half-finished sayings, anacolutha, parentheses—all this betrays a fiery impulse of mind, a deep emotion, and an anxiety to convince or terrify, which even so rich and copious a language sometimes fails to satisfy; and logical argument passes with a sudden turn into a lyrical cry of joy, or a solemn ecclesiastical doxology.

Everything had conspired to make the Greek language, that master-piece of human speech,—and at its highest point of development, as the creation of a literature unrivalled for richness and mental power in the ancient world,—to make that queen of languages the first instrument for receiving Christian ideas, and giving them form and colour. The idiom the Apostles wrote in was not, indeed, the language of Plato and Xenophon, with its Attic grace and refinement; it was the so-called "common speech," which arose after Alexander out of the dissolution and fusion of the old dialects, and in its Hellenistic form, that is, as the Jews then scattered over the Heathen world had learnt it from the mouth of the people, and adapted it for oral use, with a mixture of old Hebraisms and new Aramaic forms. It was, therefore, more like a provincial dialect than the language of books. But the widely-spread Alexandrian version of the Old Testament, with its strongly marked Hebraist character, had made this dialect into a vehicle for literature. Its vocabulary supplied the foundation for the language of the Apostles and early Christian writers. They could adopt the Septuagint use of certain Greek words, to express such notions as faith, righteousness, repentance, sanctification, and the like, strange as the words would sound to one versed in Greek and Roman literature. But this previous terminology could not suffice; the richness, depth, and speciality of Christian ideas constrained them to form a new one, not so much by coining new words, as by giving a new sense to old ones. If we find the word that in classical literature means "gracefulness" ($\chi\acute{\alpha}\rho\iota\varsigma$) used by the Apostles in the sense, wholly new to the Heathen, of Divine grace, we may infer the distance, or rather gulf, between classical Greek and the language as made subservient to Christian purposes, and penetrated with the light of the Christian spirit. The notions either newly introduced into the then world, or revolutionised, corrected and transfigured by Christianity —holiness as a divine operation in man, humility, conscience, the world, the distinction of soul and spirit—these, and many more, had to be clothed in a suitable Greek dress. We can only approximately conceive the impression made on educated Heathen of that and the following age by reading the Apostolic writings. It must certainly in most cases have repelled them, if only from the speech and terminology; and much would be simply unintelligible to them.

The Old Testament passed from the Jewish into the Christian Church as a sacred document, henceforth her's of right, which bore witness to Christ and His Church, and which both had been fulfilled and would be further fulfilled through Him, and the institution He founded. He had appealed in His own defence to the Old Testament books. He says; "The Scriptures, in which ye think ye have eternal life, are they which testify of Me;" "Moses wrote of Me."[1] He reproached the Jews with not knowing the Scriptures, and not being ready to believe them. He had come into the world to fulfil the indivisible whole of the Old Testament, the Law and the Prophets. He did not mean to abolish it; on the contrary, His whole life, His teaching, the founding of His Church, His sacrificial death, and His resurrection, were to be a fulfilling of the Law and the promises; and this process was to continue through the whole period of His Church, till its final accomplishment. He derived from Judaism the whole doctrinal and ethical substratum of His Church. Only those exclusively national limitations which were inconsistent with the universality of the Church, and the ritual shadows which were abrogated by fulfilment, and whose place was supplied by realities, were to cease; Christianity was to become the development and spiritual fulfilment of Judaism for all mankind. In this sense, He could say that not any, the least, iota of the Law should pass away, while heaven and earth remained.[2]

[1] John v. 39, 46.  [2] Matt. v. 18. Luke xvi. 17.

The primitive Church received from the Synagogue the collection of Jewish sacred books in their then threefold division, Law, Prophets, and Hagiographa (*Ketubim*), which name, however, came later into use. This collection of sacred writings was by no means closed at the time of Christ; there were different views about some parts of the Hagiographa; even long after the destruction of Jerusalem there was much dispute among the Jews about the value of the so-called three books of Solomon, Proverbs, Ecclesiastes, and the Canticles, and about receiving the book of Esther into the Canon. The school of Shammai wished to exclude Ecclesiastes, and the new Synagogue founded at Jamnia after the Jewish war had an examination of witnesses about the extent of the third part of the Hebrew Canon.[1] The Alexandrian and Hellenistic Jews included in their collection of sacred writings the books written or preserved only in Greek, whose origin dates from the four centuries between Malachi and John the Baptist, and these, as being incorporated in the Alexandrian version, passed with the rest into the use of the Christian Church. These books—Sirach (*i.e.* Ecclesiasticus), Wisdom, Tobias, Judith, Maccabees, and Baruch[2]—filled up the gaps, in a doctrinal and historical sense, left between the Captivity and the Roman dominion in the Hebrew collection; they were partly the result of the marriage of the Jewish and Greek mind, and the contact of Mosaicism with Greek philosophy, and thus acted as connecting links to prepare and pioneer the way for Christianity, and, if not quoted by name in the Apostolic writings, they are often used word for word. The Old Testament writings, generally, are quoted in the New Testament under the common designation of the "Law and the Prophets."[3]

Christ and the Apostles moved in the spiritual atmosphere of these books, which required a thousand years for their gradual formation; from them the first Christians derived the tradition, that the Lord and His Church were the fulfilment and proper continuation of the old promises

---

[1] Grätz. *Geschichte der Juden*, iv. p. 41 sqq.
[2] [These books, with the Greek portions of Daniel and Esther, and the third and fourth of Esdras and Prayer of Manasses—which last three are rejected from the Tridentine Canon also—make up the Anglican Apocrypha.—Tr.]
[3] Luke xvi. 29, 31. Acts xxiv. 14.

and old Covenant. Christ had admitted to the Pharisees, that "the Scripture cannot be broken." St. Paul says, "All that was written before (our time) was written for our learning (viz. the Old Testament), that we through patience and consolation of the Scriptures may hold fast the hope" (of future salvation).[1] In the New Testament, besides Isaiah, Jeremiah, Daniel and the Pentateuch, the Psalms are quoted with particular frequency; most of the other Prophets, Job and Proverbs are used. But Obadiah, Nahum, Ecclesiastes, Canticles, Esther, Ezra and Nehemiah are never quoted. These Old Testament citations or references and arguments are not strictly a deduction and demonstration of particular doctrines from that source; as a rule, they only show that what was now a Christian certainty had been already attested there, or might be found in kindred and corresponding forms of expression. Christ Himself had not formed His teaching from these books, but possessed and proclaimed it from a higher original source, from His own immediate vision of God. The Apostles and disciples did not use and expound the Old Testament according to any fixed hermeneutic system they had received or had themselves formed; they were convinced that in their knowledge of Christ and His history they had a key to the Biblical promises, that much hitherto obscure in these books had become clear to them by their faith, and that the then existing gift of prophecy was certainly in part to be applied to the interpretation of Scripture prophecies. They kept free from the tricksy and purely arbitrary exegetical devices already prevalent in the Rabbinical schools, though their method of interpretation was inherited in many respects from the Jews. Starting from the consideration of the Bible as a great prophetical whole, they saw everywhere types and promises of Christ, of His present kingdom and its future glory; and the Old Testament was to them an inexhaustible mine of types, of historical parallels and applications. Looking back from the time of fulfilment to the preparatory period of Judaism, they regarded persons, events, institutions, sayings, in the light of the world-wide dispensation of God, ordering and harmonizing all things, and thus in the present—in the acts and

---

[1] John x. 35. Rom. xv. 4.

events they themselves witnessed—they recognised antitypes corresponding to those types of the past; they read all as a prophecy and shadow of the future, and were so much the more confident of the ultimate victory of their cause.

A more precise exposition of the relations of the Scriptural books to that Divine guidance to which they owed their typical and prophetical character, or of the nature of their authors' illumination, will be sought in vain from Christ and the Apostles. Taking the Pharisees' standpoint, while appealing to a word in the Psalms to justify an expression He had used, Christ says that the Scripture cannot be loosed, according to the belief of His opponents themselves; implying that it must also in this passage be right.[1] What the Lord says of the abiding force of the Law, until every letter be fulfilled, applies simply to the future fulfilment of the old Law in Him and His Church.[2] There is no reference meant to the legal code, or the whole collection of Scriptural books. St. Paul refers Timothy to the (Jewish) sacred writings which he had known from childhood, and which (through faith rooted in Christ) could lead him to salvation; and adds, in a general way, without reference to any particular documents, that every Scripture, breathed through or inspired by God, is useful for instruction, correction, and improvement.[3] And lastly, St. Peter's observation, that the prophetic promises did not come of man's will, but that the Prophets spoke, being moved by the Holy Ghost, is confined to the Prophecies.[4] At the same time, the Apostles often quote the Old Testament with the formula, "God," or "the Holy Ghost, says." And St. Paul recognises a prophetic purpose of God in many passages or facts of the Old Testament, which he does not therefore scruple to affirm were written for the requirements of Christians.[5]

The Apostles generally availed themselves of the Alexandrian version of the Old Testament, already widely spread among the Jews, and used even in Palestine.[6] This version differs constantly, and in matters of importance, from the

[1] John x. 35.  [2] Matt. v. 18. Luke xvi. 17  [3] 2 Tim. iii. 15, 16.
[4] 2 Pet. i. 21.  [5] Rom. iv. 23, 24; xv. 4. 1 Cor. ix. 10; x. 11.
[6] Of about 350 O. T. quotations in the N. T. only about 50 differ from the Septuagint. Cf. Grinfield's *Apology for the Septuagint*. (London, 1850), p. 145.

Hebrew text, or at least from the form given to it several centuries later by the Jewish " Masoreth." The text on which the Greek version was founded had no vowel points, accents, directions for reading or division of words. For the whole present arrangement of the Hebrew text, the vocalisation, division of words, verses and paragraphs, is the product of the labours of much later Jewish schools many centuries after the introduction of Christianity. And thus the Greek translators, having to deal with a dead language, only understood by the learned, were left in numberless cases to their own judgment, or referred to the tradition of their own circle.[1] They laboured, too, in a period and situation standing in complete contrast to the earlier needs and circumstances of Israel, first for the Jewish dispersion outside Palestine, then for the Gentiles. They wished above all not to leave a mere literal translation, giving word for word;—the profound and fundamental distinction of the two languages forbade that. They frequently softened the harshnesses of the original, which contradicted later habits of thought, especially the anthropomorphisms; they exchanged figurative for ordinary language, and intercalated explanatory passages into the text. The Septuagint thus formed is the creation and monument of the first interpenetration of the Hebrew and Greek spirit, which took place at Alexandria. It was, together with the Alexandrian school whose views are mirrored in it, an instrument in the hands of Providence for setting free the Jewish spirit from its narrow, national exclusiveness, and pioneering the way for Judaism to pass into a world-religion, which was to be accomplished in Christianity. This school desired to intimate that in the history, laws, worship and faith of Judaism was contained the kernel of a Divine universal truth, and a purer philosophy, exalted above all national religions, and common to all peoples. It had a decided influence on the mental culture and manner of expression of the first preachers of the Gospel, which is seen in St. Paul and St. John and above all in the Epistle to the Hebrews.

[1] The reading of the unpunctuated text was not left to individual caprice, or entirely uncertain; there was a traditional interpretation; still that must have left much doubtful, and the Alexandrian translators cannot have always known it, and in other cases would reject its principles.

In the use made by New Testament writers of Old Testament passages they display a freedom which cannot be measured by the rule of strict exegetical argument. They generally quote by the sense and not by the letter, according to the use they want to make of the passage. They combine several, sometimes widely separated passages into one,[1] or make a compound of different passages,[2] or quote so freely as to explain and adapt the passage to the event specified as its fulfilment.[3] St. Paul uses the greatest freedom of any; he commonly quoted simply after his own view of the sense, as the many departures from the text, greater or less, prove; he sometimes used the Alexandrian version, sometimes translated himself, where the Hebrew was fresher in his recollection, or served his purpose better. He often gets more out of a passage than the words or historical sense convey,[4] or ascribes to it a typical and symbolic meaning;[5] once he gives and applies to his argument a meaning precisely opposite to that of the passage quoted.[6] He not seldom adopts Scriptural language to express his own ideas, and thus allows himself to make additions or changes, or applies the words in a new relation. It must be ascribed to the Greek translator, that in St. Matthew's Gospel, originally written in Aramaic, all the passages from the Pentateuch and Psalms, and some from the Prophets, follow the Septuagint text. Only some Messianic passages of the Prophets, where the Messianic reference of the Hebrew text was lost in the Greek translation, are quoted independently of the Alexandrian version. The author of the Epistle to the Hebrews goes furthest; he not only adheres so closely to the Alexandrian version that he seems to have had the text before him, but he founds his argument upon it in passages where it completely departs from the Hebrew text, or makes additions to it.[7]

Nor can it be said that the Apostles kept strictly to the

---

[1] e.g. Matt. xxi. 5. Acts xiii. 22.
[2] e.g. Rom. ix. 33. Cf. Is. xxviii. 16; viii. 14.
[3] Matt. xxvii. 9. [4] Gal. iii. 8. Rom. iv. 11—13; ix. 25, 26.
[5] 1 Cor. ix. 9, 10.
[6] In Eph. iv. 8, for, "Thou receivedst gifts among men," St. Paul reads, "He gave gifts to men." Cf. Ps. lxvii. 19 [lxviii. 18. E. V.]
[7] In Heb. x. 5—7, for the Hebrew, "Mine ears hast Thou opened; Ps. xxxix. 7—9 [xl. 6—8 E. V.] the Greek reads, "A body Thou hast prepared Me." St. Jerome says this was made an objection to the Pauline authorship of the Epistle.—*Ad. Is.* vi. 9, *Opp. Ed. Mart.* iii. 64.

canonical books of the Old Testament, using older texts. Christ Himself quoted from writings now lost, and not comprised in the Canon;—thus He spoke of the rivers of living water which shall flow from the believer, adding, "the Scripture saith;" and the "Wisdom of God," from which He applied to Himself the passage about the Prophets sent to the Jews, and their fate, must be a book not found in the Canon.[1] St. Paul, with the same formula he uses of canonical citations, "as it is written," adopts from another lost document, the "Revelation of Elias," the words, "Eye hath not seen, nor ear heard, nor hath it entered into man's heart, what God hath prepared for them that love Him."[2] Again, in the Epistle to the Ephesians, a passage from some lost religious document is quoted with the usual formula.[3] Thus, again, St. James in his Epistle appeals to an expression which occurs nowhere in the Bible, with "the Scripture saith." And St. Jude in one short composition quotes two books not in the Canon, the Anabasis of Moses and the Book of Enoch.[4]

There is no trace of a collection of Apostolic writings, or the formation of a New Testament Canon, being attempted in the Apostolic age by St. John or any other influential Christian. We do not possess all that the Apostles wrote; two of St. Paul's Epistles, one to the Corinthians and one to the Laodiceans, had already in the early Church been lost.[5] Nor do we hear that they or their immediate successors took any steps to provide all Churches with accurate copies of Apostolic writings. Only once in the whole New Testament is mention made of the doctrine and writings of another Apostle, when St. Peter reminds the Christians of Asia Minor that his "beloved brother," Paul, has given them similar advice, to lead a holy life, waiting for the appearance of the Lord; but he adds the warning that St. Paul's Epistles contain matter hard to understand, and already perverted by ignorant and unstable persons, as also they twisted to their own destruction "the other

---

[1] John vii. 38. Luke xi. 49—51.
[2] 1 Cor. ii. 9. This is not taken from Is. lxiv. 4, as St. Jerome thinks (*ad Pamm* Ep. 101), for except in the chance coincidence of two words there is no similarity in the passages [?]. Origen says, it stood in the book named above; *Comm in Matt.* xxvii. 9, Cf. *Coteler. ad Const. Apost.* vi. 17, p. 346.
[3] Eph. v. 14. [4] James iv. 5. Jude 9, 14. [5] 1 Cor. v. 9. Col. iv. 16.

Scriptures," *i.e.*, those then used in the Christian communities.[1]

It was thus openly admitted even in the Apostolic age that important doctrinal passages of St. Paul's Epistles were hard to understand; and especially to Gentile Christians much in his writings must have continued to be difficult and unintelligible in itself. For, even if many among them had once been "Proselytes of the Gate," or attendants on the Synagogue, still they would mostly be without the deeper Old Testament training of Jews and familiarity with Jewish ideas. In the Synagogues the Bible was read from the Hebrew text, which few Jews and no Gentiles understood; in some, however, it was afterwards read in Greek, or interpreted. But it was long before hearing these lessons could suffice to make Proselytes familiar with a circle of ideas so entirely new and strange to them. Still less could the numerous Gentiles who came straight into the Church without any previous acquaintance with Judaism follow the course of thought and argumentation in the Apostolic writings. For the Apostles retained their Jewish education and way of looking at things, though transfigured and spiritualized by Christ; and their whole writings are penetrated by this line of thought. The very proofs the Apostle of the Gentiles found in the Old Testament must have seemed scarcely comprehensible to a Greek Christian. Only after years spent in Christian communion, and after having *lived into* the Apostolic habit of thought, could he find himself at home in these Epistles.

The New Testament Scriptures do not attest their own inspiration; the authors never tell us what they thought of their own writings. No one says anywhere that he wrote by Divine suggestion. But they felt, whether teaching orally or writing, as men under the guidance and suggestion of the Holy Ghost. Through Him, they said, is the revelation given us; it is He, sent from Heaven, who speaks through us; our office is a ministry of the Holy Ghost, a continuation of the teaching of Christ.[2] St. Paul, indeed, distinguished between commands of the Lord which he proclaimed in His name, and such precepts as he derived

---
[1] 2 Pet. iii. 15, 16.
[2] Eph. iii. 5. 1 Cor. ii. 10. 2 Cor. iii. 8; v. 20. 1 Pet. i. 12.

from his own insight and his judgment of the then condition and needs of the Churches; but he knew that even these originated under the influence of the Holy Ghost communicated to him, and they were thus in his eyes precepts of the Lord.[1]

The writings which make up what afterwards became the New Testament were composed between 54 and 98 A.D. The Church, therefore, had been guided by oral teaching, under the immediate influence of Christ and the Apostles, for more than twenty years, before a word of it was written; and what was written grew up in her bosom, out of the fulness of doctrinal and practical knowledge she already possessed. It was nowhere said or assumed in these most ancient documents, which do not bear testimony to themselves, that men were to take the writings of the Apostles and their disciples for the sole rule of faith and discipline, and to seek in them alone the knowledge of God's revelation. Neither was it anywhere said or hinted that the Apostles had written down all that was essential for believers, or all they had taught by word of mouth. At the end of his earthly course, St. Paul referred his disciple Timothy, not to his Epistles or the writings of other Apostles, but to what he had heard him teach orally; that teaching he was to hand on to trustworthy men, to be faithfully preserved and imparted.[2] It was, then, this oral tradition which appeared to St. Paul the fittest means for securing Christian doctrine pure and genuine to after generations, when the first generation of disciples was passed away. Even when he did refer them to an earlier Epistle addressed to them, to whose contents they were to adhere, he did not forget to mention first what they had been taught by "word," as the richer source of information.[3]

But at the same time we must maintain, in accordance with the frequently repeated testimony of the Fathers and other writers of the ancient Church, that there is no point of Christian doctrine which is not attested and laid down in the Apostolic writings. The Church cannot and dare not receive any teaching which does not find its justification in

---

[1] 1 Cor. vii. 10, 12, 25, 40; xiv. 37.   [2] 2 Tim. ii. 2.
[3] 2 Thess. ii. 14.   [15 E. V.]

the Bible, and is not contained somewhere in the New Testament, in a more or less developed form, or at least indicated and implied in premises of which it is the logical sequel, and thus shown to fit into the harmony and organic whole of Christian doctrine.

The dogmatic tradition of the Jewish necessarily passed into the Christian Church. Christ Himself had recognised it, taught out of it, and referred His disciples to the authority of the Pharisees who sat in Moses' seat, who were its organs.[1] And if He sharply denounced their arbitrary interpretations of the Law, and reproached them with making God's law of none effect by their own inventions, put forth as traditions of the fathers,—as in forbidding works of charity on the Sabbath, or allowing a son to let his parents starve, that he might put the money he had saved into the temple treasury,—those were perversions of individuals, or at most of entire schools; the dominant teaching was independent of them, and was rather confirmed or implied in the discourses of Christ and the Apostles. From tradition came the common teaching about the resurrection, the judgment, Paradise and Gehenna, without any distinct evidence from the Hebrew Canon. A good deal in the New Testament about the angels and fallen spirits comes, not from the Bible, but tradition.[2] The assertions of St. Peter and St. Jude about the sin and punishment of the fallen angels are similarly drawn from Jewish tradition.[3]

Thus the religious consciousness of Judaism, in which the Apostles, the first Christian teachers, and most of the first believers, had been brought up and had lived a longer or shorter time, flowed in unbroken stream into the Christian Church; and the Jewish became the Christian tradition. There was no violent break or formal renunciation; Christianity claimed to be, not merely a reformation, but a fulfilment of Judaism, expectation passing into possession,

---

[1] Matt. xxiii. 3.
[2] St. Paul has got from the same source his notion of a heavenly Jerusalem (Gal. iv. 26, Heb. xii. 22) and of a third heaven (2 Cor. xii. 2). The statements in the Epistle to the Hebrews about the contents of the ark and certain details of the sacrificial ritual are further proofs that the first Christians did not confine themselves to the use of canonical books, to the exclusion of traditional notices or uncanonical writings.
[3] 2 Pet. ii. 4. Jude 6.

the worship of a Redeemer who had come instead of looking for a future one, the Law spiritualised into the Gospel, a world-religion and universal Church opening its gates to every nation, instead of a mere fellowship of blood and race, a Church (*Ecclesia*) instead of a Synagogue. The Christians were conscious of being in communion with all pious Israelites up to that time, and if they threw aside as having no significance for them the Pharisaic tradition about the use of the ceremonial Law, the "hedge of the Law," and the like, they claimed for themselves all its real benefits, the sacred books, the tradition of doctrine, the moral law as expanded by Christ, and even the ritual law in its principles, with a priesthood, altar, and sacrifice, divested of their former typical and carnal character. The Psalms were their manual of prayer and praise, Baptism took the place of circumcision, the Paschal feast was transfigured into the Eucharistic celebration of sacrifice and communion, and the Jewish priesthood, with its descent from father to son after the flesh, when brought to an end by the destruction of the temple, was replaced by the spiritual succession of the teaching and priestly ministry among Christians. Thus the Christian consciousness and life were an outgrowth of the Jewish. For the first quarter of a century from the Lord's Ascension, when the Church existed without any written documents, she lived on the recollections of Christ, the spoken words of His Apostles and disciples, and the Jewish Scriptures and tradition. In the bosom of the Church, as an expression and embodiment of the Spirit that ruled and the tradition laid up within it, the New Testament Scriptures were written in the course of fifty years. By the light of this Spirit, filling the Church and guiding her from generation to generation, both people and pastors read, understood and expounded these writings. Whatever difficulties certain passages might even then suggest, on the whole men did not miss any thing in them, or find any thing obscure, uncertain, or doubtful, while they possessed the living commentary and requisite supplement in the Church's oral traditions, in the intellectual and moral convictions which lived in the hearts and on the lips of believers. And if we consider how strange and obscure whole paragraphs of the Epistles to the Romans and Galatians and the whole Epistle to the Hebrews must have appeared to the Greek converts, who had no previous training to help them, we may well say that the second generation of Christians, partly brought up in the bosom of the Church, understood the New Testament better than was possible for the Greek contemporaries of the Apostles.

The crucified Christ, whom the Apostles preached, was "to the Jews an offence, to the Gentiles foolishness." Yet troops of converts thronged into the Church, because they believed the Apostles, *i.e.* were convinced that they were the messengers and plenipotentiaries of One higher, and their message true. As soon as they had become members of the Church, they were ready to learn and to obey, to submit inwardly and sincerely to the whole teaching proclaimed by an Apostle, and laid up in the Church. They had not come in to wrangle and to choose, to take one article and reject another which displeased them; that would only be a sign that they were wanting in real faith. St. Paul thanks God that the Thessalonians had received the word he preached, not as man's, but as God's word.[1] Those who demanded belief in this word were a handful of uneducated Galileans, and a Pharisee who himself described his teaching as folly in comparison with what then passed for truth.[2] But they were the only persons of that day who believed themselves, and therefore won belief. By them the Church was built on faith, and became a school of faith. Much as there was in Christian doctrine repulsive and burdensome, dark and mysterious, for the natural man, every one learnt in the Church to bow his mind and will under her authority, and to regard her as the embodiment of the Holy Ghost instructing the nations of the earth, bearing outward witness to what the Spirit taught within, and holding her mission from Christ as He held His from the Father. And thus Christians found release from false confidence in men, from the labour and insecurity of searching, and the torment of doubt and uncertainty. They had not a book handed them from which they were to extract a summary of *credenda* with painful uncertainty, and at the risk of misconception, but were referred to a living ever-speaking authority, open and accessible to all. This belief,

[1] 1 Thess. ii. 13.   [2] 1 Cor. i. 21.

that God had spoken first by the Apostles, and still spoke in His Church, gave them rest in its certainty, and formed the rule and support of their whole lives; and thus all their powers were directed to action, and their one aim was to make their life a genuine reflection of the faith by whose power they were possessed.

From the year 68, after the death of St. Peter and St. Paul, the greater part of the Church found itself deprived of the personal authority of Apostles. Yet the Church increased rapidly; Jews and Gentiles were eager to be received and instructed. To the question, What is your faith? what must I believe and do? the rulers of the Church answered, not by pointing to a collection of Apostolical writings, for the sufficient reason that no fixed collection existed for a long time, each community having some fragments only, more or fewer. The catechumen was referred to oral tradition. Thus, he was told, have the Apostles received from Christ, and we from them and their disciples. A brief summary of the chief articles of faith was given him, such as is comprised in the oldest creed reaching back into Apostolic times; living in the Church, intercourse with elder believers, taking part in worship and hearing sermons,—all this supplied what he needed, and completed his Christian education. He believed on testimony, while its actual truth shone upon him. "We here," they told him, "are but a fraction of the whole great Church spread already over Asia, Africa and Europe. As we believe and teach, so believe and teach all Churches founded immediately or mediately by Apostles or their disciples. We write to each other, send charitable gifts, are visited by believers of other communities; there is everywhere one and the same doctrine. Whether, as in Ephesus, an Apostle still teaches, or, as elsewhere, the third or fourth successor sits already where once an Apostle sat, the contents and the certainty of the witness borne is everywhere the same. In believing our words you believe the teaching of the whole Church, and, therefore, of the Holy Ghost. For Christ has promised and given to His Church this Spirit of truth, and therefore, so far as concerns the substance of saving faith, she can teach nothing but truth. For us, our Church is a member of the Body quickened by this Spirit; this connection and membership is our guarantee for the purity and genuineness of our doctrine, and the elder members of our community who have heard our predecessors the earlier teachers, or even the Apostles themselves, testify to the younger that the same doctrine is still taught." This was the tradition of the Church. Thus every community had its own tradition witnessed and handed on from generation to generation, from bishop to bishop, from father to son; but this brook, while constantly enriching and refreshing itself from the broad stream of universal Church tradition, gave back its own contents again into that. So every one knew whom he believed, and on whose testimony he staked his salvation. He did not believe in himself or his own independent study of certain documents, nor build his faith on conclusions drawn according to his own gifts and acquirements from comparing passages in those documents, but in the last resort on the testimony of the Church, whereof Christ said that He would found it on a rock, and place it under the protection and guidance of the Spirit of Truth.

Thus the faith of individuals was based on the double testimony of the Church, human and Divine, the testimony received by the younger generation from the older in every community, and the concurrent testimony each particular Church received from the rest, and thereby from the universal Church. In the Apostolic succession of her bishops the Church had a certainty, like that of the contemporary philosophical schools as to the continuity of their doctrine, that her teaching was identical with that proclaimed at the beginning; only the succession of so many Churches in living spiritual intercourse with each other made the security much greater. But every Church had besides a higher certainty of its own, which excluded all doubt or possibility of error, in its membership with the body of the universal Church. Enlightened, confirmed and set at rest by this testimony, and already possessed by a fixed conception of faith, individuals whose zeal so inclined them read what they could procure of the Gospels and Apostolic Epistles, and found there a confirmation of what they had been taught. They read these writings as part of the general tradition of the Church, its first written part. As the oral teaching consigned to her and rooted in her was here first embodied in written memorials, so was it also in the next and subsequent generations. The Church in every period produced a literature consisting of monuments of her contemporary tradition, and thus a part of what lived in the minds of believers was constantly fixed in writing, though, of course, the whole matter of belief existing and energizing in her bosom did not attain full expression in literature and ecclesiastical records; for it is impossible to reduce to writing the whole life, thought and mind of a great community like the Church. The living belief of every generation or period, again, was nourished from the records of former ages, above all from those of the Apostles. And thus every period of her history felt the influence of those which had gone before, through the living organism which bound together her past and present by the unfailing power of the Divine promise, "I am with you to the end of the world," by her inheritance of laws and customs, by the teachers who being dead yet lived and spoke in their writings.

What the Apostles transmitted to the Church by writing or by word of mouth was no compendium of ready-made articles of belief, no catalogue of dogmas fixed in matter and form, which it would have been her sole office to guard carefully in her memory and in the documents committed to her, and thus to preserve the heirloom of doctrine, a lifeless property once for all made up. The first deposit of doctrine was a living thing, which was to have an organic growth, and expand from its roots by a law of inward necessity and in a manner corresponding to the intellectual needs of believers in different ages, and to find its adequate expression. It consisted mainly of facts, principles, dogmatic germs, and indications containing in themselves the outline and capability of successive developments and doctrinal formation, since they held dynamically a rich store of dogma. In conformity with the historical character of Christianity, and analogous to the common life of the Church, there was also to be a corresponding progressive development and building up of doctrine, without change of its essence. It was the work of the co-operative mental toil of the most enlightened Christians, lasting on through centuries and always building on the foundation laid by their predecessors, and of a deepening search into the holy Scriptures, by which the intimations and germs of truth contained in them were gradually unfolded, first to enlightened inquirers and teachers and then to the great body of believers. This expansion from within resulted from the very nature of a Divine communication designed to penetrate and control, not only the moral domain, but the whole mental life of man, and bearing in itself an inexhaustible treasure of implicit consequences; it resulted equally from the ineradicable craving and tendency of the human spirit to sink deeper into this doctrine, to shape it into a coherent system, and to appropriate it in all its ramifications to the satisfaction of the scientific understanding. To this was added an external necessity, arising from the endeavours of heretics gradually to change or decompose all Christian doctrines, for strengthening the points that were menaced and surrounding them, as it were, with bulwarks of wider and deeper definitions, for guarding the doctrinal deposit against every attempt of a one-sided or thoroughly perverse interpretation and wrong development, and thence for mapping out its details and exhibiting its full contents secured and fixed by ecclesiastical decision. In such cases Church tradition, represented by the common sentiment of Christians which was injured or threatened, raised a loud and unanimous protest, and demanded positive definitions. The whole history of the Church displays an advancing process of doctrinal development, in which the human mind necessarily takes part, not, indeed, unaided or left to its natural movements, but guided by the Paraclete, the Teacher given to the Church And thus, in the last resort, this rearing and consolidation of the doctrinal fabric was the work of the same Spirit to whom are due the doctrinal contents of the New Testament; and whatever of narrowness, error or passion was mixed with the process, from the fault of its human instruments, was, in the long run, remedied through the higher energy of the Divine indwelling Spirit, and consumed, as in a purifying spiritual fire.

Christian doctrine, from its mental and moral elevation, its mysteries transcending vulgar comprehension, and its strictness inexorable to vulgar weaknesses, is exposed more than any other religious system to the destructive assaults or modifying influences of human inclinations, whether selfish appetite or narrowness of mind, and thus incurs the danger of being deformed and degraded into an instrument of self-seeking or short-sighted passion. This peril which menaced her dearest treasure, her very principle of life, the Church met by her possession and use of the Apostolic writings and other records of faith, new or old, by her strong position as the necessary organ for guarding tradition and cutting off impure or destructive elements, and by the protection and abiding illumination of the Holy Ghost. Through that period the prevalent doctrine or tradition of the Church was a product at once human and Divine, resulting from the co-operation and interpenetration of Divine powers and human teaching and belief, the outcome of the faith and life of all past generations. The inward growth and gradual unfolding into their consequences of the germs and principles of Christian dogma, the gradual expansion in the mind of the Church of isolated and hitherto undeveloped truths, the multiplication and widening scope of ecclesiastical decisions and formularies,—all this took place through the combined operation of three forces and forms of activity at work within her pale, the logical faculty, the learned investigation of Scripture and ancient ecclesiastical literature and tradition, and an enlightened devotion feeding on Scripture and contemplation of the mysteries. So, too, in the ages before Christ, religious knowledge required above a thousand years to advance from the simple facts and articles of the Patriarchal creed to the elaborate doctrinal system of His Jewish contemporaries,—Pharisees such as Gamaliel, or St. Paul before his conversion. And this development was the common result of a growing Revelation, and of the action of the human mind confined to one nation only, whereas the most gifted nations of three quarters of the world have taken part for eighteen centuries in the development of Christian doctrine.

And thus in no age of the Church, from Christ and the Apostles till now, could her faith and teaching differ to-day from what it was yesterday. At a later period, indeed, theological opinions might rise and pass away, and many popular beliefs which had gained a temporary ascendancy in one age, be again submerged by the advancing waves of time. But the continuity of the stream of tradition allowed neither the sudden nor gradual submersion of a doctrine by its opposite; never could a truth once thoroughly acknowledged and believed in the Church be lost, or sink from the dignity of an article of faith to a mere tolerated opinion. The right understanding of doctrine and the corresponding interpretation of the Apostolical writings went on like the links of an unbroken chain. The criticism which guarded it belonged in principle to every faithful Christian, preeminently to the organised hierarchy which inherited the Apostolic office. Their rejection of every strange doctrine resulted simply from the perception that it directly or by implication contradicted that handed down from their forefathers. Every one, layman or clergyman, could take part according to his talents in the inquiry, and offer his contribution to the common stock in the great process of forming and developing Christian doctrine; he could do so with the more confidence as knowing he was carried on and secured by the body of which he was a member, the Church whose judgment, spoken or implied, favourable or unfavourable, would sooner or later decide on the merit or demerit, the truth or error of his interpretations and views, if only he and his adherents had a fixed and humble faith, so as not to desire to set their minds above that of the Church.

# CHAPTER II.

## DOCTRINE OF THE HOLY TRINITY, THE INCARNATION AND REDEMPTION.

WHEN the Apostle of the Gentiles said, "It pleased God to reveal His Son in me," he meant that the inward Being of the glorified Jesus had been disclosed to him by an immediate communication from heaven. Christ Himself had repeatedly appeared to him, so that he bears witness of what he has seen. According to his view, Christ "from heaven" is the antithesis to our earthly father, Adam; for he saw the glory of God shining in the face of Christ.[1] Between the Son and the Father there is an inward and unshared fellowship of Being, so that the whole Substance of the Father is expressed in the Son, and He as His Image reveals the otherwise invisible Father, as the brightness of the sun is manifested in its rays.[2] By Him and in Him (by a creative act of His Person) were all things made; as the Mediator of the Divine work He has formed the whole universe, and is Himself the First-born of all creation, begotten not created, from the substance of God. With the glorified Body of the ascended Christ before him, the Apostle uses the expression, "the whole fulness of the Godhead dwells bodily in Him," the fulness of the Divine essence, not of Divine grace.[3] Though speaking here of the Incarnate Son, St. Paul has in his eye the Son in His eternal nature

---

[1] Gal. i. 15, 16. Acts xxii. 17 sqq. 1 Cor. xv. 47. 2 Cor. iv. 6.
[2] Heb. i. 3. Col. i. 15. [χαρακτὴρ τῆς ὑποστάσεως αὐτοῦ ("figura substantiæ Ejus," Vulg.) means "image of His *Substance*," not *Person* as in E.V. That use of the word ὑπόστασις is much later.—TR.]
[3] 1 Cor. viii. 6. Col. i. 16; ii. 9.

too, while he says of Him that He was in the form of God (the possession of Divine glory) but thought not this equality with God "a spoil," *i.e.*, did not look on it as man regards and jealously watches over property he has stolen and is always fearing to be deprived of, but, rather, emptied Himself by His Incarnation and His taking the form of a servant.[1] Therefore the whole world of spirits must bend the knee to His Name. St. Paul designates alike the Incarnate Redeemer in His earthly pilgrimage or heavenly exaltation, and the Divine pre-existent Person whom God sent down from heaven, as the Son, the Only Son of God, the Son of His love. He calls Christ, God, directly in two places, once in the Epistle to the Romans, "Christ, who is over all, God blessed for ever," once in the Epistle to Titus, where he speaks of "the appearing of our great God and Saviour, Jesus Christ."[2]

St. John, at the beginning of his Gospel and in the Apocalypse, calls that Divine Person who was incarnate in Jesus the *Logos* or "Word," not "Reason." In the time and place where he wrote his Gospel the word *Logos* was notoriously in use to signify a Divine Mediator, a second Person next to God or the "Father." The sources whence this notion and title were derived, and from which St. John directly or indirectly adopted them, are to be sought in Genesis, in the deutero-canonical books, and in the religious philosophy of the Alexandrian Jews. The Apostle had learnt from the very mouth of Jesus that He had His glory with the Father before the world was made, and that the Father had given to the Son to have life in Himself. In the Apocalyptic vision Jesus appeared to Him as the Author of all creation, the Beginning and the End. In the beginning of Genesis he found the Word of God spoken of as the medium of creation; in the deutero-canonical books he read of Wisdom sitting as a foster-child and companion by the Father's throne from the beginning, before the worlds were, fashioning all things, being the Brightness of

---

[1] Phil. ii. 6—8. [The E. V. is clearly incorrect in translating οὐκ ἁρπαγμὸν ἡγήσατο, "thought it not robbery," and the whole force of ἑαυτὸν ἐκένωσε is lost in "made Himself of no reputation."—TR.]

[2] Gal. iv. 4. Rom. viii. 3.; ix. 5. Tit. ii. 13. [Here the E. V. misses the point from ignoring the article.—TR.]

the Eternal Light, which pierces and gives life to all, having a dwelling-place among all nations, but a special inheritance in Israel.[1]

The teaching of the Alexandrian Philo suggested the right expression for all this, though, indeed, the *Logos* of Philo is far other than that of St. John. The *Logos* of Philo is a second God, only improperly called God; and Philo commends the Jews for not worshipping the representative Revealer, the *Logos*, but the Almighty God who is exalted over all "nature of the Logos."[2] His *Logos* is properly the Platonic ideal, the archetype of order and harmony in the material world; not the Creator, but the pattern and archetype after which God has created and ordered the world. But the *Logos* of St. John is not the instrument or subject of the Divine thought, the idea, but a personal self-existent *hypostasis*. He is neither pattern nor archetype, but self-creative; by Him the worlds were made. With Philo the *Logos* is the fountain of all light, the spiritual in man's soul, and the physical; with St. John He is only the intellectual and moral Light, that lightens every man, and strives with the moral and mental darkness of the world. Philo acknowledges no closer relation of his *Logos* to the Messiah, nor any incarnation of it; for his *Logos*, whose personality he failed to grasp, and which was ever fading into an abstraction, could not become man. The *Logos* of St. John is made flesh, and revealed as the Messiah.

But St. John names the pre-existent Lord the *Logos*, not only because he found the title ready to hand, but because it served best to express the nature and office of the Son. The Son is the "Word," because, as words are the expression of thought, so He is the Expression of the Father's Substance and the Reflection of His glory, having His Being from the Father, as a word is the formed utterance of the speaker's thought. St. John says, in the "Revelation," of the Rider appearing on a white horse (Christ), that He bore a name secret and unspeakable, which none but Himself knew; but he adds that His name was called the "Word of God," as though he would say, this name

---

[1] Prov. viii. 22 sqq. Ecclus. xxiv. 1—16. Wisd. vii. 26.
[2] Phil. *Opp. Ed. Mangey* i. 413; ii. 625.

ame nearest among men to that Divine Name which adequately expresses the Being of the Son.[1]

In his Prologue St. John describes the Divine Word as well in His Divine nature and His operations before all time, as in His human manifestation. But He ascribes Sonship, not first to the incarnate, but to the pre-existent Christ. "In the beginning was the Word," that is, from all eternity, not in the beginning of creation; He was God, and with or near God,[2] not an emanation from God, or a second substance outside Him, or a second God, but all which belongs to God is His; He has part in the fulness of God's glory, and, before the worlds were made, God, the Father, is the object of His energy, His vision and His will. He is the Only-Born of the Father, for He is the Word the Father has outspoken into separate personal existence out of the fulness of His Being, and by whom alone He speaks.

This *Logos* was, and now is, the organ and medium of creation; by Him all was made, and He alone is Life, and gives life, of body or of soul; for in Him all life is contained as its Principle and Fountain. As the Light of man He shone into the darkness which grew out of man's alienation from God, even before He was incarnated; but the darkness comprehended Him not, and when He came as Man to His own people the multitude of them rejected Him. The world, as the Apostles teach, was created not only by, but for, the Son, and for His sake; for He is its immediate End, in Him its every end is realised, and therefore has God given it Him for an inheritance, and put all things under His feet.[3]

Christ had already frequently mentioned the Holy Ghost, before He more clearly indicated His nature and office in promising His disciples Another in His place, a Paraclete, a Divine Comforter and Helper. But He said it was only after His departure, and when He was glorified with the Father, that He could and would send to them this Spirit, who would compensate for the loss of His bodily presence.[4] The whole work of the Incarnation must first be accomplished, redemption wrought, the way re-opened to the

---

[1] Apoc. xix. 11—13.
[2] πρὸς τὸν θεόν. John i. 1.
[3] Col. i. 16. Heb. i. 2. Eph. i. 22.
[4] John xiv. 16; xv. 26.

Father, and human nature exalted and glorified in Christ; the disciples must first be made ready to receive Him, and the material prepared for building up the future Church, before Christ could send the Holy Ghost, who would then make the disciples into living stones of that edifice, and take up His abiding habitation in it. As the Son by Incarnation bound human nature to Himself, the Spirit by indwelling carried on and completed His work, and erected a Kingdom on earth which, as a living organisation, has Christ for its Head and King, Himself sent from the Father and the Son for its animating Soul, Christians for its members. He, therefore, is the Principle of Church communion and unity; He glorifies the Son in the Church, which is the perpetual manifestation of the life of Christ, Christ being the Head, the Church the collective body of His members.[1] He convinces the world of sin, of righteousness, and of judgment. For, as Spirit of the Church, He is an abiding Revelation and unceasing Witness of the sinfulness of the world at irreconcilable enmity with the Church, so that the world, as the domain of the natural life under the power of delusion and sin, displays itself in all its emptiness and falsehood. He, further, testifies of the righteousness of Christ's cause, the Redeemer now exalted to the glory of the Father, and thence invisibly ruling the Church; and of the judgment already accomplished upon Satan and his worldly dominion.[2]

This Spirit is the Spirit of Truth;[3] as such He exhibits His power in the Church, imparting to her truth by imparting Himself. He reminds the Church of all that Christ had said, He teaches her what the disciples could not bear while Christ was personally with them, and by enlightening and sanctifying her members gives them a living apprehension of what they before had not understood, and fits them for full and perfect knowledge. And, by combining gradually into a whole in the Church's mind the scattered intimations in the words of Christ, He leads her into all the truth.[4] It is thus His office to preserve in the Church pure and perfect the tradition of Christ and of His entire teaching. He speaks not, Christ says, of Himself, but only

---

[1] 1 Cor. xii. 12.
[2] John xvi. 8—11.
[3] John xiv. 17; xv. 26; xvi. 13.
[4] John xiv. 25; xvi. 12—15.

what He has heard from the Father and the Son, as Christ said of Himself, that He only spoke what He had heard of the Father, only acted and spoke after the Father's will and suggestion.[1] As the Son can do nothing of Himself, but what He sees the Father do, *i.e.* as in word and work He only proclaims and embodies the Divine thought He sees in the Bosom of the Father, so too the Holy Ghost works not alone, standing apart and independently,[2] but He "receives of the Son." Thus there is a personal distinction and living mutual inherence of Father, Son and Spirit.[3]

All Christ had predicted of the mission and operations of the Holy Ghost was abundantly fulfilled. The disciples felt His power and energy in themselves, as bearers of the Apostolic office, in the believers, and in the Church. Thus the lie of Ananias and his wife seemed to them not merely a sin against man, but against the Holy Ghost, who energised in the Apostles, as Christ's representatives, and in the Church; and St. Paul describes the Corinthians as inhabited by the Holy Ghost, and therefore a holy temple of God that may not be defiled.[4] To this Spirit belongs pre-eminently the seeking out the deep things of God, the knowledge of His innermost being and most hidden thoughts and counsels, and He alone can possess and communicate this knowledge, just as none but his own Spirit knows the counsels and designs of a man.[5] In individual believers sanctification, or love, with its fulness of works and virtues, is a fruit of the Holy Ghost.[6] It is He too who, when He has perfected these operations in a man, assures him of being a child of God, while the testimony of his own conscience corresponds with that of the Divine Spirit.[7] And, therefore, He is also the Pledge of our perfection in heaven.[8]

---

[1] John v. 19; viii. 28; xii. 49.   [2] ἀφ' ἑαυτοῦ. Ib. xvi. 13.
[3] [The περιχώρησις, or as it is called in Latin Theology "Circuminsession," of the Persons in the Holy Trinity is defined, "intima existentia Unius Personæ in Alterâ, sine confusione Personæ seu Personalitatis." *See* Compendium of Perrone's *Prælect. Theol.*, vol. 1, p. 391, where St. Fulgentius is quoted as saying (*De Fid.* i. 4) "Totus Pater in Filio et Spiritu Sancto est, et totus Filius in Patre et Spiritu Sancto est, totusque Spiritus Sanctus in Patre et Filio est." Cf. also Newman's *Arians of Fourth Century*, pp. 189, 190 (ed. 1).—TR.]
[4] Acts v. 3, 4. 1 Cor. iii. 16, 17. Cf. Eph. ii. 19—22. 1 Pet. ii. 5.
[5] 1 Cor. ii. 9—11.   [6] 2 Thess. ii. 13. 1 Pet. i. 2. Gal v. 22, 23. Rom. xv. 30.
[7] Rom. viii. 16.   [8] 2 Cor. i. 22; v. 5. Eph. i. 14.

The Divine Trinity, or Godhead, unfolding Itself in Three Subjects, is proclaimed in the baptismal formula prescribed by Christ as the foundation doctrine of Christianity.[1] Every one received into the Church was to confess his belief in the Father, the Son, and the Spirit, and to come into communion with the Father through the Son, with the Son through the Holy Ghost. The Trinity is always spoken of only from its economical side, that is in relation to the method of human salvation.[2] But the ontological relationship of the Divine Persons to each other lies at the root of this, and is implied; and, where the Apostles only name the Lord or the Spirit as the Giver of grace, we must understand the common operation of Father, Son, and Holy Ghost.[3] Thus St. Paul distinguishes gifts as conferred by the Son, and ministries by the Spirit, operations (gifts and ministries) as wrought by the Father (God), yet refers all notices of these gifts to the Holy Ghost; such, again, is the drift of his threefold farewell salutation to the Corinthians, the grace of Christ, the love of God (the Father), and the fellowship of the Holy Ghost.[4] St Peter, in his opening salutation, comprehends the economy of salvation in election, according to the foreknowledge of the Father, sanctification, through the Spirit, and sprinkling with the blood of Christ, *i.e.* admission into the covenant of His atoning death.[5]

The history of Jesus and the Apostles contains frequent mention of Angelic appearances, at the birth of the Lord, in Gethsemane, at the grave, at the Ascension, in St. Peter's prison, and elsewhere. The existence of these lofty beings is also spoken of in the discourses of Christ and the Apostolic Epistles, as a thing well known and assumed, and the Sadducean denial of it appears something so strange to religious Jews, as not to call for notice. According to the statement of Christ and the Apostles, the angel-world is an ordered spiritual Kingdom with many gradations; it contains angels who excel in strength and power, or Archangels.[6] St. John sees seven angels of the highest rank standing before God's

---

[1] Matt. xxviii. 19.
[2] [Economy (οἰκονομία) is a favourite term with the Greek Fathers for the Incarnation.—TR.]   [3] 2 Thess. iii. 18. 2 Tim. iv. 22.
[4] 1 Cor. xii. 4—6. 2 Cor. xiii. 14.   [5] 1 Pet. i. 2.
[6] Eph. i. 21. 2 Pet. ii. 11. Jude 9. 1 Thess. iv. 16.

throne, one of whom, Gabriel, says himself that he stands before God, and the Prophet beholds myriads of myriads in wider circle around God and the elders.[1] They are all creatures who have attained their perfection, and are in peaceful enjoyment of blessings offered to the future expectation of men, holy, immortal,[2] in the abiding communion and immediate neighbourhood of God; they minister before Him, and are sent forth by Him, and He honours them by letting them take part in His own acts. Yet their knowledge is finite, and their understanding capable of progress; they long to look into the Divine economy of redemption.[3]

At the beginning of His ministry Jesus said to His disciples, "Ye shall see angels ascend and descend upon the Son of Man." They bow their knees at the Name of Jesus, and all, the very highest, who serve Him, minister to them that believe. They are interested in the destiny and circumstances of His Church; its Divine foundation and guidance is for them a mirror which reflects anew the wisdom of God. They rejoice over the repentance of but one sinful soul. St. John salutes the Churches of Asia Minor in the name of the seven angels before the throne of God; Michael is now the Protector of the Church, and St. Paul adjures Timothy by God, by Christ, and by the angels, to fulfil his duties. Every man has his own guardian angel; even the least among the regenerate, as Jesus said, have their angels, who always behold the face of God.[4] When first the disciples saw St. Peter on his release from prison, they thought it was his angel. In the Apocalyptic vision, the angels unite their prayers with those of the pious on earth, and present them before God; an angel mingles heavenly incense with the prayers of the Saints, which ascend like incense smoke, to make them acceptable to God. Angels and men form one great organisation, and God has united all in heaven and on earth into one, for His service and glory, under Christ as Head, and by virtue of His atonement.[5]

---

[1] Apoc. i. 4; v. 11. Luke i. 19.   [2] Luke xx. 36.   [3] 1 Pet. i. 12.
[4] [It is not of course meant that guardian angels are confined to the regenerate. The testimony both of Scripture and Tradition confirm the author's statement that "every man has his guardian angel."—TR.]
[5] John i. 51. Phil. ii. 10. Heb. i. 14. Eph. iii. 10. Luke xv. 7, 10. Apoc. i. 4; xii. 7; viii. 3. 1 Tim. v. 21. Matt. xviii. 10. Acts xii. 15. Eph. i. 10.

But the New Testament often speaks also of a Kingdom of Evil Angels, to which the Incarnation of the Word, His earthly work, and the Church with its institutions and gifts, are opposed. Christ came to destroy the works of the devil. There is no Prince or Head of the whole kingdom of good angels mentioned, but there is constant mention of a mighty ruler of the kingdom of darkness, and of evil spirits subject to him. It is he, in whose being and life is no truth, who began the great apostasy, and by whose free choice evil entered into that world which God had created good. He appears as one hardened in fixed contradiction and irreconcilable enmity against God, a spirit that hates all good, whose kingdom is everywhere thwarting, destroying and tempting to apostasy the kingdom of God. He is the great dragon, the old serpent, the lying spirit hating truth, who sinned from the beginning. Man found evil in existence; it originates not with him, but he is tempted to it, and because through deceit of Satan sin, and with it death both of soul and body, came upon mankind, therefore is Satan called the ruler of death, and a murderer from the beginning.[1]

The spirits who belong in fixed ranks and gradations to the kingdom of this master kept not their original power and glory, but left their proper sphere in the realm of light, and were therefore thrust down into the place of darkness, where they are reserved in chains of darkness for a last decision of their fate.[2] The darkness of this world is the region to which and by which they are bound, and where they rule. They are lords of the world, whose element is the darkness belonging to its then condition, the whole moral and religious state of the Heathen world; they are the "spirits of wickedness," who have their dwelling in the air surrounding this earth, impure spirits banished from the kingdom and service of God, and become slaves of Satan, the instruments and ministers of his hostility to God and man.[3] They believe that God is, but being apostates from His love and hardened in selfishness, tremble before Him, knowing or suspecting that He will take away their dominion over the Heathen world, and judge them.[4] The

---

[1] 1 John iii. 8.   John viii. 44.   Heb. ii. 14.
[2] Jude 6.   2 Pet. ii. 4.      [3] Eph. vi. 12.         [4] James ii. 19.

"demoniacs," or possessed, who existed in considerable numbers in Palestine and throughout Heathendom, many of whom were delivered by the word of Jesus and His Apostles and disciples, were conspicuous examples of the power of these spirits at a time when they collected all their strength in vindication of their menaced dominion. Their condition, as was commonly believed among the Jews, was the result of a demoniacal influence exerted over their bodily nature, and its usual symptoms were epilepsy, madness, melancholy and deafness; they felt themselves in bondage, and their body and its organs subjected to an alien mastery.[1]

The moral and religious condition of that age explains why Satan is named the Prince of this world, or the god of the present world, that is of the era characterized by Heathen dominion.[2] His spirits receive the Heathen worship. The idol sacrificed to, St. Paul says, is nothing, a mere work of men's hands, with no corresponding reality, of which it is a representation; but the gods of the Heathen are actually existing, not powerless beings; they are demons, and sacrifices offered to them are offered to demons. "There are many gods, and many lords, in heaven, and on earth, but we Christians have one God, the Father, and one Lord, Jesus Christ."[3] Thus, Satan's kingdom is of wide extent, for not only fallen spirits, but men estranged from God by sin and error, belong to it. But the kingdom of Christ is opposed to it, and through His redeeming work Satan will be driven from the domain he has hitherto ruled; his power to mar the Lord's work, by sowing tares among the wheat and mixing poison with the fountains of health, is decreasing and destined at last to vanish before the power of God.[4] Till then, he knows how both by violence and cunning—for he can transform himself into an angel of light—to attack men on their weakest side, so as to bring them under his power or hold them fast in his snares through sin and unbelief.[5]

---

[1] Luke vi. 18; ix. 39; xiii. 16. Matt. xvii. 15. Acts viii. 7; xvi. 16.
[2] John xii. 31; xiv. 30. 2 Cor. iv. 4. Cf. Eph. ii. 2.
[3] 1 Cor. viii. 4—6; Cf. Ib. x. 19, 20. 1 John v. 19.
[4] Acts xxvi. 18. Col. i. 13. John xii. 31. 2 Tim. ii. 26. Matt. xiii. 28. Apoc. passim. Rom. xvi. 20.
[5] 2 Cor. xi. 13. Eph. vi. 11. 1 Pet. v. 8.

The Word became Flesh; that Divine Being who existed long before the birth of Jesus, yea, before creation, was born on earth "in man's likeness." He appeared at the predestined time sent forth from God, in the likeness of our sinful nature, only that in Him it was and remained sinless.[1] In His outward appearance, attitude, and mien, all was human; but he was not *a* man, like all others, He was the incarnate Son of God, who had entered on a condition of abasement and humility, so that it may be said, "He emptied Himself," exchanging for the form of a servant His Divine form and the glory He had with the Father. Though rich and the Ruler of the world, for our sakes He became poor.[2] The Apostolic Epistles do not dwell on His supernatural generation without earthly father, but it is always assumed, and St. Paul intimates it in saying that he was born of a woman.[3] According to St. Paul's teaching, Christ could not be a descendant of Adam by race, because He is opposed to him as the Second Adam, the Father of a new race.

Christ came as Mediator, Reconciler, and Redeemer. He is Mediator, from the fact of being Man, for in Him human nature in its sinless purity was exalted to the closest personal fellowship with the Godhead, and He, as the Second Adam, has the office and the power and means to cleanse men from sin and unite them to Himself.[4] For, in His full union, on one side with God, on the other with humanity, He, and He alone, is in a position to put away the enmity of man against God, by the real removal of the sin which divides them. Therefore did He not only devote His whole earthly life, without any personal reserves, to that great mission, by a continuous self-oblation, but crowned and closed it by the sacrifice of a voluntary death for the sins of men.[5] Thus His whole life was an atonement; all its moral acts were a chain of propitiatory acts for the sins of men. Through the atonement the Mediator also wrought the reconciliation of man with God, and became the Author of a new covenant between man and God, based on His sacrificial death.[6]

---

[1] Phil. ii. 6—8. Rom. viii. 3. Heb. ii. 14.     [2] 2 Cor. viii. 9.
[3] Gal. iv. 4.     [4] 1 Tim. ii. 5. Heb. ix. 15. Eph. v. 29, 30. 1 Cor. x. 16, 17.
[5] John x. 17, 18.     [6] 1 Cor. xi. 25. Gal. iv. 24. Heb. vii. 22; viii. 6; ix. 15.

Thus God Himself is the highest Cause of Redemption; He reconciles men with Himself through Christ, and is, therefore, called Saviour.[1] He has reconciled us, the whole race of men, and thereby made each individual of it meet for grace, when we were His enemies, children of wrath, and the objects of God's displeasure.[2] But, as this displeasure is nothing else than the holiness of God in its relation to men, the reconciliation comes from the love of God. He so loved the world—while hating its sin and moral corruption—that, to unite His love with His holiness and righteousness, He gave up His Son and sent Him into the world.[3]

And thus the Incarnation of the Son, and His willingly endured death on the Cross, reveal and harmonize in act the love and the righteousness of God. God first loved us; we have not become the objects of His love in consequence of Christ's atonement, but rather the sending of the Son was itself an act and most conspicuous evidence of His original love, a love not evoked by ours, but preceding it while we were estranged from Him. "While we were yet sinners, Christ died for us." "We have seen what love is, and how far it goes in self-sacrifice, as St. John says, in Christ giving up His life for us.[4] As in the time before Christ, God, in His long-suffering, had connived at the sins of men; at last, in the fulness of time, He revealed the righteousness which had been misunderstood and concealed by that forbearance, in openly presenting Jesus as a Sin-offering; so that Christ made Himself an offering through the voluntary shedding of His blood, and men appropriated through faith its atoning and sanctifying power.[5] St Paul expresses the same great fact in saying that Jesus became sin for us;[6] that is, without being the least sinful Himself, but of perfect innocence and sanctity, He took our place in love and was treated as a sinner, regarded by the world as a criminal and executed as such; so that He was wrapped up, clothed, and covered, as it were, with sin and its consequences, and bore its whole weight.

It was thus an offering, an act of self-surrender forming

---

[1] 2 Cor. v. 18, 19.  Rom. iii. 25.  Luke i. 47.  1 Tim. i. 1.  Tit. iii. 4.
[2] Rom. v. 10.  Eph. ii. 3.     [3] John iii. 16, 17.
[4] Rom. v. 8.  1 John iii. 16; iv. 10.    [5] Rom. iii. 25.    [6] 2 Cor. v. 21.

the centre-point of all human history, by which redemption was accomplished. Therefore was the Son sent forth to fulfil what was the bounden duty of man, but what through sin he was unable to perform—to offer that full and free-will oblation to God which was man's supreme and proper obligation, and thereby to restore the communion with God which sin had broken; so that in the dignity and infinite worth of His Person as God-man, and in the character of Surety and Representative of the whole race, as its Head and the Second Adam, He might offer this sacrifice to God for atonement and remission of human sin, by enduring the bitterest sufferings and death in the struggle with a world dominated by sin.

"I have given you the blood upon the altar, to atone your souls," was said to the Israelites.[1] Thus were the sin-offerings of the Old Testament, wherein the life of the animal in the blood was offered up, feeble shadows of the offering on Calvary. For "without shedding of blood is no remission."[2] Christ Himself had said, "I sanctify Myself for them (as a sacrifice), that they also may be sanctified," and had ascribed to the shedding of His blood the meaning and power of remission.[3] So, again, St. Peter says that Christ (as our Priest and Sin-offering) has carried our sins on His body to the wood of the cross, as to an altar, "by whose wounds you were healed;" and St. John calls Him the Lamb slain as the antitype of the Paschal Lamb, who "has washed us from our sins in His blood;" the blessed "have washed their robes and made them white in the blood of the Lamb."[4] Here the cleansing from sin won for us by the death of Christ, and realised by a believing self-surrender to Him, is represented under the sensible image of washing stains out of a garment.

St. Paul, again, says that Christ is offered as our Paschal Lamb, like it faultless and atoning, a sign and pledge of our Exodus from the land of bondage, and offering Himself to the taste in communion for nourishment of the Christian life.[5] Christ is expressly called in the Epistle to the Hebrews, the great High Priest, who presents Himself as an offering for us. As in the priesthood and sacrifice of

---

[1] Levit. xvii. 11.   [2] Heb. ix. 22.   [3] John xvii. 19.
[4] 1 Pet. ii. 24. Apoc. i. 5; vii. 14.   [5] 1 Cor. v. 7.

the Old Law all was external, preparatory, carnal and imperfect, in Christ, at once Priest and Victim, all is perfected. He only is the Priest, infinitely separated from sinners through His holiness, yet indissolubly linked to them by sharing their nature. Being One with God through His Divinity, and with us through His Humanity, He binds together in His Person God and man; He is the Bridge that spans the immeasurable abyss that divided us from God, and the Eternal Spirit—that is, His heavenly and immortal nature—gives to the offering of His blood and death an infinite worth. He is also such a Priest as we need, having passed through the school of temptations and bitterest pains, and thus, though without sin, shared our circumstances, sufferings, and trials; whence for every need and every temptation He offers us the right remedy.[1] And now, having entered into heaven, He continues there for all time the priesthood and sacrifice He began on earth; His glorified estate has changed nothing in His relations and offices to us; sitting Co-equal at the Father's Right Hand He is for us what He was on earth.

We are further taught, in the Epistle to the Hebrews, that the Old Testament priesthood is abolished. As the offering of the New Covenant is far exalted over those of the Old, which were but prefigurements adapted and designed to arouse a desire for the full reality they foreshadowed, so, too, is the Priest, who is Mediator of a better covenant richer in promises, highly exalted above the Levitical priesthood, which was neither perfect nor tending to perfection but subject to constant change of persons through death. He is a Priest after the order of Melchisedech, for this ancient Priest and King was a type of Christ, by uniting in his person the royal and sacerdotal dignity, by his name (king of righteousness and of peace), and by the universality of his priesthood which, unlike the Levitical, was neither lineally transmitted, nor tied to one family or nation, nor liable to be abrogated. Thus the order of Aaron was abolished, and replaced by the eternal and unchangeable priesthood of Christ.[2]

The power of Christ's sacrifice to atone is necessarily limited by its power to sanctify. By this offering once

[1] Heb. ii. 17, 18.   [2] Ib. vii.; viii.

made He has wrought an eternal sanctification.¹ In becoming sin (a sin-offering) for man He broke the power of sin, against which the Mosaic Law was impotent; He has condemned and dethroned it in act in the flesh, the human nature it had hitherto ruled.² This was begun by the first appearing of the Son of God in the flesh. He is the Head of Humanity and second Father of believers; and from His human nature, in which the Godhead dwells, proceed those powers which make possible to Christians the victory over sin they could not obtain by the Law. Henceforth men are bound and able to overcome the law of sin and death in their flesh by the law of the spirit, the powers of life dwelling in Christ.³ The question follows, how and by what process this work of atonement and sanctification is applied to individuals, or under what conditions each partakes of its fruits and attains to true righteousness and salvation.

Reconciliation and justification are accurately distinguished by St. Paul. The death of Christ on the Cross is a great work of universal redemption; it is a making of peace, not only for earth and the human race, but for higher regions and their inhabitants also; it is a reconciliation which embraces the universe, in which even unconscious nature has a part.⁴ This was accomplished once for all on Calvary. Thereby mankind, as a race, is restored to its true relationship with God, forgiveness of sins is won for all men; God has turned His Countenance in kindness and mercy upon them, and re-opened the treasures of His gifts of grace. It is Christ who has purchased these gifts, who has paid the price, and who offers them now to us. We were still enemies of God when our redemption was wrought out;⁵ and thus we are redeemed or reconciled before we are individually justified. Christ did that for us, and without our aid. Justification—the actual change from the state of sin and God's displeasure to the state of renewal and grace—was first made possible by the act of reconciliation, and is fulfilled by Christ in us, and with our aid.

All men are deficient in righteousness before God; they are sinners. The predominance of the lower sensuous impulses over the higher, self-love degenerated into self-

---

¹ Heb. x. 11—14.  ² Rom. viii. 3.  ³ Ib. viii. 1, 2.
⁴ Col. i. 20. Eph. i. 10. Rom. viii. 19—22.  ⁵ Rom. v. 10.

seeking, freedom perverted into wilfulness,—in this consists the natural corruption innate in men, a kind of inherent principle of sin in the present condition of our nature, or, as St. Paul describes it, a law of sin dwelling in our members, our natural powers.[1] The historical origin and operating cause of this common sinfulness is that first transgression of the Divine command, into which our first parents were seduced by their enemy Satan, the author of evil and sin in the world.[2] Through the lineal transmission of human nature ordained by God sin has spread from thence as a natural power, a condition innate in every one and displeasing to God, over all mankind. It is not the act once done by Adam that is simply imputed to each individual, while yet it is not his own, but the condition of mankind which resulted from that act is a permanent and inherited one, producing sin in the whole race. Every one, through the disorder and evil condition of his nature, is unpleasing to God; sin is in him, not as an act but as a passion or state, the germ of a moral disease that developes itself with time, before it has yet shaped itself into actual sin. Thus, sin and death as its consequence have passed on all men born of the flesh.[3]

All men are, therefore, represented by the Apostle as sinners, as well physiologically as historically, sold under sin and children of wrath, the objects of that displeasure God's holiness necessarily feels against evil.[4] But this corruption of our moral nature by the Fall is not a complete destruction of it, so that no spark of good and power for doing good remains. Man is wounded as a moral being, not killed; he is capable of redemption, and earnestly desires it.[5] The death under whose mastery sin has brought him is not only bodily but spiritual;[6] redemption is a quickening of dead humanity through faith in the Crucified and Risen Redeemer; and the Apostle understands under the figure of death the whole condition of sinful humanity, turned away from God, and powerless for good or for conversion of itself. But the higher powers of man created after the image of God survive the Fall; he

---

[1] Rom. vii. 12 sqq.    [2] Ib. iii. 23. 1 John i. 8.
[3] 1 Cor. xv. 21 sqq. Rom. v. 12. John iii. 6.    [4] Rom. ii. 3; vii. Eph. ii. 3.
[5] Rom. i. 19; ii. 14, 15; vii. 7 sqq.    [6] Eph. ii. 1. Col. ii. 13. Rom. vii.

retains the rudiments of Divine knowledge, a slumbering consciousness of God only capable of developing itself in the contemplation of nature; he might, by obeying this knowledge and the inner law and voice of conscience, restrain the germ of sin within him from unfolding itself.[1] There are thus in the natural man points of contact for God's converting grace to seize upon; he has an inborn perception of truth, more or less darkened by sinfulness of life, but not extinguished, whereby he can meet on his side the message and grace which calls him to faith; and when grace has begun its work in him, then arises in him that intermediate and transitional state St. Paul speaks of, where he inwardly longs for conversion, but oscillates between two opposites in the conflict of flesh and spirit.[2] From this condition man must advance to real righteousness and attainment of the Divine promises. And this is done not by the Law and its works, but by faith. Christ stands related to the off-spring of Adam as the generous graft to the wild tree whose juices it ennobles. As sin is derived to all from Adam, so righteousness from Christ, but the instrument for receiving and appropriating it is faith.

By the Law, which he excludes from the office of justifying, St. Paul means the Law of Moses, such as he had always found it by experience, and such as it confronted him among his fellow-countrymen,—that complex system of political, ritual, and moral precepts embracing the whole mind and life, which formed the great and impassable barrier between Jew and Gentile. He felt that men were shut up in this law as in a prison. A Jew felt himself equally bound by all parts and details of it; he neither made, nor could make, any distinction between what was purely moral and unchangeable, and what was only temporary, adapted to former relations, or such as were passing away. To him all commands were on a par, as so many revelations of the Divine will binding him to a strict and literal fulfilment. He regarded all morality and piety primarily from the historical stand-point of national right, as a service of external obedience which he paid as a member of the Israelite people and state to the law of his nation, and which ensured him a rightful claim on the Divine

---

[1] Rom. i. 20; ii. 14.   [2] Rom. vii. 17 sqq.

favour and the enjoyment of the blessings promised to obedience.

Of this written Law, closely connected in all its parts, given of old to the Jews, St. Paul maintains that it is abolished—abolished, that is, in its formal relations, its speciality as a national statute embracing political, moral, and liturgical codes.[1] We preach, he says, another long promised law, stripped of all national limitations and Jewish specialities, whose contents are spiritual and consist of principles and realities in place of typical shadows. But St. Paul joins and mingles the external Mosaic with the internal moral law in the conscience of men, which is God's voice in the soul, and however feeble, dark, or fallible in its utterances, is yet a law to the Heathen. This law had the same office and significance for the Gentiles as the Mosaic law for the Jews in pioneering the way for Christ.[2] Thus the Apostle's statements about the law apply sometimes to the law generally, as well the external and positive as the internal, sometimes, and indeed oftenest, to the former or Mosaic Law. The law in itself, and apart from its results in fallen man, is good, right, holy, spiritual; it exhibits and condemns the contradiction of the human will to the Divine; by its threats and terrors it curbs and restrains the grosser outbreaks of human perversity. By the law comes the knowledge of sin; it discloses to man his indwelling evil, and thus rouses a sense of the need of redemption.[3]

On the other hand, sinful inclination is evoked by the Law as a contradiction to the will of God contained in it. Its requirements and monitions kindle our evil tendencies and propensities into full and conscious energy, and make the Law of no effect. Its very presentation keeps up vividly the consciousness of sin and sin itself, for the command which checks and opposes it impels to disobedience. It is "the strength of sin," and so far a law of death.[4] At the same time, it requires that all commands without exception be obeyed; he who transgresses one is guilty of the whole Law, and under the curse it threatens to transgressors.[5] It is implied, again, in the nature of the Law, or rather of fallen man, that the obedience enforced is only a slavish and

---

[1] Gal. iii. 19.  [2] Rom. ii. 14, 15.  [3] Rom iii 20; vii 13.
[4] Ib. vii. 8. 1 Cor. xv. 56.  [5] Gal. iii. 10; v. 3. James ii. 10.

extorted one, creating a slavish feeling, and hindering real confidence, true and child-like obedience.[1] It promises life, indeed, to those who perfectly fulfil its precepts but it does not fulfil the promise, for it cannot make alive—faith alone can do that. The Law can only condemn.

Thus the Law occupies a position antithetical to that of the Christian. Faith and the promise of redemption were earlier than the Law; it was something transitional and intermediate, introduced on account of transgressions, not directly promulgated by God, but through angels, as a system of training for infancy, to elicit first in men the consciousness of the misery of sin. It is by no means to have force for ever, but its end is Christ; with His appearance, and the coming in of His new dispensation of faith, its educational office ceases, and believers are no more under it.[2] Christ has changed for His followers the dispensation of the Law into the dispensation of grace, which could only be introduced when the former dispensation was taken away, and so the Apostle teaches that the whole Mosaic Law in its previous form, without distinction of ritual or moral precepts, has no further binding force. Thus he opposes to the blessing of Abraham, consisting in the promise of the Spirit received through faith, the curse which presses on every observer of the Law through the Law itself; from that curse Christ has redeemed the Jews who believe on Him, because by the manner of His death —hanging on a tree—He made Himself a curse in the eyes of men, according to the expression of the Law, by enduring a death which it regarded as a curse and object of abhorrence.[3] In another connection St. Paul designates the Law a hand-writing that testified against us, which, at the death of Christ, was nailed with Him to the Cross, and thereby taken away.[4] The law of commandments and precepts is thus done away for believers;[5] no study of a mass of maxims and precepts often uncomprehended, often only capable of scientific application, is required of them; the

---

[1] Rom. viii. 15. Gal. iii. 19; iv. 1—3. 1 Tim. i. 8—10. [2] Gal. iii. 19 sqq.
[3] Gal. iii. 13, 14. Deut. xxi. 23. He appeared as a curse before men, not with God, for to Him the death of Christ is a sweet odour ὀσμὴ εὐωδίας. Eph. v. 2. St. Paul has, therefore, purposely omitted the ὑπὸ θεοῦ of the Septuagint and Hebrew. [This, it will be remembered, is also the interpretation of the early Fathers.—Tr.]
[4] Col. ii. 14. [5] Eph. ii. 15.

letter of the written law, with its threats, its curse, and its anger, has no more dominion over them. But if the legal dispensation has ceased, if the Law has no power to substitute life for death, that is, to infuse into sinful men the love of God, and give them strength to subdue their evil desires, and to fulfil its own requirements, then it is clear that no man can be made righteous by the Law, and the works of the Law.

The Jew was proud of what he was and did, proud of his descent, his birth-place, his temple, his sacrifices and ceremonies, proud of his legal works—all this was his righteousness, whereby he was to stand blameless before God. Thus he held the rags of his poverty and nakedness for the purple robe of a righteousness whose hem he never touched once. For all these things—sacrifice, washings, circumcision, sabbaths and the rest—could not put away sin, or give new moral powers, or make men righteous within. Therefore to all alike without distinction or preference, Jews and Gentiles, justification through faith was preached, excluding all works of the Law. Salvation by faith alone—that means, by God's grace alone. Thereby above all was man humbled, and reminded that nothing he could do of himself could please God. Not by the works of the Law—that means, not by works done only in consequence of the Law, and by merely legal knowledge and assistance—could he be saved. St. Paul excludes from justifying all the Jew did by virtue of the Mosaic covenant law, or the Gentile by the moral law, made known in conscience, though the work be a moral one in conformity to the letter of the law.

The Apostle distinguishes constantly the righteousness of the Law or its works, which is not a true one, and the righteousness of faith, which is, indeed, a righteousness of the Law, in so far as by faith man has the mind which truly fulfils it. God looks not at the act, but at the intention and bent of the will it proceeds from. By this He judges men; where He finds it, He declares men righteous before, as yet, it has shown itself in outward acts, or taken the practical shape of real righteousness and conformity to law. Therefore to the word "justify" the Apostle adds the expression of God "imputing righteousness" to man.[1]

---

[1] λογίζεσθαι Rom. iv. 3—6.

He recognizes in justification a moral judgment pronounced on the worthiness or unworthiness of man, the worth or guilt of his will and deed. God imputes to man either sin or righteousness, whether generally, when his whole direction of will as devoted to God or revolting from Him is brought under the Divine judgment, or particularly, when some isolated act is brought under it.[1] God imputes to man what He has imparted as a gift and man has appropriated, the indwelling might and principle of free obedience, as though it were already a full performance and perfected righteousness, which it only becomes by degrees. Thus a lustful gaze is reckoned as adultery, and hatred cherished in the heart as murder. And, as man is condemned before God for the mere intent and aim of the will as for an accomplished act, so faith is reckoned for righteousness to one not working but believing.[2]

The works which gradually appear as the fruits of this faith contain nothing not substantially contained in the faith; they are only a continuation and expansion of the germ wrapped up in it. The faith dynamically includes the works, whence St. Paul constantly speaks of the obedience of faith, and makes the righteousness of man simply a service of obedience.[3] Faith, the inward obedience, contains the outer obedience in germ. It is evident that the notions of "righteousness" and "justification" are most intimately connected in St. Paul's mind. He uses the latter term for God's judgment on men; justified means with him declared just by God, but "the judgment of God is according to truth."[4] God only judges and declares him just who is such inwardly, for before God and in Christ nought avails but faith working by love, a new creature, the observance of God's commandments.[5] This is that "gift" of righteousness,[6] proceeding from the heart and penetrating the whole life in all its powers and energies till it has fought its way to mastery, with whose entrance sin in man is crucified, or, in other words, dies in painful conflicts and sufferings.[7] He who has this gift fulfils by the grace of the Gospel the righteousness of the Law, which

---

[1] Rom. iv. 8. 2 Tim. iv. 16.  [2] Matt. v. 28. 1 John iii. 15. Rom. iv. 4, 5.
[3] Rom. i. 5; vi. 16; xvi. 26.  [4] Rom. ii. 2.
[5] Gal. v. 6; vi. 15. 1 Cor. vii. 19.  [6] δῶρον, δώρημα. Rom. v. 16, 17.  [7] Gal. v. 24.

the Law could not do. St. Paul names it again "the law of righteousness," which the Jews did not attain to, because they sought it in a perverse way, "by the works of the Law."[1] It is further in his view a new, creative, life-giving law, the law of the life of Christ, which opposes and dethrones in men the law of sin, not imperiously domineering from without but passing into the will. Therefore he also calls it the "righteousness of God," or "from God," and opposes it to our own righteousness or that righteousness of the Law, for this gift is something really dwelling in man, implanted in him by God.[2] It springs originally from the grace of God, but immediately from the grace of the Man, Jesus Christ, and on receiving it our salvation depends.[3]

This indwelling principle or gift must, as St. Paul again and again reminds us, be raised to full dominion over all our faculties; we must "make our members, which before were instruments of sin, instruments of righteousness," and renouncing the service of sin pass, through obedience, to the service of righteousness.[4] Every man serves one of two masters; he is either a slave of sin or a servant of righteousness, that righteousness which together with peace and joy in the Holy Ghost constitutes the kingdom of God, in which the new man is created after God, and whose fruits or reward God will increase, for it is imparted by Him and akin to his nature; "He that doeth righteousness is righteous, as He is righteous."[5] That alone avails before God, and when St. Paul speaks of human righteousness as acceptable and well-pleasing to God, he reminds us that God works in us what is pleasing to Him, for that he alone is pleasing to God and approved to man who serves Christ in "righteousness and peace and joy in the Holy Ghost."[6] That alone can counteract and subdue the principle of sin which has enslaved all men from Adam downwards, and made them wretched. The second Adam, the God-Man, is powerful to cleanse and deliver, as the first was to corrupt and enslave. The one is the fountain of death, physical and moral, the Other of life. As by the Fall and its con-

---

[1] Rom. viii. 4; ix. 31.  [2] Rom. iii. 21; x. 3, Phil. iii. 9.  [3] Rom. v. 15.
[4] Rom. vi. 13—16.  [5] Ib. vi. 20. Eph. iv. 24. 2 Cor. ix. 10. 1 John iii. 7.
[6] Heb. xiii. 21. Rom. xiv. 17, 18.

sequences man became a sinner, not by imputation merely but inwardly and truly, and a principle of evil was imparted to the whole race, even so is the righteousness, which strictly corresponds as a remedy to the evil it is directed against, a condition wrought in men through an inward moral change. "By the obedience of One the many shall be made righteous."[1]

Christ appeared in the world to become the Second Adam and new Beginner of the human race. Adam and Christ are typically related as Heads of the old and new humanity. As Adam was of the earth, earthy, and could only beget what was earthy, Christ our second Father is from heaven, and His seed is heavenly, though His body is not from Heaven but of the seed of David. But, as a new link in the chain of humanity, He is its spiritual Representative, realising its true idea. He has become for it the quickening Spirit, giving heavenly life to men, and the life-stream that proceeds from Him can and shall overspread the whole race.[2] He said on the Cross, "It is finished," for, as the Representative Man, He had finished once for all what must gradually take effect in individuals in the course of the world's history. Hence St. Paul says, that God has quickened with Christ those dead in sins, and made them sit in the heavenly world.[3] The sufferings and the glory of the Lord, His death and His resurrection, are alike the source of righteousness to man. Only he that is dead is justified from sin, as St. Paul says;[4] and this points to the necessity of completely dying to sin, after the example of Jesus and by the power of His death, and excludes the idea that a mere sentence of forgiveness without a real inward death to sin is meant. "We judge that if One died, all died,"—suffered death in and with Him.[5] Those alone who are dead to self-seeking and practice self-denial like the dying Christ, whose whole life is determined by love to Him, are Christians. The sufferings and misfortunes of the redeemed are inwardly united to the sufferings of Christ; communion with Christ implies communion with His Passion, suffering and dying with Him. The Christian's life is

---

[1] Rom. v. 19, κατασταθήσονται, "constituted" Cf. 2 Pet. i. 8. James i. 8.
[2] 1 Cor. xv. 47. Rom. v. 14—21. [3] Eph. ii. 5, 6.
[4] Rom. vi. 7. [5] 2 Cor. v. 14.

a being implanted in Christ through conformity to His death, which is realised in believers through profound and living contemplation.[1] In this contemplation the believer condemns his former life and becomes dead to it.

So, again, by the assimilative power which proceeds from the glorified Christ, the believer becomes like Him as well in His life as in His death. The life of the Risen Christ is as mighty as His death. The whole process by which the true life of believers is perfected is both an effect and a copying of the Resurrection. St. Paul is very emphatic in making Christ's Resurrection the cause of our justification. He "was delivered for our sins, and raised for our justification."[2] Not simply because we are made righteous by faith, which again depends on the Resurrection, but because the risen and ascended Christ by the powers that flow from His glorified Body, as from an inexhaustible storehouse, is mighty to form Himself a body among men whose Head He is and to which believers belong as so many separate members drawing spiritual life from Him.[3] St. Paul shows that where Christ's death is operative, by our dying to sin, His risen life must operate also, for Christ was raised that we might bear fruit to God. Were He not risen we were yet in our sins; but by His death while yet enemies we were reconciled, by His life redeemed or justified.[4] In harmony with this view, St. Paul describes justification as a process of imparting life; and life with him is that moral renovation going out from the risen and glorified Christ, by which man dies to sin, and the "law of the Spirit of life" enters into him in place of the law of sin and death. He calls that process "justification of life," whereby man, through inward renewal, is changed from the state of sin to that of life, for "the carnal mind is death, the spiritual mind is life."[5] Such is the richness and overflowing fulness of God's grace towards us, that He has made us alive with Christ who were dead in sins, and has given us the presentiment and expectation of taking part in His heavenly glory, making us "reign in life," or clothing

---

[1] Gal. ii. 19. Rom. vi. 5, 6; viii. 17. 2 Tim. ii. 11. [2] Rom. iv. 25.
[3] Eph. iv. 15, 16; v. 29—32. 1 Cor. xii. 12 sqq.; xv. 42 sqq. 2 Cor. iii. 18; iv. 10. Phil. iii. 21. [4] Rom. vi. 4, 5; vii. 4; v. 10. 1 Cor. xv. 17.
[5] Rom. v. 18, (δικαίωσις ζωῆς) viii. 2, 6.

us with the royal robe of true righteousness; for life and righteousness are, in St. Paul's mind, identical.[1]

It is the same thought differently applied, when the Apostle represents justification as wrought in men by the Holy Spirit. In contrasting with the Old Testament ministry of death and condemnation that of the New Covenant, he calls the latter indifferently "the ministry of the Spirit," and "the ministry of righteousness," and gives as its result freedom and the communication to believers of the glory of Christ, under whose abiding influence they shall be at last completely transformed into His likeness.[2] And, again, it is the Holy Ghost, with the name—the being and power—of Jesus, from whom believers obtain forgiveness, sanctification and righteousness.[3] Justification is thus again set forth as a gift of grace conferred by the Holy Ghost, but won by Christ, of whose fulness we receive it; for it is the very work and office of the Holy Ghost to restore to the condition of God's children those who were estranged from Him by sin, and build them up by degrees to the "perfect man of God."[4] Thence the justification of man is in the Apostle's eyes above all a manifestation of Divine *power*. The Gospel—the message of God's kingdom and salvation therein to be obtained—is a "power of God," and, because he was sure of the powerful working of this message on believers, the Apostle says he was not ashamed of it.[5] As contrasted with the Greek philosophical systems and the Jewish law, it is a power of God, the instrument of what only Divine omnipotence can effect on man, namely, his freedom from the yoke of sin and inward renewal, the powerful and operative medicine which never fails to heal the sick when received by faith.

But this power of the Gospel is most vividly expressed in the two leading facts of the Evangelical history, the Crucifixion and Resurrection of Christ. As the Gospel generally, so especially Christ Crucified, to the Jews indeed a stumbling-block and foolishness to the Gentiles, but to believers the power of God, is the instrument whereby the

---

[1] Eph. ii. 4—6. Rom. v. 17.     [2] 2 Cor. iii. 8, 9, 17, 18.
[3] 1 Cor. vi. 11.     [4] John i. 16. 2 Tim. iii. 17.
[5] Rom. i. 16.

Divine omnipotence and love make men free from moral and spiritual slavery.[1] And therefore, by faith in the death or, as St. Paul says shortly, the blood of Christ man is made righteous.[2] The Apostle shows by his own example wherein this faith peculiarly consists, and what it does. He is so absorbed with all the powers of his thought and will into the death of Jesus, that he can say he is crucified with Christ, he does not so much live as Christ in him, the world is crucified to him and he to the world.[3] His inward being was so possessed and ruled by this fact, so penetrated by the spirit of the crucified Lord, that the all-pervading aim to copy those virtues Christ showed on the Cross and the fulness of the mind of Christ in him overcame and killed every earthly desire and passion.

Thus, faith in the Lord's death and resurrection, quickened and confirmed in us by Divine grace, becomes our righteousness. Of all events in human history that death is adapted to make the deepest impression on every mind, and to exert the greatest power over the thoughts and feelings of men. In this sense, Jesus Himself had pointed to the type of the brazen serpent, by gazing on which the Israelites in the wilderness were healed of the bites of deadly serpents.[4] Thus He, too, was uplifted before the eyes of the world and of all coming generations, and by looking on Him hanging on the Cross the poison of sin—which is for the soul what the serpent's bite was for the body of the Israelites—was to be made harmless, and man's moral sickness healed. Distance of time and place does not affect it. The spiritual sight of the Crucified is as powerful to heal after eighteen centuries, the magnetic attraction of His sufferings and death is as great, as it was for St. Paul. This greatest act of self-devoted love, this abasement of the God-Man, to our eyes immeasurable, includes all that by the laws of human nature could exert the most powerful constraint on us and stifle at birth the movements of fleshly lust, of worldliness and of pride. In the clear light of His Passion, and while the pattern of His

---

[1] 1 Cor. i. 23, 24.
[2] Rom. iii. 25. [It is a question whether $\dot{\epsilon}\nu\ \tau\hat{\wp}\ a\ddot{\iota}\mu a\tau\iota$ here does not go with $\dot{\iota}\lambda a\sigma\tau\acute{\eta}\rho\iota o\nu$, rather than with $\pi\acute{\iota}\sigma\tau\epsilon\omega s$. Cf. Vaughan *in loc. Ep. to Romans*. Macmillan.—Tr.]
[3] Gal. iii. 20. [4] John iii. 14, 15.

self-sacrifice and patient meekness is reproduced and preserved in our souls through the abiding influence of the Holy Ghost, all self-pleasing presumption appears a delusion, all pursuit of temporary pleasure a folly.

But the Lord's death is ever closely bound up with His resurrection, and considered as completed in it; both are looked on as equally needed and equally effective for our healing and justification. As the power of Christ's death is to be mirrored in the Christian's life, so must that life be also a continuous revelation of the power of His resurrection.[1] Christ in His exaltation and glorified Humanity, and by virtue of His relation to the Father and to man, is the Source of all power imparted to men through the Incarnation, and brings them to salvation by an energy flowing from His divine Manhood, piercing flesh and spirit. For He forms Himself a body from among men, whose quickening Head He is; and all, who by faith and baptism are incorporated into that body, receive the gifts and powers which flow from Him as its Head; whence St. Paul makes justification consist specially in faith in His resurrection and exaltation.[2] Man believes in Christ when he comes into fellowship with Him, and is made partaker of His death and resurrection, by so dying to sin that it has no more dominion over him, and by becoming a member of His body and sharer of the life He gives through regeneration and spiritual birth. When in this manner the principle of sin is cast out by the principle of righteousness, and the latter has become active and powerful in him, the Divine judgment recognising him as righteous is realised. This life-giving principle St. Paul calls the Spirit, and contrasts with the ministration of death and condemnation—the Law—the ministration of the Spirit—of righteousness—as he ascribes our righteousness to the influences of the Spirit working in us, who writes the law in our hearts.[3]

Justification is so distributed among the Persons of the Trinity, that the Father from His eternal love has reconciled the world with Himself, the Son by His Incarnation has become the Instrument of reconciliation and the Source

---

[1] Phil. iii. 10.
[2] Eph. iv. 15, 16; v. 29—32. 1 Cor. xii.[12 sqq. Col. ii. 19. Rom. iv. 24; x. 9.
[3] 2 Cor. iii. 7 sqq.

of our righteousness, the Holy Ghost, sent forth from the Son, perfects justification in us actually. Therefore, St. Paul represents Christ's appearance on earth and the existence of the Christian Church as a great revelation of Divine righteousness at the present time.[1] In former ages, God's attitude towards human sin had rather manifested His long-suffering and mercy than His righteousness, that is His holiness in relation to man. He had connived at men's sins and passed them over;[2] thereby, and from the moral state of His chosen people, His holiness was darkened in the eyes of many. The heavy and continuous sins of Israel had caused His name to be dishonoured among the Heathen, as though He were not a holy and righteous God. Thence that remarkable prophecy, "I will sanctify My great name, which is profaned among the Heathen, which ye have profaned in the midst of them; and the Heathen shall know that I am the Lord . . . and I will give you a new heart, and a new spirit I will put within you; and I will take away the stony heart from your flesh, and will give you an heart of flesh. And I will put My spirit within you, and will make you to walk in My precepts, and to keep My judgments and do them."[3] The later revelation of His righteousness, then, consisted in substituting for the mere passing over or leaving alone of sin (πάρεσις) its forgiveness (ἄφεσις) with inward renewal of men, for the proper efficacy of the blood shed for remission of sins is shown in cleansing from sin.[4] The righteousness of God was further revealed in that now, first, the utterance of His holy will to man in the Law was rightly established, and its right internal fulfilment made possible to him by the powers and means of grace flowing from the work of redemption, and thus God declared the Heathen righteous who before were unrighteous, because He also made them inwardly righteous.[5]

[1] Rom. i. 17.    [2] πάρεσις. Rom. iii. 25.
[3] Ezek. xxxvi. 23—27.    [4] 1 John i. 7. Heb. ix. 13, 14.
[5] Rom. iii. 31; iv. 5. δικαιοῦντα τὸν ἀσεβῆ. From the beginning of Jewish Hellenism ἀσεβής is the regular expression for the Heathen, as εὐσεβής for Jews. So Josephus, Philo, the Sibylline books. Cf. 1 Maccabees iii. 15; ix. 73. In writing to the Roman Jews whom he had never seen, St. Paul could not have used the word—which only occurs three times at all in his Epistles—in any other than the usual sense; no Jew could have understood it of himself and his countrymen who, before becoming Christians, were pious Jews. In Rom. v. 6 again, ὄντων ἡμῶν ἀσθενῶν refers

St. Paul comprises under the idea of faith the two factors of human righteousness,—the gift and operation of the Holy Ghost in men, and their corresponding action in receiving and appropriating it. A righteousness of God is offered to man; he appropriates it by faith, and the form it takes in him the Apostle also calls faith. Thus man becomes righteous by faith, and His righteousness is nothing else than faith. For faith is the means of receiving God's gifts, and the instrument for performing the works of the Holy Ghost. This faith, which already existed in germ and as a want in the common desire of man for the satisfaction of his being by God, is in its essence, on one side self-devotion to God, on the other a seizing and appropriating of what He offers in Christ, which can only be received and possessed by such an act of self-surrender. It is not an isolated act of human knowledge, feeling, or will, but a complex action, something only consummated through the co-operation of all the powers of the soul. Hope, love, fear, trust, humility, obedience, steadfastness and zeal—all are comprised in justifying faith. But, above all, it is a state of soul wrought by God, who first brings light out of darkness, harmony out of confusion, in the heart of man, and then blesses this His work as He blessed the world at its creation.

On the whole, the faith whereby man is justified, means with St. Paul the receptivity of man, his willing self-surrender to Divine truths and influences. Man lives a new life in and by faith; Christians firmly and immovably grounded in faith and hope are holy, blameless and unreprovable before God; elsewhere the Apostle ascribes to love this being "firmly grounded and rooted," and to faith Christ's indwelling in our hearts, for only faith working by love avails with Christ and makes just.[1] Where he describes more accurately justifying faith in Christ, it is especially the obedience whereby He gave up His life as an

to the Jews, as ἡμῶν shows, while ὑπὲρ ἀσεβῶν refers to the Gentiles. St. Paul could not in the same breath call men ἀσθενεῖς and ἀσεβεῖς, the latter signifying in common acceptation godless, or betrayers of God. The ἀσθενεῖς are weak persons who, before they were Christians, lacked the power of the Spirit to co-operate with a good will, and fulfil the requirements of the Law. Between the ἀσθενὴς and ἀσεβὴς is a great gulf, but St. Paul says that Christ died for both Jew and Gentile. There is a further reference in his language to Abraham's former idolatry, recorded by Jewish tradition, as Grotius has observed. [διὰ χειρῶν ἀνόμων, Acts ii. 23, is similarly a reference to the *Gentile* executioners of Cerist.—Tr.]

[1] Gal. ii. 20; v. 6. Col. i. 22, 23. Eph. iii. 17.

atoning sacrifice, His blood or death, and His resurrection, which are named as the objects of this faith. It is these facts, intensely realised by faith, that make the strongest and most lasting impression on the heart of man, changing its whole inward being. He cannot take in the full significance of the death of Jesus, without at the same time recognising the true character of sin, hating and dying to it; he cannot contemplate the Resurrection, without being raised to a new life. What Christ did and suffered, becomes the great motive power of our whole life. That is justification by faith, and thus "grace reigns through righteousness," the righteousness whose servants we are to be, and our members its instruments. Here grace is not merely the assurance of Divine favour, but also a higher power bestowed by God, the imparting of a gift; the grace that trains us to a godly and righteous life, and the denial of all worldly desires. Thus "Christ is become to us Wisdom from God, Righteousness, Sanctification, and Redemption," as being the Type and Source of all this.[1]

St. Paul and the writer of the Epistle to the Hebrews adduce as patterns of righteousness gained by faith two men, Noah and Abraham. The former built the Ark, believing the Divine intimation given him about the approaching judgment of the Flood and the deliverance of himself and his family, and thus "became heir of the righteousness by faith." The faith of the latter in the Divine promise of an heir of his body, and a seed like the stars of heaven for multitude, was counted for righteousness. Wherein then lay the justifying power of this faith in Noah and Abraham? In its moral application; "Abraham was not weak in faith," and though old, and with body now dead, doubted not, but believed firmly, that the promise would be fulfilled. This faith was anew counted to him for righteousness, after he had long before become righteous before God through his act of believing obedience in leaving his home at the call of God. The Apostle recognises in this faith a mind resting wholly upon God, involving an entire and willing submission to every manifestation of the Divine will; and thus he deduces from faith, as a state of soul which makes the future present and the invisible visible, all that was good

[1] Rom. v. 21; vi. 4, 5, 16, 19. Tit. ii. 11, 12. 1 Cor. i. 30.

and great in the men of the Old Covenant and their whole condition of acceptable service before God.[1] Faith in Christ, which now alone justifies, is only a higher degree of the same quality. If the Patriarchs showed their strength of faith by hoping against hope, and believing firmly, and trusting against all contrary appearances, that same energy and firmness of faith is now claimed in a higher degree; for, veiled under the form of a slave and a carpenter's son, dead upon the Cross, the Christian must acknowledge his Lord and Redeemer, and that acknowledgment cannot be separated from the idea and resolution of, in a certain sense, undergoing the same process of suffering and death. While, then, man believes unto righteousness, or is made righteous by faith, he thereby makes the strongest and most decisive use possible of his freedom; he humbly accepts the sentence which declares him a sinner without power of his own and then forgives him; he renounces all righteousness of his own and all attempts after it; he confesses that righteousness is only with God, and from Him alone can be received; he completely abandons himself to the will and devotes his life to the service of God. And thus faith contains the whole energy of a will directed upon God and Christ.

St. Paul means by faith, what Christ meant when He ascribed its absence in the Jews to their vain seeking after honour, and their hearts being without love of God.[2] As the faith Christ requires is a moral habit of mind perfectly pure and free from all self-seeking, so is that faith which, according to the Apostle, God reckons for righteousness. Man, indeed, is made righteous by faith without the works of the Law, but this doctrine, St. Paul says, does not abolish but establish the righteousness of the Law. For this faith is a ruling principle which originates or determines every human act, the righteousness implanted by God as an actual living quality, the law of life of the Spirit taking the place of that sin which reigned before; and by virtue of it the requirements of the law are now really fulfilled in man and by him. For, therefore, righteousness comes not by the Law, because it cannot make alive, or

---

[1] Rom. iv. 19—21. Heb. xi.   [2] John v. 41—44.

give power to fulfil its own precepts.[1] That only the Crucified and risen Christ can do through faith in Him; He has done what the Law could not, by becoming for all the Source of life; but only those are justified before God in whom the mind that fulfils the law really rules, that is, faith working by love, for love is the fulfilling of the law.[2] Thus, the Gospel is a new revelation of the righteousness and the grace of God; of righteousness, because now the sinner really leads a righteous life by his faith, and gives proof of the Divine righteousness actually indwelling in men; of grace, in so far as this is a free gift of God, unmerited and not dependent on previous works. For that man can only be saved by faith, means that it is a gift of undeserved grace. This doctrine humbles man by reminding him that of himself he can do nothing pleasing to God, and must receive all from God. It also exhibits in its true light the holiness of God, as not satisfied with this or that outward work, or with a mechanical service, but requiring in and with faith the whole mind of man, the complete surrender of His spirit and will.

All, then, according to St. Paul, is given freely and of grace. As God forgives man's sins, so He cleanses and sanctifies their hearts, by faith. Neither our absolution from sin nor our sanctification is by works. For it is a contradiction for a thing to be of works and of grace; what is given by works is given by obligation or merit.[3] St. Paul calls the whole Christian religion "faith," and generally in the New Testament Christianity, as distinguished from Judaism and Heathenism, is named "faith."[4] "Now that faith is come we are no more under a schoolmaster," as St. Paul says; and he speaks of the faith first to be revealed, and introduced as a religious institution into the world, when the time of training under the Law was run out.[5] Faith and believers existed before Christ, but "faith" then was not this new system, this Divine economy and order, where faith is one and all and includes everything distinctively Christian. Thus faith and the Law are con-

---

[1] Rom. iii. 31 ; viii. 4. Gal. iii. 21.    [2] Rom. viii. 3 ; xiii. 10.
[3] Rom. xi. 6 ; iv. 4.    [4] Acts vi. 7 ; xiii. 8. Rom. i. 5 ; x. 8.
[5] Gal. iii. 23—25. [The παιδαγωγὸς was not a "schoolmaster," but a servant who accompanied his young master to school and carried his books; and thus Judaism handed down the Sacred Books which only Christianity can interpret.—TR.]

trasted by St. Paul as the two parts or halves of the order chosen by God. Man must become righteous by faith, and not by the Law; that means, that no one can henceforth become truly righteous and pleasing to God as a Jew, but only as a Christian, for the Law is fulfilled in Christ, and all the higher gifts are now bestowed only in the Christian Church. "The Law was given by Moses, grace and truth came by Jesus Christ." Israel, the mass of the nation, followed after a law of righteousness and attained it not, because they sought it by works and not by faith. Their end was right, for they wished to become really holy and righteous, but their means were wrong. But the converted Gentiles have attained this end of righteousness by the grace of the Gospel, so that now the righteousness of the law is fulfilled in them, and they walk not after the flesh, but after the Spirit.[1]

St. Paul distinguishes a false and true righteousness. He had a righteousness of the Law himself before his conversion, proceeding from the Law and conformed to it, and perfected in legal works through the purely human medium of an unassisted will. He was blameless after the Law; man's judgment could lay nothing to his charge. But the Law cannot make alive, and the works that proceed from it are dead and worthless. Therefore he accounts all this dung, and strives after a better righteousness, flowing from God and His imparted power, which is faith,—an experience of the power of His resurrection, a share in His sufferings, and conformity to His death.

The legal spirit of contemporary Judaism was the great opponent St. Paul had constantly to fight against, as Christ had before denounced it in the Pharisees. He knew it well, that self-righteousness which, having no love, has no moral standard; that legal spirit, which makes every thing written of equal weight and obligation, since all rests on positive law, and puts arbitrary ritual ordinances before the eternal laws of morality. He knew them, those strict legalists, how they took the bare letter for their motive and rule of action, how they strove to square accounts with that letter most conveniently in their selfish hypocrisy, and were

---

[1] John i. 17. Rom. ix. 31, 32; viii. 4. [2] Phil. iii. 4—11.

skilful in substituting their own pleasure for God's will in its interpretation.

Therefore he preached so energetically the abolition of "the law of commandments in ordinances," but he declares at the same time that the Law is not abolished, but confirmed, by the doctrine of righteousness through faith, which replaces a mere outward and literal by an inward observance of it. The Law itself is originally good and spiritual, given for life and not for death; it is only done away with in so far as it had become a letter that killeth. As a law of the Spirit it continues, and in the very Epistle where he is so intent on showing that man is justified by faith, and not by the works of the law, the Apostle yet declares emphatically that the doers of the law, not the hearers, shall be justified.[1] He recognises a law whose works always justify, because they spring from a believing mind and grow as fruits of love, as he also recognises a righteousness which excludes the works of the law and yet cannot be conceived without works,—the works of love fulfilling the law.

There is, then, a law of Christ which as King and supreme Legislator He has prescribed for His Church; that is the law of faith, the law of the life-giving Spirit, which brings with it the power to fulfil its requirements and which, unlike the Mosaic Law on tables of stone, is written in the minds and hearts of men—what St. James calls "the perfect law of freedom."[2] By that law St. Paul declares himself bound, though free from the law of the Old Covenant, and they fulfil it who bear one another's burdens. St. John says the commandments of Christ are not grievous, to him, that is, who loves God; for the whole law has regard to Christ, it is obedience and love.[3] If love were made perfect and the flesh strove not continually against the spirit, God's will and ours would be one, duty and pleasure would always coincide. But that perfection is an ideal in this life never fully reached, though always to be aimed at.

In Christ and His Kingdom there is no contradiction, no

---

[1] Eph. ii. 15. Rom. vii. 10, 12; ii. 13.
[2] Rom. iii. 27; viii. 2. Heb. viii. 10. James i. 25.
[3] 1 Cor. ix. 21. Gal. vi. 2. 1 John v. 3.

partition wall between Law and Gospel. The Gospel has a legal side, for its promises are conditional on the observance of Divine obligatory commands with the sanction of reward and punishment. The law of Christ, again, is wholly evangelical, for all it requires it also gives power to fulfil; it passes into our will as the love of God, embracing and satisfying the whole range of human duties. St. Paul always emphatically excludes the works of the law, or, as he often says shortly, works, from all part in justifying or saving men, but he means first the works of the Mosaic Law, and next all merely natural and human works springing from the unaided will. He contrasts grace and works as mutually destructive.[1] Not he who works (in legal observances) is justified, but he who believes; God pronounces him just who before was estranged as a Gentile, when he believes.[2] Abraham, like the Apostle himself, might have praise of men for his works done after the flesh (before faith and without grace;) with God they had none. Not by the Law, but the righteousness of faith, Abraham won the great promise, that in him and his seed all believing humanity should be incorporated, and his spiritual children go forth to inherit the world. By the righteousness of faith St. Paul here understands that greatest act of Abraham springing from unshaken faith and obedience, the giving up his only son.

The righteousness of faith, then, consists in works, but they are not legal works, even though corresponding to the requirements of the Law, but works of faith and grace. St. Paul describes it as the inward and spiritual circumcision of the heart wrought by Christ through His Spirit, the moral purification and renewal of man, the new creature.[3] To such works he ascribes what he denies to works of the law, he makes them indispensable for justification; by them God's commandments are fulfilled, and that fulfilment, not circumcision, avails before Him; in them faith working by love operates, which alone avails; they have praise with God, the works of the law with men; those alone who bring forth such works are the true doers of the

---

[1] Rom. xi. 6.      [2] Rom. iv. 5, τὸν ἀσεβῆ.
[3] Rom. iv. 1, 2, 13. Cf. Gen. xxii. 16—18. Col. ii. 11. Phil. iii. 3.

law, and are justified.[1] It does not occur to him who has done such works to boast of them, for he has not done them in his own strength, but received strength for it, for what is good in them comes from God. And, therefore, justification and sanctification, or righteousness and holiness, are substantially the same condition, only viewed from different sides, or according to its higher or lower stage of development. Holiness is righteousness, considered in reference to its acceptableness to God and His judgment upon it. St. Paul only once mentions being sanctified in connection with being justified, and there he puts it first; elsewhere, in reckoning up the links in the chain of salvation or order of the gifts of grace through which God leads men to eternal glory, he places glorification immediately after justification without any mention of sanctification.[2]

The transition from Judaism or Heathenism into the Christian Church St. Paul generally designates a "being delivered," understanding thereby the change from a state of misery and corruption to one where salvation could be attained. All Christians are "delivered." To be justified and delivered is the same thing, only the former term indicates the condition in relation to God's judgment, the latter in relation to the position and prospects of men. And so, in speaking of deliverance, the Apostle contrasts grace and works, namely, works done of one's own will and pleasure which are not fruits of grace and which one may be tempted to boast of, and, again, works and good works. "By grace ye have been saved through faith, and this not of yourselves; it is the gift of God; not of works, that none should boast. For we are His workmanship created in Christ Jesus to do good works, which God has prepared that we should walk in them."[3] It is a gift of God, first, that He has re-created us and enabled us instead of works valueless before God to do works well pleasing to Him; next, that He has prepared all needful to that end for us, so that we lack nothing on His part for the continual performance of good works. But works that have no bearing on our salvation precede our re-creation or new birth. Still more clearly it is said in the Epistle to Titus, "When the

[1] 1 Cor. vii. 19. Gal. v. 6. Rom. ii. 29, 13.
[2] 1 Cor. vi. 11. Rom. viii. 30. [3] Eph. ii. 8—10.

goodness of God our Saviour and His love toward man appeared, not from works of righteousness we had done, but according to His own mercy, He saved us, by the laver of regeneration and renewal of the Holy Ghost, whom He poured out upon us abundantly through Jesus Christ our Saviour, that, being justified by His grace, we might be made heirs in hope of eternal life."[1] Here we have a short account of the whole method of salvation—baptism, communication of the Holy Ghost, renewal by Him or sanctification, and with it passing into the state of salvation, justification, and heirship of eternal life. Justification is the aim and effect of the inward renewal of the Spirit which cleanses and sanctifies. God first makes man just by re-creation or new birth, and then declares him just; but all is grace, not merit of our previous works. Works done in the living condition of righteousness—and such alone are meritorious—we simply had none, for we were in no condition to perform them. And thus St. Paul teaches that we are sanctified without works of the Law, as we are justified without them.

It is clear that, in contrasting faith as that which alone justifies with the Law and its works, the Apostle indicates by this term the whole process of man's conversion and reconciliation with God, as he passes, under the co-operation of Divine grace and human freedom, into the various stages of repentance, conversion, trust, hope, and love. Man cannot make a beginning of his own conversion; the grace of God must first call him with a "holy calling," which naturally enough often remains ineffectual through his sin and hardness of heart.[2] Where it takes effect, it first produces enlightenment in the hitherto darkened and variously deluded soul of man; grace opens his eyes and heart, awakens him, and brings him to himself. With the keener intuition of grace he recognises the holiness of God, the nature of sin, and his own sinfulness; and is convinced by the message of the Redeemer, His works, His offers, and His promises, that there is a sure remedy for his ailment,

---

[1] Tit. iii. 4—7. Cf. 2 Tim. i. 9.
[2] 2 Tim. i. 9. Acts xiii. 46; xxiv. 25. Heb. iv. 7 sqq.

strength for his frailty, deliverance from an otherwise inevitable destruction.[1]

But man not only can at the beginning resist this knowledge, and the cleansing and transforming power it exerts over his will; he can continue to do so even after he has in some degree opened his heart to it; he can contest every step of its onward march in his soul, so that knowledge already gained may by his fault become dead and unfruitful. In a word, he may be enlightened and yet remain unconverted. But in so far as he admits the transforming influence of the truths of salvation on his feelings and his will, his knowledge, too, will be increased, purified and strengthened. In proportion, too, as he discovers and recognises in the mirror of Evangelical doctrine and of the pattern of Jesus the depth of his fall, the extent of his departure from these requirements and models, the contradiction between what he is and what he ought to be, and the impotence of his will to bridge over the chasm, there arises in him a sense of shame and displeasure at his state. Hatred of sin, desire for pardon, for restored communion with God and freedom from the yoke of sin,—and a resolution to renounce its service, succeed.[2] It is faith in the Redeemer and His reconciliation of man with God, already accomplished objectively, which prevents these feelings of remorse from leading to despondency, demoralisation, and despair. This faith takes in him the form of trust. He is confident that the act of Christ has broken Satan's power, and opened to him, as to all men, an approach to God; in spite of all sense of personal unworthiness he trusts the omnipotence, truth, and goodness of God, who will verify His promises, and secure to him the aid of grace to obey His laws; he is confident that the atoning and sanctifying power of the sufferings, death, and resurrection of Christ will be manifested in him also, that to him also his ascended Lord will impart, through His Holy Spirit, the fulness of His gifts and powers, unless by his own fault he rejects those gifts.

When he perceives how God first loved us, who were sinners and alienated from Him, and gave in the death of

---

[1] Acts xxvi. 18; xvi. 14. Eph. v. 14. Tit. i. 2.     [2] 2 Cor. vii. 8—11.

His Son the supreme evidence of that love,[1] and when he is absorbed in contemplation of that undeserved kindness and love, that grace so ready to give and to forgive, a corresponding love is kindled in his own heart; and thereby faith is perfected. To live by faith, means simply to love by faith, and in that love to obey and suffer. "Faith working by love" is the shortest summary of all Christianity.[2] The rays of Divine love concentrated in Christ, as in a focus, kindle in men's hearts, through faith in Him, love to God as the absolutely Holy One, our Father and Deliverer. The soul laden with guilt cannot love a holy and righteous God who hates sin, but it can love a loving, reconciled God, ready to forgive and offering the fulness of His gifts,—in a word, God revealed in Christ. Only in and with this love is there an earnest acceptance of the Divine promises and gifts, which necessarily implies a proportionate use of them. And this acceptance is, at once, a full and unconditional self-surrender to Christ, and a free and willing obedience and zeal for keeping His commandments. This is the process of man's conversion. When he has got so far, and before the inward transformation has yet been shown in outward acts, he can look on himself as in the grace of God or justified, notwithstanding the sin which yet clings to him but no longer rules him, for it is overcome in principle by penitence and love; his sins are forgiven him, he is already renewed and "created for good works."

In Justification are included and indivisibly bound together forgiveness of sin—acquittal, that is, from the condemnation of God—and actual making righteous. Forgiveness of sin is never separated from subjugation of sin, for to forgive is to remove the penalty of sin, and its worst penalty is its dominant power and the enmity with God which that implies. That, in itself, is already Hell in the breast of man. Sin is its own punishment, and only by destroying it can its punishment be taken away. Hence, forgiveness of sins is sometimes used to express the whole blessing of the Gospel, which consists in putting away the chief effects of sin—spiritual death or separation of the soul from God—and therefore, in restoring spiritual life and re-uniting the soul with God. And thus, while St. Paul

[1] 1 John iv. 19. Rom. v 6, 8  1 Pet. i. 18—20.   [2] Gal. v. 20.

always looks on the Christians to whom he writes as already justified, he yet speaks of righteousness as something future, an object of hope which he and they must strive after, because it is not something settled and done with, once for all, but, in some sense, to be always won and worked at anew,—the being holy and the pleasing God.[1] And he adds, that only faith working by love avails, a developing, ever-growing and therefore, in part, only hoped-for righteousness.

Conversion, then, which is the decisive turning point in man's life, is the beginning of an advancing renewal and transformation from the innermost mind and spirit, the spirit's entrance on a struggle for its proper lordship over the flesh and the lower motions, and on a continuous process of effacing the remnants of the old dominion of sin, in which man makes all the occurrences of life minister to an increased purity and holiness.[2] All depends on his not withdrawing himself from the influence of Divine grace. By virtue of the mediatorial office between God and man, predestined from all eternity to the Son, all Divine love and grace is given only in Him and through Him.[3] But the Holy Ghost proceeds from the Crucified and Risen Son, and imparts to men, as the principle of a new life, the true power to abolish sin, and forms in them a godly life. For man cannot of himself turn to God, with his moral powers weakened and disordered by the common sinfulness of the race and his own personal sins superadded: the grace of God must prevent him. As Christ said to His disciples, "Without me ye can do nothing," so St. Paul says, that no man can call Christ Lord, and enter into communion with Him, but by the Holy Ghost.[4] The operations and gifts of the Holy Ghost, which are variously imparted as it pleases God in His wisdom, embrace the whole course of conversion and sanctification.[5] God works in us both to will and to do, the power of acting, and therefore we must work out our salvation with fear and trembling, for we are able to resist the action of His grace and make it void.[6] Faith, repentance, hope, love—all these are "fruits of the Spirit," who cleanses and enlightens us within, our feelings, under-

---

[1] Gal. ii. 17; v. 5.   [2] Eph. iv. 23. Rom. xii. 2.   [3] 2 Tim. i. 9.
[4] John xv. 5. 1 Cor. xii. 3.   [5] Heb. ii. 4.   [6] Phil. ii. 12, 13.

standing, will; in short, all that concerns Christian life, its commencement, development, growth, and consummation, is referred back to God or the Holy Ghost as its Author.[1] Therefore, St. Paul calls man's body the temple of the Holy Ghost, because the soul that dwells in that bodily tabernacle is the theatre and object of His operations and gifts.

And hence, when believers fulfil God's law, it is not their own work, but His work in them; for the Spirit who sets them free from the law of sin and death puts another law in its place,—His own power and law of life in Christ.[2] But His power does not act forcibly, with physical and irresistible determination of the will; man can and must in each case either yield to it or shut it out, accept or reject it.[3] But the gift of the Divine Spirit already received, the power which enables us to fulfil God's commandments, the shedding forth of His love in our hearts, the consciousness of being heirs by hope of eternal life—all this assures the Christian that he already has part in the love of God, and is in real communion with Christ.[4] As the Apostle words it, the Spirit is the Seal and Pledge in our hearts of the firmness of His covenant, the truth and certainty of His promises.

By security, by want of watchfulness, by lazy neglect of offered graces and helps for Christian advance and strengthening, the regenerate may fall back into His former sinful condition, and even under the full dominion of sin; and then a second conversion is harder than the first. Hence, St. Peter's vigorous warning against a complete hardening of the heart: "Their last state is worse than the first, for it were better never to have known the way of righteousness." The Epistle to the Hebrews speaks of a falling away connected with the unpardonable sin against the Holy Ghost, or identical with it, and leaving no further possibility for conversion.[5] This has immediate reference to certain unstable Jewish converts who had been highly favoured in not only receiving faith, but also the miraculous spiritual gifts of that period, and had become living members of the mystical body of Christ; when such persons utterly fall

---
[1] Gal. v. 22, 23.  2 Pet. i. 5 sqq.  Rom. xv. 15.  2 Tim. ii. 15.  Phil. i. 6.
[2] Eph. ii. 8—10.  Rom. viii. 2.  [3] Heb iii. 12, 13.
[4] Rom. v. 5.  Tit. iii. 7.  1 John iii. 24.  2 Cor. i. 21, 22.
[5] 2 Pet. ii. 20, 21.  Heb. vi. 4—6.

away and revile as a lie and delusion the operations of the Holy Ghost they have themselves experienced, and even go so far as to blaspheme Christ, they naturally sink into a condition of judicial blindness and hardness from which there is no further deliverance.

The whole life of a believer, shaped and ruled by grace, consists of a series of separate acts which, as the common product of grace and the human will, as "good works" and a fulfilment of God's commandments, have high promises. Such works proceed from the heart, wherein dwells faith working by love. Christ Himself had connected the abiding in His love and enjoying His friendship with the keeping of God's commandments.[1] So the Apostles say that love is the fulfilling of the law; that His commandments are not grievous; that he who says he knows Christ, and keeps not His commandments, is a liar; that God has prepared us to walk in good works, to be rich in them, and thereby lay a foundation of future blessedness, for Christ has promised it as their reward.[2] They are fruits of the Spirit, ascribed to God as their Author; the power comes from Him, and without Him we can do nothing. Yet the believer who produces them by grace as His instrument co-operates in their goodness, whereby they are an object of His complacency and ground of His promised recompense, and is "a good and faithful servant" in his patient well doing, a vessel fitted for every good work and worthy of honour, deserving the happiness of the glorious and perfect kingdom.[3] These shall walk with Christ in white raiment, "for they are worthy;" and St. Paul, when looking back on the good fight he had fought, and the fidelity he had kept, could say that his reward was already prepared for him, the crown of righteousness which the Lord the righteous Judge should repay to him in that day, nor only to him but to all who await His return in love.[4] For eternal happiness is a blessing conditioned on a life of faith fruitful in good works, and therefore a reward, pre-supposing the moral capacity of the receiver, that is, his merit. But this very moral capacity, this treasure of good works, is a gracious gift of God

---

[1] John xv. 10, 14.  [2] 1 Tim. vi. 18, 19.  Matt. xvi. 27.
[3] 2 Cor. iv. 7.  Matt. xxv. 21.  2 Tim. ii. 15, 21.  2 Thess. i. 5.  Luke xx. 35.
[4] Apoc. iii. 4.  2 Tim. iv. 8.

merited by Christ, as He also merited for us that our works should deserve increase and advance of grace in this life and the crown of glory in the life to come, that they should be capable of reward.[1]

If St. Paul combated that perverse confidence in the Mosaic Law, which sought righteousness and salvation only in its observance, and not in believing self-surrender to Christ, St. James, at a somewhat later period, had to contend against an apparently opposite error, though really springing out of the same root,—the error of those who thought to be righteous before God by faith alone. This notion appeared under various forms among Jews, Christians, and heretics. St. John, also, had to warn against false teachers who preached a righteousness of mere faith, and was obliged to insist that only he is righteous who does righteousness; that real Christian righteousness is a complete, moral new birth of man.[2] In fact, Simon Magus and his adherents taught that men obtained salvation only by grace—by faith or believing knowledge, *gnosis*,—and not by good works.[3] There were those among the Jews in Justin's time who said that, if they were sinners, their sins would not be imputed to them, in consideration of their knowledge of the true God; and the Judaizing Gnostics, whose views are given in the Clementines, held that "monarchical" souls (*i.e.*, those believing in One God) had this advantage over the Heathen, that even if they led vicious lives they could not be lost, but would at last attain happiness after a purifying punishment.[4]

St. James and St. Paul connect with the word, "Justification," the same idea, viz., of being found and declared just in God's judgment on the human character which further implies being children of God and heirs of eternal blessedness. At first sight, they seem to contradict each other, for St. Paul says that man becomes righteous by faith without works of the law, while St. James says that man becomes righteous by works and not by faith alone.[5] But the difference is only a seeming one. St. James teaches that

---

[1] John xv. 4, 5. Phil. ii. 13.
[2] Rom. xiii. 10. 1 John v. 3; ii. 4. Eph. ii 10. Phil. ii. 13.
[3] 1 John ii. 29; iii. 7 sqq. Iren. v. 20. Theodoret. *Hær. Fab.* i. 1.
[4] Just. *Dial c Tryph.* 141. Clem. *Hom.* iii. 6.
[5] Rom. iii. 28. James ii. 24.

two factors must combine in man's justification, his faith and his works, meaning such works as are only produced by faith. By these works justifying faith first reaches its true form, and displays itself in its full truth and reality. Without works it is indeed faith, but a dead, not a living faith, as being without that life consisting in good works which alone has decisive worth before God. In these works it is perfected. Abraham's example shows how faith and works are necessary and inseparable in justification, neither availing without the other. And thus the very example St. Paul relies on for excluding dead works of the law from justification is used by St. James against an unfruitful and unworking faith. He quotes Abraham's last and most decisive work of faith, the giving up his son Isaac as a sacrifice. It was only when Abraham's faith was thus conspicuously proved, as an unshaken trust in God's promises and unconditional obedience, that, in the words of Scripture, his faith was counted to him for righteousness and he was called a friend of God.[1]

Thus did St. James combat a new Pharisaism rising in the bosom of the early Church, proud of its pure and professedly blameless faith and dispensing itself from troublesome works. When he makes works necessary for justification and St. Paul excludes them, they do but supplement and explain each other. St. Paul means works of the law done in the flesh; he never calls them "good works," but rather distinguishes works, or works of the law, from "good works," and is always careful to add the epithet, "good," when not speaking of dead works of the law, which he also calls simply "works."[2] He means works where the mere outward act, and not the principle or motive, is the thing considered, done indeed from obedience to a command but from a selfish, blind, slavish obedience; works, again, which the unenlightened man left to himself does from his own natural powers, and so he impresses on the Gentile Christians at Ephesus, that they owe their deliverance and state of salvation, not to their works—those done before conversion—but to the gift of God, that they must first be created

---

[1] James ii. 14 sqq.
[2] 2 Cor. ix. 8. Eph. ii. 10. Col. i. 10. 2 Thess. ii. 17. 1 Tim. ii. 10 ; v. 10, 25 ; vi. 18. 2 Tim. ii. 21 ; iii. 17. Tit. i. 16 ; ii. 7, 14 ; iii. 8, 14 ; Heb. x. 24 ; xiii. 21.

in Christ unto good works, and the Holy Ghost be implanted in them as a principle of life.[1] And such works alone justify, according to St. James, works of a law by which we shall be judged, a "law of liberty" entering and penetrating man's inmost soul, not simply giving external commands, but eliciting a free and spontaneous obedience, through its accompanying power to give life. This is what St. Paul calls the law of the life-giving Spirit in Christ, which has freed him from the law of sin and death.[2] The truth which St. James speaks out, that justifying faith must be completed and made perfect by works, St. Paul clothes in this form,—that if he had all, the very strongest, faith, and had not love, he would be nothing, therefore not righteous before God. In the same sense, he makes love greater and more precious than faith, attaching salvation and righteousness in a higher degree to love than to faith. For, as St. James says, faith is first perfected through love, or the works of love, so as to justify.[3]

If it is now clear how entirely the Apostles are agreed in their account of the conversion, justification, and glorification of man, they are equally at one in affirming that none are excluded from this scheme of salvation, that grace is even more abounding than human sinfulness. St. Paul asserts distinctly the *universality of redemption*. God wills all men to be saved, and come to the knowledge of the truth; He wills to have mercy upon all. The salvation proceeding from Christ as the Second Adam, and offered by Him, is as all-embracing as the sinfulness of the first Adam. Christ has made atonement for the whole world, as St. John says.[4] If all do not actually attain the blessing, it is their own fault; there is no defect or limit on God's side; His whole dispensation for the fallen race is one of mercy. When the New Testament writers look up from the act of redemption fulfilled in time to its Author, who first determined and then carried it out, they speak of the eternal

---

[1] Eph. ii. 8—10.   [2] James i. 25; ii. 12. Rom. viii. 2.
[3] 1 Cor. xiii. 2, 13. The last attempt at a distinction (Huther *Exeget. Handbuch über den Brief Jacobi*, p. 130), to the effect that St. James speaks of a different justification from St. Paul, viz., only of a later one in the last judgment, while St. Paul is dealing with man's first entrance into the state of grace, is groundless. St. James understands δικαιωθῆναι as synonymous with φίλον θεοῦ κληθῆναι, or λογίζεσθαι εἰς δικαιοσύνην; he clearly knows of no justification by faith *alone*.
[4] Rom. v. 18, 21; xi. 32. 1 Tim. ii. 4. 1 John ii. 2.

counsel of God before time was. The Lamb is slain from eternity. God chose us out before the foundation of the world, to be holy and blameless before Him.¹ That does not refer so much to the destiny of individuals, as the objects of a special determination of God, as to the work of redemption and the institution of the Church as a whole. It is the calling of the Gentiles into the Church, which is the mystery predestined from the beginning of time and of the world's history, but kept secret with God, and now brought to its accomplishment.²

When God chose out a people for Himself, as the bearers and organs of His preparatory Messianic dispensation, neither their fathers nor their descendants had done good or evil and their election could not have depended on their deserts. But God foresaw in their fathers, Jacob and Esau, the characteristic dispositions of the two peoples who should spring from them, the Israelites and Edomites, and therefore He "loved Jacob and hated Esau," that is, He chose not Esau and his people for the instruments of His plan of salvation. God hates nothing that He has made, for God is Love.³

How even the rejection of the Gospel by the multitude of the Jews falls into God's designs for the religious guidance of mankind, and must ultimately promote the salvation of men and the glory of God, St. Paul shows by the example of Pharaoh, who was only hardened by all Divine commands and warnings, and yet with this obstinacy of a perverted will was but an instrument in the hand of God, to proclaim His power against his own will, and to confirm the feeble confidence of Israel. If the Apostle uses the expression, "God hardens," it is only that, in his energetic way of speaking, the result of those dispensations through which Pharaoh's pride developed itself is referred immediately to God, without noticing any secondary causes. In the Old Testament passage which he had in his eye, it is Pharaoh who hardens himself.⁴

St. Paul admits no valid contradiction between the universal scope of redemption, and the fact, already sufficiently clear, that the great majority of that people whose origin,

---
¹ Eph. i. 4; iii. 9.  ² Rom. xvi. 25, 26.  ³ Wisdom ii. 23.
⁴ Exod. viii. 15, 32.

promises, and former privileges gave it a special call, remained shut out from Messiah's kingdom. Priding themselves on their descent and their legal works, the Jews were wont to regard salvation and its conditions as something that belonged of right to them, and to them alone. Hence their conclusion that Christ cannot be the true Messiah, nor faith in Him what God requires, for that would be shown in the unanimous and willing assent of the whole nation, but clearly the very reverse is the fact. St. Paul's answer is twofold. First, it is not lineal descent, or belonging to a particular nation, that is the point; not all members of the Israelite people are Israelites in the higher spiritual sense of the word. Secondly, man's will and act has as little to do with the matter as bodily descent, but only the counsel of God, who foresaw all and directs all with a supreme wisdom and justice, inscrutable to us short-sighted mortals. The Apostle here rests on that Divine necessity which is not limited by our aims or acts, but by the eternal decree of God. It is God who fixes for nations, as for individuals, their eternal relations and condition and their whole outward course of life, who in this sense chose Isaac before Ishmael, Jacob before Esau, and, from their children, the Israelites before the Edomites. But he leaves every one free to follow out his own nature; only it is not the particular outward acts, good or bad, but the foreseen motive and temper from which they spring by which his decisions are ruled. The subtle intellect which questions the why of God's dispensations for the position, circumstances, and conditions of life of individuals, is warned back by St. Paul to its proper limits, with the remark that the potter has power to mould of the clay what vessels he will for honour or for dishonour.[1] And so, indeed, to the question—why am I thus formed? thus gifted? thus placed?—every one can but answer, that it so pleased God, that he is a vessel formed by God to serve Him as His instrument, either in high and honourable matters, or in what seem small and are of no repute with men.

And so, as the Apostle expresses it, the Gospel to one is an odour of death unto death, to another of life unto life, and there are among men "vessels of wrath fitted to

---

[1] Rom. ix. 6—21.   [2] 2 Cor. ii. 14—16. Cf. 1 Cor. i. 18.

destruction," but only such because they would not become vessels of grace; and these God bears with patiently, partly to leave them time for conversion, partly that they may be instrumental to the good of others, as the obstinacy of the Jews is said to be a gain to the well-disposed among the Gentiles. In one section of the Jews St. Paul saw vessels of wrath, but he shows that God has not yet rejected His people. It is in his thoughts, though he does not expressly state it, that the conversion of the whole nation would rather have increased than lessened the difficulties of converting the Gentiles. But Israel is only for a time cast off, and only for its unbelief and faithlessness to the grace offered in Christ. The time will come, after the multitude of the Heathen are converted, when the hard-heartedness of Israel will cease, and the whole remnant of them be saved by coming into the kingdom of Messiah. St. Paul never speaks of arbitrary Divine decrees about the salvation or destruction of men, or of a Divine predestination which fixes their belief or unbelief, the change or hardening of their hearts; on the contrary, he always assumes the freedom of the individual and the responsibility of his actions. The Jews incurred their exclusion from Messiah's kingdom by their own unbelief, and the one will endure as long as the other. When St. Paul speaks of men being hardened by God, he is thinking of that state of superinduced stupidity and hopeless obduracy against truth and grace, which is the inevitable result of a chronic struggle against the force of Divine warnings and the voice of conscience.[1]

---

[1] Rom. ix., xi.

# CHAPTER III.

### DOCTRINE OF THE CHURCH AND THE SACRAMENTS.

THE Christian Church was to be formed out of two great races of men previously divided, Jews and Gentiles. They did not enter it as two rivals of equal birth, rights and privileges, but the one party were those long favoured and chosen out, "whose were the adopted sonship, and the glory, and the covenants, and the giving of the Law, and the worship, and the promises, whose are the Fathers, and from whom is Christ according to the flesh." But the others were without Christ, who had long dwelt spiritually among the people of Israel as the Eternal Word of the Father and the Messiah who was to come; they were strangers shut out from the citizenship of Israel, aliens to the covenants of promise, without hope and without God in the world.[1] But now is the partition wall broken down, and the strangers are brought nigh; they are engrafted on the chosen people as branches of the wild olive, engrafted on the parent tree and made partakers of its living sap. Both now are joint citizens of the one kingdom of Israel, both form one household of God, and the whole building, harmoniously fitted together, "increases to a holy temple in the Lord." This image of a temple often recurs with the Apostles, for to them the Christian community is the dwelling-place of the Holy Ghost, as before the Shekinah of the Jewish temple was; and thus St. Peter calls believers the living stones of which the temple was built.[2]

---

[1] Rom. ix. 4, 5. Eph. ii. 12. Cf. Col. i. 21.
[2] Rom. xi. 17, 24. Eph. ii. 19—22. 1 Pet. ii. 5.

From one family sprung a pilgrim band, from that a people first of slaves, then of warriors and conquerors, with its sanctuary in a movable tabernacle, then in the house of Shiloh, then in the temple of Jerusalem. Once carried away into distant captivity, then after return and national restoration made the plaything of the Heathen, it was now leading a double life, one of civil nationality in Judæa, another in the dispersion, where Israel, Hellenized and surrounded by a circle of Gentile proselytes, after a century and a half was ripening for the office of converting the Gentiles and forming with them one vast Church. That the great majority would reject this call was to be expected and did not hinder the continuity of the Church. The Prophets had only promised to a "remnant" glorious triumphs and successes among the Heathen; and St. Paul knew it, for he said in reference to the seven thousand who had not bowed the knee to Baal, "thus is there a remnant according to His gracious choice."[1] In fact many, nay all, were called, only few chosen. But the Church remained; and when the great body of Jews rejected the universal religion, now become a world-wide kingdom, the quickening Spirit withdrew from them. The animated body still held the members together, but the power of religious fecundity was withered; all that stirred in the corpse was casuistry, Talmud, Rabbinical lore. All the life was in the Church, where law was changed into grace, fear into love, types and symbols into realities. There, shadow had turned to substance, and God's sanctifying power was not simply displayed but given; all that was accidental or temporary in the institutions and precepts of the ancient people passed away, all that had an universal and permanent human significance was retained, enlarged and elevated. Christ had so arranged that His death and resurrection coincided with one great annual festival and the descent of the Holy Ghost with the other; He had given His Church the form of a well-ordered kingdom, preserving an hierarchical and liturgical character, and thus being not a mere continuation of the Synagogue—for the mighty event of the Incarnation and the powers derived from it intervened—but the ancient Church maintained in substance and raised to a higher

---

[1] Joel ii. 32. Mic. v. 8. Zach. viii. 12. Rom. xi. 2—5.

stage of life by the threefold process of elevation, confirmation and improvement.

Thus was the Christian Church at first enclosed in the Jewish, like the unborn child in its mother's womb. The time allowed to the Synagogue was not yet run out, even after the authorities and their adherents at Jerusalem had rejected the Messiah. The Apostles did not wish either to separate themselves or their converts from communion with the indissolubly united civil and ecclesiastical polity of Judaism; they visited the temple and took part in its sacrificial worship; even the first Gentile converts, when they came to Jerusalem, might worship the true God in the temple. So stood the Church of Christ in its preparatory and transitional period, with its first and more honourable part, the Jewish, abiding within the Synagogue, but with its younger and second part, the Gentile, already outside the Synagogue and independent of it.

Christ spoke of His Church as a kingdom, great and powerful, superior to all hostile attacks, with the keys consigned to Peter; He told His Apostles they would sit as princes and judges in that kingdom on thrones judging the tribes of (the bodily and spiritual) Israel, and that their judgment would hold good in heaven. His Kingdom, as being the perpetual revelation through all history of His power and glory, would not be of this world, not related in origin and constitution to other earthly kingdoms, but founded directly from above and destined to outlast all other kingdoms. After having come to the Jews, its born heirs, it shall be taken from them, as a people, and given to nations who will receive it. But the kingdom of Christ is also one in warfare; it shall not only never be destroyed according to Christ's promise, but it shall crush and consume all kingdoms that oppose it; its King shall rule the nations with an iron sceptre and break them in pieces as a potter's vessel.[1] He shall break what will not bend, His Church shall come into contact with all national kingdoms, into conflict with many, but shall always conquer in the end; it will either work an internal change in those king-

---

[1] Matt. xvi. 18, 19; xii. 28; xxi. 43. John xviii. 36. Dan. ii. 44. Cf. Isa. lx. 12. Apoc. xix. 15. Ps. ii. 9.

doms, or, if they refuse change and renewal, it will overset and dissolve them.

By degrees all peoples will be incorporated into this Church. It will not vegetate as a hidden sect, nor prolong its existence as a silent company of individual souls deeming themselves elect, but will be wide and capacious enough as a world-church to assimilate and ennoble every nationality, every disposition and energy of human nature. It was to be the great institution for educating mankind, and was to penetrate and purify by its spirit, civil polity and right, marriage and morals, civilization and science, every form of moral life, every principle and product of national and individual life and activity. Originating from a people whose very existence was created and sustained by religion only, it had from the first to maintain and develope itself in bitter conflict and struggle with that tough nationality so firm and so exclusive, and afterwards to expand into a world-kingdom built on the ruins of conquered nationalities and transcending all their limits. Thus the Church escaped the danger of being confined to a narrow and repulsive form of nationality in its youth, and of being thereby estranged from its universal mission and rendered unfit for it.

Christ had chosen for His Church the significant image of the mustard-seed, the smallest among the seeds of the fields and gardens of Judæa, from which grew a shrub which often there became a tree; even so was His Church, from the smallest circumference, from a tiny germ which yet included in itself dynamically and substantially its whole successive development, to expand into a mighty tree overshadowing the peoples. He added the image of leaven, which quietly, secretly and irresistibly, not without a process of fermentation, by degrees leavens the whole mass of humanity.[1] But the richest and most instructive image is that which St. Paul prefers, of an organised body, the body of Christ and filled with His Spirit, where type and antitype partly coincide.[2] The multiplicity of members in this body does not affect its unity, but is rather necessary for constituting and preserving it. And with unity is joined,

[1] Matt. xii. 31, 33. Mark iv. 31.
[2] Rom. xii. 5. 1-Cor. x. 17; xii. 12, 20, 27. Eph. i. 23; v. 23. Col. i. 18.

by God's will, the greatest variety of vocations and gifts, of offices and participation, greater or less, in the common life of the whole. All are thus closely connected with each other and with the whole body, which is penetrated by the life of Christ. All are to work together in harmony, each according to his own speciality and office; no member may separate itself, wish to stand alone, and follow selfish ends, or usurp the functions of others. Particular members, and many of them, may be diseased and corrupt, so that the body becomes disfigured and its vital force withdrawn from those suffering or dislocated members; but unless they actually divide themselves they remain under the healing, or at least health-offering, influence of the sound members and the whole organic body.

It is said by St. Paul to be the end and office of this body to grow to the maturity of "a perfect man."[1] It is being continually "built up," or is in constant growth, till its members finally reach that measure or stage of progress where they are made partakers of the fulness of Christ. This expresses a movement of the Church, constantly advancing throughout the course of the world's history,— a growing maturity up to that age when Christ, who filleth all in all, will impart to her the whole riches of His being and His gifts and fill her with Himself as a vessel containing nothing else.[1]

While St. Paul speaks of Christ loving His bride, the Church, and giving Himself for her, he represents the Lord's action on the Church as a constantly advancing purification and adornment, so that His bride may appear worthy of Him in blameless beauty, without spot or wrinkle.[2] Therefore she is always holy, because Christ is always sanctifying her and in Him, as her Head, she always possesses the Source of sanctity; because her indwelling Spirit is the "Holy" Ghost; because, in doctrine, means of grace, discipline and authority, every instrument of holiness is given her; because this fulness of moral powers and mighty equipment of the Church is in constant warfare with sin and can never be overcome by it. However great the power of evil and the number of evil men in the Church, they cannot destroy her objective sanctity, darken the light

[1] Eph. iv. 13. εἰς μέτρον ἡλικίας τοῦ πληρώματος τοῦ Χριστοῦ.　[2] Eph. v. 27.

of her teaching, or kill the living power of her ordinances and means of grace. The representation of the Church as the Bride of Christ indicates her relation to Him as already a nuptial one; although the great marriage feast will not be solemnised till the end of the world, when, as the chosen consort of the Lord, she will take her proper part in His glory.[1] She has received for her dowry the powers and means of grace she now administers as His steward. As woman is taken from man and in marriage is corporally made one with him, so that in loving his wife he loves himself, so is it with Christ and the Church. It is a chain of few but sure links that binds believers indissolubly to Christ. Every Christian can say he is a member of the body of the Church, which is the body of Christ and is also the bride of Christ, possessing and enjoying the goods of her spouse; that he has part in all her privileges, means of grace and wealth of healing powers. All is yours, says the Apostle, but ye are Christ's, and Christ is God's.[2] That "all" can at any moment be lost, and he who was a member of Christ's body may by his own fault become a castaway.

From sin, self-seeking, the wilful and unregulated understanding and imagination of man left to himself, sprang the number and diversity of religions; from the holiness and unity of God sprang the unity of the Church in faith, morals, and Divine worship. What man put asunder God joined together. In the unity of His Church was recognised the seal impressed on His creation, whose being is unity, whose will is order and love, whereby He has bound into one the centrifugal forces in men. The organic unity bestowed on the Church is, as a Divine work, indestructible; persons, parties, whole communities and portions of the Church, might depart,—they could not take away with them at their departure, in whole or in part, her promises and gifts, or the Spirit who ever dwells in her; they could not divide the Church, or introduce a number of Churches or bodies of the Lord, or take up a position as rival Churches of that which is ever one, steadfast in her continuity and the ordered succession of her Apostolate. They fell off, as many branches from one tree,—the

---

[1] Apoc. xii. 1 sqq.; xix. 7, 8; xxi. 2, 9. Eph. v. 29 sqq.
[2] 1 Cor. iii. 22, 23.

tree remained and bore new shoots with inexhaustible vitality.

The visible and invisible elements are indivisibly united in the Church, and do not form two Churches. Christ came Himself as a Light into the darkness of the world, and founded the Church, to be seen and accepted as the common teacher and educator of all peoples, the city on a mountain, which could not be hid,—the candlestick not to be put under a bushel, but to give light to all; her word, her institutions, her ordinances, her pastors and teachers, her usages and instruments—all were to be visible and tangible. But she was also to have her invisible side; above all, her Head, Christ, was an invisible One, and she herself, militant in this world, triumphant in the next, belonged with her other half to the invisible domain.[1] Her continuity and identity with the Church of earlier ages and generations, her lofty prerogatives, as the body of Christ and organ of the Holy Ghost, and the power of her ordinances, lay beyond the reach of sensible perception and could only be experienced as a result of faith. And yet the Church guaranteed and witnessed to herself. Her testimony consisted in her peculiar gifts, her appearance, voice, the impression she made upon men, and her power over spirits; these were her credentials, the guarantee of her claim, her lofty origin and her mission. Christ spoke "as One having authority,"[2] and so her word, too, was authoritative and irresistible; men often did not believe her till after long resistance, but they *felt* her, and both understanding and will had to bend before the majesty of a Queen who won souls alike by love and by reverence.

The old prophecies met in the assurance that Messiah's kingdom would be an everlasting kingdom, His dominion and glory have no end. The Founder of the new Church did not omit to renew the assurance to those who believed on Him, that the house He built for them would be one that could not be shaken, and had every security against destruction, and that in it they would be guaranteed against every danger of error or of being misled. He had before praised him as a prudent man, who built his house not on the sand, but on the rock, where alone it could brave all

---

[1] Matt. v. 14, 15. Eph. iii. 15. Heb. xii. 22.   [2] Matt. vii. 29.

storms. He declared that His own house, the Church, should be built on a rock, and that the law of decay, death and dissolution, to which everything else is liable (the gates of Hell), should have no power over it. When about to leave the earth, He added in solemn and majestic manner to His commission, given to those ordained for its administration, a promise whose terms are so distinct, unconditional and comprehensive that it became the Magna Charta of His Church. "All power is given to Me in heaven and on earth ; go, therefore, make disciples of all nations, baptizing them—teaching them to observe all that I have commanded you. And lo, I am with you always, to the end of the world."[1] Such words have only once been spoken to men, and, after eighteen centuries, they have an echo still in the soul of every believer. He to whom all earthly power is committed, will not forsake His Church; He will let no enemy subdue, no persecutor destroy, no error darken it; for her teaching and her office of handing down revealed truth, pure and uncorrupted, to all peoples and all generations He has promised her for ever His presence and almighty aid. He has explained more exactly the manner and kind of that presence; while He goes to the Father, the Paraclete, the Spirit of Truth, descends sent by Him to dwell for ever in the Church, whose office is to guide her into all the truth, to bring to remembrance all that Christ has spoken and to make known His teaching.[2] Thus, since the first Pentecost, the Church has a Divine Teacher and Guide, and is the organ whereby the Holy Ghost instructs believers. This gives the Christian Church a great superiority over the Jewish, which was not the body of the Incarnate Son, and neither had Him for Head nor was filled and taught by the Holy Ghost.

St. Paul recognises a house of God on earth, but it is no more the people of the Old Covenant; Israel is no longer the community where God has His dwelling, but the Christian people, "the Church of the living God," which is the "pillar and ground of the truth."[3] Outside this Church is falsehood and deceit, or truth defenceless, mixed with error

[1] Matt. vii. 2 ; xvi. 18; xxviii. 19, 20.   [2] John xiv. 26; xvi. 13—15.
[3] 1 Tim. iii. 15.

and left a prey to human caprice, alteration and disfigurement. But the one Church, and that alone among earthly institutions, is the vessel where the truth will be ever preserved unadulterated, for Christ is her indivisible Head and the Holy Ghost, the Spirit of Truth, is her Lord, her Light and Life. And thus the stream of truth, as of grace, flows for ever in the Church. The substance of what Christ taught and His Apostles preached, is become an abiding illumination, a light that never leaves the Church and never turns to darkness. Outside, not within the Church, is that state realised which St. Paul described, where men "are carried about by every wind of doctrine," given over to "the deceitfulness and cunning craft of men." In the Church Christ has appointed a ministry, for the edification of His body, till we all come to the unity of the faith and knowledge of the Son of God, to man's estate and the full measure of Christian maturity.[1]

Christ took upon Himself for our salvation the threefold office of Prophet, Priest and King; in each He is alone and unapproachable, and each He continually exercises. Raised to heaven, and free from all limits of time and space, He is the One great Prophet of His Church, who sustains what He has once created, who by His Spirit and His abiding presence with His Church till the end of the world continually teaches and guards the truth and purity of her doctrine. He is the One High Priest, who presents before the Father His sacrifice completed on earth, who stands ever before the Father to intercede for men and bestow grace upon them. He is lastly, the One King and Lord of the world and the Church, who has all things under His feet, who rules the Church with almighty power and omniscient wisdom and carries out all within it to the great result.[2] All believers of all ages are disciples of that Prophet, subjects of that King, partakers in the sacrifice of that High Priest. But they are such through the ministry of His earthly representatives, who exercise His prophetic office by constant preaching of His doctrine, His royalty by governing His Church, His priesthood by presenting and

---

[1] Eph. iv. 11—14.
[2] Heb. iv. 14; vi. 20; viii. 1 sqq. Rom. viii. 34. 1 Cor xv. 24—27.

dispensing His sacrifice. This threefold office is united in the Apostolate, for the Church is His body, the fulness fulfilled of Him "who filleth all in all."[1]

Christ alone has suffered for men, yet St. Paul could say that he filled up what was wanting of the sufferings of Christ, and every Martyr or sufferer for the truth and weal of the Church could say the same. He is the one Mediator and Intercessor, yet the Church is bidden to make intercession for all men. He alone can forgive sin, yet "whose sins ye forgive they are forgiven."[2] He alone can regenerate men, yet the ministers of His Church do it in baptism. He alone can give the Bread of Life, yet human hands dispense it in His Church. For that end has Christ formed the Church, His Body, that all her instruments do in His name, by His power and authority, may be His act; that every minister of priestly and ecclesiastical functions may know he can only supply the outward form, while the power and truth of the act belongs to the one Prophet, Priest and King, and the roots of all self-seeking and self-glorification of men may thus be cut off.

And thus their priesthood who are the organs of His Body is on one side the making visible and applying of Christ's priesthood, on the other the representative fulfilment of the common priesthood of believers. In relation to the people, the Apostles and their successors represent the Lord; in relation to God, the people. Their earthly organic priesthood is the guarantee and witness at once of the abiding, ever active High-priesthood of Christ, and of the common and acceptable priesthood of all believers. The Church possesses all the blessings of the old Covenant—the Synagogue, temple and throne of David—in the teaching office, royalty and priesthood, divided there, first united in the Person of Christ, and thus transmitted to those to whom He said, "As My Father hath sent Me, so I send you." In a higher and peculiar sense Christ delivered to the Apostles, as He Himself possessed it, that union of spiritual powers, the priestly kingship or royal priesthood. When He took occasion from their strife for pre-eminence

---

[1] Eph. i. 23. τὸ πλήρωμα, the body wholly filled by Christ with His gifts, offices and powers, containing the fulness of Christ.
[2] Col. i. 24. 1 Tim. ii. 1. John xx. 23.

to declare that there would always be a "greater" and a "leader" among them, who yet was to behave as servant of all, He added that they would all have royal and sacerdotal dignity and a supreme rank in His kingdom, "I appoint you a kingdom, as My Father hath appointed Me, that ye may eat and drink at My table in my kingdom, and sit on thrones judging the twelve tribes of Israel," which includes the Gentile boughs to be engrafted on the Israelite stock.[1] The two chief rights and offices included in this constitution of the kingdom are the priestly celebration of the Eucharistic feast and sacrifice, and the royal and judicial authority in the Church.

And accordingly St. Paul infers the right of the Christian ministry to be supported by the laity from the right and usage for those who served the temple to live of the temple, and for the ministers of the altar to partake of the altar.[2] For the Church to him is the true temple of God. But as yet the ancient temple stood, the whole Old Testament sacrificial worship was performed, the High Priest sat in Jerusalem and the whole Aaronic and Levitical ministry was in untouched, unchallenged possession of its influence, rights and functions, recognised by Christ Himself. The Church was but an expansion of Judaism. Its Jewish members did not cease to be Jews, members of the Church and commonwealth of Israel on becoming Christians. Till the city and temple were destroyed, the time had not come for the Apostles to proclaim openly the substitution of the Christian for the Jewish priesthood, and be able to use without scruple the name of priest; the use of the word would only have given offence and caused mistakes, it would have been taken in the legal instead of the Evangelical sense. But when the temple fell and the Levitical priesthood lost its office and object, the time was come to proclaim aloud the Christian priesthood; then St. John, at Ephesus, assumed the golden mitre-plate which had been the peculiar ornament of Aaron's successors.[3]

As the Church shares the threefold office of her Head, and is at once temple and priesthood, St. Peter calls believers

---

[1] Luke xxii. 29, 30.   [2] 1 Cor. ix. 13, 14.
[3] Polycrat. *ap. Eus.* v. 24. Epiphanius says that St. James, as Bishop of Jerusalem, had worn this ornament of the High Priest before the destruction of the City.—[Cf. Exod. xxix. 6. Lev. viii. 9.—Tr.]

a "spiritual house" and "holy priesthood," called to offer spiritual sacrifices pleasing to God through Christ, and applies to the Church of the new Covenant what was said of the people of Israel, "Ye are a chosen generation, a royal priesthood, a holy nation, a purchased people." And in the hymn sung by the Saints in the Apocalyptic vision we read, "Thou redeemedst us to God by Thy blood from every tribe, and tongue, and people, and nation, and madest us kings and priests to our God, and we shall reign upon earth."[1] As the Israelite people was named in common "a kingdom of priests," so the whole Christian community, which inherits all privileges and prerogatives of ancient Israel, is called, and is, a nation of kings and priests; it has at present royal dominion over the world and sin and the enemies of salvation, in the future the hope of sharing royal honours. "To him that overcometh I will give to sit with Me on My throne;"—" If we suffer with Him, we shall also reign with Him;" nay, according to a strong expression of St. Paul's, believers already in their inward consciousness, and so far as they know how to rule their passions, are seated with and through Christ in heaven.[2] From its priesthood the Christian community has the power and obligation of presenting that offering called by St. Paul "the reasonable worship," the sacrifice of ourselves, the complete surrender of body and soul to God. This great and all-embracing sacrifice includes that of prayer, of praise —" the fruit of the lips praising His name"—and that of love for our neighbour expressed in deeds of kindness and mercy.[3] In this sense every Christian has a priestly vocation, as every citizen of the Old Covenant had; but the common priesthood of Christians is more excellent and a higher dignity, for it is also exercised in the Eucharistic sacrifice of the Church, where the self-oblation of the believer is most intimately united with the oblation of the Person of Christ and sustained by it. But, as besides the universal priesthood of all Israelites there was the special and peculiar priesthood of the sons of Aaron and Levi, so that one limited and completed the other, so was it also from the first in the Christian Church. All believers had

---

[1] 1 Pet. ii. 5, 9. Apoc. v. 9, 10.   [2] Apoc. iii. 21. 2 Tim. ii. 12. Eph. ii. 6.
[3] Rom. xii. 1. Apoc. viii. 3, 4. Heb. xiii. 15. James i. 27.

the call and dignity of priests, but the actual office of serving the altar was confined to the Apostles and those they appointed to assist them. Since the Eucharistic celebration was appointed, there was a special priesthood in the Church, an "altar" from which they who served the tabernacle had no right to eat; from thenceforth the fulfilment of the old prophecy had begun, that God would take of strange nations for priests and Levites and that, while David's seed should last, there should never want a priest to offer daily sacrifice.[1] Thus St. Paul called himself an Evangelical priest of Jesus Christ among the Gentiles, called to present them as an offering sanctified by the Holy Ghost, acceptable to God. He does not use here his common word, minister, but that used in the Epistle to the Hebrews of the priesthood of Christ, and applies to the priestly ministry of the Gospel another word of exclusively sacerdotal significance.[2]

The institution and transmission of priestly powers was attached to the rite of ordination by laying on of hands, as every act of transference—such as the substitution of the victim for the offerer—was done by laying on of hands; and, again, as the same form was used in blessings and healings as real communications of spirit and life. The Lord healed the sick by the laying on of hands; but when, after His resurrection, He bestowed the Holy Ghost on His Apostles—in this case power to bind and loose—He did not lay on His hands, but breathed on them with His glorified Body.[3] This beseemed the Lord only, not the Apostles; He gave out of the fulness of His own spirit.[4] But the Apostles who could only bestow certain gifts of the Spirit laid on their hands, as well to impart those gifts to new baptized converts as for the grace of priesthood. Church offices, with their attributes of remitting sin, teaching, administering sacraments and sacrifice, required such an endowment with power from on high, for they rested wholly on the appointment and authority of God, and where He gave a mission He gave His power and blessing to discharge it. A special gift was conferred from

---

[1] Heb. xiii. 10. Is. lxvi. 21. Jerem. xxxiii. 17, 18. Rom. xv. 16.
[2] λειτουργὸν, ἱερουργοῦντα. Cf. Heb. viii. 2, and see *Suiceri Thes.* and *Schleussneri Lex.* in verb. [3] Luke iv. 40. Mark vi. 5. John xx. 22.
[4] Cyril *in Joann.* Opp. T. iv. p. 1,095. τὸ ἴδιον πνεῦμα διδοὺς δι' ἐπιφανοῦς ἐμφυσήματος.

which the priest could always, like Timothy, draw fresh power for the worthy and successful administration of his office.[1]

All offices in the Church depended on Divine mission; as the Apostles were sent, so were all who shared or inherited their functions. All could say, "Christ has sent me, directly or indirectly, and I speak because I am bidden of Him, in His name." The community did not make its rulers, but the Apostles; they and those they sent formed the communities and gave them overseers. "We are ambassadors for Christ, as though God exhorted through us." The pastors of the Church must be regarded as servants of Christ, stewards ordained by God to administer mysteries in His house, the Church. The other members of the body neither can nor ought to usurp their office any more than the hand can discharge the functions of the eye or mouth.[2] On the contrary, in the ever-living and organic body of the Church that subordination and mutual relationship and co-operation must be maintained which its Founder established from the beginning.

St. Paul says that if the ministry of the Old Testament Law, which condemned, was glorious, much more must the Christian ministry of righteousness exceed in glory. That Levitical priesthood was but a shadow of the new one. Of that it is said, "None taketh to himself this honour, but he that is called of God, as Aaron was."[3] The Christian ministry could not be behind the Jewish, which had an unbroken succession and Divine authority, wholly independent of the popular will. The type cannot excel the fulfilment. The stream of succession proceeding from the Apostles descends from generation to generation. Christ said for all times, "He that receiveth whomsoever I send receiveth Me, and he that receiveth Me receiveth Him that sent Me;" He gave to all ordained in regular succession the power to bind and loose.[4] And, therefore, the Church has a sure and unvarying doctrine, withdrawn from human caprice, because Christ Himself has appointed her pastors and teachers. St. Paul, indeed, clearly foresaw the approach of a time when men after their own selfish lusts would provide themselves

[1] 2 Tim. i. 6.
[2] 2 Cor. v. 20. 1 Cor. iv. 1; xii. 21.
[3] 2 Cor. iii. 9. Heb. x. 1; v. 4.
[4] John xiii. 20. Matt. xvi. 19.

teachers who should preach smooth things, but that was a time of apostasy.[1] Only outside the Church and in revolt against her authority could man form a ministry for himself, ordered to deliver a new and more flattering doctrine.

St. Paul exalts his Apostolic office and power with the solemn protestation, "I speak the truth in Christ, and lie not," that by virtue of it he may entrust His full powers to His disciples Timothy and Titus for certain portions of the Church, Timothy for Ephesus and Titus for Crete. They were to teach and watch over purity of doctrine, to ordain overseers or presbyters, and to provide for the planting and dissemination of the doctrine received from him through fit men qualified for the ministry.[2] But this appointment and commission to discharge Church functions was no mere human precaution or act of fitness. With mission grace also was conferred on those called to the ministry; the Holy Ghost ordained them through human instruments. "Take heed to yourselves and the whole flock in which the Holy Ghost hath made you overseers, to feed the Church of God which He hath purchased with His own blood," were St. Paul's words to the Ephesian overseers at Miletus; and he warned St. Timothy not to leave unused the grace bestowed on him by the laying on of hands of himself and the presbytery, but to re-awaken it to activity in himself.[3]

Christ desired to have in His Church offices, rights, and powers, but not lords to domineer over it. When the Apostles strove among themselves for pre-eminence, He told them beforehand that one would always be the first and greatest in His Kingdom, but His Kingdom was not to be like the contemporary Gentile kingdoms, nor rank and power in His Church like that of worldly rulers, but the greatest among them must become as the least, the ruler as the servant, even as He became the servant of His disciples.[4] St. Peter warned the presbyters to be not tyrants, but patterns of the flock.[5] There was to be none of that despotic, arbitrary, selfish authority, no utilizing of the people for the pleasure or convenience of their lords, in the

---

[1] Eph. iv. 11.  2 Tim. iv. 3, 4.   [2] 1 Tim. i. 3, 4.  2 Tim. ii. 3.  Tit. 6. sqq.
[3] Acts xx. 28.  1 Tim. iv. 14.  2 Tim. i. 6.
[4] Luke xxii. 24—27.        [5] 1 Pet. v. 3.

Church of Christ; rulers were to impose no capricious burdens and commands. The authorities Christ ordained were for guidance; they were to fulfil their ministry as pastors and educators, not as lords over the Christian people, in the fear of God and with abiding consciousness of having to give account for it, making the salvation and spiritual growth of their congregations their sole aim, being humble and ready to serve others, but always putting the known will of God above man's will and not courting human favour; they were never to forget that it was their one peculiar privilege to be willing and devoted instruments of God for the benefit of their brethren. On the other hand, they were not to regard their authority as derived from the people, but as coming immediately or mediately from Christ. As the Lord said to His Apostles; "Ye have not chosen Me, but I have chosen you," so could the Church's office-bearers say to their people; "It is we, God's messengers and instruments, who taught, converted, baptized you; before you were what you are, we were."

At first the Apostles had to use much patience and forbearance with weak and erring members of the Church, even as the Lord had had much patience with them and had borne in meekness their narrow Jewish prejudices. "If ye be in anything differently minded from the perfect, God will reveal this also to you," St. Paul says to the Philippians; and he tells the Thessalonians that he prays night and day to see them in person, that he may supply the defects of their faith.[1] Individuals and whole communities had to be treated as infants, who, for a long time, have no solid food given them, but only milk, who could only receive the first elements of Christian doctrine.[2] But in two points they tolerated no weakness and insisted on enforcing their requirements;—the duty of confessing the faith, and the exclusion of every heresy. Without confession there was no salvation; "With the heart man believeth unto righteousness, with the mouth he confesseth unto salvation," St. Paul says, referring to the words of Christ, that He will only confess those before His Father in heaven who have confessed Him before men. The Hebrew converts are bidden to hold fast their confession without

[1] Phil. iii. 15. 1 Thess. iii. 10.   [2] 1 Cor. iii. 2.

wavering.[1] The chief substance of this confession was Jesus, the Son of God and High Priest manifested in flesh and raised from the dead, the resurrection, judgment, repentance, and baptism.[2] But it meant more than the mere utterance of a formula; a Christian's whole life was to be a continual confession in act, a living mirror of the truth his lips professed. In this sense St. Paul says, that no man can call Jesus Lord, except by the Holy Ghost; and St. John, that every spirit which confesses Jesus to have come in flesh is of God.[3]

All members and all portions of the One Church must confess the same truth. The very existence of the Church involved this; a Church with dissimilar and contradictory confessions could never have been held together during the Apostles' lifetime, still less after their death. Unity of doctrine, and therefore of creed, was the first condition of the unity of the Church. Hence the earnest exhortation to have the same speech and the same confession and to be established in the same mind and judgment.[4] Of sects, schools, views and systems, the then world was full; all was in ferment and in motion, attesting and repelling by turns, theory following theory in endless confusion and revolution; all forms of Heathenism, of Pharisaic, Alexandrian or Gnostic Judaism, courted and catered for the applause of men. There was plenty of room for trial and choice; every one in the proud consciousness of intellectual freedom and self-glorification could try these systems, schools and sects, one after another, and run riot to his heart's content in the doctrines and forms of knowledge, the pompous promises and views unfolded to him. There was but one thing wanting—certainty, authority, faith. That could only be found in the Church. When once it was clear and certain to a man that Christ was what He claimed to be, the Truth; that in Him was revealed the nature of God, that in His Church the will of God was represented—then he gladly gave up all reserve, all bargaining with the doctrine of the Church, and made it his one aim

---

[1] Rom. x. 9, 10. Matt. x. 32. Heb. iv. 14; x. 23.
[2] 1 John ii. 23; iv. 2, 15. 2 John 7. Heb. iii. 1; iv. 14.
[3] 1 Cor. xii. 3. 1 John iv. 2, 15. [4] 1 Cor. i. 10.

that his mind and will should be ever increasingly penetrated with the truths he believed.

The Apostles knew of no patience or indulgence towards false teachers. The word, "Heresy," which had come into use in the Church and was already adopted in this sense by St. Peter, is first applied by St. Paul in the general sense of divisions and parties, but in the Epistle to Titus he means by the "heretical man," whom his disciple is to avoid after one or two admonitions, a false teacher. In the sentence of rejection against every heresy, every doctrine departing from that of the Church, all were agreed. The opponents of Apostolic doctrine were "taken captive in Satan's snare," and lost, unless they repented; they sinned willingly and, after admonition had failed, must be expelled from Church communion. St. Paul formally excommunicated Hymenæus and Alexander, and gave them over to Satan—took from them, that is, all rights and safeguards of Church communion, so that they fell back under the demoniacal influences prevalent outside the Church, "that they might be taught not to blaspheme." And such an exclusion was always to be adopted, for religious error had, as the Apostle expresses it, "an energetic power of deceit," like a strong poison or intoxicating drink, and to guard her children from this disease, was among the first and most imperative duties of the Church.[1] The Apostles, therefore, held false teaching to be more mischievous than evil example, because, as a later writer words it, the latter poisons the stream, the former the fountain. St. Paul says emphatically, "If we or an angel from heaven preach to you another Gospel than that we have preached, let him be accursed." St. John, with all his gentleness, forbids the community to show hospitality to false teachers, or even to salute them; he calls them Antichrists, and says of those who have fallen away from the Church, "They never really belonged to us, or they would have remained with us."[2]

There could accordingly be no doubt for believers as to the general relations of freedom and obedience towards the Church. Those really converted entered it to obey, and

---

[1] 2 Pet. ii. 1.  1 Cor. xi. 19.  Gal. v. 20.  2 Tim. ii. 26.  Tit. iii. 10, 11.  1 Tim. i. 19, 20.  2 Thess. ii. 11, ἐνέργειαν πλάνης.
[2] Gal. i. 8, 9.  2 John 9, 10.  1 John ii. 19.

not to rule. Being told expressly that they were members of a body, they knew that it was a self-evident duty and necessity for them, as members, to obey the impulses emanating from the higher organs of the Ecclesiastical body. They knew, as the Apostle says, that they were bought for a great price, and were not to become slaves of men; but they recognised and preserved the freedom they had gained with the faith, in that having become servants of Christ, they submitted humbly and trustfully to the ordinances and laws of His Church, being convinced that Christian freedom consists not in caprice, idiosyncracy and licence, but in yielding to the law ordained for sanctification, and that they would be not weaker but stronger from intimate dependence on the Church, as being upheld and supported by its Divine organisation. They knew that the Lord had said, he should be taken for a Heathen and a publican who would not hear the Church, and that St. Paul had forbidden all communion with one who despised the word of the Apostles, while the Hebrew Christians were bidden to reverence from their hearts those ruling over them.[1]

It follows from the nature and design of the Church, that all its members are under a continuous educational influence. The Church is a moral power, holding together all its members in a real fellowship, even those not inwardly good, where on the whole the purifying and sanctifying influences are stronger than the indwelling evil in individuals. It is a great educational institution, not for one particular period of man's life but for the whole of it, receiving him as a child and constantly acting on him, cleansing, instructing, building up, and sanctifying through teaching, example, common prayer and worship, and means of grace; constantly nourishing and enlightening his mind and seeking to strengthen his will, and only leaving him at his death, without even then regarding him as cut off or renouncing its influence over him. In the Church, all are called; all, however sinful, are capable of salvation and subjects of her educational action; all are intended, by taking and giving, to hold at once active and passive relations. All are to be prayed for and to pray for others. All are to set an example to their fellow-members of the body, and to take example

[1] 1 Cor. vii. 23; iii. 23. Matt. xviii. 17. 2 Thess. iii. 14. Heb. xiii. 7.

from them. None can sink so low that the Church need despair of him, or is not bound to stoop to him and seek to lift him up again. While he lives, he is not given over, and the Church relies on the means of grace entrusted to her, which can fan into a bright flame the spark of life remaining, in spite of all sin, in the baptized, however near extinction.

None, then, in the Church is hopelessly lost, or predestined to damnation. Nations, like individuals, may be healed ;[1] and the Church is the great institution for healing and improvement, which despairs of no moral sickness, passes no sentence of death, pronounces none evil but only a sinner, who may always be converted while his day of grace, his earthly life, lasts. For sinners' sakes the Church was founded, as her Lord and Master came as a Physician, not for the whole but for the sick.[2] And so, even the unworthy, who had fallen into great sins, were regarded and treated as members of the body of Christ ; so long as they did not leave the Church, but remained in her and discharged at least some functions and duties of membership, she sought to heal them and exercised an educational influence over them, by teaching, example and warning. Even if they were so far dead or maimed members of the Lord's body, that they shut themselves out for the time from the healing influences streaming on them from the rest of the body and from its Head, yet no one could say that those influences would always be vain and fruitless; the Church hoped and prayed for them, and the sinner of to-day might be the converted of to-morrow. Only when the danger of the sound members being infected was greater than the hope of the sick being healed, they must be cut off.

Therefore, in a series of Parables bearing on the condition of the members of His kingdom, the Church, Christ prepared His disciples for finding a great number of the unconverted and impure in it ;—in the parable of the floor with wheat and chaff, of the wheat and tares in the field, of the fishing net, the royal marriage, the wise and foolish virgins, the Good Shepherd, and the vine.[3] For He fore-

---

[1] Wisd. i. 14. [2] Mark ii. 17. Luke v. 31.
[3] Matt. iii. 12; xiii. 24—30, 47—50; xxii. 2 sqq.; xxv. 1 sqq. John x. 1 sqq. Luke xv 4 sqq. John xv. 1 sqq.

saw that one of the greatest temptations and most seductive errors would be the wish to set up a Church composed entirely of the pure and perfect. The field of the Church is sown with wheat and tares and the first separation will be made at the harvest, the day of judgment. In the net are good fish and bad, as the Church, God's kingdom, includes evil men and righteous. The good Shepherd sees sheep of His own among the wanderers, and follows them into the wilderness. Christ, the true Vine, has unfruitful branches, only then to be rejected and burnt when they are fallen off. St. Paul again says that in the great household of the Church are not only gold and silver vessels but wooden and earthen, vessels for honour and for dishonour in the using; but he will not have these last cast out of the house, but only that men should keep themselves pure and undefiled by them, so as to become holy vessels of honour to the Lord.[1] Thus in the Church there are at once manifold gradations and a close interdependence of all. All believers are a priestly generation, and each in his way is a medium and organ for imparting moral influences to others, and the most advanced are the salt and leaven for the rest.

The Apostles speak most emphatically of the privileges and prerogatives of members of the Church over the rest of the world. The "Saints" at Ephesus are in a condition of grace, and enjoy higher rights; they are already blest with all spiritual blessing in heavenly things through Christ. They need a special enlightenment to understand aright their high and glorious inheritance; they are fellow-citizens of the Saints and of the household of God, who were darkness but are now light in the Lord.[2] Yet the Apostles, who described the state of the Church and its members as one of such high grace, prerogatives and glory, held it necessary to denounce gross sins and excesses in the whole community and to warn men against them constantly.[3] Close upon the mention of the Church's privileges and gifts follows the reference to their possible and often actual misuse. St. Paul thanks God for the grace bestowed on the Corinthian Christians, that through Christ they are rich in all knowledge and every gift, but then immediately follows

[1] 2 Tim. ii. 20, 21.     [2] Eph. i. 3, 18.
[3] Heb. vi. 4—6; x. 26—29. 2 Pet. ii., iii.

a severe censure of their divisions and quarrels; he tells them they are still carnal, and heaps a long catalogue of reproaches and accusations upon them. He knew that God's gifts to the Church are without reservation or repentance, that great faults may long exist side by side with great privileges within her domain, and he looked on those communities not only as they were in the present, but as they would be in the future.[1]

It was the glory of the Christian as compared with the Jewish Church, that shadows were transmuted to substance, symbols to means of grace, types to instruments of salvation, rituals to channels of higher powers. What before was a pious usage—an intimation, a memento, a suggestion only—was now become the medium of Divine power and an instrument of sanctification. The simplest materials and acts which subserve the needs of daily life were chosen by the Lord as vessels and instruments of Divine gifts, conductors of sanctifying power,—water, bread and wine, oil, imposition of hands. To the symbolic matter and acts were added corresponding words, which, perfecting the action and concentrating the grace into a given moment, wrought what they expressed and what the act signified, so that they remained in the mind and memory of the recipient, as decisive facts, monuments of his religious life and points for confidence to cling to.

These means of grace were ordained for beings composed of body as well as soul, and by Him who appeared on earth as Redeemer with the bodily as well as spiritual nature of man. They were not to be mere signs, pledges or symbols of grace, but an actual communication of it, wrought by the risen and glorified Christ on the men He would convert and sanctify, bonds to unite the body of the Church with its Head, nourishment to sustain and medicines to restore its life. By opening the eyes of the blind with earth and spittle, and bidding His disciples anoint the sick with oil, Christ had Himself announced that He would connect higher powers with sensible signs, in order to accustom men to look beyond the simple matter or sign and the human minister to the Divine Redeemer concealed under that material veil and using man as His instrument.

[1] 1 Cor. i. 5 sqq. Rom. xi. 29.

Jesus bade all nations be baptized in the Name of the Father, the Son, and the Holy Ghost, which bound them to believe and confess the Three Divine Persons, and brought them into fellowship with His own death and resurrection, so that the old man was buried and the new man raised up in them, and they experienced in themselves the power of the Lord's death and resurrection. St. Paul makes the idea of men being buried and rising with Christ in Baptism the great point in the sacrament; by Baptism man is incorporated with Christ, and puts on Christ, so that the sacramental washing does away all natural distinctions of race;—Greek and Jew, slave and free, men and women are one in Christ, members of His body, children of God and of the seed of Abraham.[1] His death and resurrection in Baptism is made ours, and the whole life of a Christian is but an expansion of what had its ground and beginning there. The Apostle not only divides man into body and spirit, but distinguishes in the bodily nature the gross, visible, bulky frame, and a hidden, inner, "spiritual" body, not subject to limits of space or cognisable by the senses; this last, which shall hereafter be raised, is alone fit for and capable of organic union with the glorified body of Christ, of substantial incorporation with it.[2] And that process takes place even now in Baptism, so that immersion in the water is immersion in Christ's body, and we there begin in principle to experience those two critical processes through which His Body passed, death and resurrection; the old Adam with his sinful inclinations is buried or crucified, and the pure body of Christ overflowing with powers of healing gradually dispossesses or absorbs his, and our whole religious life is built up on this foundation.[3]

Thus Christ becomes by Baptism the Father of a new family, and all individuals of it are made members of His Body through the sacrament; in all is implanted the principle, power and beginning of a death to the old life of sin, and of a gradual though laborious development of the new life, together with the germ of the future bodily resurrection. To make Baptism really a laver of regeneration, a covenant of good conscience towards God and means of

---

[1] Rom. vi. 4. Gal. iii. 27—29.
[2] Rom. vii. 22. 1 Cor. vi. 14. Eph. iii. 16; v. 30.
[3] Col ii. 12, 20; iii. 1.

forgiveness and sanctification, the Holy Ghost works through the rite on man's mind and will, and moves him to conscious acceptance of the imparted gift. Hence St. John calls Spirit, water and blood, (the power of Christ's blood communicated in baptism,) the three witnesses to the certainty of our salvation.[1]

The right and full communication of the Spirit promised by Christ to His followers was to be given by a separate action after baptism. When Philip the Evangelist had baptized the Samaritan converts, St. Peter and St. John went down from Jerusalem to Samaria to impart to them the Holy Ghost by the laying on of hands, to give them what they had not received in Baptism, but what Christ promised as a baptism of the Holy Ghost and of fire.[2] Not only extraordinary and miraculous gifts were imparted by the Laying on of Hands, but powers of knowledge, faith and holiness,—power and courage to make confession, gifts of the Spirit required generally and in all ages for fulfilling the vocation and common priesthood of Christians. The gifts poured out on the little company of the first believers at Pentecost were to be imparted ordinarily to new converts by an ecclesiastical ceremony after Baptism. Whether or not it was accompanied by extraordinary gifts, was an accident, and as the miraculous signs Christ specially promised to believers afterwards ceased, without prejudice to faith or involving any inference that it was feeble or unreal, so, too, were the miraculous gifts at laying on of hands able and sure to cease, while the essential inward operation of enlightenment and strengthening remained.

The doctrine of Laying on of Hands is numbered in the Epistle to the Hebrews among the elementary and chief articles of the Christian religion, from which Christian life begins and which the believer finds at his entrance on the very threshold of the Church. Those mentioned are, repentance from dead works, faith in God, baptism, laying on of hands, resurrection from the dead, and eternal judgment.[3] The laying on of hands is the same as that spoken of in the following parallel passage as imparting the Holy Ghost. It is, therefore, a common ordinance designed for all be-

---
[1] Tit. iii. 5. 1 Pet. iii. 21. 1 John v. 8.
[2] Acts viii. 14—17; i. 5.     [3] Heb. vi. 1, 2.

lievers, having a Divine promise and meant always to endure, for else it could not belong to the first and elementary principles of Christian doctrine and life. In reference to it, St. Paul tells the Christians he addresses that they were sealed with the Holy Ghost and had His first-fruits. He calls Him the Spirit of Promise because already promised in the Old Covenant as a Gift to be bestowed alike on sons and daughters, old and young, men servants and maid servants. "On you is this promise (of the Spirit) and on your children, and on those afar off whom God shall call," St. Peter said at Pentecost.[1] The miraculous gifts which announced the presence of the Spirit were only signs and pledges of a gift afterwards recognised by faith alone, but then requiring outward manifestations to secure recognition and belief.

The other imposition of hands, whereby persons were consecrated to Ecclesiastical functions, had also the character of a means of grace. Twice in his two Epistles St. Paul reminds St. Timothy of the grace received in and through his ordination. The Apostle had himself laid hands on him, but the Presbytery had joined in the act, and he exhorts him not to neglect the grace thus conferred, but rather to stir it up by prayer and by exercising it.[2] This laying on of hands took place "by prophecy," just as the Ordination of St. Paul and St. Barnabas in Antioch was by prophetic inspiration. In the same Epistle the Apostle had referred to the earlier prophecies about St. Timothy, charging him to fight a good fight, as being conscious of them. One or more of these gifted with prophecy had designated him as called to a higher office in the Church, where his ministry would be blest, and thereupon he was dedicated to it. But the grace, or *charisma*, did not consist in the extraordinary gifts imparted by general imposition of hands to the baptized of that day; the hands of the Apostle, without the Presbytery, sufficed for that. Nor did those miraculous gifts require being "revived" or "rekindled." The prophetic choice of St. Timothy was in this case extraordinary, but the subsequent Ordination, which imparted an abiding and indwelling grace, belonged to the regular

---

[1] Eph. i. 13, 14; iv. 30. Rom. viii. 23. Joel ii. 28, 29. Acts ii. 39.
[2] 1 Tim. iv. 14. 2 Tim. i. 6, ἀναζωπυρεῖν.

order of the Church and was a grace of ministry, giving higher capacities and strength for the worthy and successful discharge of his office. So the seven at Jerusalem, who just before had shared the outpouring of the Spirit at Pentecost, had the Apostles' hands laid on them when appointed to an ecclesiastical function.

St. James in his Epistle has ordered a special means of grace for the sick in the Church. A sick man was to call for the presbyters of the Church, and they were to pray over him and anoint him with oil; God would either grant recovery or strengthen and revive him, and his sins would be forgiven.[1] This is no gift of healing, for that was not confined to the presbyters; and for that Christ prescribed not unction, but laying on of hands. Had he meant that,[2] St. James would have bidden or advised the sick to send for one who possessed the gift, whether presbyter or layman. And the sure operation of such a gift would have been in direct contradiction to a fact before the Apostle's eyes, viz., that a generation had then died off, according to natural laws, just as was the case before or afterwards. What was to be conveyed by this medium was, therefore, only sometimes recovery or relief, always consolation, revival of confidence and forgiveness of sins, on condition, of course, of faith and repentance; the form is Unction with prayer. This anointing was not for any medicinal purpose, which could not be thought of in most internal diseases, though the frequent anointing for a remedy against diseases among the Jews suggested this Christian unction as a means of grace, just as Jewish baptism and the Jewish Passover formed the ground-work for Christian baptism and the Eucharist.

The Apostolic conception of the Eucharist is laid down in the first Epistle to the Corinthians, and in that to the Hebrews. St. Paul wished to make the Corinthians understand that taking part in Gentile sacrificial feasts, and eating meat offered in sacrifice, was by no means an indifferent thing. It was the aim and effect of sacrificial feasts to

---

[1] James v. 14, 15. Once σώσει, then ἐγερεῖ αὐτὸν ὁ κύριος.
[2] Mark xvi. 18. [The *subordinate* function of the Sacrament, for bodily healing, is recognised in the rubrics and prayers of the Roman Ritual, and in the Tridentine Decrees and Catechism.

enter into real fellowship with the deity who received the sacrifice, to become a feaster with him. And although, says the Apostle, the gods of the Gentiles are dead idols, it is the demons who appropriate the sacrifices offered to them, and with whom the guests at these banquets come into fellowship. There are those, too, among the Jews who eat of the sacrifice, partakers of the altar, who are thus brought into communion with God by the altar and by virtue of the Covenant. But the Christian has his own sacrificial feast, where the bread is the communion of the Body of Christ, and the chalice the communion of His Blood; and so, by at once eating the flesh of Gentile sacrifices and partaking the bread and chalice of the Eucharist, he would enter, on the one hand, into communion with demons, on the other, into the communion of the Body and Blood of Christ, which were an abomination. This fellowship with demons would also be an offence against the unity of the body of Christ, an attempt to rend it, for precisely because we all eat of the one Eucharistic bread, and so receive the Lord's Body, do we all become one body, or as St. Paul says elsewhere, we become members of His body, of His flesh and His bones.[1] We are nourished by communion with the substance of His flesh and blood, and so bound to the unity of His body—the Church; and thus what was begun in baptism is continued and perfected in the Eucharist. The office of the Second Adam to heal the corruption of the First must be discharged towards men's bodies also. The glorified flesh of Christ, with its purifying powers and blessings, is to be inwardly received by Christians, and to counter-work the flesh derived from Adam—the seat of sin and impure desires.

The abuses that had crept in at Corinth into the observance of the *agape*, which was connected with the Eucharist, led the Apostle to speak again more particularly in the same Epistle of the institution and meaning of that sacrament.[2] He says that the Lord's death is proclaimed by its celebration. As the celebration of the Paschal sacrifice was a continual setting forth of the deliverance from Egypt, and of the covenant between God and Israel then made, so is the Eucharistic Sacrifice the continual setting forth of the

---

[1] 1 Cor. x. 16 sqq. Eph. v. 30.   [2] 1 Cor. xi. 23—30.

death of Christ in its eternal efficacy and abiding presence. Whoever eats the Body of the Lord unworthily—by stupidly and thanklessly confounding it with common food, approaching it without that penitent and believing disposition which alone befits an observance of the Redeemer's death—sins against the Body and Blood of the Lord, and draws on himself a judgment for sacrilege, for the Lord's Body has power to bless and to punish; and at Corinth sicknesses and even death followed from an unworthy partaking of it. Among Old Testament sacrifices St. Paul brings forward the Paschal Lamb as most like the offering of Christ, being the only Jewish memorial sacrifice. Christ, he says, is slain as our Passover; and, indeed, the Lord died as the true Paschal Lamb at the exact hour of the legal Passover. In His desire to eat the Passover with His disciples yet once more, He held the feast with them in a private house, not a consecrated place, without the victim being slain in the sanctuary, and several hours before the legal time, on Thursday evening.[1] Here was already a separation from the communion of the observers of the Law, which was all the more natural, as immediately after eating the Passover He ordained with bread and wine His own New Testament and Paschal sacrifice, whereby He substituted fulfilment for type, substance for shadow, and gave the flesh and blood of the Divine Lamb in a form that could be eaten.

The Old Covenant, with the Paschal sacrifice, pledged to Israel immunity from the Plagues of Egypt, deliverance from bondage, and entrance into the Promised Land; the New Covenant, with its new sacrifice abrogating and replacing the whole temple service, pledged and secured redemption from sin and its consequences, and the sacrifice bestowed on the believer all which the various Mosaic sacrifices, sin-offerings, burnt-offerings, peace-offerings and thank-offerings, typified. Thus was the prophecy of Malachi fulfilled; this was the pure oblation, the *Mincha* which was to be offered to the Name of the Lord everywhere, from the rising to the setting sun. And that other prophecy was also fulfilled, that God would receive no more offerings from the hands of the Levitical priesthood, that He would create

---
[1] Luke xxii. 15.

a purer and better priesthood, a new priestly race succeeding by spiritual not bodily descent, and would purify the sons of Levi, as gold and silver, to bring an offering to Him in righteousness—a prophecy and promise immediately connected with that of John the Baptist's mission and of the Lord coming to His temple.[1]

The Lord Himself, in the Sermon on the Mount, which comprehended the moral substance of His teaching for all time, had brought out in His precept about reconciliation with enemies the permanent existence of an altar, and therefore a sacrifice, in His Church. "If thou bringest thy gift to the altar, and there rememberest that thy brother hath aught against thee, leave there thy gift before the altar, go and first be reconciled to thy brother, and then come and offer thy gift."[2] He did not mean to give the Jews a new command, not found in the Mosaic Law, for the few years their sacrifices were to continue; but to impart by anticipation an unchangeable law and instruction to His Church on the necessary and indissoluble connexion between Christian brotherly love and the Eucharistic Sacrifice, as celebrating the brightest act of divine love. At the moment when the Christian is commemorating the love and mercy of God, he should above all display those qualities towards others.

When the Apostles treat of the sacrifice of Christ, their point of departure is, that He began on His entrance into the world to offer His Person for the salvation of men, that He continued and recapitulated the offering in the institution of the Eucharist and in His Passion on the following day, and consummated it in His resurrection and glorification. The leading idea of the Epistle to the Hebrews is that Christ continues His priestly office in the heavenly sanctuary, in His state of eternal glory. He has died once, and can die no more, but His self-oblation is no passing event, but abiding and imperishable. His priesthood and sacrifice endure as long as His Incarnation. "He is a Priest for ever," and therefore brings a continual offering; He has entered the heavenly sanctuary with His own blood, and stands evermore before God as our High Priest and Sacrifice; but the sacrifice He offers is still the same which

---

[1] Mal. i. 11; iii. 1—4.  [2] Matt. v. 23, 24.

has reconciled all, and "perfected for ever them that are being sanctified."[1] In Him sacrifice and redemption meet, for by His offering He has wrought redemption for the whole human race, from the beginning to the last man who shall be born on earth. But the work is not yet finished in individuals; their redemption and sanctification is an advancing process and living continuation in the Church of the act done on the Cross, for all Christ does for men is by virtue of His sacrifice, whose fruits He applies separately to each believer.

Christ died on the Cross as the Great Sin-offering to restore the broken communion between man and God. In that supreme act of self-denying love, the surrender of His Person and life, He showed the world the true meaning of sacrifice, the nature and end of all sacrificial worship. All Heathen and Jewish sacrifices were thereby abrogated; the offering of all alien and remote material borrowed from the animal kingdom, which is given over to man for use, was set aside. Man could not but bring such offerings before, as shadows, substitutes and types of the one true and availing sacrifice, while the partition wall of sin still stood between him and God, and the Divine Mediator, whose Person was the true oblation, had not yet appeared. But thenceforth, when God had bestowed His highest and noblest Gift, there could be but one offering, which enabled, nay obliged, men to give all to God without division, mingling, reserve or limit of devotion, for the measure of their obligations is the measure of His gifts.

As heaven and earth are one kingdom of God, the heavenly and earthly Church are one coherent, indivisible whole. The earthly Church is the ante-chamber of the heavenly, and the heavenly stretches into it; prayer and its answer, sacrifice and its acceptance, ascend and descend, the earthly corn-fields ripen for the harvest of the Church above. Christ is the High Priest of both portions of the One Church. He has entered, as it is said, into the heavenly sanctuary, with His own blood, as the Mediator of good things to come, the High Priest of an everlasting order; and there St. John saw him in the midst of the

---

[1] Heb. vii. 3; ix. 12; x. 14.

throne, as the Lamb that had been slain and bore the marks of His death.[1]

"We have an altar, of which they that serve the tabernacle have no right to eat."[2] This is said, to make the Hebrew converts understand the perversity and uselessness of trusting to the Levitical sacrifices, and the wide difference and great superiority of the Christian priesthood and sacrifice. The Jews are forbidden by their law to taste of the sin-offering brought on the day of atonement, but we Christians have a new sacrifice and a feast attached to it. Thus altar is compared with altar, sacrifice with sacrifice, the Christian communion attached to the new sin-offering with its absence among the Jews.

The prerogatives of the priesthood and offering of Christ are contrasted by the writer with the defectiveness of the Levitical and Aaronic priesthood. While the Jewish High Priest presents an offering vain and perishable in its own nature, the blood of animals which cannot really cleanse men's souls or be pleasing to God, an offering which needs constant repetition, Christ has offered a higher and more availing sacrifice, and administers a nobler priesthood. He offers blood which is intimately allied to our own and therefore pleads for us before God with power, for it is His own blood, that of the new, everlasting Covenant. With that He has entered into heaven, the true sanctuary, the house of God, which He has built and rules. Thenceforth His priestly function is discharged in heaven, and is therefore exalted above the priesthood and sacrifices of the Law, with

---

[1] Heb. ix. 11, 12, 24; vi. 20. Apoc. v. 6.

[2] Heb. xiii. 10. The altar to be eaten from is explained by Commentators outside the Church, even the most recent (Bleek, de Wette, Lüneman, Delitzch) of the Cross, while Tholuck in despair thinks nothing in particular is meant. If it is incredible in itself that the writer should have obtruded on the Hebrews this notion of eating from the Cross, which could only be realised through several intermediate links, without any explanation, we may add that all through the Epistle, and where the sacrifice of Christ is expressly discussed, the Cross is not once named, nor is it anywhere in the New Testament called an altar, though holding such a position in the eye of faith. How, then, could the reader here have understood the long buried Cross by "we have an altar to be eaten from?" (*i.e.*, what is both altar and table of sacrificial feast). It is precisely the close connection of the Eucharistic action with the heavenly oblation and its dependence on it that is here insisted upon, as throughout the Epistle the reader's eye is directed, not to the Cross, but to the heavenly sanctuary as the place of priestly ministration. Why could not the servants of the Jewish tabernacle eat of the Christian altar? Because the thing there eaten is the Sacrifice of Christ, and He is the Minister of the true tabernacle, not built by men's hands but by God. (Heb. viii. 2). It is altar against altar, tabernacle against tabernacle, one sacrificial feast against another.

their earthly and typical sanctuary. His blood has a real power to cleanse and sanctify, and the offering of His death and passion could be made but once, for in its eternal and all-sufficient perfection it cleanses all. All sins are taken away by one offering, which in its power and inexhaustible efficacy can bring all to perfection and beatitude, which has opened to us a new way of access to God and imparts to us the gifts of the Holy Ghost, the blessedness of the world to come, and the inheritance of heaven.[1]

The Levitical priesthood, therefore, is not abolished, but only changed and committed to other hands. Christ, the Lamb, offers Himself continually on that heavenly altar; He is the Priest for evermore, who has wrought the reconciliation of the human race, and the Victim who applies to us in the fulness of His gifts the fruit of the reconciliation He has won. And here the Church on earth was not to be poorer than the Church in heaven. Therefore, on the eve of His Passion He ordained in His Church the offering of His Body and Blood, whereof He would here as there be Himself the Priest, only that here both priesthood and sacrifice, in accordance with the present order and economy of faith, are veiled from the eyes of men, His Body concealed under the form of earthly nourishment, His priestly act under the ministry of men called by the Church to represent Him.

As the Church was founded by the Incarnation of the Word and His dwelling among men, so is her continuance, her constant blossoming and increase on earth, dependent on the abiding Presence of His living Body in her midst, hidden, indeed, but indicated and pledged by sensible signs. But where He is present, there He is and must be continually offering Himself and discharging by that oblation His office as our Intercessor;[2] so that on the earthly altar of the Church is the same presence and the same performance as in the heavenly sanctuary, here concealed on the altar from the believer's gaze, there unveiled. For since the Incarnation unites the Son for ever indivisibly to man's nature, His sacrifice is also everlasting. God and Man for ever, with a true though glorified body which has suffered and died, He is Victim and Priest for ever, High Priest and Minister of

[1] See Heb. *passim.*   [2] Heb. vii. 24.

the sanctuary, sitting on the right hand of the throne of Majesty.[1] In this unbroken celebration His death once suffered, over whom death hath no more power, is but a single moment, a moment that lives in the commemoration of the past but ever-energizing fact; and thus the sacrificial rite of the earthly Church represents and typifies that act of love of which it is the appointed memorial.

Christ has become Man, that He may gradually draw mankind to Himself in His exalted and glorified state. His words, "I in My Father, and ye in Me, and I in you," He Himself explained by ordaining His sacrifice, and St. Paul by saying that He has made the Church His body and Himself its Head.[2] All types of the Old Covenant were to be abundantly fulfilled in Him in the perfect satisfaction of all our wants and in a manner transcending all our hopes. If the Jewish sacrificial feasts expressed the need and desire for drawing nigh to God and holding communion with Him, the Eucharist is the means for realising the closest fellowship and union possible for men on earth, while it has also enabled us to present continually to God the sole worthy oblation. As, then, the flesh of the Jewish peace-offering had first to be prepared by fire for eating, so has His flesh and blood been made capable of being received under the form of bread and wine; and He has thereby given us the noblest and most powerful thing we could receive, that by tasting and partaking of His mind we may be united with Him and offer the One great Sacrifice alone acceptable to God. God will not receive Christ from us without ourselves, nor ourselves without Christ. Only that oblation where the self-sacrifice of Christ and His members is united, is pleasing to Him, and befits the disciples of the Crucified.

The Eucharistic offering of the Church is a recapitulation and summary of the whole Christian religion. As our Brother and our Head, our Redeemer and High Priest, our Food and our Victim, Christ is here present and energizes in us and for us. "He that eateth My flesh and drinketh My blood, abideth in Me, and I in him."[3] The Apostle describes all individual Christians and Christian communities of the world as one bread and one body, for the

---

[1] Heb. viii. 1, 2; xii. 2.   [2] John xii. 32; xiv. 20. Eph. i. 22, 23.
[3] John vi. 56.

Eucharistic bread, under which the Lord's Body is veiled, makes the many into one body;[1] and thus the Church as the body of the Lord, fed with His substance and joined with Him, is offered to God together with His natural body, and the Eucharistic sacrifice is the product of this unity of the Head and members, and the means through communion of upholding, nourishing and strengthening it.

Thus the offering of Christ in the Church is both peace-offering and thank-offering; it contains all which was wanting to the oblation of the Cross. As in the Old Covenant the peace-offering was not only allowed but commanded to be eaten of, so now is communion added as a sign of peace and reconciliation wrought, as the consummation and seal of the sacrifice. The event which actually took place on Calvary was hidden from the comprehension of men; the offering was dishonoured, without partakers, without public testimony to its dignity and power. But in the Church it is the object of unceasing veneration, the centre of her worship and her solemnities. It is as well a sin-offering as an offering of memorial and thanksgiving, for He who wrought the great reconciliation is present here in His quality as Sin-offering, and the memorial of His accomplished atonement, celebrated by those who need constantly fresh forgiveness, is necessarily a constant renewal of the reconciliation. In offering Christ to the Father as her sin-offering, the Church is but imploring Him in the most effectual way to grant to believers pardon and power over sin by cleansing and strengthening their will, directed to Christ and joined with His, through Him our Mediator and Intercessor, and in virtue of His atoning death once suffered on the Cross. In so far as the general reconciliation has once for all been accomplished, mankind restored to its true relations with God, and the way of access to Him again laid open, in this sense all was accomplished by the sacrifice on Calvary, and the sacrifice of the Church can claim no similar end or significance, for it neither is or can be a supplement or repetition of the offering on the Cross. But in all that concerns the individualizing, applying and imparting the blessings and gifts of God there won, and inasmuch as constant forgiveness is not the

[1] 1 Cor. x. 17.

least of those gifts, so far the Church's sacrificial celebration has the meaning and power of an atoning sacrifice.

The author of the Epistle to the Hebrews repeatedly asserts, that Christ has offered Himself but once, and needs not to offer Himself often.[1] In fact His sacrifice can neither be supplemented by another—for it would then appear inadequate—nor be repeated, for it would then lose its unity and sink to the level of the sacrifices of the Mosaic Law. But Jesus has an eternal priesthood, not as a mere titular dignity with no corresponding function, but as being engaged in an abiding act of sacrifice; and the Church's offering is a solemn participation in that abiding act, the earthly reproduction and representation of the sacrifice proceeding in "the tabernacle not made with hands."[2] It is a single service both here and there, a service wherein living Christians take part in the worship of the Blessed. Both here and there, as once on Calvary, is the same Priest, the same Victim, the same one immolation; there was the Cross, an altar in the eyes of the denizens of heaven, here is the altar, one with the Cross in the eyes of earthly believers, and He is present on it in that quality of a hidden Victim now inseparable from His Body. How, indeed, could that showing forth and celebration of His sacrificial death, wherein He who died and is now glorified is Himself present, be anything else but a sacrifice, in which the Lord's Body is held up before the Father in heaven as an offering of atonement and thanksgiving under the symbols of His Passion and outpoured blood, given and received in communion as a token of peace and reconciliation? To celebrate without sacrifice the sacrifice of His death, one must violently exclude His humanity, believed to be there present, from its essential relation to God. To the true believer it is simply impossible not to offer Christ, whom he knows to be bodily present on the altar, to God, or not to unite himself in very deed with the act of intercession even now proceeding in the Church above, to be content with a mere retrospective glance at the sacrifice accomplished more than a thousand years ago.

Thus the Christian Sacrifice is at once permanent and single; its unity does not contradict its duration, nor its

[1] Heb. ix. 25—28.     [2] Heb. vi. 20; viii. 4; ix. 11.

duration prevent its being ever one and indivisible. The offering of that sacrifice is, indeed, divided into numberless acts, according to the conditions of time and space in our earthly life, but they are brought into unity and held together through the Person of Christ, with whom and in whom His ministers do all their acts. It is precisely in this multiplicity of the oblation, whereby the One everliving Victim is offered and the sacrifice of the Cross constantly applied anew in its effects to the whole body and its individual members, that the perfection and indissoluble power of that sacrifice reveals itself. To the Christian's retrospective glance the multitude of sacrificial acts on the altars of the Church at once take their place as dependent on that one heavenly offering, which again depends on that of the Cross as one single celebration of sacrifice. "For Jesus is entered into heaven itself, now to appear for us before the presence of God."[1] No new immolation takes place; only that once made on Calvary is exhibited to the Christian people in a symbolic act, sensibly representing the separation of body and blood in death. The Cross has grown into a living Tree, ever green and ever fruitful, under whose shadow the Church of all times and all places finds rest.

[1] Heb. ix. 24.

# CHAPTER IV.

### THE LAST THINGS, AND THE FUTURE OF THE WORLD AND THE CHURCH.

SINCE the time when the seed of death entered with sin into man's nature, and the body of every one, however spiritually minded, became dead or mortal on account of sin, the universal law of death has shown itself a benefit, though it be the wages and the penalty of sin. To die is to lay aside a heavy garment, to leave a fragile shell, the going forth of the soul from the earthly house it dwelt in. For death, as man's enemy, is overcome; Christ has destroyed its power, and made it but a passage from life to life, an entrance for His own on the inheritance prepared for them.[1] They, if they have alike in life and in death preserved their fellowship with His death, and have willingly accepted death in whatever form it comes upon them, are set free from strife with the world and earthly sufferings; they rest from their labours, and are ripening for perfection through the renovation of the whole man, and his intimate union with his Lord.[2] "It is appointed for men once to die, but, after that, judgment."[3] Human life, then, cannot be repeated, as in the Pythagorean scheme, in another body. The course is finished with death, and man's lot determined according to his relations with Christ.

The happiness to which Christ introduces His own is described as an exceeding great glory, yet suited to the nature and deepest needs of man.[4] It is eternal life, there-

---

[1] Rom. viii. 10.   2 Cor. v. 1—4.   2 Tim. i. 10.
[2] Matt. x. 38, 39.   Apoc. vii. 15, 16; xiv. 13.
[3] Heb. ix. 27.   [4] 2 Cor. iv. 17.   John vi. 35.

fore energy. In the Apocalypse, the Blessed in heaven are before God's throne, and serve him without interruption; they feel neither hunger, thirst, nor heat; the Lamb feeds them, guides them, and dries their tears. Gathered from all times and all nations, they form one heavenly choir united to God and the Son of Man, and serve Him day and night in their priestly ministry of praise and adoration.[1] They share the glory and even the dominion of Christ, and rejoice in a knowledge that is ever growing. "We shall be like God, for we shall see Him as He is;" in the bold language of St. Paul, "we shall know as we are known"— by God; but this must be taken with a limitation, for even in that kingdom the knowledge of the Blessed cannot bridge over the infinite chasm which divides the creature from the Creator.[2]

The Apostle points to the antithesis between the knowledge of the Blessed, and the piecemeal, fragmentary, limited range of man's knowledge here.[3] As yet we see the highest things as it were in a dark mirror; here only mystical symbols are shown us, there our knowledge will be an intuition commensurate in kind, though not in degree, with the Divine knowledge, a seeing face to face. The Blessed will there be like the Angels, even in their manner of perception, and when our Lord tells us that there is joy in heaven over one converted sinner, this indicates an acquaintance with what passes on earth among the inhabitants of heaven.[4] And as the gift of prophecy in the Apostolic age often included a knowledge of the spiritual state of individuals, that is true in a higher degree of the Blessed, for here, St. Paul says, "we know and prophesy in part," but there, where the veil is removed and we see all in the light of God, "what is partial shall be done away."[5] In the Revelation of St. John, the souls of the Martyrs under the heavenly altar know the condition of the Church on earth, they pray that their blood may be avenged and the sufferings of the Church be ended; and it is said to them, that

---

[1] Apoc. vii. 15—17.
[2] Rom. v. 17. 2 Tim. ii. 12. 1 John iii. 2. 1 Cor. xiii. 12.
[3] 1 Cor. xiii. 9—12.
[4] Matt. xxii. 30. Luke xv. 7.   [5] 1 Cor. xiv. 25; xiii. 9, 10.

the time is not yet come, that the number of their brethren must first be fulfilled.[1]

The first condition of seeing God is perfect purity, and thereby likeness to God. "We know," St. John says, "that when Christ appeareth, we shall be like Him, for we shall see Him as He is." And, from the promise of seeing God, he infers a purity which can really be called a likeness to God; "Every man who hath this hope purifieth himself, as He is pure."[2] And as in this life the measure of our sanctification and purity is the measure of our likeness to God, the sight of Him in Paradise, "as He is," requires perfect purity, for "there is no fellowship between light and darkness," nothing of human impurity shall enter His kingdom, and "without holiness no man shall see the Lord."[3] Therefore, neither secret nor open, habitual or actual evil, may cleave to the soul; so long as it retains any moral defect, any vestige of sin and its consequences, it cannot really attain to the beatific vision of God, and, if the cleansing process is not completed in this life, it must be carried on in the interval between death and resurrection. God disciplines us that we may partake of His holiness, and "whom He loveth He chastiseth," so long as the soul requires this means of purification.[4] These purifying chastisements are expressly declared to be signs of His favour, but since the roots of evil implanted by separate sins in the soul must be rooted out, they cannot in our human state be other than painful. This is implied in the very condition of the soul when unclothed by death of its bodily integument, for, as its powers of sensation were partly deadened and laid to sleep under the weight of an earthly and material body, they are greatly excited and intensified when those bands are relaxed. Even that inalienable self-knowledge which yet is so little realised in this life, but to which the soul will gradually wake in the next—the knowing ourselves as God knows us, the soul's mere perception and consciousness of its indwelling evil and impurity and its defective goodness—will in that state of elevated sensibility be a painful but purifying suffering.

The Apostle says that, at the name of Jesus, not only all

---

[1] Apoc. vi. 10, 11. [2] 1 John iii. 2, 3.
[3] 2 Cor. vi. 14. Apoc. xxi. 27. Heb. xii. 14. [4] Heb. xii. 10, 6.

in heaven and on earth but also those under the earth, the dead in Hades, shall bend their knees in adoration. They will thankfully worship Him as their Redeemer, for only by virtue of His blood poured out for men is their cleansing in that state fulfilled; it is the blood of Christ which cleanses us from all sin. St. Paul, therefore, speaks of the work the Lord has begun in believers being carried on, not only till death, but after death, till "the day of Christ"—that is, the last great and decisive judgment—thus implying a salutary process in the interval, which can only be a continuation of cleansing. And Christ Himself, with unmistakable reference to that interval after death, spoke of a prison whence men should not be released till they had paid their whole debt to the uttermost farthing. He said, that the sin against the Holy Ghost should be forgiven neither in this life nor in the life to come.[1] There is, then, a forgiveness in the other life, and multitudes enter it in a condition that needs forgiveness; for complete remission, or removal of all consequences of sin, involves its entire ejection from the soul and a complete purification.

This condition of man is locally designated Hades, a word corresponding in the Apostolic writings to the Old Testament *Scheol*, and expressing generally the place and condition of men before the resurrection and universal judgment.[2] In the Apocalypse, death and Hades are always distinguished; Christ has power over both; the sea, death and Hades give up the dead that are in them at the last judgment, and finally death and Hades are cast into the lake of fire, which means that, when death is destroyed, the kingdom of the dead shall have an end, partly swallowed up in heaven, partly in hell.[3] In this Hades or intermediate state there was what St. Peter calls a preaching of the Gospel to the dead of earlier generations there reserved. During the three days' interval between His death and resurrection Christ went there, while His body lay in the grave, and preached to those who of old disbelieved and perished in the Flood the glad tidings of redemption. But St. Peter says, again, quite generally, that the Gospel was preached to the

---

[1] Phil. ii. 10; i. 6. 1 John i. 7. Matt. xviii. 34; v. 26; xii. 32.
[2] Acts ii. 27. 1 Cor. xv. 55.
[3] Apoc. i. 18; vi. 8; xxii. 13, 14; 1 Pet. iii. 19; iv. 6. Heb. xi. 39. 40.

dead, "that they may be judged according to men in the flesh," (having incurred bodily death as a common punishment) "but may live according to God in the Spirit." The victims of the Flood, therefore, are only quoted as an example. With this agrees the statement in the Epistle to the Hebrews that the believers of the Old Covenant were not to be perfected without those of the New, inasmuch as Christ's atoning death, and His appearance, for which they were waiting, is the decisive moment of their being made perfect.

Christ said, "In My Father's house are many mansions."[1] That points to the great variety in those regions, the separate divisions in the great heavenly home according to the moral state and development of those received into it. Under figures borrowed from earthly things there is distinguished in the "heavenly Jerusalem" the City of the Living God, a most holy place where is the throne of God, or full revelation of the Trinity and manifestation of Divine glory, and a holy place, or heaven, where the Angels and Saints dwell.[2] But elsewhere, when the state and dwelling of the Blessed is spoken of, especially with St. Paul, local ideas fall in the background. He rather makes heaven a different manner of existence suited to spiritual bodies than a different place, the condition of being in God's presence.[3] Heaven and earth, in the theological sense of the terms, are not so removed from each other that heaven is to be looked for somewhere in universal space, but rather do heavenly powers surround and penetrate the earthly domain, and Christ, even when on earth, could be living in heaven.[4]

As the Church is both visible and invisible, having a home in two worlds, and as Christ her Head is in both of them, so are the members of both united together. Their union is not dissolved because some have already entered that glorious and spotless Church, the inner Temple whereof this is the outer Court. St. Paul says that all members of Christ's body should care for one another, that if one suffers all should suffer with it, and if one is glorified all rejoice with it.[5] There is a real communion of living and departed

---

[1] John xiv. 2.
[2] Heb. xii. 22; ix. 12. Apoc. xi. 19; xiv. 17; xv. 5; iv. 5.
[3] Eph. i. 3; ii. 6. 2 Cor. v. 1, 6, 8.  [4] John iii. 13.  [5] 1 Cor. xii. 25, 26.

Christians through Christ, to whose body both alike belong, nor can we doubt that the Blessed who see God, as being members of Christ's body, share His knowledge of the Church militant on earth so far as He is pleased to impart it to them. They accordingly take part by their prayers in His great work and the accomplishment of His judgments on earth. The Apostles and Prophets in heaven rejoice over the fall of Babylon. Christ declared the conversion of one single sinner to be a feast of joy in heaven, and the four and twenty Elders are said to present the prayers of the Saints in golden vials before God.[1] If love is the highest of earthly powers, and survives when faith and hope are extinguished, and the Saints are like minded with Christ towards their earthly brethren, it cannot but be that by interceding for us they should conform to the pattern of their Head, our great High Priest and Intercessor.

Meanwhile the brotherly love of the living, which reaches beyond the grave, must take the form of intercession for the departed. St. Paul himself gives an example of such a prayer. The Ephesian Onesiphorus, mentioned in his second Epistle to St. Timothy, was clearly no longer among the living. St. Paul praises this man for his constant service to him but does not, as elsewhere, send salutations to him, but only to his family; for him he desires a blessing from the Lord, and prays for him that the Lord will grant he may find mercy with Christ at the day of judgment.[2]

Between death and the resurrection the soul is in a disembodied or naked state, as compared with its present existence, whereof the Apostle feels a horror, though he elsewhere speaks of the believer longing for redemption from this "body of death," in which the law of sin rules and which is so often felt as a weight pressing down the spirit. But "we know that if our earthly house of this tabernacle be dissolved, we have a building of God, a house not made with hands, eternal in the heavens," and we long, instead of the unclothing of our soul by death, to partake of that overclothing where the mortal is swallowed up by life.[3] But that will only be their lot who live to see the Second Coming of Christ, who will then suddenly have

---
[1] 1 Cor. xii. 25, 26. Apoc. vi. 10, 11; xviii. 20; xix. 1—4; v. 8. Luke xv. 7.
[2] 2 Tim. i. 16—18; iv. 19. [3] Rom. vii. 24. 2 Cor. v. 1—4.

their bodies changed and be clothed upon, as it were, or transfigured; they will put on their new and heavenly dress without the former being destroyed by death, which implies their having then a corresponding place to dwell in. But that nakedness of the soul, when separated by death from its earthly body, is not to be conceived of as a purely spiritual existence without any corporal substratum or organ. The twofold personality wherein man is created, the continuity of his consciousness, and the bodily or organic power which substantially inhabits the soul, all this necessarily leads to the notion that the soul, though it has no body of its own, has some covering in place of one; that it does not lack that bodily organ, without which no receptivity of influences, no manifestation or energy can be conceived, even in the intermediate state before the resurrection. And from this organ as its germ the new and immortal body will be developed at the resurrection. For St. Paul illustrates the doctrine of the resurrection by the figure of a seed-corn putrefying in the earth and thereby ripening to living fruit, where there is the same continuity as in man's body.[1] While, then, we must believe that the soul remains in continual relation with its body which is undergoing constant change and is nourished and interpenetrated by Christ's body, and that this relation supplies a continual bodily power, yet, in the middle state before the resurrection, the psychical side of existence predominates, and thus in the Apocalypse only the *souls* of the risen are spoken of.

Very different from Hades is Gehenna, the "fiery furnace" or "bottomless pit," the proper Hell or place of the reprobate.[2] The word signified, first, that valley of Hinnom or Tophet, desecrated by the abominations of idolatry and therefore purposely defiled by Josiah, where Israel had offered children to Moloch, and where afterwards malefactors' corpses were burnt and a fire constantly smouldering in the place consumed the filth and abominations of all kinds cast into it.[3] In the time of Christ it had become the popular expression for the place of punishment of the condemned; and He said of the dwellers in Gehenna, in words borrowed from Isaiah, that their worm dieth not,

---

[1] 1 Cor. xv. 35 sqq.      [2] Matt. xiii. 50. Apoc. ix. 1. Luke viii. 31.
[3] 4 [R. V. 2.] Kings xxiii. 10. Jerem. vii. 31; xix. 6; xxxii. 35.

and their fire is not quenched.[1] Here and elsewhere, the lot of the condemned is symbolically described as a being cast into the outer darkness, as a second and eternal death, an ever-dying life: St. Paul calls it destruction from the presence of the Lord, and ever-abiding corruption.[2] These and other intimations show the condition of those who are irreclaimable, and therefore shut out from the Blessed, to be an abiding consciousness of having missed the end of life, a loss of all the heart before clung to; it is an absolute powerlessness and want of all energy, because the powers of life are withdrawn, and the will is now empty and unfruitful and only fixed on evil; the constant burning of unsatisfied passions, and the gnawing pain of a conscience which cannot again be laid to sleep. The outward sphere of this internal misery is Gehenna, and even material nature, in the dregs and stagnant pool left as the precipitate of the process of regeneration, supplies its place and substance.

The doctrine of the resurrection of the dead was a distinguishing and fundamental doctrine of the Apostles, and to acknowledge it was a mark of a disciple of Jesus. St. Paul concludes, that if there was no resurrection Christ could not be raised, and then the preaching of the Apostles and their faith were in vain; they would be false witnesses.[3] Christ is thus the Pledge of our future renovation, His resurrection the assurance and the seal of ours, for He rose as the Head of His body—the Church. He is but the First-fruits of them that sleep;[4] as He had power to take up again His bodily life, so, too, can He bestow glorified bodies on us; and He has actually shown by His deeds—by raising some dead persons, by calling out Lazarus when already given over to corruption from the grave—that He has both the will and power, as Conqueror of death, to break its dominion over man and force it to give up its prey.[5] And, since it is sin which wrought bodily death, the final annihilation of death and restitution of our decom-

---
[1] Mark ix. 43, 44. Cf. Isa. lxvi. 24.
[2] Matt. viii. 12; xxii. 13. Apoc. xxi. 8. 2 Thess. i. 9. Cf. Gal. vi. 8. 2 Pet. iii. 7. Jude 7.
[3] 1 Cor. xv. 13, 14.
[4] 1 Cor. xv. 20 sqq.; vi. 14. Phil. iii. 10. 1 Thess. iv. 14. Eph. ii. 5; i. 22. Col. i. 18.
[5] Heb. ii. 14.

posed bodies belongs to the integrity of His redeeming work. Thence He is called the First-begotten from the dead, who shall be followed by many brethren.[1]

By Christ's resurrection we are certainly assured that we, too, shall rise in like manner with a spiritual body like His—strong, glorious, incorruptible. For as in our earthly body, subject to corruption, dishonour and shame, we are like the first Adam and united to him, so shall we be in our glorified body like the Second Adam, and shall bear His image. There is only this difference that Christ did not first lay aside the veil of His natural body or need to sow the corruptible, but changed His mortal for a glorified body immediately. Flesh and blood, says the Apostle, cannot inherit the kingdom of God, nor the corruptible attain to incorruption. The body formed of gross and animal matter is perishable and destined to pass away, and in the future spiritual body shall be no "flesh and blood."[2]

It follows that we are to look not for a mere re-animation of the body, to be wrought by Divine Omnipotence, but a changing of it which will overcome death and corruption fully and for ever. St. Paul contrasts with the decay and feebleness of our present body, this "earthly tabernacle," the prerogatives of the "heavenly house, not made with hands" which we shall then inhabit. The renewed body will have a richer measure of unshackled living energies, will be a spiritual body, as compared to our present body composed of gross matter and pertaining to the earthly order, free from pain and suffering and from all destructive influences, and without distinctions of sex; its corporeal elements will be refined and transfigured, through communication of heavenly glory, to a body of light, fit for the conditions and destiny of life in a higher order of the world and a glorified sphere, and gifted with the power of rapidly penetrating solid matter.[3] The Apostle had before his eyes the risen body of his Lord, such as it had appeared to him, whence he says that Christ, according to His power of subjecting all things to Himself, will change our corruptible bodies to the likeness of His own glorious body.[4] The unrighteous,

---

[1] Apoc. i. 5.
[2] 1 Cor. xv. 42—50.
[3] Matt. xxii. 30. John xx. 19.
[4] Phil. iii. 21.

who will equally rise to judgment, will of course be clothed with a totally different, nay opposite, kind of body.[1]

The Lord will return to take unto Himself His own who, through faith and love, are united to Him and raised by His power to the full integrity of human nature, and to hold the judgment of the world. For the Redeemer is also the Judge of mankind. As He came the first time into the world for judgment, to separate the incurably evil and the dead from the great fellowship of life, and to overthrow the previous ruler of the world, so will He appear the last time, not veiled, indeed, in form of a servant but in the majesty of His glory, and with His appearance the present epoch of the world will close. "The Father judgeth no man, but hath given all judgment to the Son," because He is the Son of Man;[2] for as only in that capacity could He be our Redeemer, so from being made like to us in all things, sin only excepted, with human feelings and human thoughts, He is our rightful Judge. His judgment will in two senses be universal—first, as extending over the whole human race, nations and individuals, men of all climes and all ages—secondly, as embracing the whole course of each one's life, his acts and omissions, thoughts and intentions, specially the latter, for it is the motive which gives to human acts their worth or their unworthiness.[3] Concerning retribution, it is intimated that punishments will be unequal, that each will be judged according to his power and his knowledge, so far as his want of them was not wilful, and that from him who has received little will little be required.[4]

St. Paul everywhere refers to a great reconciliation of the universe at the final appearance of the Lord, when, death being overcome and creation regenerated, God shall no more be as a Stranger or an Enemy in this world, but be All in all.[5] He speaks of all being made alive in Christ, all things comprehended under one Head; and St. John says, that Christ is a Propitiation for the whole world.[6] But this does not point to any universal restitution (ἀποκα-

---

[1] John v. 29. Acts xxiv. 15.     [2] John xii. 31; v. 22, 27.
[3] 2 Cor. v. 10. Rom. ii. 16. 1 Cor. iv. 5; Matt. x. 40 sqq; vii. 21—23.
[4] Matt. xxv. 14 sqq. Luke xii. 47, 48.     [5] Col. i. 20. 1 Cor. xv. 24—28.
[6] Eph. i. 22. Phil. ii. 10, 11. 1 Cor. xv. 22. 1 John ii. 2.

τάστασις);[1] but only, on the one hand, to the universality of redemption, from which they alone are excluded who exclude themselves; on the other hand, to the harmony and perfection of God's kingdom. And when it is said in the Revelation, "There shall be no more curse"[2]—nothing which the curse of God rests upon—this only means that all evil shall be excluded from the Company of the Saints in the heavenly Jerusalem, and the punitive justice of God have no object there. For the utterances of the Lord are clear enough about the eternal fire prepared for Satan and his angels, the worm that dieth not, and the sin that shall not be forgiven in this world or the next, as besides what St. John says about the sin unto death which may not be prayed for.[3]

In the Revelation of St. John, God predicts of the perfection of the latter days, "Behold, I make all things new."[4] The whole visible world, or heaven or earth, shall be consumed and purified by fire. As unconscious nature sympathised with the fall of man, and through his sin, who was her keeper and preserver, was made subject unwillingly to "vanity" and "the bondage of corruption," and became a "groaning creature," so shall she undergo a process of cleansing through the element of fire, and partaking in the glorification of men shall be renewed and exalted to a higher state.[5] The heavenly and earthly Church shall melt into one, the earthly become heavenly and the heavenly earthly. The outward and the inward, the spiritual and the bodily, shall exist in pure untroubled harmony; the body, in its spiritual qualities and its freedom from earthly desires, shall be a perfect organ of the spirit. The whole of nature is bound up in solidarity with man, and therefore the royal priesthood of Christians which embraces all nature shall then first appear in all its brightness.

Of the fire, which will encompass the Redeemer when He comes from heaven and burn up the present fashion of the world, St. Paul says, with immediate reference to the contemporary teachers of the Gospel, but clearly also in a sense applying to all believers, that the true character of

---

[1] [The author refers to Origen's theory of the final restitution of all things.—Tr.]
[2] Apoc. xxii. 3.   [3] 1 John v. 16.   [4] Apoc. xxi. 5.
[5] 2 Pet. iii. 7—10.  Rom. viii. 20—22.

every man's work or building shall be manifested on the day of judgment by the trying and consuming fire. What any man has built (in deed or teaching) on the good foundation (faith in Christ) will either be recognised as suitable to the foundation, and will endure the cleansing fire, or will prove to be foreign matter and be consumed by the fire, as wood or stubble. The author will receive a reward, if his work endures; if not, he will forfeit it, but will himself be saved, yet so as by fire (like a man who escapes out of the fire alive, but with the loss of all his property and not unscathed by the flames).[1] Thus the Apostle represents the last burning of the world as an ordeal for accomplishing in the shortest time the cleansing of those found alive when the Lord appears, while it closes the trial of those already dead.

When all is now fulfilled, when the earthly and heavenly Church are become completely one, when every strife is extinguished by the perfect victory over all hostile powers of the world, and death, the last enemy, is overcome by the general resurrection, then the royalty of Christ ceases; for there is no longer any Church that needs a Mediator, Protector and Champion. The Son will give up to the Father the kingdom He has hitherto ruled for the Father's glory and according to His will, "that God may be all in all."[2] As Man, of common nature with those whose Head He is and who are members of His body, He will be subjected to the Father; but, as the Divine Word, He will be consubstantial with Him. Thus the glory of the Blessed will be that of their Head, and the glory of Christ will be His Father's. While it dwells in Him by virtue of His eternal generation from the Father, it will communicate itself to His human nature, and through that to His members, and thus will God be all in every being, without extinction or limitation of individuality—all, through the two radical powers of men, the intellect and will, being fixed on Him alone and satisfied by Him—all, through the Divine glory shining through their very bodies.

The prophetic portions of the Apostolic writings referring to the future fate of the Church are based on the predictions of Christ, and especially on the discourse St. Mat-

[1] 2 Thess. i. 8. 2 Pet. iii. 10. 1 Cor. iii. 12—15.     [2] 1 Cor. xv. 24—28.

thew records about the last things. The Apostles assume a knowledge of its contents in believers, and sometimes make verbal references to it. Christ had taught in many parables and sayings, that after the destruction of Jerusalem would follow a period, necessarily long, for the conversion and Christian development of the Gentiles; He had declared that "the kingdom"—the possession and use of God's kingdom on earth—hitherto entrusted to the Jews, would be taken from them and given to a ruling Heathen nation that would bring forth the true fruits of faith. He had further announced that He would return in Person, in sight of all men, and had bidden His disciples look for His coming with lively hope and constant watchfulness; adding, that the time of His coming was hidden from all, and would so continue till its accomplishment, for it was not for them to know the seasons the Father had put in His own power. There was, therefore, no sign given of His return to judgment; He would come suddenly at a time when they looked not for Him, perhaps before they expected Him, perhaps after a long time and yet unexpectedly. But He would certainly come at a time of carnal security and thoughtless levity; He had foretold in connection with His coming a series of events which would fall within the lifetime of His contemporaries, and of which the judgment hanging over Jerusalem was the centre. On its destruction the "times of the Gentiles" were to follow, and not till those times were fulfilled would His Second Coming take place.[1]

Christ had specially characterized the physical horrors and moral abominations that would precede and usher in the destruction of Jerusalem, in order to guard His followers against being seduced by false prophets, who would then appear in great numbers. He had foretold that it would be almost impossible under the circumstances to withstand their deceits, and that very many would fall away.[2] He at the same time described this judgment on Jerusalem in the symbolic language of prophecy as connected with His (invisible) presence, and bade His disciples await His coming and recognise it in that event; for the fate of the holy city was a type of the last general judgment, and this His first

---

[1] Matt. xxiv., xxv.; xxi. 43. Mark xiii. 32. Acts i. 7. Luke xxi. 24.
[2] Matt. xxiv. 5, 24.

appearing of the second at the end of the world. He said to the Jewish rulers at His trial that hereafter they would see the Son of Man come in the fulness of Divine power.[1] Thus His presence, which he called in prophetic language a coming on the clouds of heaven, would consist in the manifestation of His Divine interposition in human affairs as the exalted Protector of His Church. This they would behold, of course only with the eyes of faith, for He had already told them that they would then first see or recognise Him, when they acknowledged and honoured him as the Messiah.[2]

The Apostles had these expressions and announcements before their eyes when they spoke of the appearance or presence of the Lord. They knew that His last return to judgment at the close of the present age of the world was concealed from all, even the angels of heaven, that the day would come suddenly and unlooked for, "as a thief in the night," an expression St. Paul borrowed from the Lord. The duration of what Christ called the "times of the Gentiles" was a secret they could not look into;[3] it might end conceivably in one generation. Their Master had said, "Watch, for you know not the day or the hour," and so they said to the Churches.[4] That many of their contemporaries would live to see that first catastrophe, in which Christians were to recognise an anticipatory and typical Coming of Christ, they knew. But when would be the Second Coming and the Resurrection? Both first and second alike they named "the day," or "the appearing of the Lord." And all they could say definitely about the latter was, that it would not be foreshown by signs, that it would come as the lightning, as a thief or a snare upon all, as well the careless as the watchful.[5] It might be in a few years, or it might be after many centuries. But they were bidden to look for Him as servants for their master, virgins for the bridegroom, and the intermediate time was always regarded as the "last time," the final period of the world's history.[6] St. Peter says in one place, "the end of all things is at hand," and elsewhere, "a day with the Lord is as a thou-

---

[1] Matt. xxvi. 64.     [2] Matt. xxiii. 39.
[3] καιροὶ ἐθνῶν. Luke xxi. 24.     [4] 2 Matt. xxv. 13. Mark xiii. 35 sqq.
[5] 1 Thess. v. 2—4. 2 Pet. iii. 10. Apoc. xvi. 15.     [6] Heb. i. 2. 1 Cor. x. 11.

sand years, and a thousand years as one day," and that if He delayed His promised Coming, it was not from dilatoriness but from long-suffering love.¹ St. Paul once wished to live till His last appearing, so as not to be "unclothed" by death, but "clothed upon" by the resurrection; but later he puts before himself the martyr's bloody death, sees his course accomplished, his fight fought out, and only awaits the just reward.² St. James says, "The coming of the Lord is nigh, the Judge stands before the door," and it has been correctly observed that this is an evidence of the Epistle being composed before the destruction of Jerusalem. With St John, again, the last hour, the Coming of the Lord, is at hand; he recognises it in its signs already beginning, the entrance of Antichristian lies and false teaching.³

It was, then, a day of the Lord, a first appearing of Christ, when Jerusalem, the temple and the whole hitherto indestructible constitution of Judaism in Church and State fell, while the Christian Church, previously entangled in its bonds, attained full freedom. Therein was revealed, as in burning and shining lightning, the majesty of the glorified Son of Man.⁴ The Apostles knew that this Coming of Christ was at hand, and thence their frequent intimations of its nearness and their expressions of hope.⁵ "We see the day approach," says the Epistle to the Hebrews,—the appearances of the time were already fulfilling what Christ foretold as signs of His Coming. But when the last decisive Advent would follow, and after what interval, of that the Apostles knew nothing. They only knew and taught that it must be continually looked and watched for, and that the possibility of its taking place at once must be kept in mind. It might follow immediately on the fall of Jerusalem, or the two events might be divided by centuries, for "a thousand years with God are as one day."⁶ But the whole period between the first appearance of Messiah on earth and His Second Coming is the "last time;" the closing period of the ages of the world has begun, whether

---

¹ 1 Pet. iv. 7.  2 Pet. iii. 8, 9.   ² Phil. iii. 10.  Cf. ii. 17.  2 Tim. iv. 6 sqq.
³ James v. 8, 9.  1 John ii. 18, 19.            ⁴ Matt. xxiv. 27.
⁵ 1 Pet. iv. 7.  1 Thess. iv. 15, 17.  1 Cor. iv. 5; xi. 26.  1 Tim. vi. 14, 15.  Heb. x. 25, 37.  James v. 8.  1 John ii. 18.      ⁶ 2 Pet. iii. 10.

it be a short or a long one. "We who are alive," St. Paul says of those who shall survive to the end, which implies the possibility—but only the possibility—that he and others of his contemporaries might witness the catastrophe.[1] He says "we," by reason of that fellowship in faith which bound together all believers, the future and the yet unborn; for he only knew that the time was hidden in impenetrable darkness from all, even the most enlightened, and would come upon all, even those who were watching, suddenly and unexpectedly, because with no signs to announce it. Elsewhere he expects and desires to be dissolved soon. Christ Himself, on whose statements all the Apostles say about His Coming, the judgment, and the end of the world, is based, has declared that the Gospel should first be preached to all nations. And St. Paul expected, after the Heathen had been evangelized, the conversion of the unbelieving Jews. But whether these two events would be realised in a longer or a shorter time was shrouded from the Apostles' view, and they saw everything, as it were, foreshortened in the future of the world and of the Church, the immediate approach of the beginning of the end. "The day of the Lord cometh as a thief in the night," and the Apostles and first believers only saw as men see by night, when the mere outlines of objects are perceived, not their relative distance. At the end of the Apostolic age, in the Apocalypse, Christians had for the first time a clearer insight given them into the details of the future and the Divine counsels; but even there it is but an account under various forms of the Coming of the Judge. At the opening of the first seal St. John sees the Lord going forth to victory, at the end He goes forth again from heaven to subdue His enemies.[2]

Christ gave as a principal sign of the approaching judgment on Jerusalem the appearance of pretended prophets and false Messiahs; they were to exercise by their magical signs and wonders a power of delusion which only the elect could withstand. When St. Paul took leave of the Churches in Asia Minor, he judged, from what he saw there, that such false teachers and ravening wolves would speedily break into the Church from without, and arise within its own bosom.[3] He described them more exactly in his Epistle to

[1] 1 Thess. iv. 15, 17.   [2] Apoc. vi. 2; xix. 11 sqq.   [3] Acts xx. 29, 30.

Timothy; and St. John, who saw them in full action with their strong delusions, recognised therein the sign of "the last hour," given by Christ. "You have heard," he said, "that Antichrist will come, your expectation is already fulfilled, the spirit of Antichrist is in the world, and many have already disclosed themselves as children of that spirit. The spirit of Antichrist is that heresy planted and fostered from the beginning by great lies, which denies that Jesus is the Christ, the promised Messiah, or Docetically deprives him of His human nature."[1] As yet believers had only been told in general to expect the appearance of an opponent or rival of Christ; the Apostle gives concrete shape to that notion or expectation, by repeatedly declaring that the new heretics who denied the God-Man, and thus laid their hands on the very foundation of faith, were not merely fore-runners of a future Antichrist, but the incarnation of the Antichristian spirit already in the world, the impersonation of the principle; every one of them was in the proper sense of the term an Antichrist. This designation is not used by the other Apostles. St. John is the only one who employs it, and that five times, clearly to characterize a heresy that denies the Person and dignity of Christ as God and Man. Antichristianism with him is a simple lie, the spirit of Antichrist is the spirit of lying and deceit; they are false prophets and tools of Satan, the father of lies, who, led by that spirit, rob Christians of the truth and of their blessing, by denying that Christ has come in the flesh.[2] He distinguishes the one Antichrist, of whose coming believers had heard, from the many already come; but the latter are closely related to the former, it is his spirit that works in them and is manifested by them.[3] It is quite conceivable, however, that the Apostle expected a chief Antichrist to go before the personal coming of the Lord, who should successfully disseminate far and wide a false teaching, denying and removing the cardinal doctrines of Christianity; but only the general idea of such a "theological" antagonist of Christ can have floated before his mind.

In the Apocalypse is found neither name nor thing.

---

[1] 2 Tim. iii. 1 sqq.   1 John ii. 18, 22; iv. 3, 4.   2 John 7.
[2] 1 John iv. 6; vi. 26; 2 John 7.   [3] 1 John iv. 3.

The beast St. John saw coming up out of the sea is the Roman Empire in its Heathen hostility to Christianity. It has a name of blasphemy on its seven heads, for in blasphemous pride it has itself worshipped, and the dragon gives it power and dominion to serve as the instrument of his fury.[1] The other beast that came up from the earth is the false prophetic system of Heathendom, as then represented by philosophers and priests, by the soothsaying and magic of conjurors and oracle-mongers. It is twice expressly named the "false prophet;"[2] it has the form of a lamb and speaks as a dragon, and deceives men by its wonder-working to worship the first beast (the Roman Empire, in the person of the Emperor and the goddess Roma), it causes images of the beast to be set up and worshipped, and all who take part in that idolatry to be marked or branded, so that none who have not the mark can buy or sell. Further on, the Antichristian Roman power is described under two forms, the beast and the harlot sitting on it.[3] The beast is the Roman Empire, and its red colour the sign of the blood it sheds, but the "great whore" is the City of Rome, where is the throne of the beast. She rules over kings, she sits on many waters, to signify her dominion over nations; she is seen in the wilderness, because of her approaching desolation. Arrayed in purple and scarlet clothing, the emblem of royal power and of the stains of Christian blood, she bears in her hand a golden cup full of abominations and filth, for she is the new Babylon, which, like the old,[4] has made kings and peoples drunk with the wine of her impure idolatry, and filled the world with her abominations. She is "drunken with the blood of the Saints and Martyrs of Jesus." But she will be laid waste and depopulated amid the lamentations of the merchants and shipmasters who served her luxury. After the city has fallen, judgment will be executed on the beast (the persecuting Empire), and its assistant, the false Prophet, as also on the inhabitants of the earth who worshipped the beast. Then follows the period of the Church's freedom and dominion indicated by a thousand years, during which the Heathen idolatry is overcome and done away, and Satan chained in the bottom-

---

[1] Apoc. xiii.  [2] Apoc. xvi. 13; xix. 20.  [3] Apoc. xvii.
[4] Jerem. li. 7.

less pit has no power to persecute the Church as before. At last he is again set free and deceives distant nations (Gog and Magog), to make a vain assault on the "beloved city," the Church, which is described as a strong kingdom or fortified city. The hostile peoples are not called Heathen, for those Satan would have no need first to deceive, and it is precisely this deceiving that is dwelt upon.[1] Neither the beast nor the false Prophet are here the deceivers, for the old Roman Heathenism is long ago extinguished, beast and prophet alike made harmless. It is another kind of deceiving, an error quite distinct from idolatry, that is alluded to. What instrument Satan could make use of is not stated, and immediately after the last deceiving and attack on the "holy City," follows the judgment of Satan and the world, and the end. There is therefore no reference to a person specially called Antichrist in the Apocalypse, nor any place for introducing him.

But in the second Epistle to the Thessalonians, St. Paul announces the speedy approach of a "Man of Sin," whom he does not himself call Antichrist, but in whom later ages have thought they saw all the characteristics of a great opponent and rival of Christ. St. Paul wanted to meet the erroneous notion that the end of all things and the day of the Lord was already come, and that the great catastrophe would immediately occur. He shows that this could not be so, because there were three events to come first, viz., a great falling away from the Church, the appearance of a mighty Antiochus, and his attempt on the temple of Jerusalem.[2] When the end would come, whether after centuries or thousands of years, he knew not; the day and hour not even angels knew. But he did know that these events must come first, and he expected them to come shortly, for he knew whose existence alone stood in the way of the approach of the "Man of Sin." What he says here about these future events, which must precede the "day of the Lord" or the last catastrophe, he drew from the announcements of Christ, the prophecy of Daniel to which Christ

---

[1] Apoc. xx. 3, 8, 10. The expression ἔθνη (vv. 3, 8) does not imply the notion of *Heathen* nations, as Düsterdieck thinks (*Offenb. Joh.* p. 548), creating thereby a difficulty on his view insoluble.
[2] 2 Thess. ii. 1—4.

referred, and from observation of certain contemporaneous events. Christ had foretold that many false prophets and false Christs would precede His coming, that they would cause many believers to fall away, through their craftiness and lying wonders, and that it would be a bitter time of oppression and persecution. He had further declared that Daniel's prediction of the abomination of desolation, or desecration, in the holy place—that is, the temple—would be fulfilled by a hostile army.[1]

St. Paul had witnessed an event fourteen years before which had undoubtedly made a profound impression on him, as on all Jews of that day. This was the order of Caligula, to set up his colossal image in the sanctuary of the temple at Jerusalem, and that henceforth it should be called the temple of Caius, the new Jupiter. The Syrian pro-consul, Petronius, at the head of a division of the army, was to superintend this erection and crush the foreseen opposition of the Jews. The whole nation was roused. They said, the Emperor must kill them all before they suffered this to be done. Philo and Josephus bear witness to the condition of things and state of feeling. Philo says, " The whole world, all cities, peoples, men and women, flattered and did homage to him, and thereby increased his inordinate pride; the Jewish people alone would take no part in the blasphemy of making a created and mortal man into an eternal God. But he would have nothing on earth, not even this one temple, left to God the Lord, that everywhere his own divinity and the gods he tolerated should alone be worshipped. Thence his hatred of the Jews, whom he treated as the basest slaves and threatened with a war of extermination."[2] The Synagogues at Alexandria had already been changed into temples or chapels of the new Emperor-god by the forcible erection of his image. When the deputies of the Alexandrian Jews came before him to implore protection, he replied, " You are those men hated of God who will not call me God, as all others acknowledge me to be, and give the preference to a nameless One," and then, rais-

[1] Matt. xxiv. 5, 15. Mark xiii. 6, 14. Luke xxi. 8, 20. St. Luke clearly refers to the same prophecy as St. Matthew and St. Mark. Christ therefore declared that the abomination mentioned by them would be the work of a hostile army, or coincide with the siege of Jerusalem.
[2] *De Leg. ad Caium.* Opp. ed. Par., 1640, 1008.

ing his hand with threatening gesture towards heaven, he broke out into words of blasphemy which even to listen to, Philo says, was sin. Shortly before his murder, when he went to Egypt, he was busied with this scheme for having his image, already prepared at Rome, carried to the temple at Jerusalem, so that, according to Josephus, the whole nation, which would have infallibly risen in revolt, was only saved from destruction by the death of Caius.[1]

St. Paul had lived through this agony and danger of his nation, and he knew how the *cultus* of the deified Emperors was constantly spreading and increasing. If Cæsar was deified after death, temples and altars were erected to Augustus during life. Eleven Asiatic cities contended for the honour of erecting a temple to Tiberius during his reign.[2] Under Caius, the worship of the living deity at Rome was organised throughout the Empire. All this the Apostle saw; he saw the Asiatic cities, where he worked, rival each other in this *cultus*, and whole communities accounting it an honour to become temple ministers and acolytes of the Emperor-god. And again, the temple at Jerusalem was as good as in the hands of the Romans; their garrison lay in the castle of Antonia, which commanded the temple, and on all high festivals the cohorts marched out to keep the people in order and remind them of their dependence and servitude even in what concerned Divine worship.[3] For a long time the sacred vestments of the high priest were kept by the Romans locked up in the castle.[4] And the Jews knew well that the Emperors gave the management of the temple at their mere caprice to whom they would, as Claudius first gave it to Herod, prince of Chalcis, at his request. They were obliged to accept the sacrificial gifts of the Emperors for offering in their temple. Since the Emperors had themselves become gods, this was viewed as a courteous acknowledgment paid by one god to his equal; and how bitterly the Jews felt the dishonour of this oppression, appeared under Nero, when

---

[1] Jos. *Archæol.* 79, 1.
[2] Tac. *Ann.* iv. 55. Cf. "*Heidenthum und Jud.*," p. 614 sqq. [Vol. ii. p. 166, *Eng. Trans.*]
[3] Josèph. *Bell. Jud.* v. 5, 8.
[4] Claudius first gave back the robes to their care at their request. Jos. *Arch.* xx. 1, 2.

the priests were persuaded by Eleazer the zealot to refuse the Emperor's gifts, and declared they would receive no more offerings from any but Jews, which was the signal for war against Rome.[1] And moreover, the unexampled splendour and beauty of the temple, which surpassed that of any other building in the Roman Empire, was a constant invitation to the Heathen to attempt to appropriate it. Its enigmatical and imageless worship of a nameless God was a standing inducement to fill up the emptiness of this sanctuary and service according to Roman notions, to put an end to the solitary anomaly of a temple without god or image, and instal the god upon earth, the living and visible Emperor-god, in a building so worthy of him. The attempt of Caius does not stand alone; Pilate had before undertaken under Tiberius to hang up in the temple several shields dedicated to the imperial deity. And his act was sure of applause and active support from surrounding nations, partly from hatred of the Jews, partly from desire to see this One God humiliated. Hence, Philo observes that, when Caligula enacted that every one should be at liberty to erect altars, temples and images to him and his in Judæa, and that any attempt at opposition should be punished with death, it was expected that the Gentiles would fill the whole land with altars and images.[2]

A profanation of the temple was as shocking to Christians as to Jews. The Lord had called it His Father's house; the first and last act of His public ministry was to cleanse it, and His disciples recognised the fulfilment of that saying, "The zeal of thine house devoured me," in His act.[3] The first Christian community at Jerusalem treated the temple as its own, and assembled there daily; St. Paul undertook one of his journeys to Jerusalem solely to perform a vow in it.[4] The Apostles and Christians, therefore, could only regard as "the Man of Sin and Son of Perdition" him whom they looked on as the author of that profanation whereof Christ had spoken. And in what light must the Jewish converts have regarded the Emperors of that day generally? Cæsar had destroyed their last semblance of national independence, and handed them over to a foreigner, the Idumean Antipater and his

[1] *Jos. Bel. Jud.* ii. 17, 2.  
[2] *Leg. ad Caium.* p. 1038.  
[3] John ii. 17.  
[4] Acts ii. 46; xviii. 18; xxi.

sons. Augustus had maintained the frightful tyranny of the odious Herod. Under Tiberius, and in his name, Pilate had given up Christ to be crucified. Caligula persecuted those who would not worship him, and Claudius had banished from Rome both Jews and Christians with them. And now all the Emperors were gods, with temples, altars and priests. Enmity against Christ, contempt of the true God, despotic persecution of His people, were their characteristics. What the beast with seven heads in the Apocalypse wills and does, one of the Emperors does in St. Paul's writings, as "the Adversary."

The description of this "Man of Sin" is borrowed, partly in the same words, from that of Antiochus Epiphanes in Daniel. The prophet says of that bloody persecutor of the Jews, who had an altar erected to the Olympian Zeus in the temple at Jerusalem and also desecrated Heathen shrines, so that Polybius saw in his horrible death a judgment on sacrilege;—" The king shall exalt and magnify himself against every god, and shall speak proudly against the God of gods; ..... he shall not regard the God of his fathers, nor the desire of women (Nanæa, the Persian Artemis), nor regard any god, but exalt himself against all."[1] Even so "the Adversary" of the Epistle "exalts himself against every so-called god, and every image" (or sanctuary.)[2] It is a new Antiochus, a Heathen monarch, that St. Paul refers to. Only such an one could be characterized as exalting himself above every god or idol, and making himself worshipped as God.[3] The statement is then intelligible, of any Jew or Christian it is not. This is self-evident, because every one exalts himself above what he despises and counts for nought, and such a deification of one's self, and exaltation over other gods, is only possible from a Heathen point of view. The "Lawless One" spoken of by St. Paul chooses

---

[1] Dan. xi. 36, 37. [The Vulgate reads in verse 37, "et erit in concupiscentiis feminarum."—Tr.]

[2] σέβασμα 2 Thess. ii. 4. The word only occurs again in Acts xvii. 23, where St. Paul says to the Athenians, "I beheld your sanctuaries," *i.e.* altars and images. Theophylact explains it, εἴδωλα. Theodoret (Therap. 2), says to the Heathen, οὐκέτι τὸ θεῖον εἰς πόλλα μερίσετε σεβάσματα. The word is used also for image in Wisd. xv. 17.

[3] The meaning of πᾶς λεγόμενος θεὸς is explained by St Paul speaking of Heathen "so-called gods," in 1 Cor. viii. 5, as opposed to the one God of Christians, with the addition, "as there are many gods and many lords," namely preternatural powers or "demons," worshipped by the Gentiles as gods.

to be one of the gods, but the chief and most powerful of them, like Caligula, Nero, Domitian and other Emperors, whose unlimited earthly authority must have really seemed to them far greater than the power of such a god as Apollo or Mercury, and who knew they were in a position to decree new gods and forbid and abolish existing worships, in a manner to annihilate a god.[1]  "Kill me, or I thee," cried Caligula, to Jupiter, whom he accused of having usurped the capitol, in the words of Homer.[2] That is to exalt oneself above every so-called god and idol, and of course this could only happen when Heathenism was still dominant and there were still idols. Since Heathenism died out, such an "exaltation" is become impossible. Therefore, St. Paul calls the new god "the Lawless," using an expression chiefly applied to Heathen lawlessness.[3]

This evil-doer will now also seize on the temple of God. This must mean the only then existing temple of the true God, that at Jerusalem, to which, in the words of a contemporary writer, both East and West looked with reverence as to a sun.[4] St. Paul had here before his eyes the prophecy of Daniel, which Christ had spoken of as shortly to be fulfilled;[5] he meant Caligula, and expected, as under the circumstances

---

[1] "Facit et hoc ad causam nostram, quod apud vos de humano arbitratu divinitas pensitatur. Nisi homini Deus placuerit, Deus non erit." Tertull. *Apol.* 5. Olshausen's statement (*Bibl. Commentar.* iv. 509) that "the Emperors did not exalt themselves *over* the other gods, but only wished to have a place *next* to them as representatives of the Roman people," is therefore quite incorrect. It was precisely exaltation over the gods that the Roman Emperors wanted. He who was himself worshipped as god, and as Pontifex Maximus settled the whole Divine cult and made or unmade gods, did exactly what St. Paul says. Under Heliogabalus, Jupiter himself had to take rank under the new Syrian deity, and the Emperor went still further, "id agens nequis Romæ Deus nisi Heliogabalus coleretur." Lamprid. Vit. Hel., p. 796, ed Lugd., 1671.

[2] Sueton. Calig. 22. Dio. Cass. 59, 26.

[3] ἄνομος. Cf. Mark xv. 28. Luke xxii. 37. Acts ii. 23. Rom. ii. 12. 1 Cor. ix. 21. So again 1 Macc. ii. 44; iii. 5. Wisd. xvii. 2. "ἄνομοι vocantur κατ'ἐξοχὴν in N. T. Gentiles, qui legem Mosaicam non habent," says Schleussner, *Lex. in verb.*

[4] *Philo. Leg. ad Caj.*, p. 1019. The explanation of ναὸς τοῦ θεοῦ as the Christian Church is now given up by every sensible commentator. What could "seating himself in the Church" mean? That could not be said of one who belonged to it, but only of one forcibly entering it from without, an enemy or persecutor. To say of a member of the Church, that he sits in it to be worshipped as God, is *contradictio in adjecto*. The expression might in itself mean the Church, as elsewhere (Eph. ii. 21) it is called "a holy temple in the Lord," but then the meaning must be fixed by the context. But here the immediate context referring to the Heathen gods and σεβάσματα necessarily implies that something cognate is designated by the temple of God, a σέβασμα or visible sanctuary, which could be profaned.

[5] Christ spoke of a new or second fulfilment. The first was accomplished by Antiochus Epiphanes. Cf. 1 Macc. I. 57, where the words of Dan. xii. 11 are so applied.

was likely, that a new attempt on the temple would be made from Rome at once. In the Gospel composed according to the oldest testimony under St. Paul's influence, the desecration or desolation, the abomination in the holy place, is connected with the siege of Jerusalem.[1] St. Paul, therefore, anticipated that the profanation would be wrought by a Roman Emperor and his army. He thought of Nero.

The Epistle is commonly supposed to have been written A.D. 53. Claudius was then on the throne. His stepson, Nero, Caligula's nephew, who had been brought up under the care of a dancer and a barber, was already married to the Emperor's daughter, adopted into the Claudian family, and proclaimed by the Senate "prince of the youth," a title then officially designating the heir of the throne.[2] It was well known that his mother Agrippina would only allow him and not Britannicus to succeed. Claudius had already commended him to the people by an edict and declared in a letter to the Senate that, in case of his death, Nero was of age to reign. Nero took his uncle Caligula more and more for a model, of whom Josephus says that only his sudden death delivered the Jews from extermination.[3] And he soon surpassed his model.[4] His reign corresponded to the Apostle's expectation; on the throne he was really the man of sin exalted over all gods and all sanctuaries. That he out-bid all the world had yet seen in shameless transgression of decency and law, and was in the fullest sense of the word "lawless," is notorious.[5] Pliny called him the enemy and common scourge of the human race. On the other hand, the Armenian king Tiridates publicly declared him before the Roman people to be his God whom he adored as the sun itself. On his entrance into Rome, on returning from Greece, sacrifices were offered

---

[1] Luke xxi. 20.
[2] Princeps juventutis. See Eckhel. *Doctr. Num.* viii. 371 sqq. Jos. Arch. 19, 1.
[4] πρὸς τὸν Γαίον ἔτεινεν says Dio ὡς δ' ἅπαξ ζηλῶσαι αὐτὸν ἐπεθύμησε, καὶ ὑπερεβάλετο. (*Excerpt. Ed. Val.* 681).
[5] It was the common view of the Fathers that by saying "the mystery of lawlessness already worketh," St. Paul meant Nero. So say Victorinus, Hilary, Chrysostom, Jerome. Augustine and Theodoret also mention it. Nero, they say, was the type of Antichrist, "cujus jam facta velut Antichristi videbantur" (Aug. Civ. Dei. 20, 19) or, "quod ille (Antichristus) operaturus est postea in isto (Nerone) ex parte completur" (Hieron. Ep. 51, ad Algas Q. 2). A great many moderns have followed this view, Lyranus, Erasmus, Gagney, Guilland, Cornelius a Lapide, &c.

to him all along the road, and he counted it a crime in Thraseas that he did not offer to his divine voice.[1] He despised all gods and worships; only for awhile he served the Syrian goddess, but her image, too, he shamefully dishonoured, and he took vengeance on Apollo and his Delphian oracle by depriving him of his lands in Cyrrha, killing men in the sanctuary, choking up the cavern, and dragging away five hundred statutes.[2]

Nero personally undertook nothing against the temple at Jerusalem, but he appointed Vespasian general in the war, and thus after his death introduced that desecration and abomination of desolation in the holy place which St. Paul, following the intimations of Christ and the prophecy of Daniel, called a sitting in the temple. The Apostle did not, of course, mean this literally, but he meant to say that the Heathen power would dominate even the temple, that even this or the holy city would be profaned by the worship of the Emperor.[3] In the Sibylline books, too, Nero is mentioned as the destroyer of the temple;[4] the Jewish author, who lived at the time or near it, knew well that Vespasian was the commander, but the real author of the war against Jerusalem was Nero. Christ gave as the fulfilment of Daniel's prophecy the appearance of Gentile troops on the temple hill; St. Paul's prophecy, that the would-be God should sit in the temple and be worshipped, was fulfilled when the Roman eagles with images of the Emperor were planted in the "holy place" of the temple,

---

[1] Suet. 25. Dio. Cass. i. 62, p. 714.

[2] "Religionum usquequaque contemptor, præter unius deæ Syriæ. Hanc mox ita sprevit ut urina contaminaret." Suet. 56. Dio. i. 63. p. 721. Pausan 813, Ed. Sieb. Lucian *Nero*, *Opp*. ed. Bipont. ix. 302.

[3] Origen long ago perceived that St. Paul's words about sitting in the temple were simply an application of Daniel's prophecy about the abomination of desolation, ὥσπερ παρὰ Παύλῳ λέλεκται, ὥστε αὐτὸν εἰς τὸν ναὸν τοῦ θεοῦ κάθισαι, ἀποδεικνύντα ἑαυτὸν, ὅτι ἐστὶ θεὸς, τοῦτο ἐν τῷ Δανιὴλ τοῦτον εἴρηται εἰς τρόπον καὶ ἐπὶ τὸ ἱερὸν βδέλυγμα τῆς ἐρημώσεως κ. τ. λ. Contr. Cels. vi. 46. To imagine a literal fulfilment of St. Paul's prophecy is to forget that he was not accurately predicting the future by virtue of any special prophetic inspiration of his own, but merely applying to the instruction of the Thessalonians the knowledge and expectation of approaching events which the Church had derived from the words of Christ. All that is essential in his description is fulfilled in Nero and the events connected with him. This, of course, no more excludes the belief afterwards prevalent in the Church, of a partial fulfilment at the end of the world, than the first fulfilment of Daniel's prophecy by Antiochus Epiphanes excluded a second by the Romans, as Christ announced.

[4] ὃς ναὸν θεότευκτον ἔλεν καὶ ἔφλεξε πολίτας. 5. 150. p. 108. ed. Friedlieb. He is before clearly described as Nero, the matricide, &c.

and the Emperor worship of Heathen Rome was regularly practised where the service of the true God had been observed.[1]

St. Paul had already given the Thessalonians more exact information, orally, about the event he is writing of. He is here reminding them of it, and at the same time recalls to their memory that he had also described to them the person who as yet stands in the way of the open appearance of the "Man of Sin." "You know," he says, "him who is now in possession, so that the Lawless One will first appear *in his own time.* But already 'the mystery of lawlessness worketh,' or is already preparing for its open manifestation; it has to wait awhile, but as soon as the present 'possessor' is out of the way, the Lawless One will be revealed."[2] Claudius is here intended, and it is very intelligible why the Apostle, in a letter which might easily fall into the wrong hands, expresses himself about the situation in so enigmatical and secret a manner. The Christians could not misunderstand him. And in fact, Claudius contrasts most markedly in this respect with his predecessor, Caligula, and his successor, Nero. He had forbidden sacrifice and divine honours to be offered to himself as a god, and had further directed that the adoration paid to Caligula should

---

[1] "Religio Romanorum tota castrensis signa veneratur, signa jurat, signa omnibus diis præponit." Tertul. *Apol.* 16. Cf. Joseph. *Arch.* vi. 32. *Herodian* iv. 4. Baur has observed, "Even after the temple was no longer standing, the place where it had stood was considered as holy as itself, as is proved by the erection of the idol under Hadrian." *Theol. Jahrb.* 1855. 158.

[2] ὁ κατέχων is commonly rendered "he that impedes," but the word does not properly mean to impede, hinder, or divide; but to possess, contain, hold, rule. See the passages collected in Dindorf's *Thesaurus.* Its meaning of κωλύειν, which Dindorf gives after κρατεῖν and συνέχειν, comes only from the senses coinciding in such expressions as κατέχειν τὴν ὀργὴν, τα δάκρυα,—to hold back. In the N.T., especially with St. Paul who most often uses the word, it always means to possess, hold; nowhere to retain, not even in Rom. i. 18, as the context shows. St. Chrysostom, indeed, interprets it τὸ κώλυον, but only from following the traditional notion that the Roman Empire is meant. Besides, the holder or possessor is here always the hinderer, he that stands in the way; when the Man of Sin is come into possession (of power) he will first come forward with his blasphemy, &c. The neuter, τὸ κάτεχον, is explained by the following masculine, ὁ κατέχων. A person is referred to who also represents a thing, the Empire. μόνον ὁ κατέχων ἄρτι ἕως ἐκ μέσου γένηται, *i.e.,* μόνον ἕως ὁ κατέχων ἄρτι, &c., as Gal. ii. 10. μόνον τῶν πτωχῶν ἵνα μνημονεύωμεν; "until the present possessor is removed." The Vulgate rightly translates ὁ κατέχων, "qui tenet," but interpolates, "teneat," which changes the sense, and has given occasion to such interpretations as that of Estius (*Comm.* ii. 195): "quicunque tenet Christum et veram ejus religionem, firmiter retineat, donec de medio Ecclesiæ fiat apostasia." So Calmet: "que celui qui a maintenant la foi, la conserve jusqu'à ce que cet homme (l'Antichrist) soit détruit." Such palpable disfiguring of the sense needs no answer.

not be continued to him, nor divine homage be exhibited when he appeared in public. But Nero and Agrippina were impatient for his death; and soon after (A.D. 54) he was "removed out of the way" by Locusta's poison, and the new Emperor-god was able to appear.

This wicked one "Christ will destroy by the breath of His mouth, and the brightness of His presence;" that is, He will execute judgment on this Man of Sin, as He will also on Jerusalem,—both alike will be an effect of His presence. It has been already observed, that St. Paul knew nothing about the time of Christ's personal coming, and made no express distinction between the first and second coming. He had a type of this wicked one in Antiochus of whom Daniel said that he should come to his end without deliverance, and whose death is treated in Maccabees as a Divine judgment on the profaner of the sanctuary of the true God.[1] And therefore the words of Isaiah, which St. Paul has here partly adopted, were already applied by the Jews to Messiah's victory over his enemy, Armillus: "With the breath of His lips He shall slay the wicked."[2]

---

[1] Dan. xi. 45. 1 Macc. vi. 13 ; 2 Macc. ix. 7.

[2] Isa. xi. 4. Of late, much trouble has been taken to force upon the writer of the Apocalypse and the early Church the fable about Nero's miraculous resurrection from the dead and appearance as Antichrist. So Ewald, de Wette, Lücke, Bleek, Baur, as before Corrodi and Eichhorn. Kern thinks the author of 2 Thess. (which is therefore spurious) also believed in this fable, and referred to Nero's future return as Antichrist. There was certainly a report spread soon after Nero's death that he was still alive concealed somewhere, and would reappear. But there is no trace for the first three centuries of the Christians having founded on it the story that he would be brought back to life by Divine omnipotence, in order that there might be a bodily Antichrist. The Sibylline Books are referred to, and Baur has quoted the passages where Nero is mentioned and his return predicted (Tübing. *theol. Jahrb.* 1852, pp. 318 sqq.). But, first, they say nothing of Nero's *death;* they make him fly and disappear, and afterwards return; next, how could it be forgotten that these fragments were composed by Jews, not by Christians? Persecution of Christians is not alluded to; besides his notorious crimes, as matricide, &c., it is Nero's war against "the holy people of the Hebrews" and destruction of this city and temple, that is put forward. Thus, I. 5, p. 574, we read, ὃs ναὸν θεότευκτον ἔλεν καὶ ἔφλεξε πολίτας, and at p. 575 Italy will be burnt, ἧς εἵνεκα πολλοὶ ὄλοντο "Εβραίων ἅγιοι πιστοὶ καὶ ναὸs ἀληθής. There is no hint in these passages of Christian belief. The first Christian who mentions the story is Commodianus, in the middle of the third century, who got it from the Sibylline books. (*Spicil. Solesm.* Ed. Pitra, i. 43). Then comes Lactantius in the fourth century, who mentions it as a fancy only entertained by some, and refers to the Sibylline books as the source (*De Mort. Pers.* 2). But he only knows the notion of a Nero still alive. Augustine first says, "Nonnulli ipsum *resurrecturum* et futurum Antichristum suspicantur." *De Civ. Dei* xx. 19, 3. But Sulpicius Severus says, "Nero is thought to have been wounded, not killed, to be alive and destined to appear as Antichrist at the end of the world." *Hist. Sacr.* i. 2, p. 373, ed. 1647. Such notions, then, commence with the close of the fourth century; the early Church knew nothing of them. In the Jewish *Martyrdom of Isaiah*, inter-

If St. Paul connects the appearance of the " Adversary " with Satanic agency, that is all the more natural, as he connects the more potent manifestations of Heathenism generally, the Heathen rejection or hatred of the faith, with Satanic operations: "The god of this world has blinded the minds of unbelievers;" "works in the sons of unbelief."[1] The use of lying wonders and signs which St. Paul foresees is, again, Satanic. And it is noteworthy, that Pliny tells us nobody was more zealously devoted to magical arts than Nero, in order that he might be able to command the gods, which he so eagerly desired that he even offered human sacrifices to them."[2] It is not, however, said that the "Lawless One" himself would work these signs, but that men would be deceived by them to their own destruction. St. Paul had before his eyes Christ's prophecy: and the false prophet of the Apocalypse, the beast from the earth, which by great wonders seduces men to worship the beast from the sea (the Emperor) is part of the same idea. Magical and theurgic arts were then inseparable both from Heathenism and from the heresies which sprung from Heathen elements.

The apostacy, which was to come first, was the falling away from faith, the seductions of false doctrine, which St. Paul elsewhere mentions and which after its entrance gave so much trouble to the Apostles. How solemnly St. Paul tells the Ephesians that after his departure ravening wolves, false teachers, will arise, as well from without as from within the Church, and lead the people astray! He meant the Gnostic heretics, whom he clearly described afterwards in his Epistles to Timothy as apostates, whose entrance in "the latter times" the spirit (of prophecy) "expressly" foretold.[3] They, by

---

polated by Gnostics, a Nero appears as Antichrist at the end, but it is Satan himself, Berial, taking the form of the matricide and "king of this world;" the Church planted by the twelve Apostles is given into his hand; all will believe and sacrifice to him, and only a few remain loyal to Christ; but after 330 days Christ will come and cast Berial into hell, &c. *Asc. Is.* iv. 2—14, ap. Gfrörer Proph. Vet. Pseudep. p. 10. It is the devil taking the form of a returned Nero. But these interpolations into the old Jewish text date from the fourth century only. Origen knew nothing of them. See Lücke's *Einl. in Offenb. Joh.* p. 297.

[1] 2 Cor. iv. 4. Eph. ii. 2. τοῦ πνεύματος τοῦ νῦν ἐνεργοῦντος, the same word as here, κατ ἐνεργείαν τοῦ Σατανᾶ; (2 Thess. ii. 9).

[2] "Primumque imperare diis concupivit, nec quidquam generosius valuit." *Nat Hist.* xxx. 5.

[3] 1 Tim. iv. 1, ῥητῶς. Acts xx. 29.

magical delusions, deceived the credulous and gained them for themselves.[1] The falling away St. Paul mentions cannot be one to be wrought by "the Man of Sin." Of him the Apostle only knew that he would make himself a god, and put down or slight all other gods. He could not mean that a great number of believers would fall away, simply to flatter the pride of this man-god and worship him. No sort of anxiety about an apostacy to this crudest, almost insane, form of Heathenism is ever expressed throughout the whole New Testament, nor any warning given against it. St. Paul speaks of a strong power of delusion working this result. But the apotheosis of a despot could so little deceive, that, as Philo remarks, all except the Jews took part in the divine adoration of Caligula, but purely out of terror and against the grain.[2] But here, again, it is only the intimations of Christ which the Apostle follows.[3] The Lord had connected a great deceiving with the period of the abomination of desolation in the holy place, and so also did St. Paul. The coming of the "Lawless One" would coincide with the apostacy wrought by miracle-mongering false teachers and magical signs. Two great judgments were to come together, the profanation and fall of the temple, and the delusion or falling away to Gnosticism of many believers. This last evil the Apostle regards as a judgment on those "who, not having believed the truth, take pleasure in unrighteousness," wherefore "God will send them a strong delusion, that they may believe the lie."

---

[1] The ancients call them Satanical arts, and use the same word as St. Paul; so Justin Martyr, of Simon, διὰ τῆς τῶν ἐνεργούντων δαιμόνων τέχνης δυνάμεις ποιήσας μαγικὰς, Apol. ii. So Eusebius iii. 36, of Menander, διαβολικῆς ἐνεργείας. John of Damascus, remarks (iv. 26) that St. Paul means feigned miracles, πεπλασμένοις καὶ οὐκ ἀληθέσι.
[2] Phil. *Leg. ad Caj.* 1008.   [3] Matt. xxiv. 23 sqq.

# THIRD BOOK.

## THE CONSTITUTION, WORSHIP, AND LIFE OF THE APOSTOLIC CHURCH.

### CHAPTER I.

#### ORDERS AND OFFICES OF MINISTRY AND SPIRITUAL GIFTS.

The Apostolic Church before the year 64 was by no means a lawless chaos; as the body of Christ, it was from the beginning a well-ordered whole, but its constitution corresponded to the double condition of a Church designed above all to spread and increase, and at the same time full of *charismata*—dominated by extraordinary spiritual gifts, which were bestowed without distinction of office. All power and authority was lodged in the Apostolate. As long as the Apostles lived it was they who ruled the Church, and in whose hands was centred all official power. Each Apostle possessed in solidarity, not a divided or partial, but a complete right of superintendence over the Christian communities; he was able and bound to use his Apostolical authority, where it was needful and useful, in every portion of the Church, whence St. Paul says the care of all the Churches was laid upon him.[1] They did not first make an agreement with their flocks, or receive rights from them, but stood over them with fatherly authority, as over their sons begotten in Christ. The very name of "Apostle" pointed back to One higher, whose messengers and ambas-

[1] 2 Cor. xi. 28.

sadors they were, so that whoever met a bearer of that title was compelled to ask or answer for himself the question, whose Apostle this man was? The Twelve gave laws, as well conjointly, as at the Synod of Jerusalem, as separately, many of them not expressly ordained by Christ. St. Paul distinguished pointedly between commands, in which he was merely the interpreter of Christ, and those he promulgated by his own authority.[1] He promised the Corinthians that he would make several regulations when he came to them.[2] He knew how to exercise his power of punishing transgressors; the Corinthians themselves received Titus, whom he deputed, "with fear and trembling;" he threatens that he will come to them with a rod; he is ready to punish all disobedience, and will not spare when he comes; he bids the Thessalonians separate from those whose conduct is disorderly, and desires that the names of such persons may be given him.[3] Where, as at Corinth, individuals or parties hesitated to recognise his authority, this was from not holding him to be a true Apostle, so that he simply maintained against them his claim to the Apostolic office, and did not contend about its extent or rights.[4]

The Apostles had their ministering disciples and subordinate helpers. Thus we find St. Paul and St. Barnabas making use of several, mostly younger men, as assistants. They were sent here and there on commissions between the Apostles and the various communities, and brought a report of the state of these communities. Certain duties were left to them; as of baptizing, which the Apostles usually committed to others, after Christ's example who did not baptize Himself but made His disciples do so.[5] When St. Peter converted Cornelius and his family, he commanded "that they should be baptized;" St. Paul declares that he had baptized none of his Corinthian converts, except Crispus, Gaius, and the family of Stephanas; for Christ sent him not to baptize, but to preach the Gospel. At Ephesus he seems to have acted in the same way, for it is said of the twelve disciples of John he found there, that "they were bap-

---

[1] 1 Cor. vii. 10.  [2] 1 Cor. xi. 34.
[3] 2 Cor. vii. 15.  1 Cor. iv. 21.  2 Cor. x. 6; xiii. 2.  2 Thess. iii. 6, 10.
[4] 1 Cor. ix. 1, 2.  2 Cor. xi. 5; xii. 11, 12.
[5] John iv. 2.

tized in the name of the Lord Jesus; and when Paul had laid his hands on them the Holy Ghost came upon them." This laying on of hands was a special prerogative of the Apostles, as appears here and in the case of the Samaritans, baptized by the Evangelist Philip.[1]

St. Peter held a pre-eminence among the Apostles, which none of the rest contested. He received the keys of the kingdom, and is the rock on which the Church is built— that is, the continuance, increase and growth of the Church rests on the office created in his person. To him was the charge given to strengthen his brethren and feed the flock of Christ. "The Gospel of the Circumcision," as St. Paul says, was especially committed to him by the Lord, as to the man of Tarsus that of the uncircumcision.[2] Christ Himself was a minister of the circumcision; His Messianic energies were devoted to the good of Israel, so that He said Himself, "I am not sent, but to the lost sheep of the house of Israel."[3] In this St. Peter followed Him; he is peculiarly the Apostle of Israel, the head of the Church of the circumcision, and he is this in a higher and more eminent sense than St. James who is doubly inferior to him, both as being confined to Jerusalem, while he included the whole dispersion in his labours, and as holding aloof from the Gentiles, while he was the first to incorporate them into the Church and also extended his ecclesiastical labours, though in a lesser degree, to uncircumcised converts. For there were not two Churches, one of the circumcision and one of the uncircumcision; but there was one olive-tree, one people of God, one Israel; and into this tree the Gentiles were grafted and thereby made partakers of the root and the juice, as adopted children of Abraham, whence St. Peter tells the Christian women of the communities he addresses, that they are daughters of Sarah.[4] And thus the Apostle, to whom Israel is specially entrusted by God, is necessarily the Head of the Apostolic College and the whole Church. The agreement between him and St. Paul regarded a division of labour, not of the Church; and St. Paul, who travelled to Jerusalem for the special purpose of spending fifteen days

---

[1] Acts x. 47, 48; xix. 5, 6; viii. 14—17. 1 Cor. i. 14—17.
[2] Gal. ii. 7. [3] Rom. xv. 8. Matt. xv. 24. Cf. xx. 28.
[4] Rom. xi. 24. 1 Pet. iii. 6. Cf. infr. iv. 3, which proves that St. Peter was addressing communities, formed chiefly of Gentile converts.

with St. Peter, knew well that he was chief among the three pillar Apostles, although he would not be dependent on him in pursuing the way shown to himself by Divine call and revelation, and opposed him at Antioch. The point on which St. Paul laid such great weight, that the Gentiles were to be converted immediately to Christ and not through the medium of previous conversion to Judaism, was first taught by special revelation, not to him but to St. Peter. Nor did St. Paul enter on his peculiar office of preaching to the Gentiles till after his fifteen days conference with St. Peter. While the Apostles remained united at Jerusalem the primacy of Peter displayed itself on all grave occasions. It was he who arranged the filling up of the Apostolic College through St. Matthias' election; he fixed the form of election, confining it to those who had been companions of Christ and witnesses of His teaching and acts. He takes up the word before the people and the Sanhedrim, and works the first miracle for confirming Christ's resurrection. The punishment of Ananias and Sapphira, the anathema on Simon Magus, the first heretic, the first visiting and confirming the Churches suffering under persecution, were all his acts. If he was sent with St. John by the Apostolic College to the new converts at Samaria, he was himself member and president of that college. So the Jews sent their high priest Ismael to Nero; and St. Ignatius says that the neighbouring Churches in Asia had sent, some their bishops, some their priests and deacons.[1] He was always and everywhere at the head of the assembly of Jerusalem, which freed the Gentiles from observing the ceremonial law; he opened it, and his motion was carried, with the conditions added by St. James.

The sentence of St. James could not but have great weight at that Synod, for St. Peter, like St. Paul, was in a manner a party concerned in the question. It was known in Jerusalem that he had ordered the centurion Cornelius and other Gentiles with him at Cæsarea to be baptized without circumcision, and this had raised great opposition on his return. And when St. Paul and St. Barnabas came to Jerusalem, and the Synod was to be held, the converted Pharisees again urged that Gentiles

[1] Joseph. *Arch.* xx. 7. Ignat. *Ep. ad Philad.* 10.

must submit to circumcision and the Law.¹ Therefore, St. James, who with his community was so faithful to the Law, was the best, and for opponents most convincing judge in this strife, and it was obvious that the decree would be made in conformity with his opinion. And hence St. Paul, when appealing in his Epistle to the Galatians to the pillar Apostles who gave him and Barnabas their right hand in token of fellowship, named James first, before Cephas;² for in that matter, and for persons who appealed unhesitatingly to the example of the Mother Church which kept the Law, the example of James had more weight than that of Peter, just as later the Ebionites laboured to make his authority appear the highest in the Church. But St. James himself acknowledged that Peter was called by God's appointment to gather from among the Gentiles a people that should bear His name, and unite them into one Church with converted Israelites; for he confirms St. Peter's words, that God had chosen him among all to preach to the Gentiles.³ And so it became the Apostle who had alone received the keys of the kingdom. St. Paul was the first to enter into the work St. Peter had begun, and build on his foundation; he could not have done so unless St. Peter, in consequence of their previous arrangement, had recognised him as a fellow-labourer Divinely called, even though he derived his mission immediately from Christ. That he stood on a lower level than St. Peter is shown by his own way of describing his relations to Jews and Gentiles; he took every way of "glorifying his office," as Apostle of the Gentiles, by numerous conversions, that through the influence thus obtained he might rouse the emulation of some at least of his people and win them.⁴ St. Peter had no need of this circuitous method; he wrought, by the weight of his office, equally on Jews and Gentiles, and it was his own free act that made him afterwards prefer confining his energies chiefly to Jews. St. Paul was far from concealing that, in his eyes, St. Peter was not simply one of the Twelve but had a peculiar position and dignity distinct from the rest, and that, accordingly, an appeal to his example had peculiar weight. He is not

¹ Acts xv. 5      ² Gal. ii. 9.
³ Acts xv. 14.     ⁴ Rom. xi. 13, 14.

content with saying, "Have I not power to lead about a sister, like the other Apostles," but he adds, "like the brethren of the Lord and Cephas."[1] And if St. Peter, in mentioning the presbyters of the Churches, calls them "fellow presbyters," he was mindful of his Lord's example who, while standing so high above the Apostles, called them "His brethren," bade him strengthen his brethren, and as greatest in the kingdom be the least and humblest.[2] He saw in the presbyters men who, like himself, served the brethren in teaching and ministration, and who, so far, were his fellow ministers.

In the constitution of the communities important changes were clearly introduced during the Apostolic age. All of them had presbyters who had come over from Judaism, but their office could only be a subordinate one, while the spiritual gifts were distributed among all and not confined to office-bearers. The extraordinary gifts conferred by laying on the Apostles' hands were so widely communicated, that nearly all, or certainly very many, for a time shared them. This was a condition singular in history which has never since repeated itself, and which, in the absence of any experience, we can only approximately conceive of. The metal of the Church, so to speak, was still glowing, unformed, in fusion, and presented a very different appearance from that of its later condition, when cold and fixed. St. Paul's Epistles show how much, during this early period, corporate organisation and interdependence was either wanting or was kept in the background. If we except the Epistles written at the close of his life to the Philippians, to Timothy and Titus, he never mentions deacons, presbyters, or bishops;[3] he has no charges, no hints or instructions about their office, to give them, and yet much which he censured in the communities or required from them must have depended on their ministry if they already held the position we find them in afterwards. St. Paul only speaks of the communities. When he counts up the teachers given by God to the Church, according to their various gradations or peculiarities, the names of

---

[1] 1 Cor. ix. 5.   [2] Matt. xxviii. 10   Luke xxii. 32.
[3] In Rom. xvi. 1, a deaconess is mentioned. Elsewhere St. Paul uses διάκονος and διακονία in a general sense, with no reference to the special office of the seven appointed at Jerusalem.

deacons, presbyters, and bishops do not occur among them. Thus he says to the Ephesians, "God has appointed Apostles, Prophets, Evangelists, Pastors, Teachers;"[1] to the Corinthians, "God has set in the Church first, Apostles; secondly, Prophets; thirdly, Teachers; then powers, then gifts of healing, helps, interpretations, kinds of tongues."[2] He is clearly speaking in these passages, not of offices but of gifts. Even the Apostles he names, not as holding Apostolic office but as miraculously gifted persons. The Apostles, prophets and teachers avail themselves of their three-fold capacity of teaching according to their respective gifts, of teaching or of wisdom, of knowledge or of faith.[3]

We see here a condition of the Church, where the whole community receives its character and dominating influence from the extraordinary gifts, in this most striking and outwardly cognisable form. What St. Paul says of the Corinthians was no doubt equally true of other communities, that they fell short in no gift.[4] These gifts were necessary; the believer had them more for the sake of others than for his own, they were to be used for the service of others or for the whole community. For that they were given, and only so was their end attained. St. Paul adds, that, since, while all gifts were good, all were not of equal value and importance for the common weal, every one should strive for the most excellent.[5] And since every one who enjoyed these gifts had to seek an appropriate sphere of action for their use, while yet this or that man often lost his gift again, partly by his own fault, or received a higher one in its place, we see how temporary were such relations and how little idea there could be of fixed cor-

---

[1] Eph. iv. 11.
[2] 1 Cor. xii 28. κυβερνήσεις occurs only in this place in the N. T., and is commonly rendered "governments" or "administrations." [So in Vulg. and E. V.] It has not that meaning in the Septuag. but "consilia, prudentia, intelligentia." The Lex. Cyrilli explains it φρόνησις; Schleussner's Glossæ ineditæ in Prov. Sal. ἐπιστήμη τῶν πραττομένων; Hesychius, προνοητικαὶ ἐπιστῆμαι καὶ φρονήσεις. The position of the word here, between ἰαμάτων and γένη γλωσσῶν, and the plural point the same way. In the following passage v. 30 μὴ πάντες διερμηνεύουσι corresponds to it, and in v. 30 διερμηνεία γλωσσῶν or διακρίσεις πνευμάτων. But if κυβερνήσεις means the gift of government, why should St. Paul, who thrice reckons up the gifts in this chapter, have twice passed this one over, which was one of the most important and peculiarly bearing on the point he had in view, of showing the necessity of co-operation for a common end? And why, again, in v. 28, should he pass over διρμηνεία which he had twice mentioned as a special gift? Truly it is very improbable!
[3] 1 Cor. xii. 8, 9.   [4] 1 Cor. i. 7.   [5] 1 Cor. xii. 7, 31.   1 Pet. iv. 10.

porate form or of definite arrangement and gradations of ecclesiastical offices and rights; nor, indeed, was any need for it as yet experienced.

But, notwithstanding this effusion of gifts, a community could easily fall into grave errors. At the very time that he mentions the gifts of the Corinthian Church St. Paul has to censure its grievous abuse of them. Among the Galatians, Jewish seductions and darkening of Christian doctrine, through the notion of its being necessary to observe the Law, had so far gained the upper hand that the Apostle calls them foolish and senseless; yet he appealed to the evidence of their spiritual gifts and miraculous powers, not derived from observance of the Law but from faith in Christ. The gifts of teaching and knowledge must, however, have been greatly weakened or extinguished in these communities, else so great a delusion would be inexplicable. But in this Epistle there is no trace of a fixed teaching office, but the "spiritual" among them are exhorted to use their office of denunciation.[1] But from thenceforward the age of spiritual gifts was more and more passing away in the Churches, though some gifts and some gifted persons remained. In the first Epistle to the Thessalonians St. Paul insisted especially, that his Gospel had not wrought as mere doctrine, but in manifestation of the power of the Holy Ghost.[2] But in the Epistles to the Philippians and Colossians, there is no hint of these gifts or any allusion to them, though in both Churches there was direct occasion for them, in Philippi on account of the Jewish adversaries, in Colossæ from the danger of heresy and the Gnostic asceticism. On the other hand, Bishops and Deacons are mentioned as Church officers in the Epistle to the Philippians.[3] The Pastoral Epistles not only contain no mention of the gifts, but exhibit a state of the Church entirely different. The communities of Asia Minor, especially the Ephesian, are partly threatened, partly thrown into confusion by Gnostic errors, logomachies, foolish controversies, sorceries, empty babbling about matters of belief, and an advancing godlessness that eats like a canker.[4] All the advice here given to St. Timothy and the line he is

[1] Gal. iii. 1—5; vi. 1.  [2] 1 Thess. i. 5.  [3] Phil. i. 1.
[4] 1 Tim. iv. 1—3; vi. 3—5, 20, 21. 2 Tim. ii. 14—18.

directed to take against this evil is so conceived as to imply that gifts were no longer common, that in place of the first spiritual outburst and fulness of extraordinary powers the dry, prosaic life of the Church was now begun. The Church offices not before mentioned by St. Paul and the qualifications for those who are to be ordained are referred to in passing, but it is no special gift he here requires for a Presbyter. That whole domain seems, as it were, now shut out from Church ministration. So, again, in the writings of St. John there is nothing to imply the continuance of the period of extraordinary gifts in the Churches of Asia Minor, though his first Epistle especially could scarcely have avoided referring to it if it still survived.

St. Paul has placed the Prophets of that early age with the Apostles, and, in some sense, on a par with them, as the common foundation whereon the Church was built. St. John puts for Christians generally Saints, Apostles, and Prophets, and elsewhere simply Saints and Prophets, including under this designation all organs of Christian revelation and preachers of the counsels of God.[1] They were Divinely inspired men who spoke before the congregation out of the knowledge communicated to them in the form of visions and ecstatic impressions, while those whom St. Paul calls "teachers" were, indeed, filled with the Spirit —for he reckons them among the possessors of a special gift—but used a quieter and more comprehensible manner of exposition. Many of them, like the Apostles themselves, had the double office of teaching and ruling; they were "pastors and teachers."[2] And if St. Paul makes separate mention of "Evangelists," he means those assistants chosen by the Apostles who went from city to city to collect congregations and to train them.[3] A later writer is, therefore, correct in saying that in those days every one taught in the Church who had received with the gift the capacity of public speaking. But the matter of his teaching was subject to the judgment of the Apostles and of those who had the gift of discerning spirits.

In the young Church at Jerusalem, soon after the out-

---

[1] Eph. ii. 20. Apoc. xviii. 20, 24; xi. 18; xvi. 6.
[2] ποίμενες. Eph. iv. 11. προιστάμενοι. Rom. xii. 8. 1 Thess. v. 12.
[3] 1 Cor. xiv. 29, 32, 37.

pouring of the Spirit, a discontent arose of the Hellenistic Jews against those of Palestine, because they thought their widows were neglected in the distribution of alms. Owing to the voluntary community of goods, the Apostles had to manage the common fund and the distribution of alms and food, and the persons whose services they used seem to have given occasion to this complaint. They knew that it was time to relieve themselves of this business and responsibility, which in a rapidly increasing community could only hinder their office of teaching. The "serving of tables" was to be taken from them and given over to others, "wise men, full of the Holy Ghost." The community sought out seven men, and the Apostles ordained them by prayer and laying on of hands.[1]

The whole Church has recognised in this act the institution of the Diaconate, but the seven are not so called separately or collectively in the New Testament. St. Luke calls Philip an evangelist, and one of the seven.[2] Care for the poor and provision for the *agape*, which were the original occasion of their appointment, became the proper office of Deacons later, when the communities were fully organised. But at that time there were no other office-bearers, besides the Apostles, in Jerusalem; the seven were the most qualified and approved men who could be selected, and two of them, Stephen and Philip, probably also others, took part in the higher Apostolic duties. While St. Luke never speaks of Deacons, he often mentions Presbyters, but says nothing of their appointment; and this silence would be very strange if the Apostles had, soon after ordaining the seven, also constituted a distinct Presbyterate, a body taking rank above the Deacons in authority and importance, but in which no single name has been preserved, while St. Luke gives the names of all the seven. Not till after the congregations scattered by persecution were reassembled in Jerusalem, is the existence of "elders" there mentioned, quite incidentally, when St. Paul and St. Barnabas gave them the alms from Antioch to distribute. And that was precisely the business of the seven. St. Luke also states that St. Paul and St. Barnabas had appointed "Elders" in Pisidia, and repeatedly speaks of the Apostles and Elders in Jerusalem.

[1] Acts vi. 1—6.     [2] Acts xxi. 8.

The Apostles, elders and brethren issued the decree of the Synod to the Christians at Antioch.¹ But if the seven were distinct from the elders, they vanish without a trace.

We are thence led to infer, that, as yet, there was no distinction of Deacons and Priests, but that the office of the seven included the two afterwards separated. In the earlier Epistles of St. Paul and St. James, there is no trace of their co-existence. They first appear as distinguished in the Epistle to the Philippians and the Pastoral Epistles, after the year 64. That was the second important step towards permanent Church organisation, falling into the later period of the ministry of St. Peter and St. Paul. Even then there was no distinction of Presbyters and Bishops; the two designations were used as synonymous. The name, "Overseer," or Bishop, is only four times used to designate an office. The Philippian Christians are addressed "with the Deacons and Bishops." When St. Paul took leave of the Ephesian elders at Miletus, he said they were appointed by the Holy Ghost as "overseers" in the flock, and to feed the Church of God. The same men whom St. Luke names elders, St. Paul calls "bishops." Thus he tells St. Titus he had left him in Crete, to appoint as "elders" men blameless and otherwise suitable, for an "overseer" must be blameless.²

It seems that originally the expression "Elder" prevailed in the Jewish, "Overseer" in the Gentile communities. St. Peter and St. James use the word "Presbyter," never "Bishop." The word "Elder" was common among the Jews, and derived from them. There were elders in the Sanhedrim as assessors of the chief priests and scribes, and every synagogue or local congregation had a chief or president.³ But the name was new to the Gentiles, and they would have thought it strange that young men, as often happened, should be ordained "Elders." In such communities, therefore, the Apostles preferred the word Bishop, which occurs in the Alexandrian version of the Old Testament, in the sense of an ecclesiastical or civil officer. In the larger cities and communities, as Jerusalem, Ephesus, Philippi and others, these Presbyters, or Bishops, were combined into a college, whence St. James bids the sick

---

¹ Acts xiv. 23; xv. 2, 6, 23    ² Phil. i. 1. Acts xx. 28. Tit. i. 5. sq.
³ Acts v. 21; γερουσία; xiii. 15. Luke vii. 3.

send for the presbyters of the Church (several, therefore), to anoint him.[1]

The office afterwards called episcopal was not, then, yet marked off; the Episcopate slept in the Apostolate. It was the last branch to grow out of the Apostolic stem. In Jerusalem it had already taken shape in the person of St. James, whose attitude towards the local Church, his renunciation of missionary work and his remaining within the holy city point him out as the first true and proper Bishop. The other Apostles discharged their Episcopal office in superintending and guiding several communities. Tradition knows only of St. Peter and St. James, one in Jerusalem, the other in Alexandria and Rome, as founders of a line of Bishops, forming themselves the first link in the chain. No Pauline Church claims St. Paul as its first Bishop; he belonged to all, and gave no such pre-eminence to any. But his martyrdom at Rome gave the Church there a right to claim him, with St. Peter, as joint founder of the Roman See. The rest of the Apostles have not so bound themselves to any particular Church as to be called its first Bishops. Ephesus was the centre from which St. John administered his Apostolic office, but he is never called its first Bishop; indeed, the Apocalypse shows that there was another there under him. But the nearer came the moment for their departure, and for the complete separation of the Christian Church from Judaism, the more urgent was the call on them to provide for the continuation of their Apostolic office, that is, to appoint Bishops. We saw what weighty grounds they had for delaying this step; but there were others besides. While the temple stood and the connexion with Judaism was not finally dissolved, the organisation of the Church was in one sense incomplete and provisional. It might in the interval have Presbyters, who were a common Jewish institution and whose appointment was no sign of separation; but the appointment of Bishops would certainly have been regarded by all Jews and by Christians also, as an act sealing the exclusion of the Church and its definitive separation from the Israelite nation and religion.[2] Therefore, the Apostles retained the Episcopal

[1] James v. 14.
[2] It may be objected that St. James appeared as Bishop in Jerusalem from the first

authority provisionally in their own hands. And again, until the two nationalities, Jewish and Gentile, were completely amalgamated, there would have been great difficulties about appointing a Bishop, who must necessarily have belonged to one of the two classes and yet have governed both. If the difference and jealousy of Hellenistic and Palestine Jews troubled the early Church and constrained the Apostles to appoint officers from both parties, how much more would this be the case with the far deeper contrasts between Gentiles and sons of Israel! The only available form of government while this division remained—in other words, while Jewish converts still observed the ritual law—was a Presbyterate gathered from, and representing both classes, subjected to the authority of the Apostles and sustained by it. A Jewish Bishop would inevitably find himself in the same predicament as St. Peter at Antioch, while a Gentile Bishop would have the greatest difficulty in dealing with the Israelites; and such difficulties were better met by the erection of domestic Churches,[1] and having several Deacons and Elders. For the pride of birth still lived among those Jews of the Dispersion who had kept from intermingling with Greeks and Syrians, in whose veins the noble Israelite blood flowed; and it would have been asking of such men more than could reasonably be expected to bid them, who from youth had been taught to regard themselves as children of grace and heirs of the kingdom, to bow to the authority of a man who but shortly before was a blind and unclean Gentile. Even St. Paul, in one of his last Epistles, had to complain bitterly of the Judaizing seducers with their "circumcision, or rather concision."[2] Moreover, there was a great difficulty in finding the right men for an office doubly difficult under the then state of circumstances. St. Paul writes to the Philippians that he would shortly send them Timothy to bring him word of their condition, because he had no other equally of one heart and mind with him; the rest sought their own, not what was Christ's.[3] Even if this severe sentence refers

and under the very eye of the authorities there. But he, from his habit of visiting the temple and his careful observance of the Law, was peculiarly qualified to dispel in the minds of Jews all suspicion of an intended separation. It was different elsewhere.

[1] Rom. xvi. 5. Col. iv. 15. τὴν κατ' οἶκον αὐτοῦ ἐκκλησίαν. Philem. 2.
[2] Phil. iii. 2, 3. [3] Phil. ii. 20, 21.

only to a temporary absence of suitable helpers, still it shows how the Apostles were forced to keep the superintendence of the communities as long as they could in their own hands. St. Paul could more easily find dozens of Presbyters than one Bishop, one man to undertake this burden with entire self-denial and self-devotion. And even this one, whom he had much rather have kept by him to send here and there on commissions, he gave up as Bishop to the Church of Ephesus, though bidding him take care that he be not despised on account of his youth.[1] So, too, St. Titus had only a charge from him in Crete to appoint presbyters in the island communities. How could men be found for Bishops in those newly-formed communities, that had only temporarily enjoyed Apostolical care and all whose members were novices? Neophytes were not even to be made presbyters.[2]

But, as these hindrances to introducing the Episcopate diminished with each year, and men gradually grew ripe for the discharge of that office, so too, as the end of the chief Apostles drew near, dangers multiplied, which forbade them to defer any longer the consolidation of the Churches. St. Peter and St. Paul saw times of persecution at hand, and also the imminent peril of false teachers rising up from within and of a great falling away.

Thus, we find in the Epistle to the Philippians, that St. Paul, who at the opening addresses the community "with the Overseers and Deacons," afterwards speaks of some one, not named, as a "true yoke-fellow," and gives him a charge.[3] It was he who received the Epistle and was to communicate or read it to the rest, and he is the only person in all St. Paul's Epistles to whom this honourable title is given. He elsewhere calls those who worked with and under him, "fellow-labourers," "fellow-soldiers," "fellow-servants."[4] All this points to a man who had no equal there in his office,—to a Bishop. So again with Archippus at Colossæ; he is the only person there whom St. Paul exhorts to administer his office carefully.[5] And, when

[1] 1 Tim. iv. 12.
[2] οὐ γὰρ πάντα εὐθὺς ἠδυνήθησαν καταστῆσαι οἱ ἀπόστολοι says Epiphanius quite correctly.—*Hær.* 75, p. 908, Ed. Colon.
[3] Phil. iv. 3. σύζυγε γνήσιε.
[4] Rom. xvi. 3, 9, 21. Phil. ii. 25; iv. 3. Col. i. 7. Philem. 1.
[5] Col. iv. 17.

writing to Philemon, in whose house the community, or a part of it, assembled, in order to reconcile him with his slave, Onesimus, he also addresses Archippus, "our fellow-soldier," though the Epistle contains no word relating to him and is wholly occupied with the private relations of Philemon and Onesimus; and this shows that the only ground for addressing Archippus, was his being the head of the Church there, who as such was to join his intercession with St. Paul's for Onesimus.[1]

St. Timothy, then, was placed at Ephesus, in the Church the Apostle of the Gentiles held dearest and most important, in a position which implied full possession of Episcopal authority. He was the Apostle's favourite; St. Paul not only calls him his true and beloved son, but his brother, he six times joins him with himself in the superscription of his Epistles, and says he has no other like-minded with him.[2] He gives over to him the full Apostolical authority he had used himself at Ephesus, as well over ministers as members of the Church; he was to rule and teach those confided to him, to arrange the solemnities of worship, not to allow women to teach in public. His office is to watch over the purity of the doctrine taught and himself to appoint trustworthy men for preaching it, to ordain Bishops and Deacons, to judge the qualifications of men for Church offices, and not "lay hands suddenly on any man," which implies the further right of deposing the unworthy from the ministry. It is also his duty to provide that fitting submission and reverence be paid to the ministers of the Church, to exercise jurisdiction, to examine and decide not only about laymen but Presbyters, and to impose proportionate punishments on offences. He is to denounce sinners publicly, that others may fear, and to show strict impartiality.[3] The man clothed with such ample authority is yet so young, that care must be taken that his youth be not despised. He is to admonish Presbyters as fathers, to judge those who are themselves rulers, and lastly—which shows how little St. Paul thought of a mere transitory office—he is to keep the Apostle's commandment unspotted and blame-

---

[1] Philem. 2.
[2] Rom. xvi. 21. 1 Cor. iv. 17. 2 Cor. i. 1. Phil. i. 1. Col. i. 1. 1 Thess. iii. 2. Phil. ii. 20.
[3] 1 Tim. iv. 11.; i. 3; iii. 1, 2. 2 Tim. ii. 2. 1 Tim. v. 17, 19, 21.

less till the return of Christ, that is, of course, he and his successors in the Episcopate.[1] Tradition accordingly makes him the first bishop of Ephesus, those who followed are called his successors, and at the Council of Chalcedon twenty-seven bishops of Ephesus from him were counted up.[2] He has been also regarded as an Apostolic delegate, one of a special class of ecclesiastical officers, but that does not prevent his being a Bishop. The authority St. Paul gave him, unless it had a defined and permanent character within a certain sphere, would have expired with the Apostle's death. The needs of the Church would have been ill supplied with mere delegates of dead men, and that too at a transition period from Apostolic to post-Apostolic times, when it needed a firm authority and a universally recognised ministry of superior teachers and pastors, to maintain and hold together its communities against the violent and pertinacious assaults of heretical disorder. Such delegates would have been everywhere resisted and told their authority was only temporary and expired with its source, that they were not, like the Apostles, immediately called by the Lord, or witnesses of His death and resurrection. St. Paul knew well when he wrote for the last time to Timothy, "Make full use of thy power," that he was himself near death, and that Timothy henceforth must stand by himself, without the great support he had hitherto enjoyed.[3]

St. Timothy, then, was Bishop of Ephesus, though not in such sense bound to that city and community as to be incapacitated from giving Apostolical assistance in the neighbourhood also. St. Paul, left almost alone, summoned him to Rome, and promised to send him to Philippi on his return to Asia. He seems once to have been sent to Judæa.[4] It was a consequence of this transition period that Apostolic legates became Bishops, and Bishops on occasion became legates again, as later also Bishops often travelled on affairs of the Church.[5] And the powers and charge St.

[1] 1 Tim. v. 1, 17, 19; vi. 14.
[2] Chrys. *Ep. ad Tim.* Photius Bibl. Cod, 254. Conc. Chalc. Ap. Labbé, iv. 699.
[3] 2 Tim. iv. 5, 6.
[4] Heb. xiii. 23.
[5] Theodoret has inferred from 2 Tim. iv. 12, "I have sent Tychicus to Ephesus," that St. Timothy was not then in Ephesus, but this does not follow, and the persons saluted in this Epistle lived at Ephesus. Cf. 2 Tim. iv. 19, with Acts xviii. 26.

Paul gave his disciple extended over all pro-consular Asia, though Ephesus continued to be his peculiar seat. Nor is it in itself conceivable that such men as St. Timothy and St. Titus, notwithstanding their frequent journeyings, should not have had some city and community which they regarded as their home, and where they spent at least the later years of their life in quieter work on the spot. Thus tradition makes St. Titus at least latterly bishop of Gortyna, though St. Paul gave him charge of all the communities in Crete. Hence we see why there are no precepts or intimations in the Apostolic Epistles about the Church being guided by the collegiate action of the Presbytery.'. The silence is significant; for St. Paul and his colleagues could not avoid creating some system which should have the necessary conditions of permanence and stability after their own departure, whether monarchical, by devolving the Apostolate on the Episcopate, or Presbyteral. This latter St. Paul clearly never thought of. He only once speaks of the laying on of hands of the Presbytery;[1] but it was he who ordained, and the Presbyters only joined, as is still the custom.

Diotrephes, who is mentioned in the Third Epistle of St. John, seems to have been in a position which must have been that of a Bishop. In his domineering pride he forbids members of the Church to receive foreign brethren, and puts those who do so out of communion; he shows contempt for the Apostle himself, and St. John saw that he must come there in person to unmask him.[2] In the Revelation the Episcopate appears clearly and unmistakably. The Lord sends written messages to the presidents of the seven Asiatic Churches, who are called in prophetic language "angels" or messengers of God, as Malachi had before called them angels, ambassadors or messengers of the Lord of hosts, and as the forerunner of Christ was also called.[3] The name comes nearest that of an Apostle, and is almost synonymous with it; those so called are messengers of God, who, as successors of the Apostles, have to proclaim God's will to the people. Christ calls these angels the seven stars

---

[1] 1 Tim. iv. 14.  
[2] 3 John 9, 10, φιλοπρωτεύων.  
[3] Mal. ii. 7. Matt. xi. 10.

in His right hand; their seven Churches are symbolised by seven candlesticks distinct from the stars.[1] One of them, the angel of Thyatira, has a wife who claims to be a prophetess, and whose Heathenish and heretical errors and evil influence in the Church he suffers with culpable weakness.[2] The angels are always spoken of in the singular number, which is then first changed into the plural when the communities are spoken of. It is said, for instance, to the angel of Pergamos, " Thou hast not denied my faith even in the days of Antipas, My faithful Martyr, who was slain among you."[3] Thus the angel or Bishop is always distinguished from the community. One message, after addressing its warnings to the Bishop of Thyatira, turns to the community in the words, " But to you the rest in Thyatira, I say," that is, to those whom the false prophetess has not been able to seduce.[4] These angels are praised for the good found in their Churches, and made responsible for the abuses, which last, therefore, they have authority to put down. The angel of Philadelphia is promised that, although he has little power as yet, a portion of the unbelieving Jews shall kneel before him—either for baptism or confirmation. Those in whose communities are Nicolaitans or Balaamites are sharply rebuked; they ought to have thrust those men out of the Church. These, then, are seven bearers of Apostolical, now become Episcopal, authority. St. John praises, blames and threatens them, not in his own name, but in the name of the Lord, who Himself bids him write these letters. The Church of Ephesus which, when St. Paul took leave of it at Miletus, was under the guidance of several Elders and the superintendence of the Apostle, is now under a successor of St. Timothy, who is praised for having proved and rejected the false Apostles and hating the deeds of the Nicolaitans.

The Epistle of Clement of Rome to the Corinthians dates,

---

[1] Apoc. i. 16, 20; ii. 1.
[2] ii. 20. τὴν γυναῖκά σου Ἰεζαβήλ. The word σου is in the best and oldest MSS., the Syrian and older Latin version (in Cyprian and Primasius, "uxorem tuam,") and is, therefore, rightly received into the text by Meyer, Lachmann, Tischendorf and Buttmann. Only Düsterdiek rejects it, manifestly on grounds other than critical, for the evidence is overwhelming in its favour.
[3] Apoc. ii. 13.
[4] ὑμῖν δὲ λέγω τοῖς λοιποῖς κ. τ. λ. Apoc. ii. 24. The agreement of the best MSS. puts it beyond a doubt that this is the right reading. On the later version καὶ λοιποῖς, which gives the plural ὑμῖν for the angel, more than one Presbyterian house of cards has been built.

like the Apocalypse, from the later years of the first century. Three deputies came with it from Rome to Corinth, to help in restoring the order and harmony there which had been thrown into confusion. Jealousy and pride had led to a shameful and godless division in that community, so flourishing and well-ordered before and so obedient to its rulers. For the sake of one or two persons they had rebelled against their " Elders," and deposed some of them who were blameless in the discharge of their office. The lower rose against the higher, the young against the old. This quarrel had caused great sorrow to Christians, and given great scandal; even Jews and Heathen were watching it. The rulers against whom the uproar was directed are twice called " Elders," but this word is so little appropriated by St. Clement to any office, that he twice uses it in the sense of elderly, as opposed to younger laymen. The office he calls that of over-seeing (ἐπισκόπη), and gives as its principal function the sacerdotal one of offering gifts. Nor does he use the name of " Overseer " more distinctively than that of Presbyter. He says, that "the Apostles preached in several countries and cities, and made of the first fruits of their converts, when proved in the Spirit, Bishops and Deacons for future believers." He makes no distinction, then, between the two names of Presbyters and Bishops, and he here means presbyters. He distinguishes from these the Apostles and their successors, saying, " In prospect of contention arising about the office of ruling, the Apostles appointed the afore-mentioned rulers, and ordained for the future that after their death other tried men should hold their office of appointing such persons." He adds, " that it was a crime to deprive of their office those appointed by the Apostles, or by other excellent men who succeeded them."[1]

St. Clement then distinguishes three degrees—the Apostolate, as exercised by the Apostles themselves and by " approved men after their death," their successors, especially in the choice and ordination of ministers—the office of Presbyter or Overseer—and the Diaconate. He quotes as a type and parallel the hierarchical organisation of the

---

[1] Ep. Clem. Rom. 47, 45, 21, (ἡγούμενοι), 43, 57, 1, 3, 44.

Old Covenant. It seems that at Corinth there were differences about the time and order of Divine service, for the writer urges it as a Divine precept that liturgical worship must be conducted at fixed times, fixed places, and by fixed persons. "They are blessed and pleasing to God who make their offerings at fixed times, for the high priest has his proper office, the priests their special place, the Levites their own ministries, the layman is bound by the precepts for laymen. Thus let each of you in his own order offer to God his thanksgiving with a good conscience, not overstepping the fixed limits of his ministry in the Church."[1] Then comes the mention of the three ecclesiastical degrees, Apostles, overseers, ministers; the name of "layman" is one peculiar to Christianity, having no Hebrew equivalent. The quarrel in Corinth probably arose at the bishop's death, and had reference to the appointment of a successor. This may be inferred from the statement that only two or three persons gave occasion for it and that the motive was envy and jealousy, as also from the advice that he who had caused it had better remove to some other place.[2] This, too, explains why St. Clement always speaks of "presidents" or "Presbyters." He knew of no Bishop in Corinth, because the chair was vacant, but he recognised three degrees, which he calls, after his manner of identifying Jewish and Christian ordinances, those of high priest, priest, and Levite. If the words "Presbyter" and "Overseer," some years later in St. Ignatius' Epistles, show their fixed sense as indicating two distinct offices, it is in accordance with the natural process of development that the thing should come before the name. There are, therefore, no fixed names of offices in the New Testament. Apostles, like St. Peter and St. John, call themselves Presbyters; St. Paul calls them Deacons; the same persons are called Presbyters and Overseers.[3] St. Paul calls Andronicus and Junia (of whom nothing further is known) "distinguished among the Apostles," and Epaphroditus "Apostle" of the Philippians, and speaks of brethren who help him as "Apostles of Churches, a glory of Christ."[4]

[1] εὐχαριστείτω, referring to the Eucharist as the chief act and centre of worship.
[2] Ib. c. 54.
[3] 1 Pet. v. 1.  2 John 1.  1 Cor. iii. 5.
[4] Rom. xvi. 7.  Phil. ii. 25.  2 Cor. viii. 23.

If we turn to particular Churches to collect the few reliable notices about Church officers of the Apostolic age, the first to be mentioned is the Roman Church. That St. Peter worked in Rome is a fact so abundantly proved and so deeply imbedded in the earliest Christian history, that whoever treats it as a legend ought in consistency to treat the whole of the earliest Church history as legendary, or, at least, quite uncertain. A few important circumstances may be mentioned here in addition to what has been quoted in a previous chapter. His presence in Corinth is obviously connected with his journey to Rome, and no one will accept the one and deny the other. The Corinthians parties which roused St. Paul's indignation assume that St. Peter no less than St. Paul and Apollos have been at Corinth. "Every man says, I am of Paul, I of Apollos, I of Cephas;" and, again, "All is yours, whether it be Paul or Apollos, or Cephas."[1] There is no hint in the Epistle that only disciples or adherents of St. Peter had preached at Corinth in his name and raised a party for him there. In the Second Epistle, where St. Paul defends his Apostolic authority against Judaizing opponents, there is no syllable hinting that St. Peter had sent these opponents or that they were his disciples.[2] Whence came the party of Cephas, if he had never been in Corinth himself? If we refer to his disciple, St. Clement, he says in his letter to the Corinthians;—"Paul has written to you of himself, of Cephas and of Apollos; for you make parties for those Apostles who minister with a good testimony, and for the man accredited by them."[3] St. Clement knows only of personal parties occasioned by the three men themselves, and Apollos was accredited not only by St. Paul but by St. Peter also, not in Judæa, whither he did not go, but in Corinth. Thence the contrast drawn by Clement, "But now only see who they be that have converted you;" then it was two Apostles and men accredited by them, now it is nameless men who have nothing in common with Apostles.

---

[1] 1 Cor. i. 12: iii. 22.
[2] 2 Cor. xi. 22, 23. The only thing mentioned in this last passage is their boasting of their Jewish descent and their character as ministers of Christ.
[3] παρεκλίθητε γὰρ ἀποστόλοις μεμαρτυρημένοις καὶ ἀνδρὶ δεδοκιμασμένῳ παρ αὐτοῖς. Clem. *Ep.* 47.

Dionysius of Corinth, then, had good right six years later to maintain that St. Peter had been there.

St. Clement, again, reminds the Corinthians of the martyrdom of Peter and Paul, and of the many who had suffered with them, without any indication of place, unless it lies in the words "among us," meaning Rome. But the very mention implies that St. Peter's martyrdom was a well-known fact, and it is inconceivable that his execution only should have been known without the place, or that the place can have been forgotten and a wrong one substituted so soon after. And when St. Ignatius writes to the Romans some years later; "I do not command you like Peter and Paul; they were Apostles, and I am a condemned criminal,"[1]—it is clear, without any explanation, that he desires to remind them of the two men who as founders and teachers had been the glory of their Church.

The Ebionite document, called *The Preaching of Peter*, must have originated about the time of St. Ignatius or very soon after, for in Hadrian's time it had been used by Heracleon.[2] It brings St. Peter and St. Paul together at Rome, and divides the discourses and utterances which took place there between the two. Origen thinks there is an admixture of genuine and spurious matter in this document, while Clement of Alexandria quotes it often without ever expressing any doubt about it. It is notoriously founded on the universally admitted fact of St. Peter's having laboured at Rome. But it is inconceivable that such a writing, claiming acceptance in the Church as a genuine product of the Apostolic age, should have put forward a groundless fable about the theatre of St. Peter's operations at a time when many who had seen him must have been still alive. St. Irenæus and Eusebius had the writings of Papias and Hegesippus before them, and these authors had certainly not been silent about St. Peter or contradicted the common view, for in that case neither would Eusebius have failed to record it, nor Irenæus have appealed so confidently, against the numerous heretics in Rome itself, to a fact by denying which those Gnostics could have shaken his whole argument. Moreover, the words of Eusebius show that Papias must have expressly

[1] Ignat. *Ep. ad Rom.* 4.  [2] Orig. *Com. in Joann.* xiii. 17. *Opp.* iv. 226.

maintained with Clement that St. Peter wrote his Epistle at Rome.[1]

In reference to the first Roman Bishops, the consentient statements of the Greeks, Irenæus, Eusebius and Epiphanius, are infinitely more trustworthy than the Latin accounts of Optatus and Augustine and the Roman catalogues of Popes. Among these, the list drawn up under Liberius from the death of Christ till his own time (352—369) is the oldest, and the source of the later ones;[2] the second part is the most valuable and is derived from the most genuine sources, the first part, up to A.D. 230, has important errors, and the contemporary consulates and Emperors are given in a random and very incorrect way; from this record all later Roman lists and accounts are copied. The next oldest document is the earlier Recension of the so-called Pontifical Books, closing under Justinian, with Pope Felix, A.D. 530.[3] Other records of the fifth and sixth centuries and further down have no weight. The statement of Optatus and St. Augustine are drawn from a common source, which is either the Liberian list or one based on it.[4] On the contrary, the statements of Hegesippus and Irenæus, who had both stayed in Rome, and those of Eusebius are of the most reliable kind.

---

[1] Euseb. ii. 15 ἣν (ἐπιστολὴν) καὶ συντάξαι φάσιν ἐπ' αὐτῆς Ῥώμης. The φάσιν refers to Clement and Papias.

[2] See Mommsen on the chroniclers of the year 354 in *Abhandl. der Sächs. Ges. d. Wiss.* ii. 583. The chief error of the first part is putting Anicetus before Pius. From this list comes the much criticised statement of the twenty-five years duration of St. Peter's episcopate. This does not mean that he was bishop *at Rome* twenty-five years, as it was afterwards misunderstood, but that from Christ's Ascension to his death was twenty-five years, during which he held his episcopate, that is his dignity in the Church. The words are, "Post ascensum Ejus Petrus episcopatum suscepit." And thus the consuls are given from the year 30 to 55. The omission of consulates after Liberius in later Recensions of the *Liber Pontificalis* shows that they are taken from this document.

[3] Schelstrate *Antiq. Eccl.* T. i. p. 401 sqq.

[4] Before, however, the blunder of making Cletus and Anacletus into two Popes came in. The false position of Anicetus before Pius is there also. Victorinus, author of the poem against Marcion found in Tertullian, forms, in a measure, an independent source. Oehler has pointed out that Victorinus, a rhetorician at Marseilles in 425, was the composer. He gives a list of Roman Bishops up to Marcion's time, and agrees with the Liberian list as to a Cletus *or* Anacletus, whom, however, he places before Clement, as also in observing that Hermas, author of the *Shepherd*, was a brother of Pius, whom he rightly places before Anicetus. There are, then, three different Western Recensions of the Roman succession, the Roman in the Liberian list, the African of Optatus and St. Augustine, and the Gallican of Victorinus. The Canon of the Roman Mass retains the original order of the Greek diptychs, "Lini, Cleti, Clementis."

Hegesippus, a Christian Jew of Palestine, having journeyed as far as Rome stayed there till A.D. 156, in order to ascertain the state of doctrine in the separate Churches, and to examine the Apostolic succession in the principal Churches. He says that in Rome he wrote down the list of the Bishops up to Anicetus.[1] Here we perceive the authorities used by Eusebius as to the oldest Roman bishops and the duration of their Episcopate; he did not go to St. Irenæus, who gives no dates, but who was enabled, from being in Rome twenty-five years after Hegesippus, to learn equally well on the best authority the succession of eleven or twelve Bishops. If we consider that Hegesippus, when he came to Rome, only required for his purpose to investigate the succession of Bishops there for the short period of about eighty-three years, that he certainly found persons there whose fathers could remember the beginning of that period, and that, except the short and not severe persecution under Domitian, the Roman Church had suffered no special disturbances, we must place the fullest reliance on his statements—the more so as they are confirmed by a man who used the same authorities and whose teacher had heard the Apostle St. John.

We have, then, for the succession of the first Roman bishops two independent and accordant witnesses, Hegesippus and Irenæus. The latter certainly did not know Hegesippus' book, or he would have appealed to it against the heretics. Both of them, and the Roman catalogues, make Linus the first bishop after the Apostles,—probably the same member of the Roman Church whom St. Paul names with Eubulus, Pudens and Claudia, as greeting Timothy.[2] St. Irenæus says: "After Peter and Paul had founded the Roman Church, and set it in order, they gave over the Episcopate of it to Linus."[3] This makes the re-

---

[1] διαδοχὴν ἐποιήσαμεν μέχρις 'Ανικήτου. Euseb. iv. 22. Soon after he uses of the succession of Soter and Eleutherius the word διαδέχεται, and adds, ἐν ἑκάστῃ δὲ διαδοχῇ καὶ ἑκάστῃ πόλει οὕτως ἔχει, ὡς ὁ νόμος κηρύσσει καὶ οἱ προφῆται καὶ ὁ κύριος. There can be no doubt, then, that διαδοχὴ means Episcopal succession. The conjecture διατριβὴ, which Savile introduces in the margin of his work and Stroth has taken without further comment into the text, comes from no MSS., and is quite worthless. See note in Routh's *Rel. Sacræ.* i. 245. The context of Hegesippus shows that he did not mean in the words cited, to say, "qu'il mit par écrit la doctrine que suivait alors l'Eglise Romaine," as Tillemont supposes (Mem. Eccl. iii. 611,) though it was his aim certainly to examine the condition of doctrine in the particular Churches.

[2] 2 Tim. iv. 21.  [3] Iren. iii. 3.

gulation of the Roman Church and the appointment of Linus a common act of both Apostles, and since then the Roman bishops have been frequently regarded as successors of both. The Roman Church was viewed as inheriting alike from St. Paul his prerogative of Apostle of the Gentiles, and from St. Peter his dignity as the foundation of the Church, and as possessing the power of the keys. Eusebius says of Linus, that he was the first Bishop after Peter, and of a later Bishop, Alexander, that he formed the fifth link in the succession from Peter and Paul;[1] and he almost always reckons the others "from the Apostles," *i.e.* Peter and Paul. Epiphanius calls Peter and Paul the first Bishops of Rome, which rests, indeed, on a peculiar notion of his to be mentioned presently.[2] The Roman Church is the seat of the two Apostles;[3] the power of Rome founded on Peter and Paul;[4] these and similar expressions are frequent later.

Anencletus succeeded Linus; both, according to Eusebius, were bishops for about twelve years, so that Clement, the third, entered on his office A.D. 79 or 80. The change of the name Anencletus into Cletus, and then Anacletus, has led to one bishop being divided into two, of whom one is placed before Clement and the other (Anacletus) after him.[5] That the Greek records which give but one Anencletus, and place him before Clement, are the only correct ones, is now acknowledged even in Rome.[6]

---

[1] Euseb. iii. 4; iv. 1.     [2] *Panar. Hær.* 27, 6, οἱ ἀπόστολοι αὐτοὶ καὶ ἐπίσκοποι.
[3] So the Council of Arles in 314 says, "In quibus (partibus, *i.e.*, Rome) apostoli quotidie sedent." *Ep. ad Silv.* Cf. Theodoret, *Ep.* 113 *ad Leonem.*
[4] Paulin. *Natal* 3.
[5] Anacletus is no name I ever heard of. But Anencletus (meaning the same as Innocentius) is found as a man's name in a Spartan inscription. Boekh. *Corp. Inscr.* T. i. p. 116, n. 1240. The Greeks always have Anencletus. In Photius, *Cod.* 113, p. 90, Bekker, the name stands Anacletus, but the *Cod. Marc.* has the right form, Anencletus, as Dindorf observes (*Thes. Gr.*). The name Cletus is equally unknown and is clearly a corruption of Anencletus, which sounded strange to Latin ears. Many things have conspired to produce an appearance of error and uncertainty in the succession of the first Roman Bishops. First, there is this corruption of the second name; then, the influence of the Ebionite *Recognitions* translated by Rufinus, Clement's *Letter to James* from the same source, and the *Apostolical Constitutions.* The Letter to St. James, which records the solemn appointment of Clement by St. Peter, was generally followed, and its chief passages were copied into the Roman Pontifical; and so Linus and Cletus were said to have been only St. Peter's assistants during life, as Rufinus had already conjectured. Then, again, Cyprian says of Hyginus, "qui in urbe nonus fuit," and it was not observed that he reckoned St. Peter as first bishop, and so Anencletus was doubled to make eight predecessors.
[6] See Lazari *Catal. duo Antiq. Pont. Rom.* Romæ 1755, p. 31, where Cletus or

Whether, as Origen and Eusebius thought, Clement is the same person praised by St. Paul in the Epistle to the Philippians, is very doubtful. It seems more likely that St. Paul's disciple belonged to the Philippian Church. Anyhow the Roman bishop, as Irenæus remarks, had seen the holy Apostles and associated with them. He is the author of that famous Epistle to the Corinthians, which Eusebius says "was read of old in most congregations."[1] St. Clement displays in this writing a mind fostered and moulded by the reading of the Old Testament. He scarcely ever quotes the New Testament, and for every reference to a word of the Apostles' one finds ten citations from the Pentateuch, the Psalms, or the Prophets. He lives and moves in the Old Hebrew history; most of his examples come from it. He talks of "our father Abraham,"[2] whence many supposed that he was a born Israelite. He was not, but he certainly speaks as if he was. He sees but one Church since Abraham, the Church of the promise is become by a natural and necessary transition the Church of the fulfilment. All that was before Christ in a sense continues, and belongs to the present Church. Jewish priests and Christian presbyters are the same institution, and both have a sacrifice to offer. In short, Clement is the most characteristic representative of Church continuity. His leading idea is: "We Christians are the true Israelites, sons of Abraham and heirs of the promises; Abraham and Jacob, Moses and David, belong to us alone."

No New Testament or subsequent writer displays so marked a preference as Clement for the Jewish and Old Testament habit of thought, outspoken as he is about Christ and His redeeming work. In this respect his Epistle is in striking contrast to those of St. Ignatius and St. Polycarp, which are thoroughly saturated and ruled by New Testament ideas, phrases and reminiscences. St. Clement, therefore, was the right man for the Ebionite or Gnostic

---

Anacletus is supposed to have been Pope twice, both before and after Clement. On the other hand, see Delsignore *Inst. Hist. Eccl. Rom.* 1837, T. i. p. 38, Saccarelli *Hist. Eccl.* ii. 212. Yet in the Benedictine *Origines de l'Eglise Rom.* (Paris, 1836), an unsuccessful attempt is made to keep Anencletus and Cletus. What makes the thing more certain is, that the Roman author of the "Little Labyrinth" (Hippolytus) knows nothing of the double Anacletus, for he reckons Victor thirteenth after St. Peter. Eus. v. 24.

[1] Eus. iii. 15.     [2] Clem *Ep. ad Cor.* 31.

Judaizing party to choose (after St. James) for their hero and founder, under whose name they might try to gain entrance and authority for their writings. A man who had known both Apostles and was a successor of St. Peter in the imperial capital, whose Epistle was read with reverence in so many Churches, and gave evidence of such a Jewish turn of mind, was fitter than any one else of the Apostolic age for being represented as the connecting link between St. Peter and the Ebionite communities. It naturally follows that his person and history would be much coloured by fiction. Thus, in the Clementines, an Ebionite production of the second century, where Christianity is exhibited as a purified Mosaism, he is the principal personage after St. Peter, and his family history forms the basis of this didactic romance. In the Clementine *Epitome*, the reason why he was so dear to the Jews is thus given, not without a certain admixture of truth,—he had spoken of their forefathers as friends of God, their Law as holy, Divine and imperishable, had declared that Palestine was their abiding inheritance, and that, if they kept the Law, their nation should never be trodden out of the land.[1] The Ebionite view of Clement re-appears later in the *Teaching of the Apostles*, which formed the substratum of the so-called *Apostolical Constitutions* as they are known to us. This also was a document of Ebionite origin.[2] Here, too, as in the preface to the Homilies, which he is said to have addressed to St. James, Clement is the bishop appointed by St. Peter himself, and the brothers ascribed to him in the Homilies, Nicetas and Aquila, are made bishops of districts, not named, in Asia.[3]

Another Ebionite document was the *Preaching of Peter*, mentioned above, which records the last discourses of the Apostle at Rome and his intercourse with St. Paul.[4] The

---

[1] This must have been written before 136 A.D., or borrowed from a writing of that date, for the war under Hadrian was so far a war of extermination ὥστε πᾶσαν ὀλίγου δεῖν 'Ιουδαίαν ἐρημωθῆναι, Dio. Cass. 69, 14.

[2] Besides the traces and proofs of Ebionite thought in the Constitutions pointed out by Rothe (*Anfänge der Kirche*, pp. 541 sqq.) there are others. Thus, (I. 1, c. 6) when the Christian is advised to read the Mosaic law, he is warned to beware of later interpolations (τῶν ἐν αὐτῷ ἐπεισάκτων). On this Ebionite view of the Pentateuch being interpolated cf. *Clem. Hom.* ii. 38; iii. 4, 5, 47.

[3] *Const. Apost.* vii. 46.

[4] The title Ebionite is here taken in a wider sense than only to include those so-called by Epiphanius, or represented in the Clementines. That, notwithstanding

appointment of Clement by St. Peter must have been found chronicled here, and hence came the parallel statements of the Clementines, the Recognitions, the Epistle of Clement to St. James and the Constitutions. The fact of the *last* discourses and ordinances of St. Peter being recorded in this document proves that it must have contained an account of the administration of the Roman Church after his death also.[1] A Latin translation of this *Preaching of Peter* gained currency early in the West; Lactantius appeals to it, and in an old writing about baptism it is pointed out as the authority for an heretical form of baptism.[2] The statement of Tertullian, that Clement was ordained by St. Peter, is derived either directly or indirectly from this document; and some later Latin writers say the same. But it was obviously requisite from the Ebionite point of view that St. Clement should be regarded as St. Peter's heir and successor, appointed by him, and that in consequence Linus and Cletus should be ignored.[3]

The fable, again, of Simon Magus being cast down at the Apostle's prayer when flying through the air, is another derived from the Petrine apocryphal writings, which were all composed in the Ebionite interest, probably from the *Judgment of Peter* which got its title from this legend. It was so far founded on fact, that Simon was really in Rome and St. Peter met him there; and then the account given by Suetonius of an unlucky attempt made in Nero's presence was made to refer to Simon. So the story got into the *Teaching of the Apostles*, and, in the West, Arnobius was the first to adopt it, 303 A.D.[4]

---

what St. Paul is made to say against the Jewish feasts, the *Preaching* represents Jewish views, is clear from its agreement with the Hebrew Gospel and its ascribing to Christ a confession of sinfulness. See Jones, *Method of Settling the Canon*. Oxf. 1827, I. 313—315.

[1] *Inst.* iv. 21.

[2] In the Bremer edition of Cyprian, p. 22, Append.

[3] Tert. *Præscr.* 34. St. Jerome, who is himself uncertain and sometimes places Clement after Anacletus, sometimes directly after St. Peter, but in his catalogue of ecclesiastical writers pronounces decisively in the latter sense, says that most Latins held him for successor of Peter. *De Vir. Ill.* 14. This is certainly an exaggeration, for Tertullian is the only extant Latin writer who says so, and St. Jerome knew very few who are now lost, viz., Rheticius, Donatus, Severus and some lost writings of Novatian and Victorinus.

[4] The *Judicium Petri* is mentioned by St. Jerome (*De Vir. Ill.*) and Rufinus (*Expos. in Symb. Ap.* 38). Hippol. *Ref. Hær.* vi. 19, mentions Simon being at Rome, but describes a wholly different kind of death elsewhere. Arnobius' book shows clearly that he got many ideas from apocryphal and Gnostic sources, widely

This is the place to mention a theory of Epiphanius which has been thought to explain much in the oldest Church history, and to settle the contradictions about the early Roman succession. He says that the Alexandrian Church never had two bishops together, "like other cities."[1] Hence it has been inferred, that at first the still unreconciled difference between Jewish and Gentile converts obliged the Apostles to appoint two Bishops in every city, a Hebrew and a Greek, for the two congregations. Thence came the further notion that Linus was appointed by St. Paul for the Roman Gentiles, Cletus by St. Peter for the Roman Jews, but that the Petrine bishop survived his colleague, and from 71 to 77 A.D. was sole bishop of Rome; while Clement succeeded him, and sat from 78 to 86.[2] There is no older authority for this notion. Epiphanius himself has not applied his view of a double Episcopate in the same city to the Roman Church, undoubtedly because he attached great authority to the fixed and consentient lists of Irenæus and Eusebius. But as he believed the *Teaching of the Apostles* to be genuine, which makes Clement ordained by St. Peter, he tried to explain matters by what he himself designates a mere conjecture,—that Clement, after his ordination by St. Peter, laid aside the episcopal office and kept quiet during the life of Linus and Cletus (Anacletus), but, after the death of Cletus, was compelled to undertake the direction of the Roman Church. Of a contemporary episcopate of Linus and Cletus Epiphanius knows nothing; he makes Cletus follow Linus.[3] But

---

different from the teaching of the Church. Cotelier perceived that the story, given by him in *Const. Apost.* vi. 9, is derived from apocryphal and unreliable sources. *Pat. Ap.* i. 341. Even at Rome the fable seems to have gained no entrance, notwithstanding so many authorities. Cotelier tells of the "silentium Romanorum Pontificum, qui sua tacere non solent," and the *Liber Pontif.* only says, "dum diutius altercarentur Simon divino nutu interemptus est." Ed. Vignol. i. 7. And this even is a later addition from St. Augustine's treatise *De Hær.*, who says himself that most Romans thought the event fabulous. *Epist.* 36 *ad Casul.* I think he means not only the derivation of the Saturday fast from St. Peter's then fasting, but the whole story.

[1] *Panar. Hær.* 68. 7.

[2] This is Bunsen's theory, as his friend Greenwood says, in his *Cathedra Petri* i. 53, London, 1856, observing that he will give further grounds for it in a future work, *Chronological Tables of Ecclesiastical History.*

[3] Epiph. *Hær.* 27. He thinks the words in St. Clement's Epistle to the Corinthians, advising the withdrawal of the person who had given occasion to the complication, refer to Clement himself, a misconception that rests only on want of memory.

Rufinus tries to save the credit of the Epistle to James on the supposition, often adopted afterwards, that Linus and Cletus only presided over the Roman Church during St. Peter's life.[1] As far as we see, he only got his notion of Clement being appointed by St. Peter from this Ebionite document.

The statement of Epiphanius about there being two bishops together in the first age stands quite alone; there is no hint or trace elsewhere of one Church having really had two Bishops. But we can point to the authority from which the uncritical and credulous Epiphanius got his view; it is the *Teaching of the Apostles*. He was the first to treat the *Constitutions* as a genuine work of the Apostles, "a divine discourse," and he often uses it.[2] What is there said about the first bishops appointed by the Apostles had accordingly full authority for him, and he found there that St. Peter appointed Evodius, and St. Paul Ignatius, in Antioch; that at Ephesus St. Paul appointed Timothy, St. John appointed John; whereas of Alexandria it is said that the first ordained by St. Mark was Annianus, and that Abilius, ordained by St. Luke, succeeded him.[3] Therefore, Epiphanius says, Alexandria had not two bishops like other cities. The element of truth in his view has been already noticed, that just at first a single bishop distinct from the Apostles was impracticable in many Churches.

Hegesippus found everywhere in the Church, so far as his researches or his travels led him, the same constitution, doctrine and succession. He certainly visited Antioch on his way westwards from Palestine, for Evodius its first bishop is mentioned, whom Ignatius succeeded.[3] Eusebius has an important statement, probably derived from Hegesippus, about the filling up of the See of Jerusalem after St. James' death; he says that after the conquest of Jerusalem the surviving Apostles and disciples and the relations of Christ assembled, and unanimously chose as Bishop Simon, son of Clopas, the Lord's cousin.[4] The Apostles

---

[1] *Præf. ad Recogn.* Coteler. i. 492.
[2] *Apost. Const.* vii. 46. Epiphanius calls them once θεῖος λόγος. He not only recognised the six first books but the seventh, which is commonly held to have a later origin. For, in appealing to the διάταξις τῶν ἀποστόλων about fasting (*Hær.* 75. 6.) he had *Const.* vii. 23 before his eyes. In the succession of Roman bishops he has included Cletus, whom the Constitutions omit, undoubtedly influenced by the testimony of Hegesippus and Irenæus.
[3] Eus. *Hist.* iii. 22, 36.  [4] Ib. iii. 11.

then living were St. John, St. Philip and St. Andrew, who came from Asia Minor to this meeting, A.D. 71. That St. Polycarp was made Bishop of Smyrna by the Apostles (immediately by St. John) is testified by his disciple Irenæus.[1] Polycrates of Ephesus, who was thirty-eight years old when St. Polycarp died (167 A.D.), relates that he was the eighth bishop in his family, and appeals to the tradition of his relatives and predecessors, which carries back the Episcopal succession in one family to Apostolic times.[2] In the Epistles of Ignatius, written a few years after the death of St. John, all the Asiatic Churches appear provided with bishops. And this is confirmed by Clement of Alexandria, the best acquainted with Christian literature of any one up to his time, who says:—" When John went from Patmos to Ephesus, his custom was to visit the neighbouring Gentile regions, partly to appoint bishops, partly to regulate whole communities, partly to ordain any one marked out by the Spirit." Here we meet with the noteworthy fact, mentioned by Clement of Rome, that, as was the case with St. Paul and St. Timothy, ordination to any function in the Church followed on a prophetic illumination, either vouchsafed to an Apostle or to other members of the Church.[3]

St. Paul ordered that women should not speak publicly in the Church; they were to obey their husbands, to learn and not to teach.[4] Yet spiritual gifts were bestowed on the female sex, as the four daughters of Philip had the gift of prophecy.[5] And in Corinth the custom had grown up that women under the influence of the gift of tongues and prophecy should pray and prophesy aloud in the assemblies. Meanwhile the Apostles knew how to find a sphere of work for women in Church life. The institution of Deaconesses was created; and Phœbe a deaconess at Cenchrea is mentioned in the Epistle to the Romans. It was the business of these women devoted to the ministry of the Church to take care of the poor, the sick, and strangers. There is further information about them in the first Epistle to Timothy. St. Paul speaks first of the provision to be made for helpless and neglected widows, but proceeds there-

---

[1] Iren. iii. 3. Eus. iii. 36. [2] Routh i. 371. [3] Clem. Ep. 42.
[4] 1 Cor. xiv. 34. [5] Acts xxi. 9.

upon to refer to a peculiar kind of widows, who had a special relation to the Church. Their names were to be marked in a catalogue, and they were to have a special ministry assigned to them. The requisite conditions were, that the widow should be over sixty years old, that she should have had one husband, should have the testimony of good works, should have brought up children, have been hospitable, and have given aid and consolation to the afflicted and sorrowful.[1] The duties of a Deaconess were accordingly such as aged women could best discharge, not requiring severe bodily exertion. Preparing women for baptism and assisting them in it so as to avoid any scandal, bringing up orphans, conveying Apostolical and Episcopal charges to individual female members of the community,—these duties and the like belonged to them. In short, they supplied to the great family of the local Church the wifely and motherly element.

It was self-evident that widows over sixty years of age would not marry again, nor was any promise required of them. But there were younger widows and virgins who became Deaconesses. The latter must, even in the Apostolic age, have been chosen by preference in some communities, for St. Ignatius, in his Epistle to the Smyrnians, salutes the virgins who were named "widows."[2] This shows that widow had become an official title of deaconesses, but that most of them, at least in Smyrna, were not really widows but virgins. There had already been evil experience of younger widows in Ephesus, or other Pauline communities. They had, like the virgins, taken a vow to serve the Lord unmarried, and St. Paul expected them to persevere night and day in prayer and in Church works of mercy. But many of them waxed wanton, made use of their position in houses for tattling, desired to marry, and broke their vow, which gave to the adversaries of Christians occasion for mockery.[3] Therefore, the Apostle wished younger widows to marry again, and only aged ones to be made Deaconesses. But since many diaconal functions required younger and stronger persons, there was the more

---

[1] 1 Tim. v. 9, 10. St. Paul could not mean that all widows under sixty were to be excluded from charitable support, and he must therefore refer to a special class of widows.
[2] Ignat. *Ep. ad Smyrn.* 12, p. 196. Dressel.     [3] 1 Tim. v. 5, 11—14.

readiness in many Churches to take virgins, who would not be led, like young widows, by their former experience of the married state to break their promise made to God and the Church.

St. Paul mentions in his Epistles to Timothy and Titus the qualifications required for the office of an Elder.[1] He lays more weight on moral character than on intellectual eminence. A new convert was not to be taken, for he was likely to become proud, if preferred to older and more tried members of the community; an arrangement which could be carried out at Ephesus, but not everywhere, not in recently planted Churches. He only is fit, St. Paul adds, who has proved himself a good master of a house and father of a family, for only he will be able to maintain his authority in the Church. It had to be a rule at first for fathers of families to be chosen for Church offices, for among Jewish converts there were no unmarried men of ripe age; and if a Gentile remained single to man's full age, he had nearly always led a wild and dissolute life, and lacked what the Apostle made an important qualification, a good report from those without. Sobriety and chastity, a seemly external conduct and deportment, and the exercise of hospitality, are equally indispensable qualifications. Hospitality was then the more highly esteemed, because Christianity was in some sense a migratory religion, and both missions and persecutions imposed on Christians the duty of keeping open house for brethren coming and going.

Only two intellectual qualifications were made essential, first that the elder be capable of teaching—that is, he must possess a certain degree of culture and the natural gift of clear and regular enunciation—secondly, that he should keep to the traditional sense of the Old Testament and the words of Christ—that is, preach the word of faith as deposited by the Apostles in the Church, not his own subjective notions, and be able to withstand gainsayers. The capacity of teaching, then, required in a Presbyter was a very limited one, in accordance with the circumstances of the period. The number of well educated men must have been extremely small in the first communities. Attendance on the Synagogue service had given Jewish converts the requisite

[1] 1 Tim. iii. 2—7. Tit. i. 6—9.

acquaintance with the Old Testament; accurate knowledge of Apostolic teaching they of course had. The rhetoric then so highly prized, and the art of word-painting and elegant periods, St. Paul had pointed out as one he declined to use and not one to be coveted; but the natural eloquence of intense conviction, increased by miraculous power, was honoured in the Apostolic communities, wherever it appeared, as a most worthy gift, and St. Paul knew well that his gift of utterance was serviceable to the cause of Christ.[1] Yet at no time and in no nation has eloquence had so pure and lofty a mission as then, when Christian preaching entered into history as a Divine institution and mighty instrument of human weal, when it had for its theme, inexhaustible and ever new, all the antitheses of human life, all the great problems of mind, all moral relations of man to man, life and death, heaven and hell, God and Satan. We may picture to ourselves the impression made on a Heathen when he first entered a Christian congregation, accustomed as he was to a dumb priesthood and a silent temple, and heard men speaking at once on the highest questions elsewhere only handled in the philosophical schools and on the daily occurrences and duties of life, in the language of confidence and out of the consciousness of a common conviction and experience.

Nothing is more prominent in the Apostolic writings than the assured conviction that the shepherd is answerable for the sheep. St. Paul calls his communities his glory in the day of the Lord.[2] There is a sacred bond of mutual love between shepherd and sheep. His sufferings are for their sake. And those who minister must serve the Church by their sufferings as well as their acts.[3] It is part of their priestly office to pray constantly for their people, apart from the Eucharistic Sacrifice. Therefore, the twenty-four elders, who represent in heaven the earthly priesthood, have "golden vials full of odours, which are the prayers of the Saints"—that is, the earthly members of the Church.[4] And thus the spirit of self-sacrifice, the freedom from all self-seeking, is to be made an indispensable qualification by Titus in choosing ministers.[5]

[1] 1 Cor. ii. 4, 5. 2 Cor. v. 11; vi. 11.
[2] 2 Cor. i. 14. Phil. iv. 1. 1 Thess. ii. 19.
[3] Col. i. 24. [4] Apoc. v. 8. [5] Tit. i. 7.

These requirements, of which men like St. Timothy at Ephesus, St. Titus in Crete and their successors, the Bishops, were to be the final judges, show that congregations could only have a very restricted right in the choice of their officers and in entire subordination to the Apostles or Bishops [1] St. Paul assumes that, as a rule, those possessed of the necessary qualifications will desire the ministerial office. In fact, the Apostles had sometimes to guard against too many wanting to become teachers, as St. James's warning indicates.[2] The Bishops were to delay ordaining candidates and appointing them to this work, as long as seemed necessary for their due probation. When St. Paul says that one who desires the office of Overseer desires an honourable work, he implies that the Bishop should not only watch for those who offer themselves, but exhort those whose fitness he knows to do so.[3] Then followed the part of the congregation; the Bishop proposed to them the man he had already tried and found qualified, and they expressed their assent. So says St. Clement; "The Apostles appointed Overseers and Deacons, approved by the whole community."[4] Of a competition between several candidates, decided by the majority of votes, there is no trace either then or afterwards, nor has such a custom ever prevailed in the Church. What occurred at Jerusalem, where the Apostles left to the Church just formed and filled with the extraordinary gifts of the Spirit the choice of its first seven ministers, has scarcely ever been repeated.[5] The Ephesian Presbyters were called by the Holy Ghost to rule the Church; St. Timothy was ordained in consequence of a prophecy, not a popular election, and he is bidden to impart to other fit and faithful men what he has received from St. Paul,[6]—which implies that he is to choose them himself, and not trust it to the chances of a public election. But still, it is certainly true that no Elder or Bishop was forced on a reluctant community. And St. Paul had made it a condition, that he should enjoy a good reputation.

The Lord Himself had ordained in the beginning that the

[1] 1 Tim. iii. 1.   [2] James iii. 1.   [3] 1 Tim. v. 22; iii. 1.
[4] Clem. *Ep. ad Cor.* 44.
[5] Acts vi. 1—6. The χειροτονεῖν of Acts xiv. 23 may apply equally well to ordination of men chosen by previous election, as of men chosen by the Apostles.
[6] 2 Tim. ii. 2.

members of the Church should support their ministers. He told His first disciples that they should want for nothing, for the workman was worthy of his meat.[1] The accompanying admonition, to give freely what they had freely received, pointed to the right mean to be observed between making a professional and covetous use of the Apostolic office, and, on the other hand, keeping silent as to the duty of the people to support them. St. Paul expressly claimed for the messengers and ministers of Christ this right to live of the Gospel, to be supported by their congregations, just as the gardener, warrior, or shepherd—he names the three positions most like the clerical—live by their calling.[2] He naturally preferred himself, in presence of his many adversaries, to avoid every appearance of gaining by his office, and so to live by the labour of his hands; and he even persisted in this, where, as at Corinth, it provoked contempt, in order to give Christians an example of the diligence in work he so stringently urged upon them.[3] But he at the same time insisted, that those who impart the greater blessings of teaching and ordinances of grace have a just claim to the lesser benefits of a livelihood. And thus he accepted the voluntary offerings of the Philippians, for there the suspicions, which elsewhere restrained him, could not be felt. When he tells St. Timothy that Presbyters who rule well, especially such as labour in teaching and preaching, deserve double honour, it is clear from the following words that he means a richer income.[4]

We gather from the Apostolic Epistles that Christians gave much and readily, though the number of poor was far greater among them than of the wealthy. Collections were frequently sent to the poor Churches in Palestine, and St. Paul could incite particular Churches by the example of others.[5] He ordered that on the first day of the week every Christian should lay aside in his house something from his earnings, first for the Mother Church of Jerusalem.[6] In what form provision was made for the support of Presbyters and other common needs, we do not know. But it is clear

---

[1] Matt. x. 10.   [2] 1 Cor. ix. 7.   [3] 1 Cor. ix. 11. 2 Thess. iii. 8, 9.
[4] 1 Tim. v. 17. Cf. the citation in v. 18 of Deut. xxv. 4. The passage Gal. vi. 6 does not refer to worldly goods, for it would be too unmeasured a requirement. St. Paul means the moral and religious κοινωνία between teacher and disciple.
[5] Acts xi. 29. Rom. xv. 26.   [6] 1 Cor. xvi. 1 sqq.

that everywhere there was a common fund, made up of free-will offerings.

St. Mark's Gospel closes with an account of the signs which Jesus promised His disciples should follow them that believe in Him. These are, casting out evil spirits, speaking with new tongues, protection against the bite of deadly serpents and poisonous drinks, and healing the sick.[1] And in fact, from the time of the first outpouring of the Spirit at Pentecost, a rich stream of these and the like gifts flowed through the young Church, partly indeed through the consecration to her service of natural powers in an exalted and highly cultivated form, but also partly through miraculous powers breaking through all natural limitations. St. Paul named them in writing to the Corinthians, but without intending to give a full enumeration of all spiritual gifts then in the Church; his object was to exhibit, amid all their diversity, their unity of origin and of scope. There were gifts of knowledge, of faith, of will, of speech; but all had this in common, that they were wrought by the same Spirit for the service of others, for the building up of the Church, for ministering to the body of Christ. Only as so used did they fulfil their proper end.[2] They formed together a treasure the Church possessed, according to the Apostle,—a spiritual wealth, in which she recognised her strength, her ornament and her glory. He reminds the Corinthians of the contrast between their old dumb Heathenism, with its silent idols and voiceless temples, and the exuberant richness of utterances and communications in their assemblies now.

But these gifts and powers were of very unequal value, and St. Paul exhorted the Corinthians to strive for the highest and best. There were gifts one might keep or lose, use or leave unused, as one chose. To misuse many was easy enough, and every one was responsible for his use of his gifts to the Holy Ghost, who gave them. How St. Paul distinguished the gift of wisdom, which he claimed for himself also, from the gift of knowledge, must remain doubtful. The special gift of faith he mentions can only have consisted in the energetic power and heroic confidence of unlimited trust in God. The gift of discerning spirits

[1] Mark xvi. 17, 18.   [2] 1 Cor. xii. 7; xiv. 12.

enabled its possessor to discriminate true prophets from false, and judge whether what was announced came from God, or was an illusion.[1] Such a gift was indispensable to the Church at a time when false prophets abounded, forced their way into congregations, and increased every year in numbers and audacity. There were false teachers, as St. John intimates, who preached their doctrine, not merely as the product of human inquiry or intuition, but as a revelation imparted to them from above.[2]

Other gifts mentioned by St. Paul are healing the sick, and power generally to perform extraordinary operations; the plural here used shows that some at least had this gift only for particular diseases and sufferings to which, doubtless, various means and methods were applied. Prophecy and teaching are distinguished as separate gifts, the former depending on revelation, the latter on knowledge. St. Paul recommended his readers earnestly to covet the gift of prophecy.[3] The prophets stood higher than the teachers, and their gift was one peculiarly serviceable for the community. The prophet exhorting and consoling in clear, intelligible language spoke something designed for all; he understood the needs of his hearers, and brought to light what lay hidden in the heart. If he did not always know the full significance of his own utterances, others understood it all the better. But the spirits of the prophets were always to be subject to the prophets, for, as the Apostle says, God is not the author of confusion, but of peace.[4] The true prophets did not allow themselves to be torn to pieces by an involuntary inspiration; they never fell, like the Heathen theoleptics, into an ecstasy which drowned their consciousness, or a delirious enthusiasm, but retained entire freedom of thought and will, and when speaking in public could break off at any moment. Many of them predicted future events, as Agabus foretold the famine at Jerusalem, and afterwards by a symbolic act the imprisonment of St. Paul; or they saw visions, and declared them, as St. John "was in the Spirit on the Lord's day" (in ecstasy), and heard a voice as of a trumpet, and saw a door opened in heaven, and beheld the new Jerusalem with the

---
[1] 1 Cor. xii. xiii. xiv. 1 Thess. v. 19—21.  [2] 1 John iv. 1 sqq.
[3] 1 Cor. xiv. 1.  [4] 1 Cor. xiv. 32.

river and tree of life.¹ Even women received the prophetic gift, like the four daughters of Philip the Evangelist. There were prophetesses also in Corinth, but St. Paul, who mentions this, forbade their exercising their gift in public.²

St. Paul estimated the gift of speaking in various tongues rather than that of prophecy, but wished that all the Corinthians possessed it, for it was wrought by the grace of the Holy Ghost, and was not without use for converting unbelievers; and he declares that he himself enjoyed it in larger degree than any one in Corinth.³ But he combated the tendency of the Corinthians to overrate this gift, which they regarded as the highest and most precious manifestation of Divine influence, and which, from its frequent and persistent introduction into their public assemblies, served rather for confusion and disturbance than for edification and use, since no one understood what was said, unless the speaker or an interpreter explained it. Now in what did this speaking with tongues consist? It was not a speaking in strange and unwonted expressions, different from the prevalent usages of language, still less an utterance of low, scarcely audible, inarticulate tones and words, or a breaking out into mere ecstatic exclamations, or a noisy exultation and cry of ecstasy.⁴ In such things, which were an ordinary result of Heathen and demoniacal inspiration, St. Paul would have recognised no gift, nor have desired that all should possess so sterile and ambiguous a power. Nor would any special gift of interpretation have been required. Nor, again, would the contrast drawn between prophecy and speaking with tongues—that the one primarily benefitted believers, while the other was useful as a sign for unbelievers—be intelligible.⁵ The speaking with tongues at Corinth was substantially the same phenomenon that appeared at Jerusalem on the day of Pentecost, in Cornelius and his family, and in the twelve disciples of St. John at Ephesus, a speaking in foreign languages, which were therefore unintelligible in assemblies where only one or

---
[1] Acts xi. 28; xxi. 11. Apoc. i. 10; iv. 1, 2; xxi. 2; xxii. 1, 2.
[2] Acts xxi. 9. 1 Cor. xi. 5; xiv. 34.
[3] 1 Cor. xiv. 5, 18.
[4] Such are the various recent explanations of Baur, Schulz, Wieseler, Bloek, Meyer, &c.
[5] 1 Cor. xiv. 22.

two languages were known to those present. They were not newly-formed languages that were spoken at Cæsarea, Ephesus, and Corinth, for that would contradict all analogy of similar phenomena later, and there must then have been as many different and instantaneously created languages as there were persons to speak them.[1] It is more conceivable psychologically, that the human mind in the state of exaltation implied in miraculous endowment, should intuitively and clearly master a foreign, but existing language, than that it should throw out, as it were, by a sudden creative act, one wholly new.[2]

But the whole condition of such a speaker was one of inspired ecstasy, whereby the discursive faculty was forcibly repressed. He poured himself forth in thanksgivings, hymns, and prayers, but so that he could not freely choose

[1] That is the view of De Wette, Rosstaüscher (*Die Gabe der Sprachen*. Marburg, 1850). Those who lay great weight on the fact, that only γλώσσαις occurs in Acts x. 46; xix. 6; 1 Cor. xii. 10, without ἑτέραις being added, as at the first mention Acts ii. 4 (*e.g.* Meyer *Comm. zur. Apost. elgesch* p. 210), forget that St. Paul, by quoting Isaiah in 1 Cor. xiv. 21, ἑτερογλώσσοις and ἑτέροις χείλεσιν, has expressly attested the identity of the two. St. Peter, and the Jews with him, evidently refer what took place in the family of Cornelius to the event of Pentecost. "They were amazed, because on the Gentiles also was poured the gift of the Holy Ghost, *for* they heard them speak with tongues and glorify God." (Acts x. 45, 46).

[2] In our own day things have ocurred in a lower sphere, and without any miraculous endowment, but in a state of strong religious excitement, which serve partly to explain partly to confirm, the phenomena of the Apostolic age, viz., in the congregations formed by the Scotch preacher Irving, or through his teaching. Robert Baxter relates how he was first violently seized in such an assembly, and adds, "At home a mighty power came upon me, but for some time no impulse to speak out; then a sentence in French came vividly before my mind, and I was constrained to utter it; soon after a Latin sentence was similarly spoken, and after a short interval sentences in many other languages, to judge from the sound and the various action of the organs of speech. My wife, who was with me, said, some were Italian and Spanish; the first she can read and translate, of the last she knows very little. But she was in no condition then to interpret or retain the words spoken." He adds, that he repeatedly experienced the most vehement impulse to speak, which overpowered him when they were inarticulate, dissonant sounds, but yielded to him when forming themselves into words or sentences, though he was ignorant to what language they belonged, except in the case of French and Latin. See *Narrative of Facts characterizing the supernatural Manifestations in Members of Mr. Irving's Congregation and other Individuals in England and Scotland, and formerly in the writer himself.* By Robert Baxter, London, 1833, p. 133, 4. Here we see an unusual phenomenon but one completely within the range of natural operations, which the gift of the Apostolic age came into, to exalt and ennoble it. The like has happened *e.g.* in magnetism. That the tongues spoken at Corinth were really foreign languages, is further proved by the continuance of the gift in the Church, for 120 years later St. Irenæus expressly describes it as παντοδαπαῖς διὰ τοῦ πνεύματος γλώσσαις λαλεῖν, and as something still existing in his own day (ap. Eus. v. 7). [The reader need hardly be referred to Mrs. Oliphant's interesting Life of Irving for these and earlier alleged miraculous events in Scotland. Archdeacon Stopford described the hysterical utterances of the converts at Irish revivals some few years ago, as precisely like those he had heard at the earlier Irvingite meetings in London.—Tr.]

his language but was constrained by an internal impulse to speak in a certain language otherwise strange to him. He had a conscious perception or a general idea of what he said, but often found it impossible or difficult to repeat it in ordinary language; and thus, while he could converse with God and edify himself, the congregation remained unmoved. For the unconverted, the phenomenon was a sign adapted to suggest further inquiry and so to lead to faith, but Christians needed no such crutch to lean upon, and, moreover, they were accustomed enough to the phenomenon. For such an out-pouring to be of any service to them, there must be a man with the gift of interpreting, who, without having learnt the language, understood what was spiritually uttered by a kindred supernatural intuition, so that he could draw matter from it to edify and instruct. Therefore, St. Paul ordered those who had the gift of tongues to pray to God for the gift of interpretation, and if they had it not and no interpreter was present, to keep silence and converse inwardly with God. He had rather himself speak five words in the congregation in an intelligible manner than ten thousand in an unknown tongue, for if he came to them speaking in tongues he should not profit them.[1] Therefore, only two, or at most three in order were to speak with tongues in the assembly, that room might be given for the far more salutary prophecy.

It is only the Corinthian Church whose life of spiritual gifts St. Paul directly lays open to our gaze; but it follows from the very nature of the case that phenomena essentially identical must have occurred elsewhere also. If, in writing to the Ephesians, he prays for his readers only the two gifts of wisdom and prophecy, he pre-supposes the lesser gifts and mentions these two as the highest. He admonishes the Thessalonians "not to quench the Spirit," as though a flame, which means that they should give free utterance and scope in their assemblies for those spiritually gifted, and especially that they should esteem the gift of prophecy. To convince the Galatians of their error, he asks them whether the miraculous powers and gifts working among

[1] 1 Cor. xiv. 13, 28, 6.

them came through works of the Law or from the hearing of faith.¹ But this condition gradually passed away, or only survived in certain gifts and certain individuals. The silence about it in the Pastoral Epistles and the Epistles of St. John, suggests that already a change had taken place.

¹ Eph. i. 17. 1 Thess. v. 19, 20. Gal. iii. 5.

# CHAPTER II.

### ORDINANCES OF DISCIPLINE AND WORSHIP AND RELIGIOUS IDEAS.

St. John had first introduced the rite of immersion in the Jordan as a symbol of the repentance and renovation whereby the whole man must be purified. This was not borrowed from the Jewish custom of baptizing proselytes, which only came in after the fall of Jerusalem;[1] St. John was *sent* to baptize for repentance. Christ adopted the rite, but made the laver of repentance a "laver of regeneration," and exalted the act to a dignity and power beyond the baptism of John, which had nothing to confer.[2] And, therefore, those who had received his baptism were re-baptized on their confessing Christ, as was done with those twelve disciples at Ephesus at St. Paul's bidding.[3] Christ Himself, according to the old tradition, only baptized St. Peter, St. Peter baptized St. Andrew, St. Andrew St. James and St. John, and they the rest.[4]

At first Christian Baptism commonly took place in the Jordan; of course, as the Church spread more widely, also in private houses. Like that of St. John, it was by immersion of the whole person, which is the only meaning of the New Testament word.[5] A mere pouring or sprinkling

---

[1] The oldest testimony for it is in the Gemara Babyl. Jobamoth. 46. 2. [Probably, however, it prevailed at least from the time of the Captivity, if not earlier. See Smith's *Dict. of the Bible*, vol. ii. p. 944 (art. "Proselytes"), and vol. iii., Appendix, p. lxxxvi., vii. (art. "Baptism").—Tr.]
[2] Luke iii. 3. Tit. iii. 5. [3] Acts xix. 1—7.
[4] Clem. Alex. *Hypotypos.* ed. Potter. p. 1016.
[5] Even in Luke xi. 38 and Mark vii. 4, βαπτίζεσθαι means dipping or taking a bath, not washing the hands. In the first passage it alludes to the Pharisees' custom of cleansing themselves from any impurities possibly contracted, after returning from market.

was never thought of.[1] St. Paul made this immersion a symbol of burial with Christ, and the emerging a sign of resurrection with Him to a new life: Baptism is a "bath."[2] Of the Ethiopian's baptism it is said, that both he and Philip went down into the water and so the evangelist baptized him.[3]

There was no long preparation for Baptism; only the universal condition of faith in the kingdom of God and its Founder was required. The Apostles had no hesitation in admitting multitudes to the Sacrament who knew very little of Christian doctrine, whose faith was but a very undeveloped sentiment, rather a desire than a fixed consciousness. The act of baptism took place by question and answer. The postulant was asked if he renounced Satan and gave himself to Christ? Thence St. Peter says that, as of old the believing and the unbelieving were separated by the Flood, which to the former brought salvation and was a seal of Divine grace, so now is Baptism not a cleansing of bodily filth but the answer of a good conscience toward God.[4]

There is no proof or hint in the New Testament that the Apostles baptized infants or ordered them to be baptized. When the baptism of whole households is spoken of, it is left doubtful whether they contained little children, and whether, if so, these also were baptized.[5] What is certain is, that it is congruous to the spirit of Christianity and the meaning and nature of the act that children should partake of this means of grace. The very fact that Christ entered into human nature, not as a full grown man, but as a Child, and that in that Child slumbered the fulness of Divine powers, proves that He came as Redeemer of childhood under the ban of original sin, and that man is not called to spend a part of his life estranged from God and the healing influences of His Church, but to be brought immediately after birth into communion with the Triune God and

---

[1] It is not said that the 3,000 converts of Pentecost were all baptized the same day, but only "on that day were added 3,000 souls," (Acts ii. 41), *i.e.*, their conversion and belief took place on that day; they were baptized on the following days, of course, gradually, and accordingly the fact of their baptism is mentioned without any time being assigned.

[2] Rom. vi. 4.  Col. ii. 12.  Eph. v. 26.  Tit. iii 5.  [3] Acts viii. 38.
[4] 1 Pet. iii. 21.  [5] Acts xvi. 15, 33; xviii. 8.  1 Cor. i. 16.

made a member of the body of the Church. The Apostles did not require of adults, as was said just now, as a condition of baptism, the full, conscious faith which implies entire self-devotion to Christ, but were satisfied with a mere confession that Jesus was the Messiah and a willingness to receive all the faith. By Baptism the convert first received aid for a deeper and more comprehensive faith, and by entering the Church he had the means of knowledge she possessed opened to him for the first time. Children, though unable to believe, are so much the fitter recipients of Baptism, that by this means of grace the capacity and inclination for receiving Christ, from which faith grows, is first implanted in them, and they are to be thereby dedicated to future belief, and are to be trained and educated accordingly.

As the Apostle said, children are already holy, if their fathers or mothers are Christians; that is, they are already distinguished from the mass of Heathen and Jews by the mere fact, which alone proclaims God's will, of having a Christian parent. They are already destined for sanctification and capable of it; from their earliest age the Christian profession and life of their family has a sanctifying effect on them; they grow up under the religious influence of a father's or mother's prayers and example: they have a right to Christian fellowship, for they are becoming Christians. The Lord confessed a peculiar predilection for children; He proposed them as patterns to the adult, whom he exhorted above all to become again as little children, that they might enter into His kingdom, to be child-like in their openness and docility, in their feeling of helplessness and confident leaning on the stronger, in putting away all prejudice, all self-righteousness and pride of knowledge. If on earth He laid His hand upon children and blessed them, He did not mean them to be excluded from that act which He ordained as the first and chiefest fountain of blessing in His Church. But, so far as we know, He left no command about it; it was one of those many things His Church was to learn in her gradual development through the Paraclete whom He had given, and before the historian decides how the Apostles acted in this matter he must take into consideration their entire silence about it, the absence of any command or counsel on the subject in their Epistles, where so much is said of the family life and relative duties of Christians, and the varying practice of the period immediately following. Still, there always remains the weighty testimony of Origen, the most learned of ancient theologians; "The Church received from the Apostles the duty of baptizing children."[1]

St. Paul mentions one peculiar custom, that of vicarious Baptism for the Dead. He urges among arguments for the resurrection, that else those who are baptized for the dead would do something quite foolish and senseless.[2] The practice must, therefore, have been a common one. Probably it was done for those who had shown an intention of being baptized, but had died without fulfilling it. A surviving relative would then be baptized for the dead, in order to give a public testimony to the Church that he had died a member of it in mind and desire, and so to obtain for him the prayers of the Church, which else were not offered for those who died unbaptized.[3]

On the day of His resurrection, Christ committed to His Apostles the judicial power of remitting and retaining sins, and for that end breathed on them and thus bestowed the gift of the Holy Ghost. This defined more explicitly the power of binding and loosing, which he had already promised them.[4] They were to bind, by depriving the impenitent sinner and false teacher of liberty to mislead and disturb the Church, by laying him under the ban of exclusion from

---

[1] Orig. *Comm. in Rom.* v. 9. *Opp. Ed. Maur.* iv. 565. Cf. ii. 130; iii. 948
[2] 1 Cor. xv. 29.
[3] It is now pretty generally confessed that all attempts to explain this much controverted passage differently are violent and untenable. See Adalb. Maier's *Com. über d. ersten. Cor. Brief.* p. 318. Who now would accept Estius' interpretation of ὑπερ τῶν νεκρῶν, "jam jam morituri?" Tertullian implies that the rite lasted to his time by saying, "Si autem baptizantur quidam pro mortuis, videamus an rationem." *De Res. Carn.* 48.
[4] John xx. 23. Matt. xviii. 18. Giving the keys of the kingdom, and giving power to bind and loose, are usually taken as synonymous figures, on the assumption that Hebrew doors were secured with bars fastened by strings and thongs, and so the key was an instrument to loose or unbind these thongs. But this is a groundless conjecture, only derived from Homer's Odyssey. The O. T. gives a different view of key and locksmith. We read in Ecclus. xxii. 33 : [27 E. V.] "Who shall put a lock upon my mouth?" and in Cant. v. 5, there is an allusion to the custom of anointing the lock and bars of the house and chamber door of the beloved, but there is no mention of tying with strings or thongs, but only of a bar. The power of the keys, then, which was given only to St. Peter, was the power of a master of the house to open and shut; but the power of binding and loosing, given to all the Apostles, is the full judicial power in the Church to remit and retain sins.

communion and from all ecclesiastical privileges. They were to loose, by restoring to the penitent what he had lost. They were to retain sins where faith and repentance were wanting, to forgive them where they found the conditions of forgiveness; and their sentence was to avail, not only before men, but before God, if they pronounced it according to truth and the Lord's command, not blinded by hypocrisy or deceived by passion. Christ chose for conveying this power the same word which is always used elsewhere for the forgiveness of sin by God Himself, or for pardoning personal grievances. The forgiveness thus bestowed was to be regarded as an act of Divine authority and wrought by Divine commission. The Lord had, indeed, foreseen the mistakes which would arise from the short-sightedness and narrowness of men; but he looked, on them no less than on the defects, corruptions and errors of preaching, which were equally foreseen, and of human instruments generally in carrying out a Divine purpose, as an unavoidable incident of His earthly economy, a something to be allowed for, and which would not counteract the far greater benefits of the institution.

The question of how to deal with moral errors in those already in the Church had a double aspect, as bearing on the Church or community, and on the inward state and conscience of the sinning individual. The community suffered a double injury, internal and external, from the grave public offences of its members; internally, from the bad example and scandal given, which required some kind of reparation or satisfaction to counteract it; externally, from the prejudice to that good reputation among Jews and Heathen so desirable and needful for the Church. This last evil was felt, as before under the Old Covenant, and even more strongly at a time when the rumour was sure to spread among the Heathen, as an aggravation of guilt. St. Paul cried out upon the Jews in the words of Isaiah; "Through you God's name is blasphemed among the Gentiles," and he warned Christian slaves, in their behaviour to their masters, to provide, "that the name of God and His doctrine be not blasphemed."[1]

As a matter of self-preservation, the sinner's exclusion

[1] 1 Rom. ii. 24. 1 Tim. vi. 1.

from the communion of the Church, which, so far as in him lay, he had injured and humiliated, must have seemed the only adequate remedy; and that exclusion must last till the scandal publicly given was as publicly atoned through undoubted tokens of penitence and change of heart;—and thus we have at once the public penance of the Apostolic Church. And further, every one regarded himself, and was regarded by others, as a member of the body of Christ, the Church. No Christian could sin for himself alone; the consequences must inevitably extend to other members, to all, though it might be in a remote manner not outwardly cognisable. "If one member suffers, all suffer with it."[1] All therefore share in the sin of one. No Christian could say to his fellow-Christian, "What is it to thee, if I sin?" Every community was a people of priests, called to serve God in common and bring to Him the sacrifice of self-devotion,—it was the bride chosen and prepared by the Lord; the sins of individuals lessened that sacrifice, and stained the bridal robe. It concerned every community and the whole Church, that sins should be repented, should not be concealed, but confessed with sorrow and forgiven, for every sin was both an offence against God and also an injury to the Church. Nor could the sinner be at rest till assured of forgiveness from the injured party, forgiveness therefore as well on the side and in the name of God, as also of the Church. And hence, the power of binding and loosing was so indispensable to the Church, and had to be made into an institution which the Old Covenant neither knew nor needed. The Church had to forgive, but she could not do so till assured that God forgave. Thus, when an Apostle or Bishop loosed the sinner in the name and by the authority of God on evidence of true repentance, he also forgave in the name of the Church; he acted in the double capacity of one bearing the commission of God and of a plenipotentiary of the Church.

On the other hand, the power to loose, ordained by Christ in His Church, was a provision for the sin-laden conscience to receive on penitent confession the assurance of pardon. The inheritors of Apostolic power were to use this right of binding and loosing, not after their own will and human

---

[1] 1 Cor. xii. 26.

pleasure, but according to God's dispensation, as organs whereby He announces His intention to forgive the Christian his sins, or applies to particular individuals His general will to forgive. Here, then, was a gift of grace and an ordinance for its administration deposited in the Church, so far related to Baptism, the Eucharist and other means of grace, that in all alike the secure communication of a certain healing and quickening operation of the Holy Ghost was connected with the sensible act of a human minister. Here, again, was a foundation laid for relations of confidence, advice, and instruction between the dispenser of the ordinance and its recipient. For "it is not good for man to be alone," in matters where self-deceit and self-love are difficult to avoid. He was not to pronounce sentence on himself and so gain rest, but to have it pronounced on him in the name and by the standard of God. Meanwhile, the confession and the self-examination which it pre-supposed had a cleansing and illuminating power not otherwise attainable; but the Church could not fulfil her office of healing the wounded and bringing back the lost, unless they made an unreserved disclosure of their state of conscience.

The ministers of the Church were appointed to dispense her mysteries and means of grace. When Christ bids His disciples not cast what is holy before dogs or pearls before swine,[1] that is said firstly of doctrine, but applies also to means of grace which are not to be wasted on the hardened and impenitent and thus profaned. As St. Paul bids individuals examine themselves lest they receive the Body and Blood of the Lord unworthily, and eat and drink their own judgment;[2] so was it the duty of pastors also to make such an examination and give or refuse to give accordingly. But this examination was only possible, if Christians were willing to confess their sins and reveal their inward state to the priest, not merely as a confidential human adviser, but as a minister of God, to whose dispensation was committed the remission of sins in the Church. One sin, indeed, there was, a "sin unto death," which could not be forgiven, the sin against the Holy Ghost; that wilful denial and rejection of Divine truth, which is the fruit of a radically evil will

---

[1] Matt. vii. 6.  [2] 1 Cor. xi. 27—29.

and hardened mind darkening the intellect.¹ But the Church could never know that any one had committed this sin, or make it a ground of exclusion. She was to assume that the penitent Christian, however deeply he had fallen, was not under the terrible ban of unpardonable sin, and was, therefore, to deal with him as with a curable patient.

In that age of small Christian communities chosen out from the mass of men, where the bond was so close and the mutual intercourse of members so living, where miraculous gifts prevailed and the prophets often saw into men's innermost hearts, individual sins and errors were undoubtedly brought before the congregation, and this was done in the form of self-accusation and a request for the intercession of the rest, as well as in prophetic warnings and revelations. In such cases even an individual Christian, who possessed the prophetic spirit, could assure a fallen brother of forgiveness in the name of God and the Church. But gradually, towards the close of the Apostolic period, the Church had to enter in these respects also on her regular course of ordered administration. In the Old Testament, the need of confessing sin and the blessing God attached to it was expressed; "He that covereth his sins shall not prosper, but he that confesseth and forsaketh them shall have mercy." "While I kept silence, my bones waxed old."² In St. James' Epistle the sick man is bidden to call for the presbyters, that they may anoint him and he may obtain remission of sins. And then these words immediately follow; "Confess your sins one to another, and pray for one another that ye may be healed."³ Healing of the sick, both bodily and spiritual, is spoken of, and the Apostle connects closely the removal of bodily disease with the remission of sin. "Confess to one another," refers to the priests called in to anoint the sick man and pray for him, and to whom he was also to confess his sins. That is what St. James directs.

There was a precept of the Lord as to the position of the community towards a sinful member. He had bidden the offended party deal thus with the offender; first to admonish him alone, then before some witnesses, and, if this

---

¹ Matt. xii. 31. Mark iii. 28, 29. Luke xii. 10. 1 John v. 16. Heb. vi. 4—6.
² Prov. xxviii. 13. Ps. xxxi. 3 [xxxii. 3, R. V.].   ³ James v. 15, 16.

failed, to accuse him before the Church,—not the multitude of believers, which would generally be impossible, but the officers of the Church. If the offender would not submit to their decision, he was to be treated as a Heathen and a publican, estranged and apostate from the Church. The commission to bind and loose immediately follows. The Apostles accordingly ordered public penance for gross and open offenders.[1] If that proved ineffectual, the sinner was to be excluded and the rest were to break off intercourse and not even eat with him, though not to view him as an enemy.[2] This exclusion was to be used as a means of reformation, and, in the case of great public faults, to be applied by the community itself. St. Paul says of the false teachers, Hymenæus and Philetus, whom he "gave over to Satan,"—that is, thrust out from the Church and her ordinances among the Heathen and princes of this world—that it was a chastisement designed to teach them not to blaspheme the doctrine of Christ.[3] The case of the incestuous Corinthian shows that the Apostles acted with independent authority. St. Paul writes word, that on the information reaching him he had pronounced judicial sentence in the name of Christ, being absent in body but present in spirit, that this sinner should be delivered over to Satan, in order that his body might be punished (with diseases) and his soul be saved.[4] He sat in spirit in their assembly and pronounced sentence as judge, they being assessors or jurymen; their only remaining duty was to carry out his sentence and separate themselves from the evildoer. In his next Epistle to the Corinthians, after his command had been obeyed, and the sinner had entered into himself and was deeply grieved, he bids them forgive and receive him back to his Christian privileges, lest he should be swallowed up by too much sorrow and fall into despair.[5] A like instance of combining Church discipline with love is related of St. John. He had commended to the bishop of a city on the coast of Asia, a youth who was baptized, but was afterwards led astray and became the chief of a band of robbers. The Apostle sought him out, converted him, and brought him back to the community.

---

[1] Matt. xviii. 15—18.    [2] 2 Thess. iii. 6, 14, 15. 2 Tim. iii. 5.
[3] 1 Tim. i. 20.    [4] 1 Cor. v. 3—5.    [5] 2 Cor. ii. 6—11.

"He prayed constantly for him, persevered in fasting with him, consoled him with many words of admonition and comfort, and did not leave the city till he had restored him to the Church."[1] Here, then, is seen a development of the institution of penance, which appears in a more settled shape in the middle of the second century in the writings of Hermas and others.

The first Church at Jerusalem continued in religious and national fellowship with Judaism, and took part in the temple service as Christ had set the example. The Christians came daily to the morning and evening sacrifice, they assembled gladly in Solomon's Porch, and out of Jerusalem attended the Synagogue service on the Sabbath, which consisted of reading and expounding the Scriptures, prayer and psalmody.[2] In all these portions of the legal worship they, with their gaze rendered keen by faith, recognised a typical and prophetic reference to the Lord, and saw the fulfilment in Him. Even St. Paul, the Apostle of the Gentiles, observed the Jewish feasts and sacrifices, and attended the Synagogues. He testifies himself to his eager desire to keep the feast of Pentecost in Jerusalem.[3] This cannot be applied to the Gentile Christian communities. Nor even in Jerusalem could believers confine themselves to partaking in this national worship. There was a sacred legacy they could only celebrate in close and secret communion together,—the new Passover which continually proclaimed the death of Jesus, the sacrifice and feast which applied its fruits. For this celebration, which was the centre of their religious life, they assembled in private houses, subdividing into smaller congregations.

And thus was the word of the Lord fulfilled, that the time would come when neither on Gerizim nor at Jerusalem would the Father be worshipped, but the true worshippers should worship Him in spirit and in truth.[4] As yet, the two went on side by side,—in the temple, the bloody annual sacrifices of the Law, local, ceremonial, unspiritual, belonging only to the past, with an only typical truth,—and beside them, in the secrecy of a quiet chamber, the celebration of the new sacrifice, all spirit and truth,

---

[1] Eus. iii. 23. [2] Acts iii. 1, 11; v. 12, 20, 42; xiii. 14; xviii. 4, 19.
[3] Acts xviii. 21; xx. 16. [4] John iv. 21, 23.

where the Victim itself was spiritual, and all rested on facts and realities, on inward surrender of spirit and heart to God. A few short years, and the temple with its sacrifices had passed away; while the new sacrifice of spirit and truth—the fulfilment, spiritualisation, and perfecting of the temple service which was now become impossible,—passed from city to city, from nation to nation, and was celebrated pure and bloodless on thousands of altars.

To the Christians of that first age the whole of life was a continuous worship, and every day a festival. They assembled constantly; reviled and hated by the mass around them, they felt keenly the need of meeting as often as possible, to gain support from the Lord and from their own hopes, to quicken their memory of His words and acts, to console and encourage one another. The rich treasure of spiritual gifts existing since Pentecost in the bosom of the Church imparted to these meetings a higher consecration; and even if no Apostle was present, there was no lack of gifted teachers and prophets whose prayers, meditations and exhortations supplied expression and nourishment to the faith and desire of the assemblage. Afterwards, St. James had to give a caution against too many seeking to be teachers.[1] Thus the worship and life of the community flowed into each other. A separation of private and social acts of devotion was neither practicable nor desirable. St. Paul announced the supreme law of public worship in saying, "Let all be done to edification."[2] For the Church is God's house, and the soul of every believer should be a temple of the Holy Ghost built on that house or temple. And this is so, when common and individual energies are alike directed to mutual growth and confirmation in faith and knowledge, in love of God and our neighbour. He who joins in this work for himself and others, builds up; he who counteracts the work by evil example and false teaching, rends asunder.

Brotherly fellowship and equality, gladness and singleness of heart, were the dominant feeling and temper of the Christian communities.[3] The common bond was almost as close as of family life. Brotherly love found expression in the *Agape*, a simple meal to which all contributed and

---

[1] James iii. 1.   [2] 1 Cor. xiv. 26.   [3] Acts ii. 46.

which all partook without distinction;[1] what remained over was applied to the poor. Connected with the Eucharistic celebration, solemnised with prayer and psalmody, and closed with a brotherly kiss,[2] these "feasts of love," or "of the Lord," had a liturgical character. The union of the *Agape* and Sacrifice into one unbroken act spread from the Mother Church of Jerusalem. The example of Christ, who ordained His sacrifice at a meal, and the custom of the Greek *syssitia*, supplied by contributions from the partakers, co-operated towards suggesting this institution. At Corinth, an abuse had crept in of the wealthy taking first the portions brought for themselves and their friends, so that, in the strong language of the Apostle, one was hungry and another drunk.[3] The party spirit there was chiefly in fault in this matter. St. Paul tells them that, if they came together to satisfy hunger and thirst, they could do that better at home, without insulting the poorer Christians by the distinction of a separate table. They were to wait for each other, and feast together, each distributing of his own without distinctions.[4]

It is not clear whether the Eucharistic oblation and communion preceded or followed the *Agape*, and the views of antiquity on the question are divided.[5] The two were, anyhow, so closely connected that St. Paul saw a profanation of the Eucharist in the conduct of the Corinthians about the *Agape*. They showed, by their loveless and greedy behaviour, that they were not in a state of soul corresponding to the dignity and sacredness of the act, and did not distinguish the Body and Blood of the Lord from common food. They received the Body of Christ without self-examination, with an impure conscience and intention, unworthily, and were guilty of profanation, so that they ate and drank judgment to themselves, and sicknesses and deaths followed as Divine chastisements.[6]

Whether the Eucharistic Sacrifice was celebrated daily in the first Christian communities, as has often been assumed, is very doubtful. There is no trace of it in the New Tes-

---

[1] Jude 12.   [2] Rom. xvi. 16.  1 Cor. xvi. 20.  1 Thess. v. 26.  1 Pet. v. 14.
[3] 1 Cor. xi. 21.     [4] 1 Cor. xi. 33, 34.
[5] St. Chrysostom, Theodoret, and Pelagius, think it came first; St. Augustine, that it came last. (*Ep.* 118 *ad Januar.*)
[6] 1 Cor. xi. 27—30.

tament.¹ If it was so, the custom very soon ceased. The *Agape* connected with the Eucharist was certainly not held daily, or it would have taken the place of household meals —which St. Paul assumes, however, to be the rule²—and have disturbed family life. From what occurred at Troas, we may conclude that the celebration was always or often in the evening, after the pattern of its institution. St. Paul desired to observe Sunday there by the Communion and *Agape*, but it was after midnight when the young Eutychus fell down asleep from the window, and not till after raising him to life did the Apostle proceed "to break bread."³

Other religious meetings were held frequently, sometimes daily, for instruction, edification and prayer. These were open to strangers who were not converts. Passages from the Old Testament were read and expounded, as in the Synagogue.⁴ When men with the requisite spiritual gifts were present, they took part in the teaching. There is no evidence that any took part in public teaching, who were not either ministers of the Church or endowed with some special gift. Psalms and hymns were chanted in these assemblies.⁵ The Psalter exactly suited the then condition of the Church. The constantly recurring complaints and hopes of the oppressed, the prayers of the poor and feeble for protection and deliverance, gave full expression to the sufferings and faith, the supplication and confidence of the first Christians. St. Paul reckons among the special gifts one of singing Psalms.⁶ They had also songs newly composed, the utterance of solemn devotion; and it is clear how familiarly they used these and with what powerful effect, from St. Paul's bidding them seek inspiration, not in wine, but in psalms, hymns and spiritual songs.⁷

The same Apostle bids them pray in their assemblies for all men; first, for their enlightenment and conversion, for

¹ [This depends on whether καθ' ἡμέραν, Acts ii. 46, applies to the whole verse or the first clause only. There is certainly some difficulty in supposing that the daily *celebration*, if it ever existed, should have fallen into disuse, as it seems to have done, for several centuries. Daily *communion*, as we know from Tertullian and others, was common enough; but it was received at home from the reserved Sacrament. Nor does this practice seem to have ceased with the ages of persecution.—Tr.]
² 1 Cor. xi. 22, 34.   ³ Acts xx. 7—11.   ⁴ 1 Tim. iv. 13.
⁵ Eph. v. 19.   Col. iii. 16.   James v. 13.   ⁶ 1 Cor. xiv. 26.   ⁷ Eph. v. 19.

God wills all men to be saved and come to the knowledge of the truth. They were to make special prayer for kings and all in authority, and at the same time to ask the blessing of a quiet and peaceful life under their protection.[1] They were to pray with pure and uplifted hands, men with uncovered, women with covered heads, and in decent clothing.[2] Offerings were made at the public service, partly to support the ministers of the Church, partly for the poor. For it was part of the agreement between St. Paul and the three chief Apostles, that the Gentile converts should support the Jews in Jerusalem and Judæa with such gifts.[3] He directs the Corinthians to lay by something every Sunday, that the sum total may be devoted to this purpose.[4]

The Jewish Sabbath was a day of rest and abstinence from all labour. It was not specifically intended as the day of worship, for the legal sacrifices bore no relation to it, but in the time of Christ the chief Synagogue worship was always held on that day, with prayer and reading and exposition of Scripture. And Christ, while declaring Himself Lord of the Sabbath, kept the day in Jewish fashion, only rejecting the severe Pharisaic restrictions about rest. In the Church, the Sabbath was observed from the first by Jewish converts; and St. Paul treats this, like other practices of the Mosaic Law, as permissible, so long as the observers of it did not interfere with the liberty of others and try to make it of universal obligation. He reckons the Sabbath, like the Jewish laws about fasts, distinctions of meats and new moons, among things whose only meaning was typical, and which must be left to the judgment of every man's conscience. He reproaches the Galatians, who sought righteousness and salvation in observing the ceremonial law, with keeping Jewish weekly and annual feasts and the Sabbath, and thus becoming again enslaved " to weak and wretched elements." To the Romans he says,

---

[1] 1 Tim. ii. 1—4.
[2] 1 Cor. xi. 10. In saying, "because of the angels," the Apostle has a similar meaning to that of Christ; "Despise none of these little ones, *for* their angels always behold the face of My Father." Matt. xviii. 10. St. Paul means that women, as to the decency of their outward appearance at Divine service, should have regard to their guardian angels and Him whom they behold; just as Christians, in their general intercourse with simple, retiring believers, should remember the guardian angels of these little ones, who are therefore highly esteemed before God.
[3] Gal. ii. 10.   [4] 1 Cor. xvi. 2.

"One maketh a distinction of days, another regardeth all days alike; let each follow his own conscience."[1]  And, in fact, the Jewish Sabbath belonged to what was done away, the "elements of this world," which have no further meaning for Christians. It was a memento of blessings bestowed on the Jews; but now a higher dispensation had entered in. Since the day of Pentecost the Church kept, and keeps, in a higher sense to the end of time one great Sabbath of spiritual rest in God. But the old Sabbath, with its rest of mere inaction, its formality of the letter, was at an end. The Church established her own weekly festival.

It is certain, then, that in the Apostolic Church the law of the Sabbath was no longer binding in the Jewish sense. Nor is it true to say that the Apostles changed the Sabbath into Sunday, the observance of the seventh day to the observance of the first. For neither is there any trace of such a transference taking place, and, moreover, the Christian Sunday differs widely from the Jewish Sabbath. There was no precept for the latter of common worship, but only of bodily rest; nor has the prohibition of lighting fires and cooking food on the Sabbath been transferred to the Sunday of the Christian Church.[2] And, indeed, but for later history and tradition, we should be completely in the dark as to the customs of the Apostolic age about this festival, for all that can be gathered from the New Testament amounts to this; first, that St. John calls the day when he saw his vision "the Lord's day," which probably means the first day of the week;[3] secondly, that St. Paul celebrated "the breaking of bread" at Troas on a Sunday,[4] which obviously does not prove that the Eucharist was not celebrated on other days also; lastly, that he recommends the Corinthians to lay up something for an offering on every first day of the week.[5]

That Sunday received its festive character as the day of the Lord's Resurrection, is beyond a doubt, and is testified at the beginning of the second century.[6] Its new name, "the Lord's day," entirely unknown to the Old Testament,

---

[1] Col. ii. 16.  Gal. iv. 9, 10.  Rom. xiv. 5.
[2] Exod. xxxv. 3; xvi. 23.  Numb. xv. 32.   [3] Apoc. i. 10.
[4] Acts xx. 7, 11. According to our reckoning it would be Monday, for the celebration came after midnight.
[5] 1 Cor. xvi. 2.   [6] *Ep. Barn.* 15.

shows that in the mind of the Church it was Christ the Lord who set upon it the seal of the New Covenant. And thus the Divine command, as well moral as liturgical, "Hallow the Sabbath," was fulfilled in the Church. The first Christians neither kept to the Old Testament day nor the legal manner of observance; they sanctified their new festival as a community for whom the Jewish sharp distinction between work day and Sabbath had no existence, who viewed the whole life of a Christian as a festival, and recognised as their essential and imperishable Sabbath the rest of the soul in God.

There is no mention of annual festivals in the New Testament, but we may safely assume that Easter and Pentecost were solemnly observed as the commemoration of Christ's Resurrection and of the Gift of the Spirit. The example of the Lord, who used to come to Jerusalem for the Passover, would suggest to Christians to keep a feast which had naturally and necessarily become a Christian festival, and indeed the chief festival of the Church, since Christ had become the true Paschal Lamb sacrificed in place of the Paschal lamb of old. And so with Pentecost. To communities which had before their eyes in the spiritual gifts the fruits of that great birthday of the Church, the annual commemoration of the event, or the change of Pentecost from a Jewish solemnity of dedicating the first-fruits of the harvest into a Christian feast of the descent of the Spirit, was a matter of course, needing no express command. We see that St. Paul laid special stress on this feast; he would not stay to keep it with the Church at Ephesus, but hastened on to Jerusalem, to be able to keep it there.[1] In the subsequent disputes about Easter, A.D. 160, Bishop Polycarp of Smyrna, and Anicetus of Rome, appealed each to the Apostolic tradition of his own Church. St. Polycarp insisted that he had himself kept Easter with the Apostle John after the Asiatic use, and that the other Apostles he had conversed with, St. Philip and St. Andrew, had agreed in this. Indeed, it is quite conceivable that St. Peter and St. Paul fixed a different time for Easter at Rome from what St. John had observed at Ephesus, where he had to consider the Jews especially.

[1] Acts xviii. 21; xx. 16.

The Christians were above all a praying people. The history of the new-born Church commences; "They were continually in the temple, praising and blessing God." The little knot of believers "continued with one accord in prayer and supplication;" "they continued daily with one accord in the temple."[1] They had their hours of prayer constantly recurring. "At the sixth hour, Peter went on the roof of the house to pray;" "At midnight Paul and Silas prayed, and sang praises to God."[2] Their frequent prayer rested on the conviction that man is united to God, called into fellowship and intercourse with Him, that the omniscient God "is not far from every one of us, for in Him we live, and move, and have our being."[3] Christians prayed, for God's will was in their hearts, His name on their lips, His kingdom their hope. They prayed, while the Gentiles knew not what prayer was; the multitude called on their gods for help and earthly blessings, but did not pray, and the student of philosophy, who deemed that all things were subject to fixed laws of an eternal and unbending course of nature, could look for no answer to petitions vainly addressed to powerless deities, themselves under the same constraint of nature.

Christians had received the Psalms as a precious heritage from the Old Covenant. In them they possessed the only true prayers then existing among men. In them they found what at once moved and satisfied them, the sense of God's presence, the yearning for a closer communion with Him, the grief of sin and the agony of repentance tempered with consolation and forgiveness. But prayer had a higher place in the Christian Church than under the Old Testament. Christians were bidden to pray without ceasing, under all circumstances, without being weary.[4] Prayer was to be for spiritual, what breath is to bodily life. The constant endeavour and desire of man's heart for eternal righteousness, the fixing of intellect and will on God, the raising of the spirit out of the narrow boundaries of the present into fellowship with that Being to whom all evil is an abomination, whose law of holiness is immutable, and who wills only

---

[1] Luke xxiv. 53. Acts i. 44; ii. 46.
[2] Acts x. 9; xvi. 25.   [3] Acts xvii. 23.
[4] Luke xviii. 1. 1 Thess. v. 17, Eph. vi. 18.

our perfection,—that is the prayer without ceasing which Christ and the Apostles commended and practised. Prayer meant for Christians—listening above all for God's voice within them, remembering His words and shaping their thoughts accordingly, questioning and looking at themselves in the light streaming from Him, letting it shine into all the dark corners of their hearts, and, while gazing on their sins and imperfections, entreating pardon and strength to purify themselves continually more and more. All that philosophy in its noblest form had promised to the Greeks—repose of mind, regulation of the affections, stilling the excited passions, moral purification—Christians gained from prayer. This practice was the school of philosophy, where they cried to God, prayed, gave thanks with childlike self-surrender, confidence and perseverance, renewing constantly this interrupted communion with him, resting from earthly cares and toils and feeding their faith and love on meditation of the sublimest truths. The Gentile wordiness and thoughtless repetition of the same form, as though some magical power lay in the words, Christ had forbidden to His followers. Christian prayer was not to consist in moving the lips, or in multiplying words, but in the heart's love and desire to please God, the hunger and thirst after righteousness, the continuous act of self-sacrifice; this prayer, and this alone, Christ promised that He would always hear.[1]

He had taught His disciples a short prayer of seven petitions, which comprehended all the teaching of His Sermon on the Mount.[2] All which a man can say when holding intercourse with God, is there contained. Yet in form and character it is an universal prayer, rising above individual needs and wishes and embracing all nations and the whole Church. It opens with expressing the consciousnes of relationship between God and man, absolute trust in His fatherly love, and the return of a childlike love to Him. Then, as he named heaven, the suppliant placed himself in the presence of God and, as it were, in sight of Him; that kingdom and dwelling-place of the unfallen and the Blessed,

---

[1] Matt. xxi. 22.
[2] [The substance of the Lord's Prayer seems, however, to have been already in use among the Jews, and adopted rather than revealed by Christ. See Möhler's *Symbolism*, vol. ii. p. 336, *Eng. Trans.* Cf. Horne's *Introd.*, vol. iii. p. 296. Wordsworth's *New Test.* Pt. i. p. 19.—Tr.]

in the midst whereof God is throned in glory and is all in all, rose before his spirit's eye. His prayer began, not with his own personal wants and complaints, but with the wants and the advancement of the Church. He felt himself above all things the citizen of a Divine kingdom, bound first to think of that great whole to which he belonged. The Church has no other office but the hallowing of God's name, the realisation of His kingdom, and the submission of mankind to His will. For the Church, therefore, is the prayer offered that in and through it God's name may be hallowed, —that He may be known and worshipped as the Holy One, His name be glorified by all in word and deed, His service conducted in the Church be a worthy ministry of the Holy Ghost. Then the prayer passes on to the coming of His kingdom, for it is the Church's mission to overshadow the whole earth with her branches; she is not only existing, but continually coming into existence, destined to grow evermore in an unfailing youth. The Church is a kingdom ever coming, having the tendency and power, while growing inwardly, to penetrate ever more and more the substance of humanity, to sink more deeply into her members' souls with her blessings, while spreading outwardly from land to land, from nation to nation, and widening her borders. Here, too, the suppliant cast his eye on the accomplishment of that kingdom and the close of its earthly period by the return of Christ. And thus, in praying for the coming of the Church, the Apostolical Christian prayed for the salvation of the world. In the third petition, he uttered the highest wish which the finite created spirit can attain to, the desire for perfect agreement between the will of the creature and the will of God. In desiring that God's will might be as perfectly fulfilled by men as it is by the blessed spirits, with as free and joyful an obedience and as unconditional an abandonment to the Divine counsels, he prayed for himself and others the noblest object that can be striven for in this life, though in this life only approximately attained; he said for himself what the Lord had said in the moment of His bitterest agony of soul, "Not my, not our will, but Thine, be done!"

By a bold and sudden transition the prayer passed from lofty petitions for mankind and the Church to individual wants, from the spiritual to the earthly. But the Christian neither desired, nor was it right he should desire, more of earthly goods than mere bodily support.[1] The prayer, therefore, included the expression of his contentment and readiness to offer up to God all beyond what was absolutely indispensable, if only he had bread, and above all had Him who called Himself "the Bread of life."[2] The consciousness of guilt warned him after earthly needs to think of spiritual, of the satisfaction of the most imperative want of a soul deeply acquainted with its own sinfulness; he represented to himself the worst among his many remembered transgressions of God's commandments, but even here, as in asking for bread, his prayer was not confined to himself but embraced the whole community; he prayed, "forgive *us*," not simply, forgive me. And the prayer was also a vow. While he penitently acknowledged his sin, and confidently looked for God's forgiveness as the consequence of his prayers, he did not forget the condition under which alone he could dare to appropriate it. He knew that only those who forgive shall be forgiven, and he declared his willingness to fulfil that hardest among the precepts of love, the renunciation of all feeling of revenge and the repayment of evil with good. But he not only prayed forgiveness of the past; that past reminded him of the present and future, that he still was and would be a weak, frail man, in constant need of the help of grace, exposed to manifold temptations. He thought how often the motions of his heart were in league with those temptations, and how powerful they were, unless checked at once; and so he prayed that God's fatherly care would keep far from him the most dangerous stumbling-blocks and assaults, and not let him be tempted to the point of yielding and beyond his power. And, lastly, he compressed the feeling of painful eagerness of one drowned, yet restored to life, into the closing all-comprehensive prayer for deliverance from evil, from the burden of sin and from eternal destruction, and for entrance into that kingdom where there is no more evil.

---

[1] ἄρτον ἐπιούσιον. This word, used nowhere else, can scarcely have any other sense than that suggested by ἡ ἐπιοῦσα, from which it is derived—"Give us to-day our bread for to-morrow."
[2] John vi. 35.

Intercession, for prayer or blessing and grace for others, was commended by Christ to His followers; "Pray for them that injure and persecute you."[1] In His great prayer as High priest He set forth an exalted model of intercession, though, of course, no Christian could apply those words to himself.[2] The Apostles often asked for the intercession of believers and highly esteemed it; St. James says that the earnest prayer of a righteous man availeth much."[3] Christians looked for a double blessing from it, both for him who prayed and those he prayed for; they remembered that saying of Christ, that the blessing pronounced by the Apostles on the house they entered would return to them again, if the inmates were unworthy.[4] So would it be with intercession.

When the attention of a thinking Heathen was directed to the new religion spreading in the Roman Empire, the first thing to strike him as extraordinary would be that a religion of prayer was superseding the religions of ceremonies and invocations of gods; that it encouraged all, even the humblest and most uneducated, to pray, or, in other words, to meditate and exercise the mind in self-scrutiny and contemplation of God. For the praying Christian, if his prayer was anything more than lip work, could not think or meditate on anything else, and the places of Christian assembly were not first and principally schools or lecture-rooms, but places of prayer. The doctrines which served to occupy the Christian mind in prayer were, the omnipresence and holiness of God, His remunerative justice, the freedom and immortality of man, sin, redemption, and the need of God's strengthening and upholding grace. This region of Christian metaphysics was open even to the mind of one who had had no intellectual culture before conversion. In this school of prayer he learnt—what philosophy had declared to be as necessary as it was difficult, and only attainable to few—to know himself as God knew him. And from that self-knowledge prayer carried him on to self-mastery. If the Heathen called on his gods to satisfy his passions, for the Christian, tranquillity of soul, moderation and purifying of the affections, was at once the preparation

---

[1] Matt. v. 44.   [2] John xvii.
[3] Eph. vi. 18, 19. 1 Thess. v. 25. 1 Tim. ii. 1.   [4] 1 Matt. x. 13.

and the fruit of prayer. And thus prayer became a motive power of moral renewal and inward civilization, to which nothing else could be compared for efficacy. It was a bond of common fellowship and brotherhood, an exercise where the intellect and will of an ever-increasing number of men, however great their original varieties of mental power and culture, found a point of contact. And, further, it was an efficacious means of peace and reconciliation, for he had to pray constantly, "forgive me," and he could never do that without himself forgiving in word and deed, and making peace with his brother. It was a constant struggle against all tendencies to greed and self-seeking, or he had to remember that saying; " Give, and it shall be given to you."[1] If he wished to pray for earthly goods with any hope of being heard, it could only be on the condition of using them for the benefit of others. He knew that all he received was but a loan, entrusted to him to be devoted according to God's will to the service of others after his own wants were satisfied. And if, finally, he was discontented with his lot, murmured at his position, and was embittered by the harshness and injustice he had to suffer under, to pray or hold intercourse with a suffering and crucified Lord was a sure means of gaining calmness and patience; the more so, because in entering the Church he was forewarned that he joined a hated and persecuted community, and must be prepared for his full share of sufferings and troubles. " The disciple is not above his master, nor the servant above his lord; ye must be hated for My name's sake." So Christ spake, and so, too, His Apostle; " All who will live godly in Christ Jesus shall suffer persecution."[2] They knew, therefore, beforehand that by the school of suffering they would be brought into the school of prayer.

And here another essential contrast between Christianity and Heathenism, and in a measure Judaism also, is revealed. A religion whose Founder died on the cross could only be a religion of suffering. There is truth in that saying; " Worldly welfare is the blessing of the Old Testament, tribulation of the New." For it is the constantly recurring teaching of the Apostles, that suffering is a blessing, one of

---

[1] Luke vi. 38.     [2] Matt. x. 22, 24. 2 Tim. iii. 12.

God's most effective and beneficial instruments for training the soul.[1] All sufferings have a general relation to sin, and are so far chastisements, but purifying chastisements, which God sends now as a Father, that He may not inflict them hereafter as a Judge. Christ is our example in His sufferings; we must drink His chalice and suffer with Him, that we may partake His glory. These ideas are always recurring, and we may observe in St. Paul a peculiar mingled feeling of joy, consolation and sorrow in his sufferings.[2] His conviction that, for those who love God, all things work together for good, upholds him under bitter tribulations in the clear atmosphere of thankfulness and love.[3] He counts it an honour to be bitterly afflicted, and expects all Christians to share his feeling, for trials are a means of perfection and pledge of Divine grace.[4]

Hence arose a virtue which first grew on Christian soil and from the root of Christian ideas,—patience, with its fruits or various forms, of equanimity, steadfastness and endurance. With the Apostles and their brethren it was so unshaken a trust in the wisdom and goodness of God, that the will of the sufferer, even in long-enduring afflictions, resigned itself without murmur or discouragement entirely to His higher will, and thought only of letting the purifying power of suffering take full effect. Here, again, St. Paul was an example; in him is seen how the comple'e incapacity to help themselves forced upon Christians an absolute surrender to the will of God. Thrice he had prayed in vain for the removal of a grievous bodily pain, and was answered, that the power of God's grace was proved in his weakness and impotence.[5] Thus patience was transfigured into hope and quiet waiting for the time when it would please the Lord to turn sorrow into joy. And from patience in sufferings grew a tolerant and forgiving view of the faults and infirmities of others and of offences received from them. But this new and purely Christian virtue was only possible through the perfection to which prayer had reached in the Church. "If any one

---

[1] Matt. x. 38, 39 ; xx. 22, 23. Luke ix. 23. Rom. viii. 18, sqq. 2 Tim. ii.12. James 1, 2, 3. 1 Pet. iv. 1. Apoc. vii. 14.
[2] Rom.viii. 17. 2 Cor. iv. 10. Phil. iii. 10. Col. i. 24. Heb. xiii. 13.
[3] Rom. viii. 28. [4] Rom. v. 3. [5] Cor. xii. 9.

among you is afflicted, let him pray," St. James had said.[1] The patience thus evoked, and built up in the soul by prayer, differed widely from the patience taught and commended by the later Greek philosophy of the Stoics; the earlier philosophers took no notice of the subject. Christians were surprised that patience was so highly valued by the most various schools of philosophy, and praised as the noblest fruit of their teaching; that in fact they were wont to put it forward as a speaking evidence of the excellence of their system, and while in conflict on all other questions were only agreed in this.[2] But in that system the philosophical ground of the apathy corresponding to Christian patience was entirely different and thoroughly unsatisfactory. If with some it was only the quiet submission to what is inevitable, which becomes the wise man,—with others, a forced mastery over the affections, or an unyielding defiance of destiny, or some kind of hope to regain former joy after transitory disturbance and mishaps,—that was commended under the name of patience; the Stoics came nearer to the Christian idea, in so far as they always spoke of resignation to the will of God.[3] But when this resignation of theirs is more closely examined, its hollowness and unnaturalness is disclosed. The sufferings of mankind are necessary for the good of the universe and happiness of Zeus, for in the great chain of cause and effect, up to the highest point, no smallest link can be dropped;[4] God must care more for the universe than for individuals, and the sufferings of a part are the welfare of the whole; if man chose, instead of resignation, to break out into impatience, he would injure or wrench off a limb of that great animal, the universe.[5] It was only Christian doctrine which could recognise alike the indestructible dignity of human personality, and the full maintenance of its rights even in suffering.

The Christian esteemed it the highest evidence of God's favour when he was counted worthy to suffer for faith, truth, and righteousness. The disciples of Jesus learnt to regard it as their proper calling to be likened to the image of the sufferings and death of Christ, in persecutions, in

---

[1] James v. 13.  [2] Tert. *De. Pat.* 1.  [3] Arrian. ii. 16. Senec. *Ep.* 107.
[4] Marc. Antonin. v. 8. Sen. *De Prov.* 3.  [5] Sen. *Ep.* 74. Max. Tyr. *Diss.* 25.

shame and contempt, in prison and in death. They knew that in the natural course of things confessing with the lips would involve confessing in deeds; that the doctrine of the Cross would rouse hatred, and hatred would pass into persecution. They must take up the Cross of Christ, and be ready to share His baptism of blood.[1] When He foretold to St. Peter His death on a Cross, He said: "Follow Me;" St. Paul grounded his hope of partaking in the glory of Christ on being conformed to the image of His death.[2] And thus grew up the idea of Christian Martyrdom, as a bearing witness to the faith. That critical moment, when the Christian had to choose between denying his profession or dying for it, was regarded as the moment of giving a solemn testimony for the Redeemer. The believer had to show before the world what value he put upon the honour of Christ; what the teaching, the grace, and the ordinances of Christ had done for him; what power lay in his hopes and his presentiment of eternal joy. His public confession was an act of truthfulness and moral courage, an act of fidelity to God and self-sacrificing love for his unconverted brethren, to whom his unshaken, and to them enigmatical, firmness and trust would be a token and a light to guide them on the path to Christ. In these witnesses of the early Church was seen that union of pride and humility, so unintelligible to all without, which was first made possible by Christianity. The Christian could not but feel proud in the consciousness of being greater and freer than the strong and mighty ones who had power over his life and his body. And yet he was truly humble, for he knew that he had not given but received this; he was ready to offer up his life to avoid giving scandal, either to believers or unbelievers, and urged to do so by feeling that the immortal souls of the unbelievers, who would be first awakened to faith by the testimony of his death, were far more precious than his life.

St. Paul calls St. Stephen the first-fruits and type of all Martyrs, a "witness" for Christ;[3] but it is in the Apocalypse that the notion of Christian Martyrdom appears in its completest form. Antipas is called by the Lord, "My

---

[1] Matt. x. 38; xvi. 24; xx. 22, 23. Mark viii. 34. Luke ix. 23.
[2] John xxi. 19. Phil. iii. 10, 11. 2 Cor. i. 5.     [3] Acts xxii. 20.

faithful Martyr;" St. John saw under the altar the souls of them that were slain for the word of God, and the testimony which they held, and the giving a white robe is the symbol of their blessedness.[1] They are under the altar, because they have offered themselves to their Lord. Thus, St. Paul compares his foreseen martyrdom to being poured out as a drink-offering; and St. Ignatius, who was conducted to the same death, desired to be a victim slain for sacrifice.[2] And St. John saw the woman clothed in scarlet (Rome) "drunken with the blood of the Martyrs of Jesus."[3] This was a clear enough intimation to the Christian communities that, as the enmity of the Heathen world increased, a great company of Martyrs would be required of them. And the thought was impressed upon them, that for a Christian there could be no fairer ornament than to pour out his blood for the Lord; that this endurance of torments and dying to bear testimony was a combat where the slain was hero and victor, where judge and executioner were the conquered; and that every Christian Martyrdom was a wound inflicted on the dominant Heathenism.

---

[1] Apoc. ii. 13; vi. 9—11.   [2] Phil. ii. 17. 2 Tim. iv. 6. Ignat. *Ep. ad Rom.* 2, 4.
[3] Apoc. xvii. 6.

# CHAPTER III.

### ECCLESIASTICAL INSTITUTIONS AND CUSTOMS.

"Make not provision for the lusts of the flesh;" "Use not your liberty as an occasion for the flesh;" "Crucify the flesh with its affections and lusts."[1] These and the like admonitions of the Apostle express a conviction that there is a strength of evil in the bodily organism of man, that his physical life, which Scripture calls "the flesh," contains the exciting, sustaining and corrupting cause of moral evil in the soul, that it kindles and fosters those passions which by consent of the will become acts of sin. In fact, the whole collective brood of corruption, even those sins whose seat is rather in the soul than in the body, like overweening egotism, are summed up under the term, "flesh," or "works of the flesh;" which includes, generally, moral weakness and decay, religious impotence or perversion, all in man that opposes God.[2] The Apostles knew full well that sins of anger, hardness of heart, sloth and self-seeking, are intimately related to the body, and that it is difficult to say of many of them whether they reside more in flesh or spirit. Experience taught them that luxurious habits and rich diet gradually alter and deteriorate the whole character. And therefore they recognised in fasting—a diminution either in quantity or quality of food—a power for purifying the soul, a means of making the spirit freer and stronger, the body more willing and submissive, and of promoting the converse of man with God, a beneficial exercise of moral self-restraint and self-mastery, and even a condition of bodily welfare.

[1] Rom. xiii. 14. Gal. v. 13, 24.   [2] Gal. v. 19—21.

The Lord Himself, when withdrawn into solitude to prepare for His ministry, fasted forty days, and He was to be in all things a model for His disciples. He had given special instruction, as well about fasting as about alms and prayer, as the three closely connected offerings of men, warning them against perverting to Pharisaical ostentation what was given as a means for sanctifying the heart. He once declared that prayer and fasting were the only sure means against certain diabolical influences. The disciples of John, who always fasted, were amazed at Jesus often accepting invitations to feasts, and at no special practices of fasting being observed in Him and His disciples. He replied, that now was a time of joy for His disciples, a continual marriage feast, while the Bridegroom was with them, but that when the Bridegroom was taken away the time of fasting would begin.[1] St. Paul reckons fasting among the evidences of a genuine devotion to the service of God, and does not forget to include in the number and variety of his acts and sufferings, as an Apostle, his frequent fastings.[2] There was prayer and fasting at the ordination of St. Paul and St. Barnabas, and of the presbyters they appointed.[3] Whether public fast-days were fixed so early is uncertain; very likely not, because for a long time Jewish converts continued to observe the Jewish fast-days. But it is clear that from the beginning the Christians were a people who fasted much.

St. Paul shows the Corinthian Christians the necessity of ascetic self-restraint by the familiar example of the candidates at the races in their public games, who prepared themselves during many months by severe diet and careful abstinence.[4] What they did for a corruptible he bids us do for an incorruptible crown. He proceeds to set himself forth as a pattern of this Christian wrestling; and in strong words, borrowed from the boxing match, describes his combat with his own body, the seat of ungodly and corrupted impulses, to break the antagonism of the slothful and voluptuous flesh and bring it into subjection, that it may become a willing and flexible instrument of the spirit.

[1] Matt. vi. 16—18; xvii. 21; ix. 14, 15.
[2] 2 Cor. vi. 5; xi 27.   [3] Acts xiii. 2, 3; xiv. 23.
[4] 1 Cor. ix. 24—27. Compare the passages quoted here by Wetstein.

Labours, exertions, privations and self-denials of all kinds, were the means he used to make his body pliant, lest after heralding the strife to others he should himself, in God's judgment, prove a castaway. And yet he had already to bear "a thorn in the flesh," a depressing bodily suffering, which he felt like the pain of a blow with the fist, and had vainly prayed to be released from.[1]

But there was meanwhile a kind of asceticism, springing from a view wholly foreign to them, which the Apostles emphatically repulsed when it sought to force an entrance into the young Church. In combating this false asceticism St. Paul follows the hint given by Christ. The Pharisaic and Gnostic tendency among the Jews agreed, in so far that both saw in many things a physical pollution, defiling body and soul, and making man an abomination to God. This led to a growingly materialistic and mechanical conception of evil and sin, and to the whole life being taken up with a constant oscillation between defilements and various washings and other necessary ceremonies of purification. But the greatest importance was attached to meats, whose defiling power washings could not remove, and which, like a destructive poison, infected the whole man into whose substance they were to be changed. It was against this error that Christ's saying was directed: "Not what goeth into the mouth defileth a man;"[2] meat and drink are digested, and cannot touch or defile the inner man; the heart with its desires, which food cannot reach, is the workshop of sin. But St. Paul had a worse error to combat than the Pharisaic exaggeration of Jewish laws about meats, since it was connected with a world-wide general system, the notion of animal food being in itself objectionable and sinful. "Touch not, taste not, handle not," said the false teachers of Colossæ, and the Apostle briefly and strongly points out the contradiction involved in the touching of such trivial things, destined to perish in the using, being considered so important and so perilous for the soul, as Christ had already said to the Pharisees. He adds, that this theory of abstinence has, of course, an appearance of zeal for God's service and disregard for the

---

[1] 2 Cor. xii. 7. [For the various interpretations of this passage, see Alford *in loc.*—Tr.]  [2] Matt. xv. 11.

body; the willing subjection to these human teachers and human ordinances had a show of humility, but at bottom there was no creditable motive, and it was but a flattering of carnal pride.¹ Indeed, the Gnostic and Christian asceticism were directly opposed in spirit, the former resting on the assumption that the creature to be eaten is evil and morally poisonous, the latter acknowledging that "every creature of God is good,"² and that we, men, are the only exception to this rule, who are therefore required to restrict ourselves in the use of what is good and blameless in itself, and to confine ourselves by abstinence and self-control to what we really need.

St. Paul passed a milder judgment on those Jewish converts at Rome who not only continued to keep Jewish festivals, but abstained from flesh and wine altogether. Here there was no radical Gnostic error, as at Colossæ; else he would not simply have called these persons weak in faith, and commended them to the forbearance and brotherly love of the rest. It was only an exaggerated scruple of the Jews, which, in a city like Rome, might arise from the difficulty of obtaining meat that was pure, or had not come from an animal offered in sacrifice, and wine that had not been used for libations. This and the observance of Jewish feasts and fast days must have caused disturbance in the Christian community life. And here the Apostle brings out a most important principle, which was to guide Christians of all ages in such cases of conscientious practical differences. He says that in such matters none must judge others, or impute sin to them, for no Christian is lord over others, but all are God's servants. Each must act according to the measure of his knowledge, as he deems it right and pleasing to God. Whatever a man does against or beside his conviction, grounded on faith, that for him is sin. *His conscience is a law for him, even if it should err in the practical application of a truth of faith,* and binds him to

---

¹ Col. ii. 21—23. This passage is confessedly one of the most perplexing and most variously interpreted, especially the words πρὸς πλησμονὴν τῆς σαρκός. The Greeks, and Estius, with many others, think St. Paul meant to assert against the ἀφειδία of the false teachers the due honour and satisfaction to be given to the body. But, if so, he would certainly not have used so strong a word as πλησμονὴ, filling or sating; and σάρξ has the moral significance of a carnal mind. Therefore Hilary has explained; "Sagina carnalis sensus traditio humana est."
² 1 Tim. iv. 4.

abstain from an act he holds to be forbidden. Others are bound to honour this tenderness of conscience, even at the cost of their own rights and sacrifice of their liberty. Hence St. Paul desires "the strong" to abstain rather from flesh and wine at common meals, lest the scrupulous brethren be led to follow their example, and so injure their own conscience. He says that he himself became weak to them that were weak, that he might win the weak.[1]

While in many relations of life Christianity opened out new paths, and both introduced and confirmed views for which hitherto Jews and Gentiles had been little if at all prepared, this was especially the case as regards the question of Continence and voluntary Celibacy. To be childless and unfruitful was a curse and reproach among the Jews. There were, indeed, among the Gentiles certain priesthoods, chiefly for women, where marriage was forbidden; but in the case of men, the Greek and Roman world did not leave the matter to moral restraint, but used the services of eunuchs for the few offices requiring celibacy, as with the hierophants of the mysteries, the priests of Cybele, and some others.[2] But this involuntary celibacy was only for the ministry of some particular deities, and did not rest on moral grounds, or on any special reverence for that state, but on nature-worship and ideas of sterility and of the death of the generative and productive powers of nature, as represented by certain gods. In most cases, continence was required of their priests only to insure sterility, that no being might derive its existence from them. No notion of connecting celibacy with the aiming at holiness could grow on Heathen soil, because the general ideas of holiness, prayer and intercourse with God, as of renunciation for the good of others, were wanting. Least of all in the then state of the Heathen world could any value be set on the unmarried state; on the contrary, just the opposite view prevailed. The legislation of Augustus had visited celibacy with heavy disabilities, for the government wished the avoidance of marriage to be regarded as a want of patriotic feeling and neglect of one of the weightiest duties of citizenship. The Greek Republics of Athens and Sparta had

---

[1] Rom. xiv., xv. 1—7. 1 Cor. ix. 22.
[2] *Heid. und Jud.* pp. 171, 347. [Vol. i. pp. 192, 375, 6. *Eng Trans.*]

before imposed penalties on celibacy; in Sparta even deferring marriage was penal.[1] There were indeed older Roman laws against celibacy, and prizes or privileges for begetting children.[2] The prevalent view was that those who remained unmarried, who were always a great number, only did so from selfish motives, to be rid of cares and save the expense of wife and children, and chiefly to be more at liberty to gratify their passions, or at best from dread of the follies and extravagances of wife and sons. No one dreamt of any higher ground, though at that time two famous philosophers, Epictetus and Apollonius of Tyana, preferred to remain unmarried. The recommendation of celibacy in the Christian Church must have increased the dislike of statesmen and patriots to the new religion, and this was afterwards a leading charge against it in Persia.

There is a remarkable prediction made by him who peculiarly deserves to be called the Evangelical and Messianic Prophet.[3] While announcing a time when the Gentile shall no more be separated from the fellowship of Israel, he turns to the eunuchs, with the promise that they shall no more say, "Behold, I am a dry tree," for God will give to them that hold to His covenant a place and a name in His house and within His walls, better than sons and daughters, an eternal, imperishable name. While the Gentile stranger is only promised that God will admit him to His altars, and accept his offering, something far higher is set before the eunuch, who is to have an office and dignity in the house of God[4]—the Church—and his want of children to be richly compensated. The prophet, in this solemn contemplation of the future greatness and glory of the Church, cannot possibly have been thinking of the few eunuchs in Asiatic courts; what would be the meaning of promising them so special a lot in the Church? He did not by eunuchs refer chiefly to the Heathen, for he distinguishes clearly enough between "the stranger" and the eunuch, and means by the latter the unmarried and childless.[5] He

---
[1] Pollux *Onom.* viii. 6. Ariston *ap. Stob. Serm.* 73. Plut. *Lysand.* 3.
[2] Cic. *De Leg.* x. 20. Gell. v. 19, where the "præmia patrum" are mentioned in a speech of Scipio Africanus. Colum. i. 8. [3] Isaiah lvi. 3—5.
[4] This is indicated by "place and name in God's house," τόπος ὀνομαστός, *Septuag.*
[5] So *e.g.* Umbreit *Com. über Is.* p. 406. On the contrary, Stier *Is. nicht Pseudo-is*, 1850, p. 573, does violence to the text, by explaining it to mean those spiritually impotent.

was gazing with prophetic eye into the inner courts of the Church, and there he saw the band of eunuchs for the kingdom of heaven's sake, whom Christ mentions, not without reference to his words.

When the disciples were alarmed at the Lord's saying, so startling to Jewish ears, about the indissolubility of marriage, and thought it were better not to marry at all, Christ said to them, " All receive not this saying, but they to whom it is given."[1] He thus confirms what the disciples said, that it is really better not to marry; but they alone take this into their heart and conviction, who have received from God a right understanding of the matter and the requisite moral capabilities. And He explains more exactly, that there are three kinds of eunuchs, those born such, those made such by men, and those who have made themselves such for the kingdom of heaven's sake. There is, then, besides those naturally or otherwise disqualified for marriage, a third class, who have voluntarily renounced it, in order to strive more securely and without hindrance for the kingdom of heaven, or to be better qualified for ministering in the Church. " Let him that can receive it," is added, that is, let him act accordingly.[2] This also shows in what sense it can be truly said that to remain unmarried is better than to marry—not in itself, or because marriage is indissoluble, as the disciples thought, but "for the kingdom of heaven's sake," the kingdom which Christ was even then founding for men to enter, and of which Peter afterwards received the keys. There are those to whom it is clear, under the guidance and light of grace, that it is better for them to serve God and their neighbour unmarried, in and for the kingdom, and who have the power to make this sacrifice. That is what Christ said. St. John and St. Paul say the same.

When St. John describes the hundred and forty-four thousand that were sealed as a chosen band, distinguished from other believers by special holiness, he praises, together with their guilelessness and blamelessness, their virginity. " These were not defiled with women, for they are virgins." And, as a special reward, they have the privilege among the Blessed of constantly following the Lamb, for they

---

[1] Matt. xix. 10, 11.  [2] Matt. xix. 11, 12.

alone are like the Lord in the continual observance of virginity.[1]

St. Paul lays down as a general principle, that it is good for a man not to touch a woman, or, in other words, to abstain from marriage; and he wishes that all, like himself, would live in voluntary celibacy.[2] But his wish is limited by the fact that God variously divides His gifts, bestowing on one the qualifications for continence and a solitary life, in order to pursue a higher calling, while He gives to another as His special grace, the disposition for family life and the capacity for fulfilling the duties of husband and father. And the Apostle knew well, and said so, that it was better to marry than to foster an impure fire of lust breaking out from time to time into sinful acts. He that marries sins not, but he that remains unmarried does better. "If thou art free from a wife, seek not a wife," for there are weighty grounds for considering celibacy a preferable condition for a Christian. First, on account of the present distress, freedom from the ties of marriage is preferable.[3] And next, there is a permanent ground, which lies in the nature of things and applies equally to all times—he that is married is variously distracted from the service of the Lord by the wish to please his wife and by worldly cares, while the unmarried can devote himself to that service with undivided heart, free spirit and full power. "The unmarried careth for the things of the Lord, how he may please the Lord; the married careth for the things of the world, how he may please his wife." And so, again, with women;

[1] Apoc. xiv. 4, 5 Many attempts have been made to weaken the force of this passage. It used to be said that abstinence from idolatry was meant? that is now given up. The new allegation that abstinence from fornication only is meant, as Bleek and de Wette explain, is contradicted by the term παρθένοι and the general expression μετὰ γυναικῶν. The evasion, that Christians of the last days only are spoken of "for whom celibacy will be a moral necessity from the peculiar circumstances of the period," (Hofmann *Schriftbeweis.* ii. 2. p. 392), conflicts with the context. They are rather an ἀπαρχὴ, "first-fruits redeemed from among men." The simplest procedure is that of Neander and Düsterdieck, who reject the whole book as spurious in consequence. Rothe (*Ethik* iii. 614) admits that, "according to our exegetic conscience, we are in no position to understand by παρθένοι anything else but literal virginity.
[2] 1 Cor. vii. 1, 7.
[3] 1 Cor. vii. 26. διὰ τὴν ἐνεστῶσαν ἀνάγκην, with reference to Matt. xxiv. 21, and the θλίψις μεγάλη, spoken of at Christ's first coming. St. Paul saw a time of great affliction for the whole Church appending, and made this one ground among many for preferring celibacy to marriage. But the whole context shows that it was not his main ground, for he alleges, before and after, much weightier motives, lying in the nature of the case and independent of these temporary circumstances, applying equally to all times, whether of peace or of distress and great commotions.

"The unmarried woman careth for the things of the Lord, that she may be holy in body and spirit; she that is married careth for the things of the world, how she may please her husband." And hence, the Apostle advises even those who are married to separate sometimes for awhile by mutual consent, in order to devote themselves to spiritual exercises.[1] This shows that the intercourse of married life is a hindrance to earnest prayer, and that those who would live in constant prayer do better to avoid it.

So distinctly is the unmarried state here put forward as the most suitable for the Christian and his high calling, that the Apostle feels bound to observe that he had no intention of "casting a snare" upon them—that he does not wish to force their consciences, which would easily lead to sins of impurity.[2] He guards himself against being supposed to lay down a general law and abuse his authority by interfering with Christian liberty. He is only advising, but he cannot but recognise in religious celibacy the nobler form of life, the more independent and worthier condition, and the opportunity of a faithful and undistracted perseverance in serving the Lord.[3] It is, in his eyes, a higher privilege, that the body of a virgin belongs solely to the Lord and remains pure from every profanation; while in marriage, where the wife "has not power over her own body," such profanation often takes place through abuse of the matrimonial relation. But purity of body, as the Apostle intimates, is to secure purity of mind, which gives it its true worth.

St. Paul has no command of the Lord in this matter; he only counsels and recommends, but he does so as one "who has received mercy of the Lord to be faithful," who is conscious according to his enlightenment that he speaks by the Holy Ghost.[4] He will not say on his own *ipse dixit* that the married state, which he well knew Christ had sanctified, is always and necessarily a hindrance to a religious life; he was quite aware that in many a marriage husband and wife mutually help each other in their Christian course. What he means to say is; first, that there are men specially

---

[1] 1 Cor. vii. 34, 5.     [2] 1 Cor. vii. 35.
[3] Ib. πρὸς τὸ εὔσχημον καὶ εὐπρόσεδρον τῷ Κυρίῳ ἀπερισπάστως.
[4] 1 Cor. vii. 25, 40. [hardly "is conscious"—δοκῶ (*Vulg.* puto) "I think," or "seem to myself."—Tr.]

called and fitted for a single life, and that, though comparatively very few, they do well to give scope to such a call; secondly, that the single are better fitted than the married for the service of Christ, and, therefore, for any Church office, and can do more in that service, when not distracted and hampered by worldly cares of wife and family in a ministry requiring the whole man; thirdly, that intercourse with God and Christ would be more easily and uninterruptedly maintained by the single than by the married. There were then, as now, many whose civil position made marriage impossible, or who could only found a family with the prospect of bitter want. Slavery, again, reduced thousands to compulsory celibacy. St. Paul taught all these how to regard their state as a holy one, and even a blessing from God. For, as he says elsewhere, "God is faithful, who will not suffer you to be tempted above your power;"[1] the Christian who uses prayer, watchfulness, moderation and the means of grace, can always check and master even violent assaults of bodily passion. The temptation to transgress is not stronger for the unmarried than the temptation to abuse what is lawful for the married.

There can be no doubt how St. Paul would have answered, if he had been asked, whether it were better for the bearer of a Church office to be married or unmarried. In commending to Timothy the conscientious discharge of his office, he says, "No soldier entangleth himself with the affairs of life, that he may please him that chose him."[2] The principle of clerical celibacy is here involved. St. Paul would accordingly have said, "Every Church officer is a combatant, who has to carry on incessantly a most difficult strife, and in order to please his Leader must copy His example, as I do myself. He should not increase the difficulties of a faithful discharge of his office by the trials, cares and distractions of the married state. The Lord to whom he belongs and the Church he serves must be the centre of his life and action, nor should he have any other centre of his affections. In every other relation and position man can and should be divided; he may be a husband and father, while he discharges a civil office or a profession. Only the service of the Church of the New Covenant, the care of souls, which is a new thing

[1] 1 Cor. x. 13.     [2] 2 Tim. ii. 4.

in the world, allows no division and will not be content with half the man. No wife and family should stand between the congregation and him to whom the Holy Ghost has entrusted it, to watch over souls and give account of them,[1]—between the spiritual father and his children. The Lord says that the good shepherd gives his life for the sheep;[2] and so his head and heart, time and strength, care and love, labour and property, belong to them. But a husband and father owes all this, first, to his wife and children, and only what is over comes to the flock." So would he have spoken, who said of himself that he was full of tenderness for his people, and willing to impart to them not only the Gospel of God but his own life.[3]

But it was neither possible nor right, at that initial and preparatory period of the Church, that those called to the ministry should be required to practice life-long celibacy. Presbyters had to be chiefly taken from among the Jews, who were seldom unmarried, because childlessness was a reproach and misfortune among the chosen people;[4] the few Jewish converts who were single had to be employed in distant missions. The unmarried Gentile converts were those who had avoided the burdens and ties of marriage, or been disqualified by their civil position, and were precisely the least fit for office in the Church. Moreover, the ministry had no attractions for the natural man; if a persecution broke out, the pastors were the first to be seized. There was no such run upon Church offices as left the Apostles and their assistants free to choose. St. Paul, therefore, contented himself with the lesser requirement, that an overseer or deacon should be the husband of one wife, and widows of one husband be chosen for deaconesses.[5] The parallel passage about widows shows that the explanation often attempted, of a prohibition only of making men living in polygamy Bishops or Deacons, is quite untenable. And it is obviously inconceivable that baptized Christians in Apostolic communities should have been living with two or more wives at once, and allowed all rights of Church communion except the ministry. Nor

---

[1] Acts xx. 28. Heb. xiii. 17.   [2] John x. 11.   [3] 1 Thess. ii. 8.
[4] 1 Kings [E. V. 1 Sam.] i. 6. Job xxiv. 21. Luke i. 25.
[5] 1 Tim. iii. 2, 12 ; v. 9.

did bigamy or polygamy then exist, either among the Jews or in the Roman Empire among the Heathen. There is no trace of polygamy being practised among the Jews in the whole New Testament;[1] and it is nowhere forbidden, for the same reason that Solon made no law against parricide, because it was not thought necessary to forbid what was unheard of. In the whole Roman Empire it was not tolerated, but punished with deprivation of civil rights.[2]

St. Paul, therefore, can only be understood as saying that Presbyters and Deacons were to be husbands of one wife, in the same sense as widow deaconesses were to have had one husband. This was grounded on his feeling that second marriages of widowers, though allowable, were something imperfect, and would be a stumbling block in one who was to be a pattern to the community. The Jewish High Priest could only marry once, and it was a common view with Greeks and Romans, that second marriages, after the death of a consort, were inconsistent with the ideal character and dignity of marriage.[3] St. Paul, then, had two grounds for making this condition—first, because a presbyter must be above reproach as well among Heathen as Christians; and, therefore, he laid great stress on no occasion being given to unbelievers to speak ill of Christians.[4] But, if what would have given offence in many Heathen priests was suffered in a Christian presbyter, it would cause scandal. And, next, St. Paul, who prizes abstinence from fleshly desires so highly that he reckons it among the noblest fruits of the Holy Ghost, and makes it a mark of a genuine Christian to have crucified the flesh with its affections and lusts, could not regard a man married a second time as a bright example of continence and a pattern for imitation, as a minister of the Church should be.[5] And

---

[1] Justin, indeed, objects to Trypho that there were Jewish teachers, who allowed men to have five wives, *i. e.*, said it was not forbidden in the Law, and was justified by the practice of the Patriarchs; but he never says that this theory of individual teachers was put in practice. (*Opp. Ed. Otto.* ii. 442.)

[2] *Cod.* i. 5. Tit. v. 2, a Prætorian and, therefore, older law.

[3] Valerius Maximus says a second marriage was considered "legitimæ cujusdam intemperantiæ signum." The much praised laws of Charondas ordered, that one who gave his children a stepmother should hold no place in the Council. Diod. xiii. 12. Cf. Liv. x. 23. Tac. *Germ.* 19, where a single marriage is highly extolled.

[4] 1 Tim. iii. 2. ἀνεπίληπτος. 1 Thess. iv. 12.

[5] Gal. v. 22, ἐγκράτεια. Cf. 1 Cor. vii. 9, εἰ δὲ οὐκ ἐγκρατεύονται γαμησάτωσαν. [The *word* ἐγκράτεια only means self-mastery or temperance, however exercised. See *Eth. Nic.* Lib. vii. passim.—Tr.] Gal. v. 24. 1 Pet. v. 3.

so this condition, of a clergyman being only once married, was always treated as an universal law even in the ancient Church by the Apostles.[1]

It has been already said that three of the Apostles, St. Paul, St. John, and St. James, remained unmarried, while the rest, and notably St. Peter, were married. Of St. John this is universally testified. Of St. James there is the same tradition, so that the Ebionites for a long while honoured virginity from his example.[2] When St. Peter said to the Lord, "Behold we have left all and followed Thee," the answer shows that wives were included; and hence it was believed in the ancient Church, that the married Apostles renounced the use of marriage in after life.[3] St. Paul's words are often quoted against it: "Have we not power to lead about a woman, a sister, as the other Apostles, and the brethren of the Lord and Cephas? Or have I only and Barnabas no power to abstain from labouring?"[4] But this does not mean that the Apostles took about wives, together with children and maidens, on their missionary journeys; that after renouncing the society of their wives, while following Christ, they afterwards were accompanied by them in frequent and often distant journeys. But, as the Fathers have observed, women followed the Apostles, according to a Jewish custom adopted by Christ Himself, to minister to them and facilitate their intercourse with the females of the families they visited.[5] This could be done without arousing suspicion or surprise by those Apostles who worked chiefly among the Jews; but St. Paul and St. Barnabas, who worked among the Gentiles, renounced the use of a right which would have scandalized them.[6]

---

[1] How Theodoret came to a different conclusion is shown in *Hippolytus and Callistus*, p. 149. [The rule against second marriages of priests still survives in the Greek Church, both "Orthodox" and Uniate.—Tr.]

[2] Epiphanius, Ambrose, Chrysostom, Paulinus, Augustine, Cassian and Jerome, say that St. John was so specially favoured by Christ, for this reason. Epiphanius (p. 1045) says that St. James died at 96, πάρθενος. See, as to Ebionites, Epiph. p. 126.

[3] Matt. xix. 27, 29. St. Athanasius calls virginity ἀποστόλων καύχημα. St. Epiphanius (p. 491) thinks Christ meant the Apostles in Matt. xix. 12. St. Jerome, (*Apol. ad. Pam.* 21,) thinks they were " vel virgines, vel post nuptias continentes." or, as he says, (*Contr. Jov.* 1, 14,) "relinquunt officium conjugale." So Isidore of Pelusium, *Ep.* 3, 176.

[4] 1 Cor. ix. 5, 6.     [5] Matt. xxvii. 55.

[6] Those who insist on these sisters being wives instead of sisters, seem to have forgotten the seventh chapter of the Epistle. For it would be strange if St. Paul, who

The custom of binding oneself by vow to God to special religious practices, passed from Judaism into the Christian communities. Just as marriage in the Christian Church became indissoluble, as involving not merely a mutual engagement but an obligation before God, so the force and meaning of a vow consisted in a man's sanctifying and securing his resolution against personal instability or change by a promise made to God. Believers entered the Church with a vow at their baptism; its scope was the most comprehensive and universal possible, for it implied no less than a complete self-surrender to God, a promise to make His will the guide of life. But room was left for particular vows referring to special acts or seasons, or binding to a special kind of work. Thus, St. Paul went to Jerusalem to accomplish a vow.[1] A vow to dedicate themselves wholly to the Lord in the service of the Church, and remain unmarried, was taken by Deaconesses even in the time of the Apostles. This is clear from St. Paul's solemn warning to Timothy, not to admit younger widows, who would wish to marry again from wantonness, and would thereby break their first vow and incur serious guilt and punishment.[2]

It may be truly said that the Christian religion is pre-eminently the religion of righteousness, in the sense that it, and it alone, respects the claim of every human idiosyncracy, condition, or need; that it never exalts one at the cost of

there puts forward his own example of voluntary celibacy for the service of Christ, and wishes all would follow it, had said afterwards, "Have I not power to take about my wife with me?" His opponents would have simply replied, that those who have no wives cannot take them about, and that he did not remain unmarried merely to avoid being chargeable for a wife, but from a higher motive, on his own showing, viz., that it was good not to touch a woman, and that the unmarried has only the Lord to please and not his wife. He meant, therefore, that he might have taken about a "sister," and claimed support for her. So Chrysostom, Theodoret, Tertullian and Jerome understand it. Only Clement of Alexandria is misled by σύξυγε, Phil. iv. 3, which he takes for wife.

[1] Acts xviii. 18. The notion that it was Aquila who had taken the vow, though very old, is quite erroneous. The Vulgate has it, and of modern writers, Hammond, Grotius, Wieseler, Schneckenburger and Meyer. Among the ancients, Didymus and St. Augustine saw that St. Paul was meant; the practical St. Luke was not likely to mention the circumstance, if it concerned so subordinate a personage as Aquila. He wants to give a motive for St. Paul's journey to Syria and Jerusalem. The Apostle himself tells the Ephesians, who wished to detain him, that he must keep the feast in Jerusalem, clearly on account of his vow. Else no object for this journey would be given, whereas St. Luke gives motives for all St. Paul's other journeys. [The Vulgate does not apparently *mean* Aquila, for it gives a reference to Acts xxi. 24, and puts Aquila and Priscilla in a parenthesis. But the construction seems to require such a meaning.—TR.]

[2] 1 Tim. v. 11, 12, τὴν πρώτην πίστιν ἠθέτησαν

another, but sanctifies and applies all to the se
To the superficial gaze of a stranger, who has ı
of its power and truth, contradictions and
appear everywhere; while the son of the house
perfect harmony and comprehensiveness, wh
the whole of life. It can exalt virginity
paraging marriage, and not only reconcile
obedience, but make obedience instrumental
preaches without inconsistency the rightfu
husband and wife, and the subjection of the
rule of her husband.

If the doctrine of Christ was proclaimed a
for all mankind, to the female portion of the hu
was doubly so. With the Church was found
tution, whereby woman was to be restored t
dignity and proper social position. She is
vessel," as St. Peter says, and physically ur
but in the Church she is his equal, having
rights of citizenship in the kingdom of grace.
is to love, honour and care for the wife, as hi
God, and to make no violent or despotic use of
that his "prayer may not be hindered"—or
fruitful—through his unworthiness.[1]

St. Paul rises higher, when he makes the rel
to the Church, the love of the Divine Head
a type of earthly marriage and of the pure lov
subsist between husband and wife. He appl
the characteristics of Christ's love, and requir
a sanctifying, self-sacrificing, purifying love c
for his wife, something widely different from s
The man is the head, who must rule, love,
quicken the woman as his own body, and both
one whole, so that their love of each other is
selves, "for no man ever hated his own
marriage is itself a Church in miniature, the
springs first the household Church, then of
composed the community, and of various cc
great edifice of the universal Church, the bri
Christ. And thus Christian marriage raises
of his own worth and dignity, and makes hi

[1] 1 Pet. iii. 7.   [2] Eph. v. 23 sqq.

is not simply an individual, but part of a higher and more sacred whole, joined in a covenant whereof the Church's union with her Lord is the type.

Closely connected with this restoration of woman's dignity is the elevation of chastity to its full moral significance, through the idea of an universal priesthood. The Christian's body is a temple of God, sanctified for His service, and inhabited by the Holy Ghost; chastity is the pure, priestly feeling, which preserves the body from becoming a mere instrument of sensual desire, and hallows it to be an organ of the Divine will in the generation of children, making it part of the one offering to be continually presented to God, as being united to the human nature of the Redeemer and destined to be raised and glorified hereafter.[1] For therein is shown the power and reality of a religion which masters the most vehement and unbridled of our passions, subject as it is to such terrible perversion, and easily degenerating from a fount of life into a deadly poison that pollutes the very sources of our being. Here Christianity gains its hardest and most beneficial victory. Dishonour of woman, contempt of marriage, celibacy and childlessness from corruption, selfishness and mutual criminality, facility of divorce and re-marriage, paiderastia, a public life of shamelessness, and the degradation of whole classes to be the contemptible instruments of lust—all these moral abominations, springing from the same root, prevailed far and wide and desolated whole provinces. The Church opposed to them her notion of chastity, her consecration of marriage, her absolute prohibition of divorce, and her praise of continence and virginity. She taught and showed that the wife is not a mere chattel of the man, an instrument for his lust or for perpetuating his family, but his equal, joined to him in a sacred and indissoluble bond. The Apostles speak of sins of unchastity as wholly alien to real Christians, simply Heathenish, and belonging only to their earlier Heathen life, not even to be named among believers.[2] Such works of darkness spring from Satan, and make the doer his slave, drawing after them curse and destruction.[3]

---

[1] 1 Cor. vi. 19.   Heb. ii. 16.   Phil. iii. 21.
[2] Col. iii. 7.   1 Thess. iv. 5.   Eph. v. 3.   1 Pet. ii. 11.
[3] 1 Cor. vi. 9, 10.   Eph. v. 5.   Heb. xiii. 4.

"Crucify the flesh, with its affections and lusts;"—
"Mortify through the Spirit the deeds of the body;"—
"Let every one preserve his vessel in sanctification and honour;"—"Will ye make your bodies, which are members of Christ, members of an harlot, and sin against your own bodies?"[1] Such are the Apostolic warnings. Chastity was considered the virtue which above all gives moral strength and self-mastery to the soul, and preserves it from being made effeminate and pressed down under the weight of the body. Nor does Christian teaching recognise in marriage love any involuntary feeling, depriving man of his liberty of will and action; such a sentiment the Apostles would have called by a very different name. The married love they hold to be a duty in Christians, is a free and conscious direction of will, grounded on high religious motives,—a feeling under their own control, not an unbridled passion—a feeling which can be made as pure and enduring as love of friends or children or country. In this sense St. Paul exhorts husbands to love their wives.[2]

Christian marriage, then, is the internal fusion of two human beings, so that each may supplement the other, and both be joined by mutual self-devotion in a perfect unity of life and will. Husbands and wives who feel themselves living members of Christ's body employ that almost irresistible power, which married love gives them over each other, for mutual sanctification and improvement; for they feel as halves of each other, and the faults of either are the faults of both. The man, in whom all desire for another woman would be adultery in the heart, purifies his love for his wife from all sensuous self-seeking, and sanctifies it through higher love to Christ.[3] The man is to the woman, what Christ is to the Church; she submits to him as her head, and willingly and trustfully accepts his guidance, while they help one another and share in bearing each others joys and sorrows.

If St. Paul forbids women to teach in public, he says that they shall be saved through child-bearing.[4] He means that God has given to them, in place of the ministry reserved for men, another office in the Church, in the

---

[1] Gal. v. 24. Rom. viii. 13. 1 Thess. iv. 4. 1 Cor. vi. 15.    [2] Eph. v. 25.
[3] Matt. v. 28. 1 Cor. vii. 29.    [4] 1 Tim. ii. 15.

faithful discharge of which they are to work out their salvation—that of peopling the Church by bearing and training children to be citizens of God's kingdom on earth. This consecration of family life and maternal duties, exalting and purifying carnal affection and natural tenderness to the dignity of a priestly office, in bringing up and forming new members of the Church and heirs of the kingdom, is the side of marriage where its highest and peculiarly Christian ends are realised and its sacramental character exhibited. Here it is the true picture of Christ's union with the Church, a sanctified and ever fruitful marriage wherein He makes her through baptism the mother of countless children. For this cause the Divine blessing is bestowed on the union of man and wife, and it is a state of grace where Christ joins them indissolubly and the Holy Ghost specially operates; for marriage is the foundation of the Church, wherein the Spirit dwells, and the source of her continual increase. And as the seal of a special grace is impressed on the priestly state, which is indispensable for the existence and duration of the Church, so is the state of marriage placed under the protection and blessing of a special grace, as being dedicated to the Church, and subserving its continual growth and expansion. Christ says that God knits the marriage bond, as it is the Holy Ghost who appoints presbyters to superintend and guide the Church;[1] both positions must be entered upon through a Divine call and consecration, and with that promise and guarantee of grace from on high, without which no office in the Church can be fulfilled. And thus marriage became a link in the chain of the Church's means of grace, though no outward sign or vehicle, as laying on of hands, use of oil or water, or the like, was ordained for it. Here, as in baptism and penance, there is a sanctification and cleansing through discipline and mastery of the spirit over the perverted animal nature, so that through it children of grace may be born for God and according to His ordinance, not children of the flesh after the will of the flesh. Marriage, again, is like confirmation, in being a consecration to a lay priesthood and a special means of fulfilling it. It is so far akin to ordination, that to enter on marriage is to enter on

[1] Acts xx. 28.

a state peculiarly dedicated to the service of the Church. It is a fruit of the Divine Incarnation, a dispensation of the New Covenant and high privilege of the Church, that where sin is strong, healing and sustaining grace should be stronger still. And thus the intercourse of the sexes, which rightly and religiously used is a continual fountain of blessing, but, when misused and unbridled, a source of corruption for whole generations, is placed under the shelter and sanctifying power of an ordinance of grace, and directed to the higher end of preserving and carrying forward the kingdom of God on earth. Only thus is marriage really what the Apostle calls it, the hallowed copy of an archetype, both Divine and human, Christ's union with the Church. For, as that union was only possible through His cleansing His chosen bride in the laver of baptism, and thus making the act of marriage an act of purification,[1] so must the Divinely ordained antitype be qualified to be a means of cleansing and sanctification.

Christ and His Apostles said nothing of the first requisite of marriage,—monogamy, because polygamy did not occur to them as possible. There was no need to command what the law and custom of the Pagan Empire secured, and what Christians would have degraded themselves among the Heathen by not observing. The New Testament accordingly contains no word of prohibition against bigamy or polygamy. So much the more needful was it to announce, as a radical principle of the new Church, that marriage was indissoluble, and no divorce, with permission to re-marry, admissible. Christ spoke four times of this, according to the three first Evangelists. The Law of Moses recognised as an existing custom the husband's right to separate from his wife and marry another, and ordered a writing of divorce to be given to the rejected wife. There was no interposition of others, or sentence of a court: the man acted wholly for himself, and only his right was allowed—the wife could not separate herself. By the time of the last Prophets the disorder of frequent divorces must have greatly gained ground, for Malachi denounces it as the cause of God's displeasure against the offerings of Israel: "The Lord hath been witness between thee and

[1] Eph. v. 26.

the wife of thy youth, with whom thou hast dealt unfaithfully; yet she is thy partner and the wife of thy covenant."[1] That it was no better at the time of Christ, is clear, from the contest between the two schools of Hillel and Shammai, —the former inferring, from the generality of the expression in the Law, "if she no longer please him," the man's absolute right to repudiate his wife for the most trivial cause, or from mere fancy; while the latter maintained, that two words added by the lawgiver limited the permission to cases where there was some evidence of the wife's unfaithfulness. Any Jew could act on the laxer theory of Hillel; and Josephus, who was of priestly family, relates that his first wife left him, and that he repudiated the second, who had borne him three children, when her conduct displeased him, in order to take a third.[2]

In the Sermon on the Mount, where He declared the perfect fulfilment of the Law to be the end of His mission and the condition of belonging to His kingdom, Christ pronounced against the writing of divorce, saying that whoever dismissed his wife, unless on account of fornication, caused her (by marrying another) to commit adultery; and that whoever married such an one, committed adultery. According to the same Evangelist, He repeated this saying, when the Pharisees, desiring to implicate Him in a contradiction either to the Law or to their interpretation of it, asked Him whether (as the school of Hillel taught) it was allowable to put away one's wife for every cause? In His answer, He passed beyond the controversies of the schools and even the Pharisaic circle of ideas, which kept to the irrevocable liberty of divorce, declaring marriage, according to God's original institution, to be so strong and indissoluble a bond that it superseded every other, even that of parents and children; and that every divorce, with one exception, was adultery and led to adultery.[3]

A teaching so sharply and decisively antagonistic to prevalent Jewish notions startled the disciples also, and they asked Him privately about it, when he declared every dissolution of the marriage bond, without exception, to be unlawful. On another occasion, only mentioned by St.

---

[1] Mal. ii. 14. Cf. Mic. ii. 9.     [2] Jos. *Vit.* 75, 76.
[3] Matt. v. 32. 32; xix. 4—9.

Luke, He said the same before the Pharisees.[1] He wanted to show the Jews, by an example, how the Law would be fulfilled in His kingdom, by being brought back to its purest and most ideal forms, and thus carried out in the utmost strictness and perfection. As a test of this, He laid down the fundamental principle, that no man can serve two masters,—God and Mammon; and this elicited the mockery of the covetous Pharisees. They meant that in the Law the possession of riches, which Jesus called the service of Mammon, was so far from being forbidden, that earthly blessings were promised by God to the pious. He replied, that such indeed was the old dispensation of the Law, which lasted to the time of John, and to obey it required no "violence" or moral effort and self-denial; men found themselves born in it, and could serve God and Mammon while still sons of Abraham. But with John began a new epoch, and the setting up of God's kingdom on earth was preached: to enter it, is difficult, and a share in it must be won by toil and combat. There the Law is taught and practised, not as before John, but in its completeness. Heaven and earth shall pass away, before the least particle shall be taken from the integrity of that Law, which is a revelation of the holiness of God, in His new kingdom. And then, in order to illustrate the setting up of that Divine Law in its primeval purity—no more to be changed or disturbed by human perversity—Christ held up before them the absolute indissolubility of marriage to be observed in His kingdom, where the previous permission of divorce would be withdrawn. And lastly, St. Paul, premising that it is not his precept but the Lord's, bids the Corinthians treat marriage as a relation that can never be dissolved.[2]

If we combine the teachings of Christ on this question, these four statements occur. First: marriage rests on a Divine institution, dating from the beginning of the human race; God ordained it for the life-long and indissoluble fusion of two persons into one moral and religious personality, and a man who enters on that state must subject his free will to this Divine appointment—for what is in every case joined together by God, it is not right or possible for man to put asunder. Secondly: the Mosaic permission of a writing of

[1] Mark x. 11, 12. Luke xvi. 18.    [2] 1 Cor. vii. 10, 11.

divorce is an after-thought, and was conceded as a temporary dispensation on account of the Jews' hardness of heart, and to preclude worse offences, as secret murder and the like. "From the beginning it was not so." Thirdly: this temporary permission of divorce is now at an end, for the original dignity and holiness of marriage is restored in the Church to its proper place; and there can be no more talk of concession to the hardness of men's hearts, since the Incarnation has opened a fresh fountain of Divine strength for believers. The very object for which the Church was founded is to supply abundant means for overcoming the hardness and frailty of man's nature, and to fulfil the ancient prophecy, that God will give His people a new, fleshly heart, instead of their hard and stony heart.[1] Those who are determined to remain obdurate and will not be healed, cannot belong to the community of the redeemed, and must consequently leave the Church. Fourthly: whoever puts away his wife, and takes another, is doubly or trebly guilty; he commits adultery against his wife, he causes her to commit adultery by marrying another, and he is responsible for the adultery of whoever marries her.[2]

Three witnesses, St. Mark, St. Luke and St. Paul, make the Lord declare marriage absolutely indissoluble; while one, St. Matthew, twice makes Him add the limitation, "except for cause of fornication." Two of the statements in St. Mark and St. Luke are not found in St. Matthew, viz., the explanation given to the disciples in the house, and the illustration before the Pharisees of the difference between the purity and perfection of the Law in the Church, and its former meaning and observance. But St. Matthew and St. Mark agree in their account of the answer given to the Pharisees before that private explanation to the disciples, only that St. Matthew inserts the exception and St. Mark omits it. It follows that Christ said twice—once in the Sermon on the Mount, once to the Pharisees—"no divorce except for fornication," and as often, especially in answering His disciples; that marriage was absolutely indissoluble. And, further, St. Mark must have had some ground for omitting the limitation in St. Matthew, and St. Paul knew

---

[1] Ezek. xxxvi. 26. Jer. xxxi. 33.   [2] Matt. xix. 9. Mark x. 11, 12.

only of an absolute prohibition of any dissolution of the marriage bond, or, if he did know of the exception given in St. Matthew, either did not think it applicable, to those he was concerned with, or did not consider it to affect the general rule.

St. Matthew is known to have written in Aramaic for the Jews of Palestine, and accordingly what is conspicuous in his Gospel is the local colouring, the Jewish line of thought, the connection of Christianity and Judaism, while St. Mark and St. Luke wrote for Gentile converts. Hence St. Mark says that Christ declared the woman also, who left her husband and married another, according to Heathen custom, an adulteress, while St. Matthew omits this, as being a thing unheard of among the Jews. It is the reverse with the exception about fornication. Christ had said that, only in one case, when a man discovers that his wife has deceived him and was unchaste before marriage, so that he has married one not a maid, he may give her a writing of divorce and put her away. That this is His meaning appears from the word used, (πορνεία), which is always applied to the sin of an unmarried person, not to unfaithfulness in a wife, which is constantly described by another word (μοιχεία) both in the Old and New Testament. The Law punished with stoning a bride who professed to be a virgin and was not. With a people who had so strong a feeling of jealousy as the Jews about a bride's virginity, deceit in the matter seemed deserving of death; and if the public conviction and execution ordered by the Law did not actually take place —of which no example is known—it was natural and in order, for a man who discovered such treachery to send back the woman who had been disgraced and had dishonoured him to her parents, with a writing of divorce after the Mosaic form.[1] If the strict law survived the period of the

---

[1] Michaelis (*Mos. Recht.* sect. 93, vol. ii. p. 118, *der Bieler Ed.*) observes, that the Jews could only have understood Christ to mean that a man was justified in divorcing his wife, if he discovered at once that she had deceived him and had been unchaste before marriage. He contradicts himself, when he adds that the Jews would have understood sin after marriage to be included in His words, for they could not with any reason have attached two wholly different meanings to the same word. The last commentator on Deuteronomy, F. W. Schultz, (Berlin 1859, p. 163), thinks "the Lord's saying, Matt. v. 32, is wide enough to recognise our case also (that of previous seduction) as a ground of divorce." So, too, Stier. (*Reden Jesu.* i. 134, 2nd Ed.) "The word extends further and does not exclude unchastity before marriage." It is

Captivity, it was certainly modified in practice, since the Jews had lived among Greeks and under Greek rule, for to stone a girl who had been seduced would appear to Greeks an unpardonable abomination and barbarity. The milder practice of divorce would first prevail in Galilee, where Christ taught, which since the time of the Maccabees had been called "Galilee of the Gentiles," and had a mixed population of Greeks and Syrians.[1]  Hence Joseph wanted to dismiss Mary, his betrothed, privately, when found to be pregnant, whether with or without the Mosaic form, does not appear.[2] By the law she was liable to death. In such cases of divorce there was properly no dissolving of the matrimonial bond, for every marriage took place under the condition recognised by the Law, that the bride should be a maid; and deception in a point so essential to Oriental notions invalidated the whole act, for in such a case the man's consent could not be supposed. It was fair that the man should thus divorce a girl he would never have married had he known of her sin, and he showed forbearance in not getting her put to death. And when Christ added for the Jews, who could only thus understand him, this one exception, where divorce was allowable, His rule, that man may not sever what God has joined, remained wholly unaffected. God only binds those who consent to be bound. And this explains why on other occasions, and especially in speaking to His disciples on the future observance of the principle of indissolubility in His Church, Christ did not name this exception. He omitted it, when not referring to the Jewish institution of divorce, but proclaiming the great and binding rule for Jewish and Gentile converts alike, that all dissolving of marriages is destroying a work of God, and, therefore, absolutely forbidden. It is clear, again, how St. Mark, in a narrative designed for Gentile converts, could omit what St. Matthew had said of the exceptional case mentioned by Christ, as something only concerning the Jews and not affecting the general question of the indissolubility of marriage.

in truth so little excluded that it is the only thing meant. The fiery jealousy of the Jews, which could not be appeased with gifts, is mentioned, Prov. vi. 34, 35. Cf. Jahn *Bibl. Archælogie* ii. 254, as to the testimony of travellers, and Jahn i. c. *Mich. Mos. Recht.* Biel. 1777, v. 217 sqq.

[1] 1 Macc. v. 15. Matt. iv. 15.     [2] Matt. i. 19.

But that expression of the Lord, "except for the cause of fornication," has been often, and especially of late, understood of conjugal infidelity; and the doctrine has been attributed to Him, that, while marriage is, indeed, indissoluble as a Divine institution, it is dissoluble, or is *ipso facto* dissolved, by unfaithfulness on either side or both, in which case divorce and re-marriage is allowable. To support this interpretation, the theory has been devised that adultery destroys the essence of marriage, that such a crime on either side *ipso facto* dissolves it, so that the formal divorce and subsequent marriage is the mere authentication and rightful consequences of an accomplished fact.

This interpretation of the words of Christ goes against language, history and logic. The language will not bear it, for Christ carefully distinguishes, as is done everywhere in Scripture, between the two words, one (πορνεία) referring to unchastity in the single, the other (μοιχεία) to unfaithfulness in the married, or what is properly called adultery. The view, that the former term is a generic one for all kinds of carnal sin, including breach of matrimonial fidelity as a species, is erroneous, and only devised to meet this case.[1] It is inconceivable that Christ, while engaged in inculcating the inviolable sanctity of the marriage bond and reducing the possibilities of divorce within the narrowest limits should have used in a crucial statement an ambiguous word, leaving ample scope to those desirous of divorce, when just afterwards He twice uses the proper word.

Moreover if by "fornication" St. Matthew means adultery, there would be a contradiction very difficult to explain between him and St. Mark, St. Luke, and St. Paul; and hence hypotheses have been adopted which throw grave suspicion on the historical fidelity and accuracy of the Scripture writers.[2] For it makes an immense difference both in

---

[1] Tholuck rightly observes (*Bergpredigt.* 4th Ed. p. 247), "The *Lexicon* meaning of the word has been variously widened in the interest of an extension of divorce." But, like nearly all his co-religionists, he has done this himself, and without bringing any proof. He quotes Stier's explanation, "every serious disturbance of conjugal union," and Marheineke's, "whatever *ipso facto* annihilates marriage;" so that no term could be more elastic than πορνεία. Yet no one adheres to *adulterium* only; one or more causes are always added. Most recently, Carlblom (*Uber Ehesch. in der Dorp. Zeitschr. für Theol.* 1859, p. 524), remarks, "At present, I think, we shall find no commentator or moralist who confidently and consistently demands that πορνεία be made the sole legal ground of divorce."

[2] So e. g. Julius Müller (*Uber Ehesch.* Berlin, 1855, p. 3) says, "The Evangelical tradition may easily have lost the clause."

practice and theory whether Christ said, "Marriage can never be rightly dissolved in the Church, for God has sealed it and placed the act of human consent beyond possibility of lawful change;" or whether He said, "Marriage, indeed, is a work of God, and must not be capriciously or lightly disturbed by man for this or that cause; still there are frequent cases—those of adultery, namely,—where the one party may separate from the other and marry again. When either has sinned against the holiness of this sacred bond, the other may wholly and finally sever it by a new marriage." In the former case, every one would marry with the consciousness that no human caprice could ever change the relationship on which he was entering. In the latter case, the married person would know from the first, and all along, that however firm his own determination, it lay in the power of the other party to dissolve the tie. And if Christ taught that marriage could be dissolved by adultery, St. Mark, St. Luke, and St. Paul withheld this important fact from their readers, and misled them by misrepresenting the case; so that the Churches had first to learn the truth from the Greek translation of St. Matthew, and thence discovered that St. Paul had, to say the least, expressed himself very inaccurately, in repeatedly describing marriage as a relation that could only be dissolved by death.

Christ could the less assign to men the right of divorcing their wives for adultery, in the Sermon on the Mount and in His answer to the Pharisees, because the adulteress was still legally punishable with death.[1] Had any relaxation of the law come into vogue, we should have found some trace of a substituted penalty; for even by Roman and Athenian law a man could kill his wife, if caught in the act, and so could her father, according to the new law of Augustus; else she was banished to an island.[2] The Romans had certainly not forced their jurisprudence and penal code on the Jews, even when limiting their right of life and death; and nobody will believe that an ordinary Jewess, convicted of adultery, was banished to an island. In fact,

[1] F. W. Schulz, in his Explanation of Deuteronomy (p. 579) has remarked, what is often forgotten, that in the disputes between the schools of Hillel and Schammai about the sense of the Mosaic *ervat dabar* there could be no reference to adultery, for that was punished with death.
[2] School Cruq. ad Hor. *Sat.* ii. 7, 61. Paull. ii. 26, 14.

the case of the woman taken in adultery, whom the Pharisees brought to Christ, clearly implies that the Mosaic punishment continued in full force, for the Pharisees grounded on it their attempt to lead Him into saying something that might supply matter for an accusation of despising the Law.[1] They knew His gentleness and condescension to the erring, and that He was accounted a friend of sinners, who ate and drank with them, and said He had come for their sake,[2] and who had not repudiated even so notorious a woman as Mary Magdalene; and so they counted on His advocating mercy to this woman, but that could only serve as a weapon against Him, if the legal punishment still held good.[3]

How in such matters were Christians out of Judæa situated in this respect during the Apostolic and subsequent period? By the Julian law, the husband or father must prosecute the unfaithful wife within a fixed time. If the husband married again without having done this, he was guilty of bigamy, and not only lost civil rights, but by the Julian law incurred, together with his second wife, the penalty of rape, which for persons of a lower class was scourging and banishment; while a woman who separated herself from her husband on account of his adultery, and married again, was punished as an adulteress.[4] But a Christian, who brought his wife before the civil courts, sinned against the good name of the community and the Apostolic prohibition of going to law before Gentile courts.[5] If he divorced his wife on any other pretext, he was anyhow considered an offender against the sanctity of marriage,

---

[1] A bethrothed maiden, who let herself be seduced, was to be stoned, but nothing is said in the Law of putting to death a married woman. Probably the penalty was the same. The later Talmud (Sanhed. f. 51, 2), which says " adultera, cum nupta, strangulanda, cum desponsata lapidanda," is of no weight here.

[2] Matt. xi. 19. Mark ii. 16, 17.

[3] In the second Appendix, I think I have proved that the Romans had then deprived the Jewish courts of power of life and death ; but even so, it would only follow that the Jews required the procurator's leave to hold a court and carry out its sentence, and ordinarily such leave would be granted. Therefore Meyer's view is untenable (*Com. in Ev. Joh.* 2nd Ed. p. 220), that the Pharisees meant to accuse Christ before the Roman courts, if He decided for stoning according to the Law of Moses. He might have decided by the letter of the law without saying a word of its execution, simply saying what the Pharisees said of Him afterwards, "We have a law, and by our law He ought to die," when, far from seeking to invade the rights of Roman authorities, they tried to thrust both judgment and execution upon them.

[4] Instit. iv. 18, 4. Paull. ii. 26, 13.

[5] 1 Cor. vi. 1.

and would be excluded from communion. And Christians were convinced by the Lord's words, that for the innocent party to re-marry, on the plea of his wife's unfaithfulness, was a grave offence, as the oldest evidence on the point we possess of post-Apostolic date testifies,—that of Hermas.

Nor is it a logical view, that Christ meant in such cases to leave to the guiltless party only the option of re-marriage. For His teaching would be involved in the reproach of a strange contradiction. He had represented the three persons concerned as guilty of adultery in a case of divorce and re-marriage, the husband who re-married, the divorced wife, and the man who married her.[1] But if He also taught that marriage was actually annulled by adultery, and that at least the innocent party might marry again, then a woman divorced for any *other* cause than adultery might take a new husband without either of them being guilty of sin, if her former husband had married again and thereby committed adultery. The words of Christ are only intelligible, when we distinguish πορνεία from adultery. For it will not be seriously maintained that while placing the rights of husband and wife on an equality, and declaring divorce on either side to involve adultery, He also taught that a man who divorced an adulterous wife might marry again, but that a wife divorced by an adulterous husband, who had married again, must remain single and defenceless all her life and consider herself still bound to him.

In course of time the Church had to proclaim that there could be no true marriage, except between Christians, and to refuse consent to an union between a Christian and a Jew or Heathen. But in the Apostolic age such mixed marriages were of course frequent, and to such cases the strict rule of indissolubility could not be applied. The unbelieving consort, who was outside the Church and its influences, could not be treated as subject to a Divine law only given for the Church. The principle of "hardness of heart" came in. Such a half Christian marriage could be no type of Christ's union with the Church. The Christian partner, however, could do nothing to dissolve it; but if the other refused to maintain the marriage on account of religion, or

---

[1] Properly four persons; for the woman who marries the divorced husband is clearly included by implication in the guilt of adultery.

made apostasy a condition of doing so, it was a different matter. In such a case, the Apostle says, a Christian is not "enslaved," or bound to force himself on a Heathen consort who insults his faith and maltreats him for its sake. Christians are called by God to a service of peace, not of constant strife; and if the unbelieving consort separates, the believing one is also free. But where the Heathen partner is not so hostile, he and the children are sanctified by being brought under the domestic influence of Christian holiness, and indirectly under that of the Church, though not members of it.[1]

---

[1] 1 Cor. vii. 12—16.

# CHAPTER IV.

### SOCIAL AND POLITICAL RELATIONS.

THE Christian idea of poverty and riches was one of those new views radically opposed to men's customary notions. There was no class so displeased by what Christ said as the rich. He calls wealth "Mammon," a god whom men worship, and whose service is incompatible with that of God. A camel will sooner go through a needle's eye, than a rich man enter into the kingdom of God. "Woe unto you rich, for ye have your consolation."[1] And the parable of Lazarus and the rich man, who without being vicious used his wealth for his own enjoyment, harmonises with these stern sayings. He taught that it was hard to be rich and not set one's heart on riches; to possess much, and not be possessed by it. There is a power of deceitfulness in riches, and none can enter the kingdom of heaven, who have not divested themselves of their riches and become poor in spirit, either by an actual and complete renunciation of property, or by an inward conversion of will from the desire and enjoyment of it; for "where your treasure is, there will your heart be also."[2] Christianity could only recognise those wealthy men who acted as stewards of God, and possessed as not possessing. For, as St. Paul says, covetousness and insatiable greed of gain is the root of all evil, and to wish to become rich leads to destruction.[3]

The Christian idea was that man is only the steward of

---

[1] Matt. vi. 24; xix. 23, 24. Luke xvi. 13.  [2] Matt. xiii. 22; vi. 21.
[3] 1 Tim. vi. 9, 10.

earthly goods, which are not an end, but a means for advancing the service of God and the good of one's neighbour, and for the use of which an account must be given. It is a leading thought with St. Paul also, that goods and possessions are no worthy object of a Christian's aim, for they only avail for this passing earthly life, the dwelling-place we must soon leave before we have got well at home there; " Having food and clothing, let us be content therewith."[1]

It was to be expected that Christian teaching would appear peculiarly repulsive and uncongenial to the wealthy, and especially to classes devoted to the pursuit of gain. The Founder of Christianity had not where to lay His head in life, and hung in death naked on a Cross. He preached His Gospel chiefly for the poor, and they were far readier to receive it than the rich. " The common people heard Him gladly."[2] So in the Apostle's time: " Not many wise after the flesh, not many mighty, not many noble (are called); but God hath chosen the foolish things of the world to put to shame the wise, and the weak things of the world to put to shame the strong."[3] In fact, nearly all the first converts were from the poorer and humbler classes. The only known exceptions are Nicodemus, Joseph, Sergius Paulus, Dionysius the Areopagite, Apollos, and St. Paul himself. That was the order of Christianity;—first came the poor, the ignorant and uneducated, slaves and the very lowest classes; gradually, and after a long interval, the powerful, the wise, the rich, were won by them, or rather were overcome and compelled to follow the general movement.

Among all nations, where there was a large slave population, manual labour, especially in industrial production and mechanical trades, was looked down upon; it was left to slaves, and in many places to women, and thence came to be held unworthy of free men. Every Greek and Roman citizen had a certain claim to be idle. It was counted honourable to shrink from labour and live at the public expense. The Christian Church produced and fostered a very different view. The old command given to the first man, " In the sweat of thy face thou shalt eat bread," was held to apply to all Christians, and regarded as something

[1] 1 Tim. vi. 8.  [2] Matt. xi. 5.  Luke iv. 18.  Mark xii. 37.
[3] 1 Cor. i. 26, 27.

they had in common with Christ and His Father, who ever work; it was remembered that Christ came to minister, and to make His humble ministry a pattern for his disciples.[1] St. Paul not only exhorted every man to work with his hands, primarily indeed, because the majority of Thessalonian Christians lived by manual work, but he added that he who would not work should not eat.[2] And this involves the general principle that every one is bound to follow some active calling, for the only difference recognised by the Church was that one man had his particular sphere of labour fixed for him by circumstances, while another was free to choose for himself. The Church first taught men to realise the great importance of time, and that no moment of it was given to be wasted, since Christian doctrine showed that time was for the sake of eternity, that every moment had a bearing on eternity, and that it was a Christian's duty to "redeem the time" and seize every opportunity of profitable work.[3] It was to show the close connection between care for souls and hard bodily labour, each supplementing and giving effect to the other, that St. Paul combined working at a trade with his high Apostolic vocation. The man who had day and night "the care of all the Churches," and whose Epistles are monuments of intense labour of mind, found time and strength to make carpets and tent covers. He added lastly as a further motive for Christian labour, that we ought to procure means thereby for relieving the necessity of others.[4]

There was no formal community of goods and abolition of private property in the first Church at Jerusalem. There was a common purse for supporting those in want, and many sold their estates and put the proceeds into it. But every one was free to keep his own property, and the house possessed by Mary, the mother of St. Mark, at Jerusalem is mentioned.[5] Nor was the distinction between wealth and poverty altogether removed even there, and in those first years. Christians were well aware that a thorough community of goods was impracticable on a large scale, and for a continuance. But so urgently had Christ

---

[1] Gen. iii. 19. John v. 17; xiii. 15. Matt. xx. 28.
[2] 1 Thess. iv. 11. 2 Thess. iii. 10. [3] Eph. v. 16. Col. iv. 5.
[4] Eph. iv. 28. [5] Acts xii. 12.

recommended active love of one's neighbour, that there was no need of formal community of goods in the Apostolic Churches. It is a theme constantly recurring in His discourses and teaching, "Give, and it shall be given to you"—"What ye do to the least, that ye have done to Me." Acts of mercy to the suffering, done or omitted, were to be the standard of acceptance or rejection at the last judgment. To the Pharisees, who attached so high a value to the ceremonial washing of vessels, He said, "Give alms of what they contain, and behold, all things are clean to you."[1] He bade the rich youth, if he would be perfect, sell all that he had, give the price to the poor, and follow Him. Brotherly love is the great, new commandment He left His disciples, and the badge they are to be known by. He does not put first the duty of helping the poor and suffering, but teaches that love of God and love of our brother, as its necessary effect, is the supreme law and dominant power of life.[2] St. John says, "He that hath this world's goods, and seeth his brother in need, and closeth his bowels against him, how dwelleth the love of God in him?"[3]

St. James calls love of our neighbour a "royal law," and makes true worship consist in visiting orphans and widows in their affliction, and keeping oneself unspotted from the world. With prophetic wrath he denounces impending judgment on the rich, who are unmerciful; their injustice cries to heaven for vengeance, and their treasures, used for wanton enjoyment, shall become a corroding fire.[4] The whole of St. John's first Epistle is like a commentary on the Lord's saying about brotherly love being a sure sign of His true disciples. He makes that love the crown of the Christian life, and the token that believers dwell no more in darkness, but in the Divine light. He recognises no intermediate state; our relation to our brethren is either that of love, ready to sacrifice itself, or of hatred, which under circumstances would become murderous.[5] He that loves his brother can always approach God and reckon on being heard by Him. But St. Paul, with his vigorous eloquence,

---

[1] Matt. xxv. 34 sqq. Luke xi. 41.   [2] John xv. 17; xiii. 34, 35.
[3] 1 John iii. 17.
[4] James ii. 8; i. 27; v. 1—6.
[5] 1 John iii. 11—18. Rom. xii. 10—13. Gal. vi. 9. 1 Cor. xiii.

and in various ways, is the chief panegyrist of active charity, commending it in all its forms and ever referring it to its pure source. And in order that it may ever flow back to its fountain, the love of God, he so often urges mutual intercession. But he insists on the possibility of doing works of mercy and benevolence without having true love, in which case such works are without blessing or profit, and proceeds to count up the outward manifestations of true love, in order to draw a picture of it as the fruitful mother of all virtues.

That love must indeed have been powerful in the Apostolic Churches, or else the welding together of such unlike and antagonistic elements as Jew and Gentile, free and slave, poor and rich, educated and ignorant, then were, would have been impossible. Indeed, in every small and isolated sect, the sense of fellowship and desire to help each other is sure to be exceptionally strong; the spirit of sect secures that, and thousands of Heathen would only see a sect in the Church, regarded from that side. Moreover, Christians were told by the Apostle to do good first to those of the household of faith.[1] But at the same time, they were to oppose decisively, and with a large-hearted love like the sun that shines upon all men, the jealous, prejudiced, national misanthropy displayed by Jews towards Gentiles; they were to show by acts of universal charity, that they were His disciples who had uttered that saying, new and unknown in the world, "God is Love,"—to show that saying to be the seal and motto of their communion.

Christians here were in a worse position than Jews, whose strongly-developed commercial spirit and unwearied industry in acquisition were constantly bringing them into intercourse with the Heathen, and plunging them into the thick of popular life, and whose national religion was sufficiently recognised by law to secure them in the courts against anything offensive to their conscience in taking oaths and similar matters and to guarantee their privileges. But the law gave no such protection to the first Christians, and it is not too much to say that none were ever placed in so difficult a position. All the incidents of public and social life,

---

[1] Gal. vi. 10.

both civil and popular, were thoroughly interpenetrated by Heathen customs, and coloured by the prevalent worship; its symbols met the Christian at every step, and he was often entangled in religious acts before he recollected himself or could draw back. If he really wished to keep pure from all contact with it, he had almost to confine himself within the four walls of his house. But Christians felt that they were the salt of the earth, the City set upon a hill, that they must let the light of their faith and life shine before the Gentiles, and that every one in his own sphere was called upon to care for the enlargement of the Church. And this constrained them to mix with the Heathen, however great the danger to their souls in the midst of so many corruptions.

The desire of a Gentile convert to separate entirely from all he had known and been connected with before, must often at first have been overpowering, and over the very cradle of the Church was uttered the reproach of hating the human race.[1] Years had to pass away before Christians could convince the Heathen by their deeds, that they not only lived in society, but stretched out a helping hand to the poor and suffering, without distinction of race or creed. And this was the less credited, because their secret assemblies, often held at night, combined with their shyness and anxiety and the charges made by Jews against them, had led the Heathen from the very first to say that they indulged criminal lusts in secret; whence St. Peter observes, "The Gentiles speak against you as evil doers."[2]

Yet Christianity had the power and the means of softening and changing this hostile feeling. It not only prompted men to deeds of neighbourly help and charity, but inspired them with a spirit of regard and tenderness which ennobled social life, but which could only originate and prevail where the inborn dignity of man, and the full right of personality to be treated as an end in itself, and not as a mere chattel, was recognised. In the widest sense, and without any exception, Christians were bidden to "honour all men;"[3] not only those worthy of special honour, but every one, simply *because* he is a man, because he is created after God's image

---

[1] Tac. *Ann.* xv. 44.   [2] 1 Pet. ii. 12.   [3] 1 Pet. ii. 17.

and is an object of His love, because he belongs to that world God loved so well that He gave His only Son for it. That is the distinctive teaching proclaimed by Christianity alone, that every human being, as bearing the stamp of a Divine creation, has a right to be honoured by his fellow man. All are called to salvation, and, therefore, all are to be prayed for.[1] And thus, while Christian doctrine exhibited so prominently the deep fall and common sinfulness of the race, it yet led to a more favourable judgment of mankind as a whole. A dark and discontented disdain and contempt of man was utterly alien to the Christian spirit, which rather sought out what was good in every man, in spite of the repulsive evil which disguised it.[2]

The Apostles went further, and wished every one to look on his own faults and his neighbours' excellences, " esteeming others better than himself."[3] And here Christ's religion was in sharp contrast with Heathen wisdom and morality. Bias used to say that the mass of men were evil, and Aristotle reckons among the attributes of his ideal character, the high-souled man, that he is open in his hatred and his love and despises others.[4] In the later, Stoic, philosophy this view was deepened, and the more earnest spirits spoke out the most clearly, whether in anger or in sorrow, their contempt of men, as did Tacitus and Seneca. Lucian professes his hatred for the great majority of mankind, who are either deceivers or deceived.[5] And how contemptuously the Pharisees spoke of their own nation! " This rabble that knoweth not the Law, is cursed."[6] With Heathen moralists, this was the natural result of aiming at virtue, for they had always a sharper and quicker eye for evil than for good, and it was part of their virtue to hate evil and evil men. The specially Christian virtues of humility and love, which alone could counteract this, were wanting.

There was the more need for urging on Christians the duty of humility and of honouring all men, because the Apostles were wont to paint in such strong colours their high privileges above the rest of the world. It was said of

---

[1] 1 Tim. ii. 1—4.
[2] [See *Christian Year*, Second Sunday after Trinity.—Tr.]
[3] Phil. ii. 3.
[4] Diog. Laert. i. 5, 88. *Eth. Nic.* iv. 4.
[5] Piscator 20, 111, 151, Lehmann. [6] John vii. 49.

them, "Ye are a chosen generation, a royal priesthood, a holy nation, a purchased people."[1] St. Paul says they needed a special enlightenment, to comprehend their high and glorious privileges; and treats them as spiritual men, who judge all things and are judged of no man.[2] But these high representations of their dignity are accompanied by the knowledge and admonition that all is undeserved grace; and that humility, the most precious and peculiar virtue of a Christian, makes him bow, not only before God but before men, and, like his Lord, prefer serving others to being served.

Hence arose an internal incompatibility between Christianity and Slavery.[3] In proportion as it gained ascendancy, and influenced and remoulded social relations, slavish bondage, in its various forms, was sure to be gradually put down. Still no Apostle required or recommended its abolition, even within the narrow circle of the Christian communities, although they certainly were not blind to its evil effects on a large scale. St. Paul advised converted slaves not to seek for emancipation.[4] This advice, of course, implied the condition of their not being hindered from discharging their sacred duties, or compelled to do anything sinful. And it must be remembered that the condition of freed men was often worse than that of slaves. They found themselves left suddenly without other means of support than the precarious proceeds of their labour, and exposed in case of sickness to the most utter want.[5] St. Paul may have seen in the large cities, freed men, now become "clients," cringing at the doors of their wealthy

---

[1] 1 Pet. ii. 9.  [2] Eph. i. 18. 1 Cor. ii. 15.  [3] 1 Pet. v. 5.
[4] 1 Cor. vii. 21. This is confessedly one of the most perplexing passages in the N. T., and every one, however familiar with the context, will have a difficulty in deciding between the two methods of interpretation, whether to understand with μᾶλλον χρῆσαι, τῇ ἐλευθερίᾳ, or τῇ δουλείᾳ. Three grounds appear to me decisive for the meaning adopted in the text.—(1) the difficulty of understanding ἀλλ' εἰ καὶ, v. 21, in any way except "even if you were able to become free, &c.;"—(2) the authority of the Greek Fathers;—(3) the injunction repeated, v. 24, for every one to remain where he was, which is unmeaning if the contrary advice had been just given to slaves. The words of v. 23, which are urged, e. g., by Olshausen, for the opposite meaning, only refer to what has gone just before; St. Paul had said that he who was called free was a servant of Christ and should not *place himself* in a position of slavery or dependence, as the helpless poor often did, ["*Become* not slaves of men," μὴ γίνεσθε, not, "*be* not," as in E. V.—Tr.] Thus the advice given to both classes follows the same rule.

[5] Juv. *Sat.* i. 95, 6; iii. 240. Martial iii. 7, 14; xiv. 125.

patrons to beg for the morning *sportula;* and he would fear their often becoming a burden to communities chiefly consisting of poor. So he contented himself with pointing the attention of slaves to their inward liberty, as freed men of Christ, and to the absence in the Church without of all distinction between slave and free, as between Jew and Gentile. He shows how serving was ennobled by Christ, who appeared on earth in the form of a slave, had declared all rank and authority among Christians to be a service, and all who ruled in His Church to be the servants of others, and, finally, had given an example to His disciples by performing the slave's office of washing their feet.[1]

It is clear, from a deeper view even of the Apostolic age, that the Christian Church was destined to become the school for educating men in true civil freedom, the very notion and meaning of which did not exist in the world before Christ; that freedom, namely, which rests on a recognition of the equality of other mens' rights, and of individual dignity and independence. What the Heathen world called freedom rested on the proportionate oppression and degradation of the great majority for the benefit of certain classes and citizens, who sought and found the freedom they desired in a democratic or aristocratic form of republic, and the absence of anything like monarchy. Among the civilised peoples of the time before Christ only the Jews had any idea and appreciation of liberty; and they had it very imperfectly, both from being unable or unwilling to dispense with slaves, and because their monarchy, notwithstanding the counteracting influence of a strongly organised priesthood, degenerated too readily into a despotism, as was the case with the Asmoneans who were supported by foreign mercenaries. And thus true liberty was first brought into the world with and by Christianity,—that right of self-determination whereby man, while equally recognising and respecting the freedom of others, and far removed from egotistically using them as mere tools for his own use or enjoyment, follows his own judgment and will, and not another's, in the whole region of human action that lies under the control of conscience.

But this freedom is limited by conditions unpleasing to

[1] Phil. ii. 7. Matt. xx. 26.

the natural and not religious man, who, while ruled by his appetites and passions, is in continual conflict with the rights and interests of others, and with right and morality generally, and the powers that guard them. He is sure to want to increase the power and influence that belong to him or are at his command, and to domineer over others, in order to compel them to serve his ends and desires. What he wants is not freedom, which would belong equally to others, but arbitrary power for himself alone, or in alliance with those who share his views and interests. The true sense of freedom could only be created by a religion, which taught and enabled men to make God's will and law their own and wrote it on their heart and mind, as the supreme law of life, that God is over all, and that they must love their neighbours as themselves; a religion, which subdued all selfish opposition to God's will on earth and to the dignity and equality of other men. There is no true freedom, but for him who has become the servant of God.

And thus, men had for the first time to be educated for freedom by the Christian Church, first individuals and then nations. Christian teaching about the brotherhood and equality of men, the dignity of women, the holiness of the family, and the duty of self-denial and of a right use of earthly goods, had to be ingrained into men's blood, and a corresponding tone of public opinion and custom grow up and prevail, before true civil freedom and equality before the law could be fully realised. For that, centuries were needed: but we see in the New Testament the beginnings of the great process of training and education.

Christ said once to the Pharisees, who were greedy and proud of freedom, "If you abide in My word, the truth shall make you free." They were offended; for this implied that they were not free, and needed deliverance from slavery. "We are Abraham's seed, and were never slaves of any man," they replied. They were unwilling even to admit the fact, that the yoke of Roman domination really pressed on them. Christ showed them, by his reply, that they needed above all deliverance from the bondage of sin, that they were servants, not sons and heirs, and would be cast out of their father's house—the Divine institution for salvation; they could only become really free by the Son making them free, and only attain, through moral, to civil and national, freedom.[1] The Apostles also laboured to arouse in believers a sense of their Christian dignity and freedom. They told them they were a chosen generation, who, from being strangers, were become citizens and members of the family in the Divine kingdom, called by Christ to freedom, children of light, whose limbs were members of Christ and their bodies temples of the Holy Ghost. They were to regard themselves as God's dearly bought property and servants, purchased back by their rightful Lord, and thereby excluded from any other service than that of free and loving obedience to His whole law and will.[2]

This was the freedom the Apostles so often spoke of. Christianity was a law of freedom: where the Spirit of the Lord is, there is liberty, but a liberty which must not be made a cloak for malice.[3] Thus, the only true liberty, in the Apostolical sense, and the condition of every other, was the right and capacity of following no will but that of God in matters of conscience,—a redemption from the yoke of sin. And while Christians were thus being educated to true freedom in the Church, they had also in their outward and social life to prove and strengthen their sense of freedom, by constant struggle against prevalent habits, saturated as they were with what was Heathenish and idolatrous, by renouncing and abstaining from many enjoyments, sinful to them, but passionately desired by others. Their strength of character and moral courage was tested day by day, in bearing the scorn or contemptuous pity of Heathen acquaintances, declining invitations to share their pleasures, and enduring the suspicion of indulging in secret excesses. They had to preach Christ, knowing that they were universally hated, and to win men's souls, at the risk of being turned out of their houses, or imprisoned, or put to death as malefactors. It was their schooling for future freedom.

But the Church itself, too, in its organisation and social discipline and order, pioneered the way and served as a

---
[1] John viii. 31-36.
[2] 1 Pet. ii. 9, 16. Eph. ii. 19 ; v. 8. Gal. v. 13. 1 Cor. vi. 15, 19, 20.
[3] James ii. 12. 2 Cor. iii. 17. 1 Pet. ii. 16.

type of future civil liberty. Within it, flourished the full and genuine equality of universal brotherhood, and in that school of willing obedience the patrician learnt to defer to a slave, who was made priest or bishop. The bearers of Church office were no wheels or screws of a great machine, but free persons; their administration was no mechanism or clerks' department, but organic life.

To prevent the idea of Christian freedom being misconceived, and the royal dignity of Christians being represented as dispensing from the duty of political obedience, St. Paul and St. Peter have insisted on its being a matter of conscience and Divine order to obey secular authorities.[1] This was quite a new doctrine in the world, but was the more needed, inasmuch as the Civil Power, when better informed about the Christian society, was infallibly certain to assume a hostile attitude, of which there were already symptoms. And there were many Christians still under the influence of a spirit of Jewish zeal, who thought that, so far from its becoming them to bend under the yoke of Heathen rulers, they had a divine right to rule all nations.

St. Paul says in so many words, "Let every soul be subject to the higher powers." Every one knew what those powers were, and the form—whether monarchical, republican, or mixed—made no difference: that was an accident, as far as the religious question was concerned. The legal exercise of sovereignty lay in the hands of the Roman Senate, through it only were the Emperors supposed to govern; and it had the right of appointing and deposing them, and of confirming their acts.[2] But in fact, the Senate was completely dependent on their will. Should a civil war arise, however, as happened soon after, when the Senate declared Nero an enemy and issued an order for his arrest, so that every one had to choose his side, Christians were bound to take part for the Senate and its Emperor against Nero.

The Apostles, then, taught, that the civil power or government, under whatever form, is the minister of God, ordained for salutary ends and wielding His jurisdiction on earth. The Christian, therefore, must respect those who

---

[1] Apoc. v. 10. Rom. xiii. 1—7. 1 Pet. ii. 13—17.
[2] See Suet. *Nero*, 19. Spartian, *Did. Julian*, Capit. *Maxim. duo* 15. Lamp. *Heliog.* 13.

hold this authority, in their own place and the exercise of their functions, without regard to their moral and religious qualities, and not from fear of punishment but for conscience sake. "All power is from God," whether parental or civil; it does not rest on contract or arbitrary agreement, even where the particular form derives its historical origin from a contract; nor is obedience matter of choice, limited by previous agreement, but a necessary obligation. St. Paul did not mean that this or that particular government was a positive Divine institution, like the constitution of the Christian Church, but merely that its authority is based on the command and dispensation of God, whatever be its form or historical origin; he meant, however, that the civil power not only has a Divine authorization, but is the minister of God, for punishing evil and promoting good. And here also he followed the teaching of the Lord.

When Pilate reminded Christ of his power, He answered, that Pilate himself was dependent on the Roman government, whose instrument he was, for ends he did not comprehend;[1] and intimated that He was not in his power, but under the higher power of God. He told the people to give to Cæsar what was Cæsar's, and to God what was God's.[2] He was speaking of the tax they had asked about, and referred them to the maxim, "He is the ruler, whose image is stamped on the coin," which included whatever belonged to Cæsar according to the existing order of things. But he spoke at the same time of duty to God, in order to show that Christians are bound to unite their obedience to the civil government with obedience to God, because the two are closely connected, and in case of conflicting claims to prefer the latter, for they must never forget that God must be obeyed rather than man, as the Apostles said afterwards.[3] The law and ordinance of God have the first claim on men, but when that is satisfied they are allowed and bound to conform to the requirements of the State. And thus Christian teaching at once widened and narrowed the range of social and political obedience,—widening it, in so far as it was brought within the sphere of the religious con-

---

[1] John xix. 11. [ἄνωθεν may certainly refer to the imperial authority, but it may refer directly to power from on high.—Tr.]
[2] Matt. xxii. 21.   [3] Acts v. 29.

science and made part of the service of God,—narrowing it in so far as it determined according to its own spirit and presented to the Church, quite independently of laws, opinions, or the will of rulers, the immeasurably wide field of moral and religious duties, the profession and preaching of revealed truths, domestic and public worship, and the obligations of philanthropy. It was an entire surrender of the old Heathen principle, which merged religion and morality in the State, so that a good citizen could have no gods or moral code but those of his country. The Heathen authorities and philosophers did not, however, for some time resent this, or understand clearly how completely the Christian Church was the rival of the Roman State, and to how great an extent Christians followed other laws and belonged to another system; or they would from the first have carried on a systematic and uninterrupted persecution till they had eradicated the Church, and not have persecuted only by fits and starts.[1]

A new kind of freedom was born with Christianity, a wide domain inaccessible to imperial or popular will was created, wherein beggars and defenceless women and slaves felt themselves free and invincible—the liberty of conscience, the right of individuality hitherto ignored. The sense of absolute dependence on God and obligation to Him formed the Christian's freedom, as against the world and the state. The conviction that man must answer to God for his every action, his time, his powers and his property, was an indelible motive for the freest self-determination in all matters of moral and religious life. The leading idea and aim of this new Christian feeling was, that man did not appertain with soul and body to the State or Commonwealth, and was not determined by it, but by God and the struggle for holiness, in his wishes, thoughts and acts. The state could no longer be the final end of his being and limit of his aims; he served his country and commonwealth by giving an

---

[1] [The reader may recall a similar observation in Arnold's Lectures on Modern History, to the effect that the Roman government did not persecute Christians because they might be dangerous to the Empire hereafter, but because they disobeyed its laws now. This, however, must be taken with some reservation, and cannot, of course, be applied to the *later* persecutions at all. Men like Marcus Aurelius and Diocletian were quite aware that it was a life and death struggle, and that the safety of the Empire required the destruction of the Church.—Tr.]

example of willing obedience; he observed the laws—so far as they did not contradict his belief or moral principles—took his share in common burdens, and prayed for the prosperity of Cæsar and the Empire. But he had another country and kingdom too, those of his heavenly Father; and his membership of that kingdom and rights of sonship in the earthly Church gave him a consciousness of freedom. And thus, while the Apostles exhort to a willing submission to existing laws and governments, they remind Christians of their own special liberty and warn them to hold it fast. Thus St. Peter says, "Submit to every ordinance of man for the Lord's sake"—as being His will—"whether to the king, as supreme, or to rulers sent by him . . . . . as free, and not having your freedom as a cloke of wickedness." And St. Paul says, "You are bought with a price ; become not slaves of men."[1] The believer felt himself free, because and in so far as he was the servant of Christ, for the service of God excludes every other. He felt himself free from the yoke of sin and from fear of men, free within, even if in body he was a slave; for the five tyrants of human life, hatred, envy, lust, covetousness, ambition, had no power over him, or, at least, he had power to overcome them.

To understand what amount of civil and religious liberty the Christians of that age were able to attain, we must get a clear idea of the social condition of the Roman Empire, which cannot be judged by the standard of a modern absolutist government. Even in the worst times of the Empire there was a great deal of liberty, and of the kind most valuable to Christians. The main props of a modern absolutist government are a powerful army spread over the country, an omnipresent police, a state monopoly of education, censorship of the press, and above all, a bureaucracy, arranged on the principle of state omnipotence and managing and meddling everywhere, with a huge net-work of paid officials spread over the whole country, and jealously keeping down every movement of combined and independent energy. In such a State the Christian Church, had it ever been able to form itself, must, humanly speaking, have perished; it would have been stifled or annihilated. But the Roman government was in marked contrast to all this, nor did the worst

---

[1] 1 Pet. ii. 13—16. 1 Cor. vii. 23.

tyrants among the Emperors adopt that method of ruling. The legions were not used to keep down the people, but placed on the frontiers; only in the capital the Prætorian cohorts were the Emperor's body guard. The modern institution of an all-embracing and elaborately organised police was unknown to the Romans. A few officials, ædiles and prefects, under the city prefect, provided by the simplest means for public order and security. There was no idea of a literary censorship, or a system of state education, or government schools. All inferior schools were private establishments. Only a few chairs of Rhetoric and Philosophy were erected gradually under the Emperors. Teaching and education on the whole were entirely free, and under private control. Indeed there was in general very little government influence. In the provinces, besides proconsuls and prætors and their secretaries and attendants, there were only commissioners of taxes and the Post-office. The administration was chiefly in the hands of communal authorities, who served without payment and accordingly had no desire to increase their business and make it more difficult by over-governing.

This state of things was obviously very favourable to the development of the Church, and in accordance with the needs and desires of Christians. Under no other circumstances could they have stood their ground against the universal hatred and suspicion felt towards them from the first, as a gang of secret miscreants. It was a further advantage to them, that there already existed a great variety of colleges, sodalities and corporations, as well for religious ends as for the common benefit or pleasure, enjoying great liberty of action, and under protection of the law; though it was a principle of Roman jurists, that in such cases civil authorisation was necessary for their legal existence, and a sharp line of demarcation was drawn between licensed and unlicensed societies. But their great number soon made it impossible to keep any strict watch over them, and thus Christian liberty had a wide field.[1] There was certainly little liberty in the sense of sharing the supreme governing and legislative authority, but that the Christian did not desire. Even had it been open to them, they must have

[1] [This point is dwelt on at length by Rénan, *Les Apôtres*, p. 253 sqq.—TR.]

withdrawn from it, as things then were, in a polity thoroughly saturated with Heathenism, as a snare and intolerable burden.

Christian equality corresponded to Christian liberty. Christian teaching rejected the prevalent view, that a portion of mankind was doomed to slavery by an eternal law of nature. All men, as descendants of the first pair created by God, are brethren; all have the same Father in heaven and on earth; all bear the indelible image of God; all, without exception, are called to be children of God, members of Christ and of His Church; and all in the Church are members of one body. "There is neither Jew nor Greek, slave nor free, male nor female;" all differences and divisions have passed away.[1] Christians must respect and observe civil ranks and gradations, and the subjection of wife to husband must remain as before, according to natural and Divine law. But before God and the Church all were to be equal in rights and duties, and there was to be only inequality of service and variety of instruments.

One special difficulty in the relations of Christians to the State was about oaths. At first sight, it is one of the most striking differences between the Old Testament dispensation and that of Christ, that an oath was there Divinely prescribed in certain cases as a religious act, whereas Christ gave a general prohibition of swearing, and required that attestations of the truth should not go beyond an emphatic "Yes" or "No."[2] His enumeration of particular forms of oath—by heaven, by earth, by one's head, by Jerusalem—was directed against the existing custom and the casuistry of the Scribes. St. James in the same way desired Christians not to swear by heaven or earth or any other oath, but to content themselves with a simple affirmation or denial.[3] There were, then, three evils and abuses, which Christ and His Apostle wished to meet; first, the danger of perjury, where oaths were so frequently and easily taken, and often of course about doubtful matters; secondly, the mistaking the essential nature of an oath, as an attestation in the name of God and an appeal to Him, and the discovery and use of

---
[1] Gal. iii. 28.
[2] Exod. xxii. 10, 11. Deut. vi. 13; x. 20. Matt. v. 33—37.
[3] James v. 12.

forms professedly less solemn and binding; thirdly, the prevalent mistrust, and the want of truthfulness that caused it, for the constant use of oaths, even in unimportant matters, only came from the presumption of falsehood in others. The command of the Lord implied above all that He both willed and expected strict truthfulness, and consequently full mutual confidence, in His Church, and assumed that none would have the uncharitableness to brand the word of a brother and fellow Christian as false by requiring an oath to confirm it. Had the Christian Church remained in its original stage of development, in the form of small communities made up of Christians intimately connected and knowing each other well, and with a corresponding system of ecclesiastical discipline, the absolute prohibition of swearing would have been maintained, and no Christian allowed to require an oath from another. But the prohibition could not be carried out in dealings with a Heathen State. As in the Church of the Old Covenant, which was both a civil and religious polity, oaths were not only allowed but expressly commanded, so the Christian was bound by his duty to the State not to refuse to take oaths, so long as they contained nothing directly Heathenish—as when taken in the name of the gods, or by the genius of the Emperor. For he could not reasonably expect the State to accept from him, and him alone, a mere assertion or denial as equivalent to an oath, while it required an oath from all who were not Christians. And thus, when the Church had opened her gates to whole nations and populations, and had established definite relations with the Civil Power based on a mutual recognition of their respective rights, she was obliged to allow political and judicial oaths, as indispensable for bringing the truth to light and vindicating its claims.[1]

How quickly and powerfully Christianity could dispossess or transform the most deeply rooted prejudices, was clearly shown in the view taken of death and dead bodies. With the Jews, it was a defilement to touch a corpse, and cleans-

---

[1] To prove the right of the Church to limit in this sense the apparently general statement of the Lord and His Apostle, we must not say, as is often done, that Christ Himself "took a solemn and formal judicial oath," (Matt. xxvi. 64,) for He did not swear, but gave the simplest and shortest answer possible to the adjuration of the high priest. But St. Paul's strong attestations come very near an oath, *e.g.*, 2 Cor. i. 23; Gal. i. 20; Phil. i. 8; and the like.

ing by sprinkling water was commanded on pain of death. Whatever was touched by one thus polluted was unclean; whoever even entered the chamber where a man had died, or touched a dead bone or a grave, was unclean. The Greeks and Romans shared this feeling. Corpses, graves and houses of the dead were unclean and polluting; the mere sight of a dead body so desecrated a solemn act of worship, that all had to be performed over again.[1] Christians believed, thought and felt quite differently. For them, the human body had a much higher value, since the Incarnation had exalted it into communion with the Godhead, and believers, as the Apostle said, were become temples of the Holy Ghost, and their bodies members of Christ, which would be summoned at the resurrection to take part in the glorification of the whole man.[2] And while on this account they shrunk with scrupulous horror from all sinful defilement of the body, the feeling of disgust and dislike towards dead bodies gave place to a feeling of reverence; they were drawn towards the places where the earthly remains of their departed brethren lay, as to fields sown with the seed of a glorious harvest. There the Saints slept, and there they would rise. Hence, too, the Heathen practice of burning the dead was revolting to Christian feeling, and they introduced burial in the Apostolic age.

Herodotus describes the impression made on the Greeks by the sight of the government and manners of the Egyptians, in these words; "This people has customs and regulations almost the precise opposite of those of other men."[1] The educated Greek or Roman, who had taken the trouble to investigate closely the inner life of the new Christian society, its beliefs and institutions, would have received a similar impression. He would have discovered a state within a state, an independent kingdom, which in the eyes of a Roman was a criminal and ephemeral creation of fanatical folly and blindness, or a dark gang of conspirators, a sect hating the light, which must be trampled, like a worm crawling on the ground, under the iron heel of the civil power, as soon as it emerged from its lurking place into the light of day. The members of this kingdom were defence-

---
[1] Jos. *Arch.* xviii. 2, 3. *Contr. Apion.* ii. 26. Numb. xix. 11—16. Hagg. ii. 14.
[2] Dio Cass. 54, 28. [3] 1 Cor. iii. 16, 17; vi. 14, 15. [4] Herod. ii. 35.

less, and determined to endure the worst without resistance, while yet they were confident of ultimate victory and of the indefectibility and permanence of their society. In this kingdom, a crucified Jew was beginning, middle, and end; He was honoured as its unseen king, and Jewish fishermen and tax-gatherers were its visible founders. It grew quietly but surely, under reproaches and injuries, through means a Heathen could not comprehend, and by powers he could neither measure nor analyse. In this kingdom, a slave ate at the same table with his master, nay, a slave might be a ruler and the master a ministering brother. The poor and humble were no less honoured than the wealthy and men of gentle blood. Jews, Greeks and Romans, who hated each other elsewhere, were all brethren here; there was no distinction of nationality any more than of rank. The greatest was he who served most, and the extent and difficulty of the service was the sole criterion of dignity. Here, for the first time, weakness, experience of human infirmity, and failure of natural power through bodily suffering, was recognised and commended as a condition and means of moral power and strength.[1] All had equal claim to the advantages of the kingdom; rights were measured by duties. The woman was on a par with the man, the virgin not less honoured than the wife and mother. There was but one weapon of defence and one threat which this kingdom had the power or will to use for its self-preservation, that of exclusion from its fellowship; but so greatly was this dreaded, that the outcast entreated re-admission at the price of the deepest humiliation. Prayer was offered in this kingdom for him who called himself "lord of the human race,"[2] but its members would rather die than allow him to meddle with its internal arrangements. And as they believed it to be both visible and invisible, stretching beyond the limits of earthly being into another world, Cicero's beautiful saying of an universal state, among whose citizens should be included both gods and men, was here fulfilled, though in a very different sense from his.[3]

---

[1] 2 Cor. xii. 10.     [2] Tac. *Hist.* iii. 68.     [3] Cic. *De Leg.* i. 7.

# APPENDIX I.

#### HISTORY OF THE INTERPRETATION OF THE PASSAGE ABOUT THE MAN OF SIN, IN THE SECOND EPISTLE TO THE THESSALONIANS.

THERE is no passage in the New Testament that has given occasion to so many and such various explanations, or is, as commonly understood, more obscure and difficult than this, viz. 2 Thess. ii. 1—12. Yet it is doctrinally and historically so important, and so essential to a right understanding of the Apostle's general line of thought, that the reader may be grateful for an historical review of the attempts to explain it, and of the notions and expectations to which it has given rise. And it is obvious that such a review will serve to justify the historical explanation developed in this book.

This explanation starts with the assumption that this prophecy, like those of Christ, contains intimations of events soon to happen, as well as of others belonging to the end of the world—that it has a double fulfilment, one just after the Apostle's time, and a second in the last days. It is another question whether St. Paul was himself distinctly conscious of this double sense and fulfilment of his words, and what idea he had about the nearness or distance of the end of the world; for it is an attribute of prophecy, that its objective and subjective meaning are by no means always coincident, and that it sometimes has a wider scope than is present to the prophet's mind, as appears in many visions of the Old Testament Prophets.[1] And this must

[1] Cf. among others Jahn's *Einleitung in die Bücher des A. B.* ii. 373 sqq.

be peculiarly the case about the last days, since Christ has emphatically told us that it is God's will for the time of the final catastrophe to remain hidden from all, as well Apostles as others; and thus none can know whether the end and the events immediately preceding it will occur tomorrow or after thousands of years. A double fulfilment of Daniel's prophecies is universally admitted, one by Antiochus Epiphanes, and a second later. Bossuet interprets the Apocalypse on the theory of a double or more than double fulfilment and appeals to "all theologians" in support of his view.[1]

It is the universal and constant belief and tradition of the whole Church, that towards the end of the present dispensation and before the Second Coming of the Lord a last and greater Antichrist, some power pre-eminently hostile to the Church, will appear and seduce many into apostasy. And this Antichrist will be like the "Man of Sin" described by St. Paul, so that in him men will see a fulfilment of the great "adversary" here foretold. Such is the constant opinion from the time of St. Irenæus and Tertullian. But is that last fulfilment the only one, or is there another already past, so that St. Paul had this first and immediately impending event chiefly before his eyes, and some of his statements refer to that alone? This is an open question, and I have felt the more bound to adopt the latter solution, because hitherto every attempt to explain ὁ κατέχων from the point of view of a future fulfilment only, has palpably failed, and must be given up as hopeless.

It will be convenient to distinguish in our review the patristic interpretation, the mediæval, the modern Catholic, and the earlier and later Protestant.

I. As to the Fathers, all or most of them agree in the following points:—1. The "Man of Sin" will appear towards the end of the world at the time of the fall of the Roman Empire, and will set up his own kingdom in its place. 2. He will appear as the Messiah expected by the Jews, and will either himself build their temple, or get

---

[1] "A celà il faut ajouter ce que dit Alcasar avec tous les théologiens, qu'une interprétation même littérale de l'Apocalypse ou *des autres prophéties*, peut très-bien compatir avec les autres." He then gives examples of Scripture prophecies which must have a past and future fulfilment. *Œuvres.* Éd. Liège, 1776, ii. 368.

possession of it when it has been rebuilt. 3. " He that letteth," is the Roman Empire. 4. " The mystery of iniquity that already worketh," is Nero.

Bossuet has perceived that one point in these interpretations has been since disproved by history, and must be given up accordingly. He says:—" Ils (les pères) ne marchent qu'à tâtons dans l'explication du détail de la prophétie, marque assurée que la tradition n'en avait rien laissé de certain."[1] He adds, that on Grotius' theory of the prophecy being completely fulfilled, with no further accomplishment to follow at the end of time, the secret St. Paul had orally communicated to the Thessalonians would have remained hidden, and tradition throw no light upon it. But that is just the question. It seems to me more likely that the old explanation, referring the mystery of iniquity to Nero, had its ground in primitive tradition; and that the Heathen rumour about his future return was adopted, because the relation of the Man of Sin to the temple of Jerusalem had not been so literally fulfilled by the historical Nero as was considered necessary.

St. Irenæus is the first Father who undertakes to explain, " sitting in the temple of God." He maintains that the language only suits the true God and the temple of Jerusalem. He adds that the Apostle's meaning is the same as that of Christ (Matt. xxiv. 15), when speaking of the " abomination of desolation in the holy place," and that the Antichrist will establish his kingdom at Jerusalem and have himself worshipped there in the temple, (v. 25, 2—4.) He must have assumed a previous rebuilding of the temple by the Jews; and this was the usual idea in the following centuries. It was well known that those whom St. Paul addressed could only understand the temple at Jerusalem, for the direct reference to Daniel's prophecy excluded any other interpretation. And thus it was pretty generally assumed that, when the scattered Jews were gathered together again and restored, the temple would be rebuilt. The Sibylline books implied this throughout; and it was the more believed, as for some time considerable remains of the temple were standing. In the fourth century, it was supposed that Antichrist himself would rebuild it, a

[1] *Pref. sur l'Apoc.* Œuvres. ii. 378.

view foreign to the older Fathers; indeed Lactantius says he would try to destroy it.[1] The difficulty of a temple built by Antichrist being called by the Apostle "the temple of God" did not trouble them.

But Irenæus, and still more Hippolytus, in his book on Christ and Antichrist, and the Greek Fathers generally from that time forward, enlarged the notion of the "Man of Sin" by attaching to it one of the two Apocalyptic beasts (Rev. xiii.) and the "little horn" of Daniel (ch. vii.) growing on the head of the fourth beast and speaking blasphemies, which roots out the other ten horns or kings and combats and overcomes the Saints. And thus the view grew up, that St. Paul spoke of a great monarch and bloody tyrant, who should rule the world and destroy the Roman Empire, but whose own should be the last universal monarchy. As the older kingdoms had been destroyed by the later, the Persian by the Greek, and the Greek by the Roman, so should the Roman be destroyed by Antichrist, and his by Christ. And this last kingdom of Antichrist was to be set up in the East, according to an old prophecy Lactantius cites, that the East should rule and the West serve. As the four kingdoms of Daniel were then understood to be the Babylonian, Persian, Macedonian and Roman, the Roman being the last, a time was looked for when this would be divided among ten kings; then Antichrist, after destroying three of them and subjugating the rest, would reign over the world for three years and a half (Dan. vii. 25). Armed with all magical arts, and as the chosen instrument of Satan, he will give himself out for Christ, the Son of God. He will not invite or seduce men to idolatry, but as a rival god will put down all other gods, as St. Chrysostom says.[2] And thus three events were expected as almost contemporary, the fall of the Roman Empire, the appearance of Antichrist, and the end of the world. The Fathers said there would be no other Empire after the Roman; all others would fall with it.[3]

---

[1] Lact. *Inst.* v. 17.  [2] Chrys. *Opp.* xi. 525.
[3] Lact. vii. 25. Hieron. *in Dan.* vii. Chrys. *in* ii. *Thess.* Tertullian (*Apol.* 32) calls the rule of Antichrist, "vim maximam universo orbi imminentem." Lactantius says, "Insustentabili dominatione vexabit orbem terrarum." St. Jerome says, "In uno Romano imperio propter blasphemantem Antichristum omnia simul regna delenda sunt."

As long as the fear of that Empire lasted, no one would willingly submit to Antichrist, according to St. Chrysostom; but as soon as it is destroyed, he will seize the vacant place and draw to himself the kingdom of God and men.

This view is seen in its most elaborate and fantastic form in the Syrian Ephrem, and in the Pseudohippolytus or author of the treatise *De Consummatione Mundi et Antichristo*, who, as Dodwell has shown, probably wrote in the middle of the seventh century.[1] Both make hypocrisy the chief characteristic of Antichrist; he will be outwardly meek and humble, and deceive the world by an appearance of piety and by the glitter of his lying wonders, and only when his dupes have proclaimed him their king will he appear in his true light, hard, terrible and shameless. The theatre of the whole drama is, of course, always laid in the East; the three kings he destroys are those of Egypt, Libya and Æthiopia; he is worshipped at Jerusalem, and the Mount of Olives is the scene of his fall. He must be a born Jew, to be accepted as the true Messiah by the whole Jewish nation; and it was inferred from the Bible account of Dan, as a serpent, (Gen. xlix. 17) that he should be of that tribe. Nor was this view affected by the circumstance that there had long ceased to be any distinction of tribes. The great point was that the temple of Jerusalem would be rebuilt, as the temple and throne of Antichrist, and hence that the Jews would be his chief adherents and worshippers. St. Irenæus says:—" To him will the widow deserted of God, the earthly Jerusalem, flee, that she may take vengeance on her enemies." It was added that he would show a special zeal for the temple, would be hailed by the Jews as their true Messiah, and would show peculiar honour to them. Some, like Theodoret, went so far as to consider him an incarnation of Satan. St. Cyril thinks Satan so filled him as to be αὐτοπροσώπως δι' αὐτοῦ ἐνεργῶν. Lactantius calls him, *malo spiritu genitus*, and St. Martin of Tours, as quoted by Sulpicius, *malo spiritu conceptus*. St. Basil thought the Apostle understood by the son of perdition, the devil.[2] Hilary, the author of a Commentary on St. Paul's Epistles, which long

---

[1] Syr. Eph. *Opp. ed. Par.* v. 303 sq. Hippol. *Opp. Ed. Fabr.* end of first vol.
[2] Iren. v. 25. Cyr. *Cat.* 15. Greg. Naz. *Or.* 57. Lact. *Inst.* vii. 17. Sulp. *Dial.* 2. Bas. *Opp.* i. 98. *Ed. Garner.*

went under the name of St. Ambrose, represents Satan, who will then for the first time come down from heaven to earth, arranging the whole Antichristian drama, and being worshipped as God under the assumed appearance of a man; and Gregory the Great takes a similar view, but St. Jerome rejects it.[1] It was commonly held enough to believe that Antichrist would be intimately allied with Satan, as his willing instrument; and Satan, as St. Ephrem says, will send his demons over all the world to announce the coming of the great king in his glory.

The Latin Fathers, Ambrose and Jerome, for the most part followed the Greek view. And so St. Augustine, who, in his work, *De Civitate Dei*, repeats the usual and widespread statements about Antichrist, the length of his persecution, his origin from Dan and the like; adding, that there were only conjectures in existence as to the "hindering" or "possessing" one, and the mystery of iniquity. "We might desire to elaborate the Apostle's meaning, but we cannot. I confess plainly that I do not know it."[2] The view of Nero being referred to, soon came into vogue among the Latins also, whether regarding him as the precursor of Antichrist, or adopting, especially under the influence of the Jewish Sybilline Poems, the old Heathen and Jewish notion of his future return, as was done after the middle of the third century,—first by Commodian, then by Lactantius and Victorin of Petabis. St. Jerome thus states the former idea: *Multis malis atque peccatis, quibus Nero, impurissimus Cæsarum, mundum premit, Antichristi parturitur adventus.*[3] Those who adopted the other view, among whom were Martin of Tours, and his biographer, Sulpicius Severus, either held that Nero would rise from the dead, or that he was still alive and concealed somewhere. St. Augustine remarks on this: *Multum mihi mirum est hoc opinantium tanta præsumptio.*[4] This "presumption" is

---

[1] "Cognoscitur ipse esse quasi eorum deus, quos prius nutu ejus ut deos coluit vulgus, quorum sit ipse primus aut summus." Ambr. *Opp. Ed. Ben.* T. ii. Append. 284. St. Gregory calls Antichrist "homo a diabolo assumptus—damnatus ille homo quem in fine mundi apostata ille angelus assumet," and, again says, "Ipse diabolus illud vas perditionis agressus Antichristus vocabitur." *Opp. Ed. Ben.* i. 422, 445. St. Jerome says, "Ne eum putemus juxta quorundam opinionem vel diabolum esse vel dæmonem, sed unum de hominibus in quo totus Satanas habitaturus sit corporaliter." Hieron. *In Dan.* vii. 8.
[2] Aug. *De Civ. Dei.* xx. 2.
[3] Hieron *Ep.* 151, *ad Algas Quæst.* 11. Cf. *Com. in Dan.* xi. 30.
[4] Aug. *De Civ. Dei.* xx. 19.

strikingly shown by the African, Commodian, A.D. 252. His Antichrist is Nero returned from the lower world, accompanied by the false prophet (Apoc. xiii. 11 sqq.), who claims to be the Messiah, and is worshipped as God. He appoints two other rulers, or Cæsars, to share with him the dominion of the world. Meantime, the Jews he has duped perceive their error and cry to God for help. Then Christ appears from heaven at the head of the ten lost tribes, and all creation rejoices at the sight. They take Jerusalem, and Antichrist flies to the north and collects the great army of Gog and Magog. But he is conquered, and thrown with the False Prophet into Gehenna; and the reign of a thousand years and the first resurrection follow in Jerusalem, which is come down from heaven. The *Carmen*, which is probably later than the *Instructiones*, gives two Antichrists; a Western, in Rome, who deceives the Christians—an Eastern, in Jerusalem, who deceives the Jews. Both share equally the work of Antichrist; Nero is worshipped at Rome, abolishes the Christian Sacrifice, and persecutes Christians to the death. Against him marches the real Jewish Antichrist from Persia, attended by four nations—Medes, Persians, Chaldeans, and Babylonians. He kills the three Emperors, destroys Rome and its inhabitants, and is worshipped in Judæa.[1] The attempt to combine Daniel, the Apocalypse, and the Pauline prophecy, led to this perversion of the Apocalypse.

No use will be made here of the poem of Crisias, which Pitra has recently edited, in vol. iv. of his *Spicilegium* (1858), though it says a great deal about Antichrist. Avevalo conjectured the author to be the African bishop, Verecundus, in the sixth century; and Pitra will not decide whether it belongs to the sixth or fifteenth. It seems to me to be clearly an Italian work of the fifteenth or sixteenth century, chiefly translated or paraphrased from the Sibyllines. Just after the taste of Italian humourists of that day for confounding Heathen and Christian elements together, the whole Greek Olympus, with its gods and goddesses, is

---

[1] Combine the two poems of Commodian, the *Instructiones*, long known, and *Carmen Apologeticum*, lately edited by Pitra (Spic. Sol. T. 1). Pitra reads in v. 974 of the *Carmen*, "Et fu (giet in rub) ore." But a comparison with the *Instruct.* I. 42, v. 38, shows it should be, "et fugit in Boream." See also *Oblatio Christi*, v. 872.

brought into play to train and educate Antichrist for his future calling. Instead of the common idea of his assumed sanctity and treacherous hypocrisy, we read: *totus per stupra nefanda Amplexusque ruet, circumdatus agmine semper Fœmineo, semper que inter lasciva volutans.* And again, *Intentusque epulis semper que intentus Iaccho*, &c.

The Fathers of the first six centuries generally viewed the episode of Antichrist as a Jewish movement; he was one of the Jewish false Messiahs who appeared from time to time, but the most powerful, bold and successful of all. The words of Christ (John v. 43,) were usually applied to him. He was expected to try and introduce the Mosaic Law and circumcision everywhere, beginning from Jerusalem. So Victorin, Cyril, Sulpicius Severus, Jerome, Augustin, Pelagius, Sedulius, Hilary, Gregory the Great, Gregory of Tours, Isidore of Seville. No one thought he would rise out of the bosom of the Christian Church; but it was held that his short reign of three years and a half would be foreign and hostile to it. Far from calling himself or his society Christian, he would ostentatiously profess his Judaism. Many Christians would fall away to him, and many Christian churches be seized by him and his; but the course and visible succession of the Church would not thereby be injured or stopped.[1] Those who applied Apoc. xii. 4 to the case, inferred that a third part of Christians would fall away. So Victorin, Gregory the Great, Hilary, &c. These notions survived in the following centuries, notwithstanding various rhetorical amplifications and fantastic distortions prevalent in the Church.[2] As the geographical range of vision grew wider and the Church spread in foreign parts, the difficulty naturally increased of conceiving a world-wide Jewish Antichristian empire ruled from Jerusalem, and so universal a persecution compressed into three years and a half. Later theologians, since the sixteenth century, became gradually more cautious and sober in what they said about Antichrist, and began to see that the

---

[1] *See e. g.* Aug. *De Civ. Dei.* xx. 8.
[2] I know but one theologian of name who, under the excitement of the sixteenth century events, exceeds all moderation in this matter,—Dominic Soto, in his Commentary on the Fourth Book of Sentences, Dist. 46, Q. 1, art. 1: "Extincta fide per discessionem ab Apostolica sede totus mundus vanus erit et deinceps in casum processurus." But Bellarmine and de Valentia have sharply blamed this perverse view.

attempt to combine the words of Daniel, of Christ, of St. Paul and of the Apocalypse, had been carried a good deal too far.

Speculations on this theme were limited, and in some sense closed, in the Greek Church, by the cautious manner of discussing Antichrist in John of Damascus' dogmatic work, which attained a classical authority. It is based on the Pauline passage, without any reference to the Apocalypse, evidently from a conviction that the "Man of Sin" has nothing to do with the two Apocalyptic beasts. He infers from John v. 43, that the Jews would receive Antichrist as their Messiah; the temple where He is worshipped as God is the old Jewish one, "not ours (viz. the Church of the Resurrection at Jerusalem), for he will come to the Jews, not to us." A man born of lust, but equipped with the whole power of Satan, he will suddenly seize the dominion and persecute the Church, but will only seduce the feeble and unstable to apostasy with his lying wonders.[1]

II. Western mediæval Christianity had a good deal more to say about Antichrist, chiefly derived from St. Augustine, St. Jerome, and St. Hilary, and, as a chief authority, from the treatise of an unknown African (composed between 450 and 455 A.D.), *De Promissionibus et Prædictionibus Dei*, with its appendix, *Dimidium Temporis, ad cujus finem implendæ sunt visiones in S. Scripturis factæ de Antichristo*.[2] This work, commonly ascribed to Prosper, was one of the best known in the middle ages. By Antichrist the author understands properly Satan, appearing either in the form of Nero or of some one else, but in any case exhibiting Nero's vices. While many, especially later writers, thought Antichrist would ape the whole history of Christ, he maintains, on the contrary, that the contrast of his appearance and works will be so complete to all that befel Christ, as to make it easy for posterity to see that he is a false Messiah. Writing at a time when the Catholic Africans were groaning under the yoke of Arian Vandals, he supposes that the persecution of Antichrist—which he thinks near at hand— will be an Arian one. From the eleventh century almost every one drew his views of this subject chiefly from a

---

[1] *Joh. Dam. Le Fid. Orth.* iv. 26, Opp. Ed. Lequien. i. 299.
[2] See Paris edition of Prosper's works, (1711). *Append.* pp. 91, 190 sqq.

short treatise composed 953 A.D., at the desire of the Frankish queen Gerberga, by the monk Adso, abbot of Montier-en-Der, from 968 A.D. It was ascribed sometimes to St. Augustine, sometimes to Rhabanus Maurus or Alcuin, and thus notwithstanding the rather fantastic and silly nature of its contents was much reverenced. Adso says that Antichrist will be born in Babylon and brought up by magicians in Bethsaida and Chorazin; and this was often repeated afterwards, in forgetfulness that for many centuries none of these places had existed. Satan takes possession of him in the womb. He settles at Jerusalem, where all Jews flock to him as their Messiah, is circumcised, sends his preachers into all the world, works many wonders, raises the dead, rebuilds the temple, and is worshipped as the Son of God. He converts all princes and through them all nations to himself; the Christians who do not join him are killed. Unlike the older fathers, Adso makes him restore idolatry (*dœmonum culturam*), and as though to make it impossible for any later writer to exceed the horror of his account, says that all the human race will be deceived and destroyed by him.[1] He adds, as an alleviating circumstance, that after his death on the Mount of Olives the judgment will not immediately follow, but God will wait for the conversion of part of those he had deceived. But the Man of Sin will not come till the secession (ἀποστασία) has taken place, *i.e.*, till all the countries under the Roman Empire are separated from it, and that will not be, so long as there are Frankish kings.[2]

Besides these writings, the so-called *Revelations of Methodius* essentially contributed to colour later mediæval notions about the last things. It first became known in the West about two centuries after Adso's work, and was ascribed to the famous bishop of Patara at the beginning of the fourth century; but it is not by him or by his namesake, the Patriarch of Constantinople (as Fabricius thought), who died 846, but by another Methodius who lived in 1240. It treats of the fate of Oriental Christendom, its sufferings under the yoke of the sons of Ismael, a great victory of

---

[1] "Totum simul humanum genus suo errore decipiet et perdet."
[2] Adso's tract is in St. Augustine's works, T. vi. Ap. p. 723, Ed. Antwerp, and in Froben's edition of Alcuin.

the Greek Emperor which was to break the Mahometan yoke, and the Mongol invasion of Gog and Magog.[1] Then the Greek Emperor is to reign twelve years and a half at Jerusalem, after which Antichrist appears, born in Chorazim, brought up at Bethsaida and ruling in Capernaum, till he marches to Jerusalem and is worshipped in the temple. It is a peculiarity of this account, that Antichrist will be unmasked by the preaching of Enoch and Elias, and afterwards universally deserted and despised.

Throughout the middle ages Christians always looked to the East for Antichrist, and when he was supposed to be at hand it was Eastern, not Western events, that suggested the notion. No doubt was felt that he would appear in the East, in Chaldæa and then in Palestine. In a wider and less strict sense particular individuals were called Antichrists, or precursors of Antichrist, to brand them as special enemies or corrupters of the Church, just as St. John had extended the use of the term; and it was natural that this designation should be chiefly given to persecutors and to the authors of schisms and heresies. St. Cyprian and St. Jerome had said before that all heretics are Antichrists;[2] as, on the other hand, the Arian author of the *Opus Imperfectum in Matthæum* called Catholics, or "Homoousians," the host of Antichrist. The notion gradually grew up that all heresies were preparations for the great revolt which would cause the persecution of Antichrist, and would be swallowed up in it like brooks and rivers in a mighty sea. Under his rule no new sects or heresies would arise; there would be but two religions in the world, the Catholic and that of Antichrist.

In the twelfth century it begun to be thought that the expositions of Antichrist and of the preceding and attendant circumstances had been carried much too far, and a protest was raised against categorical assertions of matters not included in the traditional teaching of the Church. The learned Provost Gerhoh, of Reichersberg, did this in his treatise *De Investigatione Antichristi*, where he wishes to show that all said in holy Scripture about Antichrist had

[1] The Latin translator always names the Turks in the titles of the chapters, but the author meant the Caliphate. The work is found in Greek and Latin in the *Orthodoxographa Basil.* 1569, Tom. i.
[2] Cypr. *Ep.* 74, 76. Hieron. *in Matt.* xxiv. 5. Opp. vii. 193.

been already fulfilled in the history of the Church and the acts of her enemies, even should no such Antichrist come hereafter, as was commonly supposed, to give himself out for Christ, be worshipped as God in the temple, bring fire from heaven, kill Enoch and Elias, and do all the rest, which is more a matter of opinion in the Church than of faith. For nothing more pertains to faith about him than what is necessary for the fulfilment of the Bible prophecies, and we are free to suppose that the former Antichrists sufficiently fulfil the Scriptures and the "mystery of iniquity," to justify the Lord, if the day of judgment should dawn at once.[1] But many were not content with representing Antichrist as at hand; they maintained that he was already born, and would appear in their generation. St. Bernard relates this of Norbert, founder of the Præmonstratensian order.[2]

Bishop Ranieri, of Florence, created a great stir by a similar statement earlier, between 1071 and 1080. Guibert, archbishop of Ravenna, afterwards anti-pope, tried to convince him of his error in a treatise, where he says that his assertion was the universal topic of conversation, and that he claimed to know what no Prophet knew; that the Roman Empire was still in full power over all Italy; and there was no trace of the "secession" announced by the Apostle to precede Antichrist.[3] And Vincent Ferrer, the Dominican, wrote to the Avignon Pope, De Luna, in 1412, that he had learnt Antichrist was born.

The Joachimite school invented the theory, which has led to so much confusion, of explaining the 1260 days in Daniel by so many years; the oppression of the Church under the mystical Babylon, or German Empire of the Hohenstaufen, was to last from 1200 to 1260, and from 1256 to 1260 the tyranny of Antichrist. But the Joachimites distinguished the *Antichristus mixtus* or *mysticus*, or

---

[1] Gerhoh says that in his day the mystery of Antichrist was often acted in the churches, which he blames as truly Antichristian. That must have constantly supplied food for fresh mythical decorations of the story. Jodok Stültz gives extracts from Gerhoh's treatise in the 22nd vol. of the *Archiv. für Kunde Oester. Geschichtsq.* Wien. 1858.

[2] "De Antichristo cum inquirerem quid sentiret, durante ea quæ nunc est generatione revelandum illum esse se certissime scire protestatus est." Bern. *Ep.* 56. Opp. Mab. ed. i. 59.

[3] See *Novelle Letterar.* Florence, 1768, p. 771, 803.

*reipublicæ*, the tyrannical worldly power with its false Pope, from the proper Antichrist.[1] When the year 1260 passed without any fulfilment of these cherished anticipations, Daniel's 1335 days were taken, and the year 1335 fixed as the date of Antichrist's destruction. So the Beguines or followers of Peter John of Olive.[2] Wicliffe made the year 1400 that of Antichrist's appearance, if he wrote *The Last Age of the Church*.[3] He elsewhere calls the Pope, Antichrist, or an Antichrist; but he, like other mediæval heretics, uses the word in a wider and improper sense, not meaning to refer the Pauline Man of Sin to the Papacy, for the notion that St. Paul referred to an individual, who should arise in the East out of the bosom of Judaism at the end of the world, was firmly held. It was only meant that the Popes were Antichrists, as many heretics and persecutors had been before, or as Wicliffe expressed it, that there was a contrast in all points between a Pope and Christ. One section of the Waldensians called Pope Silvester Antichrist, not of course meaning that the last and proper Antichrist had appeared in the fourth century, but only that by accepting Constantine's gift Silvester poisoned the Church, and showed himself its enemy and an heretical forerunner of Antichrist. So the Beguines saw in Pope John xxii. who rejected their pet doctrine about perfect poverty, the *mysticus Antichristus*. But they said this of the particular Pope, not of the Papacy, which they considered a Divine institution.[4] Some of them thought the real Antichrist would come from the most perfect order, the Franciscan, as Lucifer came from the highest rank of angels.

III. The schism of the sixteenth century introduced a change in the interpretation of this passage (2 Thess. ii. 1—12), which is, in fact, one of the most remarkable occurrences in the whole history of Biblical criticism. For 1500 years every one had understood the Apostle to mean a certain *individual*, by the adversary or Man of Sin; not one Father had doubted this. It was now suddenly discovered that St. Paul meant nothing of the kind, but a long succession of persons extending through many centuries, viz., the

---

[1] See *e.g.* Joachim, *In Hierem.* p. 329.
[2] See Limborch, *Hist. Inquis.* pp. 298, 303.
[3] It is edited by J. H. Todd. Dublin, 1840.
[4] See Limborch, *Hist. Inquis.* p. 308.

Bishops of the Roman See. He meant to foretell that the Church itself for at least fifteen centuries would be the kingdom and seat of a chronic Antichrist, so that there would be a regular dynasty or succession of Antichrists, though with short breaks,—for whenever the Roman See was vacant there was no Antichrist, but as soon as it was filled there was one again, nor would Christendom ever be without one to the end of the world. The temple of God, where the adversary would sit, could be nothing else than the Christian Church.[1] The view of Antichrist appearing at the fall of the Roman Empire was retained, only there was a question when that fall took place, whether it was that of the Western or the Byzantine Empire, or whether both should be included. The 1260 days of Daniel, which had been made into years, were now taken to define the duration of the Antichristian Empire, and according to what Pope was chosen as the first Antichrist, it was extended into the eighteenth, nineteenth, or twenty-first century. The so-called gods, over whom "the Adversary" sets himself, are princes and kings, whom the Popes have maintained to be subject to their ecclesiastical authority. This explanation, first devised by Luther, was received into the Smalcaldic Articles, and thus obtained a place as a formal dogma, and was eagerly seized and kept to by all Protestant theologians. Calvin declared it to be so true and evident that a boy of ten years old must see its truth. It was dangerous to understand the passage differently; one of the charges against Archbishop Laud on his trial was his refusal to recognise the Roman Bishop as the "Man of Sin."[2] But as this view is now given up everywhere, where there is a scien-

---

[1] The difficulty of the Church, which recognised Antichrist as her head, being at the same time called "the temple of God," and "apostate," (for so ἡ ἀποστασία was understood), was not thought of. That all adherents of the "Man of Sin" are called ἀπολλύμενοι, irrevocably lost, caused no hesitation in the Reformation period, when that consequence was gladly admitted; but it did later, whence Koppe remarks, "Plerosque interpretum hanc Paulinæ orationis partem prorsus silentio præteriisse animadvertimus." De Wette observes that the metaphorical sense of the temple, as the Christian Church, does not agree with the notion of "sitting;" but there was of course no taste or appreciation for such refinements in that age.

[2] It seems to have become a traditional view that Catholic divines understand Luther and his work by Antichrist. One writer copies it from another. Cf. Olshausen, iv. 521, and Lüneman, p. 210. But no one has really done so; and if any theologian in the heat of controversy had been driven to adopt such an absurdity, it would have been rejected as contradicting the whole tone of the Church's mind. Lüneman quotes Estius, Fromond, and Bern. a Piconio; but none of them say anything of the sort.

tific theology and exegesis, it is enough to have mentioned it. Kern says rightly; "It is so obvious to the unprejudiced that our text speaks as distinctly as possible of an individual, that it could never have been doubted, but for the wish to avoid that interpretation at any price from certain ulterior grounds, dogmatic and other."[1]

The first to see the necessity of a different explanation, and to perceive that the Apostle referred to persons and events of his own day, were Netherlanders and Englishmen. Grotius thought Caligula was the Man of Sin, and the apostasy the profligacy of his court, but that from the eighth verse onwards Simon Magus was spoken of. Witsius and Wetstein understood Titus by the man of sin, and the revolt of the Roman armies under Nero and after him by the apostasy. Hammond referred all to the Gnostics and their head, Simon Magus. These views were easily assailable. Equally unsatisfactory was another explanation, which made the Man of Sin the unbelieving Jews, who persecuted Christians.[2] While Benson and Macknight unthinkingly repeated Luther's view, Whitby's Commentary—the sharpest of the older English critics—is a medley of right and wrong. He saw that Claudius was meant by ὁ κατέχων, but he thinks "the Adversary" is the Jewish people, with its tendency to tumult and hatred of Christian Churches, which only Claudius kept from apostasy. Rösselt agrees with him in principle.[3]

The first German Protestant theologians who rejected the older view, Döderlein, Eckermann and Kleucker, tried to refer the passage to Jewish mutinies against the Romans, and the false Messiahs and agitators of the period. Koppe, Stolz and Kuinöl thought it referred to a succession of opponents of God and Christ, who would rise up in the Church. Berthold thought the Antichrist of St. Paul was a mere Jewish fancy of the time, in which the Apostle was entangled.[4] Baumgarten-Crusius thinks he merely repeated the images of the old Prophets, especially Daniel's; a particular person is out of the question, and the κατέχων is

[1] *Tüb. Zeitschr. für Theol.*, 1839. No. II., p. 158.
[2] This appears first in La Roche, *Mem. Lit.* Sept. 1726.
[3] Whitby *Paraph. and Comment. on N. T.* London, 1718; ii. 470; Ross. *Opusc.* ii. 292.
[4] Berthold. *Christol. Jud.* i. 16.

"the young Christian spirit," or "Christ in believers." Olshausen follows those who go furthest in embellishing the figure of Antichrist. He is to work secretly for a long time, but will at last appear conspicuously in the body as an incarnation of Satan. It goes evidently against the writer's critical sense to make the Christian Church the temple of God, but he sees no alternative.[1] The κατέχων is the Roman Empire, or the Emperor as its representative.

One special class of modern Protestant theologians and critics has taken up the view that the prophecy refers in its full and proper sense to our own days, the middle of the nineteenth century, and that everything is leading more and more to the appearance of the true and proper Antichrist. Thus O. von Gerlach; "In our days, powers of lying of the opposite side (to the Church of Rome) are roused, which point far more strongly and decisively to the approaching fulfilment of this Apostolic prophecy." And he counts up the deification of the human race, the doctrine of the rehabilitation of the rights of the flesh, the loosening of ecclesiastical and social bonds, the loss of respect for authority, and attacks on the foundations of Christian faith. As soon as these powers of evil are summed up and concentrated in one highly-gifted man, who makes the world believe that in him the Spirit Himself is completely incarnated, St. Paul's prediction is fulfilled.

Heubner's view comes very near this. "The Man of Sin must be considered as collective, as a generation, though the generation may have a typical representative."[2] He thinks men will be ruled by a spirit proceeding from within the Church, and will fall into deification of nature and of self, naturalism, worship of reason and Autotheism. This spirit appeared in the Gnostics in St. Paul's day, and in the first centuries the check to its full outbreak was the dominant power of the Christian Apostolic spirit, after the fourth century the civil power, which then favoured Christianity.

---

[1] Olsh. *Bibl. Comm.* iv. 506 sqq. Olshausen gives two grounds for this; (1) In the temple at Jerusalem was no image or throne of Jehovah, except the Ark. How this proves that the Christian Church must be substituted is not obvious. (2) The temple is not to be rebuilt, as we learn from Matt. xxiv. 2 and John iv. 21. But neither passage says so; and if they did. the words of St. Paul must be taken in their most direct, and here only possible sense.

[2] Heubner, *Praktisch Erkl.* N. T., vol. iv. p. 176.

When the civil power is seized by this spirit of the age, it will break out. In the new *Zellers. Wörterbuch der Bibel* (ii. 44,) we read : " Among the judgments of God, advance the Apostasy and the Lawlessness, so that the predicted appearance of the Man of Sin will not be long delayed." At p. 704 it is more exactly described. Under the conduct of the two witnesses (Apoc. xi., Mal. iii. 1), a new Christian temple will be built in Jerusalem, and defended for some time against Antichrist, but taken by him when he has conquered the witnesses, and he will then have the human spirit alone worshipped there as God. So Rudelbach sees the whole appearance of the Antichristian period in gigantic form before us.[1] Many other recent writers, on the contrary, have maintained that St. Paul was mistaken. Düsterdieck thinks he gave a wrong date for the personal appearance of Antichrist. De Wette says that from human infirmity the Apostle wished to foreknow too much, and was influenced by Jewish Apocalyptic writings, and a misconception of the sense of Daniel. Wieseler came to similar conclusions. " The κατέχων (James, or the Christians at Jerusalem). is long removed, but the Man of Sin is not yet come." Schrader sees in the Man of Sin the same image we find in Simon Magus, and infers that the Epistle is spurious. Krehl is content with observing that an accurate account of the Apostle's exact meaning is not possible, as he has spoken of future and obscure matters. Lüneman, who equally understands the Roman Empire by κατέχων, implies by his interpretation that the Apostle was mistaken. He thinks that St. Paul, "impelled by his individuality," wished to settle more about the occurrences and conditions of the closing catastrophe than is given to man to know, even though he be an Vpostle filled with the spirit of Christ. Lechler leaves the whole passage unexplained, and is content with these results,—that the adversary is the Antichrist, only the name is not expressed, and, (against Kern) that the appearances will be in the religious, not the political domain. But Baur agrees with Kern in attributing to the writer of the Epistle, who is not St. Paul, the fancy about Nero's return ; " There is nothing to prevent our understanding the same person by the Antichrist of the

[1] See *Zeitschr. für Luth. Theol.* 1859, p. 255.

Epistle, as in the Apocalypse," *i.e.* Nero, and he too makes Vespasian the κατέχων.[1]

Ewald has devised an explanation which as yet stands alone. "We have here a secret which in the first Apostolic ages believers were only willing to talk of and propagate among themselves, so that St. Paul did not venture to speak openly about it." And he explains this secret which had grown up in the Mother Church of Jerusalem to be, that the κατέχων is Elias, who will return before the appearance of Antichrist, and will have to be put out of the way by him.[2]

Of recent English theologians, I know but three who have expressly dealt with this passage. Burton understands by the "Man of Sin," Christians who, soon after St. Paul's time, renounced their faith and became Gnostics; he can find nothing in the passage which need restrict the fulfilment of the prophecy to a period just before the end of the world. The Apostle may have meant himself and the other Apostles, by κατέχων.[3] Alford refers all to the future, finds the mystery of iniquity in all persecutions of Christians—in Mahomet, the Popes, Napoleon, Mormonism —and the κατέχων in secular states and rulers.[4] Jowett has recently expressed himself most fully in a special dissertation *On the Man of Sin*.[5] But he leaves all dark and uncertain, giving as the likeliest conjecture, that the Man of

---

[1] Düsterdieck, *Johann. Brief.*, 1852, i. 330. De Wette, *Exeg. Handbuch*, vol. ii. Pt. III. p. 133. Wieseler, *Chron. apost. Zeitalt*, 1848, p. 273. Schrader, *Der Apost. Paulus*, Pt. v. p. 46 sqq. Krehl, Wörterbuch, N. T., p. 638. Lüneman, *Krit-exeg. Handb. über Thess-Brief.*, 1859, p. 220.—Lechler, *das apost. und nachapost. Zeitalter*, 1857, p. 132. Baur, *Theol. Jahrb.*, 1855, p. 150 sq.
[2] *Jahrb. Bibl. Wissensch.* iii. 251.
[3] Burton, *Inquiry into Heresies of the Apostolic Age.* Oxf. 1829, p. 400.
[4] Alford's *Gr. Test.* vol. iii. London, 1856.
[5] Jowett's *Epistles of St. Paul*, vol. i. pp. 168—182 [pp. 178—194. 2nd edition. London, 1859.] . [In his notes on the passage itself, Jowett explains the "temple of God" to be the temple of Jerusalem, *as an image of* the Christian Church. "Antichrist, ὁ ἀντικείμενος, is *not without, but within* the Church;" he is not a person, but "the concentrated and personified might of evil, possessing it by force;" ... "a form of evil, springing out of the state of the world itself, to which mankind are ready to give homage." In the dissertation on the subject the author says, "we know of no person or power existing in the lifetime of the Apostle," to which "most of the features" in the description of the Man of Sin will apply (as Caligula, Nero, &c.) He thinks τὸ κατέχον may be the Roman Empire, or more probably the Jewish Law, or both,—certainly not a person. But he disclaims the intention of adding "another to the multitude of guesses that exist already," as to any specific fulfilments of the prophecy, and treats it as having a broad spiritual significance, applicable more or less to all periods of the Church, and corresponding to what is said in Rom. vii. of the individual soul. This does not of course exclude some

Sin might be merely a personification of the abomination of desolation mentioned in Daniel, suggested to the Apostle's mind by the prevalent worship of the Emperors.

IV. Catholic Commentators of the sixteenth and seventeenth century confined themselves to following the earlier interpretations for the most part, but showed more and more their dissatisfaction with them. Hardouin's view and that of his scholar, Berruyer, stand alone; the falling away is according to them a mingling of Judaism with Heathenism and idolatry at Jerusalem, in which a considerable fraction of the people take part, led by the Sadducean High Priest, Ananias (Acts xxiii. 2), who is the "Man of Sin," and the κατέχων is the existing high priest.[1] That no word of his theory is found in the history, causes Hardouin as little scruple here as elsewhere. But we see that even he and Berruyer felt compelled to seek an interpretation in contemporary history, which drove them to this desperate device. Since their failure, theologians seem to have had a shrinking from meddling with this Epistle, and this crucial passage in it. For one hundred and thirty years I know of but two Catholic divines who have tried to solve the riddle. So complete a silence from 1730 to 1818, when Jahn's treatise appeared, and again from 1818 to 1858, indicates that the case was thought hopeless, and men neither found the common explanation tenable, with the Roman empire restraining Antichrist, nor could discover any other. Jahn, at Vienna, after eighty years, was the first to undertake the task. With his true critical tact, he saw that St. Paul could only be speaking of the temple at Jerusalem, and cannot understand this being overlooked by all interpreters; (since 1818 it is different). But—and here he comes on Hammond's traces—St. Paul speaks of a revolt of the Jews, which was already secretly approaching, and the "lawless one" signifies the chief conspirators, who had their prophets, magicians and conjurors.[2] No one has adopted this unsatisfactory explanation since. And thus

more minute and detailed fulfilment during the Apostle's lifetime, (such as that given, *e.g.*, in the text), or in the future, still less does it imply that contemporary events may not have contributed to suggest its forms and imagery, so far as it is not borrowed from Daniel.—TR.]

[1] Hardouin, *Comm. in N. T.* Amst. 1741, p. 613. Berruyer, *Paraphr. Lit. des Epît. des Apôtr.* Amst., 1758, iv. 62.

[2] Jahn *Erkl. der Weissag Jesu, &c.*, in Bengel's *Archiv. für Theol.* ii. 376 sqq.

rested the interpretation of 2 Thess. and this *crux interpretum* till 1858, when Professor Bisping's *Erklärung* appeared in Munster. He returned to the unhappy view which all sensible critics seemed to have abandoned, and which has nearly all the Fathers against it—that the temple of God, in which the adversary is to sit, is the Christian Church. He seems to have looked at the end for a complete ruin of the Church; for he explains, " Antichrist will banish the true God, the one object of worship, from the Church, and put himself in His place." I assume that he does not mean these words to be literally taken, and that Christ's promises to His Church are to fail when the adversary appears, as would certainly be the case if he succeeded in banishing God from the Church.[1] " The isolated and scattered movements of vice and godlessness which appear here and there, but are only recognised by a few as heralds of Antichrist, are the mystery of iniquity." This is a common but thoroughly unhistorical view. (1). It resolves itself into a common place, which I cannot attribute to the Apostle, that sins and errors have existed and will grow— for two thousand years or more, as experience teaches—till they culminate in Antichrist. (2). If St. Paul really gave out the movements of sin and ungodliness in his own day for heralds of Antichrist, then, limit and soften it as we may, we must admit that he was wrong. It contradicts all logic, to make events under Claudius and Nero heralds of another event which, after eighteen hundred years, is still to come; without some connection of cause there can be no talk of harbingers. (3). The movements of evil St. Paul meant, must have been either within or without the Church. If without, in the wide field of Heathendom there were not only isolated movements of wickedness, but everything was full of it; the abominations were conspicuous, and could not be connected with an Antichrist to come long after Heathendom had perished. But if they were sins and errors within the Church, St. Paul could not deal with them as a "mystery," but would be bound to mention

---

[1] [If, however, Daniel's prophecy is to be referred to Antichrist, he is expressly said to "take away the perpetual sacrifice," which is the characteristic "worship of the true God" in the Church. Dan. viii. 11, 12; ix. 27. But cf. infr. p. 415.— TR.]

them, as in all other such cases, for the warning of his people, and not keep them thus secret.

Of the κατέχων Bisping says, that even after the fall of the German Empire, in 1806, he thought he must keep to the old interpretation of the Roman Empire, and in a wider prophetic view the Christian State, which, as a restraining power, opposed the universal falling away from God and delayed the appearing of Antichrist. Did he really think it conceivable that St. Paul, who nowhere else shows the least trace of any such distant prophetic gaze over the Roman Empire, made statements to the Thessalonians about the Christian State?

And now let us review the attempts made at various times to explain the κατέχων, the apostasy, and the temple of God, where the adversary will seat himself. By the apostasy, which must come first, the Greeks—Chrysostom, Theodoret, Theophylact, and Ephrem—understood Antichrist himself, who will cause many to fall away; and St. Augustine joined them, for in his version he read *refuga*, and therefore adds *quem (Antichristum) refugam vocat, utique a Domino Deo*.[1] The Apostle was supposed to mean a great separation from the Church, wrought by Antichrist. Others, as St. Cyril of Jerusalem, understood apostasy from the faith. It was still oftener interpreted of the subject nations rebelling against the Roman Empire. So Jerome, Hilary, Sedulius, Primasius, and the Commentary in St. Anselm's works. But this last gives a choice of two other interpretations, *sive ut multitudo ecclesiarum discedat a Pontifice Romano aut multitudo hominum discedat a fide*. According to Thomas Aquinas, the whole world must first be converted to Christianity, and then many will fall away.[2] There is to be, therefore, a double apostasy, from the Roman Empire and from Catholic belief. As Christ came at the time of the universal dominion of the Roman Empire, so is its break up the sign of the coming of Antichrist. The two glosses, *ordinaria* and *interlinearis*, as also Cajetan and Cornelius à Lapide, hold to the sense

---

[1] Aug. *De Civ. Dei*. xx. 19.
[2] "Futurum erat ut fides a toto mundo reciperetur. Istud ergo præcedit, quod nondum est imp'etum, et post multi discedent a fide." Thom. Aq. *Comm. in Paul. Ep.* Antworp 1591, 193.

of a falling away from the Roman Empire. Engelbert, of Admont, makes a three-fold falling away, of countries and nations from the Roman Empire, of Churches from the Pope, of believers from God.¹ It has been shown that in the ancient Church the temple at Jerusalem was understood by the "temple of God." St. Cyril rejects as inadmissible, the view of its being the Christian Church, where Antichrist would be worshipped.² But soon afterwards some Greek and Latin Fathers thought Christian churches (buildings) were meant, which Antichrist would get possession of, and be worshipped in. So say St. Jerome, St. Chrysostom, and Theodoret. St. Jerome seems to have understood Christian churches only, without the temple, St. Chrysostom both, and the Arian author of the Commentary on St. Matthew expresses an anticipation that Antichrist is *obtinere loca ecclesiarum sancta sub specie Christi*.³ St. Augustine, who is altogether more cautious than other Fathers about the Pauline prophecy, and more ready to acknowledge his ignorance, leaves it doubtful what temple of God Antichrist will sit in, and only mentions the opinion of some, that St. Paul is not speaking of any particular person, but of a number of Antichristian men with their chief Antichrist, who will make themselves God's temple, *i.e.*, a Church.⁴ This view had but few supporters. The Fathers who understood Christian churches thought of such occurrences as took place in the East under Mahometan rule, where they were turned into mosques.

Estius is quite wrong in supposing that the view of some Fathers that Antichrist will get possession of Christian churches is identical with another, that the temple of God is a symbol of the Christian Church, where he will place his throne.⁵ On the contrary, there is a broad distinction; the one would be a mere act of violence and oppressive persecution, the other would require the consent of at least a great part of the Church. Fromond, one of the best Commentators of the seventeeenth century, saw that

---

¹ Eng. *De Ortu et Interitu Rom. Imp.* c. 18.
² μὴ γένοιτο γὰρ τοῦτο ἐν ᾧ ἐσμέν. Cyr. Cat. xv. 15.
³ *Opus Imperf. in Matt.* T. vi. Append. p. 6 in Montfaucon's Ed. of Chrys.
⁴ Aug. *De Civ Dei.* xx. 19. They said, according to the Greek, it was not "in tem*plo*," but in tem*plum* Dei sedet, tanquam ipse sit templum Dei quod est Ecclesia."
⁵ Estius *Comm.* ii. 192, Ed. Duac.

the temple of God could not be the Christian Church, and maintained that it was one of the two ancient Christian churches at Jerusalem which had been turned into mosques, either that of the Holy Sepulchre or of the Minorites.[1]

The application to Antichrist of what Daniel says about Antiochus Epiphanes, led to the Prophet's words about the taking away, for a time, of the daily offering in the temple being referred to an universal abolition of the Eucharistic Sacrifice in the Church; whence it followed again, that the power and persecution of Antichrist and his adherents would extend over the whole world and all nations, especially if, as was often supposed, he was not to appear till the Gospel had really been preached to all nations, as the Lord said, and the Church was spread over the whole earth. This seemed quite possible to the older Fathers, Irenæus and Hippolytus, who only knew the beginnings of the Church, and saw persecutions which, if extended, must lead to an actual cessation of the Church's sacrifice and worship. The Arian writer already mentioned thought Christians would fly into the deserts, and none be left to attend churches or offer sacrifice.[2] Ephrem, Primasius and the Pseudohippolytus, equally mentioned an universal desertion of churches and cessation of the sacrifice during the 1260 days. Pseudoprosper anticipates the same from the united tyranny of the Arians, Goths and other peoples breaking in upon the Roman Empire. But the more illustrious Fathers, Augustine, Cyril, Chrysostom, John of Damascus, know nothing of it.[3] As to the κατέχων, the Greeks could not well understand it, like the Westerns, of the Roman Empire. Theodore, of Mosuestia, thought the Apostle meant the "dispensation of God;" Severian understood rather by the term the gifts of the Spirit.[4] As the

---

[1] From. *Comm. in Epist. Apost.* p. 315.
[2] *Opus. Imperf. in Matt.*, found in *Chrys. Hom.* vi. 49.
[3] It is the stranger, therefore, that so many moderns—Bellarmine, Acosta, Valentia, Saunders, Viegas, Suarez, Malvenda—equally affirmed this ceasing of the Liturgy. We cannot conceive a world-wide power strong enough to close all churches and put down all worship at once in Europe, Asia, Africa and America, and all islands. Malvenda himself thinks we must draw a line somewhere. The holy sacrifice will be celebrated still in crypts, catacombs, caves, hiding places and deserts (*De Antichr.* ix. 11). He does not see that this destroys the whole point of the passage in Daniel. For he does not believe in an universal apostasy, but affirms that under Antichrist, "plurimi *ubique gentium* fortes et invicti in religione permaneant." Ib. ix. 22.
[4] *Catena* Cramer. p. 389.

dissolution of the Roman Empire was immediately to precede the appearance of Antichrist and the end of the world, all this was thought to be close at hand, and every fresh severity of persecution increased the expectation. Nearly all the older Fathers speak in this sense, the Alexandrians only being more reserved. In the palmy days of Arianism the disturbed state of the Church was supposed to indicate all the signs of Antichrist's near approach.[1] Then came the great popular migrations; and as the weakness and dissolution of the Empire became still more conspicuous, the Man of Sin was all the more confidently looked for. In 409 A.D. St. Jerome says, "That which withheld is removed, (*i.e.* the Empire is fallen to pieces) and shall we not perceive that Antichrist is near?" St. Augustine spoke more cautiously, since Christ did not intend the time to be known.[2] But Gregory the Great was not deterred by the mistakes of earlier Fathers from confidently proclaiming that in his own time, the beginning of the seventh century, the last things were approaching;[3] and Theodore Studita (in 813) thought he saw before his eyes the apostasy which, according to St. Paul, was to come first, and consequently the approach (τὰ εἰσόδια) of Antichrist.[4]

The application of κατέχων to the Roman Empire was naturally seized upon with eagerness by the adherents of the Reformation theory about Antichrist, though it was impossible to think of a Greek masculine which St. Paul could have used in this sense; for if the succession of Emperors were meant, he must have used the plural. These divines assumed the Empire to have been long destroyed, while the Church commentators generally held it to continue in the German Empire, impossible though it was to point out the continuity. Such a man even as

---

[1] So Hilary, "Necesse est in ipsam nos Antichristi ætatem incidisse." *Cont. Aux.* v. p 1615, ed. 1693. He calls the Arians "imminentis Antichristi prævii ministrique," p. 1263. So Greg. Naz. *Or.* 14, T. i. p. 618, ed. 1630. Ephrem *Opp. Græc.* T. i. p. 44, Romæ. 1732. Cyril of Jerusalem says, "The apostasy is here already; men are fallen away from right belief, and we must look for the enemy's approach" *Cat.* xv. 9, p. 228, ed. Bened.
[2] Hieron. *ad Ager.* Ep. 123. 16. Aug. *Ep.* 199 *ad Hesgch.*
[3] He quotes a vision or dream of Redemptus of Ferentinum, and adds, "Quid in aliis mundi partibus agatur ignoro. Nam in hac terra in qua nos vivimus finem suum mundus jam non nuutiat sed ostendit." Greg. Mag. *Dial.* iii. 38. Opp. ii. 368, ed. Bened.
[4] Theod. Stud. *Epp.* ii. 17. Opp. Sirmondi, v. 410.

Stapleton did not scruple to affirm, that the Church and Roman Empire were so intertwined that both would fall together.[1] Meanwhile, as on the Protestant side the exigencies of the system compelled men to refer the beginning of the series of Antichrists back to the first centuries, they came to a time when the Roman Empire was still actually existing. Yet some Protestant writers as early as the sixteenth century felt the common view to be untenable. Tilenus maintained that St. Paul meant himself by ὁ κατέχων; Du Jon (Junius) generalised it into all good preachers of the Gospel. On the Catholic side, too, some other interpretation was sought for, or the enigma was left as hopeless. Ambrose Catharinus, after St. Augustine's example, confessed his uncertainty, and said no explanation he had met with satisfied him.[2] He urges the difficulties of referring the mystery of iniquity already working to a future Antichrist, as was commonly done, and seems to have felt that making a long series of persecutors and heretics the harbingers or pioneers of an Antichrist to come after two thousand years, was at bottom a mere shift and evasion; still he acquiesces in the view that Satan himself, working for awhile through various instruments, is meant. Estius and Justinian saw clearly that it was an unhistorical perversion to make the Roman Empire the κατέχων, whence the former suggested the apostasy, which must come first, instead, but feeling the weakness of this view, preferred with St. Augustine to acknowledge his ignorance. But Cornelius à Lapide and Calmet stuck to the view of the Roman Empire; the former thinking it would certainly be the last, and would endure till the end of the world, when it would pass into the kingdom of Antichrist; Calmet maintaining that even in 1730 the Roman Empire survived, though immensely weakened, in the German Empire, but that this very weakness, and the separation of so many Churches (become Protestant) were sure signs the end was near.

Bossuet thought Theodoret's view the most probable, that the κατέχων is the immutable counsel of God withholding Antichrist's coming till the end of the world; Picquigny thought God did not mean us to understand it; Mauduit

---

[1] Stapleton, *Opera*, Paris, 1610, ii. 422.
[2] Cath. *Comm. in Pauli Epp.* Paris, 1566, p. 385.

that it was the public profession of orthodoxy.¹ The author of *Les Sept Ages de l'Église*² held that a great religious revolution preceding Antichrist, and admitting the Jews into the Church while excluding the Gentiles who had become unbelievers, is what St. Paul means by the apostasy and the κατέχων. As long as the Gentiles possess the faith they hinder the coming of Antichrist. Alcasar adopts the usual interpretation of the Roman Empire, but thinks that as in Scripture it is always considered a Heathen power and an enemy of the Church, the Apostle meant to say that it discharged the office or took the place of Antichrist by persecuting the Church, till the Church conquered it under Constantine.³ Thorndike, who saw rightly that by the "adversary" must be meant a Roman Emperor, and that the "so-called gods" could only be Heathen deities, gives a very forced explanation of κατέχων; it is the Jewish Law, whose observance saved the Christians from persecution, (the mystery of iniquity,) and the apostasy is their release from it.⁴

Koppe, Heidenreich, Reiche and Schott, understand by ὁ κατέχων St. Paul himself, who only out of modesty, as Heidenreich thinks, does not name himself. So, too, Böhmer.⁵ Wieseler understands collectively "the pious at Jerusalem, especially Christians;" but if an individual must be taken, the Apostle James. John Peter Lange, on the other hand, thinks from the context it can only be the ancient social order (Church and State, chiefly the latter.) So Lütterbeck, all lawful authority in the world. Flörke says it "can only be the angel of Divine fitness in the order of creation," but says nothing further as to who that angel is. Otto of Gerlach, premising that there can be only conjectures, thinks it may be " the supreme authority built on a religious basis, at first that of the Roman Emperors, in the middle ages that of Christian sovereigns as opposed to the Pope, at present most Christian governments." Finally,

---

¹ Bossuet, *Avertis. au Prot.* 49. *Œuvres* iii. 83. Picquigny, *Explic. des Epît. de S. Paul.* 9 ed. Paris, 1839, iii. 400. Manduit, Analyse des Epîtr. de S. Paul. Lyon. 1710 p. 86.
² Vol. i. p. 311. (Rome, 1783).
³ Alcasar *Vestig. Arc. Sens. Apoc.* p. 540; (Lugd., 1618).
⁴ Thorndike's *Works,* Oxf. 1844, vol. i. p. 748.
⁵ See *Jahrb. für deutsch. Theol.* vol. iv. No. 3, p. 452.

Messner says that St. Paul undoubtedly meant a power of his own day by ὁ κατέχων, but what power cannot be determined, or whether it was an institution or a person. And he makes an observation, correct in itself, that as the great prophecies of Scripture have several fulfilments, the last and complete fulfilment of this one, like the Coming of Christ which it precedes, must be looked for in the future.[1]

[1] Lange *Dogmat.* Heidelberg 1851, p. 1270. Lütterbeck *Neutest. Lehrb.* Mainz. 1852, ii. 231. Flörke. *Lehre von tausendjahr. Reiche*, p. 186, Marburg, 1859. Otto, *Das N. T. mit Anmerk.* Berlin, 1854. Messner, *Lehre der Apost.* p. 287, Leipzig, 1856.

# APPENDIX II.

### THE RIGHT OF THE SANHEDRIM OVER LIFE AND DEATH.

WHEN Pilate told the Jews to condemn Christ themselves, instead of demanding that he should do so, they replied, according to John xviii. 31; "It is not lawful for us to put any one to death." This answer is taken by De Wette as implying that the Roman government had deprived the Sanhedrim of the power of life and death.[1] Josephus is appealed to in proof of this, as saying that the Sanhedrim could not hold a court without the procurator's consent;[2] and the Talmud, as saying that forty years before the destruction of Jerusalem, Israel lost the power of life and death; and, lastly, there is the analogy of Roman law. As the question has also an importance in reference to Christ's teaching about marriage, it shall be briefly examined here.

It would certainly be strange if Pilate, in telling the Jews to judge Christ themselves, publicly insulted the people and their rulers, yet so it must have been, if he knew they could not do what he told them. Indeed, he must have twice mocked them in this way, for he says again (John xix. 6), "Take ye Him, and crucify Him." Any one acquainted with Roman history and manners would think this repeated insult of a nation by its Roman governor at least very improbable; doubly so here, for Pilate was afraid of the Jews, and condemned Christ from fear of their denouncing him to the President of Syria or the Emperor. And again, this view is inconsistent with the Gospel narrative, which makes the fulfilment of Christ's prophecy about the manner of His death a result of the refusal of the Jews to

---

[1] *Erklärung des Johan.*, 4th ed., p. 269.  [2] Jos. *Arch.* xx. g. 1.

try Him themselves, instead of being (as it then would be) the inevitable result of existing circumstances, so that there would be no prophecy at all. The "analogy of Roman law" is no evidence that the Jews had lost their autonomy, for the cities and countries which retained it were numerous. Strabo observes that Marseilles was not subjected to the Roman provincial legates, nor, again, Nemausus and the whole tribe to which it and twenty-four other towns belonged. Claudius first deprived the Syrians of their freedom, because they had put Roman citizens to death,[1] and the Rhodians were likewise deprived of it for crucifying Romans, for this freedom and autonomy could always be taken away at the will of the Emperor and Senate, and often was. It was for the sake of this free use of their law that the Jews, after Herod's death, so earnestly desired to have their land made a Syrian province, and a procurator of their own sent them. They hoped thus to be more independent, as regarded their laws and magistrates, than they had been under Herod;[2] and, had they been disappointed of this hope, Josephus would certainly have mentioned it. His silence justifies us in assuming that it was not so. And he makes the High Priest, Ananus, and Titus himself declare that the Romans had confirmed the laws of the Jews and allowed the free administration of them to remain in their own hands; even after war broke out Titus offered them autonomy, if they would submit, which they, therefore, clearly had not lost before.[3]

Josephus mentions, on occasion of St. James's condemnation and execution under the High Priest, Ananus, one limitation, viz., that the Sanhedrim could not hold a judicial court without the procurator's leave. But that very occurrence and the mention of this disability prove that the Sanhedrim certainly had the power of death. For else the complaints against Ananus for arbitrary exercise of power, made by the "moderates" to Albinus, would have taken a very different shape, and would have been based on his carrying out the sentence of death, not on his summoning the council by his own authority. Most likely the High

[1] Strabo *Div.*, I. 60, pp. 676, 681.
[2] Jos. *Arch.* xvii. 9, 4, Cf. 13, 1. All Jewish writings of that date speak of "autonomy" as the great thing.
[3] Jos. *Bell Jud.* vi. 6, 2; vi. 3, 5.

Priest had to get power to summon it once for all, from every Procurator, when entering upon his office. Anyhow the execution would have been a serious aggravation of Ananus' guilt, and a charge against the whole Sanhedrim, whereas he alone was accused, and punished by deposition.

Josephus observes on this procedure, that the Sadducees exceeded all other Jews in harsh and shocking sentences. The Jews had then been towards forty years under direct Roman rule, with the four years' break of Herod Agrippa's reign. He also says that the Essenes punished every contempt of the Mosaic Law with death.[1] Add to this what Titus testifies, that even Gentiles who offended against the Jewish religion, e. g. by entering the inner temple court, were put to death, and that by Jewish authorities, and it becomes the more incredible that they had not the power to judge their own countrymen by their own laws.[2] In all cases of uproar, high treason and disturbance of public order, the Roman authorities could judge and punish, but in religious matters and what concerned the law of Moses, full power was left to the Jewish authorities to pronounce and execute sentence of death. Hence Pilate said to the Jews, "I find no fault in Him, take ye Him and crucify Him;"[3] i. e. "I find no proof of sedition or high treason, which are the crimes I have to punish. Whether he has offended against your religion and law I know not, or leave unsettled; if you think so, punish Him yourselves." It is quite unnatural and against history to assume that this was a mere mockery of the weakness of the Jews.

Nor is the attitude of Jewish authorities towards the Apostles intelligible, except on the assumption of their full autonomy and power of life and death in religious matters. We read, in Acts v. 33, that the Sanhedrim in great wrath was resolving to kill them, when Gamaliel changed its decision, but not from any doubt of its power. St. Stephen's death was the result of a formal trial, in which witnesses were heard, however passionate the execution; nor does it stand alone, for St. Paul says afterwards, "Many of the

---

[1] *Bell Jud.* ii. 8, 9.
[2] Ib. vi. 2, 4. Titus says, ὑμῖν ἀναιρεῖν ἐπετρέψαμεν. The criminal was therefore not condemned by the Roman authorities, but given up to the Jews.
[3] John xix. 6.

Saints I put in prison, having received power from the high priests, and when they were executed, I gave my vote against them."[1] The Pharisees wanted to put Christ Himself to death for breaking the Sabbath.[2]

The testimony of the Talmud, that the Jews were deprived of the power of life and death forty years before the fall of the capital, cannot be accepted, for the date is wrong. Judæa became a Roman province not forty, but sixty years before Jerusalem fell, and then, if at all, this must have taken place. Selden quotes a passage from the Gemara to the effect that, during those forty years before the destruction of Jerusalem, four kinds of capital punishment were in use; and he thinks the Talmud only means that this jurisdiction was often interrupted during that period, especially under Pilate.[3]

What then do the words of the Jews in John xviii. 31 mean? They wanted Jesus to be *crucified*, and therefore wanted Pilate to pronounce sentence; for they would have had to condemn Him to be stoned themselves, as they did St. Stephen afterwards. Therefore, they charged Him with aiming at royalty, for that was a political crime which only the Roman government could judge. They also wished Him to die, not after Easter, when the crowds who came to visit the temple had turned homewards, but during the festival, before the eyes of the multitude gathered from all countries, and by the most shameful death suffered at the hands of the Heathen.[4] For them to execute the punishment themselves at that sacred season, and by their own hands, would have been a criminal desecration of the feast.[5] But if they had said this distinctly, Pilate would have answered, "Then wait till the feast is over." To preclude that, they said equivocally, "We can kill no one," *i. e.* (1) on a charge of high treason; (2) now, during the feast.

---

[1] Acts xxvi. 10.
[2] John v. 18; vii. 1, 25. What happened to St. Paul in the temple shows that both Jews and Romans were aware of this right. The Jews say they took and meant to judge him for profaning the temple, when Lysias tore him out of their hands; and Lysias justifies himself only because St. Paul was a Roman citizen (Acts xxiii. 27; xxiv. 6, 7.) If the Jews had no autonomy, it was Lysias's duty to protect any one, citizen or not, from their threats of punishment.
[3] *Gem. de Synedr.*, ii. 15, 11.
[4] [Hence St. Peter's words (Acts ii. 23), διὰ χειρῶν ἀνόμων προσπήξαντες.—TR.]
[5] We learn this from Philo's words. *In Flaccum*, p. 976. Ed. Paris, 1640.

# APPENDIX III.

## ON CHRIST'S TEACHING ABOUT MARRIAGE.

THOSE who think that, in His two statements about marriage given by St. Matthew, Christ meant that it was dissolved or made dissoluble by adultery on either side, are compelled (1) to maintain, that the word πορνεία may mean adultery, (2) to find a ground for its being used by Christ in a crucial passage instead of the ordinary word μοιχεία, which He uses elsewhere, (3) to maintain the principle that one act of adultery on either side *ipso facto* dissolves marriage. These three points require proof. The first assertion must be most emphatically contradicted; πορνεία always means incontinence in the unmarried, never, either in the New Testament or the Septuagint or in profane authors, adultery. Thus πορνεία and μοιχεία are always distinguished, as in Matt. xv. 19, Mark vii. 21; and the adulteress in John viii. 3 is called ἐν μοιχείᾳ κατειλημμένην. There is no ground for making πορνεία a generic term including adultery; when more than simple fornication is meant, either μοιχεία or ἀκαθαρσία are used with it, as in Mark vii. 21; 2 Cor. xii. 21; Gal. v. 19; Eph. v. 3; Col. iii. 5; Heb. xiii. 4. And Meyer, in proof of his view, that πορνεία in Matt. v. 32 means adultery, can only cite two passages, John viii. 41 and 1 Cor. v. 1. In the former the Jews say, "We are not born of fornication (are not idolaters) we have one Father, God;" in the latter St. Paul calls the cohabiting of a man with his father's widow πορνεία, for there is no Greek word for incest, so he could only call a connection which was no true marriage, πορνεία. Both passages are further evidence that πορνεία is *not* adultery. So in the Old Testament, both Hebrew and Septuagint, πορνεία (Heb. *senut* or *tasnut*) and μοιχεία (Heb. *naphuph*) are always distinguished; the last is never used of the unmarried, or the first of a wife. The one exception (Amos vii. 17), confirms the rule, for it says, "Thy wife shall be violated (πορνεύσει) in the city" *i. e.* by force, which is not adultery. Both words are put together in Ecclus. xxiii. 33, ἐν πορνείᾳ ἐμοιχεύθη, for emphasis. Kuinöl and others quote, besides Amos, Hosea iii. 3, where it is said of a wife, called μοιχαλις before, καί οὐ μὴ πορνεύσῃς, but it is added, " Thou shalt not be any man's." The woman was bought by the Prophet for a slave, as a type of Israel; he does not marry her; she is his property, not his wife; meanwhile, she is to be continent, and πορνεύσῃς is properly used. The Greeks always urge that πορνεία expressly excludes adultery, and is only used of the unmarried. So Gregory of Nyssa says,[1] πορνεία ἐστὶ καὶ λέγεται ἡ χωρὶς ἀδικίας ἑτέρου γενομένη τισὶ τῆς ἐπιθυμίας 'ἐκπλήρωσις, and Balsamon, (p. 1048.) πορνεία λέγεται ἡ χωρὶς ἀδικίας ἑτέρου μίξις, ἤγουν ἡ πρὸς ἐλευθέραν ἀνδρὸς γυναῖκα. Only in Greek, as in all languages, πορνεία and πορνεύω is used of a wife who has become a common prostitute. Thus Dio Cassius, (60, 31,) says of Messalina, ὥσπερ οὐκ ἐξαρκοῦν οἱ ὅτι καί ἐμοιχεύετο καὶ ἐπορνεύετο, for she actually did both; she contracted adulterous ties, and she went to a regular house of ill fame. So Clement of Alexandria, when showing the analogy between fornication and idolatry, says of this sort of prostitution, ὡς εἰδωλολατρεία ἐκ τοῦ ἑνὸς εἰς τοὺς πόλλους ἐπινέμησίς ἐστι θεοῦ, οὕτως ἡ πορνεία ἐκ τοῦ ἑνὸς γαμοῦ εἰς τοὺς πόλλούς ἐστιν ἔκπτωσις,[2] where the comparison obliged him to give up the common meaning of πορνεία. Tholuck says πορνεία is used for μοιχεία in the *Itala* and by Ulfilas, but he is wrong. See Sabatier's Edition of the *Vetus Itala*, iii. 27, which reads, *exemptâ causâ fornicationis*, and so most manuscripts read as well as St. Jerome and St. Augustine, who appeals to the agreement of those he knew.[3] Only two manuscripts of the *Itala* (*Cod. Clarom.* and *Cantab*) render *adulterium*, as Tertullian did before and after him Zeno of Verona.

[1] Greg. Nyss. *Ep. Can.* T. ii. p. 118.
[2] Clem. *Strom.* iii. p. 552, ed. Potter.
[3] Aug. *De Conjug. Adult.* Opp. vi. 393.

But, supposing πορνεία could be used for *adulterium*, that does not explain why Christ, or St. Matthew, should have used the word, where it was essential to define accurately the one ground for dissolution of marriage. Christ more than once uses μοιχεία here; what should have induced Him suddenly to change the word for "fornication," if, as our opponents maintain, He meant adultery, and that only? Most prefer to pass over this difficulty in silence. De Wette, Gerlach and Weiss say, that it is because μοιχᾶσθει is used in the same passage in a wider sense, for the re-marriage of a divorced wife.[1] But that contradicts the obvious meaning of Christ. He calls marrying a second wife or a divorced wife most strictly and properly, "adultery;" and it is the right term, if marriage be indissoluble. The connection of a married man with another woman, or of a single man with a married woman, is then, not in a wider and improper, but in the strictest and most proper sense, μοιχεία.

To make it intelligible that Christ, while declaring marriage an indissoluble bond, as being a Divine ordinance and independent of human caprice, should yet have annulled His own rule and allowed divorce and re-marriage in all cases of adultery, the principle has been set up that one or more acts of adultery destroy the essence of marriage, so that the formal dissolution and re-marriage is only the recognition and natural consequence of an accomplished fact. Julius Müller says: "The binding force of marriage is broken for the injured party by adultery, according to Christ's meaning; he does not break it by re-marriage, for it has been already broken by the other partner;" Olshausen says πορνεία is itself dissolution, not a ground for it; Meyer, that adultery destroys, *eo ipso*, the essence of marriage; Liebetrut, that marriage is actually destroyed by it; Sartorius says adultery breaks actually and fully the bond, both spiritual and bodily; Weiss, that this sin creates an actual dissolution, not a ground for it; Gerlach, that divorce simply announces what has already taken place without any co-operation of the innocent party; Tholuck consistently adds that the guilty party has thereby con-

---

[1] See *Zeitschr für christl. Wissenschaft*, 1856, p. 259.

tracted a new marriage.[1] Similar statements occur everywhere, and this is, at least, in Protestant Germany, the prevalent theory, and claims to agree with the Protestant Exegesis of the sixteenth and seventeenth century, for Gerhard said that adultery destroyed the *unitas carnis*, and thus annulled marriage, *quoad substantiam*. But till now there was a scruple in carrying out the theory consistently. When that is done in good earnest, a view of marriage and a treatment of questions connected with it very different from the teaching and practice of the Christian Church follows.

According to the teaching of Christ and the Apostle Paul, there are three factors of marriage, God, the husband, and the wife; to separate from a husband is to separate from God; a bond made fast by the Divine will constitutes a Divine right, and this can the less be annulled by the act of one party, since even the desire to annul the marriage relation cannot always be assumed. No human act can annul a Divine right, nor human sin dissolve a bond Divinely ratified. From the moment when Christ declared that God ratifies and seals the marriage bond, and that what He has joined together man may not put asunder, it is a law for the Church that marriage *cannot* be dissolved. And so the Lord understood it, when He Himself denounced on the three persons concerned in such a transaction the curse God has laid on adultery; and St. Paul, when he treated the marriage bond as a type of the indissoluble union of Christ and the Church, and therefore as itself indissoluble. It is a contradiction to make a generally transient error able to dissolve a bond embracing the whole life and all its relations, a sin against the lower and physical side of marriage, which is merely subservient to its higher ends, destroy what is above all a spiritual fellowship and an institution for the common bringing up of Christian children. Such a sin makes no chief end of marriage impossible. Even the Heathen view of it as a "*consortium* of the whole life, and common sharing of rights, human and divine,"[2] is higher

---

[1] Müller, *Uber Ehesch. und Wiederwerehl*, Berlin, 1855, p. 22. Olshausen, *Comm.* in N. T. i. 718. Meyer. *Exeg. Handb über Matt.* 1848, p. 151. Liebetrut, *Entwickl. der Ehe*. 1856, p. 104. Sartor. *Lehre heil. Lieb.* iii., ii. 69 Weiss, *Schriftlehr. Ehesch.* i. c. 261. Gerlach. *Das. N. T.* p. 73. Tholuck, *Bergpred*, 4th ed., 1856, p. 246.

[2] *Digest. de Rit. Nupt.* Lib. 1.

than this professedly Christian view, which, in order to make adultery destroy marriage, places its essence in carnal union. The really Christian view of the question requires that the wound inflicted by adultery on a covenant sealed by God should not be incurable, but, if a temporary separation follows, that the door should always be left open for repentance on one side and true forgiveness on the other. Christ showed that forgiveness should not be denied to the fallen wife, by His way of treating the adulteress brought before Him, and inculcated it by saying we should forgive our brother, not seven times, but seventy times seven. And finally, if adultery is a real dissolution of the bond, we may infer the greater from the less. Stier says correctly, "Whatever is a shameful act of any sort in Christian marriage, is as good a ground of divorce as carnal sin."[1] There is an unfaithfulness of mind, without any carnal sin, still more opposed to the essence, inward character and ends of marriage. Incongruity of temper, if reaching to hatred, is at least as good a ground of divorce as the seduction of a wife, or the momentary offence of the husband, if divorce be allowable at all.

The perverse and revolting character of this view is clearly seen, if we only consider that the single, often bitterly repented, act of a man is to have an effect often not intended, and to destroy a bond of relationship whose speciality is its being something objective, withdrawn from all human caprice, independent of the changes and uncertainties of individual taste and will, and designed to endure for life. On this theory, either party can at any moment destroy the marriage, and, if feeling it a burdensome yoke, or violently enamoured of another person, is strongly tempted to annul by one act a contract formed for life, while the innocent party, however anxious to forgive and preserve the marriage relation, must recognise and accept the actual dissolution of the marriage, and let the children of the guilty party be left fatherless or motherless.

Christ indeed only speaks of a man divorcing his wife, but it is quite indifferent, on the new theory, on which side adultery takes place. The *unitas carnis*, and therefore the substance of marriage, is of course equally destroyed in

---

[1] Stier, *Reden des Herrn, Jesu*, 2nd ed. 1851, I. 137.

either case. One sin breaks the husband's union with the mother of his children, and joins him in *unitas carnis* perhaps with his servant maid, who has therefore a better claim to his hand and home than his former wife. Far from hindering or forbidding the formal union of the adulterer and adulteress, one should on this theory seek to facilitate it; for *in fact* the new marriage is accomplished already, and the old destroyed, and a public formal marriage does but ratify a bond already contracted inwardly and really, and is more moral, or rather less immoral, than for the adulterer, who is separated from his first partner and hindered from marrying his second, to form a third *unitas carnis* with another person. These are but some results of the new theory about the substance of marriage; it would be easy to name several others which would inevitably follow. Every thinking man can discover them for himself.

# INDEX.

Abgar, king of Osroene, 138.
Abomination of desolation in the temple, 265, sq.
Abraham, as pattern of faith, 191.
Acts of Apostles, 132.
Adulteress brought before Christ, 370.
Adultery does not dissolve marriage, 365 sqq. Cf. Append. iii.
Agabus, the prophet, 74.
Agape, the, and its connection with the Eucharist, 328 sq.
Agrippa I., 76.
Alexander, false teacher, 227.
Alexandrian school, its view of Judaism as a world religion, 148.
Alphæus or Clopas and his sons, 102 sqq.
Altar and sacrifice of New Covenant in Sermon on Mount, 238; in Heb., 240.
Ananias, 44, 167.
Ananus, high-priest, 105, 421.
Andrew, Apostle, his call, 5, 10; his labours in Scythia, 137.
Andronicus, 295.
Anencletus, bishop of Rome, 300; not bishop with Linus, 304.
Angels, doctrine of N. T. concerning, 168 sq.; angels of seven churches, 117, 292, 293.
Antichrist, in St. John's epistles, 127, 262; not found in Apocalypse, 264; as "Man of Sin," in 2 Thess., 264 sq. (Cf. Append. i. 7).
Antinomian heretics, 126 sq.
Antioch, beginnings of Gentile Church there, 50; its first bishops, 305.
Antiochus Epiphanes, in Daniel, 268.
Antipas, martyred at Pergamos, 116.
Apathy of heathen philosophy, compared with Christian patience, 341.
Apocalypse, 113 sqq.
Apollos, at Ephesus and Corinth, 67.
Apostasy from faith, unpardonable in Heb., 202; will precede return of Christ, in 2 Thess., 274.
Apostles, their call, 5, 10; first sending forth, 11; training, 12; number of Twelve fixed, 55; their plenary powers, 30 sqq., 276; relation to communities, 276; Council of, 59, 278 sqq.; their assistants, 277; apostolic delegates, 291; marriage and celibacy of, 356; ministering sisters, 356; biographical notices of, 137, 138. See also under their names.
Aquila, in Corinth, 65; in Rome, 73, 96.
Archippus, bishop in Colossæ, 289, 290.
Aristarchus, 77.
Asceticism, Christian, 344; false, 346.
Athens, St. Paul's presence there, 65.
Atonement, (see Reconciliation).
Authority of Church officers, divine, 223.

Babylon, means Rome, in 1 Pet. v. 13, 97; also in Apocalypse, 121, 263.
Balaamites, 128.
Baptism, of John, 2, Cf. 318; of Christ, 2; its meaning, 3; teaching of Apostles on Christian baptism, 232; they seldom baptized themselves, 277; its relation to St. John's, 318; way of administering, 318; baptism of children, 319; for the dead, 321.
Barnabas, St., his labours at Antioch, 50; ordination and apostolate, 55; goes with St. Paul on first journey, 56; and to Council of Jerusalem, 59; his conduct at Antioch and separation from St. Paul, 64; death at Cyprus, 137; Epistle wrongly ascribed to him, 137.
Bartholomew, St., the Apostle, his calling, 5, 10; labours in India, 137.

Beast of Apocalypse, the power of Roman Empire, 120 sqq., 263.
Beatitude, teaching of Apostles on, 246 sqq.
Berœa, 65.
Bible, (see Scriptures).
Binding and loosing, power of, given to Peter, 28; to Apostles generally, 30, 321 sqq.; distinguished from power of keys, 321, note; its object and effects, 322 sq.
Bishops, why not appointed at first, 287; difficulty of choosing, 288; first indications of in St. Paul's Epistles, 289; duties of, 290; in Apoc., 292; in Clement of Rome's Epistle, 294; never two together, 304; first Bishops of Rome, 296 sqq.; of Antioch, Jerusalem, Smyrna and Ephesus, 305, 306; not chosen by popular election, 310.
Blessed, the, knowledge of, 247.
Brothers of Jesus, 10, 102 sqq., 305.
Burial of dead, first introduced by Christianity, 391.
Burning of Rome, 100.

CALIGULA, his desecration of the temple, 265.
Canon, the, of O. T. as received by Christians, 145; of N. T. not formed in Apostolic age, 152.
Catholicity of Church, 210.
Celibacy, Christian as distinguished from Heathen, 348 sqq.; in bad repute among Heathen, 348, 349; prophecy of Isaiah about, 349; sayings of Christ, 350; of St. John and St. Paul, 350, 351; celibacy of Clergy, 353 sqq.; of Apostles, 356.
Ceremonial law, dispute about it, 57; observed at first by Jewish converts, 108.
Cerinthus, heretic, 112, 132.
Chastity, its Christian aspect, 359.
Christians, origin of name at Antioch, 50; persecution of by Jews, 47; under Herod Agrippa, 54; under Nero, 101; under Domitian, 116 sqq.
Christianity, its relation to Judaism, 23 sqq., 57 sqq., 153 sqq., 327, 331 sqq.; its antithesis to Heathenism, 334, 338 sqq., 373 sqq., 379, 389; to Judaism and Heathenism together, 348, 390 sqq.; the religion of righteousness, 357.

Christology of N. T., 162 sqq., 172.
Church, teaching of Christ upon, 25 sqq.; His legacy to, 31; its connection at first with Synagogue, 27, 43, 211 sqq.; teaching of Apostles, especially St. Paul, on its Catholicity, 210 sqq.; relation to Synagogue, 211 sqq.; Cf. 278; to the world, 212; its growth as body of Christ, 213; holiness as bride of Christ, 214; unity, 215; visibility and invisibility, 216; infallibility and indefectibility, 216 sqq.; profession of faith, 225; attitude towards heresy, 226; authority, 223; Cf. 227; training and healing office, 228; privileges of members, 230; communion with unseen world, 250; prophecies of Christ and Apostles on future state of, 32, 257 sqq.; early constitution of, 281 sqq.; miraculous gifts, ib. (Cf. also Ministry, Sacrament, Sacrifice).
Civil power, relation of Christians to, 384 sqq.; obedience how far due to, 385 sqq.
Claudius Cæsar drives the Jews out of Rome, 96; is the κατέχων of 2 Thess., 272.
Clement of Rome on Church offices, 293 sqq.; his addition to O. T. and reverence felt for him by Ebionites, 301.
Clementines, the, an Ebionite work of second century, 302.
Clergy (see Ministry).
Cletus (see Anencletus).
Colossæ, false teachers there, 124.
Colossians, Epistle to, 77.
Commandments of God, necessity and power of fulfilling, 22; (see Law and Love).
Communion (see Eucharist).
Community of goods, no formal institution in primitive Church, 375.
Confession of sins, necessity of, 324; Ecclesiastical form and Scriptural grounds, 325; public penances, 325, sqq.
Confirmation at Samaria, 47; at Ephesus, 67; a means of grace, 233; a prerogative of Apostles, 278.
Conscience, a law to Heathen, 179; St. Paul on its supremacy, 347.
Continuity of doctrine in Church, 160.

# INDEX. 433

Conversion, its process, 191 sq.; a work of Holy Ghost, 201.
Corinth, founding of Church there, 65; St. Peter there, 296.
Corinthians, first Epistle to, 70; second, 72; Clement of Rome's Epistle to, 293 sq.
Cornelius, centurion, received into Church, 48 sq.
Corpse, Christian reverence for, 391.
Council of Apostles at Jerusalem, 59.
Creed of Apostles, 156.
Crescens, companion of St. Paul, 81.
Crete, St. Paul there, 81.
Crispus, 66.

DEACONS (see Diaconate).
Deaconesses, 306 sq.
Dead, state of, 248; prayer for, 251; baptism for, 321.
Death, teaching of N. T. upon, 246, 391; power of Sanhedrim over, Appendix ii.
Demas, 77, 81.
Demoniacs in N. T., 171.
Development of Church, 213; of Christian doctrine, 158 sq.
Devil, the teaching of Christ upon, 20; of Apostles, 170 sq.; binding of him in Apoc., 122.
Diaconate, institution of, 285; not distinguished from priesthood at first, 286; as treated by Clement of Rome, 294; ordination of seven at Jerusalem, 235; Stephen and Philip, 46, 47.
Dionysius, the Areopagite, conversion of, 65.
Dionysius of Corinth, on St. Peter's founding Roman Church, 95; on the death of St. Peter and St. Paul, 99.
Diotrephes, 113, 292.
Divorce, teaching of Christ upon, 362 sq. (Cf. Appendix iii.)
Dogmatic contents of Apostolic writings, 140 sq.
Domitian, in Apocalypse, 116.

EASTER, as a Christian festival, 333.
Ebionites, their writings, 302.
Eloquence, Christian (see Preaching).
Epaphras, 76.
Epaphroditus, 295.
Ephesians, St. Paul's Epistle to, 76; St. John's in Apocalypse, 117.
Ephesus, St. Paul and Apollos there,

67; St. Paul there again, 81; false teachers there, 126.
Epiphanius, his view of there being two bishops in one place criticised, 304 sq.
Episcopate (see Bishops, Ministry).
Equality, Christian idea of, 389.
Essenes, the, 125.
Eucharist, the, its institution, 35; both sacrifice and sacrament, 36; Apostolic teaching on, in 1 Cor, 235 sq.; in Heb., 238 sq.: time and manner of celebrating in Apostolic age, 329 sq. (see also Sacrifice).
Evangelists, in 1 Cor. xiv., 284 (see also Gospels).
Evodius, first bishop of Antioch, 305.
Excommunication, 322, 326.

FAITH, a condition and object of Christ's miracles, 15; a condition of salvation, 21; its grounds, 156; justifying faith, as treated by St. Paul, 181, sq.; by St. James, 204; its nature, 191 sq.; its relation to good works, 182, 196 sq.; 204; to the Law, 194 sq.; Noah and Abraham patterns of it, 191 (see also Justification and Good Works).
Fasting, teaching of Christ and St. Paul on, 344 sq.
Felix, 76.
Festivals in Apostolic Age, 331 sq.
Festus, 76.
Fire of purification in 1 Cor. iii. 256.
Fornication, in connection with Christ's teaching on divorce, 365 sq.: 371 (Cf. Appendix iii.)
Freedom of man's will, weakened but not destroyed by sin, 177; its relation to process of justification, 198; and to justifying faith, 192; to obedience towards the Church, 227; to conscience, 347, 386; true civil freedom introduced by Christianity, 381 sq.; training for it in the Church, 382; how both enlarged and limited by Christianity, 385; favoured by condition of Roman Empire, 387.

GALATIANS, Epistle to, 68.
Gamaliel, 46; teacher of St. Paul, 51.
Gehenna, 252.
Gentiles, first received into Church, 48; Gentile Church at Antioch, 50; their place in the Church, 210 sq.; times of the, καιροὶ ἐθνῶν, 259, 261,

28

Glaucias, translator for St. Peter, 94.
Gnosticism, 125 sq.
God, teaching of Christ about His fatherhood, 16; God all in all, 257 (see also Trinity).
Godhead of Christ, 16 (see Jesus Christ and Trinity).
Gods, so-called ($\pi\hat{a}s$ $\lambda\epsilon\gamma\delta\mu\epsilon\nu os$ $\theta\epsilon\delta s$), 268, note.
Gospels, the Synoptic, 129 sq.; St. John's, 132 sq.; Gospel of Hebrews, 135.
Good works, fruits of faith, 182, 196 sq.; required for justification, 196; wrought in us by God, 202; fruits of Holy Ghost, having high promises, 203; distinguished from works of the Law, 205; agreement of St. James and St. Paul upon them, 204 sq.
Grace, a divine power, 191; grace and justice in justification, 193; grace and merit, 203; grace can be lost, 202, 215.
Greek language, the instrument of Christian teaching, 143.

Hades, 249.
Harlot, the, in Apoc., 116, 121, 263.
Heathen, dominion of demons among them, 171, 274; their hostility towards Christians, 378.
Heaven, teaching of N. T. about it, 250.
Hebrews, Epistle to, 82 sq.; Gospel of, 135.
Hegesippus on succession of Roman bishops, 299; of bishops of Antioch, 305.
Hell (see Gehenna).
Heresy, its beginnings, 123 sq.; its exclusion from Church, 225; described by St. John as Antichrist, 262; St. Paul's prophecy of it at Ephesus, 274.
Herod Agrippa persecutes Christians, 54: his death, 55.
Herod Antipas imprisons the Baptist, 4; mocks Christ, 38.
Holiness of God revealed in Christian dispensation, 175, 189; of the Church, 214.
Holy Ghost, descent of at Pentecost, 42; teaching of Christ and Apostles on His Person and work, 18, 165 sq.; His office in justification, 186; in conversion, 201; in fulfilling the Law, 202.

Humility, a Christian virtue, 144; its ground, 342; contrasted with Pagan and Jewish Ethics, 379.
Hymenæus, a false teacher, 126, 227.

Idol sacrifices and feasts, participation in, forbidden by Council of Jerusalem, 60; by St. Paul in 1 Cor., 72 Cf. 129; they are offered to devils, 171.
Imputation of righteousness in justification, 181.
Incarnation, teaching of Apostles on, 172 (Cf. Jesus Christ).
Infallibility (see Church).
Inspiration of O. T. Scriptures, 147; of N. T., 151.
Intercession for the dead, 251; for others generally, 338; a duty of priesthood, 309.
Irenæus, St., on succession of Roman bishops, 299.
Izatas, king of Adiabene, 59.

James, St., the elder, Apostle, son of Zebedee, his call, 10; martyrdom, 54.
James, St., the younger, Apostle, son of Alphæus, his call, 10; his eminence among Apostles and kinship to our Lord, 102 sq.; bishop of Jerusalem, 103: his ascetic life, 105; his martyrdom, 105; his Epistle, 106, 141; his agreement with St. Paul in doctrine, 204 sq.; his relation to St. Peter and St. Paul at Council of Jerusalem, 279 sq.
Jerusalem, destruction of, and the results, 108 sq.; prophecy of Christ concerning, 258; its destruction a Coming of Christ, 260; its first bishops, James, 103, 287; Simon, 305.
Jesus Christ, His life, ministry and teaching till the Ascension, 2—40 (see Table of Contents); teaching of Apostles on His Godhead, 162 sq.; is the Logos, 164 sq.; the incarnation, atonement and redemption, 172 sq.; influence of His death and resurrection on Christian life, 186 sq.; Christ as Head and Bridegroom of the Church, 214; His threefold office, 218; His priesthood, 239; His return to judge the world, 255; His giving up the kingdom to the Father, 257.

INDEX. 435

Jews, the, their settlement in Rome, 96; in Babylon, 97; their aversion to Christianity, 110; their hatred of the Gentiles, *ib.*
Jezabel, in Apoc., 129, 293.
John, St., Apostle and Evangelist, his call, 5, 10; his life, 111; his Epistles, 112, 113; his Apocalypse, 113 sq.; his Gospel, 132 sq.; general subject of his writings, 141; their individual character, 142; his appointment of bishops, 306; story of his converting the robber youth, 326.
John the Baptist, 1 sq.; origin and meaning of his baptism, 318; his disciples at Ephesus, 67.
John the Presbyter, reputed author of Apoc., 113.
Joses, son of Alphæus and brother of the Lord, 102, 103.
Jude, St., (Thaddæus or Lebbæus), Apostle and brother of the Lord, his call, 10; his Epistle, 107; its relation to 2 Pet., 93; false teachers spoken of in it, 126.
Judaism, Pharisaic, 58; Gnostic, 125 (see also Law, Tradition).
Judaizers at Jerusalem and Antioch, 57 sq.; in Galatia, 69; at Corinth, 70 sq.
Judas Iscariot, his call, 10; prophecy of betrayal, 35; betrayal, 38.
Judgment, the last, 255.
Judgment of Peter, an Ebionite document, 303.
Justification, teaching of Christ concerning, 21 sq.; teaching of Apostles, especially St. Paul, 176 sq.; how distinguished from reconciliation, 176; how related to faith, 181; to good works, 182, 196, 204; its process, 183 sq.; is a fruit of Christ's death and resurrection, 184 sq.; an imparting of life, 185; a work of the Holy Ghost, 186; a manifestation of divine power, 186; a new revelation of divine justice, 189; identical with sanctification, 197; with deliverance, 197; conditioned by human freedom, 198; St. James and St. Paul agree in their doctrine of it, 204, sq.
Justus, a proselyte at Corinth, 66.

Κατέχων, ὁ, in 2 Thess., 272, note 2.
Keys, power of (see Binding and Loosing).
Kingdom of God, 27 sq.

Labour, its Christian aspect and duty, 374.
Lamb of God, Christ, 20; the true Paschal Lamb, 174, 237.
Last things, the, doctrine of N. T. concerning, 122, 246 sq.; prophecies of Christ and the Apostles concerning, 257 sq.
Law, the Mosaic, Christ on its fulfilment in Himself, 23 sq.; dispute about its observance, 57; St. Paul's teaching about it, 178 sq.; righteousness of the Law and of faith, 181 sq.; abrogation of Law, 179 sq.; its establishment by faith, 189, 192, 195; as Law of Christ or of freedom, 195; Law and Gospel, 196; fulfilment of Law through grace of Holy Ghost, 202 (Cf. Justification).
Lawless one, the, 272 sq.
Linus, a disciple of St. Paul, 82; bishop of Rome, 300; not joint bishop with Anencletus, 304.
Logos, of St. John and of Philo, 163 sq.
Love, the chief commandment, 22; its universality, 25; its relation to faith and justification, 200; love of our neighbour as taught and practised in Apostolic Church, 376 sq.
Lucius of Cyrene, a prophet, 55.
Luke the Evangelist accompanies St. Paul, 64; is with him in Rome during his first imprisonment, 77; and his second, 81; his Gospel, 131; and Acts, 132.

Magna Charta of Church, 31.
Man of Sin, the, 264 sq. (Cf. Appendix i.)
Manahen, a prophet at Antioch, 55.
Manhood of Christ, real, 19.
Mark, St., the Evangelist, separated from St. Paul and accompanies St. Barnabas, 64; translates for St. Peter, 94; his life and Gospel, 130, 131; founds Church of Alexandria, 138.
Marriage in its Christian aspect represents union of Christ with the Church, 358; is a sacred ministry in Church, 360; its sacramental character, 361; its indissolubility, 362; teaching of Christ thereon, 363 sq. (Cf. Appendix iii.); mixed marriages, 371; second marriage of clergy forbidden, 354 sq.

Martyrdom, Christian estimate of, 341 sq.
Mary, wife of Alphæus, 102.
Mass (see Sacrifice).
Matthew, St., Apostle and Evangelist, his call, 10; his Gospel, 129; its relation to Gospel of Hebrews, 136; his ascetic life, 137.
Matthias, St., the Apostle, his election, 41; a saying of his, 137.
Melchisedech, a type of Christ, 175.
Merit of good works, 203 sq.
Millenium, the, 118, 122, 263.
Ministers of Church, their qualifications, 308 sq.; appointment, 310; support, 311; celibacy desirable, 353; but not enforced, 354; second marriage forbidden, 354 sq.
Ministry of Christ in the Church threefold, 218 sq.; universal priesthood, 220; special priesthood transmitted by ordination, 222; dependent on divine mission, 223: for the people's sake, but not derived from them, 224; special ministries in Apostolic age, the Apostolate, 276 sq.; the primacy of Peter, 278 sq.; extraordinary ministries, 281 sq.; prophets, 284; evangelists, 284; deacons and presbyters not distinguished at first, 285; nor presbyters and bishops, 286; Episcopate as a distinct office, 287; Clement of Rome upon it, 294; no fixed names of offices in N.T., 295.
Miracles of Christ, 14; their object, 15.
Mystery of iniquity, the, 272 sq.

Nazarites, their Gospel, 136.
Neighbour, love of (see Love).
Nero, persecutes Christians, 101; is "Man of Sin," 270 (Cf. Appendix i.); fable of his return to life, 273, note 2.
New Testament (see Scriptures).
Nicodemus, his conversation with Jesus, 7.
Nicolaitans, a sect of heretics, 128.
Nicolas, the deacon, 128.
Noah, a pattern of faith, 191.

Oaths, why forbidden by Christ, 389; in what cases allowed afterwards, 390.
Old Testament (see Scriptures).
Onesimus, 290.
Onesiphorus, comes to St. Paul at Rome, 81; is prayed for by him after his death, 251.
Ordination, of Paul and Barnabas at Antioch, 55; of Timothy and others, 305, 310; its sacramental character, 222, 234.
Original sin (see Sin).

Parties, in Corinthian Church, 70 sq.
Passover, the Christian, its relation to Jewish Passover, 237.
Patience, as a Christian virtue, 340.
Paul, St., the Apostle, his conversion, 50 sq.; his life and Epistles, 52—82 (See Table of Contents); his character and teaching, 84 sq.; his relation to the other Apostles, 90 sq.; to St. Peter especially, 278 sq.; his martyrdom at Rome, 99; general character of his writings, 141 sq.
Pentecost, the first, 42; observance of the festival in the Church, 333.
Pergamos, the Nicolaitans and Balaamites there, 128.
Persecution (see Christians).
Peter, St., chief Apostle, his call, 5, 10; his life after the Ascension, 43—49 (see Table of Contents); his meeting with St. Paul at Antioch, 61 sq.; his Epistles, 92 sq.; his relation to Roman Church, 94 sq.,; cf. 296 sq.; his martyrdom at Rome, 98; doctrinal contents of his writings, 140; his presence in Corinth, 296; his primacy, 28 sq.; 278 sq.; his second meeting with Simon Magus in Rome, 303; relation to St. Paul and St. James, 278 sq.
Pharaoh, St. Paul on his hardening of heart, 207.
Pharisees, the, their attitude in relation to Christ, 11.
Philemon, Epistle to, 77; cf. 290.
Philetus, a false teacher, 126.
Philip, St., the Apostle, his call, 5, 10; his labours in Phrygia, and death, 137.
Philip, St., the deacon, baptizes chamberlain of Queen Candace and preaches in Samaria, 47.
Philippi, founding of Church there, 65.
Philippians, Epistle to, 78.
Philo, his doctrine of the Logos, compared with St. John's, 164; his account of profanation of temple, 265.

Pilate, procurator of Judæa, 1; condemns Christ to death, 38; profanes temple, 267.
Police in Roman Empire, 388.
Polycarp, St., bishop of Smyrna, 306.
Polycrates, bishop of Ephesus, 306.
Poverty and wealth, Christian aspect of, 373.
Prayer, zeal of the first Christians in it, 334; the Lord's prayer, 335 sq.; prayer a distinctive feature of Christianity, 338.
Preaching, its requisites and character in Apostolic age, 308.
Preaching of Peter, an Ebionite document, its early date and mixed character, 297; its influence and popularity in the West, 303.
Predestination, of God, its nature, and relation to human freedom, 206 sq.
Presbyter, meaning of word in 2 and 3 John, 113; not distinguished at first from deacon or bishop, 286; nor by Clement of Rome, 294; derived from Jewish usage, 286; qualifications of the office, 308 sq.
Presbyterate, not possessing any corporate authority, or power of ordination, 292.
Priesthood of Christ, as taught in Heb., 174, 218 sq., 238 sq. (Cf. Sacrifice).
Priesthood, the Christian, its relation to Christ's, 219; to the Jewish, 220; universal and special, 220 sq.; the latter transmitted by ordination, 222; exercised in intercession as well as sacrifice, 221, 309.
Primacy (see Peter).
Profession of faith, a duty, 225; its unity, 226.
Privileges of Christians, as members of the Church, 230.
Property, Christian aspect of, as a stewardship, 373 sq.
Prophecies of Christ, generally, 16; on the last days, 257 sq.
Prophet, the false, in Apoc. is a revival of Heathen philosophy and magical arts, 121, 263.
Prophets, in Apostolic age, their gifts and functions, 284, 313.
Prophetesses, in Apostolic age, 314.
Proselytes of the gate, distinguished from proselytes of righteousness, as not being required to observe the ceremonial law, 48, 58.

Psalter, the, its special fitness for Christian worship, 330; a bequest from Jewish to Christian Church, 334.
Purgatory, 248.

RECONCILIATION (or Atonement), teaching of Christ upon, 21; it is a fruit of His incarnation and death, 172 sq.; its connection with sanctification, 175; and justification, 176.
Redemption, teaching of Christ upon, 20; of Apostles, especially St. Paul, 172 sq.; its universality, 206 cf. 256.
Repentance, a condition of entering God's kingdom, 21. (Cf. Conversion and Confession.)
Reprobation, in what sense taught by St. Paul, 208 sq.
Resurrection of Christ, 39; its influence on justification and sanctification, 185, 188; it is an earnest of our resurrection, 253.
Resurrection of dead, a chief doctrine of Christianity, 253; nature of the resurrection body, 254; first and second resurrection, 122, 123.
Righteousness of God, revealed anew in justification, 189.
Righteousness of men, in what consisting according to Christ's teaching, 23; teaching of Apostles on righteousness by faith, 181 sq.; it is a gift of Holy Ghost, 190; true and false distinguished, 194; the true identical with holiness, 197.
Roman Church, its founding by St. Peter, 94 sq.; 296 sq.; St. Paul's relation to it, *ib.*; succession of its first bishops, 298 sq.
Romans, the, Epistle to, 72.
Rome, settlement of Jews there, 96; meant by Babylon in 1 Pet. v. 13, 97; in Apoc. 122.

SABBATH, the, teaching of Christ on, 24; its observance by Jewish converts allowed, at first, 331.
Sacraments of the Church, in general, 231; in particular, 232 sq.
Sacrifice, the, of N. T., bloody on cross, (see Redemption), unbloody in Eucharist, its institution, 35 sq.; Apostolic doctrine of, 235 sq.; its relation to Passover and Jewish sacrifices, 236 sq.; its permanence

in Church, 238, 241 sq.; its relation to Christ's heavenly priesthood, 239 sq.; to His incarnation, 241 sq.; its significance, 242 sq.; its abiding unity, 244.
Samaria, preaching of St. Philip there, 47.
Sanctification, its relation to atonement, 175; to justification, 197. (Cf. Justification.)
Sanhedrim, the, sits at Jamnia after fall of Jerusalem, 111; its power of life and death. Appendix ii.
Satan (see Devil).
Scribes, their relation to Christ, 11.
Scriptures, the holy, 139—155 (see Table of Contents).
Second coming of Christ, prophecies concerning, 258; time uncertain, 259; prefigured in fall of Jerusalem, 260.
Seven, mystic number in Apoc., 118.
Seven Churches of Asia Minor, 117; heresies in them, 123; their angels, 292.
Septuagint, the, its composition and use in N.T., 147 sq.
Sick, gift of healing them, 313.
Silas, attendant of St. Paul, 64; carries St. Peter's first Epistle, 92.
Similitudes of kingdom of heaven, 25.
Simon, son of Alphæus, 102; chosen second bishop of Jerusalem, 305.
Simon Magus rebuked by St. Peter, 47: father of heresy, 127; his doctrine, 204; fables about him, 303.
Simon Niger, a prophet of Antioch, 55.
Simon Zelotes, St., the Apostle, his call, 10.
Sin, original and actual, Christ's teaching on, 20; the Apostles', 176 sq.; its forgiveness and subdual, 200; sin against Holy Ghost, 202.
Sisters, ministering to Apostles, 356.
Slavery, Christian view of, 380.
Smyrna, mentioned in Apoc., 117; Polycarp made bishop of by St. John, 306.
Social position of Christians in Roman Empire, 377, 387 sq.
Soul, the disembodied, state of, 251.
Spirit the holy (see Holy Ghost).
Spiritual gifts, their abundance and variety, 281 sq., 312 sq.; their exercise in the Church, 312 sq.; their early withdrawal, 283, 317; their kinds, 312.
Stephen, St., first martyr, 46.

Succession of Roman bishops, 298 sq.
Sufferings, of Christ, 37 sq.; of Christians, viewed as blessings, 341 sq.
Sunday, a Christian festival, not derived from Sabbath, 332; how kept, 333.
Synagogue, its relation to Apostolic Church, 27, 47, 211 sq.

TALMUD, its gradual formation, 111.
Temple, the, cleansed by Christ, 6, 34; profaned by Caligula, 265 sq.; by Nero, 271 sq.; its fall, 109; meaning of in 2 Thess., 269 sq.; cf., 271 note 1, and 414.
Thaddæus, St., the Apostle (see Jude).
Thaddæus, one of the seventy, converts king Abgar, 138.
Theophilus, a noble Roman, 131, 132.
Thessalonians, founding of their Church, 65; Epistles to, 66.
Thomas, St., the Apostle, his call, 10; doubts resurrection, 40; his labours and death in Parthia, 137.
Thyatira, mentioned in Apoc., 117; seat of Gnostic prophetess, 129; its angels, 293.
Time, Christian view of, 375.
Timothy, joins St. Paul at Lystra, and is circumcised, 64; is with St. Paul in Rome, 77; first Epistle to him, 79; second, 82; is favourite of St. Paul, 290; Apostolic delegate and bishop of Ephesus, 291.
Titus, goes with St. Paul to Council of Jerusalem, 59; not circumcised, 60; Epistle to him, 81; his death in Crete, 138; was bishop of Gortyna, 292; cf. 289.
Tongues, gift of, 314 sq.
Tradition, 152—161 (see Table of Contents).
Trinity, teaching of Christ upon, 16 sq.; of Apostles, 162 sq., 168; relation of Trinity to justification, 189.
Trophimus, an attendant of St. Paul, 75, 81.
Tychicus, is with St. Paul in Rome, 77.

UNCTION of the sick, 235.
Unity of Church, 215; of the faith, 226.
Universality of offer of salvation, 206; of judgment, 255.

VIRGINITY (see Celibacy).
Virgins, employed as deaconesses, 307.

Vision of God, 247.
Voluntary offerings in Apostolic age, 311, 331.
Vows, adopted from Judaism into Christian Church, 357.

Widows, employed as deaconesses, 307.
Women, their position raised by Christianity, 358. (Cf. Celibacy, Marriage.)
Works (see Good Works.)
World, the, Christ's teaching on, 20; judgment of, 255; its renewal by fire, 256.
Worship, Christian, teaching of Christ on, 7, 25; its co-existence with Jewish at first, 327; its general character, 328; the agape, 328; the Eucharist, how often celebrated, 329; frequent services, 330; intercession, 330; festivals, 333; continual prayer, 334; the Psalter, 334; Lord's Prayer, 335 sq.; Christian prayer contrasted with Heathen, 338.

# RECENT WORKS BY THE AUTHOR OF THIS TRANSLATION.

*Recently published in* 1 *vol.,* 8*vo., price* 8*s.* 6*d.,*

THE CATHOLIC DOCTRINE OF THE ATONEMENT: An Historical Inquiry into its Development in the Church; with an Introduction on the Principle of Theological Developments.

### EXTRACTS FROM REVIEWS.

" It is written with some learning, with great clearness, with much grace, and the Author has happily avoided that prolixity which is the besetting sin of theologians."—*Pall Mall Gaz.*

" This is the most liberal and generously written treatise on a great doctrinal question which we ever read from the pen of a Roman Catholic. Mr. Oxenham does not revile or misrepresent his opponents, and he has a calm and judicial mind."—*British Quarterly Review.*

" Of Mr. Oxenham's treatise we desire to speak in high terms of praise. We are not aware of any book in which so much information on so important a subject is condensed with equal precision and method. We cannot discover a single point in which his sympathies have misrepresented any opinion held by fathers, schoolmen, reformers, or modern theologians. Mr. Oxenham writes like a scholar and a man of taste, and his readers will find more than one passage of no inconsiderable eloquence."—*London Review.*

"We welcome this volume for many reasons. . . . It surely cannot lead to anything but good when the central truths of Christianity are discussed with learning and reverence, as is the case in this treatise. . . . Although compelled sometimes to differ from Mr. Oxenham's views, we are heartily grateful to him for his monograph on this great Christian verity."—*Guardian.*

" The book is a fair mirror of the author's many-sided mind. It is no dry didactic treatise that is brought before us, but one full of illustrations from most varied sources—one unlike any other kindred book it has ever been our fate to meet with. . . . . There is hardly any important fact bearing upon the development question which does not receive some notice in the preface."—*Church Review.*

" Mr. Oxenham's is the work of a scholarly divine, and is worthy both of his first training at Oxford, and of the countenance of his eminent Roman Catholic friend, Dr. Dollinger."—*Westminster Review.*

" It appears to us to show throughout a devout and reverent spirit, much thoughtful reading, and in point of style is a good model of clear, refined, and nervous English ; and lastly, we think the author shows a gift of dealing fairly by the views of opponents not altogether common."—*Weekly Register.*

" Probably no recent volume of English theology will so well repay careful reading as Mr. Oxenham's. Full of careful and wide research, masterly in style, accurate in scholarship, and of the soundest order of divinity, it cannot fail to take a high place among the standard authors of the Church."—*Church and State Review.*

---

DISHONEST CRITICISM. Some Remarks on Two Articles in the *Dublin Review.* Price 1s. 6d.

"That Mr. Oxenham has met with scant courtesy or fairness is not only his own view, but that of others also who have come forward in his defence, and is made out (so far as we can judge without seeing the whole of the articles) by his argument."—*Guardian.*

"We have no hesitation in saying that Mr. Oxenham has proved his case; . . . . we think that men of all opinions should join in reprobating such criticisms, equally offensive to the sense of justice and of propriety."—*Spectator.*

"The *Dublin Review's* abuse is unfair, insulting and arrogant. Mr. Oxenham is, as it appears to us, very ill-used, and says no more than is strictly true ; . . . his retorts are perfectly fair, and his exposure of his ill-treatment is complete."—*Pall Mall Gazette.*

---

DR. PUSEY'S EIRENICON CONSIDERED IN RELATION TO CATHOLIC UNITY. A Letter to the Rev. Father Lockhart of the Institute of Charity.—8vo., Price 3s. 6d.

" Distinguished for its calm, charitable tone, its thoroughly manly avowals, and for the largeness of its concessions. It is important, not merely because of the ability which conspicuously marks it, but for the indication which it gives of the growth of a school in the bosom of the Roman Catholic Church, the members of which can approach the subject of the present divisions of Christendom in a candid temper, not to say an impartial spirit."—*Churchman.*

"As the representative of an actually existing element in the Roman Catholic Church, Mr. Oxenham affords the most hopeful evidence of the possibility at least of Catholic reunion. He points out with characteristic force and eloquence, and with considerable learning, the arguments and reasonings bearing on the subject, especially those which relate to the overpowering practical evils arising out of the present distracted state of Christendom."—*John Bull.*

" Mr. Oxenham's Letter is very interesting and well worth reading. . . . . All will agree with the eloquent words in which he dwells on the grand theme of an united Christendom."—*Weekly Register.*

" Mr. Oxenham's beautiful pamphlet."—*Christian Remembrancer.*

"Clear argument and a brilliancy of thought and expression rarely to be met with abound on its every page."—*Church Review.*

" By far the ablest portions of the pamphlet is from page 7 to page 85. . . . . We cannot, indeed, concur with every individual expression contained in these pages, but on the whole we can sincerely recommend them to our readers."—*Dublin Review.*

---

*In the Press.*—*To appear shortly.*

THE SENTENCE OF KAIRES AND OTHER POEMS. 2nd Edition, Revised.

www.ingramcontent.com/pod-product-compliance
Lightning Source LLC
Chambersburg PA
CBHW030323020526
44117CB00030B/737